Communications Systems and Networks,

Second Edition

Ray Horak

M&T Books
An Imprint of IDG Books Worldwide, Inc.

Foster City, CA • Chicago, IL • Indianapolis, IN • New York, NY

Communications Systems and Networks, Second Edition

Published by
M&T Books
An imprint of IDG Books Worldwide, Inc.
919 E. Hillsdale Blvd., Suite 400
Foster City, CA 94404
www.idgbooks.com (IDG Books Worldwide Web site)

ISBN: 0-7645-7522-8

Printed in the United States of America

10 9 8 7 6 5 4 3 2

1B/QT/RR/ZZ/FC

Distributed in the United States by IDG Books Worldwide, Inc.

Distributed by CDG Books Canada Inc. for Canada; by Transworld Publishers Limited in the United Kingdom; by IDG Norge Books for Norway; by IDG Sweden Books for Sweden; by Woodslane Pty. Ltd. for Australia; by Woodslane (NZ) Ltd. for New Zealand; by TransQuest Publishers Pte Ltd. for Singapore, Malaysia, Thailand, Indonesia, and Hong Kong; by ICG Muse, Inc. for Japan; by Intersoft for South Africa; by Le Monde en Tique for France; by International Thomson Publishing for Germany, Austria and Switzerland; by Distribuidora Cuspide for Argentina; by LR International for Brazil; by Galileo Libros for Chile; by Ediciones ZETA S.C.R. Ltda. for Peru; by WS Computer Publishing Corporation, Inc., for the Philippines; by Contemporanea de Ediciones for Venezuela; by Express Computer Distributors for the Caribbean and West Indies; by Micronesia Media Distributor, Inc. for Micronesia; by Chips Computadoras S.A. de C.V. for Mexico; by Editorial Norma de Panama S.A. for Panama; by American Bookshops for Finland.

For general information on IDG Books Worldwide's books in the U.S., please call our Consumer Customer Service department at 800-762-2974. For reseller information, including discounts and premium sales, please call our Reseller Customer Service department at 800-434-3422.

For information on where to purchase IDG Books Worldwide's books outside the U.S., please contact our International Sales department at 317-596-5530 or fax 317-596-5692.

For consumer information on foreign language translations, please contact our Customer Service department at 800-434-3422, fax 317-596-5692, or e-mail rights@idg-books.com.

For information on licensing foreign or domestic rights, please phone +1-650-655-3109.

For sales inquiries and special prices for bulk quantities, please contact our Sales department at 650-655-3200 or write to the address above.

For information on using IDG Books Worldwide's books in the classroom or for ordering examination copies, please contact our Educational Sales department at 800-434-2086 or fax 317-596-5499.

For press review copies, author interviews, or other publicity information, please contact our Public Relations department at 650-655-3000 or fax 650-655-3299.

Library of Congress Cataloging-in-Publication Data

Horak, Ray.
    Communications systems and networks / Ray Horak. --2nd ed.
        p. cm.
    Includes index.
    ISBN 0-7645-7522-8 (alk. paper)
    1. Telecommunication systems. 2. Computer networks. I. Title.
TK5101 .H665 1999
621.382'1--dc21   99-048104

This work is published with the understanding that M&T Books and its authors are supplying information, but are not attempting to render engineering or other professional services. If such services are required, the assistance of an appropriate professional should be sought.

Trademarks: All brand names and product names used in this book are trade names, service marks, trademarks, or registered trademarks of their respective owners. IDG Books Worldwide is not associated with any product or vendor mentioned in this book.

 is a registered trademark or trademark under exclusive license to IDG Books Worldwide, Inc. from International Data Group, Inc. in the United States and/or other countries.

 is a trademark of IDG Books Worldwide, Inc.

ABOUT IDG BOOKS WORLDWIDE

Welcome to the world of IDG Books Worldwide.

IDG Books Worldwide, Inc., is a subsidiary of International Data Group, the world's largest publisher of computer-related information and the leading global provider of information services on information technology. IDG was founded more than 30 years ago by Patrick J. McGovern and now employs more than 9,000 people worldwide. IDG publishes more than 290 computer publications in over 75 countries. More than 90 million people read one or more IDG publications each month.

Launched in 1990, IDG Books Worldwide is today the #1 publisher of best-selling computer books in the United States. We are proud to have received eight awards from the Computer Press Association in recognition of editorial excellence and three from Computer Currents' First Annual Readers' Choice Awards. Our best-selling ...For Dummies® series has more than 50 million copies in print with translations in 31 languages. IDG Books Worldwide, through a joint venture with IDG's Hi-Tech Beijing, became the first U.S. publisher to publish a computer book in the People's Republic of China. In record time, IDG Books Worldwide has become the first choice for millions of readers around the world who want to learn how to better manage their businesses.

Our mission is simple: Every one of our books is designed to bring extra value and skill-building instructions to the reader. Our books are written by experts who understand and care about our readers. The knowledge base of our editorial staff comes from years of experience in publishing, education, and journalism — experience we use to produce books to carry us into the new millennium. In short, we care about books, so we attract the best people. We devote special attention to details such as audience, interior design, use of icons, and illustrations. And because we use an efficient process of authoring, editing, and desktop publishing our books electronically, we can spend more time ensuring superior content and less time on the technicalities of making books.

You can count on our commitment to deliver high-quality books at competitive prices on topics you want to read about. At IDG Books Worldwide, we continue in the IDG tradition of delivering quality for more than 30 years. You'll find no better book on a subject than one from IDG Books Worldwide.

John Kilcullen
Chairman and CEO
IDG Books Worldwide, Inc.

Steven Berkowitz
President and Publisher
IDG Books Worldwide, Inc.

IDG is the world's leading IT media, research and exposition company. Founded in 1964, IDG had 1997 revenues of $2.05 billion and has more than 9,000 employees worldwide. IDG offers the widest range of media options that reach IT buyers in 75 countries representing 95% of worldwide IT spending. IDG's diverse product and services portfolio spans six key areas including print publishing, online publishing, expositions and conferences, market research, education and training, and global marketing services. More than 90 million people read one or more of IDG's 290 magazines and newspapers, including IDG's leading global brands — Computerworld, PC World, Network World, Macworld and the Channel World family of publications. IDG Books Worldwide is one of the fastest-growing computer book publishers in the world, with more than 700 titles in 36 languages. The "...For Dummies®" series alone has more than 50 million copies in print. IDG offers online users the largest network of technology-specific Web sites around the world through IDG.net (http://www.idg.net), which comprises more than 225 targeted Web sites in 55 countries worldwide. International Data Corporation (IDC) is the world's largest provider of information technology data, analysis and consulting, with research centers in over 41 countries and more than 400 research analysts worldwide. IDG World Expo is a leading producer of more than 168 globally branded conferences and expositions in 35 countries including E3 (Electronic Entertainment Expo), Macworld Expo, ComNet, Windows World Expo, ICE (Internet Commerce Expo), Agenda, DEMO, and Spotlight. IDG's training subsidiary, ExecuTrain, is the world's largest computer training company, with more than 230 locations worldwide and 785 training courses. IDG Marketing Services helps industry-leading IT companies build international brand recognition by developing global integrated marketing programs via IDG's print, online and exposition products worldwide. Further information about the company can be found at www.idg.com.   1/24/99

Credits

ACQUISITIONS EDITOR
Michelle Baxter

DEVELOPMENT EDITOR
Elyn Wollensky

CONSULTING EDITOR
Mark A. Miller, P.E

TECHNICAL EDITOR
Rick Luhmann

COPY EDITORS
Victoria Lee
Julie M. Smith

PROJECT COORDINATORS
Linda Marousek
Tom Debolski

**GRAPHICS AND
PRODUCTION SPECIALISTS**
Jude Levinson
Dina Quan
Ramses Ramirez

QUALITY CONTROL SPECIALIST
Chris Weisbart

ILLUSTRATOR
Margaret Horak

PROOFREADER
York Graphic Services

INDEXER
Ray Horak

COVER ILLUSTRATION
© Nicholas Wilton/SIS

About the Author

Ray Horak is an internationally recognized author, lecturer, and consultant. In addition to this book, he has authored well over 100 articles for major publications, and is Contributing Editor for *Newton's Telecom Dictionary*, and serves on the Editorial Advisory Boards of several leading technology periodicals. Ray lectures before thousands of communications professionals annually, both in the United States and around the world. As an author and a lecturer, he is well known for his ability to explain the most complex technologies in plain English, using common-sense terminology . . . and with more than just a dash of humor, just to keep things in perspective.

Ray's 30 years of experience in the networked world began with Southwestern Bell Telephone Company (now part of SBC Communications), which was part of the AT&T Bell System (which no longer exists) at the time. Toward the end of his nine-year Bell System career, Southwestern Bell loaned him to AT&T and Bell Telephone Laboratories in a failed attempt to make him fit the mold. Ray then spent nine years with Contel (since acquired by GTE, which is in the process of merging with Bell Atlantic), where he founded several successful companies that were later sold to or merged with other companies. When Contel failed to straighten him out, he worked for another company or two. Finally, and in a desperate attempt to make a living on his own terms, he founded The Context Corporation, an independent consultancy. That worked so well that he's been independent ever since. Ray hopes for continued success, since he figures that he's been on his own for so long that he now is unemployable, for all practical purposes. Borrowing and modifying a quote attributed to Groucho Marx, Ray claims that he wouldn't want to work for any company that has poor enough judgement to hire him. He also claims no responsibility for the fact that most of the companies for which he worked no longer exist as such.

Ray met his lovely wife, Margaret, during his Contel days. They lost touch for a number of years, but were reunited through an article he wrote in 1990, which attests to his skills as an author. Ray and Margaret claim to be the two happiest people on the face of this Earth.

Ray Horak, President
The Context Corporation
1500A East College Way, PMB 443
Mt. Vernon, WA 98273
Tel: 360.336.3448
Fax: 360.336.3759
E-mail: ray@contextcorporation.com

To Margaret,
for whom my love and devotion are boundless

Foreword

If you're involved in telecom, datacom, networking, the Internet, or the Web (or all five), you owe it to yourself to read this book.

This is the best book to give you a quick or in-depth (your choice) overview of all the important technologies. Though this book is technical, I seriously recommend it for managers, who (theoretically) don't need the technical expertise because they can rely on their technical staffs instead. The reality is that things are changing so fast in these exciting fields, that no one can be an expert in or even stay up to date with everything. The more people in your company who know enough to be dangerous, the better network and the better deal your company is going to get out of its vendors.

I like this book for three reasons: First, its logic and flow make sense to me. Ray starts with the most basic concepts and works up to the most complex technologies, and their real-world implementations.

Second, Ray has written the book in plain business English. Someone like me, who's not technical (but wishes he were) can understand all the technologies — even the most complex ones. Ray explains how these technologies work, what they do and their pros and cons.

Third, Ray's book doesn't bore you to tears, like so many books on this subject. He's actually a "cool guy" and his style reflects that. (So does his haircut — he sports a cute graying ponytail.)

I've known Ray for eons. He's spoken at my conferences and has written in my magazines. One of his articles was so popular that an impressed reader sought him out and contacted him. *He* was so impressed that he married her. And they have lived happily ever after. By the way, this is a true story — her name is Margaret Horak, and she is lovely.

Ray is also a contributing editor on my best-selling *Newton's Telecom Dictionary*. This is no mean achievement. I searched for over five years before I found Ray — someone whom I felt had in-depth technical understanding of the field and superb writing skills. Over the years, he has defined the most difficult words in my dictionary and has written both mini and major essays on the most complex of topics. What constantly amazes me about Ray, is that if I ask him if he's heard of some obscure term, within hours he sends me a full explanation of it and all its associated terms. Even better? Ray seems to know about new technologies before they even get close to the mainstream. *Ray's been there, done that.*

So if you're looking for a companion book to this one (and you really should have one), you may want to try *Newton's Telecom Dictionary*, available (I'm hoping) at the same place you bought this. If not, try my Web site, www.HarryNewton.com, which will lead you directly to my dictionary.

By the way, if you find things you don't understand in our books, you should e-mail us. We're both obsessed with making our books be the absolute best they can be. And since they're always going into a new, updated edition, there's always an opportunity to fix up the last edition's screw-ups. Mine, for example, is at its 15th edition, going on for its 20th. Ray's is into its second. So help us make them better for everyone.

Harry Newton

Harry@HarryNewton.com

Harry Newton is the author of the best-selling "Newton's Telecom Dictionary" and founder of leading telecommunications and networking ad technology magazines — Call Center, Computer Telephony, LAN (now Network), Technology Investor and Teleconnect.

Foreword by the Consulting Editor

Although you have probably noticed, the landscape of telecommunications technologies is changing at an ever-increasing pace. Computing power is increasing so rapidly that the obsolescence of some platforms is now measured in months, not years. On the communications front, high speed technologies, such as ATM, xDSL and cable modems, have replaced more traditional dialup or leased circuits, such as T1 lines, that were projected to last for many years.

These changes come in the "good news — bad news" category of stories. The good news is that the price performance of both computing and communications has dramatically improved in the last few years. The bad news is that with these technology advances, the challenges given to network managers have increased in direct proportion. (Some might even claim that their challenges are increasing faster than technology!). But in any event, most of us have to run pretty hard just to keep up, and sometimes we wonder if that simple goal is even attainable.

To address this dilemma, Ray Horak in *Communications Systems and Networks* presents solutions to the challenges that network administrators, designers, and managers face. Ray provides a concise, yet complete, chapter-by-chapter discussion of the technologies that will shape our business communication strategies into the next millennium. I have known Ray for many years, and consider him to be a good friend. He is a respected veteran and consultant in the industry. Undoubtedly many of you have read his journal articles or research reports, or have attended his excellent seminars. This book attempts to capture his vast experience in printed form — the only thing that is missing is his deep Texas accent!

Our hope is that your journey into this exciting industry blending communications and computing technologies will have fewer memory shortages and no packet retransmissions. Make sure to pack this text in your overnight bag as a guidebook along the way.

mark@diginet.com
October 1999

Preface

I was a civil engineering student in Berlin. Berlin is a nice town and there were many opportunities for a student to spend his time in an agreeable manner, for instance with the nice girls. But instead of that we had to perform big and awful calculations.
Konrad Zuse, 1910.

Those of us who have been involved in communications technology for any number of years have witnessed a transformation that truly is revolutionary. The *big and awful* calculations got even bigger and more awful, as the technologies became more complex. Yet, the old voice network remained much the same from the late 1800s through the 1960s — Alexander Graham Bell would have recognized it clearly and understood it completely. Around the time of World War II, however, dramatically new technologies started to make their presence felt. Radio systems began to make their appearance and the foundation for electronic computer systems was laid. Soon thereafter, serious computer systems began to emerge and the need to network them became obvious. Over time, the networks themselves gradually became computerized. During the 1940s, the groundwork also was laid for the development of fiber optics transmission systems, which have the ability to transport incredible volumes of information over very long distances, and with crystal clarity. Videoconferencing systems began to emerge in the 1960s, although they became practical only in the last few years.

The rate of development of the underlying system and network technologies gathered speed in the last 20 years, to the point that it has become difficult for even the most technically astute to keep pace with the rate of change, much less the depth and breadth of its impact. Copper wires have yielded to glass fibers. Rather than flowing through networks in continuous streams over connections, information often moves in packets, frames, and cells . . . sometimes on a connectionless basis. Data rules; but data now includes voice data, video data, image data, and even multimedia data, in addition to traditional *data-data.* The networks not only connect telephones and computers, but also have become networks of computers, themselves. Wired networks are no longer just supplemented by wireless network technologies, but in many applications are being challenged by them, especially where portability and mobility are advantageous. Regulation has yielded to deregulation, most especially with the Telecommunications Act of 1996. Monopolistic companies have been torn apart in the interests of increased competition, only to be reconstituted in altered states when the regulators became convinced that the market, indeed, is the best regulator. Competition has become rife in virtually every sector of the communications world, bringing with it the inherent advantages of alternative choice, improved performance, greater creativity, enhanced technology, lower cost, and a bewildering range of options. CATV providers have entered the fray, offering voice services and Internet access over coaxial cable systems put in place for entertainment TV. The Internet has been commercialized and now is available in virtually every corner of the world, supplanting more traditional means of communication and even threatening more traditional voice and data networks. Underlying Internet technologies and protocols have become the foundation for next-generation networks that promise to replace the circuit-switched network that served us so well for over 100 years. Audio, images, animated images, and even video clips are attached to electronic mail, which only recently became available to all but the technically elite. Voice network technologies are under development that can translate languages in real-time – as we speak.

This book delivers a comprehensive overview of a wide range of communications systems and networks, including voice, data, video, and multimedia. It is written in plain English and provides a commonsense basis for understanding system and network technologies, their origins and evolutions, and the applications they serve. Further, it discusses the origin, evolution, and nature of many relevant standards, and explores remaining standards issues. It also provides a view of the evolution and status of regulation and examines a number of key regulatory issues, which await resolution. From fundamental concepts through the convergence of voice and data networks, and the Information Superhighway, this book offers a single source of information for those who need to understand communications networking. Reserving discussion of volts, amps, ohms, algorithms, and the like for a later date and another book, it weaves a fabric of understanding through a complex set of technologies that underlie meaningful contemporary and future applications. Further, this book is, in effect, a language primer, providing a short course in the vocabulary and syntax of the language of telecommunications – having read this book, you will be conversational in telecommunications techno-speak. Finally, you will understand how networks work, and why.

How This Book is Organized

Let all things be done decently and in order. Bible, 1 Corinthians 14:40

This book is organized into 15 chapters, each of which addresses closely related areas of telecommunications technology and applications, with an eye toward the development of meaningful and cost-effective solutions to legitimate communications requirements. Taken as a whole, this document is a discourse on the origins, current status, and foreseeable future of the networked world. As I weave a bit of a story throughout, it is best read from cover to cover. Those who are either impatient or highly focused, however, will find that each chapter is fully capable of standing on its own.

The first several chapters set the stage for understanding the fundamental nature of systems and networks. Chapter 1 offers a set of basic concepts and provides a set of definitions that apply, fairly universally, across all communications and networks. Chapter 2 offers a detailed explanation of the essentials of transmission systems, both wired and wireless, and including twisted pair, coaxial cable, microwave radio, satellite radio, infrared light, and fiber optics. Each transmission system is explained in detail, and is compared and contrasted with others along a number of critical dimensions.

Chapter 3 is devoted to discussion of communications systems that primarily support voice applications, although they increasingly support data and even video communications. It begins with an examination of the several generations of Private Branch Exchanges (PBXs), their capabilities and applications, as well as emerging trends. This chapter also examines Key Telephone Systems (KTSs), Hybrid systems, and Centrex, the old standby that refuses to fade away. Automatic Call Distributors (ACDs) are profiled and discussed, as well. I conclude with an examination of Computer Telephony (CT) and client/server systems, recent developments that provide tremendous value and efficiency in the processing and management of voice calls.

I dedicate Chapter 4 to electronic messaging technologies and systems, including facsimile, voice processing, and electronic mail. Increasingly, these technologies are viewed as converging into a unified suite of messaging systems, if not a unified information stream. Indeed, we see the beginnings of such unification in the Internet, the World Wide Web (WWW), and next generation IP-based networks.

Chapter 5 provides the initial treatment of voice networks. Concentrating on the Public Switched Telephone Network (PSTN), I address the origin, evolution, and contemporary nature of the traditional voice network. The underlying technologies, regulatory and standards domains, carrier/service provider domains, and functional domains all are discussed. This chapter also defines the nature and specifics of signaling and control systems, which manage and control the operation of the various network elements in order to ensure that the network functions as a whole. A wide variety of voice network services are defined and illustrated. I conclude the chapter with discussion of a number of critical PSTN issues, including numbering plan administration, portability, equal access, and the impact of developing IP-based voice networks.

Chapter 6 begins the discussion of data communications, where I address a number of basic concepts. Data terminal equipment, data communications equipment, communications software, and the network are explained as the various functional domains in a data communications network. Protocols are explained, both as a concept and in terms of certain specific, baseline examples.. I discuss a number of key elements of a data communications protocol, and include specific examples. Network architectures are examined, with concentration on layered operations models such as that of the OSI (Open Systems Interconnection) reference model, which sets the framework for interconnectivity and interoperability. Discussion follows of the various influential standards organizations, with security techniques and issues serving as the conclusion.

Chapter 7 centers on conventional digital and data networks, which are based on the voice network model. I discuss dedicated and circuit-switched networks in the context of both private and public data networks. Specific data network options, presented in rough order of deployment, include DDS, Switched 56 and classic

Virtual Private Networks (VPNs), T-carrier, packet switching, and ISDN. While several of these network options (e.g., T-carrier and ISDN) also support voice and video communications, they are particularly distinguished in their support of data communications in the realm of the Wide Area Network.

Chapter 8 steps back from the traditional wide area network to explore the world of the Local Area Network (LAN). The concept of a LAN was first formally expressed in 1973 and the first standard was published in 1982. Since that time, LANs have grown like kudzu. This chapter defines LANs in terms of fundamental dimensions such as acceptable transmission media, physical and logical topologies, baseband vs. broadband, and medium access control. I also discuss LAN network and internetworking devices, including hubs, bridges, switches, routers, and gateways. Network Operating Systems (NOSs) are presented in the context of the client/server model, and the fundamentals of LAN internetworking are discussed, with emphasis on the Transmission Control Protocol/Internet Protocol (TCP/IP) protocol suite. I finish the chapter with a discussion of recent developments including virtual LANs, remote LAN access, and high-speed LAN technologies and standards such as 100BaseT and Gigabit Ethernet.

Chapters 9 and 10 deal with broadband networking: the high-speed future of communications. I dedicate Chapter 9 to discussion of the physical infrastructure being built in support of broadband networking. The initial focus is on recently developed local-loop technologies, including both wired and wireless alternatives to traditional twisted pair; considerable discussion is devoted to xDSL (generic Digital Subscriber Line) and Wireless Local Loop (WLL) options. The transformation of CATV networks also is discussed in detail, as those coaxial cable networks are being upgraded to support two-way voice and Internet traffic, as well as entertainment TV. I present SONET fiber optics, perhaps the ultimate in broadband, backbone wireline networks, in detail. Chapter 10 focuses on broadband fast packet network services in the forms of Frame Relay, Switched Multimegabit Data Service (SMDS), and Asynchronous Transfer Mode (ATM). The future of broadband networking is projected through examination of the concepts of Broadband ISDN (B-ISDN) and Advanced Intelligent Networks (AINs).

Chapter 11 explores the world of wireless communications — not traditional wireless transmission systems such as microwave and satellite, but rather specialized network alternatives. Popular options I examine include Trunk Mobile Radio (TMR), paging, cellular and PCS, packet radio, and wireless LANs. Low-Earth Orbiting satellites (LEOs) provide a glimpse into one dimension of the future of wireless communications.

Chapter 12 profiles the Internet, which, in fact, has become the first version of the Information Superhighway. The origins of the 'Net are examined, with a profile of its basic nature and structure. I examine Internet access options, equipment, and costs, and discuss issues of regulation and security. Also in this chapter, I explain the TCP/IP protocol suite in considerable detail. A sample of the more interesting and legitimate applications is explored, most especially that of the World Wide Web (WWW).

Chapter 13 provides a view of the world of video and multimedia systems and networks. The addition of a visual dimension enhances communications to a very significant extent, although it places great demands on the supporting networks. As video and multimedia networking is highly capacity intensive and as broadband networks are by no means fully deployed, cost-effective applications remain few. However, the future beckons ... and the future includes video and multimedia.

Chapter 14 addresses network convergence, the coming together of voice, data, video, and entertainment networks. As the networked world becomes increasingly deregulated and as users develop an ever-increasing appetite for ever-more exotic and bandwidth-intensive applications, a host of companies vie to satisfy that hunger. Many consider the Local Exchange Carriers (LECs), or local telephone companies, and IntereXchange Carriers (IXCs) to be the logical providers. Yet, they are being challenged by Community Antenna TeleVision (CATV) providers, data carriers, electric power providers, Competitive Access Providers/Alternative Access Vendors (CAPs/AAVs), and others to deliver voice, data, video, entertainment, and other services. Internet Telephony Service Providers (ITSPs) recently have built networks for the transmission of voice and fax over IP (Internet Protocol); these emerging VoIP networks promise greater efficiencies and lower costs than their circuit-switched predecessors. The stakes are enormous in magnitude, as the outcome will shape the future of the networked world. This chapter explores the status, issues, and likely outcomes.

Chapter 15 rounds out the tour of the networked world with a profile of regulation, both domestic United States and international. The origins, evolution, and current status of regulation are tracked through key legislative, judicial, and agency events. I explore current regulatory issues with emphasis on deregulation and privatization, most especially in the context of the Internet and convergence.

Finally, there are two appendixes. The first provides a complete listing of every germane acronym and abbreviation mentioned in this book — and there are hundreds of them. Consider this appendix to be your "secret decoder ring." It also provides you with a tool for finding your way through the Index, because I don't list subject matter by acronym or abbreviation there. Rather, I list things in the Index in order of the terms, themselves, spelled out fully. The second appendix is a listing of all the standards bodies and special interest groups that I consider relevant. Each listing includes full and current contact information.

What's New in the Second Edition

This second edition is more than just an update of the first, which was published in 1996. In only three short years, such an incredible array of technologies emerged that this book is as much a total rewrite as it is an update. While the basic concepts have remained much the same for the last 100 years or so, thousands of brilliant scientists have taken them to levels that challenge the imagination. The first edition barely made mention of a number of technologies that now is available widely. For that matter, a number of those technologies didn't even exist three years ago. In that context, consider the examples of client/server PBXs, IPv6, 100BaseT, Gigabit Ethernet, 56-Kbps modems and cable modems, Digital Subscriber Line (DSL), Local Multipoint Distribution System (LMDS), Low-Earth Orbiting (LEO) Satellites, Dense Wavelength Division Multiplexing (DWDM), and Voice over Internet Protocol (VoIP). Other technologies, such as Frame Relay and Asynchronous Transfer Mode (ATM), have evolved considerably and are enjoying great success in the marketplace. The Internet and World Wide Web (WWW) have evolved to the point that they bear little resemblance to their 1996 versions.

Acknowledgments

I am a hoarder of two things: documents and trusted friends.
Muriel Spark, "Introduction," *Curriculum Vitae*, 1992.

I owe so much to so many who gave so freely of their knowledge, experience, expertise, time, effort, and technical resources to make this second edition a reality.

The book began, and continued to evolve, as a course manual for my public seminars that were sponsored by *Network World*, as the cornerstone of its Technical Seminar series. Bill Reinstein of *Network World*, with the encouragement of Mark Miller of DigiNet Corporation, had the courage to depart from his highly successful model and to sponsor a series of seminars on network essentials. The result was a seminar designed to introduce datacommunications and its underlying technologies to a new generation of communications professionals. We also updated more than a few old-timers in the process. Bill Reinstein, Deb Mahler, Bill Bernardi, and, Steve Engel made it all happen for me at *Network World*. They are great, and I'll always be indebted to them.

Mark Miller, further, saw a book in that first seminar manual. As a first-time author, the first edition (1996) of *Communications Systems & Networks* nearly killed me, or so it seemed at the time. I thought that this second edition would be much easier, but that wasn't the case at all. In the intervening three years, many of the technologies, their applications, and the service providers all have changed so as to be almost unrecognizeable. So has the regulatory environment changed. This book is a condensation of 30 years of my knowledge and experience, hundreds of years of the knowledge and experience of my professional associates (who, thankfully, also are my friends), and dozens of books and thousands of articles written by others. I am a hoarder of paper, and I forever will owe those authors a debt of gratitude for putting their thoughts and observations on paper and on the Web, so that I could draw from them. Mark was invaluable in the development of this work. As Consulting Editor, he unselfishly applied his unmatched technical expertise to ensure its absolute integrity. Mark put his name on this book, which gives me great pride, for he insists on technical perfection. His 18 or so published books are among the most respected in the industry, and he kindly allowed me to draw from them extensively during the course of this work. Thank you, Mark, for your friendship, your guidance, and your technical brilliance.

Rick Luhmann, as Technical Editor, provided a great deal of guidance across a wide range of technologies and applications. Rick is perhaps as knowledgeable as anyone in the area of Computer Telephony, and he is a prolific writer with an uncanny sense for the applications side of techology. Thank you, Rick, for your honest friendship, your help in so many ways, and your quirky sense of humor.

Elyn Wollensky, of IDG Books Worldwide, has acted as Development Editor on this second edition. It has been such a joy to work with her. My thanks also to

Victoria Lee, my copyeditor; Julie Smith, my in-house copyeditor; Linda Marousek and Tom Debolski, my production coordinators.

During the course of these several editions, a number of other individuals provided me with free and easy access to their extensive libraries. I owe John Bray, Don Hiatt, Dr. Heather Hudson, Rick Luhmann, Jeff Owen, and Gerry Ryan a deep debt of gratitude.

I also am indebted to the tens of thousands of people who have attended my public and private seminars over the past dozen years. I never taught a seminar that I didn't learn something about a technology, or an application, or a way to phrase a concept to make it more understandable. The same thing goes for my hundreds of consulting engagements over the past years. It is such a pleasure to do something that you love, to work with people who are enthusiastic and giving, to learn at the same time that you teach, and to get paid for all of it. Thank you all so very much.

Most of all, I am forever indebted to Margaret Horak, my lovely wife. We met some 20 years ago, but circumstances caused us to lose each other for some 16 years. Quite by accident, we found each other again through an article I wrote for Rick Luhmann, who then was Editor-In-Chief of *Teleconnect* magazine. That article, quite clearly, was my greatest literary achievement. Margaret's love and devotion have translated into long hours of graphics development in the late hours of the night and on the weekends. Her graphic interpretations of my words have added immeasurably to this work. Also, her commonsense, level-headedness, good nature, and wonderful sense of humor kept me focused, and helped me put this all in perspective. Her love for me made me work ever harder to make her proud. I can only hope that I succeeded, for Margaret truly is a treasure. Margaret, you are my heart and my soul.

It is not enough to wire the world if you short-circuit the soul. Technology without heart is not enough. Tom Brokaw in a speech at commencement exercises at the College of Sante Fe (NM), May 15, 1999.

Contents at a Glance

Contents

Figures

Tables

Chapter 1

Fundamentals of the Technology: Concepts and Definitions

I see no reason why intelligence may not be transmitted instantaneously by electricity.
Samuel Morse, 1832

Telecommunications is the transfer of information (*communications*) from a transmitter or sender to a receiver across a distance (*tele*). Some form of electromagnetic energy is employed to represent the data, usually through a physical medium, such as a copper wire or a glass fiber. A wireless medium, such as radio or infrared light, also may be employed. Additionally, a number of intermediate devices are typically involved in setting up a path for the information transfer and for maintaining adequate signal strength.

The information transfer must be established and maintained at acceptable levels in terms of certain key criteria such as speed of connection, speed of information transfer, speed of response, freedom from error and, finally, cost. The information can be voice, data, video, image, or some combination of these – in other words, multimedia. The information can transmit in its original, or native, form. Alternatively, the data can be altered in some way in order to effect compatibility between the transmit and receive devices, and/or with the various elements of the network. Examples include analog voice or video converted to a digital (data) bit stream, digitized voice or video converted to analog voice or video, and digital data converted to an analog format. Additionally, the information can be, and often is compressed through what effectively is some form of data "shorthand" in order to improve the efficiency of information transfer.

The electromagnetic energy employed to carry the data can be in the form of electricity, radio, or light. The medium employed can include copper wire (e.g., twisted pair or coaxial cable); space, or airwaves (e.g., microwave, satellite, cellular, or infrared); and glass or plastic fiber (fiber optic cable). In a network of substantial size that spans a significant distance, a combination of transmission media typically is involved in the information between transmitter and receiver. In fact, an intercontinental voice or data call might involve a combination of many media.

Additionally, you might use a wide variety of intermediate devices in order to establish the connection and support the information transfer. Such devices may include an appropriate combination of modems or codecs, controllers, concentrators, multiplexers, bridges, switches, routers, gateways, and so on.

This chapter examines a number of concepts and defines a fundamental set of elements that apply universally to communications networks. Distinctions are drawn among dedicated, switched, and virtual circuits, with two-wire and four-wire circuits defined and illustrated. The concept of bandwidth is explored in both analog and digital terms, with the advantages and disadvantages of each explained. The concept of multiplexers is discussed in detail, with variations on the theme detailed and illustrated. Finally, this chapter explores the nature and evolution of various types of switches, including circuit, packet, frame, and cell.

Fundamental Definitions

Developing a solid understanding of communications networking requires that one grasp a number of fundamental definitions. The following terms are significant and are applied fairly universally across all voice, data, video, and other systems and network technologies.

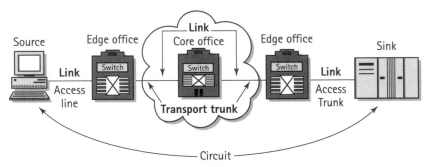

Figure 1-1 Simple circuit between transmitter and receiver across a network, involving multiple links and switches.

Transmitter The *transmitter*, also known as the *sender* or *source,* is the device that originates the information transfer. Transmitters include voice telephones, data terminals, host computer systems, and video cameras.

Receiver The *receiver*, also known as the *sink*, is the *target* device, or *destination* device, which receives the information transfer. Receivers can include telephones, host computers, and video monitors. Note that most devices have both transmitter and receiver functions contained under the skin of the same box; exceptions include broadcast radio and TV devices.

Circuit A *circuit* is a communications path, over an established medium, between two or more points, from end-to-end, between transmitter and receiver. *Circuit* generally implies a *logical connection* over a *physical line*. Further, the term circuit often is used interchangeably with *path*, *link*, *line* and *channel*, although such usage can be specific to the underlying technology, the context and other factors. Circuits are either *two-wire* or *four-wire*, depending on the requirements of the specific application and the fundamental nature of the network. Circuits also may be for purposes of either transport or access. *Access* circuits are from the customer premises to the edge of the carrier network, while *transport* circuits are employed in the core of the network for purposes of long-haul transmission. Circuits may be *simplex* (one-way), *half-duplex* (two-way, but only one way at a time), or *full-duplex* (simultaneous two-way).

Link A *link* is a two-point segment of an end-to-end circuit (e.g., from terminal to switch, or from switch to switch). Typically, a circuit comprises multiple links. Also, a circuit may consist of a single link, as often is the case between a host computer and a peripheral, such as a printer. *Link* sometimes is used interchangeably with *line* or *circuit*.

Line The term *line* has several definitions, which may result in confusion. In a PBX environment, a *station line* refers to the connection between the PBX switch and the station user's terminal equipment, represented in the form of an analog or digital telephone, or a computer workstation. In rate and tariff terminology, *line* refers to a *local loop* connection from the telephone company Central Office (CO) switch to the user premises in support of Customer Premise Equipment (CPE) other than a switch. For example, such CPE may be in the form of a single-line residence or business set, a multiline set, or the common control unit of a key telephone system. In either event, *line* refers to a *voice grade* circuit; in other words, a circuit serving a single physical location and terminating in a relatively unsophisticated device with a single associated telephone number and, generally, supporting a single transmission. In telco (telephone company) parlance, *line* describes the user side or local loop side of the connection; in other words, the *line side* is the side of the network to which users connect to access the network. The *trunk side* involves the high-capacity trunks, which interconnect the various telco switching centers inside the carrier network.

Trunk A *trunk* is a communications circuit, available to share among multiple users, on a pooled basis and with contention for trunk access managed by an intelligent switching device. Therefore, trunks connect *switches*. For example, *tie trunks* connect PBX switches in a private, leased line network, *central office exchange trunks* connect PBXs to telephone company central office exchange switches, and *interoffice trunks* interconnect central office exchange switches. *Trunk groups* are groups of trunks serving the same special purpose; examples include WATS (Wide Area Telecommunications Service) and DID (Direct Inward Dial) trunk groups. Trunks are directional; i.e., they can be one-way outgoing (originating), one-way incoming (terminating), or two-way (combination).

Channel In formal standards terms, a *channel* is a means of one-way connection between transmitter and receiver; therefore, a one-way *circuit* or *path*. In data processing terminology, particularly IBM, a channel is a high-speed connection between mainframe and peripheral. In common usage, a channel is a *logical* connection over a *physical* circuit to support a single conversation. You can configure a physical circuit in such a way as to support one or many logical conversations. Multichannel circuits always are four-wire in nature – either physical or logical four-wire.

Switch A *switch* device establishes, maintains, and changes logical connections over physical circuits. Common examples of switches include PBXs and Central Office Exchanges (COs or COEs), both of which are circuit switches. Circuit switches establish connections between circuits (or links), on demand and as available. While developed to support voice communications, circuit switches can support any form of information transfer (e.g., data and video communications). Packet, frame and cell switching recently evolved in more sophisticated networks, primarily in support of data and image transfer. *Edge switches* are positioned at the edge of the network; the user organization gains access to the edge switch via an access link. *Core switches*, also known as *tandem switches*, are high-capacity switches positioned in the core of the network and serving to interconnect edge switches.

Network A *network* is a fabric of elements which work together to support the transfer of information. In the extreme sense, a network includes everything from the transmitter to the receiver, including all links, and all involved switches and other intermediate devices. The wide area carrier network (Figure 1-1) commonly is depicted as a *cloud*, which originated in sales presentations of the 1970s for data communications networks. The thought behind the *cloud* simply was that the specific internal workings of the networks could be many and various, change from time to time, and vary from place to place. The *cloud* served to obscure those internal workings from view. The *cloud* was the consummate conceptual sale – data simply popped in on one end of the network and popped out on the other.

Dedicated, Switched, and Virtual Circuits

Circuits can be provisioned on a dedicated, switched, or virtual basis, depending on the nature of the application and the requirements of the user organization. Ultimately, issues of availability and cost-effectiveness determine the specific selection.

Dedicated Circuits

Dedicated circuits involve dedicated physical circuits, which directly connect devices (e.g., PBXs and host computers) across a network (Figure 1-2). Dedicated circuits make use of access circuits, in the form of local loops, to access the carrier's Point of

Presence (POP) and the edge of the carrier network. Rather than accessing a switch port at the POP, a dedicated circuit terminates in the carrier *wire center*, where cross connections are made to long-haul transport circuits. Dedicated circuits serve a single user organization only, rather than serving multiple users. Dedicated circuits offer users the advantage of a high degree of availability, as well as specified levels of capacity and quality. You can condition dedicated circuits to deliver specific levels of performance, whereas you generally cannot with switched circuits. Additionally, dedicated circuit costs are not usage-sensitive; that is to say that you can use them continuously and to their full capacity without additional costs. However, the reservation of a circuit for a specific customer has a deleterious effect on the network provider (carrier), since that circuit was taken out of shared public use and, therefore, is unavailable for use in support of the traffic of other users. As a result, dedicated circuits tend to be rather expensive with their costs being sensitive to distance and capacity. Additionally, the process of determining the correct number, capacity, and points of termination of such circuits can be a difficult and lengthy design and configuration process. Further, long lead times often are required for the carrier to configure (provision) or reconfigure such a circuit. Finally, as dedicated circuits are susceptible to disruption, backup circuits often are required to ensure effective communications in the event of either a catastrophic failure or serious performance degradation. Traditionally, dedicated digital circuits have connected large data centers which communicate intensively; similarly, many large end user organizations with multiple locations have used dedicated circuits to tie together multiple PBXs. In both cases, the advantages of assured availability, capacity, and quality often outweigh considerations of configuration difficulty and risk of circuit failure. Dedicated circuits often are known as *nailed-up circuits* because the twisted-pair copper circuits were hung from nails driven in the walls of the carrier's wire centers.

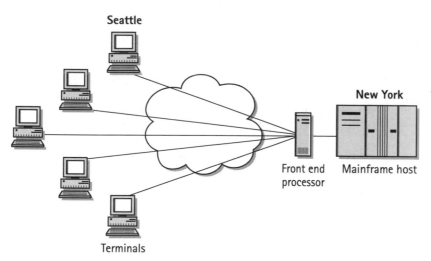

Figure 1-2 Dedicated circuits between Seattle data terminals and a New York mainframe, through a Front-End Processor (FEP).

Switched Circuits

Switched circuits are connected through the network on a flexible basis through one or more intermediate switching devices. Traditionally, the switches were in the form of the telephone company Central Office exchanges, as illustrated in Figure 1-3. As each switch serves as a contention device, switched circuits are shared, on demand and as available, among multiple users. As a result, the network providers clearly realize significant operational efficiencies, which are reflected in lower costs to end users. The end users realize the additional advantages of flexibility and redundancy because the network generally can provide connection between any two physical locations through multiple alternate transmission paths.

Figure 1-3 Circuit-switched connectivity between single-line telephone sets and data terminals through a Central Office switch.

In the voice world, all local, regional, and national networks are interconnected; however, a similarly high level of interconnection typically is not provided in the data world. The cost of establishing switched circuits traditionally is sensitive to factors such as the distance between originating and terminating locations, duration of the connection, time of day (prime time vs. non-prime time), and day of the year (business day vs. weekend day or holiday). Yet, switched circuits offer great advantage for calls of short duration, connection between specific locations that communicate relatively infrequently, in cases where network redundancy is important, and at times when a high degree of flexibility is advantageous. Currently, the vast majority of voice calls are carried over switched circuits.

Virtual Circuits

Virtual circuits are logical, rather than physical, circuits. Virtual circuit connectivity is provided over high-capacity, multichannel physical circuits, such as fiber optic transmission facilities. Virtual circuits are established through the network based on options defined in software routing tables. *Permanent Virtual Circuits* (PVCs) are permanently defined in routing tables, until such time as the carrier permanently redefines them. *Switched Virtual Circuits* (SVCs) are determined at the time the communication is requested, with relatively sophisticated devices making highly informed decisions about the best path available in support of the specific requirements of the communication to be supported. In either case, a virtual circuit provides connectivity much as though it were a physical circuit. Such a physical circuit often can support a great number of logical circuits, or logical connections. In the high-capacity, fiber optic backbone carrier networks, dedicated circuits are provided to users on a virtual basis; the capacity and other performance characteristics of the circuit performing as though the circuit were dedicated.

Now, it is worth pausing to further define and contrast the terms *transparent* and *virtual*. Transparent means that a network element (e.g., hardware or software) exists, but appears to the user as though it does not. Virtual means that the network element does not exist, but appears to the user as though it does. In this context, a user can access a virtual circuit on a transparent basis.

It also is necessary to further define a *logical circuit* or channel, as opposed to a physical one. A logical circuit refers to the entire range of network elements (e.g., physical circuits, buffers, switches, and control devices) which support or manage communication between a transmitter and receiver. In order to establish and support the information transfer, a physical path must be selected for the information transfer. The transmission facilities in the physical path may be in the form of copper wire (e.g., twisted pair or coaxial cable), radio (e.g., microwave or satellite), or glass or plastic fiber (fiber optic) [1-1].

Two-Wire versus Four-Wire Circuits

Early telegraphy and telephony communication circuits originally were metallic one-wire, which proved satisfactory even for two-way communications. Soon after the invention of the telephone, however, two-wire circuits were found to offer much better performance characteristics, due largely to their improved immunity from electrical interference. Four-wire offers still better performance, although at higher cost. Both two- and four-wire circuits are widely used, although the trend points toward using four-wire.

Two-Wire Circuits

Two-wire circuits carry information signals in both directions over the same physical link or path. Typically, such a circuit is provisioned through the use of a single twisted pair, copper wire connection. Within such a two-wire circuit, two wires are required to complete the electrical circuit, and both wires carry the information signal. A common example is a local loop connection between a telephone company's Central Office (CO) switching center and an individual single-line-or multi-line residence telephone set, or a business Key Telephone System (KTS), as depicted in Figure 1-4.

Two-wire circuits generally cover a short distance; for instance, the vast majority of two-wire local loops are less than 18,000 feet [1-2]; longer loop lengths require some form of amplification in order to maintain signal strength. Additionally, such a circuit offers relatively little bandwidth or capacity, and is single-channel in nature (i.e., supports only a single conversation). Finally, two-wire circuits, generally speaking, are analog in nature; therefore, error performance (quality) is relatively poor. Two-wire circuits often are characterized as *voice grade* – good enough for voice communications between humans, who are capable of adapting to errors in transmission over a circuit of relatively poor quality. A voice grade circuit also will support data transmission through a modem, which has internal mechanisms for dealing with errors in transmission.

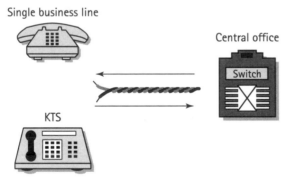

Figure 1-4 Two-wire, twisted pair, local loop connection between a
            Central Office Exchange and a single-line set or Key
            Telephone System (KTS).

Four-Wire Circuits

According to the most basic definition, *four-wire circuits* carry information signals in both directions over separate physical links or paths, and in support of simultaneous, two-way transmission. Traditionally, such a circuit was provisioned through the use of two copper pairs, one for transmission (*forward path*) and one for reception (*reverse path*); such a circuit is known as *physical four-wire*. However, current technology accommodates four-wire transmission over a single physical link or path, and over a variety of transmission media, including twisted pair, coaxial cable, or fiber optic cable. In other words, the circuit may be physical two-wire (or even physical one-wire) and *logical four-wire*, performing as a four-wire circuit but employing fewer than four wires. In fact, a four-wire circuit can be established without the use of any wires at all, as in the case with a circuit established over microwave, satellite, or infrared transmission systems.

Although the absolute cost of four-wire circuits is higher than that of two-wire circuits, they offer considerably improved performance. Four-wire circuits accommodate multiple, simultaneous communications in a two-way, or conversational, mode – all multichannel circuits are four-wire. Additionally, such circuits typically offer much greater bandwidth, or capacity, and typically are digital, rather than analog, in nature. As a result, error performance generally improves. Long-haul circuits (traditionally defined as equal to or greater than 50 miles, or 80 km) usually are four-wire [1-3], as the carriers, or service providers, typically aggregate large volumes of traffic for transport over multichannel facilities. Figure 1-5 illustrates typical examples of cost-effective applications of four-wire circuits, specifically to interconnect PBX, CO, and tandem switches in a voice environment.

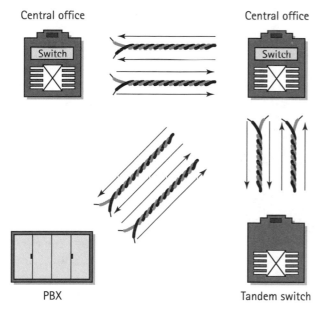

Figure 1-5 Four-wire, twisted pair trunk connections between a Central Office Exchange and a PBX, Tandem Office Exchange, and Central Office Exchanges

Bandwidth

Bandwidth is a measure of the capacity of a circuit or channel. More specifically, it refers to the total frequency on the available *carrier* for the transmission of data. There is a direct relationship between the bandwidth of a circuit or channel and both its frequency and the difference between the minimum and maximum frequencies supported. While the information signal (bandwidth usable for data transmission) does not occupy the total capacity of a circuit, it generally and ideally occupies most of it. The balance of the capacity of the circuit may be used for signaling and control (overhead) purposes. In other words, the total *signaling rate* of the circuit typically is greater than the effective *transmission rate*. The more information you need to send in a given period of time, the more bandwidth you require.

Carrier

Carrier is a constant signal on a circuit that is at a certain frequency, or within a certain frequency range. While the primary value of the carrier is in its support of the information-bearing signal, it also can support signaling and control information, used to coordinate and manage network operation.

Hertz (Hz)

Hertz, named after Heinrich Rudolf Hertz, the physicist who discovered radio waves, is the measurement of bandwidth over analog circuits. *Hz* refers to the number of electromagnetic wave forms (signals or signal changes) transmitted per second. Although some applications operate in very low-capacity environments, measured in Hz or hundreds of Hz, the frequencies generally are much higher. Hence, you can measure analog bandwidth in kHz or kiloHertz (thousands of Hz); MHz or MegaHertz (millions of Hz); or GHz or GigaHertz (billions of Hz).

Baud

Baud is an olde term which refers to the number of signal events (signals or signal changes) occurring per second over an analog circuit. In contemporary usage, baud rate describes the signaling rate of a modem for data transmission over an analog circuit, and is roughly equivalent to Hertz. *Baud rate* and *bps* (bits per second), often and incorrectly, are used interchangeably. Chapter 6 explores the distinction in more detail.

Bits Per Second (bps)

Bps is the measurement of bandwidth over digital circuits, referring to the number of binary data bits transmitted per second. Over an analog circuit, you can manipulate the sine wave to allow multiple bits to be transmitted at a given baud rate, even without the application of special compression techniques. A thousand (1,000) bps is a kilobit per second or *Kbps,* a million (1,000,000) bps is a Megabit per second or *Mbps,* a billion (1,000,000,000) bps is a Gigabit per second or *Gbps,* and a trillion (1,000,000,000,000) bps is a Terabit per second or *Tbps.*

Transmission Facilities

The level of bandwidth, in the contemporary digital context, falls into three categories: narrowband, wideband, or broadband.

Narrowband	Narrowband is a single channel of 64 Kbps or less, or some number of 64 Kbps channels (N x 64 Kbps), but less than wideband.
Wideband	Wideband is capacity between 1.544 Mbps (T-1) and 45 Mbps (T-3), according to North American standards, and between 2.048 Mbps (E-1) and 34 Mbps (E-3), according to European and international standards.
Broadband	Broadband is capacity equal to or greater than 45 Mbps (T-3), according to North American standards (equal to or greater than 34 Mbps, according to European and international standards).

Analog versus Digital

Along one dimension, communications fall into two categories, analog and digital. In the analog form of electronic communications, information is represented as a continuous electromagnetic wave form. Digital communications represents information in binary form (*1*'s and *0*'s) through a series of blips or pulses of discrete values.

Analog Sine Waves: The Starting Point

Analog is best explained by examining the transmission of a natural form of information, such as sound or human speech, over an electrified copper wire. In its native form, human speech is an oscillatory disturbance in the air which varies in terms of its volume or power (amplitude), and its pitch or tone (frequency). In this native acoustical mode, the variations in amplitude cause the physical matter in the air to vibrate with greater or lesser intensity; the variations in frequency cause the physical matter in the air to vibrate with greater or lesser frequency. As native voice air compression waves fall onto a transmitter, *analogous* (approximate) variations in electrical waveforms form over an electrical circuit. Those waveforms maintain their various shapes across the wire until they fall on the receiver or speaker, which converts them back into their original acoustical form of variations in air pressure.

A similar, but more complicated, conversion process transmits video over networks. In its native form, video is a series of still images, each comprising reflected light waves. Transmitted in rapid succession, the series of still images creates the illusion of fluidity of motion. Analogous variations in electrical or radio waves form in order to transmit the video image information signal over a network from a transmitter (i.e., video camera) to a receiver (i.e., monitor), where an approximation (analog) of the original information is presented.

Information which is analog in its native form (voice and image) can vary continuously in terms of intensity (volume or brightness) and frequency (tone or color). Transmission of the native information stream over an electrified analog network involves the translation of those variations into amplitude and frequency variations of the carrier signal. In other words, the carrier signal is *modulated* (varied) in order to create an *analog* of the original information stream.

The electromagnetic sinusoidal waveform, or *sine wave*, can be varied in amplitude at a fixed frequency, using Amplitude Modulation (AM). Alternatively, the frequency of the sine wave can be varied at a constant amplitude, using Frequency Modulation (FM). Additionally, both frequency and amplitude can be modulated simultaneously to create an analog of the native signal, which generally varies simultaneously along both parameters. Finally, the position of the sine wave can be manipulated (actually, can appear to be manipulated), adding the third technique of Phase Modulation (also known as Phase Shift Keying or PSK) and providing additional benefits which will be discussed in Chapter 6.

Bandwidth, in the analog world, is measured in Hertz (Hz). The available bandwidth for a particular signal is the difference between the highest and lowest frequencies supported. For example, a 3.3 kHz voice channel can be provided through a band-limiting filter supporting transmission at frequencies between 200 Hz and 3,500 Hz. Similarly, a 3.3 kHz channel can be provided at frequencies between 7,000 Hz and 10,300 Hz. *Passband* refers to the upper and lower cutoff frequencies at which the filters operate [1-2].

Voice

The signaling rate of a voice grade channel is approximately 4,000 Hz, or 4 kHz. Approximately 3.3 kHz (200 Hz-3,500 Hz) is used for the voice signal itself; the remaining bandwidth is used for network signaling and control, and for maintaining separation between information channels, each of which is supported over a separate carrier frequency range. While human speech can transmit and human hearing can receive a much wider range of frequencies, 3.3 kHz is considered sufficient for voice communications and certainly is more cost-effective than if full-fidelity voice were to be supported. Band-limiting filters employed in carrier networks constrain the amount of bandwidth provided for a voice application [1-3] and [1-4]. Figure 1-6 illustrates an analog local loop supporting voice communications.

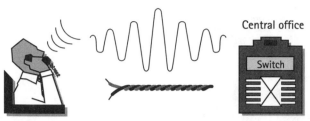

Figure 1-6 Analog voice transmission over a two-wire local loop.

Video

A CATV video channel is approximately 6,000,000 Hz, or 6 MHz. Approximately 4.5 MHz is used for transmission of the video signal, while the balance is used for guard bands to separate the various adjacent channels riding the common, analog coaxial cable system.

Digital Bit Streams: Ones and Zeros

While the natural world is analog in nature, the decidedly unnatural world of computers is digital in nature. Computers process, store, and communicate information in *binary* form. That is to say that a unique combination of *1*s and *0*s has a specific meaning in a computer alphabet, or coding scheme. A *bit* (*binary digit*) is an individual *1* or *0*. The output of a computer is in the form of a *digital bit stream*.

Digital communications dates to telegraphy, in which the varying length of making and breaking an electrical circuit resulted in a series of *dots* and *dashes* that, in a particular combination, communicated a character or series of characters. Early mechanical computers used a similar concept for input and output; contemporary computer systems communicate in binary mode through variations in electrical voltage.

Digital signaling, in an electrical network, involves a signal that varies in voltage to represent one of two discrete and well-defined states. *Unipolar* signaling makes use of a positive (+) voltage and a *null*, or zero (0), voltage; *bipolar* signaling makes use of a positive (+) or a negative (-) voltage. The receiver monitors the signal, at a specific carrier frequency and for a specific duration (*bit time*), to determine the state of the signal. Various data transmission protocols employ different physical states of the signal, such as voltage level or voltage transition. Because of the discrete nature of each bit transmitted, the bit form is often referred to as a *square wave*. Digital devices (Figure 1-7) prefer digital transmission facilities.

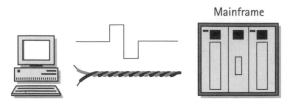

Figure 1-7 Digital communications between a terminal and mainframe.

Digital signaling in an optical network can involve either the pulsing on and off of a light stream, or a discrete variation in the intensity of the light signal. Digital transmission over radio systems (e.g., microwave, cellular, or satellite) can be accomplished by discretely varying the amplitude of the signal.

Bandwidth, in the digital world, is measured in bits per second (bps). The amount of bandwidth required depends on the amount of raw data to be sent, the desired speed of transmission of that set of data, and issues of transmission cost. Prior to its presentation to the circuit, and in order to improve the efficiency of transmission, reduce the transmission time, and thereby reduce transmission costs. Additionally, analog voice commonly is converted to a digital bit stream, requiring a maximum of 64 Kbps for acceptable fidelity, or quality.

Analog versus Digital Transmission: Which Is Better?

Although analog voice and video can be converted to digital bit streams, and digital data can be converted to analog, each format has its advantages.

Analog Advantages

Analog transmission offers advantages in the transmission of analog information. Additionally, it is more bandwidth-conservative and is widely available.

ANALOG DATA

Analog has an advantage with respect to the transmission of information that is analog in its native form, such as voice and video. The process of transmission of such information is relatively straightforward in an analog format, as the continuous flow of the native signal is easily and fully represented in the continuous flow of the carrier signal. Conversion of analog data to a digital bit stream requires special conversion equipment. Such equipment adds cost, contributes additional points of failure, and can negatively affect the quality of the signal through the conversion process itself. The impacts on analog and digital conversions are discussed fully in the explanation of T-carrier in Chapter 7.

BANDWIDTH

A raw analog information stream consumes less bandwidth in analog form than in digital form. This is particularly evident in CATV transmission, where 50 or more analog channels routinely are provided over a single coaxial cable system. Without the application of compression techniques,many fewer digital channels could be supported.

PRESENCE

Finally, analog transmission systems are in place, worldwide. All aspects of the standards are well understood and easily implemented, and the interconnection of analog systems is routine. As voice comprises the majority of network traffic and as the vast majority of voice terminals are analog devices, voice communications largely depends on analog networks at the local loop level; conversion to digital networks requires expensive, wholesale conversion of such terminal equipment and local loops.

Digital Advantages

Digital transmission is advantageous for the transmission of digital information. Additionally, such data can be compressed effectively and easily. Security of the data can be more readily ensured and the error performance of digital networks is much improved over their analog counterparts. Finally, the cost-effectiveness of such networks is improved by virtue of the greater bandwidth they provide, especially since they can be more easily upgraded as well as more effectively managed.

DIGITAL DATA

Just as it often is better to transmit analog information in an analog format, it is better to transmit digital information in a digital format. Digital transmission certainly has the advantage when transmitting binary computer data. The equipment required to convert the information to an analog format and send the digital bit streams over an analog network can be expensive, susceptible to failure, and error-laden.

COMPRESSION

Digital data can be compressed relatively easily, thereby increasing the efficiency of transmission. As a result, substantial volumes of voice, data, video, and image information can be transmitted using relatively little raw bandwidth.

SECURITY

Digital systems offer much improved security. While analog systems can offer some measure of security through the *scrambling*, or intertwining, of several frequencies, you can fairly easily defeat that technique. Digital information, conversely, can be *encrypted* to create the appearance of a single, pseudo-random bit stream. Thereby, the true meaning of individual bits, sets of bits, or the total bit stream cannot be determined without the key to unlock the encryption algorithm employed.

ERROR PERFORMANCE

Digital transmission offers much improved error performance (quality) in comparison with analog. This is due to the nature of the devices that serve to boost the signal at periodic intervals in the transmission system to overcome the effects of *attenuation*. Additionally, digital networks deal more effectively with *noise*, which always is present in transmission networks.

Attenuation Electromagnetic signals tend to weaken, or *attenuate*, over a distance; this is particularly true of electrical signals carried over twisted pair copper wire, due to the level of resistance in the wire. It also is true of microwave radio and other terrestrial radio systems, due to the physical matter in the air. Attenuation is sensitive to carrier frequency, with higher frequency signals attenuating more than lower frequency signals.

Noise Signals also tend to pick up noise as they transverse the network. Again, this is particularly true of twisted pair, copper wire systems. Such wires tend to act as antennae and, therefore, absorb noise from outside sources of *ElectroMagnetic Interference (EMI)* and *Radio Frequency Interference (RFI)*. Thus, the quality of the signal degenerates as it is distorted by the noise.

COST

The cost of the computer components required in the digital conversion and transmission process has dropped to a considerable extent, while the ruggedness and reliability of those components has increased over the years.

UPGRADEABILITY

Since digital networks comprise computer (digital) components, they can relatively easily be upgraded. Such upgrades might increase bandwidth, improve error performance, and enhance functionality. Some such upgrades can be effected through a software download over the network, thereby eliminating the need to "roll a truck," i.e., dispatch a technician.

MANAGEMENT

Generally speaking, digital networks can be managed much more easily and effectively because they comprise computerized *Network Elements* (NEs). Such components can be endowed by their creators with the abilities to determine their status (i.e., on or off), sense their own levels of performance relative to programmed thresholds, isolate and diagnose failures, initiate alarms to upstream management systems, respond to queries, and respond to commands to correct the failure condition. Further, the cost of so enabling these devices is dropping rapidly.

Amplifiers versus Repeaters

As we have noted, electromagnetic energy attenuates over a distance through either a conductor or the air. Therefore, you must place some sort of device at regular spatial intervals in a network to overcome this phenomenon. These boosting units receive a weakened incoming signal and transmit a stronger outgoing signal, which propagates across the network until it reaches another boosting unit, and so on. Analog networks make use of devices known as *amplifiers*, while *repeaters* are employed in digital networks.

> *On long lines the current often becomes so reduced by leakage, and from other causes, that it is insufficient to work an electro-magnet, either to mark paper, or give audible sound. It is therefore usual on such lines to interpose an instrument called a relay. A current weakened by distance, although unable to effectively work the receiving instrument, may have enough force to cause a light armature to be attracted by a small magnet. This movement may be made to bring a local battery into circuit so as to strengthen the current, and such an arrangement constitutes a relay.* Source: *Wonders of the Universe.* The Werner Company. 1899. [1-5]

Amplifiers (Analog)

The boosting devices in an analog network are known as *amplifiers*. Amplifiers are unsophisticated devices that simply boost, or amplify, the weak incoming signal, much as does an amplifier in a radio or TV. In addition to attenuating, the signal accumulates noise as it transverses the network; the amplifier boosts the noise along with the signal. This effect is compounded through every step of the transmission system and through each cascading amplifier, thereby creating the potential for significant accumulated noise at the receiving end of the transmission. Theresulting *signal-to-noise ratio* can produce unacceptable results. Amplifiers are spaced every 18,000 feet or so in a typical analog network.

> *If you take a bale of hay and tie it to the tail of a mule and then strike a match and set the bale of hay on fire, and if you then compare the energy expended shortly thereafter by the mule with the energy expended by yourself in the striking of the match, you will understand the concept of amplification.* William Shockley, co-inventor of the transistor [1-6].

The impact of amplification on voice communications generally is tolerable, as humans are relatively intelligent receivers who can filter out the noise or at least adjust to it. In the event of a truly garbled transmission, the human-to-human error detection and correction process simply involves a request for retransmission – the *Huh?* protocol. Should the quality of the connection be totally unacceptable, you can terminate and re-establish the connection. Computer systems, however, are not so forgiving, and garbled data is of decidedly negative value.

The exception to this broad characterization of amplifiers is that of Erbium-Doped Fiber Amplifiers (EDFAs), used in high-speed, fiber optic systems. EDFAs amplify light signals falling in a narrow optical frequency range, performing much more cost-effectively than optical repeaters. Note that high-speed, fiber optic transmission systems are noise-free; therefore, the use of amplifiers generally is not a significant issue. Chapter 9 discusses EDFAs in more detail.

Repeaters (Digital)

Digital systems replace periodic amplifiers with *regenerative repeaters*, which regenerate the signal, rather than simply amplifying it. In essence, the repeater guesses the binary value (1 or 0) of the weak incoming signal based on its relative voltage level (in an electrically-based system), and regenerates a strong signal of the same value, without the noise. This process enhances the signal quality immensely. Repeaters are spaced at approximately the same intervals as amplifiers, although spacing is sensitive to the carrier frequency, which affects both the transmission speed, or bandwidth provided, and the level of attenuation experienced.

The performance advantage of digital networks can be illustrated by comparing the error rates of amplifiers and regenerative repeaters. For example, a twisted-pair, analog network yields an error rate on the order of 10^{-5} [1-3]. In other words, digital data sent across an analog network will suffer 1 errored bit for every 100,000 bits transmitted (Figure 1-8). The very same twisted-pair network, if digitized and equipped with repeaters, will yield an expected error rate of 10^{-7}, or 1 errored bit in every 10,000,000 — an improvement of two orders of magnitude. Digital fiber optic systems, currently considered to be the ultimate, yield error rates in the range of 10^{-11}-10^{-14}, or an error rate as low as 1 bit for every 100,000,000,000,000 transmitted, which is virtually perfect [1-4].

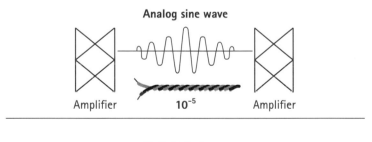

Analog sine wave

Amplifier 10^{-5} Amplifier

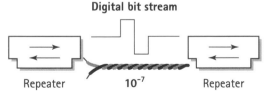

Digital bit stream

Repeater 10^{-7} Repeater

Figure 1-8 Comparative error performance of analog vs. digital transmission over twisted pair.

The Conversion Process: Modems and Codecs

Regardless of the relative merits of analog and digital transmission, both technologies are in place. Local loops, which connect the user premise to the central office exchange, generally are analog, at least in residential and small business applications. Medium and large-sized businesses typically make use of digital local loops in the form of either T-carrier or ISDN. Most U.S. cellular radio networks are analog, although digital networks are increasingly available. High-capacity, backbone carrier transmission generally is digital. Analog-to-digital and digital-to-analog conversions take place routinely.

Digital-to-Analog: Modems

As local loops often are analog, computer communications across such circuits is not possible without the assistance of a device to accomplish the digital-to-analog conversion. Of course, one might gain access to a more expensive digital circuit, by so specifying, if available.

The device which accomplishes the D-to-A (Digital-to-Analog) conversion process is known as a *modem*. Modems *mo*dulate and *dem*odulate the analog sine wave in order to represent digital bit streams across the analog local loop, reconstructing the digital signal on the receiving end through a process of an A-to-D (Analog-to-Digital) conversion (Figure 1-9). A variety of techniques, explained in Chapter 6, are used to accomplish this process.

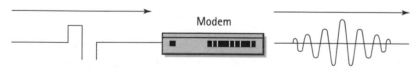

Figure 1-9 Modem: Digital-to-Analog conversion.

Analog-to-Digital: Codecs

The reverse conversion process is necessary to send analog information across a digital circuit. Certainly, this occurs often in carrier networks, where huge volumes of analog voice are digitized and sent across high-capacity, digital circuits. This requirement also exists where high-capacity digital circuits connect premise-based, PBX voice systems to Central Office exchanges or to other PBXs, assuming that the PBXs or COs have not already performed the conversion. As video also is analog in its native form, a similar process must be employed to send such information across a digital circuit.

The device that accomplishes the A-to-D conversion is called a *codec*. Codecs code an analog input into a digital (data) format on the transmit side of the connection, reversing the process, or *decoding* the information, on the receive side, to reconstitute an approximation of the original analog signal (Figure 1-10).

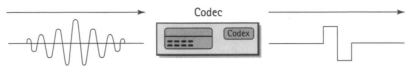

Figure 1-10 Codec: Analog-to-Digital conversion.

Encoding is the process of converting an analog information stream (e.g., voice or video) into a digital data stream. The voice or video signal is sampled at frequent intervals and each sample of amplitude is expressed in terms of a binary (computer) value, usually a 4-bit or 8-bit byte. The reverse process of *decoding* takes place on the receiving end, resulting in recomposition of the information in its original form, or at least a reasonable approximation thereof.

Multiplexers (MUXs)

The term *multiplex* has its roots in the Latin words *multi* (many) and *plex* (fold). Multiplexers (MUXs) act as both *concentrators* and contention devices which enable multiple, relatively low-speed terminal devices to share a single, high-capacity circuit (physical path) between two points in a network. The benefit of multiplexers is simply that they enable carriers and end users to take advantage of the economies of scale. Just as a multilane highway can carry increased volumes of traffic in multiple lanes at higher speeds and at relatively low incremental cost, a high-capacity circuit can carry multiple conversations in multiple channels at relatively low incremental cost.

> *The modern saying, "Time is Money," is indeed most of all true when applied to telegraphic signalling; and many endeavours have been made, not only to transmit signals with celerity, but also to transmit more than one communication at the same time along the same wire. This has been successfully done in the duplex system — by which a message is sent from either end of the same wire simultaneously; in the diplex system — in which two messages can be sent simultaneously in one direction; and in the quadruplex system, which combines the two former methods, and by which it is possible to convey four signals along the same wire at the same moment. This last method was invented by Mr. Edison....* Wonders of the Universe, 1899. [1-5]

Contemporary multiplexers rely on four-wire circuits, which enable multiple logical channels to derive from a single physical circuit, and which permit high-speed transmission simultaneously in both directions. In this manner, multiple communications (either unidirectional or bidirectional) can be supported. Multiplexing is used commonly across all transmission media, including twisted pair, coaxial and fiber optic cables, and microwave, satellite, and other radio systems.

Traditional multiplexing comes in several varieties, presented in chronological order of development and evolution. Included are Frequency Division Multiplexing (FDM), Time Division Multiplexing (TDM), and Statistical Time Division Multiplexing (STDM). Wavelength Division Multiplexing (WDM), a recent development, is used in fiber optic cable systems.

Frequency Division Multiplexing (FDM)

Frequency Division Multiplexing (FDM) takes advantage of the fact that a single twisted pair, copper circuit can carry much more than the 4 kHz guaranteed for individual voice conversations. Even in the early days of vacuum tube technology, up to 96 kHz could be supported over a set of two copper pairs (a four-wire circuit, with two wires supporting transmission in each direction), thereby enabling the support of up to 24 individual voice channels separated by frequency guard bands [1-3]. In terms of a commonly understood analogy, multiple frequencies can be supported over a single, four-wire electrical circuit much as multiple radio stations and TV channels can be supported over the airwaves through frequency separation.

Through a FDM (Figure 1-11), conversation #1 might be supported over frequencies 0 Hz-4,000 Hz; conversation #2 over frequencies 4,000 Hz-8,000 Hz; conversation #3 over frequencies 8,000 Hz-12,000 Hz; and so on. Small slices of frequency within each channel are designated as subchannels, or *guard bands*, which separate the carrier channels used for information transmission. The guard bands serve to minimize the likelihood of interference among conversations riding in adjacent information channels over the same physical circuit. Of course, the individual channels are not separated spatially; rather, they are overlaid, with all sharing the same space on the wires.

Frequency Division Multiplexers typically are not particularly intelligent. Specific devices or groups of devices often are tuned to using designated frequency bands for communications. As noted in Figure 1-11, the bandwidth associated with those devices is unused if the communication is inactive for some reason, even though other devices could make effective use of it.

FDM served its purpose well, at the time, for long-haul voice transmission. Data communications over FDM, however, requires sets of special low-speed modems, one for each channel, with one set at each end of the facility. FDM currently is used in broadband Local Area Networks (LANs), which support multiple simultaneous transmissions. FDM also is used in cellular radio networks and in certain digitized voice applications. As we have noted, however, (all else being equal) digital generally is better, especially when data traffic is involved, since this rapidly is becoming a data world.

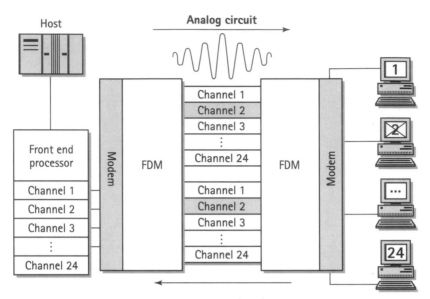

Figure 1-11 Frequency Division Multiplexing (FDM) in a data communications application.

Time Division Multiplexing (TDM)

Time Division Multiplexing (*TDM*) offers all of the advantages of digital transmission, namely improved bandwidth utilization, enhanced error performance, improved security, and upgradeability.

At the transmitting end of the connection, the TDM scans the buffers associated with the ports to which individual devices are attached. Each device port is allocated a channel, or *time slot*, for transmission of data. Device #1 transmits through Port #1 and over Time Slot #1, Device #2 transmits through Port #2 and over Time Slot #2, and so on, in a serial fashion. The transmitting TDM typically accepts an 8-bit sample of data from each port and byte-interleaves those data samples into a *frame* of data. (Note: *Byte* generally refers to an 8-bit value, or data *word*, although some bytes comprise more or fewer bits. The term *octet* is more precise, and frequently used in telecommunications standards to describe an 8-bit unit of data.) As the MUX completes a scan of the ports and transmits a set of such data samples, it will prepend each frame with some number (usually one) of *framing bits*. The framing bits delineate one frame from another, and are used by the multiplexers and other intermediate devices for purposes of synchronization. Some more sophisticated multiplexers also use the framing bits for purposes of signaling and control.

At the receiving end, the process is reversed. Each channel in each frame is identified, the individual transmissions are de-multiplexed, and each is forwarded over the port to which the intended receiving terminal device is attached. Clearly, the MUXs must be carefully *synchronized* in time, in order for the receiving MUX to determine the proper separation of frames and channels of data. The framing bits typically provide the mechanism for synchronization.

The primary constraint of a basic TDM is that of static configuration. In other words, Channel #1 is always reserved for Port #1, over which Terminal #1 always transmits. Terminals that are idle, turned off, unplugged, or on fire are still allocated valuable bandwidth, thereby having a deleterious effect on the cost-effectiveness of the facility, as noted in Figure 1-12. As a result, TDMs are no longer held in favor.

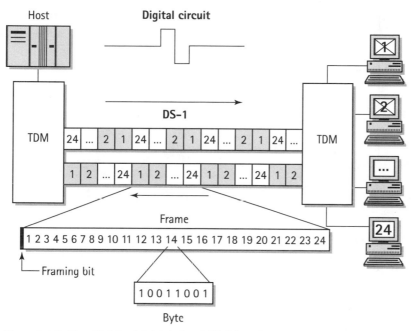

Figure 1-12 Time Division Multiplexing (TDM) in a data communications application.

Statistical Time Division Multiplexing (STDM)

Statistical Time Division Multiplexing (*STDM*) shows much improvement over TDM, because the MUXs are intelligent. STDMs, or *Stat MUXs*, offer the advantage of dynamic allocation of available channels and raw bandwidth. In other words, STDMs can allocate bandwidth, in the form of time slots, in consideration of the transmission requirements of individual devices serving specific applications (Figure 1-13). Further, an intelligent STDM can dynamically adapt to the nature and associated requirements of the load placed on it, and in consideration of the available capacity of the circuit.

Stat MUXs can recognize active vs. inactive devices, as well as priority levels. Further, they can invoke *flow control* options that cause a transmitting terminal to cease transmission temporarily, in the event that the MUX's internal *buffer*, or temporary memory, is full. Flow control also can restrain low priority transmissions in favor of higher priority transmissions. Additionally, STDMs may offer the advantages of data compression, error detection and correction, and reporting of traffic statistics.

T-carrier, discussed in detail in Chapter 7, relies on STDMs. The high-speed, four-wire digital circuit typically is divided into multiple time slots to carry multiple voice conversations or data transmissions. For example, T-1 (North America) provides 24 time slots to carry 24 conversations, each of a maximum of 64 Kbps. E-1 (European and international) provides 30 time slots to carry 30 conversations.

Additionally, the individual channels can be grouped to yield higher transmission rates (*superrate*) for an individual, bandwidth-intensive communication such as a videoconference. The individual channels also can be subdivided into lower speed (*subrate*) channels to accommodate many more, less bandwidth-intensive communications, such as low-speed data. Also, many MUXs allocate bandwidth on a priority basis, providing delay-sensitive traffic (e.g., real-time voice or video) with top priority to ensure that the resulting presentation of the data at the receiving end is of high quality.

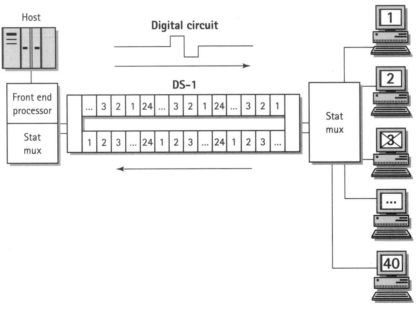

Figure 1-13 Statistical Time Division Multiplexing (STDM) in a data communications application.

Wavelength Division Multiplexing (WDM)

Wavelength Division Multiplexers (*WDMs*) enable multiple high-speed channels to be supported over a single fiber optic transmission system. This is accomplished through the transmission of multiple frequencies (wavelengths) of light, much as multiple electrical frequencies can support multiple, simultaneous conversations in a FDM transmission system. A number of carriers now routinely deploy *DWDM* (*Dense Wavelength Division Multiplexing*) on fiber optic systems, with four *windows* (lightwave frequencies), each running at approximately 10 Gbps, for a total yield of 40 Gbps per fiber strand. Recently, demonstrations have been conducted with as many as 32 windows, each running at approximately 10 Gbps, for a total yield of approximately 320 Gbps per fiber strand. As some carriers deploy many hundreds of fiber strands along a given path, the bandwidth potential is incredible.

Inverse Multiplexers

Inverse Multiplexers perform the inverse process, as do traditional MUXs. In other words, they accommodate a single, high-bandwidth data stream by transmitting it over multiple, lower-bandwidth channels or circuits. The transmitting MUX segments the data stream and spreads it across the circuits on a consistent and coordinated basis, and the receiving MUX reconstitutes the composite data stream. Clearly, the two devices must synchronize carefully with each other and with the transmission characteristics of the individual paths and channels in order to minimize errors and delays. An individual communication might spread over multiple switched circuits, dedicated circuits, or channels on multichannel circuits. For instance, a broadcast quality videoconference requires a full T-1 (1.544 Mbps). Assuming that a full T-1 is unavailable between two locations at the moment, the signal might split across multiple T-1's, and recombine at the receiving end.

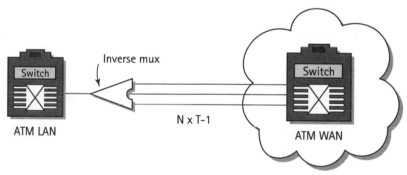

Figure 1–14 Inverse Multiplexing over ATM (IMA).

Inverse Multiplexing over ATM (*IMA*) fans out an ATM (Asynchronous Transfer Mode) cell stream across multiple circuits between the user premises and the edge of the carrier network. ATM LAN (Local Area Network) switches commonly operate at speeds of 155 Mbps or 622 Mbps, and generally are positioned as a backbone switching technology for the interconnection of lower-speed hubs, switches, and routers. Where significant levels of ATM traffic are destined for the WAN (Wide Area Network), a single circuit of appropriate bandwidth either may be unavailable, or may be too costly. In such a circumstance, multiple physical T-1 circuits can be used as a single, logical ATM pipe. The IMA-compliant ATM concentrator at the user premise spreads the ATM cells across the T-1 circuits in a round robin fashion; the carrier edge ATM switch scans the T-1 circuits in the same fashion in order to reconstitute the cell stream (Figure 1-15).

Data Over Voice & Voice Over Data

A large number of manufacturers now offer MUXs which enable data to be sent over voice lines and voice to be sent over data lines. For instance, a digital data circuit also can accommodate voice (for which it was not intended) through the use of a special MUX that digitizes the voice signal and transmits it; the reverse process takes place at the receiving end. The voice and data conversations share the same circuit sequentially, rather than simultaneously. Bandwidth is allocated as appropriate, with priority provided to the delay-sensitive voice traffic.

While such an approach is somewhat unusual, it enables the user to take advantage of excess capacity on a dedicated circuit. It also can support both voice and data communications over a single circuit-switched analog circuit. There is, of course, an investment required in the multiplexing equipment, although such equipment, increasingly, is quite affordable.

A number of manufacturers have developed MUXs and routers which enable voice to share excess capacity on a Frame Relay network. While the quality of Voice over Frame Relay (VoFR) can suffer from delay due to network congestion, the voice conversation essentially is free. Voice over IP (VoIP) can be supported over the Internet, although the quality generally is poor. Several next generation carriers recently have deployed high-speed IP (Internet Protocol) networks optimized for voice, rather than for the data traffic for which the protocol was developed. While these networks are not fully proven now, their potential is quite significant. VoIP promises to support toll-quality voice at much lower cost, due to the inherent efficiencies of packet switching as compared to circuit switching. These networks also are designed to support voice, data, video, and image traffic over the same infrastructure; such an integrated network offers inherent efficiencies and a single point of service management.

Switches and Switching:
The Basics . . . and Then Some

Switches serve to establish transmission paths between or among terminal devices (transmitters and receivers) on a flexible basis. They effectively serve as contention devices, managing contention between multiple transmit devices for access to shared circuits. In this manner, the usage and cost of expensive circuits can be optimized, based on standard traffic engineering principles. Without switches, each device would require a direct, dedicated circuit to every other device — a *full mesh topology.* Such an approach clearly is resource-intensive, impractical, and even impossible, as early experience proved. This discussion of switches and switching is presented in chronological order of development, beginning with circuit switching and its evolution, and progressing through packet, frame, and cell switching.

Circuit Switching: Optimized for Voice

In the classic sense, circuit switches establish connections between physical circuits. On demand and as available, the circuit switch establishes such connections through the switching matrix, and provides continuous and exclusive access between the physical circuits for the duration of the conversation. In other words, from circuit to circuit and through the switching matrix, the transmission path between the terminal devices dedicates the prescribed level of bandwidth to that one transmission. Contemporary circuit switches provide continuous access to logical channels within the shared internal bus of the switch. The user may gain access to the switch over a single-channel, voice-grade circuit. Alternatively, the user may gain access through a high-capacity, multichannel physical circuit such as T-1 or ISDN. The high-capacity, multichannel circuits which interconnect the circuit switches in the carrier network are known as *Intermachine Trunks* (*IMTs*), which generally are in the form of fiber optic transmission systems. While circuit switches originally were developed for voice communications, much data traffic also is switched in this fashion. Typical examples of circuit switches include PBXs and Central Offices (COs).

MANUAL (CORDBOARD) SWITCHES

These switches involved an operator who manually established the desired connection at the verbal request of the transmitting party. A unique physical and electrical connection was established, on a *plug and jack* basis (Figure 1-15), for the duration of the call. When either party disconnected, the operator was alerted and manually disconnected the circuit, which then became available for other use. The size of such switches, the complexity of interconnecting long distance calls across multiple switches, and the labor intensity of this approach all contributed to their demise. Note, however, that many thousands of such switches remain in service, largely in developing countries.

The term *tip and ring* came from the cordboard plugs that established the connection between both local loop wire pairs. One set of wires connected electrically through the *tip* of the plugs, while the other set connected through the *ring*, or seat of the plugs. The New Haven District Telephone Company in New Haven, Connecticut installed the first such switch on January 28, 1878, at a cost of U.S. $28.50. The system connected 21 subscribers referred to by name, rather than telephone number. As was typical in those days, the operators were young boys, most of them experienced as messengers and telegraph clerks—they soon proved too boisterous and unreliable, and were replaced with women [1-7].

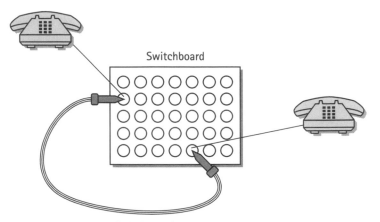

Figure 1-15 Manual Switching: Cordboard.

STEP-BY-STEP (SXS) SWITCHES

SxS switches are electromechanical in nature. Almon B. Strowger, a Kansas City undertaker frustrated with the behavior of the local telephone company operator, invented and patented the first such switch in 1891. According to legend, the operator was directing Mr. Strowger's calls to a competing undertaker, who also happened to be the operator's husband. Building on earlier Bell system inventions, Strowger invented a system that served 99 subscribers. That patent served as the foundation for the company he founded, Automatic Electric Company, which later became the manufacturing subsidiary of General Telephone and Electric (GTE) [1-7].

SxS switches consist of a large number of *line finders* to which groups of individual subscribers are assigned for dial tone. The transmitting party dials a series of numbers, originally with a rotary telephone terminal, which causes the making and breaking of an electrical circuit. As noted in Figure 1-16, those electrical pulses cause successive mechanical *line selectors* to click across contacts to set up the conversation path as the complete number is dialed [1-8].

While such switches are still in use (in 1986, approximately 38% of all U.S. switches were based on SxS), they clearly are not desirable because they are slow, expensive, large, maintenance-intensive, and capacity-limited [1-3]. Large numbers of SxS switches remain in service, mostly in developing countries.

CROSSBAR (XBAR) SWITCHES

The first *common control* switches, Xbar switches are electromagnetic in nature. While the original concept was developed at Bell Telephone Laboratories (now Lucent Technologies), the Ericsson company (Sweden) accomplished much of the early practical development work. The first such switch installed in the United States was a Central Office exchange in Brooklyn, New York (1938) [1-6]. Such switches quickly became predominant.

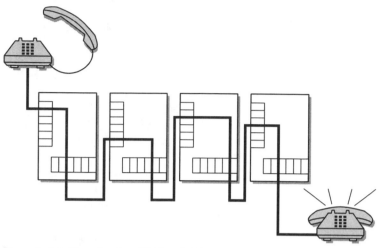

Figure 1-16   Step-by-Step (SxS) switching
              (Source: AG Communications Systems Corporation)

In an XBar switch (Figure 1-17), a request for dial tone is recognized by a *marker*, which directs a *sender* to store the dialed digits. A *translator* is then directed to route the call, reserving a path through a *switching matrix* [1-3]. Once the call connects, these various components become available to serve other calls. Compared to the SxS switch, the XBar has relatively few moving parts. XBar switches offer the advantages of increased intelligence, common control, greater speed of connection, smaller physical footprint, lower maintenance, and greater capacity.

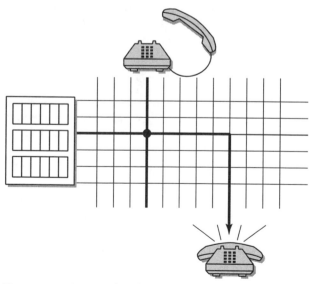

Figure 1-17 Crossbar (XBar) switching
             (Source: AG Communications Systems Corporation)

ELECTRONIC COMMON CONTROL (ECC) SWITCHES

ECC switches reflect the marriage of computer technology and telephony. While the first ECC switches were analog, contemporary switches are, in fact, fully digital. Voice conversations are digitized and switched over high-speed digital circuits, with all processes accomplished through programmed logic. ECC switches are microprocessor controlled, with the total processing power of such a switch often rivaling that of a general purpose, mainframe computer. The first ECC switch was developed (with the assistance of Western Electric) by AT&T Bell Telephone Laboratories. It was based on the invention of the transistor in 1948 and involved a development effort that began in earnest in the early 1950s. That first Electronic Switching System (ESS) CO began service in Succasunna, New Jersey on May 30, 1965, connecting 200 subscribers. By 1974, there were 475 such offices in service, serving 5.6 million subscribers. The development effort was estimated to involve 4,000 man-years and a total cost of $500 million [1-7].

ECC switches (Figure 1-18), as compared to the previous generations of switching technology, offer the advantages of further increased intelligence, greater speed of call set-up and overall call processing, and a still smaller footprint. Additionally, they offer lower maintenance costs, and can be monitored and managed from a remote location. Many contemporary ECC switches are unmanned, in favor of control from a centralized *Network Operations Center* (*NOC*). ECC switches offer greater capacity, and on a *scalable* basis — capacity can be increased through the addition of various system modules, or cabinets, with a reasonably graceful relationship maintained between increases in capacity and associated costs. As specialized, software-controlled computer systems, their functionality and feature content often can be upgraded through additional software and/or firmware. Such switches generally possess the ability to switch data and video, as well as voice. Finally, they interface with various application processors to further increase the range of services provided; such application processors (applications) might include voice processors (e.g., voicemail and language translation) and fax servers (fax mail).

Packet Switching: Optimized for Data

First deployed in 1971, *packet switching* grew out of the U.S. Advanced Research Project Agency (ARPA) network. Commonly referred to as *ARPAnet*, the network was established to support interactive, asynchronous computer-to-computer communications between the defense and university communities.

Rather than employing circuit switching, which is far too expensive for intensive, interactive computer communications, ARPAnet, and its successors such as the Internet, make use of packet switching. Packet switching involves the transmission of data in *packets* of fixed length across a shared network. Each packet, or *datagram*, is individually addressed, in order that the packet switches can route each packet over the most appropriate and available circuit, and each packet can survive independently. Each packet may represent an individual set of data, or a larger set of data can fragment into multiple packets, each of which works its way through the network independently. Packets offered to the network by large numbers of users make use of the same switches and transmission facilities; such a highly shared network offers dramatically lower costs of data transmission in comparison to circuit switching.

Traditional packet switching offers the advantage of having mature and stable technologies as its base. Additionally, it is widely available, both domestically and internationally, and is low in cost. Its disadvantages include the fact that it can support only relatively low-speed data transmission. As the switches assume a 1960s-vintage analog network environment of twisted pair, each switch must examine each individual packet for errors created in transmission. Further, each switch must resolve identified errors through a request for retransmission. These factors, in combination, result in unpredictable, variable levels of packet *latency* (delay). Therefore, packet switching traditionally has been considered to be unsuitable for stream-oriented communications such as real-time voice and video.

X.25 (an international standard packet switching interface, discussed in Chapter 7) offered great advantage in terms of its ability to support the interconnection of virtually any computer systems through its ability to accomplish protocol conversion. This highly desirable feature caused X.25-based packet networks to be characterized as the first *Value-Added Networks* (*VANs*).

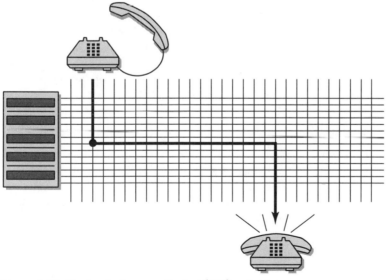

Figure 1-18 Electronic Common Control (ECC) switching

Frame Switching (Frame Relay): Optimized for LAN Internetworking

A relative newcomer, *frame relay* became commercially available in 1992 by Wiltel (United States). Much like packet switching, each *frame* is individually addressed. Frame relay also makes use of special switches and a shared network, of very high speed. Unlike the original packet switching technology, frame relay supports the transmission of virtually any computer data stream in its native form; frames vary in length (up to 4,096 bytes). Rapidly gaining in popularity, frame relay is widely available in developed nations; international frame relay service is also becoming widely available. Disadvantages include the fact that frame relay, like packet switching, is oriented towards data transmission; frame latency is variable and unpredictable in duration. While increasingly satisfactory techniques have surfaced for support of voice and video, frame relay was not designed with those applications in mind.

Cell Switching: Optimized for Everything

Clearly, cell switching is fundamental to the future of communications. Encompassing both *Switched Multimegabit Data Service* (*SMDS*) and *Asynchronous Transfer Mode* (*ATM*), data is organized into *cells* of fixed length (53 octets), shipped across very high speed facilities and switched through very high speed, specialized switches. SMDS proved very effective for data communications, although it was short-lived. ATM will be pervasive in the future.

Currently, ATM is employed primarily in data networking. Although designed to support voice and video, as well, those standards were finalized only recently. ATM's ultimate value lies in its ability to support any type of data stream (e.g., voice, data, video, image, and multimedia), providing each with the appropriate level of Quality of Service (QoS). ATM is unique in this respect.

Photonic Switches

Although still in development, *photonic switches* are yet another dimension in the evolution of switch technology. Capable of supporting circuit, packet, frame, and cell switching, photonic switches will eliminate the requirement for optoelectric conversion when connected to a fiber optic transmission system. Clearly, they also will offer advantages in terms of speed and error performance. While prototype photonic switches currently appear in testbed environments, it likely will be a decade or so before they are commercially viable; it is highly unlikely that they will find application in the PBX world in the foreseeable future. Notably, however, DWDM is a form of photonic switching, and recently has been widely deployed in carrier networks.

Signaling and Control

Signaling and control comprises a set of functions which must take place within any network in order ensure that it operates smoothly. In this context, various elements within the network must identify themselves, communicate their status, and pass instructions. Fundamental examples include on-hook and off-hook indication, dial tone provision, call routing control, busy indication, and billing instructions. Further examples include dialed digits, route availability, routing preference, carrier preference, and originating number or circuit [1-3].

In more sophisticated, contemporary networks, the responsibility for overall signaling and control functions resides within a separate *Common Channel Signaling (CCS)* and control network. Such a sophisticated CCS network involves highly intelligent devices capable of monitoring and managing large numbers of lower order devices in the communications network that it controls. From a centralized *Network Control Center (NCC)*, the network can be monitored, and faults or performance failures can be identified, diagnosed, and isolated. Finally, the lower order devices in the communications network oftentimes can be addressed and commanded to correct the condition.

References

[1-1]   Shelly, Gary B. and Cashman, Thomas J. *Introduction to Computers and Data Processing*. Anaheim Publishing Company, 1980.

[1-2]   Doll, Dixon R. *Data Communications: Facilities, Networks and Systems Design*. John Wiley & Sons, 1978.

[1-3]   *Engineering and Operations in the Bell System*. Bell Telephone Laboratories, Incorporated, 1977.

[1-4]   Bates, Bud. *Introduction to T-1/T-3 Networking*. Artech House, 1991.

[1-5]   *Wonders of the Universe*. The Werner Company, 1899.

[1-6]   Augarten, Stan. Bit by Bit. Ticknor & Fields, 1984.

[1-7]   Brooks, John. *Telephone: The First Hundred Years*. Harper & Row, 1976.

[1-8]   AG Communications Systems. *Introduction to Telecommunications*. AG Communications Systems Corporation, 1990.

Chapter 2

Fundamentals of Transmission Systems: Technologies and Applications

It was early declared by Professor Morse, and by other distinguished investigators of the nature and powers of the electric current, that neither the ocean itself, nor the distance to be traversed, presented any insuperable obstacle to the laying of submerged oceanic lines from continent to continent, and the confident prophecy that such lines would eventually be undertaken was freely uttered and discussed in learned circles.
Source: Our First Century or the One Hundred Great and Memorable Events in the History of Our Country During the One Hundred Years of Its Existence, 1876.

Information is of considerably increased value if you can convey it clearly to others, a basic principle that is well understood in this Information Age. The conveyance, or transmission, of information across a distance necessarily involves some form of transmission medium. In this chapter, the terms transmission medium, transmission system, and transmission facility will be used interchangeably, as they are in the real world. The selection of a physical transmission medium which serves to transport that information is critical to its successful conveyance. Particularly in an interactive communication, the medium can, indeed, be critical to the message.

This section addresses all transmission media commonly used in traditional voice, data, video, and image networks, whether analog or digital in nature. Those media fall into two distinctive categories, the first of which includes all wired media, also referred to as conducted, guided, or bounded media. The second category includes all traditional wireless media, also referred to as radiated, unguided, or unbounded.

Wired transmission systems employ tangible physical media. In other words, they can be seen, felt, and perhaps even smelled and tasted (I do not recommend the last two options, as the results might well be unpleasant). Also known as *conducted* systems, wired media generally use a metallic or glass *conductor* which serves to *conduct*, or carry on, some form of electromagnetic energy. For example, twisted pair and coaxial cable systems conduct electrical energy, employing a copper medium. Fiber optic systems conduct light, or *optical*, energy, generally using a glass conductor. The term *guided* media refers to the fact that the signal is contained within an enclosed physical path. Finally, *bounded* media refers to the fact that some form of twisting, shielding, cladding, and/or insulating material binds the signal within the core medium, thereby improving signal strength over a distance and enhancing the performance of the transmission system in the process. Twisted pair (both unshielded and shielded), coaxial, and fiber optic cable systems fall into this category.

Wireless transmission systems do not make use of a physical conductor, or guide, to bind the signal. Therefore, they also are known as *unguided* or *unbounded* systems. Rather than relying on electrical energy, such systems generally make use of radio waves; hence the term *radiated* often is applied to wireless transmission. Finally, such systems employ electromagnetic energy in the form of radio or light waves that are transmitted and received across space. Such systems often are referred to as *airwave* systems, although *spacewave* is a more accurate term, as the air in the space between transmitter and receiver actually serves to weaken the signal.

Each specific transmission system is distinguished by unique properties and limitations, and each has appropriate applications. The application to be supported, clearly, must be of primary consideration in designing a network and in selecting the transmission medium, assuming you have the freedom of choice. As the application ultimately must support users effectively, it places certain demands on the network, in general, and on the transmission medium, specifically.

Traditional transmission systems addressed in this section include twisted copper wire, coaxial cable, microwave, satellite, infrared, and fiber optics, the order of discussion roughly chronological. Chapter 12 discusses cellular radio, packet radio, wireless LANs, and other application-specific systems.

Frequency Spectrum

While human voice frequencies mostly fall in the range of 100 Hz-8,000 Hz, the energy in the speech spectrum peaks at approximately 500 Hz, with most articulation at higher frequencies. The human ear can distinguish signals as low as 20 Hz and as high as 20 kHz, and is most sensitive in the range of 1,000Hz – 3,000Hz. Public switched telephone networks, as discussed previously, reliably provide raw, voice-grade bandwidth at a signaling rate of 4 kHz; with 3,300 Hz (200 Hz-3,500 Hz) used for voice transmission. This range of frequencies provides a band of intelligibility which is considered to be good, although not complete. In an electrical cable system, the range of carrier frequencies depends on the nature of the medium and the requirements of the applications supported. For instance, twisted pair can support bandwidth of 10 Hz-10^6 Hz, and coaxial cable 10^6 Hz-10^8 Hz. The actual range of frequencies supporting a given communication are known as a *passband*, which is established through the use of band-limiting filters [2-1], [2-2], and [2-3].

Frequency and wavelength are inversely related – as the frequency of the signal (number of cycles per second) increases, the wavelength (length of the electromagnetic waveform) of the signal decreases. In other words, the more waveforms per second, the shorter the length, or cycle, of each individual wave. Table 2-1 defines the frequency and wavelength of various types of radio and light-based communications systems as they relate to the electromagnetic spectrum [2-2], [2-3], and [2-4]. Note that the higher the frequency of the carrier signal, the more raw signal material exists, and the greater the potential level of bandwidth available. However, the higher the frequency of the carrier signal, the greater the extent to which it suffers from signal attenuation. The impact of signal attenuation dictates the maximum allowable spatial separation between any two devices such as transmitter, amplifier or repeater, and receiver.

Table 2-1 FREQUENCY SPECTRUM: BAND DESIGNATIONS, FREQUENCY RANGES, WAVELENGTHS AND EXAMPLE COMMUNICATIONS APPLICATIONS

Band Designation	Frequency Range*	Wavelength**	Usage
Audible	20 Hz–20 kHz	>100 Km	Acoustics
Extremely/Very Low Frequency (ELF/VLF) Radio	3 kHz–30 kHz	100 Km–10 Km	Navigation, Weather, Submarine Communications
Low Frequency (LF) Radio	30 kHz–300 kHz	10 Km–1 Km	Navigation, Maritime Communications
Medium Frequency (MF) Radio	300 kHz–3 MHz	1 Km–100 m	Navigation, AM Radio
High Frequency (HF) Radio	3 MHz–30 MHz	100 m–10 m	Citizens Band (CB) Radio
Very High Frequency (VHF) Radio	30 MHz–300 MHz	10 m–1 m	Amateur (HAM) Radio, VHF TV, FM Radio
Ultra High Frequency (UHF) Radio	300 MHz–3 GHz	1 m–10 cm	Microwave, Satellite, UHF TV, Paging, Cordless Telephony, Cellular and PCS Telephony, Wireless LAN
Super High Frequency (SHF) Ratio	3 GHz–30 GHz	10 cm–1 cm	Microwave, Satellite, Wireless LAN

Continued

Continued

Extremely High Frequency (EHF) Radio	30 GHz–300 GHz	1 cm–.1 mm	Microwave, Satellite
Infrared Light	10^3–10^5 GHz	300 μ–3 μ	LAN Bridges, Wireless LANs
Visible Light	10^{13}–10^{15} GHz	1 μ–.3 μ	Fiber Optics
X-Rays	10^{15}–10^{18} GHz	10^3μ–10^7 μ	N/A
Gamma & Cosmic Rays	>10^{18} GHz	<01^7 μ	N/A

*k = Kilo = 1,000 (1 thousand)
*M = Mega = 1,000,000 (1 million)
*G = Giga = 1,000,000,000 (1 billion)
*T = Tera = 1,000,000,000,000 (1 trillion)
**cm = centimeter (1/100 meter)
**mm = millimeter (1/1,000 meter)
**μ = micron (1/1,000,000 meter)

Selection Criteria

The selection of the most effective transmission system for a given application must be made in the context of a number of key design considerations. Such considerations include general transmission characteristics such as bandwidth and error performance, both of which affect throughput. Additionally, you must consider the allowable distance between devices, as well as issues of propagation delay, security, mechanical strength, and physical dimensions. Finally, and perhaps most importantly, consider local availability and cost, including cost of acquisition, deployment, operation and maintenance, and upgrade or replacement.

Transmission Characteristics

The basic transmission characteristics of a given medium are of primary importance. Those characteristics include bandwidth, or capacity, error performance, and distance between network elements. These three dimensions of a transmission system, in combination, dictate effective *throughput*, the amount of information you can put through the system.

Bandwidth, in this context, refers to the raw amount of bandwidth the medium supports. *Error performance* refers to the number or percentage of errors introduced in the process of transmission. *Distance* refers to the minimum and maximum spatial separation between any two devices over a link, in the context of a complete, end-to-end circuit. Clearly, the attractiveness of any given transmission system increases to the extent that you receive greater available bandwidth, fewer errors, and a greater maximum distance between various network elements (e.g., amplifiers and repeaters).

Note that bandwidth, error performance, and distance are tightly interrelated. In a twisted pair network, for example, more raw bandwidth requires more raw material in the form of Hz, which translates into higher transmission frequencies. Unfortunately, higher frequencies attenuate (lose power) more rapidly than do lower frequencies. This fact results in more errors in transmission, unless the amplifiers/repeaters are spaced more closely together. For instance, a four-wire ISDN BRI (Integrated Services Digital Network Basic Rate Interface) circuit supports three channels comprising a total bandwidth of 144 Kbps in each direction over a distance of up to 18,000 feet between the carrier Central Office and the customer premise, with no requirement for repeaters. In comparison, a digital T-1 circuit typically is provisioned over four-wire twisted pair, with a pair providing bandwidth of 1.544 Mbps in each direction. T-1 error performance is excellent through the placement of regenerative repeaters approximately every 6,000 ft to overcome the effects of signal attenuation at the substantially higher carrier frequency. A somewhat better grade of twisted pair can be deployed in a Local Area Network (LAN) to support transmission rates of 100 Mbps between a workstation and a LAN hub or switch, with excellent error performance as long as the device separation is equal to or less than 100 meters. In each application, you must take measures to avoid high levels of ambient noise, and you must consider other factors such as the gauge of the conductors. While this comparison is simplified, it clearly demonstrates the close and direct relationship between bandwidth, distance, and error performance.

Also note that radio systems are limited in terms of bandwidth. As the laws of physics tell us that there is only so much raw bandwidth in the frequency spectrum, the FCC and other national regulatory bodies apportion frequency ranges on the bases of application and geography. The regulators also limit the power levels at which such systems operate to ensure that the signals do not exceed a certain range, or assigned radio cell, and, therefore, do not affect licensed users in adjacent geographic areas. As a result, licensed frequency bands are site-specific and may not always be available on demand. Given the limited availability of radio spectrum, it is especially important that it be used with maximum effect. Therefore, users prefer digital systems, as they support data compression and, thereby, are more efficient in their use of the precious resource of radio spectrum.

Further, we must consider that radio systems are highly susceptible to the quality of the atmosphere (air) between the transmitter and the receiver. Dust, smoke, haze, and humidity have decidedly negative effects on signal performance. Precipitation (e.g., rain, sleet, snow, and hail) cause substantial degradation in performance; this phenomenon is known as *rain fade*.

Finally, take note that the nature of the application has significant impact on the selection of the appropriate radio frequency range. For example, pager and cellular telephony networks generally operate in the 900 MHz band. At this frequency, the signals can travel relatively long distances at low power levels, and can penetrate dense physical matter (e.g., walls, floors, ceilings, and windows) without serious loss of signal strength. Microwave and other signals in higher frequency bands must have line-of-sight connectivity between antennae, as they cannot penetrate dense physical matter. As radio frequencies approach the light spectrum, the signals behave more like light than radio, as we normally think of it; in other words, they are reflected and dispersed by physical matter.

Propagation Delay & Response Time

Propagation delay refers to the length of time required for a signal to travel from transmitter to receiver across a transmission system. While electromagnetic energy travels at roughly the speed of light (186,000 miles per second) in a vacuum (e.g., the vacuum of space), it travels at a slower rate through a wire, a fiber, or the atmosphere of earth. The specific nature of the transmission system impacts the level of propagation delay to a considerable extent, and the total length of the circuit directly impacts the length of time it takes for the signal to reach the receiver. That circuit length can vary considerably in a switched network, as the specific circuit route will vary in length from call to call, depending on availability of individual links. Dedicated networks offer the advantage of a reliable and consistent level of propagation delay. In either case, the number of network elements (devices) in the network affects the level of delay, as each device (e.g., amplifier, repeater, and switch) acts on the signal to perform certain processes, each of which takes at least a small amount of time to accomplish. Clearly, the fewer devices involved in a network, the less delay imposed on the signal. A great many network elements and applications depend on relatively precise and consistent timing of the received signal; in other words, they do not tolerate significant levels of *jitter*, or variation in the timing of the signal.

Geosynchronous Earth Orbiting (GEO) satellite systems best illustrate propagation delay. As the fact that the radio signals must travel approximately 22,300 miles up to the satellite and the same distance on the return leg, the resulting delay is approximately .25 seconds. Note that most of the distance is through the vacuum of space, with the signal having to contend with only a few miles of atmosphere on the uplinks and downlinks. Considering the amount of time required for processing on board the satellite, as well as at the earth stations, the total delay for a one-way transmission is about .32 seconds. Therefore, the delay between signal origination and receipt of response is approximately .64 seconds, assuming an immediate response. Hence, highly interactive voice, data, and video applications are not effectively supported via two-way satellite communications.

Security

Security, in the context of transmission systems, addresses the protection of data from interception as it transverses the network. Clearly, increasing amounts of sensitive data are being transmitted across wide, metropolitan area networks, outside the range of physical protection on the user's premises. Therefore, security is of greater concern than ever before; that level of concern will heighten as nations and commercial enterprises seek to gain competitive advantage and as they apply even more sophisticated means. In hearings (May 1996) before the U.S. Senate, a statement revealed that 120 nations either have or are in the process of developing sophisticated computer espionage capabilities.

Further, note that airwave systems (e.g., microwave and satellite) are inherently insecure, as unauthorized entities can gain access to that data through the use of a properly tuned and placed antenna, without the necessity of physically tapping a wireline circuit. Finally, and as we discussed in Chapter 1, digital systems are inherently more secure than their analog counterparts by virtue of the fact that the data can effectively *encrypt*, or encode, to conceal its true meaning. Particularly in the case of data networking, access to a remote system and the data resident on it must be limited to authorized users; therefore, you must employ some method of *authentication* in order to verify the legitimacy and authenticity of the access request.

Mechanical Strength

Mechanical strength applies especially to wired systems. Twisted pair, coaxial, and fiber optic cables are manipulated physically while deployed and reconfigured. Clearly, each has certain physical limits to the amount of bending and twisting (*flex strength*) it can tolerate, the amount of weight or longitudinal stress it can support (*tensile strength*) without breaking (*break strength*), and the maximum severity of the bend it can tolerate (*bend radius*). Fiber optic cables are notoriously susceptible in this regard. Additionally, cables hung from poles expand and contract with changes in ambient temperature. While glass fiber optic cables expand and contract relatively little, twisted pair copper wire is more expansive [2-5].

The issue of mechanical strength also applies to airwave systems, as the reflective dishes, antennae, and other devices used in microwave, satellite, and infrared technologies must be mounted securely to deal with the stresses of wind and other forces of nature. Additionally, the towers, walls, and roofs on which they typically are mounted must be constructed and braced properly in order to withstand such forces, and must flex as appropriate.

Physical Dimensions

The physical dimensions of a transmission system must be considered, as well. This is especially true in the case of wired systems. Certainly, you must consider the sheer weight of a cable system as you attempt to deploy it effectively. Additionally, the bulk (diameter) of the cable is of importance, as conduit and raceway space often is at a premium. Also, bear in mind the physical dimensions of airwave systems, as the size and weight of the reflective dish and mounting system (e.g., bracket and tower) may require support.

Cost

Cost issues abound in the selection of an appropriate transmission medium. Such issues include the cost of acquisition, deployment, Operation and Maintenance (O&M), and upgrade or replacement. Without a lengthy discussion of each cost issue, it is particularly noteworthy to compare the costs of deployment of wired vs. wireless media.

Wired transmission systems require that legal right-of-way be secured, trenches dug, holes bored under streets, poles planted, conduits and manholes placed, cables pulled and spliced, amplifiers or repeaters placed, etc. Such costs, clearly, are not trivial. Wireless systems, on the other hand, require that right-of-way be secured, antennae placed (perhaps in orbit), spectrum licenses secured, and so on. While it is difficult to make hard-and-fast generalizations, the deployment of wired systems certainly involves a set of cost issues that can be problematic. Further, wired systems tend to be more susceptible to the forces of man (e.g., cable-seeking backhoes, posthole diggers, and trains) and nature (e.g., earthquakes and floods) than are their wireless counterparts.

Twisted Pair: An Introduction to Telephone Wire

The lines of telegraphic communications which now, like a web, traverse the length and breadth of the republic, and which, indeed, connect and cover as with a net-work the four continents of the globe — these attest the vastness, influence and power, of this amazing invention [the telegraph]. Source: *Our First Century or the One Hundred Great and Memorable Events in the History of Our Country During the One Hundred Years of Its Existence,* 1876.

Metallic wires were used almost exclusively in telecommunications networks for the first 80 years, certainly until the development of microwave and satellite radio communications systems. Initially, uninsulated iron and steel telegraph wires were used although copper was soon found to be a much more appropriate medium. The early metallic electrical circuits were one-wire, supporting two-way communications with each telephone connected to *ground* in order to complete the circuit. In 1881, John J. Carty, a young American Bell technician and one of the original operators, suggested the use of a second wire to complete the circuit and, thereby, to avoid the emanation of electrical noise from the earth ground. In certain contemporary applications, copper-covered steel, copper alloy, nickel- and/or gold-plated copper, and even aluminum metallic conductors are employed. The most common form of copper wire used in communications is that of *Unshielded Twisted Pair* (UTP), which has no shield, or outer conductor, to protect the signal from outside sources of electromagnetic interference [2-6].

A twisted pair (Figure 2-1) involves two copper conductors, generally solid core, although stranded wire is used occasionally in applications that involve frequent flexing of the wire. Each conductor is separately insulated by polyethylene, polyvinyl chloride, flouropolymer resin, Teflon[r], or some other low-smoke, fire-retardant substance. The insulation both separates the conductors so that the electrical circuit is not shorted, and serves to reduce electromagnetic emissions to improve signal strength over a distance. Both conductors serve for signal transmission and reception. As each conductor carries a similar electrical signal, twisted pair is considered a *balanced* medium [2-1] and [2-3].

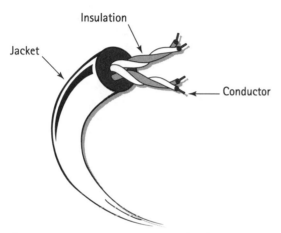

Figure 2-1 Unshielded Twisted Pair (UTP) configuration.

The Twisting Process

The separately insulated conductors are twisted 90° at routine, specified intervals;hence the term *twisted pair*. This twisting process serves to improve the performance of the medium by containing the electromagnetic field within the pair. Thereby, the radiation of electromagnetic energy reduces and the strength of the signal within the wire improves over a distance. Clearly, this reduction of radiated energy also serves to minimize the impact on adjacent pairs in a multi-pair cable configuration. This is especially important in high-bandwidth applications, as higher frequency signals tend to lose power more rapidly over distance. Additionally, the radiated electromagnetic field tends to be greater at higher frequencies, which impacts adjacent pairs to a greater extent. Generally speaking, the more twists per foot, the better the performance of the wire [2-1].

Gauge

Gauge is a measure of the thickness of the conductor. The thicker the wire, the less the *resistance*, the stronger the signal over a given distance, and the better the performance of the medium. Thicker wires also offer the advantage of greater break strength.

American Wire Gauge (*AWG*) is a commonly used standard measurement of gauge, although others are used outside the United States. The gauge numbers are retrogressive; in other words, the larger the number, the smaller the conductor. Originally known as Brown and Sharp (B&S) Gauge, the AWG number indicates the number of times the copper wire is drawn through the wire machine, with each draw serving to reduce its diameter a bit more. As an example, a 24-gauge (AWG) wire has a diameter of .0201 in. (.511mm), a weight of 1.22 lbs./ft. (1.82 kg./km.), a maximum break strength of 12.69 lbs. (5.756 kg.), and D.C. resistance ohms of 25.7/1000ft. (84.2/km.). Twisted pairs commonly employed in telco networks vary from 19 to 28-gauge, with the most common being 24-gauge. Table 2-2 provides an abbreviated comparison of the various UTP categories [2-7].

Table 2-2 UNSHIELDED TWISTED PAIR (UTP) CATEGORIES OF PERFORMANCE, AS DEFINED BY THE ELECTRICAL INDUSTRY ALLIANCE (EIA)

Category (Cat) of Performance	Gauge (AWG)	Performance	Typical Applications
Cat 1	Various	Unspecified; under 1 MHz	Analog voice-grade, ISDN BRI, other applications requiring less than 1 Mbps
Cat 2	22 & 24	1 MHz	4 Mbps Token Ring LAN
Cat 3	22 & 24	16 MHz	POTS, ISDN, T-1, 4/16 Mbps Token Ring LAN, 10BaseT LAN
Cat 4	Various	20 MHz	4/16 Mbps Token Ring LAN
Cat 5	Various	100 MHz	4/16 Mbps Token Ring LAN, 10/100BaseT LAN, 100VG-AnyLAN

Cat 5E (Enhanced) UTP is a developing, non-standard cabling system. Intended for manufacturing according to very tight specifications, it supports data rates of 100 Mbps (100BaseT), 155 Mbps (ATM), and 1 Gbps (Gigabit Ethernet) over distances up to 100 meters. Cat 5E specifications will support 200 MHz through a tighter twist ratio, electrical balancing between the pairs, and few cable anomalies, such as inconsistency in conductor diameter.

Cat 6 is a developing cabling specification for SFTP (Shielded Foil Twisted Pair) or ScTP (Screened Twisted Pair) intended to support signaling rates up to 200 MHz. Cat 6 comprises four twisted pairs separately wrapped in foil insulators and twisted around one another. The group of four pairs is contained inside an extra insulating shield that is contained within a flame-retardant polymer jacket. Applications will include 100BaseT, ATM, and Gigabit Ethernet.

Cat 7 is a developing SFTP technology intended to support signaling rates up to 200 MHz in support of Gigabit Ethernet at distances up to 100 meters. Developers of this technology intend to extend the specification to support signaling rates up to 600 MHz.

Configuration

In a single pair configuration, the pair of wires is enclosed in a sheath or jacket, also of polyethylene, polyvinyl chloride, or Teflon®. Oftentimes, multiple pairs are bundled in the same sheath to minimize deployment costs associated with connecting multiple devices (e.g., electronic PBX or KTS telephone sets, data terminals, and modems) at a single workstation. PBX telephone sets require as many as four pairs, and some LAN technologies (e.g., 10BaseT and 100BaseT) require multiple pairs between the LAN hub and the attached terminal device.

Larger numbers of pairs are bundled into large cables to serve departments, quadrants of a building, or floors of a high-rise office building – such cables may contain 25, 50, 100, 500, or more pairs. While twisted pair cables of up to 3,600 pairs are still used in outside plant applications, such continuing use is decidedly uncommon. In large cables, pairs combine into *binder groups* of 25 pairs for ease of connectivity management. Each binder group is wrapped (bound) with some sort of plastic tape to separate it from other groups. Each pair within a binder group is uniquely color-coded for further ease of connectivity management [2-5].

Bandwidth

The effective capacity of twisted pair cable depends on several factors, including the gauge of the conductor, the length of the circuit, and the spacing of the amplifiers/repeaters. One must also recognize that a high-bandwidth (high frequency) application may cause interference with other conversations on other pairs in proximity.

While a voice-grade channel is guaranteed at 4 kHz, standard copper can support much greater bandwidth. A single twisted pair, in a typical telephone installation, can provide up to 250 kHz, or 1-4 Mbps compressed, assuming amplifier or repeater spacing every 2-3 km [2-1]. Additional examples follow:

♦ T-1 connections (1.544 Mbps) are routinely provided over specially conditioned, four-wire twisted pair circuits, with repeaters spaced at approximately 6,000 ft.

◆ Category 5 (Cat 5) copper, in a Local Area Network (LAN) environment, provides bandwidth of 100+ Mbps (100 MHz) over twisted pair at distances of up to 100 meters.

◆ Asymmetric Digital Subscriber Loop (ADSL), a recently developed local loop technology involving highly advanced compression techniques, provides as much as 6.144 Mbps in the downstream direction, a bidirectional channel supporting as much as 608 Kbps, and a voice channel over a single physical two-wire, logical four-wire, twisted pair local loop at distances up to 2 miles. Standards-based ADSL specifications define considerably higher speeds, although over shorter distances.

Error Performance

Signal quality is always important, especially relative to data transmission. Twisted pair is especially susceptible to the impacts of outside interference, as the lightly insulated wires act as antennae and, thereby, absorb such errant signals. Potential sources of ElectroMagnetic Interference (EMI) and Radio Frequency Interference (RFI) include electric motors, radio transmissions, and fluorescent light boxes. As the carrier frequency of a transmission increases, the error performance of copper degrades significantly, with signal attenuation increasing approximately as the square root of frequency [2-8]. Further, a high-frequency transmission radiates a strong electromagnetic field, which is absorbed by adjacent pairs in a multi-pair cable and which affects the adjacent pairs' error performance.

Distance

UTP contains some distance limitations. As the distance between network elements increases, attenuation (signal loss) increases, and error performance degrades at a given frequency. Even low-speed (voice grade) analog voice transmissions require amplifiers spaced at least every 2-4 miles. As a result, local loops generally are 10,000-18,000 ft. in length. As bandwidth increases, the carrier frequency increases, attenuation becomes more of a issue, and amplifiers/repeaters must be spaced more closely. T-1 transmission, for example, requires repeaters spaced at intervals of approximately 6,000 feet.

Security

UTP is an inherently insecure transmission medium. It is relatively simple to place physical taps on UTP, and fairly simple to detect the presence of a tap. Through the use of an antenna or inductive coil, you can intercept the signal without the placement of a physical tap.

Cost

The acquisition, deployment, and rearrangement costs of UTP are very low, at least in inside wire applications involving only a few pairs (e.g., between a terminal and a switch or hub). In high-capacity, long-distance applications (e.g., interoffice trunking), however, the relative cost is very high due to the requirements for trenching or boring, placement of conduits or poles, and splicing of large, multi-pair cables. Additionally, there are finite limits to the capacity and other performance characteristics of UTP, regardless of the inventiveness of technologists. Hence, the popularity of alternatives such as microwave and fiber optic cable.

Applications

Generally speaking, UTP is no longer deployed in long-haul outside plant transmission systems; satellite, microwave, and fiber optic cable are the media of choice in such applications. However, its low cost, coupled with recently developed methods of improved performance, have increased its application in short-haul distribution systems. UTP is still the medium of choice in most inside wire applications due to its overall ease of handling. Current and continuing applications include the local loop and inside wire and cable.

Shielded Copper

Shielded Twisted Pair (STP) differs from UTP in that a metallic shield or screen surrounds the pairs, which may or may not be twisted. As illustrated in Figure 2-2, the pairs can be individually shielded, a single shield can surround a cable containing multiple pairs, or both techniques can be employed in tandem. The shield is in the form of a metallic foil or woven mesh made of aluminum, steel, or copper; and is electrically grounded. Shielding sometimes occurs through electroplating the individual conductors with nickel and/or gold, although this approach is less effective.

Shielded copper offers the advantage of enhanced performance, for reasons of reduced emissions and reduction of electromagnetic interference. The primary advantage of STP is in the protection it offers from outside sources of electromagnetic interference such as electric motors, other cables and wires, and radio systems. The shield absorbs that energy and conducts it to ground, thereby protecting the transmitting signal through the center conductor. A byproduct of the shielding process is the reduction of emissions from the center conductor. As a result, the electromagnetic field is confined within the conductor, signal loss reduces, and the strength of the signal maintains over a longer distance. This reduction of emissions also provides additional security and minimizes the potential for causing interference in adjacent pairs or cables.

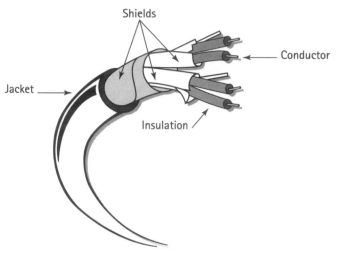

Figure 2-2 Shielded Twisted Pair (STP) configuration.

Shielded Twisted Pair, conversely, has several disadvantages. First, the raw cost of acquisition is greater because the medium costs more to produce. Secondly, the cost of deployment is greater because the additional bulk and weight of the shield makes it more difficult to deploy. Also, the electrical grounding of the shield requires more time and effort. The continuity of the shield must be protected from end-to-end; flexing or a severe bend radius will compromise the integrity of the shield.

Applications

The additional cost of shielded copper limited its classic application to inside wire in high-noise environments. It also is deployed where high frequency signals are transmitted and where interference with adjacent pairs presents a concern. Category 6 (Cat 6) is an non-standard twisted pair cabling system suggested for use in support of high-speed LANs (e.g., 100BaseT and Gigabit Ethernet) at up to 600 MHz. The Cat 6 SFTP (Shielded Foil Twisted Pair) system comprises four twisted pairs separately wrapped in foil insulators and twisted around one another, and contained in an extra insulating shield contained within a flame-retardant polymer jacket.

Coaxial Cable

Coaxial cable (Figure 2-3) is a very robust shielded copper wire. The center conductor is much thicker than a twisted pair conductor, and is surrounded by an outer shield/conductor that serves to greatly improve signal strength and integrity. A layer of foam or solid insulation generally separates the two conductors. The entire cable is then protected by a layer of *dielectric* (electrically non-conductive) material, such as PVC or Teflon[r]. The two conductors share a common axis, hence the term *coaxial*. Reportedly invented by AT&T Bell Telephone Laboratories in 1934, the first coaxial cable was placed into service in New York City in 1936. Such a cable was used in New York City to televise the 1940 Philadelphia Republican National Convention at which Wendell Wilke was nominated [2-6]. While Wilke was unsuccessful in his bid for the presidency, coaxial cable proved a big winner.

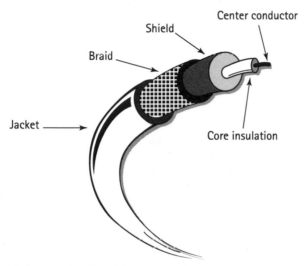

Figure 2–3 Coaxial cable configuration.

Configuration

A coaxial cable, or coax, typically consists of a single, two-conductor wire, with a center conductor and an outer shield/conductor. The outer shield generally consists of solid metal, although a braided or stranded metal screen sometimes is used. *Twinaxial cables* contain two coax cables contained within a single cable sheath. The center conductor carries the carrier signal and the outer conductor generally is used only for electrical grounding and maintained at 0 volts. Therefore, coax is described as an electrically *unbalanced* medium. A *balun* (*bal*anced/*un*balanced) connector can interconnect (balanced) twisted pair and (unbalanced) coax cables.

Gauge

The gauge of the cable is much thicker than a twisted pair. While this increases the available bandwidth (higher frequency signals) and increases the distance of transmission (less resistance), it also increases the cost (more copper). Traditional coax is quite thick, heavy, and bulky — Ethernet LAN coax (10Base5) for example. *ThinNet*, or *CheaperNet*, (10Base2) coax has many fewer dimensions, but offers less in terms of performance.

Bandwidth

The effective capacity of coaxial cable depends on several factors, including the gauge of the center conductor, the length of the circuit, and the spacing of amplifiers and other intermediate devices. Since the bandwidth available over coax is very significant, it often was used in high-capacity applications, such as data and image transmission. Note the following examples of coax standards for classic Ethernet LANs; 10Base5 involves a much more substantial cable, with a thicker center conductor than 10Base2:

- ◆ 10Base5: 10 Mbps; Baseband (single channel); 500m maximum link length

- ◆ 10Base2: 10 Mbps; Baseband (single channel); 200m (180 m, rounded up) maximum link length

As in the case of UTP, 100 Mbps is possible over coax, and over longer distances with better error performance. In CATV and other applications, coax routinely supports transmission of multiple channels at an aggregate rate of 500-750 MHz.

Error Performance

Coax offers excellent error performance due to the outer shielding. As a result, coax was used extensively in classic data applications, e.g., mainframe to Front-End Processor to cluster controller to terminal. However, the end-to-end integrity of the shield is crucial; either physical damage or poor splicing will result in awful error performance. The shield also must be grounded properly.

Distance

Coax does not have the same distance limitations as UTP, because the thicker center conductor offers less resistance to the carrier signal. Amplifiers or other intermediate devices must be used to extend high-frequency transmissions over significant distances.

Security

Coax is inherently quite secure. It is relatively difficult to place physical taps on coax. As little energy is radiated through the outer shield, radio antennae and inductive coils offer little use in gaining access to the raw carrier signal.

Cost

The acquisition, deployment, and rearrangement costs of coax are very high, compared with UTP, due to increased bulk and weight, as well as the requirement for grounding the outer shield. In high-capacity data applications, however, its positive performance characteristics can outweigh that cost.

Applications

Historically, coax often was used in telco interoffice trunking applications, as a superior option to twisted pair cables. That is no longer the case, as satellite, microwave and, particularly, fiber optic cables are the media of contemporary choice in such applications. The superior performance characteristics of coax favored its use in many short-haul, bandwidth-intensive data applications. Current and continuing applications include host-to-host, cabinet-to-cabinet (e.g., PBX and computer), host-to-peripheral (e.g., host-to-Front-End Processor), and LANs (e.g., classic Ethernet). Recent developments in UTP and fiber optic transmission systems, however, have rendered coax largely obsolete in such applications.

Coax also is used extensively in CATV networks due to its overall performance characteristics. Coax-based CATV networks commonly provide bandwidth of either 330 MHz in support of up to 40 channels, or 750 MHz in support of up to 116 channels. Such analog, one-way downstream networks support each analog TV signal over a 6-MHz channel, with the channels frequency division multiplexed at the *head end*, or point of signal origin. The signals are de-multiplexed at the set-top box, or converter. Much coax remains in place in CATV application, although it is being replaced with fiber optics in the backbone, with the existing coax used for the last leg of the connection to the premise. Such a hybrid network will support one-way entertainment TV, two-way Internet access, two-way voice, and other applications.

Microwave Radio

Ah, here's the problem—the keyboard and hard drive are fine. The trouble seems to be that your monitor is a microwave. From the comic strip *Bizarro* by Dan Piraro.

Microwave radio, a form of radio transmission which uses ultra-high frequencies, developed out of experiments with *radar* (*ra*dio *d*etecting *a*nd *r*anging) during the period preceding World War II. The first primitive systems, used in military applications in the European and Pacific theaters, could handle up to 2,400 voice conversations over five channels. Developed by Harold T. Friis and his associates at Bell Telephone Laboratories, the first public demonstration was conducted between the West Street lab and Neshanic, New Jersey in October 1945 [2-6].

There are several frequency ranges assigned to microwave systems, all in the GigaHertz (GHz) range — in other words, billions of cycles per second. The *wavelength* is in the millimeter range; that is, each electromagnetic cycle or wave is in the range of a millimeter, with billions of such cycles generated during a second of transmission. This very short wavelength gives rise to the term *microwave*. As such high-frequency signals are especially susceptible to attenuation, they must be amplified (analog) or repeated (digital) frequently. Therefore, if a considerable distance separates the originating and terminating microwave radio antennae, there must be intermediate antennae at periodic intervals in order to boost the signal.

In order to maximize the strength of such a high-frequency signal and, therefore, to increase the distance of transmission at acceptable signal levels, the radio beams are highly focused. Much as a light bulb in a flashlight is centered in a mirror which serves to focus the light beam, the microwave transmit antenna is centered in a concave, reflective metal dish which serves to focus the radio beam with maximum effect on the receiving antenna. Similarly, the receiving antenna is centered in a concave metal dish, which serves to collect the maximum amount of incoming signal and reflect it into the receiver.

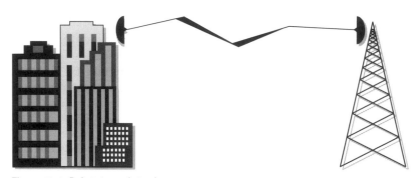

Figure 2-4 Point-to-point microwave

The requirement to so tightly focus the signal clearly limits the application of microwave. It is a *point-to-point*, rather than a *broadcast*, transmission system. Additionally, each antenna must be within the line-of-sight of the next antenna; as such high-frequency radio waves will not pass through solid objects of any significance (e.g., buildings, mountains, or airplanes). Given the curvature of the earth, and the obvious problems of transmitting through it, microwave hops generally are limited to 50 miles (80 km).

While all the various microwave frequency bands suffer from these limitations, the higher frequencies suffer to a greater extent. Those higher frequencies, set aside for digital microwave in the United States, suffer more from environmental interference including dust, smog, agricultural haze, and precipitation. The following Table 2-3 lists example U.S. frequency bands set aside by the Federal Communications Commission for commercial microwave [2-9].

Table 2-3 EXAMPLE MICROWAVE FREQUENCY BANDS (UNITED STATES)

Frequency Bands	Maximum Antennae Separation	Analog/Digital
4-6 GHz	20-30 miles (32-48 km)	Analog
10-12 GHz	10-15 miles (16-24 km)	Digital
18-23 GHz	5-7 miles (8-11 km)	Digital

The several frequency bands set aside for microwave are protected by regulatory authority in most countries and regions. Additionally, the placement of the antennae and the power level of transmission is regulated, with licenses granted to individual carriers and end users. However, difficulties have developed over time in certain areas (e.g., Europe and Asia) due to factors which include the small size of the individual nations; conflicting regulations, or the lack thereof; conflicting commercial and military applications; and unwillingness of national regulators to govern the use of radio frequencies on a coordinated, regional basis.

Configuration

Microwave radio consists of antennae centered within reflective dishes, which are attached to structures such as towers or buildings and generally take the shape of either a parabola (bowl) or horn (cornucopia). While the antennae often are quite small, larger horns yield great *gain*, or signal power, as they collect more incoming signals; therefore, larger antennae perform better. Hollow cables or tubes, known as *waveguides*, serve to guide the radio microwaves between the electronic transmit/receive equipment and the antennae.

Bandwidth

Microwave offers substantial bandwidth, often in excess of 6 Gbps. T-1 (1.544 Mbps) capacity is routine – even in end user applications – with many private microwave networks operating at T-3 (45 Mbps) rates. Note that the issue is not so much the bandwidth provided in the microwave radio spectrum as it is the fact that spectrum is licensed to users on a geographic basis. Once a slice of microwave spectrum is licensed to a user, it becomes absolutely unavailable to other users in proximity.

Error Performance

Microwave, especially digital microwave, performs well in terms of error performance – assuming proper design and deployment. Physical obstructions must be avoided at all costs, even grazing the smallest obstructions has a decidedly negative impact on signal strength and error performance. However, such high-frequency radio is particularly susceptible to environmental interference (e.g., precipitation, haze, smog, and smoke) -- *rain attenuation*, or *rain fade*, is a factor, especially at frequencies above 8 GHz. At frequencies above 11 GHz, rain attenuation can be especially serious, because the level of attenuation react is sensitive to the rate of rainfall, the size of the raindrops, and the length of exposure. Note that microwave operates at very high frequencies, many of which near the upper limit of the radio spectrum, and border on the lower edge of the light spectrum. Therefore, microwave behaves more like light than it acts like radio, as we normally think of it. In other words, it is absorbed, refracted, and reflected by physical matter – the more dense the matter, the worse the effect. Generally speaking and assuming that the system is designed properly, however, microwave performs on a par with UTP networks in terms of error performance.

Distance

Microwave clearly is distance-limited, especially at the higher frequencies (see Table 2-2). This limitation can be mitigated through complex arrays of antennae incorporating spatial diversity to collect more signal.

Security

As is the case with all radio systems, microwave is inherently insecure. If the microwave path is known, a radio antenna can easily capture the raw signal.. Security must be imposed through encryption (scrambling) of the signal at the transmitting end, with the signal decrypted (unscrambled) on the receiving end.

Cost

The acquisition, deployment, and rearrangement costs of microwave can be high. However, it often compares very favorably with cabled systems, which require extensive right-of-way, trenching, conduit systems, splicing, etc. Additionally, microwave is not affected by *backhoe (digger) fade*, as are cabled systems.

Regulation

Microwave, generally speaking, must be licensed on a case-by-case basis to avoid interference between adjacent systems; this process can be lengthy and costly. Additionally, local zoning ordinances and health and safety regulations may affect the placement of antennae.

Applications

Microwave originally was used for long-haul voice and data communications. Competing long distance carriers, first in the United States, found microwave a most attractive alternative to cabled systems, due to the high speed and low cost of deployment. Where feasible, however, fiber optic technology currently is used in long-haul applications. Contemporary applications include private networks, carrier bypass, temporary disaster recovery, interconnection of cellular radio switches, and as an alternative to cabled systems in consideration of difficult terrain.

Satellite Radio

Satellite radio, quite simply, is a microwave transmission system utilizing a non-terrestrial relay station positioned in space. The concept initially was offered in an article entitled "Extra-Terrestrial Relays" published in *Wireless World* in February, 1945 by Arthur C. Clarke, then a physicist at the British Interplanetary Society and since the author of *2001: A Space Odyssey* and many other science-fiction books. Since the launch of the Earlybird I satellite in 1965 proved the effectiveness of the concept of satellite communications, satellites have proved invaluable in extending the reach of voice, data, and video communications around the globe and into the most remote regions of the world. Exotic applications such as the Global Positioning System (GPS) would have been unthinkable without the benefit of satellites [2-10].

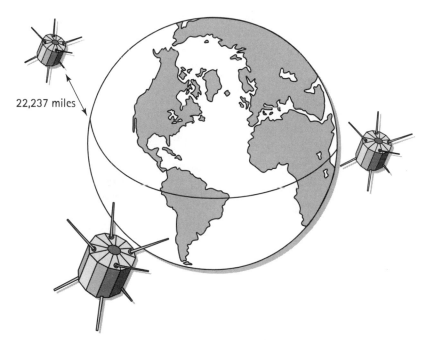

22,237 miles

Figure 2-5 Satellites in Geostationary Earth Orbit (GEO)

Geostationary Satellites

Traditional satellite communications systems involve a satellite relay station which is launched into a *geostationary, geosynchronous,* or *geostatic* orbit, also known as a *Clarke* orbit. Such an orbit is approximately 22,237 miles (36,000 km) above the equator (Figure 2-5). At that altitude and in an equatorial orbital slot, the satellite maintains its synchronization with the revolution of the earth. In other words, the satellite maintains its relative position over the same spot of the earth's surface. Consequently, transmit and receive earth stations (microwave dishes) can be pointed reliably at the satellite for communications purposes. Geosynchronous Earth Orbiting (GEO) satellites are also known as *Fixed Satellite Systems (FSSs)*.

The popularity of satellite communications has placed great demands on the international regulators to manage and allocate available frequencies, as well as the limited number of orbital slots available for satellite positioning. As in the case of terrestrial microwave radio, there are a number of frequency bands assigned to satellite systems, most of which fall in the MegaHertz (MHz) or GigaHertz (GHz) ranges. Due to the wide *footprint*, or area of coverage of a satellite, the frequencies must be managed carefully at national, regional, and international levels. Generally speaking, geostationary satellites are positioned approximately 2 degrees (2() apart to minimize interference from adjacent satellites using overlapping frequencies [2-10]. There currently are approximately 192 GEOs in operation. In an article entitled "A Short Pre-History of Comsats, Or: How I Lost a Billion Dollars in My Spare Time", Arthur C. Clarke lamented his failure to patent the concept [2-11].

Although such high-frequency signals are especially susceptible to attenuation in the atmosphere, they can *propagate* (travel) infinite distances in the vacuum of space with no signal loss. Attenuation can, however, be problematic within the few miles of atmosphere on the *uplink* and *downlink* segments. The uplink and downlink generally utilize different frequencies for transmission, to avoid interference between incoming and outgoing signals. As suggested in Figure 2-8, the higher of the two frequencies is used for the uplink; the increased effect of signal attenuation at the higher frequency can be overcome through the application of higher signal power — inexpensive power from the surface of the earth. At a much lower power level, the lower downlink frequency can better penetrate the earth's atmosphere and electromagnetic field, which can act to bend the incoming signal much as light bends when entering a pool of water. Table 2-4 provides a set of example frequencies and spacecraft serving various applications, with *LEO* referring to *Low-Earth Orbiting* satellites. Chapter 12 discusses LEOs in detail.

Table 2–4 EXAMPLE SATELLITE COMMUNICATION FREQUENCIES
SOURCE: INTERNATIONAL TELECOMMUNICATIONS UNION (ITU) AND
COMSAT

Frequency Range	Band Designation	Example Spacecraft
136-137 & 148 MHz	VHF	NOAA (LEO Weather)
400 MHz	UHF	Orbcomm
1610-1625.5 MHz 2483.5-2500 MHz	L-band	Big LEOs
2310-2360 MHz	S-band	Civil Defense Radio
3700-4200 MHz 5925-6425 MHz	C-band	Galaxy, Satcom, Telstar, Intelsat, etc.
4 GHz-6 GHz	C-band	Intelsat, Comsat, etc.
11.7-12.2 GHz 14.0-14.5 GHz	Ku-band	Globalstar, etc.
20 GHz & 30 GHz	Ka-band	ACTS

UPLINK

In order to maximize the strength of such a high frequency signal, as well as to direct the uplink transmission to a specific satellite, the uplink radio beams are highly focused. The transmit antenna is centered in a concave, reflective dish which serves to focus the radio beam with maximum effect on the receiving satellite antenna. Table 2-5 provides example uplink and downlink frequencies, with mention of standard applications.

Table 2–5 EXAMPLE UPLINK/DOWNLINK SATELLITE FREQUENCIES

Frequency Band	Uplink/Downlink Frequency Range	Example Application
C-band	6 GHz/4 GHz	TV, Voice, Videoconferencing
Ku-band	14 GHz/11-12 GHz	TV, DBS/DSS
Ka-band	30 GHz/20 GHz	Mobile Voice

DOWNLINK

The downlink transmission is focused on a particular *footprint*, or area of coverage. Although a satellite can see roughly one-third of the earth's surface from its vantage point, the signal would weaken so as to be unusable at the fringes of such a footprint, were the signal not shaped or focused. *Spot beams*, even more tightly focused downlinks, serve specific applications over smaller regions.

Broadcast

The wide footprint of a satellite radio system enables a signal to *broadcast* over a wide area. Thereby, any number (theoretically, an infinite number) of terrestrial antennae can receive the signal, more or less simultaneously. In this manner, satellites can serve a *point-to-multipoint* network requirement through a single uplink station and multiple downlink stations.

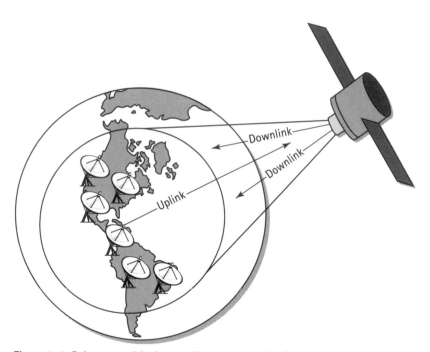

Figure 2-6 Point-to-multipoint satellite network with footprint.

Recently developed satellites can serve a *mesh* network requirement, whereby each terrestrial site can communicate directly with any other site through the satellite relay station. Previously, all such communications were required to travel through a centralized site, known as a *head end*. Such a mesh network, of course, imposes an additional level of difficulty on the network in terms of managing the flow and direction of traffic.

Configuration

Satellite radio systems consist of antennae and reflective dishes, much like terrestrial microwave. The dish serves to focus the signal from a transmitting antenna or to a receiving antenna. The send/receive dishes that make up the earth segment vary in size, depending on power levels and frequency bands. The dishes generally are mounted on a tripod or other type of brace, which anchors to the earth, a pad or a roof, or attached to a structure such as building. Waveguides guide, or channel, the radio signal between the antennae and the transmit/receive electronics. The terrestrial antennae support a single frequency band (e.g., C-band, Ku-band, or Ka-band). A hybrid satellite may support a number of frequency bands for various applications, such as radio, TV, paging, voice, and data. The higher the frequency band, the smaller the possible size of the dish, as the higher-frequency dishes can achieve greater signal gain at a smaller size. Therefore, C-band TV dishes tend to be rather large, while Ku-band DBS (Direct Broadcast Satellite) TV dishes tend to be very small. Additionally, flat, mechanically passive, phased array dishes are being built in very small sizes and at very low cost for DBS TV and other applications. Such phased array antennae employ an array of small antennae that work together to logically focus on the point of maximum signal strength, rather than requiring that the reflective dish adjust mechanically. As a point of reference, the Intelsat I (1968) dishes measured 30 meters in diameter.

The space segment antennae are mounted on a satellite, of course. The satellite can support multiple transmit/receive antennae, depending on the various frequencies which it employs to support various applications, and depending on whether it covers an entire footprint or divides the footprint into smaller areas of coverage through the use of more tightly focused spot beams. Satellite repeaters are in the form of *transponders*. The transponders accept the weak incoming signals, boost them, shift from the uplink to the downlink frequencies, and retransmit the information to the earth stations. Contemporary satellites, such as Intelsat VI, commonly support as many as 46 transponders.

VSATs

VSATs, or *Very Small Aperture Terminals*, are a breed of satellite system involving terrestrial dishes of very small diameter (aperture). Operating in the C-band and Ku-band, VSATs are digital and designed primarily to support data communications on a point-to-multipoint basis for large private networks, in applications such as retail inventory management, and for credit verification and authorization. While some newer systems also support mesh networks and compressed voice communications at rates as low as 2.4 Kbps, they are unusual at this time. Bandwidth commonly is in channel increments of 56/64 Kbps, generally up to an aggregate bandwidth of 512 Kbps, although some newer systems provide bandwidth of as much as 1.7 Mbps on the downlink and 20 Mbps on the uplink [2-12]. By far the largest concentration of users lives in North America, claiming about 75% of the market. According to Telecom Applications Corp., Mobil Oil and Shell Oil each installed a network of approximately 5,000 sites [2-13] and [2-14]. Worldwide, approximately 920,000 VSAT terminals are expected to be installed by 2001, according to MegaTech Resources [2-15].

Bandwidth

Satellites can support multiple transponders and, therefore, substantial bandwidth, with each transponder generally providing increments of up to 36 MHz. The level of bandwidth, the number of frequency bands supported, the number of transponders, and the specific area of coverage all influence the size and power requirements of the satellite.

As in the case of other transmission systems, the higher frequency bands offer greater raw bandwidth. In this sense, C-band is the most limited, while Ka-band is the most attractive of the commercial satellite frequency bands. As a point of reference, Intelsat I could accommodate only 240 voice circuits, while Intelsat VI supported 120,000 voice circuits and three TV channels, with total bandwidth of 3.46 GHz [2-16].

Error Performance

Satellite transmission is susceptible to environmental interference, particularly at frequencies above 20 GHz. Sunspots and other types of electromagnetic interference particularly impact satellite and microwave transmission. Additionally, some satellite frequency bands (e.g., C-band) compete with terrestrial microwave (see Tables 2-2 and 2-4), again illustrating the requirement for careful frequency management. As a result of these several factors, satellite transmission requires rather extensive error detection and correction capabilities [2-17].

Distance

Satellite, generally speaking, is not considered to be distance-limited, as the signal largely travels through the vacuum of space. Further, each signal travels approximately 22,300 miles in each direction, whether you communicate across the street or across the country, and assuming that only a single satellite hop is required. However, larger earth stations and additional power are required to serve areas far removed from the equator (e.g., New Zealand and South Africa). In such instances, the signals must travel a longer distance through substantial atmosphere and they are more likely to be deflected by the earth's magnetic field at such a severe angle.

Propagation Delay & Response Time

GEOs, by virtue of their high orbital altitude, impose rather significant propagation delay on the signal and, therefore, doubly affect response time(see Figure 2-6). Given the fact that the radio signals must travel approximately 22,300 miles up to the satellite and the same distance on the return leg, the resulting delay is about 250 milliseconds (.25 seconds). Considering the amount of time required for processing on board the satellite, as well as at the earth stations, the total delay for a one-way transmission lasts about 320 milliseconds (.32 seconds). Therefore, the delay between signal origination (transmission) and receipt of response is about 640 milliseconds (.64 seconds), assuming an immediate response requiring only a single satellite hop. Hence, highly interactive voice, data, and video applications are not effectively supported via two-way satellite communications.

Note that satellite commonly supports interactive videoconferencing. However, it generally is accomplished in broadcast lecture mode, with the video signal sent from the central location to the satellite, which broadcasts it to multiple receive-only earth stations. The participants at the distant locations interact with the lecturer via landline connections. This hybrid approach mitigates the impact of propagation delay, an intolerable situation if the conference made use of satellite links in both directions. This approach also reduces the overall cost, as receive-only earth stations are much less expensive then transmit-receive stations. Interactive Internet access is being offered via satellite, on a limited basis, by DBS providers; again, through implementation of a hybrid approach.

Security

As is the case with all microwave and other radio systems, satellite transmission is inherently insecure. Satellite transmission is especially vulnerable to interception, as the signal is broadcast over the entire area of the footprint. Therefore, the unauthorized user must know only the satellite location and the associated frequency range. Encryption or scrambling must enforce this security.

Cost

The acquisition, deployment, and rearrangement costs of the space segment of satellite systems can be quite high (easily U.S. $200 million). However, a large number of users can share the satellite, with each user organization perhaps connecting a large number of sites. As a result, satellite networks often compare very favorably with cabled systems or terrestrial microwave systems for many point-to-multipoint applications. Cost elements include leasing capacity from a satellite provider (e.g., GE Americom, Hughes Communications Inc., and AT&T Skynet), as well as the acquisition cost of the terrestrial antennae. Note that the acquisition cost of receive-only dishes is relatively low, while transmit/receive dishes are considerably more expensive. As is the case with microwave, satellite transmission is not affected by *backhoe (digger) fade*, which plagues cabled systems.

Regulation

National, regional, and international bodies more or less carefully regulate the space segment of satellite communications. Additionally, local zoning ordinances and health and safety regulations may affect the placement of terrestrial antennae. While satellite network technology is widely available in North America and other countries, it is not widely available to end users, worldwide. Many countries in Asia and Europe have rejected *open sky* policies, in support of the incumbent carriers, commonly known as *PTTs* (Post, Telegraph, and Telephone agencies) or *TOs* (Telecommunications Organizations). Developing countries, particularly, depend heavily on the imbalance of trade in telecommunications services as a source of hard currency; in fact, many of them intentionally price originating traffic at very high levels in order to suppress outbound traffic and, therefore, to suppress the amount of hard currency outflow. As private satellite transmission bypasses the national network, it has a negative impact on that trade imbalance (depending on one's perspective) and, therefore, is discouraged strongly.

Applications

Satellite applications are many, and increasing rapidly, as the traditional voice and data services have been augmented with more exotic applications such as GPS (Global Positioning Systems) and ATMS (Advanced Traffic Management Systems). Traditional international voice and data services have been supplanted, to a considerable extent, by submarine fiber optic cable systems.

Traditional, and still viable, applications include international voice and data, remote voice and data (e.g., island nations, isolated areas, and sparsely populated areas), television and radio broadcast, maritime navigation, videoconferencing, inventory management and control (VSATs), disaster recovery, and paging. More recent and emerging applications include air navigation, Global Positioning Systems (GPS), mobile voice and data (LEOs and MEOs), Advanced Traffic Management Systems (ATMS), Direct Broadcast Satellite (DBS) TV, Integrated Services Digital Network (ISDN), and Internet access.

Infrared

Infrared light transmissions have existed for many years in something of a backwater in the world of transmission systems — their use limited to remote controls for TV sets, slide projectors, and the like. However, they now assume a position of some, if still limited, importance. Infrared systems use the infrared light spectrum (TeraHertz, or THz, range) to send a focused light beam to a receiver, much as would a microwave system, although without the use of a reflective dish. Rather, a pair of lenses is used, with a focusing lens employed in the transmitting device and a collecting lens in the receiving device (Figure 2-7). Infrared is an *airwave*, rather than a *conducted* transmission system. Although generally used in short-haul transmission, they do offer substantial bandwidth, but with risks of interference.

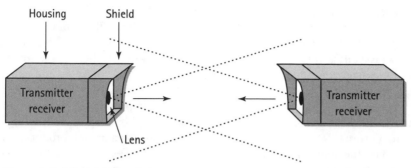

Figure 2-7 Infrared transmission system.

Advantages include rapid deployment; unlike microwave, there are no licensing requirements. Contemporary infrared systems offer substantial bandwidth at relatively low cost; infrared LAN bridges operate at rates of 1.544 Mbps (T-1), 45 Mbps (T-3), and 155 Mbps (OC-1). Like microwave systems, however, infrared systems require line-of-sight and suffer from environmental interference; under optimum conditions, error performance is in the range of 10^{-8} [2-18]. Additionally, infrared transmission typically is limited to distances of two miles. However, infrared often is an attractive alternative to leased lines or private cabled systems for building-to-building connectivity in a campus environment. Certain wireless LAN systems employ infrared transmission, as do some PDAs (Personal Digital Assistants).

Fiber Optics

Alexander Graham Bell originally trialed the concept of using light waves for communications. In the late 1800s, Bell invented and experimented with the *photophone*, a system utilizing sunlight and mirrors for audio transmission. While his experiment was successful in transmitting very poor quality voice over very short distances, the technique was clearly impractical. During World War II, the Nazi military experimented with similar but more advanced systems, which also proved impractical [2-6].

The 1940s saw the first experiments with *waveguides* conducted, with both microwave radio and optical transmission systems. Such waveguides were rigid, insulated pipes, which served to contain the electromagnetic energy and channel it from end to end, while offering protection from outside interference. While significant transmission speeds can be realized through this process, it is seldom used because of its impracticality.

Flexible glass wires offered much more potential as a transmission medium for light. As early as the 1950s, the efforts of the American Optical Corporation resulted in optical fiber cable that could carry light signals a few feet. It was at Standard Telecommunications Laboratories in 1966 that Charles Kao and George

Hockman developed the first practical conceptual breakthrough – the purity of the glass was the issue. During the early 1970s, the first practical fiber optic systems were developed. These systems were made possible by the manufacturing of pure glass fibers with a silica content high enough (few impurities) to permit the transmission of light over long distances with little signal loss. At roughly the same time, AT&T Bell Laboratories invented *laser diodes*, which serve as high-speed transmit devices. Since then, fiber optic development has progressed to the point that virtually all high-speed networks are based on fiber optic technology. According to Corning Telecommunications Products [2-19], a major producer of fiber optic cables, the demand for fiber optic technology was estimated at 14.5 million miles in 1995, an increase of 20 to 25 percent over the previous year.

Fiber optic transmission systems are *opto-electric* in nature. In other words, they involve a combination of optical and electrical electromagnetic energy. The signal originates as an electrical signal, which is translated into an optical signal, which subsequently is reconverted into an electrical signal at the receiving end. Optical repeaters also go through this opto-electric conversion process as they boost the signal at various points in long-haul transmission systems. Chapter 9 presents a detailed discussion of SONET (Synchronous Optical NETwork) fiber technology.

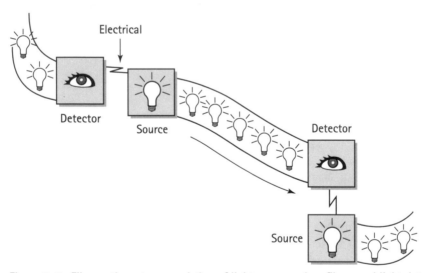

Figure 2-8   Fiber optic system, consisting of light sources, glass fibers, and light detectors.

Configuration

Fiber optic systems consist of light sources, cables, and light detectors, as depicted in Figure 2-8. In a simple configuration, one of each is used. In a more complex configuration over longer distances, many such sets of elements are employed. Much like other transmission systems, long-haul optical communications typically involves a number of regenerative repeaters. In a fiber optic system, repeaters are optoelectric devices. On the incoming side of the repeater, a light detector receives the optical signal, converts it into an electrical signal, boosts it, converts it into an optical signal and places it onto a fiber, and so on. There may be many such optical repeaters in a long-haul transmission system, although typically far less than would be required using other terrestrial transmission media. Optical repeaters essentially are fiber terminals (light detectors/sources) mounted back to back.

LIGHT SOURCES

Light sources consist of two types: *Light Emitting Diodes* (*LEDs*) and *Diode Lasers* or Semiconductor Lasers. Each has its advantages.

- ◆ **Light Emitting Diodes (LEDs)** are commonly used semiconductor components, found in clocks, calculators, and a plethora of other devices. The LEDs used in fiber optic transmission are, of course, much more sophisticated. LEDs predominated in early fiber optic systems, largely because of their much lower costs of acquisition and operation. However, they provide less bandwidth and generate infrared light waves capable of traveling only relatively short distances with acceptable error performance. LEDs also generate broadly-defined optical signals; in other words, the signals include a broad range of the light spectrum. LEDs have found continuing application in short-haul transmission systems such as LANs. As LEDs are the less capable light sources, they are matched with the less capable fiber (MultiMode) and detector (PhotoIntrinsic Diode) technologies.

- ◆ **Diode Lasers** resemble LEDs in structure, although they are much more difficult and expensive to manufacture. They also are associated with more expensive and complex supporting electronics, which require careful control of ambient temperature. However, they generally offer much more bandwidth, as they can pulse on and off in a fraction of a *nanosecond*, one billionth of a second. Diode lasers offer significant *coupling efficiency*; in other words they can tightly focus a high-speed light signal for presentation to the axis, or core, of a very thin SingleMode Fiber (SMF), which offers much better performance. Diode lasers also generate signals at optical frequencies that attenuate much less; as a result, the signal can travel much farther without being repeated. Finally, diode lasers generate tightly-defined optical signals; in other words, they are confined to very specific frequencies of the visible light spectrum. In carrier-class transmission systems, this tight definition allows the multiplexing of a number of light frequencies through a process known as *Wavelength Division Multiplexing* (*WDM*) or *Dense WDM* (*DWDM*), which is Frequency Division Multiplexing (FDM) at the optical level. As each frequency *window* is added, the bandwidth of the system increases by a factor of one. For example, a system operating at 2.5 Gbps enjoys a bandwidth increase of 2.5 Gbps as each DWDM frequency is added. As diode lasers enjoy a high level of coupling efficiency, they can be used in conjunction with either MultiMode or SingleMode fiber. Since diode lasers are the more capable light sources, they generally are matched with the more capable fiber (SingleMode) and detector (Avalanche PhotoDiode) technologies.

OPTICAL FIBERS

While plastic wires are used in some specialized, low-bandwidth, short-haul applications (e.g., automobiles and airplanes), glass predominates. Generally speaking, fiber cables contain a large number of fiber strands because the additional cost of redundancy is relatively low. Oftentimes, only a few of the fibers are active, with the remaining fibers left *dark* for backup or future use; such a system is known as *dim* fiber, as it is neither dark nor fully lit. For example, companies such as Nextlink deploy fiber systems with as many as 620 strands along a single route, with each fiber supporting as many as four DWDM optical frequencies, each of which operates at as much as 10 Gbps. While current technology can support two-way transmission over a single fiber, two fibers generally are used, with one transmitting in each direction.

The mass production of glass fiber employs several techniques, all of which take place in a vacuum environment. First, silica is heated to the point that it vaporizes. The ultra-pure glass vapor is deposited on a designated surface to create a glass cylinder. That cylinder is then reheated and collapsed into a *preform* cylinder. The preform cylinder is reheated and drawn, in a process known as *broomsticking*, into fibers which can measure as long as 10 km in length.

The light pulse travels down the center *core* of the especially pure glass fiber. Surrounding the inner core lies a layer of glass *cladding*, with a slightly different *refractive index*. The cladding serves to reflect the light waves back into the inner core. Surrounding the cladding is a layer of protective coating, such as Kevlar, which seals the cable and provides mechanical protection (Figure 2-8). Typically, multiple fibers are housed in a single sheath, which may be heavily armored. Glass optical fibers consist of two basic types: *MultiMode* (*MMF*) and *monomode*, or *SingleMode* (*SMF*).

MULTIMODE FIBER (MMF) *MultiMode Fiber* (*MMF*) is designed to support relatively low-speed transmission over relatively short distances. MMF is less expensive to produce, but lacks in performance because the inner core is larger in diameter (typically 50-125 microns). As the light rays travel down the fiber, they spread out due to a phenomenon known as *modal dispersion*, with portions of the light signals taking different *modes*, or paths. *Step-index* MultiMode Fibers are distinguished by an abrupt change in the refractive index between the core and the cladding. Although reflected fairly instantly back into the inner core by the cladding, those portions of the light pulses travel a longer distance from point to point than do the portions which travel more or less down the center of the fiber.

As the distance of the circuit increases and as the speed of transmission increases, the pulses of light tend to lose their shape and overrun each other in a phenomenon know as *pulse dispersion* (See Figure 2-9). At that point, the light detector cannot distinguish between the individual pulses. As a result, MultiMode Fiber is relegated to applications involving relatively short distances and lower speeds of transmission (e.g., LANs and campus environments).

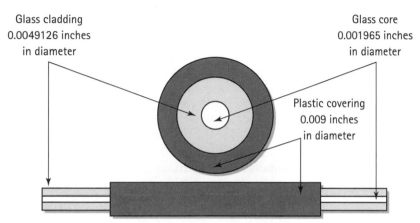

Glass cladding
0.0049126 inches
in diameter

Glass core
0.001965 inches
in diameter

Plastic covering
0.009 inches
in diameter

Figure 2-9 Glass fiber optic cable, side view and cross section.

The phenomenon of pulse dispersion is analogous to a convoy of very small automobiles (light pulses) traveling at a high rate of speed (Mbps) and tailgating (small separation) each other down a multilane (large diameter) interstate highway. While each of the cars begins in the center lane, some of them drift from shoulder to shoulder, thereby traveling a longer distance from point to point. Not only does the convoy lose its shape over a long distance, but collisions occur frequently.

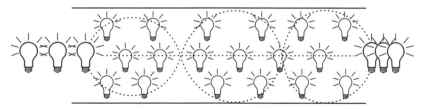

Figure 2-10 Modal dispersion and pulse dispersion within an optical fiber.

Graded-index fiber is MultiMode Fiber that reduces the impact of pulse dispersion. Graded-index fiber is distinguished from step-index by both its gradual change in refractive index between the core and the cladding, and its smaller diameter core. The gradual change in refractive index enables the errant light signal to move with greater speed through the inner edges of the cladding in order to compensate to some degree for the longer distance that it must travel. The thinner inner core serves to reduce the distance that even the most errant light signals travel. Graded-index fibers can support transmission rates up to 100 Mbps over relatively short distances; they are commonly used in LAN applications [2-20].

SINGLEMODE FIBER (SMF) Also known as *monomode*, *SingleMode Fiber* (*SMF*) has a thinner inner core, typically 10 microns or so, which reduces modal dispersion and the resulting pulse dispersion. Therefore, it performs better than MultiMode Fiber over longer distances at higher transmission rates. Although more costly, monomode fiber is used to advantage in long-haul, and especially in high-bandwidth, applications [2-18]. The thinner inner core renders SMF unsuitable for use in conjunction with LED light sources because their *coupling efficiency* produces an unacceptable level; in other words, they are incapable of tightening their focus sufficiently to present the light signal to the axis of the small SMF fiber.

Using the same analogy of a convoy of automobiles traveling down a highway, the SMF strand is a single lane wide. Even though the individual cars may drift from shoulder to shoulder, the total distance they travel is not significantly greater than that of the cars that traveled directly down the center of the lane. Even at a very high rate of speed and over a very long distance, the convoy maintains its shape, with resulting collisions unlikely.

LIGHT DETECTORS

Detectors consist of several basic types, the most common being *PhotoINtrinsic diodes* (*PINs*) and *Avalanche PhotoDiodes* (*APDs*). The light detectors serve to reverse the process accomplished by the light sources, converting optical energy back into electrical energy. APDs, although more expensive, are preferable, because they use a strong electric field to accelerate the electrons flowing in the semiconductor. This results in an avalanche of electrons. Thereby, a very weak incoming light pulse will create a much stronger electrical effect. Although more sensitive, APDs require more power and prove more sensitive to extremes of ambient temperature.

Analog or Digital?

Fiber optic systems can either be analog or digital in nature, although digital is much more common. Analog systems simply vary the intensity (amplitude) of the lightwave. Digital systems pulse on and off to represent 1s and 0s; differences in the length of the pulses can represent multiple 1s and 0s. Since digital systems offer significant advantages (e.g., error performance and compression), all long-haul fiber systems used in carrier networks are digital. While CATV providers currently deploy significant amounts of analog fiber for purposes of cable TV delivery, those systems are intended to be upgraded to digital technology when practical. Clearly, digital fiber will be required in a convergence scenario, where the CATV providers support not only TV, but also voice and high-speed data.

Bandwidth

Fiber offers, by far, the greatest bandwidth of any transmission system, often in excess of 2 Gbps in long-haul carrier networks. Systems operating at 10 Gbps are now routinely deployed. Through Dense Wavelength Division Multiplexing (DWDM), carriers routinely introduce four optical windows (light frequencies), thereby achieving bandwidth of 40 Gbps per strand; at this bit rate, a single fiber strand can support approximately 600,000 voice conversations. Sprint was the first carrier to commercially deploy a DWDM system running 40 channels at 2.5 Gbps, for a total yield of 100 Gbps. Systems have tested at 20 Gbps and introduced 55 windows, yielding a total bandwidth of 1.1 Tbps. While such systems have tested only over very short distances under laboratory conditions, the potential is staggering. The theoretical limit of fiber is thought to be in the Terabit (Tbps) range.

Error Performance

As fiber is *dielectric* (a nonconductor of *di*rect *electric* current), it is not susceptible to EMI/RFI; neither does it emit EMI/RFI. Assuming you have properly powered and grounded repeaters and other devices, interference is not an issue. The optical signal does suffer from attenuation as it transverses the fiber, although not to nearly the same extent as do other transmission systems. Such optical attenuation can result from scattering of the optical signal, bending in the fiber cable, translation of light energy to heat, and splices in the cable system. Error performance, depending on factors such as the compression scheme utilized, ranges between 10^{-9} and 10^{-14}, one errored bit in every 100 trillion [2-21]. For all practical purposes, fiber is error-free.

Fairly recently, it has been noted that fiber optic systems have suffered from *diurnal wander*, as do copper and coax. Diurnal (daily cycle) wander is a loss of signal synchronization in digital cable systems caused by temperature variations over the course of 24 hours. As the ambient temperature can vary considerably from the heat of the day to the cool of the night, the cable stretches and contracts, with the overall length of the cable changing, if ever so slightly. As the length of the medium changes, the speed of signal propagation is affected, and the number of digital pulses effectively stored in the medium changes. As a result, the network elements (e.g., repeaters and multiplexers) can get out of synch. Diurnal wander most especially affects cables strung on poles, rather than buried under ground, as the exposure to ambient temperatures is greater and as weight of the cable magnifies the effect [2-22].

Distance

Monomode fiber optic systems routinely are capable of transmitting unrepeated signals over distances in excess of 200 miles (322 km). As a result, relatively few optical repeaters are required in a long-haul system, thereby both reducing costs and eliminating points of potential failure or performance degradation. Long-haul systems, and especially submarine systems, often employ a process of amplification, achieved by chemically doping a section of the cable with a substance such as erbium, a metallic rare earth element. When the laser pulse strikes that section of the cable, the erbium is excited and, in turn, amplifies the light pulse. As certain light frequencies suffer minimally from attenuation and modal dispersion over monomode fiber, pulse dispersion is slight; therefore, multiple amplifiers can replace repeaters over long distances. In fact, tests indicate that unrepeated signals can travel distances of up to 8,000 miles (12,900 km). *Erbium-Doped Fiber Amplifiers* (*EDFAs*), or *light pumps*, are used to maximum effect in conjunction with DWDM systems, as they simultaneously can amplify multiple light frequencies, which must be in the range of 1550 nanometers. While EDFAs are more expensive than repeaters, fewer of them are required; EDFAs can be spaced at intervals of 80-120 kilometers, while optical repeaters often must be spaced at intervals of 50-100 kilometers [2-23]. The exact spacing of the repeaters or amplifiers is sensitive to a number of design factors.

Security

Fiber is intrinsically secure because it is virtually impossible to place a physical tap without detection. Since no light radiates outside the cable, physical taps are the only means of signal interception. Additionally, the fiber system supports such a high volume of traffic that it is difficult to intercept and distinguish a single transmission from the tens, or hundreds, of thousands of other transmissions that might ride the same fiber strand. Additionally, the digital nature of most fiber, coupled with encryption techniques frequently used to protect transmission from interception, make fiber highly secure. In fact, a number of U.S. government agencies recently lobbied Congress and the FCC to require that the carriers place physical taps on existing fiber optic systems in order to ease their ability to place wiretaps, assuming that an enabling court order is issued.

Cost

While the acquisition, deployment, and rearrangement costs of fiber are relatively high (approximately 130% the cost of Cat 5 copper), the immense bandwidth can outweigh that cost in bandwidth-intensive applications. At Gbps speeds, a single set of fibers can carry huge volumes of digital transmissions over longer distances than alternative systems, thereby lowering the transport cost per voice conversation to a small fraction of a penny per minute. The cost of transporting a single bit, therefore, is essentially zero; for that matter, the cost of transporting a multi-megabit file is essentially zero.

Durability

While fiber certainly does not have either the break strength or flex strength of copper or coax, it does enjoy the same tensile strength as steel of the same diameter. In vertical riser cable applications (i.e.; between floors), the integrity of the fiber often is protected through the use of aramid fiber (i.e., Dupont's Kevlar", the same material used in bulletproof vests) strength members; at some point, both steel cables and glass fibers cannot support their own weight. When covered by a protective jacket or armor, fiber can be treated fairly roughly without damage. Note, however, that you must respect limits of bend radius, as the integrity of the data stream can suffer and the glass fiber can break under a severe bend. Additionally, fiber is more resistant to temperature extremes and corrosion than alternative cable systems. Notably, and in consideration of the huge number of conversations supported over a typical fiber optic cable, a train derailment, earthquake, or other traumatic event can have consequences of catastrophic proportions.

Applications: Bandwidth-Intensive:

As you might expect, bandwidth-intensive applications are the most cost-effective fiber optic transmission systems. Such applications include backbone carrier networks, international submarine cables, backbone LANs, interoffice trunking, computer-to-computer or cabinet-to-cabinet (e.g., mainframes and PBXs), distribution networks (e.g., CATV), and fiber to the desktop (e.g., Computer Aided Design, or CAD).

Hybrid Transmission Systems

While each transmission medium/system has its own unique properties and applications, clearly digital fiber optic cable offers the most potential. However, its cost and fragility are limiting factors. In fact, the selection of the most appropriate transmission medium is sensitive to the criteria mentioned at the beginning of this chapter. Namely, those considerations include bandwidth, error performance, throughput, distance between elements, propagation delay, security, mechanical strength, physical dimensions, and a number of cost factors. In fact, a given long-haul transmission typically will transverse a number of transmission systems, perhaps both wired and wireless, and typically including twisted pair in the local loop and fiber optics in the backbone.

The true concept of a *hybrid transmission system*, however, generally involves a local loop connection deployed in a well-planned *convergence* scenario. Such a scenario involves one or more providers deploying a communications grid designed to deliver voice, data, and entertainment information to the premise. Hybrid systems (Figure 2-11) usually are described as involving *Fiber-To-The-Neighborhood* (*FTTN*), *Fiber-To-The-Curb* (*FTTC*) or *Fiber-To-The-Home* (*FTTH*). Although conventional wisdom suggests that cost considerations will dictate that the last link of such a hybrid network involve either coaxial cable or twisted copper pair, various wireless technologies currently challenge that concept.

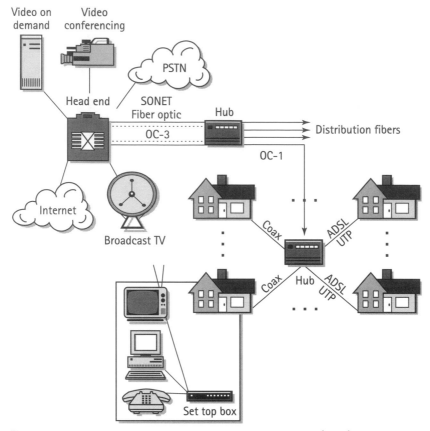

Figure 2-11   Hybrid network with Fiber-To-The-Neighborhood (FTTN): The
convergence scenario.

While many of the traditional telephone carriers and CATV providers have made dramatic announcements about their plans to install fiber optic cable to the curb or even to the premise, their ardor has cooled as the economics of such an approach have become apparent. It is likely that CATV providers will deploy FTTN, and use the embedded coaxial cable for connection to the premise. It is likely that the Incumbent Local Exchange Carriers (ILECs) also will deploy FTTN, and use the embedded twisted pair cable for connection to the premise through emerging local loop technologies such as Asymmetric Digital Subscriber Loop (ADSL). Into the future, Wireless Local Loop (WLL) technology may seriously challenge the traditional wired approach.

References

[2-1]   *Engineering and Operations in the Bell System*, Bell Telephone Laboratories, Inc., 1977.

[2-2]   Keen, Peter G.W. and Cummins, J. Michael. *Networks in Action*. Wadsworth Publishing Company, 1994.

[2-3]   Gelber, Stan. *Introduction to Data Communications: A Practical Approach*. Professional Press Books, 1991.

[2-4]   Sherman, Kenneth. *Data Communications: A Users Guide*. Reston Publishing Company, 1981.

[2-5]   Chiquoine, Walter A. and Hist, Elizabeth R. *The Connectivity Management Handbook*. Transport Management Group, Inc., 1995.

[2-6]   Brooks, John. *Telephone: The First Hundred Years*. Harper & Row, 1975.

[2-7]   *LAN Cable*. Underwriters Laboratories Inc., 1995.

[2-8]   Doll, Dixon R. *Data Communications: Facilities, Networks, and Systems Design*. John Wiley & Sons, 1978.

[2-9]   Bates, Bud. *Introduction to T-1/T-3 Networking*. Artech House, 1992.

[2-10]   Hudson, Heather E. *Communications Satellites: Their Development and Impact*. The Free Press, A Division of Macmillan, Inc., 1990.

[2-11]   Nelson, Robert A. The *Art of Communications via Satellite*. Via Satellite, July 1998.

[2-12]   Pappalardo, Denise. *GE Spacenet Turbocharges Satellite Network*. Network World, November 17, 1997.

[2-13]   Schuerholz, Katherine A. *VSATs: An International Phenomenon*. Via Satellite, December 1995.

[2-14]   Gareiss, Robin. *Down to Earth and Ready for Business*. Data Communications, December 1997.

[2-15]   Llana, Andres. *VSATs Fill in The Telephony Gaps*. Satellite Communications, August 1997.

[2-16]   Held, Gilbert. *Understanding Data Communications*. SAMS Publishing, 1994.

[2-17]   Paetsch, Michael. *Mobile Communications in the US and Europe: Regulation, Technology, and Markets*. Artech House, 1993.

[2-18]   Gasman, Lawrence. *Manager's Guide to the New Telecommunications Network*. Artech House, 1988.

[2-19]   Jones, Del. *Corning: Productivity Soars While Customer Returns Plummet*. USA Today, October 17, 1995.

[2-20]   Hecht, Jeff. *Understanding Fiber Optics, Second Edition*. SAMS Publishing, 1993.

[2-21]   Sexton, Mike and Reid, Andy. *Transmission Networking: SONET and the Digital Hierarchy*. Artech House, 1992.

[2-22]   Newton, Harry. *Newton's Telecom Dictionary*. Flatiron Publishing, 1998.

[2-23]   Finneran, Michael. *DWDM and New Switching Architectures. Business Communications Review*, July 1998.

Additional Suggested Readings:

Bates, Regis J. *Wireless Networked Communications*. The McGraw-Hill Companies, Inc., 1994.

Calhoun, George. *Digital Cellular Radio*. Artech House, 1988.

Coming: Faster, Cheaper Optical Data Links. Byte, February 1996.

Davidson, Robert P. and Muller, Nathan J. *The Guide to SONET: Planning, Installing & Maintaining Broadband Networks*. Telecom Library, 1991.

Derickson, Dennis. *Measuring ASE in Fiber Optic Systems*. Communications Systems Design, January 1996.

Gangisetty, Ramesh and Jehanian, Karen. *Can VSATs Unlock Gridlock?* Satellite Communications, May 1995.

Gifford, James M. *Going Up*. Satellite Communications, February 1996.

Haas, Lou. *Going On-Line with Your Micro*. Tab Books Inc, 1984.

Jenkins, Mark. *Fiber Optic Cable for High-Fiber Interactivity*. Inter@ctive Week July 10, 1995.

Llana, Andres, Jr. *Buying Satellite Communications by the Spoonful*. Satellite Communications, March 1996.

Lopez, Steve. *The Magic of Fiber Networks*. Internetwork, March 1995.

McClimans, Fred. *Be Wary of Wiring Standards*. Internetwork, May 1995.

McElroy, Mark W. *The Corporate Cabling Guide*. Artech House, 1993.

Paone, Joe. *SilCom Delivers Infrared Link.* Internetwork, July 1995.

Pelton, Joseph N. *The "How To" of Satellite Communications.* Design Publishers, 1991.

Saunders, Stephen. *Category 5 UTP: Going, Going, Gone.* Data Communications, March 1996.

Supermarkets Use VSAT Networks for Data Communications. Communications News, November 1994.

Williams, Veronica A. *Wireless Computing Primer.* M&T Books, 1996.

Yokell, Larry. *New Services on your Old Network: Telcos.* Convergence, June 1995.

Chapter 3

Voice Communications Systems: PBX, ACD, Centrex, and KTS

If you could make one good invention in the telegraph, you would secure an annual income...and then you could settle that on your wife and teach Visible Speech and experiment in telegraphy with an easy and undisturbed conscience. Excerpt from a letter dated March 13, 1876, to Alexander Graham Bell from Gardiner Hubbard, Bell's future father-in-law. Source: *Telephone: The First Hundred Years.*

In the beginning, there were only telephone sets and wires between them. The first commercial sets, offered by the Bell Telephone Company in May 1877, consisted of a single piece of wood (black walnut or mahogany) with a single piece of equipment serving as both transmitter and receiver. Power was supplied by a permanent magnet contained within the device, rather than by a battery or external power source. Each telephone set connected to another set directly through a private line, which Western Union generally leased to the telephone company. The first advertisements offered the use of two telephones and a line connecting them for $20.00 per year for social purposes, $40.00 per year for business. Free maintenance was guaranteed. By the Fall of 1877, over 600 telephones were in use. As the popularity of the invention grew, visions developed of rooms full of telephones and skies full of wires [3-1].

In order to improve the usefulness of the telephone device and reduce the associated costs, circuit switches were developed. George W. Coy of New Haven, Connecticut developed the first practical exchange switch, that was placed into service on January 28, 1878. This manual exchange, or *cordboard*, allowed the flexible interconnection of 21 subscribers. The number of exchanges grew quickly and although Western Union, not Bell, handled most of the initial installations, the Bell System network grew quickly and soon outpaced the networks of Western Union and other providers [3-1].

These first exchanges, housed in Central Offices, allowed circuits to be connected manually, on demand and as available. Through these central points of interconnection, each subscriber required only one terminal device and one wired connection to the central switch. Central Office Exchanges (COs or COEs) handled all switching of calls; even calls across the hall or between employees in the same office all connected in this manner. When such centralized exchanges were automated, a number of factors made it clear that this approach was less than ideal for serving businesses of any significance and with any appreciable number of terminal devices. Those factors included the following:

◆ **Labor Intensity:** Manual switchboards were labor intensive, because telephone company operators were responsible for making and breaking all connections. The early electromechanical exchanges also were maintenance intensive, as were the electromagnetic offices and the early electronic common control exchanges, although to successively less degrees.

◆ **Capital Intensity:** Central Office Exchanges were costly. In fact, the more subscribers that connected and the more functions performed by the exchange, the larger and more costly it became. Additionally, the cost of individually connecting each telephone terminal to the exchange was considerable, as each local loop connection required an individual pair, in a multi-pair cable, either placed in conduits and trenches or suspended on a series of poles.

◆ **Physical and Functional Limitations:** Central Office Exchanges were highly limited in the number of ports and, therefore, local loops they could support. Also, there were finite limits to the number of pairs which could be packed together in a cable and either pulled through a conduit or hung from a pole.

◆ **Personalized Service:** Quite simply, personalized service was not available. In other words, the telephone company operator could not handle the call as courteously and efficiently as would an employee of the user organization. Also, the telephone company was much more likely to misdirect calls due to lack of familiarity with users and their associated station numbers.

Clearly, extending a partition of the Central Office Exchange to the customer premise presented a better approach. The subscribing organization could rent the equipment, thereby yielding incremental revenue to the telephone company. Additionally, the cost of labor, cost of switch capital, and responsibility for connection errors would shift to the customer. Further, the subscriber's operators could provide more effective and personalized service to both inbound and outbound callers. Significantly, the equipment also could act as a contention device, allowing multiple calls to share a single, pooled group of local loop connections. This approach would considerably reduce the cost of cabling, as well as reduce the number of ports required to connect those local loops to the switch. The shift to the user organization of the functional responsibility for switching calls would also relieve the telco of that burden, allowing the exchange switch to serve more end users. Finally, internal (station-to-station) calls could be connected through the premise equipment, without requiring a connection through the telco's Central Office.

The first devices to accomplish this feat were *Private Branch Exchanges* (*PBXs*) in 1879. *Key Telephone Systems* (*KTSs*) did not arrive on the scene until 1938.

Centrex, a Central Office-based solution, was christened in the 1960s. *Automatic Call Distributors* (*ACD*s) didn't make an appearance until 1973. Rather than exploring these systems in chronological order, we will begin this discussion with KTS, as it is in many ways the least complex. We will then progress through PBX, Centrex, and ACD systems. This chapter will conclude with *Computer Telephony* (*CT*) solutions, which take system control out of the hands of the manufacturers and put it in those of the user organization. Indeed, users can build some Computer Telephony systems from industrial-strength PCs, standardized component boards, and shrink-wrapped application software operating on a general-purpose client/server computing platform.

Originally, the telephone company owned all *Customer Premise Equipment* (*CPE*) and, in turn, was rented to the end user. CPE comprises all devices connected to the network, including single-line telephones, and KTS and PBX systems, and all telephone sets connected behind them. When answering machines and other peripheral devices appeared, they too were rented to the user by the telco. In concert, the regulators and telcos maintained that any privately-owned equipment could conceivably cause damage to the network switches and even to telco personnel by introducing uncontrolled levels of electrical current. Further, such devices might well be incompatible with the highly standardized network and, therefore, cause uncontrollable disruption. Interestingly, even acoustically coupled devices were banned, unless provided by the telco. After a series of lengthy legal battles (Chapter 15), the Federal Communications Commission (FCC) reversed that policy through the 1968 Carterphone decision. That decision permitted user ownership through a special interconnecting device, or *coupler*, which allowed interconnection but protected the network from damage. Currently, customers own virtually all such equipment; in fact, incumbent telcos in the United States are barred from owning such equipment. The rest of the world more recently has followed this lead, with few exceptions.

Key Telephone Systems (KTSs)

Key Telephone Systems (*KTS*s) are business communications systems intended for small businesses. *Key Telephone* dates to the beginnings of telegraphy and telephony when mechanical *keys* were employed to open and close a circuit. The buttons on a key telephone set, also referred to as *keys*, mechanically opened and closed the line circuit. While contemporary KTSs provide much the same feature content as small PBXs, and while they also act as contention devices for network access, KTSs are not switches. That is to say that they do not possess the intelligence to accept a call request from a user station, determine the most appropriate circuit from a shared pool of circuits, and set up the connection through common switching equipment. Rather, the end user must make the determination and select the appropriate facility (e.g., local circuit, WATS circuit, or FX circuit) from a group of pooled facilities. KTS control relies on grayware (i.e., gray matter, or human brain power), rather than software.

1A1 and 1A2 KTSs

As was the case with early PBXs, KTSs originally were electromechanical in nature. The common control unit, known as a *Key Service Unit* (*KSU*), housed multiple circuit packs, known as *Key Telephone Units* (*KTUs*). Connections among KSU components and among the KSU and the key telephone sets were hardwired. Early KTS feature content was limited to hold, intercom (highly limited), speakerphones (separate units) and auto dialers (mechanical card dialers).

The first standard key system, known as the *1A*, was a hardwired system developed by the Bell System and first marketed in 1938. The *1A1 KTS* systems, first were introduced in 1953 and also were truly hardwired, with components wired together to form a complete system. 1A1 systems added a few features, including line status lamps that lit steadily to indicate a line in use and flashed to indicate a line on hold. *1A2* systems, introduced in 1963, were modular to some extent, as hardwired circuit packs plugged into a pre-built chassis, which included cable connectors for attaching station equipment [3-2]. You could add a limited number of enhanced features through common control cards in the form of circuit packs. In either case, wiring between the KSU and the sets required a labor-intensive *home run* (i.e., direct connection) of expensive 25-pair or 50-pair cable between each device and the KSU.

Electronic KTSs

Electronic KTSs entered the small business market in the 1970s, offering many of the same advantages of Electronic Common Control (ECC), as did contemporary PBXs. While these systems added considerable feature content accessible from sophisticated electronic station sets, at heart, they remained key systems, rather than switches. Currently, few companies manufacture such systems, as they have been replaced by *Hybrid KTSs*.

Hybrid KTSs

Hybrid Key Telephone Systems possess the unique ability to function as either a Key System (direct circuit selection) or a PBX (switched access to pooled facilities). Hybrids also simultaneously can function as both a KTS for one workgroup and as a PBX for another. Just as is the case with contemporary PBXs, Hybrids are digital systems comprising microprocessors, printed circuit boards, memory, software, and so on (see Figure 3-1). They also can be upgradeable and expandable, within finite limits determined by the manufacturer. Cabling is reduced to that required of PBXs, i.e., 1-4 pair. Hybrid port capacities generally do not exceed 256 ports, most of which can be configured as either station ports or trunk ports.

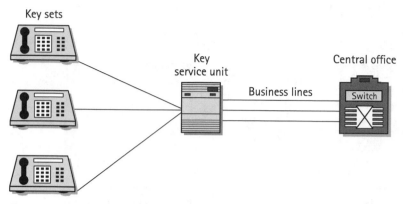

Figure 3-1 Hybrid Key System configuration

Electronic KTSs and Hybrids offer a relatively significant set of features – virtually everything a small business might require. Features can include a non-blocking switching matrix, call transfer, voice-over paging, authorization codes, ACD, SMDR, voicemail, call park, ISDN and direct T/E-Carrier interfaces, wireless sets, and display sets. Data communications commonly is supported at rates of 19.2 Kbps asynchronous and 64 Kbps synchronous. As we traditionally associate these features with PBX systems, we will discuss them in more detail later in this chapter. Leading manufacturers include Comdial, Ericsson, Executone, Lucent, Nortel, Siemens, and Toshiba [3-3].

Private Branch Exchanges (PBXs)

While KTSs effectively address the communications requirements of small user organizations, they encounter limitations in terms of both feature content and capacity. Clearly, a better approach for the larger user organization would involve effectively moving a partition of the Central Office Exchange to the customer premise, as portrayed in Figure 3-2. This *Private Branch* of the Central Office *Exchange* (*PBX*) would yield significantly improved results for both the telephone company and the user organization.

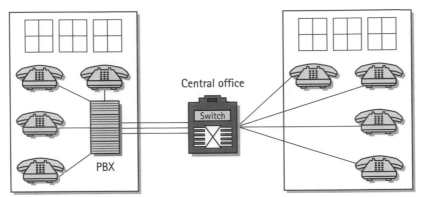

Figure 3-2 PBX vs. individual telephone set connections to a telco Central Office
Exchange (COE)

The first PBX reportedly was placed into service in the Old Soldiers' Home in Dayton, Ohio in 1879. While the first systems were little more than non-standard modifications of telephone company Central Office switches, AT&T offered a standard PBX (No. 1 PBX) in 1902 [3-4]. PBXs evolved in the same order as Central Office Exchanges. Note their designations in Table 3-1.

Table 3-1 PBX GENERATIONS

Designation	Nature of Technology
Cordboard	Manual Switchboard
PBX* (Private Branch eXchange)	Electro-Mechanical Step-by-Step (SxS)
PABX* (Private Automatic Branch eXchange	Electro-Magnetic Crossbar (XBar)/Crossreed
EPABX* (Electronic Private Automatic	Electronic Common Control (ECC) Analog/Digital
Branch eXchange)	Stored Program Control (SPC)

*The terms PBX, PABX, and EPABX often are used interchangeably.

You can characterize contemporary PBXs as Electronic Common Control (ECC), *Stored Program Control* (*SPC*), digital computer systems. They commonly support the switching of data, as well as voice. PBXs vary from 10 stations to 10,000+ stations, or extensions, with the average falling in the range of 200 stations. U.S. market share leaders include Lucent Technologies, Nortel, and Siemens [3-3]. The market continues to grow in terms of both lines shipped and revenues, with market leadership remaining fairly stable [3-5].

PBX Components

Modern PBXs are specialized computer systems that include a circuit-switching matrix for the primary purpose of connecting voice calls, although many also handle a limited amount of data exceptionally well. PBXs serve large numbers of station sets, which may include fully featured electronic terminals. PBXs primarily serve voice terminals on a wired basis, although wireless appliqués often serve as an available option. Otherwise, PBXs are much like any other computer, consisting of cabinets, shelves, printed circuit boards, power supplies, and so on. The primary physical and logical components (Figure 3-3) of a PBX include common control, switching matrix, trunk interfaces, line interfaces, and terminal equipment.

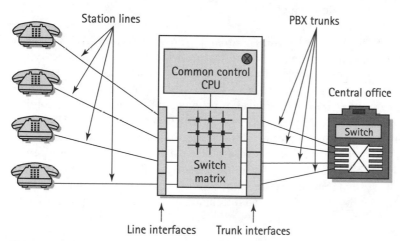

Figure 3-3 PBX components, including Common Control, switching matrix, trunks and trunk interfaces, stations, and line interfaces

COMMON CONTROL

Common Control is a common set of stored program logic that controls the activities of the system and all of its various elements. In reality, it consists of multiple microprocessors operating under a stored program, secured as *bulletproof*, according to the manufacturers. As in any computer, the control processor consists of memory, input/output equipment, bulk memory equipment, and software.

Central Processing Units (CPUs) are microprocessors that control the operation of the system. They may be centralized, but generally are distributed among cabinets, shelves, or even cards (printed circuit boards) for purposes of effectiveness, efficiency, and survivability. The CPUs control functions such as call setup, call maintenance, call release, performance monitoring, system diagnostics, and storage of operational data for analysis and report presentation. *Processor redundancy* commonly appears in contemporary PBXs. Not only are the processing functions distributed among multiple microprocessors at the cabinet, shelf, and card levels, but also many PBXs feature *hot standby* processors, available instantaneously should a primary processor fail.

Since the systems largely are software controlled, you can relatively easily upgrade them. As new software generics are released, associated functions and features are released in the form of programmable functions; the system software can be upgraded as required, although the cost of doing so can be significant. Additionally, you can fix *bugs* (program errors), by downloading corrections over the public network. Notably, traditional PBXs are highly proprietary, closed computer systems. The manufacturers control all aspects of the systems, with the end user organization having little ability to affect the operational characteristics of the system. The manufacturers also determine all features and functions, enhancements, and upgrades. Examples of the hundreds of such programmable functions and features include the following:

AUTOMATIC ROUTE SELECTION (ARS) *Automatic Route Selection* (*ARS*), or *Least Cost Routing* (*LCR*), is an optional software feature which enables the user to program the system to route individual calls over the most appropriate selection of carrier and service offerings. Routing factors typically might include the nature of the call; the *Class of Service* (*CoS*), or level of privilege, of the user; the time of day; and the day of the year (e.g., weekends and holidays). In this fashion, executives and other high-priority users with no calling restrictions can connect on a priority basis, even if restricted by availability to a high-cost carrier and service offering. On the other hand, clerks and other low-priority users are forced to queue for a low cost facility; the system remembers their requests and rings their telephones to alert them when that facility is available, and automatically connects the previously requested call.

CALL PICK-UP GROUPS *Call pick-up groups* enable users within the same workgroup to answer calls for one another. Authorized users can invoke this option by entering a code on the set keypad or by depressing a designated feature button on an electronic set.

CALL FORWARD *Call forward* enables a user either to predefine or selectively and flexibly define an extension to which a call will be transferred in the event of a *busy* or *no answer* condition.

CONFERENCE CALLING *Conference calling*, set up by the user or by the console attendant, makes use of a special *conference bridge* card in the system. Such a bridge typically supports as many as 8 or 16 parties to such a call.

CALL DETAIL RECORDING (CDR) *Call Detail Recording (CDR)*, or *Station Message Detail Recording (SMDR)* information provides detail on all incoming and outgoing calls (see Figure 3-4) so the system administrator might develop network usage reports. Information typically includes the originating and terminating station, outgoing and incoming trunk or trunk group, time of connection, time of termination (or elapsed time), access code dialed (e.g., 9 for an outside line or 8 for a private line), telephone number dialed, and account code or authorization code used.

The inclusion of an originating telephone number helps to provide the most complete incoming call detail. This level of detail requires that the incoming PBX trunks support either *Automatic Number Identification (ANI)* or *Calling Line Identification (CLID)*, services that carry additional charges from the service provider. ANI requires a *trunk side* connection, also known as *Feature Group D*, in order that the PBX trunk appear to the network as an internal, carrier *InterMachine Trunk (IMT)*. When so equipped, the PBX trunk receives the same originating call information which is passed internally within the carrier networks for telephone company billing and tracking purposes; the calling party cannot block ANI information. CLID, a feature of *Signaling System 7 (SS7)*, provides essentially the same information over an *Integrated Services Digital Network (ISDN) Primary Rate Interface (PRI)* trunk. CLID information is available only if SS7 is present throughout the entire network, from calling party to called party, and then only if the caller does not block its transmission. Both ANI and CLID information are passed in advance of call connection.

Starting Time	Elapsed Time	Orig. Sta.	Digits Dialed	Access Code Dialed	Trunk Used	Date	Account Code
12:30	0:01	431	360-336-3448	9	0003	718	
12:35	0:06	421	415-428-9081	9	0002	718	4538
12:45	1:09	411	268-9826	9	0001	718	
13:03	0:11	322	463				

Figure 3-4 Example CDR outgoing call records

Many contemporary PBXs contain adjunct software which allows the generation of a number of reports including usage costs by cost center (e.g., station, account code, workgroup, department, and division). This critical feature assists in cost control and fraud control, as well as permitting the user organization to recover the costs illby billing to clients or projects. As such software generally demonstrates limited capability, most users prefer to acquire more substantial *telemanagement* software residing on an adjunct computer, which accepts CDR output from a special PBX port, processes the data, and creates user-definable reports. Such software typically includes a number of other modules which share a common database for purposes of cost allocation, traffic analysis, equipment inventory management, wire and cable management, service order management, and numerous other critical administrative functions. Leading manufacturers of such software include The Angeles Group and Stonehouse & Company [3-6].

AUTOMATIC CALL DISTRIBUTION (ACD) *Automatic Call Distribution (ACD)* software serves to route incoming calls to the most available and appropriate agent. Incoming call centers make extensive use of such specialized software to enhance customer service. A front-end voice processor answers the calls, enabling users to make menu selections. Calls then can be queued by a specialized agent group, and routed to an available agent. The routing of the call to an agent can be on the basis of next available, longest time since last call, least number of calls answered, or some other *fairness* routing algorithm. While a specially equipped and partitioned PBX often delivers such capability, the PBX also can be specially configured as a standalone ACD. Intensive call center applications typically make use of specialized ACDs, which function as highly intelligent switches for the processing of incoming calls; specially-designed high-speed interfaces to the PBX permit the systems to function on an integrated, networked basis.

UNIFORM CALL DISTRIBUTION (UCD) *Uniform Call Distribution (UCD)* is a standard feature of many PBXs; standalone units exist, as well. While UCD serves many of the same functions as an ACD, it lacks the same level of intelligence. Therefore, it is much less capable, although much less costly. A UCD simply routes incoming calls to the next available agent, scanning agent ports in a predetermined and never-varying hunt pattern. The unfortunate agent who is first in the hunt pattern definitely earns his paycheck, while the lucky agent who is last in the hunt pattern has a very easy time of it.

SWITCHING MATRIX Contemporary PBXs employ Time Division Multiplexing (TDM), a concept we explored briefly in Chapter 1 and will discuss in great detail in Chapter 7. Through this process, multiple conversations are sampled, converted to a data format, and transmitted sequentially over a shared electrical *bus*, or common physical path.

TRUNK INTERFACES Trunk Interfaces are in the physical form of specialized circuit boards that serve to interface the PBX switch to trunks connecting it to other switches. Trunks can be one-way outgoing, one-way incoming, or two-way (*combination* trunks). Often a PBX will employ all three variations in order to serve various specific applications, to maximize system performance, and to ensure a minimum acceptable level of both incoming and outgoing network access. ISDN, offers dynamic call direction on a channel-by-channel basis, which is much more flexible and potentially more cost-effective. Chapter 7 discusses ISDN in detail.

Trunks may be single-channel (seldom used) or multichannel. Because high-capacity, multichannel trunks will support multiple conversations, they generally are much more cost-effective. Examples of multichannel trunk facilities include T-Carrier and ISDN Primary Rate Interface (PRI), also known as Primary Rate Access (PRA). Trunks of the same directional type and which serve the same purpose are organized into *trunk groups*. The PBX will *hunt* for available channels and trunks within a trunk group, based on a predetermined, user-definable hunt sequence. Trunk interfaces provide access to the following specific types of trunks:

CENTRAL OFFICE EXCHANGE *Central Office Exchange (CO, or COE)* trunks connect the PBX to the LEC exchange. These trunks serve for access to the local calling area, and to all other areas served by the local telco. They also serve to provide switched access through the LEC to IXCs for long distance calling where the user organization has not made special arrangements for direct IXC access. In the event of a failure in a trunk facility providing direct IXC access, the Central Office trunks provide a very effective level of redundancy.

INTEREXCHANGE *Interexchange* trunks provide direct access to an IXC, bypassing the LEC Central Office switch. Such trunks generally are intended only for long distance network access to geographic areas outside the LEC calling area.

FOREIGN EXCHANGE (FX OR FEX) *Foreign Exchange (FX or FEX)* trunks connect directly to a foreign Central Office Exchange. They are used for more cost-effective access to and from a distant geographic area where a high volume of traffic originates and terminates. For example, a user organization with a high volume of traffic between its Dallas, Texas offices and the area immediately surrounding Denton, Texas might choose to avoid long distance calling charges by installing a FX trunk. Since the FX trunk is priced on a flat-rate basis, regardless of the level of outgoing traffic, the user organization avoids long distance charges to that area. Callers from the Denton area dial a local Denton telephone number associated with that FX trunk, similarly avoiding long distance. As a side benefit, the organization in Dallas creates the illusion of having established a local presence in Denton.

DIRECT INWARD DIALING (DID) *Direct Inward Dial (DID)* trunks are for incoming traffic, only. Each station is assigned a DID number which roughly corresponds to the internal station number. As a call is placed to a 7-digit DID number, the CO recognizes that fact, and connects the call over a special DID trunk. The DID number is passed to the PBX in advance of the call by virtue of a special signaling and control arrangement that exists between the PBX and CO. With that information, an intelligent PBX with the proper generic software load automatically can route the call directly to the station, without the intervention of an attendant. The service provider rents DID numbers in groups (e.g., 50, 100, and 250).

TIE *Tie* trunks directly interconnect, or tie together, PBXs in a private network configuration. Through the use of ARS/LCR software, the systems will route calls between offices over leased-line tie trunks, avoiding toll charges in the process.

Coordinated, abbreviated dialing plans, programmed within each PBX, cause the various PBX systems to interact on a networked basis, appearing to the user as though they were a single system. Tie trunks and other dedicated circuits are sometimes referred to as *nailed-up circuits*, because they literally once were nailed-up on the Central Office wall and specially tagged in order to distinguish them from typical shared circuits.

WIDE AREA TELECOMMUNICATIONS SERVICE (WATS) *Wide Area Telecommunications Service (WATS)* trunks allow for discounted long distance access in defined service areas.

INCOMING WATS (INWATS) *InWATS* trunks serve INcoming WATS calls. The called party bears the charges, at a discounted cost per minute or fraction thereof. Domestic U.S. InWATS numbers originally were accessed by dialing 1-800-xxx-xxxx. Since the 800 area code was exhausted some years ago, 888 and 877 numbers were made available. Outside the United States, the InWATS dialing pattern differs greatly (e.g., 0800 and 0500). InWATS often is characterized as *toll-free*, which is correct only as far as the calling party is concerned.

DIRECT INWARD SYSTEM ACCESS (DISA) *Direct Inward System Access (DISA)* trunks allow access (generally toll-free) to the PBX system and, subsequently, to connected resources (e.g., e-mail servers, voice processors, computer systems, and outgoing toll trunks) through the entry of authorization codes. While DISA trunks are useful to authorized users, they often are targeted by hackers who seek unauthorized access to the same resources. Therefore, the integrity of the organization, its toll network, its various networked systems and the resident databases can be compromised. You should avoid DISA trunks, and, where in place, you should disconnect them, unless you take extreme security measures to ensure their valid use.

STATION INTERFACES

Station Interfaces are in the form of printed circuit boards, which can support multiple stations of the same general type through multiple *ports* on a single interface card. For instance, analog line cards with analog ports support analog sets, in which case the signal is digitized at the line card level. Digital line cards support digital telephones, in which case the analog signal is digitized at the set level. Digital line cards also support computer workstations, printers, and other digital devices.

TERMINAL EQUIPMENT

As PBXs are designed primarily to support voice traffic, the user terminal equipment generally is in the form of a telephone set. Terminal equipment often includes data terminals, as well.

TELEPHONE SETS PBXs typically support both dial and tone single-line sets of a generic nature. They also support highly functional electronic sets, which may offer easy access to a number of system features. Although such sets are proprietary to the system manufacturer and are considerably more expensive, they enable the station user to invoke system features by depressing a single designated button. Programmable sets enable either the station user or the system administrator to program the individual feature buttons, or *soft keys*. The proprietary electronic sets, generally digital, having the codec embedded in the set, rather than in the station interface card in the PBX cabinet. The codec, as we discussed previously, handles the processes of analog-to-digital and digital-to-analog signal conversion. ISDN (Integrated Services Digital Network) sets provide a highly functional ISDN connection to the desktop, through an ISDN-compatible PBX, connected to an ISDN circuit. ISDN sets generally are proprietary to the PBX manufacturer.

INTEGRATED VOICE/DATA (IVD) TERMINALS These terminals combine a highly functional *featurephone* with a computer workstation. For the most part, such terminals have failed stunningly, because of their expensive and impractical nature, and because their workstations invariably are well behind the curve of computer technology. More commonly, digital telephone sets offer an EIA-232-E standard, 25-pin computer connection port in order to allow a computer workstation and telephone set to share a common, twisted-pair link to the PBX. (EIA-232-E also is known as RS-232, referring to Recommended Standard 232, identical in function to the ITU-T Recommendation V.24/V.28.)

ATTENDANT CONSOLES These provide attendants with the ability to answer and extend incoming calls, provide operator assistance to outgoing callers, and establish conference calls. They also often provide alarm indications in the event of a performance failure. When associated with a computer workstation, they often provide electronic directory information and other functionality through an enhanced user interface. In a large, private network scenario, attendants and attendant consoles often are centralized to enhance attendant performance and minimize associated costs. *Centralized Attendant Service* (CAS) is a feature offered by manufacturers of large, network-capable PBX systems.

MAINTENANCE AND ADMINISTRATION TERMINALS (MATS) *Maintenance and Administration Terminals* (*MATs*) are PC terminals connected directly to a maintenance port on the system, generally via a RS-232 connection. Authorized users can access the system software for purposes which might include *Moves, Adds, and Changes* (*MACs*); *Class of Service* (*CoS*) changes; ARS/LCR programming; requests for traffic and usage statistics; requests for status reports; and diagnostic testing and analysis. Remote maintenance generally can be accomplished over the PSTN via a modem connection.

System Configuration and Capacity

You must consider carefully the capacity of the PBX in order to ensure that the organization does not outgrow the system over a reasonable period of time. The system initially should be configured and installed to serve current and near-term requirements, as subsequent software and hardware additions are more costly. Additionally, the system should have the ability to grow to meet long-term needs, in terms of hardware, software, feature content, etc. The following sections describe the capacity and configuration dimensions of PBXs.

CENTRALIZED OR DISTRIBUTED

PBXs generally are configured as centralized systems, with all cabinets and peripheral devices collocated for ease of administration. However, a large campus environment may opt for a decentralized approach, with multiple intelligent cabinets located in campus quadrants and interconnected with high-capacity circuits. Very large organizations with multiple, distant locations may require the capability to network multiple PBXs over either a private, tie-line network, or a Virtual Private Network (VPN) [3-7].

PHYSICAL CAPACITY

Physical capacity is the measure of the number of lines and trunks that can be supported through additional line and trunk cards, and additional cabinets. Every system has a finite limitation to the number of cabinets and ports that it will support.

TRAFFIC CAPACITY

Traffic capacity is the measure of the number of simultaneous conversations that can be supported. This measurement is critical, especially when both voice and data are switched. You must consider the capacities of both the processors and the busses. Processor capacity is measured in terms of the maximum number of *Busy Hour Call Attempts* (*BHCAs*) that can be supported, whether or not the calls are completed. Bus capacity usually is measured in terms of *Centum Call Seconds* (*CCSs*), with a *centum* call second being 100 call seconds. One hour contains 36 CCSs (60 seconds times 60 minutes).

Blocking switches (Figure 3-5), typical in a voice-only application, are engineered in such a way as to support a reasonable level of traffic, with some call attempts blocked during periods of high activity. Thereby, system capacity can be engineered to optimize the relationship between cost and availability, or *grade of service*, which is measured based on the peak busy hour. Voice-only systems particularly lend themselves to optimization, because voice traffic characteristics are well understood and as voice is not particularly bandwidth-intensive. Specifically, voice calls are occasional, short in duration, and require bandwidth of 64 Kbps or less.

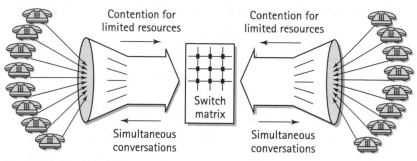

Figure 3-5 Blocking PBX

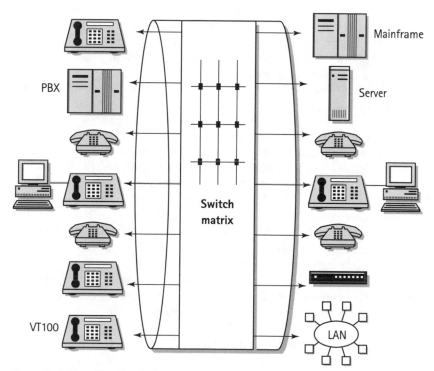

Figure 3-6 Non-blocking PBX

Non-Blocking switches (Figure 3-6) provide a non-blocked (guaranteed) talk path for every terminal; in other words, there exists a 1:1 relationship between line ports and time slots. Especially critical in data applications, characterized by insistence on immediate connectivity and very long communications sessions, this admittedly expensive approach ensures access to critical host computing resources within the organization. Notably, traditional PBXs are circuit switches, which are inherently wasteful for many data communications applications; packet switches (Chapter 7) are much more cost-effective for such applications. Access to trunks rarely is provided on a non-blocking basis, as such a high level of trunking adds significant costs in terms of trunk interfaces and the trunks, themselves.

APPLICATION PROCESSORS (APs)

Application processors often are interfaced with PBXs over high-speed links in order to provide specialized functions such as voice processing, computer host access, e-mail, and facsimile. Generally speaking, the PBX manufacturer supports interfaces either to proprietary application processors or to those developed by third parties with which there is a strong, strategic relationship. While this approach is limiting, it ensures that the systems and the interfaces between them function successfully, and remain so as the PBX system and the application processors evolve. The ability of the PBX to support such processors is critical, as they can greatly enhance the performance of the organization.

PBX Enhancements and Trends

Manufacturers increasingly have positioned the PBX as a communications server for voice, data, video, and image communications [3-3]. Some manufacturers are building such capabilities into the PBX, itself. Lucent Technologies, for instance, in October 1995 announced its Multimedia Communications eXchange (MMCX) Server in support of all customary PBX telephone features on multimedia calls. Such calls can involve voice, data, and video from any form of private or public network. The typical approach, however, involves high-speed interfaces to a variety of applications processors. This latter approach allows specialized processors, often developed by strategic partners, to perform their various functions maximizing advantage on the most effective platform, while providing application integration through the PBX. The following PBX developments and trends exclude computer telephony, which we discuss at the end of this chapter.

REDUCED INSTRUCTION SET COMPUTING (RISC)

RISC processors provide for faster call processing through the use of a reduced set of operations commands, as compared to traditional *CISC*-based (*Complex Instruction Set Computing*) processors. Although the set of executable commands reduces, the increased speed of processing is thought by many manufacturers to enhance system performance. RISC-based processors increasingly are being incorporated in PBX system design, with Lucent's Definity ECS systems enjoying notable acclaim in this regard [3-8].

PBX-TO-HOST/LAN

Such links enable users to access computer applications through the PBX, sharing the same cable and wire plant between computer and telephone terminals. Connectivity between the PBX and a host computer or LAN can be accomplished via means such as ISDN links or 10 Mbps Ethernet links [3-9]. While such capabilities have existed for a number of years, they recently advanced to very significant levels in the form of client/server Computer Telephony systems, discussed later in this chapter.

DATA COMMUNICATIONS

Data communications is increasingly important. PBX manufacturers have long supported modem pooling and low-speed data through terminal interfaces. Several manufacturers have supported X.25 packet-switching interfaces for a number of years. Although at considerable cost, Intecom and other manufacturers also support high-speed connectivity, including Ethernet, Token Ring, and FDDI. A number of PBX manufacturers (e.g., Lucent and Siemens) recently developed interfaces for ATM (Asynchronous Transfer Mode).

WIRELESS

Selected users currently can access wireless communications through a special PBX wireless appliqué. Special PBX ports support wired connections to antennae distributed throughout a large office complex or campus. Selected users who require mobility can take advantage of special cordless telephones to communicate as they roam through the organization, as long as they remain within the limited range of the antennae. Manufacturers of such appliqués include Ericsson, Lucent, and Motorola. Recently, several small manufacturers have released small PBX systems that are entirely wireless in nature; such systems have application in environments that allow the users to enjoy a high level of mobility within the office, campus, or factory. The advantages of wireless PBX technology include increased mobility, increased call completion, decreased call-back costs, and increased productivity due to decreased voicemail messages. Disadvantages include increased cost, lack of feature content at the set level, and concerns about security.

Also known as *Wireless Office Telecommunications Systems* (*WOTS*), wireless PBX technologies may employ any of a number of standards, most of which are digital in nature. Those standards range from cordless telephony to *PCS* (*Personal Communications Services*). Chapter 11 discusses WOTS in more detail.

FAX MESSAGING

Select manufacturers, including Nortel and Lucent Technologies, support fax messaging. Through voice processing system prompts, the user can download a fax message, stored in a user-specific fax mailbox. The user can access the fax message onscreen at a workstation, much as he would access a voice message from a telephone terminal.

VIDEOCONFERENCING

Manufacturers such as Fujitsu, AT&T, Nortel, and Siemens offer videoconferencing through the PBX [3-7] and [3-8]. At relatively low speeds over the PSTN, the circuit switched connections are often less costly than dedicated videoconferencing links.

Although generally based on international standards, the terminal equipment typically is proprietary, with the trend being towards more substantial standardization.

ASYNCHRONOUS TRANSFER MODE (ATM)

ATM, discussed in detail in Chapter 10, is a cell-switching technology developed for Wide Area Network application in support of a wide range of information streams, including voice, data, video, and fax. Recently, ATM has found application in LAN switching, and has been introduced by manufacturers of larger, more capable PBXs. Lucent's Definity ECS (Enterprise Communications Server) Release 6 software generic, for example, supports an ATM interface card for integration of voice traffic over an ATM campus backbone. The ATM backbone runs at speeds up to 5 Gbps, in support of integrated voice, data, video, and fax traffic.

The Siemens Hicom 300E switch supports an integrated ATM Interworking Unit (IWU), which enables a connection either to ATM switches in a private network scenario, or to public carrier-based ATM services. Nortel's Meridian Passport supports integrated access in support of voice, frame relay, ATM, and transparent data (e.g., native LAN and SDLC) through a carrier-based ATM network. Numerous manufacturers of next-generation CT (Computer Telephony) PBXs interconnect application servers via ATM over fiber optic links.

While it remains unusual to find a PBX switch which is fully ATM-based, the success of ATM in the WAN is virtually assured. As ATM finds its way into the LAN world, and as manufacturers of LAN switches and hubs increase their support of voice and video, the PBX manufacturers increasingly will feel the pressure. At the very least, they likely will incorporate ATM switching matrices alongside the standard STM (Synchronous Transfer Mode) matrices currently used to support voice traffic. The yield likely will be a PBX/ATM router combination [3-10], positioned as a multimedia communications controller.

INTERNET PROTOCOL (IP)

IP, discussed in detail in several following chapters, is part of the TCP/IP (Transmission Control Protocol/Internet Protocol) protocol suite developed for use in packet-switched Wide Area Networks (WANs) such as the Internet. TCP/IP also has found wide application in support of LAN, frame relay, and other data traffic. IP, specifically, has found recent application in next-generation, packet-switched voice WANs. While such networks are only beginning to emerge, they promise tremendous efficiencies and, therefore, much lower costs than the traditional circuit-switched networks. Further, IP telephony promises to allow the integration of voice, data, and video over a single set of access and transport facilities; in other words, access to a single packet-switched broadband WAN through a single high-capacity local loop. In anticipation of the popularity of these next-generation WANs, a number of PBX manufacturers (e.g., Lucent and Mitel) have developed IP interfaces, either in the form of an IP gateway module or a direct IP interface. When a call is offered to the PBX, it will examine the grade of service over the IP network at the moment, and either present the call to that network, or route it over a more expensive and more traditional circuit-switched alternative.

Currently, supporting IP-based packet-switched voice traffic within the PBX domain presents no clear advantage; (i.e., for internal station-to-station traffic). The main advantages offered include the use of a single wiring plan for both voice and data, and the ability to access both voice and data LAN servers through common Ethernet switches. A common voice/data infrastructure certainly is an attractive concept. The drawbacks include the loss of voice quality associated with running IP-based, packetized, compressed voice over a collision-prone shared Ethernet LAN. Another drawback is the requisite prioritization of voice over a LAN, and the resulting de-prioritization of the data for which the LAN was installed. Lucent, NBX Corp. (acquired by 3Com), Nortel, and Selsius Systems (acquired by Cisco) have developed client-server, IP-based PBX systems [3-11], [3-12] and [3-13].

PC-BASED PBXS

Also known as *dumb* or *programmable* switches, PC-based PBXs have been around for quite some time, but generally have not been well accepted. They typically consist of a dedicated Pentium PC, program logic, a switching matrix card, and a *port expansion unit* that provides 16 or more ports. While most such systems have been positioned for the small-to-medium line size market, some can expand to 4,000+ ports and reportedly can handle more than 500,000 call completions per hour. Traditionally, PCs have not been considered reliable enough for such a mission-critical application; neither have general-purpose computers proven stunningly capable of switching calls or providing significant feature content. Those limitations are lifting. Indeed, some strongly suggest that the PC, PC LAN, or client/server computer will be the PBX of the future. The low cost of such systems ($200-$300 per port) works in their favor, at least in the Key System and very small PBX markets, where the costs of traditional systems commonly range from $250-$500 per port. Manufacturers of these systems include AltiGen Communications, Mitel Corp., and NBX Corp (acquired by 3 Com) [3-14].

SECURITY

Security is of increasing concern, as hackers have penetrated PBXs (easily), voice processors (very easily), and other systems to gain unauthorized access to networks and various information resources such as critical databases. PBX, computer, and peripheral manufacturers have added security measures through enhanced software and hardware which can act on either a passive or active basis to deny or terminate such access or, at least, to recognize its occurrence and alert the system administrator [3-15]. While such products are widely available at reasonable cost, relatively few PBXs are properly protected. Researchers estimate that unauthorized network access via the PBX resulted in fraud of approximately $4.5 billion in 1997 in the United States alone [3-16].

Centrex

Centrex (central exchange), is something of a conceptual step back in time, providing PBX-like features through a special generic software load in the Central Office Exchange. Typically, each Centrex station is connected to the CO via an individually twisted pair local loop (see Figure 3-7). While multichannel local loop connections are available, they require an expensive remote CO line shelf to be installed at the customer premise; therefore, multichannel access is cost-effective only in applications that have large numbers of users at a single site. All switching of calls is accomplished in the CO, which also serves all features to the user population.

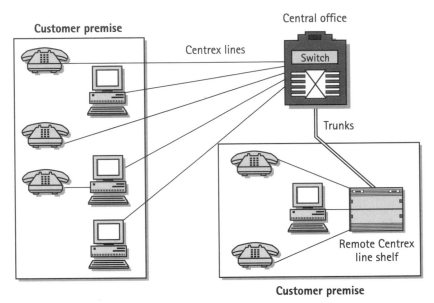

Figure 3-7 Centrex CO, with individual local loops to Centrex stations and with remote CO line shelf

Centrex first was made available in the United States and Canada in the early 1960s, through SxS offices. In the United States, AT&T and GTE de-emphasized it in the 1970s, in favor of PBXs. This shift in direction was largely to impending deregulation and divestiture, which took full effect on January 1, 1984 through the Modified Final Judgement (MFJ). In particular, AT&T reportedly anticipated that it would spin off its local exchange operating companies, but retain its CPE business. In the grand scheme of things, therefore, it was decidedly to AT&T's advantage to de-emphasize Centrex in favor of PBXs, and well in advance of divestiture – the comparative merits of Centrex and PBX had nothing to do with the strategy.

Modern Centrex became available in 1984 through the first generation of digital COs [3-17]. AT&T immediately reversed its position, developing sophisticated digital Centrex software for marketing to its former subsidiaries, the Regional Bell Operating Companies (RBOCs) and the independent telcos. In addition to Lucent Technologies (previously AT&T), Nortel and Siemens are notable manufacturers of Centrex COs [3-3].

Although most commonly provided by Incumbent Local Exchange Carriers (ILECs) such as the RBOCs, Centrex service recently has been offered by Competitive Local Exchange Carriers (CLECs), many of which previously were IntereXchange Carriers (IXCs) or Competitive Access Providers (CAPs). Traditionally a U.S. domestic phenomenon, Centrex recently has found market acceptance in the U.K., Europe, Japan, and much of Asia. Carriers find Centrex attractive because it effectively competes against PBX and KTS systems provided by third parties. Lucent Technologies (5ESS) and Nortel (DMS-100) manufacture the great majority of CO Centrex systems installed in the United States [3-18].

Centrex Features

Centrex is capable of offering the same feature content as PBX technology. Indeed, the platform inherently is much more substantial in terms of traffic capacity, processing power, memory, and virtually every respect. Ultimately, however, the carrier must consider the general market for such features, given an appropriate pricing strategy. Additionally, you must consider the impact of features on the switch in terms of limitations such as processing power, memory, and traffic capacity. Finally, the regulators all too often get involved in determining pricing, availability, impact on the rate base, and other factors. Therefore, not all technically feasible Centrex features are available, certainly not on a consistent basis. Centrex features can include Direct Inward Dialing (DID), Automatic Route Selection (ARS)/Least Cost Routing (LCR), call pick-up groups, call forward, conference calling, Automatic Call Distribution (ACD), and Call Detail Recording (CDR). Centrex also generally is capable of data switching, which more or less effectively delivers CO-based LAN functionality. Additionally, the Centrex CO generally houses a voice processing system or provides remote access to one, thereby delivering highly effective voicemail and other related functionality [3-17] and [3-19].

The Centrex CO also may offer access to a large number of CLASS (Customer Local Access Signaling Services), which you can best describe as advanced custom calling features. Such services might include Name Delivery, Calling Number Delivery, Calling Number Blocking, Continuous Redial/Repeat Dial/Automatic Recall, Distinctive Ringing, Call Return/Automatic Callback, Call Trace, Selective Call Screening, Selective Call Forwarding, Selective Call Rejection, and Anonymous Call Rejection [3-19].

Finally, Centrex offerings increasingly include *customer rearrangement* capability. This feature permits the user organization to manage its Centrex service much as it might manage its own PBX. Through a computer terminal located on the customer premise, access is afforded to the switch database on a logically partitioned basis. Thereby, the system administrator can accomplish Moves, Adds, and Changes (MACs); disconnect Centrex stations; change Class of Service (CoS); file trouble reports and work orders, and monitor their status; and perhaps even perform various system and network diagnostic tests. Leading providers are Telcordia (previously Bellcore) with the CCRS system and CommTech Corporation (previously AT&T) with the Macstar system [3-20].

Centrex Advantages

The carrier provides Centrex, which resides on a very robust computer platform — also an integral part of the network. As a result, Centrex offers a number of unique advantages, including reduction of investment and operating cost and avoidance of responsibility for system acquisition and management. Additionally, system capacity generally is not an issue, and the systems often can network to great advantage.

As the capital investment in the switching platform and associated application processors is the responsibility of the carrier, the user organization avoids the financial pain and associated risks of acquiring a potentially substantial capital asset in a premises-based system. Generally speaking, however, the user organization remains responsible for the acquisition and deployment of associated station equipment, and inside wire and cable systems. The user organization avoids a host of operating responsibilities and related costs, as those burdens are shifted to the carrier. Such responsibilities and costs can include those of system maintenance, system administration (MAC activity), system upgrade, insurance, physical space, physical and network security, power and backup power systems, fire suppression systems, and redundancy.

Since the risk of ownership is shifted to the carrier, issues of obsolescence and replacement are obviated. Further, COs are relatively unlimited in scope in terms of port, memory, and processor capacities; therefore, it is unlikely that a typical user organization might outgrow the system. This characteristic of Centrex can be extremely important to businesses that tend to expand and contract, perhaps on a seasonal basis. Rather than investing in a PBX switch designed to accommodate the maximum size of the organization, additional Centrex lines can be added as required and disconnected as that requirement relaxes, with the associated capacity and telephone numbers perhaps being reserved until such time as the requirement resurfaces.

Finally, Centrex permits the user organization to network a number of locations through the serving CO, without the requirement for leasing tie line circuits to connect multiple PBX or key systems. In fact, multiple Centrex COs of the same type can network to provide *virtual Centrex*; this approach offers the advantage of allowing multiple, distant offices to communicate as though they were collocated and served by a single switch. Notably, GTE and the RBOCs are restricted to LATA boundaries in providing virtual Centrex.

Centrex Disadvantages

While Centrex offers a number of unique and very significant advantages over PBXs, there also exist clear disadvantages, including certain cost issues and considerations of control. The recurring charges for the circuits and features continue forever, although special tariffs for very large customers can serve to mitigate this factor. Further, a *Subscriber Line Charge (SLC)*, also known as a *Customer Access Line Charge (CALC)*, applies to each local loop circuit or defined group of loops. Because Centrex generally involves a separate voice-grade local loop for each Centrex station, the typical Centrex user pays a higher price for local access than a PBX user organization. Finally, rate stability has always been a Centrex issue, as all local rates are subject to regular review and adjustment. In many jurisdictions, rate stability plans have served to mitigate this concern, at least in the short term. Rate changes affect PBX users to a lesser degree because relatively few circuits of high capacity are shared on a pooled basis.

As we noted, standard Centrex feature content is determined by the service provider, based on market demand, and in consideration of the resources available in the serving CO switches. The state regulatory agencies provide oversight in terms of capital investment, operations expenses, and rate levels, at least for the regulated ILECs. Since the offered features are geared toward the average user, the overall feature set tends to be much less complete than that of the typical PBX. Therefore, user organizations with requirements for more exotic features may find Centrex an unacceptable alternative. Additionally, feature content and feature access may well vary by carrier, regulatory jurisdiction, exchange CO, switch origin (i.e., manufacturer), and generic software load. Features such as ACD are unusual, while certain features such as message waiting generally are not well presented. Still other features, such as voice-over paging, are not available at all. As a result, some users still place small PBXs, Hybrid KTSs, and other CPE (Customer Premise Equipment) systems on premise to interface the station equipment to the Centrex lines, thereby extending more exotic features to select workgroups.

Perhaps the most significant disadvantages of Centrex revolve around issues of control, as the carriers and regulators jointly determine the nature of the offerings. Special features require lengthy tariff approval processes, assuming that the user organization can successfully negotiate the support of the carrier and assume that the regulators are sympathetic. Certainly, the user is dependent on the carrier for switch administration, maintenance, and enhancement. Considering that many ILECs have a less than stunning reputation for responsiveness, this absolute level of dependency is of great concern to many companies.

Centrex CPE

Proprietary voice terminals (*P-phones*) generally are required, although the manufacturers finally have yielded to user pressure recently and provided interfaces to non-proprietary sets. As P-phones are switch-specific, a multilocation company can face additional inventory costs associated with the requirement to stock multiple set types. User confusion also results when users must deal with multiple user interfaces.

The inherent cost and flexibility limitations of Centrex have given rise to a new breed of Centrex CPE that significantly enhances Centrex capabilities. Although the equipment must be matched carefully to the Centrex switch, such CPE includes Centrex-compatible electronic voice terminals (i.e., telephones), ACDs, voice processors, paging systems, attendant consoles, and message lamp controllers. Recently, *set handlers*, or *mediation devices*, have been developed which act as protocol converters to effect a proper interface between desired electronic station sets and the Centrex system.

Centrex Applications

Meaningful and cost-effective applications for Centrex are increasing, especially as the carriers respond to heightened competitive pressure. The carriers clearly are becoming more responsive to end users, deploying more features on a more consistent basis, and extending limited network management capabilities to the end user. Additionally, they increasingly are designing rates to attract smaller businesses. Typical applications include multilocation organizations within a single metropolitan area, seasonal businesses, and business that tend to locate only on a temporary basis (e.g., contractors). Additionally, the government, educational, and not-for-profit markets are heavy users of Centrex due to capital and expense budget limitations and restrictions.

Centrex Trends and Futures

Many industry analysts anticipate that Centrex will increase in popularity in most developed nations, for reasons which include increased competitive pressure, enhanced feature content, improved pricing, enhanced networking capability, ISDN availability, and broadband network access. Additionally, Centrex manufacturers and providers increasingly are applications focused – offering and developing capabilities that include enhanced data communications, videoconferencing, and integrated messaging. Centrex currently is growing at a rate of approximately 2.95%; most users (43%) are 1,000+ lines, although a significant number (35%) are in the range of 1-100 lines, with smaller users growing at the fastest rate (3.5%) [3-3].

Perhaps the most exciting development in Centrex deals with its potential to serve as a means of internetworking multiple PBXs of disparate origin. The City and County of San Francisco recently worked with Pacific Bell (Centrex), Siemens (PBX), and Lucent (PBX) to integrate Centrex and PBX systems through a series of Central Offices. The COs serve as protocol translators between the PBX systems, and also serve to integrate the Centrex and PBX users.

Automatic Call Distributors (ACDs)

ACDs function as incoming call switches, primarily serving call center applications. As call centers are highly active, with relatively large numbers of callers queued for a much smaller number of agents, ACDs generally are non-blocking systems. Call centers may be specific to the user organization, but often set up on a service bureau basis. A service bureau might answer calls for a large number of clients, on either a primary or overflow basis, with specific software and scripting to support the individual client's requirements. You can identify the call by the telephone number called, with a separate telephone number or set of telephone numbers associated with a specific client, a specific service offering, or a special subset of each client's customers. The specific telephone number called is identified through *Dialed Number Identification Service* (*DNIS*), a service offered by the carriers, and generally associated with toll-free numbers (800, 888, and 877). The DNIS information is passed to the ACD in advance of the call.

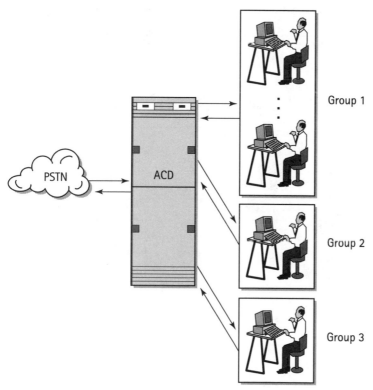

Figure 3-8 Automatic Call Distributor (ACD)

The process, as depicted in Figure 3-8, typically involves a front-end voice processing system, which prompts the caller through a menu for call routing purposes. Based on factors such as the originating telephone number, the specific number dialed, the menu option selected, and information input by the caller (e.g., account number), calls then can be routed to an appropriate agent group, queued if an agent is not available, and delivered to the first available agent. Multiple call centers can network in a *virtual call center* configuration, with calls routed to the call center in proximity to the caller, in consideration of network costs. In the event that the closest call center's queue length exceeds user-definable parameters, the call would then be served to the next nearest call center. Recent developments allow the first call center to examine the queue lengths of all call centers in the network, determine each call center's ability to handle a call in consideration of service-level parameters, and forward the call to the call center most likely to satisfy those objectives based on *look-ahead routing* logic. This approach reduces unnecessary levels of congestion and unacceptable numbers of unhappy customers.

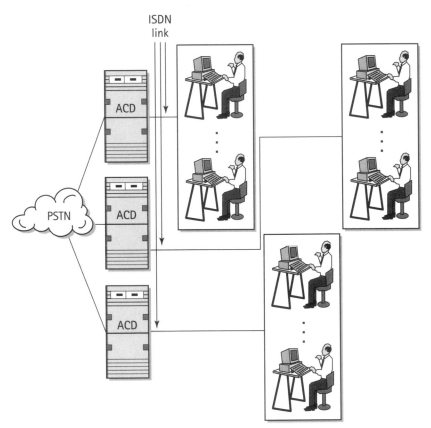

Figure 3-9 Networked ACDs, connected via ISDN links

A recent, improved alternative allows multiple call centers to logically connect as portrayed in Figure 3-9. The first appropriate available agent in any of a number of call centers can be identified and reserved via ISDN signaling technology; the call then is connected over an ISDN link.

You can employ various techniques to route the call; options include tone input, calling number, or called number. Regardless of the technique, the process of customer-programmable call handling and routing is known variously by terms such as *call vectoring* and *custom control routing.* Once a call center accepts the call, the identification of the caller can be determined through several means, including a Personal Identification Number (PIN) or Automatic Number Identification (ANI). The identification number then can be matched against a computer database in order to deliver the caller's profile to the agent in advance of the connection of the call, resulting in what is known as a *screen pop.* In this manner, the most available, appropriate, and capable agent has access to full account information and, therefore, can provide the highest possible level of service. This capability is known as *skills-based routing.* Should the agent need to transfer the call to another agent or to a supervisor, the screen pop typically travels with the call, thereby providing each successive party with the same information to assist in processing the call in the most effective manner.

In addition to agents working at formal call centers, remote agents or even agents-at-home can be networked to an ACD, often over ISDN connections. ISDN technology enables the remote agent to engage in a voice conversation with the caller, while simultaneously maintaining a data session with the centralized host computer and its associated databases. Service bureau call centers in the United States even make use of inmates in correctional facilities (e.g., federal prisons) — security concerns aside, inmates apparently make extremely good employees, as they have relatively few distractions and seldom call in sick. The ACD commonly is interfaced to a PBX, so calls can be transferred to other departments [3-21].

Benefits of ACD technology include increased productivity, because the agents are served incoming calls from a queue of waiting callers. Additionally, the incoming callers realize enhanced customer service because they are directed to the call center with the shortest queue, and held in queue until an agent is available. While the holding time may be rather long, this approach is preferable to encountering busy conditions that require repeated attempts to reach an agent. In fact, holding time can be used for advertising, promotional, or customer-service messages. Should calls be queued from both local trunks and toll-free long distance trunks, the ADC may place the toll-free callers at the head of the queue in order to minimize long distance costs. More substantial ACDs provide rather substantial workforce management reporting, which enables the system administrator to view and trend calling patterns, average queue lengths, average holding times, and so on. Through the use of such a tool, management can better anticipate future incoming call loads and, therefore, can more accurately schedule the number of agents required to handle that load based on customer service objectives.

Customer service is enhanced further when the ACD supports skills-based routing. A credit card company, for instance, might capture the originating telephone number of incoming callers, or request that callers enter their account number. Through matching that information to a database of customers, the company might determine that a particular caller holds a platinum card, prefers to deal with a Spanish-speaking agent, and has failed to make a payment with the past two billing cycles. Based on that information, the ACD might direct the call to the closest call center with a readily available, multilingual agent capable of initiating collection action involving such a privileged customer [3-22], [3-23], and [3-24].

Applications for ACDs in call center environments include reservations centers such as hotels, auto rental agencies, and airlines. Financial institutions such as stock brokerages, commodities traders, and banks make heavy use of ACDs, as do ticket agencies.

Rockwell, the company credited with inventing the ACD (Galaxy, 1973), remains the leading manufacturer of standalone ACD systems, competing with Aspect Telecommunications, Teknekron, and others. PBX manufacturers such as Lucent Technologies, Nortel, and Siemens recently captured a large share of the ACD market [3-25] and [3-26]. Some 38,000 systems currently are installed, with the vast majority (67.2%) serving the larger line sizes (500+ lines). The market for ACDs increased from $285 million in 1987 to $905 million in 1995, and was forecast to exceed $1 billion in 1997 [3-3] and [3-27].

ACD Enhancements and Trends

ACDs no longer are intended only for large, isolated incoming call center applications. In response to general organizational trends towards downsizing, ACDs now are highly cost-effective in relatively small configurations. In fact, a number of manufacturers offer highly scalable ACD systems based on a client/server computing concept. Additionally, organizations increasingly network call centers, as well as take advantage of agents-at-home, remoting access to the ACD, and associated databases via ISDN links. Further, skills-based routing often is employed to direct the incoming caller to the most capable and available agent, whether situated in the call center or working from home [3-28].

Call-back messaging, a relatively recent enhancement, enables incoming callers to register their desire to be called back by an agent should they grow weary of waiting in queue. Once the queue has been satisfied and an agent becomes available, the system will call the customers back and connect them to agents, automatically.

Call blending, another recent development, permits call centers to improve their cost-effectiveness by serving both incoming and outgoing calling functions. Through the use of a *predictive dialer*, the system will monitor the status of incoming calling activity and the level of availability of the agent pool. The system will introduce outgoing calls when it determines that the level of incoming calling activity has dropped to the point that the quality of the service to incoming callers will not be affected adversely. The predictive dialer will search a database of customers to be called, statistically predict the availability of an agent, dial the associated telephone number, detect when the call is answered, and connect the call to an available agent. (You certainly have experience with a predictive dialer. If you answer the telephone at home and experience a noticeable pause before the caller comes on the line, a predictive dialer likely called you. When the system detected your answer, it searched for an available agent, presented the agent with a screen pop, and then connected the call.) If the predictive dialer senses an answering machine at the target telephone number, it simply hangs up and dials the next number in the database. Predictive dialer software logic may be contained within the ACD or it may reside on a PC platform with a LAN connection to the ACD [3-29].

The Web-enabled call center represents an exciting ACD development. Customers accessing a company's Web (World Wide Web) site through the Internet increasingly have the option of clicking a button to request that an agent call back, with the Web site perhaps indicating the approximate length of time until that return call can be launched. The customer can receive the call while remaining connected to the Web site if a second line is available. Therefore, both the customer and the call center agent can view the same information onscreen during the ensuing telephone call. In the not-too-distant future, it is quite possible that the customer may be able to connect directly to an agent during the data session established with the Web site. Assuming that the customer has a voice-enabled PC and a multifunction voice/data modem, and assuming that the call center is properly enabled, a Voice over Internet Protocol (VoIP) conversation can be established and maintained while both parties simultaneously view the same data presented on the Web site. Multimedia queuing logic will allow incoming calls to be queued, regardless of how they call the center, but prioritized based on the method. For instance, toll-free callers might be placed in a priority queue, as those calls cost the call center sponsor; VoIP calls over the Internet might be placed in a queue of lower priority based on the assumption that those calls are free to both parties.

Computer Telephony (CT)

Computer Telephony (CT) can be defined as the true blending of telecommunications switching, and computer processing power and programmed logic. Computers have long been used to program and manage PBXs, Hybrids, and Central Office Exchanges (COs). Yet the systems' interfaces were proprietary and tightly linked, with one computer associated with one set of databases and programs residing on one switching system, one voice processor, etc. The system manufacturers ruled this world of *heavy metal*. During this period, users received only the features the manufacturers deemed worthy, and in a presentation they felt appropriate.

More recently, it became clear that a single computer system could control and integrate multiple telephony devices, taking advantage of the programmed (and programmable) PC's intelligence and the real-time call processing power of the telephony switch. By way of example, a PBX, ACD, and voice processor could integrate to provide a more effective set of solutions for the processing of incoming calls; additionally, *call blending* could be achieved through the application of a *predictive dialer* to improve the productivity of the call center.

While users and third-party software developers have long coveted access to PBX, ACD, and CO Exchange switches, the manufacturers had no real incentive to provide it on an *open* basis. Claiming the risk of potential corruption of the switch databases, their real reason was more one of erosion of their very lucrative market for application software. Over time, they did enable software developers to access expensive and difficult Application Programming Interfaces (APIs) to accomplish these feats. Recently, and under pressure from end users, these manufacturers opened the systems to APIs developed and standardized by various industry groups. Those APIs are available at very low cost and are much easier to use. In fact, every major PBX vendor now ships products that include one or more API interfaces.

The concept evolved much as did computers and their application, in general. The field initially was dominated by IBM, DEC (since acquired by Compaq), and other manufacturers of very substantial hardware and with the clout to garner the attention of the PBX manufacturers. More recently, PC and client/server approaches have captured the market. CT now is available even to the great unwashed masses of small- and medium-sized businesses [3-30].

At a minimum, the concept of CT involves the use of PCs to facilitate user access to PBX and Centrex switch features (e.g., call answer, call transfer, conference calling, call hold, and call hang-up) through a GUI (Graphic User Interface) on a workstation. Taken a step further, the concept involves stripping the switch of much of its intelligence, then placing it in an adjunct computer system. The adjunct computers then effectively become the PBX or Centrex feature server and call control platform, while the switch becomes just that — a high-performance switching matrix. Additionally, users gain access to complex information and invoke complex features through a workstation. In other words, the PBX, ACD, or Centrex system is rendered *dumb*, or *dumber* (i.e., *programmable*). The adjunct computer contains all the generic feature content, which either a third party or the user organization can customize. Service providers write the applications in accordance with interface standards or specifications. Those applications then are uploaded to the switch, which makes procedure calls to the adjunct computer controller, as required [3-31] and [3-32].

Taken to the contemporary extreme, a CT system can be based on a true client/server architecture (Figure 3-10). A single server supports internal voice and data switching, provides access to and from the voice and data WANs, and provides call control functions. Voice communications is provided over telephone sets, although multimedia PCs equipped with headsets or handsets also can be used. PC data terminals are connected to the server via a LAN (typically Ethernet, although ATM provides improved performance). The LAN provides typical data communications capabilities among terminals, mainframe and midrange hosts, and servers; and supports communications between the PCs and the server for call control purposes.

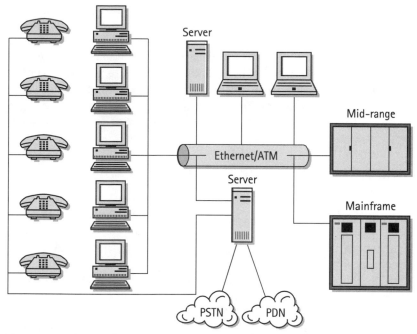

Figure 3-10 CT voice/data system based on client/server architecture

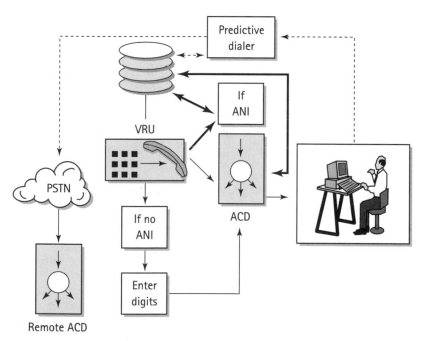

Figure 3-11 CT employed in conjunction with an ACD, in a call center environment
(Reprinted with permission from Call Center Magazine, June 1995)

As depicted in Figure 3-11, CT employed in call center applications effects enhanced functionality. Not only can the call be transferred and conferenced through computer keyboard and mouse commands, but the incoming call identification (calling number or PIN number) can match a caller profile contained in a computer database. Through a *screen pop*, a caller's profile is presented to the agent in advance of the call, thereby improving customer service. Should the original agent need to transfer the call to another agent, the user profile and all other relevant data transfers along with the voice call. The earlier discussion of Automatic Call Distributors (ACDs) presented this application in greater detail [3-33].

Technology, Standards, and Specifications

The technology concept involves Electronic Common Control (ECC) switches, computer systems, and application software. The switches can be PBXs, electronic KTSs, Hybrids, ACDs, or Centrex COs. Third-party developers write the application software in accordance with *Application Programming Interfaces (APIs)*. Defined and supported by the equipment manufacturers, such interfaces permit a great deal of flexibility, incorporating user-definable call handling parameters. The computers can be in the form of mainframes, midranges, or PCs; LAN-based client/server configurations are commonplace. IBM's CallPath Systems Architecture (CSA), Digital Equipment Corporation's Computer Integrated Telephony (CIT), and Hewlett-Packard's Applied Computer Telephony (ACT) comprised the first generation of APIs — all of which still are used widely. Early implementations involved little more than switch-to-host request and status links. More recently, CT has progressed to the point that it offers robust workstation-based intelligence.

The specifics of both the internal busses and the links between the adjunct computer and the switch are many and various. While a number of industry initiatives have launched, no single standard or specification has gained overwhelming acceptance to date. Therefore, Computer Telephony largely remains applied only in a large call center environment, where it yields maximum benefit and where the difficulties of non-standard solutions can be justified. Standards initiatives and specifications that have gained some level of acceptance include CSTA, TSAPI, TAPI, MVIP, SCSA, and JTAPI [3-7] and [3-34].

COMPUTER SUPPORTED TELEPHONY APPLICATIONS (CSTA)

These applications, developed by the European Computer Manufacturers Association (ECMA), were the first truly open CT development standard for link-level protocols. CSTA was improved and formally standardized on an international basis by the ITU-T, incorporating the U.S.-developed Switch-to-Computer Applications Interface (SCAI). CSTA is a full protocol stack that requires an open system interface to a PBX, ACD, or Centrex CO Exchange. A growing number of manufacturers, including Alcatel, Comdial, Ericsson, Inter-Tel, Siemens, and Tadiran have implemented CSTA. Closely aligned with CSTA are Lucent Technologies' Adjunct/Switch Applications Interface (ASAI) and IBM's CallPath Services Architecture (CSA).

TELEPHONY SERVICES APPLICATION PROGRAMMING INTERFACE (TSAPI)

Developed jointly by AT&T and Novell and released in March 1994, the TSAPI specification is strongly oriented toward PC platforms. TSAPI is a lesser protocol stack that does not require that the switch manufacturer fully open the switch interface. Although a number of PBX manufacturers supported TSAPI, which runs on Novell NetWare servers and other systems, the cost of TSAPI PBX drivers is quite high, and, as a result, its widespread use has been discouraged. Additionally, many suggest that it is limited in capability and cumbersome to use; TSAPI has received criticism for being a CSTA translator for AT&T Definity switches and as a means of promoting AT&T's and Novell's interests. Release 2 (1995) extended the API to other PBXs and computer systems, including OS/2, Macintosh, UnixWare, and Windows NT [3-35] and [3-36]. Newer versions of TASPI extend compliance with CSTA, and support a Windows NT client and a TCP/IP network [3-37].

TELEPHONY APPLICATION PROGRAMMING INTERFACE (TAPI)

Microsoft and Intel jointly developed this specification in response to the problems associated with TSAPI. As an integral part of Microsoft's Windows Open Services Architecture (WOSA), TAPI runs in a Microsoft Windows NT environment. Since it is Windows client/server-based, TAPI involves limited additional cost to the user organization [3-35] and [3-36] and [3-38]. New versions also support third-party call control.

MULTI-VENDOR INTEGRATION PROTOCOL (MVIP)

MVIP, an ad hoc standard developed in September 1990 by Natural MicroSystems, is supported on a multinational, multivendor basis. MVIP provides a set of telephony hardware and software standards for integrating diverse telephony technologies, network interfaces, and applications in a single adjunct computer system. MVIP was designed to overcome the limited call handling capabilities of PC busses, providing the ability to connect multiple telephony cards in a single PC – and handle 256 simultaneous calls over 8 MVIP busses of 2 Mbps each. Multi-Chassis MVIP (MC-MVIP) extends MVIP to allow the interconnection of resources in up to 20 PCs, thereby providing additional flexibility and scalability. High-capacity MVIP (H-MVIP) is in the development stages.

A number of vendors have linked together to support MVIP through the Global Organization for MVIP (GO-MVIP). Well over 50 manufacturers, including Mitel, have announced support for MVIP, and well over 200 products exist. Compatible products include Lotus Phone Notes and Nortel's H.320 Desktop Video.

SIGNAL COMPUTING SYSTEM ARCHITECTURE (SCSA)

More than 200 suppliers and developers support SCSA (developed by Dialogic). A LAN/Server-based architecture, it is hardware independent at the client, host, and media processing systems levels. Originally developed to support TAPI, it currently is interoperable with both TAPI and TSAPI. SCSA's SCbus (Signal Computing bus) permits the creation of up to 2,048 time slots per MVIP bus, thereby providing sufficient capacity for support of full-motion video and high-fidelity audio.

JAVA TELEPHONY APPLICATION PROGRAMMING INTERFACE (JTAPI)

JTAPI is a Java-based solution developed jointly by Sun Microsystems, Lucent Technologies, IBM, and Nortel. Similarly characteristic of Java, JTAPI is a cross-platform, multivendor solution that uses highly efficient applets, which are small sets of application program code, for network-based CT operation. JTAPI adds Internet/intranet functionality to CT, thereby enabling the creation of Web-based applications that integrate browser applications with call center functionality [3-37].

Forums and Consortia

Several forums and consortia exist that actively promote open system architectures and standard APIs for the development of CTI technologies and applications. In addition to the ECMA, they include the Enterprise Computer Telephony Forum (ECTF) and the International Multimedia Teleconferencing Consortium, Inc. (IMTC).

ENTERPRISE COMPUTER TELEPHONY FORUM (ECTF)

ECTF promotes interoperability and standard approaches to CTI. Members include Dialogic, Digital Equipment Corporation, Ericsson Business Networks, Hewlett-Packard, and Nortel. The ECTF has developed a highly sophisticated framework, or model, for both carrier-class and end-user level systems. In the future, the ECTF appears well positioned as the leading authority with respect to CT standards.

INTERNATIONAL MULTIMEDIA TELECONFERENCING CONSORTIUM (IMTC)

IMTC is a not-for-profit organization comprising more than 150 member companies. The stated mission of the IMTC is to promote, encourage, and facilitate the development and implementation of interoperable multimedia teleconferencing solutions through open standards. IMTC focus is on the T.120 and H.320 standards suites for data conferencing and video telephony, respectively.

Applications

Applications for CT initially were limited to telephony-intensive call centers, often serving for inbound and outbound call handling. Security Pacific Bank, for instance, installed a 24-hour customer service capability in 1988 at a cost of approximately $7 million. All information requests and branch functions consolidated into a single service center, where 450 agents now handle about 5 million calls a month. Prior to the CT implementation, representatives logged on to 3 different systems in order to access multiple databases to handle a typical call. The CT installation enabled a single workstation application interface to support customer queries, problem resolution, information trace and verification, establishment of new accounts, and so on. Additionally, they sell a variety of financial products through inbound and outbound sales programs. The systems run on Tandem NonStop computer systems and Telephone Delivery System software from Early, Cloud & Company. Key benefits reported include extension of business hours to 24 hours a day, reduction of staff costs by 33%, simplified access to multiple host systems and databases, and improved service quality and agent efficiency [3-32].

CT application in an ACD environment offers the advantages of automation of *screen pops*, skills-based routing, interactive intelligent queuing, call center networking, unified messaging, and call blending. In a typical PBX environment, it offers the advantages of electronic directories, call logs and reminders, integrated message waiting notification (voice, electronic, and fax mail), and dial-by-name. The end result is improved call handling and, ultimately, enhanced staff productivity.

More recently, you may have witnessed a great deal of activity in the area of Web-enabled call centers. Perhaps soon, a caller can access a Web site, browse that site, click a "Talk to an Agent" button, and launch an IP voice call to a call center agent over the Internet. While the agent and the caller are engaged in the *VoIP* (*Voice over Internet Protocol*) conversation, they simultaneously view the same Web site screens. In other words, both simultaneously engage in both a voice and a data session over the same Internet connection. The call center agent's screen pop includes both the screen from the Web site and the caller's profile data. The caller must have a suitably equipped multimedia PC and a voice/data modem, and must be running the TCP/IP protocol suite. The yield is that the call center agent can handle the call in a much more productive fashion. A decidedly low-tech alternative involves the caller's clicking a "Have an Agent Call Me Back" button on the Web site. This approach makes use of the PSTN to launch the return voice call and requires that the caller have two lines available, one for the Internet call and one for the return voice call. WebLine Communications notably provides *such e-commerce* (electronic commerce) solutions.

A particularly notable application initiative is that of Tadiran, a PBX manufacturer, and Novell. The Tadiran PBX (Coral ISBX) includes an optional CoraLink CTI interface which supports multiple simultaneous server-based CTI applications. The Coral's CTI/OAI (Open Architecture Interface) interface is CSTA-compatible. The Tadiran/Novell relationship initially yielded the Coral Telephony Server, which enables TSAPI-based application development for the Coral system [3-39].

Futures

Clearly, CT has a bright future. Never before have third-party software developers and end users had the ability to write their own application software to blend single-function devices into a high-performance, integrated solution set. As the PBX, ACD, voice processing, and CO manufacturers increasingly open their proprietary systems and as the APIs become increasingly platform-independent, the future of CT will be ensured. Whether the switches ultimately will be rendered completely *dumb* remains to be seen and, in fact, is highly unlikely. Nonetheless, many of the applications will be developed on and delivered through software residing on an adjunct computer platform. Otherwise, the increasingly exotic and customized applications required by contemporary businesses threaten to overwhelm the traditional PBX, Hybrid KTS, and Centrex CO.

The cost of CT software has dropped from the original $15,000-$20,000 per seat (agent position) in a mainframe implementation to only a few hundred dollars in a contemporary LAN-based client/server environment. In a telephony-intensive call center environment, this and other associated costs easily can be justified and recouped through improved agent productivity and enhanced customer service. According to Dataquest and The Aries Group/MPSG, market leaders include Lucent Technologies, Nortel, and Siemens in the arena of telecom manufacturers; leading computer manufacturers include IBM, Digital Equipment Corporation (DEC), and Hewlett-Packard, in that order [3-3], [3-33], and [3-40]. A number of PBX manufacturers also have gotten into the game, developing their own service-provider software, albeit for their own switches. For instance, Comdial's wideopen.office is a LAN-based CT solution that is relatively uncomplicated and supports most operating systems. It also supports both the TSAPI and TAPI programming interfaces. As discussed earlier in this chapter, the PC-based PBX is beginning to make a real impact in the small- and medium-sized PBX market. Whether truly PC-based, client/server-based, or in the form of a PBX in a box, these small, highly programmable CT systems offer tremendous flexibility. Generally through a Windows interface, you can customize the functionality of the system to the best advantage of the user organization; self-reliance, rather than reliance on the manufacturer, is a significant advantage. The client/server systems offer markedly improved ease of use for call control through the Windows interface at the user's client workstation. While reliability remains an issue, contemporary industrial-strength PCs act as highly dependable servers for call control and feature content. The generic nature of the various components (e.g., client workstations, PC-based servers, software, and printed circuit boards) permits the user organization to literally build a low-cost system from scratch, and to enhance it as requirements dictate. Although current limitations dictate the maximum size of many such systems, they tend to be easily expandable, and increases in cost tend to bear a graceful relationship to increases in size and functionality. Many CT systems support an integrated suite of functionality that includes voice telephony, voice messaging, ACD, and Internet access through a single server [3-41].

Dataquest forecasts that, while only 558 new CT systems were installed in 1992, that number grew to 9,311 in 1995 and will reach 502,000 in 1999. By then, some 23 million agents will be added to the network each year at an average cost of $213 for software and links, compared to $609 in 1995 [3-3]. Given its low and rapidly dropping cost, in combination with the obvious benefits of customized user control, CTI saves money and makes sense [3-42].

In collaboration with the computer manufacturers and software developers, and with the support of the various standards initiatives, the leading manufacturers of traditional PBXs all have taken steps to position the PBX as a robust communications controller for voice, data, fax, and multimedia traffic. In some cases, ATM has become an integral part of the traditional PBX; in other cases, ATM capability is delivered in the form of an adjunct switching matrix for data traffic. Virtually all manufacturers have added IP capabilities to the traditional PBX for voice and fax traffic, as well as data. All of the major manufacturers also have added server-based CT call control capability. The traditional PBX, essentially a mainframe computing system, likely will remain dominant in the high end of the market, although its basic nature will drift toward CT over the next decade. This combination of traditional mainframe reliability and client/server application flexibility will be a powerful combination.

References

[3-1]   Brooks, John. *Telephone: The First Hundred Years*. Harper &
             Row, 1976.

[3-2]   Rees, Diane and English, Michelle K. "Key and Hybrid Systems:
             Overview." *Datapro Communications Analyst*. Datapro Information
             Services Group, March 1995.

[3-3]   *1996 MultiMedia Telecommunications Market Review and Forecast*.
             MultiMedia Telecommunications Association, 1996.

[3-4]   Gasman, Lawrence. *Manager's Guide to the New Telecommunications
             Network*. Artech House, 1988.

[3-5]   Sulkin, Allan. "PBX Market Perks Up." *Business Communications
             Review*, January 1995.

[3-6]   Horak, Ray. "Telemanagement Systems and Software: Overview."
             Datapro Communications Analyst. Datapro Information Services
             Group, January 1995.

[3-7]   Costello, Rich. "PBX Systems: Technology Overview." *Datapro IT
             Continuous Services*. Datapro Information Services Group. August 10,
             1998.

[3-8]   Sulkin, Allan. *PBX System Technologies Overview*. ACUTA Spring 1996
             Seminar – PBX Technologies, March/April 1996.

[3-9]   Liebowitz, Ed. "SRX's Switch-to-Host Vision." *Teleconnect*, November
             1994.

[3-10]   Kaufman, Harvey. "PBXs, Computers and the Trend Toward ATM."
             Telecommunications, December 1995.

[3-11]   Cray, Rendleman. "IP PBXs: Open Questions." *Data Communications*,
             March 1999.

[3-12]   Rendleman, John. "Cisco to Unwrap IP PBX." *PC Week*, March 1, 1999.

[3-13]   Rybxzynski, Tony. "More Connectivity, New Applications: IP PBXs Point to IP Telephony's Future." *CTI*, March 1999.

[3-14]   Costello, Rich. "Communications Servers: Technology Overview." *IT Continuous Services*. Datapro Information Services Group, September 28, 1998.

[3-15]   Rohde, David. "Northern Telecom to Bring Security, Savings Back to PBXs." *Network World*, May 1, 1995.

[3-16]   Horak, Ray. "Voice Network Fraud." *Datapro IT Continuous Services*. Datapro Information Services Group, July 22, 1998.

[3-17]   Abrahams, John R. *Manager's Guide to CENTREX*. Artech House, 1988.

[3-18]   Horak, Ray. "PBX versus Centrex Comparison." *Datapro Communications Analyst*. Datapro Information Services Group, January 1995.

[3-19]   Costello, Richard A. "Centrex: Overview." *Datapro Communications Analyst*. Datapro Information Services Group, May 1996.

[3-20]   Horak, Ray. "Centrex: Technology Overview" *IT Continuous Services*. Datapro Information Services Group, November 3, 1998.

[3-21]   Doren, Donald van. "CTI: Moving Into High Gear." *TeleProfessional*, February 1996.

[3-22]   Bodin, Madeline. "ACD Features at Work." *Call Center Magazine*, May 1995.

[3-23]   Klenke, Maggie. "ACDs Get Skills-Based Routing." *Business Communications Review*, July 1996.

[3-24]   Klenke, Maggie. "ACDs Get Skills-Based Routing." *TeleProfessional*, March 1996.

[3-25]   Sulkin, Allan. "ACDs: Standalone vs. the PBX Vendors." *Business Communications Review*, June 1995.

[3-26]   Frydman, Isaac. "The Year of the ACD." *TeleProfessional*, February 1996.

[3-27]   Rosenberg, Arthur M. and Outlaw, Joe. "Automatic Call Distribution Systems: Market Overview — North America." *Datapro IT Continuous Services*. Datapro Information Services Group, February 24, 1997.

[3-28]   Womack, Audrey Y. "Automatic Call Distribution Systems: Overview." *Datapro Communications Analyst*. Datapro Information Services Group, June 1994.

[3-29]   Dawson, Keith. "Out Of The Box, Onto The Phones." *Call Center Magazine*, May 1995.

[3-30]   Rudd, Susan. "Where Do CTI Applications Really Belong?" *Business Communications Review*, February 1996.

[3-31]   Grigonis, Richard. "PBX Survival Techniques." *Computer Telephony*, July 1995.

[3-32]   Lau, Delina; Xue, Cindy; Paetamai, Poonpon; and Ghani, Muhammad Usman. *Computer Telephony Integration*. University of San Francisco, December 4, 1995.

[3-33]   "Computers On Call: Computer-Telephony Integration (CTI)." *Datapro Communications Analyst*. Datapro Information Services Group, December 1995.

[3-34]   "Smart, Programmable Dumb-Switch Apps." *Computer Telephony*, July 1995.

[3-35]   King, Rachael. "CTI Up Close: Analyzing the API Angle." *Data Communications*, October 1995.

[3-36]   Taylor, Kieran. "Distributed PBXs: Big Benefits, Little Boxes." *Data Communications*, October 1995.

[3-37]   Rosenberg, Arthur M. "Call Center Computer Telephony: Technology Overview." *Datapro IT Continuous Services*. Datapro Information Services Group, December 10, 1997.

[3-38]   Burton, James. "CTI: The View from Windows 95 and NT." *Business Communications Review*, January 1996.

[3-39]   Horak, Ray. "Tadiran Coral ISBX." *Datapro Communications Analyst*. Datapro Information Services Group, November 1995

[3-40]   Costello, Richard A. "Computer Telephony Integration (CTI): Overview." *Datapro Communications Analyst*. Datapro Information Services Group, March 1996.

[3-41]   Marguiles, Ed. *The UnPBX: The Complete Guide to the New Breed of Communications Servers*. Telecom Library/Miller Freeman, 1997.

[3-42]   Claypool, Loren. "Company Saves $465,000 per Year with Computer Telephony Integration System." *TeleProfessional*, September 1995.

Chapter 4

Messaging Systems: Facsimile, Voice Processing, and Electronic Mail

Press one for sales. Press two in a hopeless effort to get technical support. Press one for answers to questions you don't have. Press two if you're gullible and pessimistic. Press two if you're willing to buy something just so you can talk to a human being.
From the comic strip *Dilbert* by Scott Adams.

Electronic messaging systems comprise facsimile, voice processing, and electronic mail. Each system deals with information in a different native form, and each serves its own unique purpose to great advantage. While these technologies differ greatly in their basic characteristics and, certainly in their application, they do share some commonalities. They all reside on a computer platform of some description and they all reap the greatest advantages when networked. Perhaps most importantly, electronic messaging systems are characterized by their abilities to provide *store-and-forward* communications. In other words, the systems can accept a message and store it in temporary memory in a mailbox, where it may be accessed at a later time, perhaps remotely. Further, you may forward the message subsequently to another user.

Store-and-forward technology adds significant value because it overcomes the requirement for a real-time communication between people or machines. The s pecific benefits of store-and-forward technologies include the fact that differences in time zones are mitigated, since you can create the message during business hours in one location and forward it to the recipient, who can access it during normal business hours at the distant location. Whether the parties are at opposite ends of the country or are separated by oceans, communications can be effected on a non-realtime basis. Additionally, you can access systems and messages typically over the network from remote locations (e.g., field offices, hotels, and client sites) at any time of the day or night, thereby offering tremendous benefits to the contemporary *road warrior*. Finally, the messages tend to be abbreviated, containing only necessary information; this is especially true of voicemail, which replaces the normal human-to-human conversational mode of communications. As social animals, humans tend to socialize before getting down to the business at hand; we are much less likely to attend to interpersonal niceties via a machine-enabled, one-way communication. Therefore, communications by messaging systems is highly efficient, if not particularly personal, in nature.

While all of these devices initially were standalone systems of a proprietary nature, contemporary systems are computer-based messaging systems that generally are networked, and based on standards which ensure their interoperability at some minimum level. Additionally, you often can access them across a Wide Area Network through a KTS, PBX, ACD, Centrex, or CO system. They also increasingly are enhanced through the application of Computer Telephony (CT) technology; in fact, voice processing inherently is Computer Telephony. Taken to the technically feasible extreme, CT enables the user to access a variety and combination of messages through the switch from a LAN-attached, multimedia PC workstation, using a single and intuitive Graphic User Interface (GUI). Finally, the separate technologies of facsimile, voice processing, and e-mail currently integrate to yield *unified messaging* systems, which allow voice, text, image, and even video messages to blend, thereby enhancing the aggregate effectiveness and impact of the individual messages. The technology currently exists to support unified messaging, but the costs are hard to justify.

Facsimile (Fax) Systems

Facsimile comes from the Latin *fac simile*, which translates to *make similar*. Traditional facsimile systems are unique as they communicate image information, rather than audio or data. Additionally, they generally are based on electrochemical processes at the receiving end. Edward Davy built the first practical facsimile machine in 1837, but abandoned the invention shortly thereafter. Alexander Bain, a Scottish clockmaker, then revived the concept in 1846. The Bain device was used commercially in the United States and England, where it competed with the Cooke-Wheatstone telegraph, which could transmit images through etching metal with a stylus. Facsimile was not widely deployed until the 1970s, when the ITU-T set interoperability standards. At that point, the devices became sufficiently affordable for the technology to find relatively significant market acceptance in commercial, educational, and government applications. The low cost of current fax technology renders it cost-effective even for widespread consumer use. IDC estimates that 45 million fax machines are installed in the United States; Gallup/Pitney Bowes estimates that approximately 100 million are installed worldwide [4-1].

The Technology

Facsimile transmission typically involves a pair of standalone fax devices that serve to both transmit and receive image documents through built-in modems, which interface these inherently digital devices to the analog Public Switched Telephone Network (PSTN). The transmitting fax scans the image document from top to bottom and from left to right, looking for dots of black and white; some systems will also support 256 levels of grayscale. Through the modem, these various dots are translated into data bits, the data bits are compressed in order to reduce transmission time, and the resulting compressed data file is translated into modulations of analog sine waves, which travel over an analog local loop to the edge of the PSTN. The receiving device reads the analog sine waves through a modem, varying the temperature of a print head on the output device to cause the image to be reproduced on chemically treated paper. In other words, fax transmission generally is an analog technology that is *electrothermochemical* in nature.

Group I and II (Table 4-1) fax machines – the first generations – employed now obsolete electrochemical processes. Each Group achieved compatibility based on international standards developed by the CCITT (now ITU-T) in 1966 and 1978, respectively. Transmission was on an analog basis, with Group I machines using Frequency Modulation (FM) – 1500 Hz white frequency and 2400 Hz black frequency. Group II machines employed Amplitude Modulation (AM) at 2100 Hz.

Group III fax machines, which account for approximately 98% of all devices currently in use, conform to the above described electrothermochemical process. Note the increasingly common plain-paper facsimile machines are essentially fax laser printers. Group III facsimile machines, manufactured according to ITU-T Recommendation T.4 (1980), obviate issues of incompatibility. Group III devices transmit compressed digital data at 2400 bps-14.4 Kbps over analog lines through the use of a ITU-T standard modem protocol and compression algorithm, and are compatible with Groups I and II. Group III devices, operating at 9.6 Kbps, transmit documents at "business letter" quality at a rate of approximately 30 seconds per page, using the *Modified Huffman* (*MH*) compression algorithm. MH compresses data on a line-by-line basis, and is supported by all Group III devices as the lowest common denominator. Group III machines, which operate at 14.4 Kbps, use the *Modified Modified Read* (*MMR*) compression algorithm, which supports transmission at a rate of as low as 10 seconds per page. MMR uses a two-dimensional compression technique that permits the transmitting modem to view multiple lines of data.

Group IV fax machines – highly specialized and relatively expensive fax computer systems – are designed to make use of digital circuits. They speed the process and improve quality through compressed digital transmission at rates up to 64 Kbps. Group IV fax machines also are Group III-compatible and can be connected to analog circuits should a digital circuit not be available. ITU-T Recommendation T.6 defines Group IV standards. Table 4-1 provides a view of the characteristics of each ITU-T fax generation [4-2] and [4-3].

Table 4-1 FACSIMILE GENERATIONS AND CHARACTERISTICS

Generation (ITU-T Group)	Transmission Speed (per page)	Compatibility	Resolution: Lines Per Inch (LPI)
Group I	4–6 Minutes	Group I	100
Group II	2–3 Minutes	Group II	100
Group III	10–30 Seconds	Groups I, II, & III	200
Group IV	3–4 Seconds	Groups I, II, III, & IV	200–400

Fax boards and *fax software*, both Group III/IV-compatible, exist for computer systems ranging from PCs to mainframes. When sending a computer-based fax document, the fax software instructs the fax board to print the document to a remote facsimile machine, rather than a printer. The computer fax board contains a fax modem, thereby enabling any computer file to be transmitted to another similarly equipped computer or to a fax machine through fax *emulation* (imitation). The cost of such boards is quite reasonable, often less than $100. Fax software and fax boards often accompany an applications suite packaged with a PC. For instance, WinFax and BitFax have been included in the suites of Microsoft Windows and Microsoft Office software pre-packaged with most IBM-compatible PCs; the cost is bundled into that of the turnkey system. Client/server versions involve fax software resident on the client workstations, with a relatively small number of fax boards residing on the fax server; the server may be a standalone (dedicated) fax server or a partition of a multifunctional server. The fax software in the client workstations sends the fax documents across a LAN to the fax server (see Figure 4-1), which queues them as required before transmission, thereby considerably reducing hardware and circuit costs [4-4], [4-5], and [4-6]. The fax server, which also may support other applications, accepts and queues faxes from multiple workstations on the basis of a *print to fax* option. The fax server takes faxes from the queue, *rasterizes* them (i.e., converts them from text to image format), adds either a default or customized cover page, compresses the data, perhaps selects the Least Cost Route (LCR) for transmission, and sends the fax. International faxes can be held in queue for transmission after normal business hours, when calling costs are lowest and traffic loads are lightest. If the fax devices are IP (Internet Protocol) enabled, the Least Cost Route options may include the Internet or a special IP-based carrier. The fax server also provides accountability — records can be kept of fax traffic through employee numbers and department codes in order that the cost of fax transmission can be billed back to the responsible cost center [4-7].

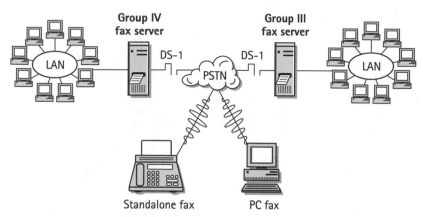

Figure 4-1 Facsimile transmission in a fax server environment

These computerized approaches contain several drawbacks, however. First, the transmitted documents either must exist as computer files, or must be scanned by peripheral equipment and converted to computer files through a rastering process accomplished by application software. Secondly, you must leave the receiving fax computers on and networked continuously to be accessible. Third and in a stand-alone PC environment, the process of fax receipt may interrupt other applications in progress at the receiving computer workstation. Finally, the received documents are memory-intensive image files, which must be converted to text files in order to achieve full effectiveness. On the positive side again, the converted documents can be fully editable text files that can be forwarded to other workstations or servers without suffering the loss of quality characteristic of documents re-faxed via the traditional approach. You also can archive the converted incoming faxes, with as many as 100,000 burned into a single CD-ROM disk [4-8]. An additional advantage to this approach is that you can retrieve the faxes over the Internet, thereby relieving the recipient of the requirement to have access to a conventional fax machine.

FAX-ON-DEMAND (FOD)

Fax-On-Demand (*FOD*) most commonly is an integration of voice processing and facsimile. The traditional FOD approach involves a voice processing front-end that answers the telephone call, then prompts the caller to select a document from a menu of options, enter a return fax number, and perhaps enter a credit card number for billing purposes. The system also may have the capability to automatically verify the credit card number on a machine-to-machine basis. Recently, FOD has integrated with Web sites for access over the Internet. Visitors can click a *fax back* button, select the requested documents, and enter a return fax number and billing information.

There exist single-line FOD systems, which work in combination with voice/fax/data modems; such systems can store as many as 999 fax documents at a cost of less than $250. The port sizes of multiline FOD systems are as small as 2x2 (incoming x outgoing) and range as large as 24x24, with the larger systems perhaps handling 2,000 calls per day and storing over 10,000 documents. The platform can be as small as a standalone PC outfitted with fax cards, voice processing cards, FOD software, and network access ports. The systems can be delivered on a turnkey basis, or the user organization can build one with a component toolkit. A number of manufacturers of voice-processing systems offer add-on FOD, which can be integrated with a PBX system. There also exist combination, single-slot PC cards that can effect both FOD and voice processing; once again, you can no longer categorize devices and their functions in discrete terms [4-8].

FOD systems also may include broadcast capabilities, which support high-speed outgoing fax transmission to large numbers of receivers through the entry of a distribution list. In larger applications, FOD systems are in the form of fax servers, typically residing on dedicated computer platforms and accessible by multiple client workstations across a LAN.

As reported by *InfoWorld*, the Ontario (Canada) Jockey Club uses Octel's (now part of Lucent Technologies) Fax Mail Plus to communicate with suppliers of its three racetracks. Additionally, trainers and horse owners can dial into the system to request fax transmission of post-positions and weekly schedules. Octel states that the automated system saves the Jockey Club $750 per month, including $325 in labor associated with manual fax transmission [4-10]. Novell, Inc. reported that its client/server FOD system pays for itself every 30 business days; the system is used for technical support, training, and to fax back product information. Octel uses a 24x24-port system to handle 1,700 calls daily and store 10,000 documents [4-11].

While e-mail and the World Wide Web (WWW) currently may be the preferred method of electronic communications, fax continues to offer advantages as the lowest common denominator. Like e-mail and the WWW, FOD is fairly instantaneous. Although in black and white, cleverly formatted documents rich in graphic content can be faxed easily and quickly; such documents sent by e-mail often are rendered unreadable if the target computer doesn't have the right application software to open or decompress the attached document. Further and very much unlike most e-mail systems, fax provides instantaneous reporting of the results of transmissions, whether successfully delivered or not.

Fax Applications

Application of facsimile technology traditionally has focused on document transfer. A key advantage, of course, is that any document can be transmitted by fax. Whether a letter, an invoice, a blueprint, or even a photograph, it can be transmitted successfully. Numerous sales-oriented enterprises now rely heavily on fax broadcast systems, in place of more traditional direct mail or other forms of advertising. Particularly in the case of time-sensitive sales situations, fax advertising very quickly positions the opportunity in front of large numbers of prospective buyers. Additionally, a faxed ad is more likely to garner attention than a similar ad in the media, a direct mailer, or an e-mail message.

Recently, Fax-On-Demand (FOD) has been used successfully by a number of customer-service and telemarketing enterprises as a replacement for fulfilling information requests generated by direct mail and other forms of advertising. By way of example, *Network World*, a leading communications-network publication, encourages prospective attendees to view detailed descriptions of its seminar and conference offerings by accessing its FOD system. Because the FOD system is completely automated, *Network World* reports substantial savings in manpower and overall fulfillment costs. Perhaps most importantly, the information faxed back to the prospect is received much more quickly and acted on more expeditiously than would in the case of more traditional means such as the United States Postal Service.

Integrated Fax Messaging, a rapidly developing technology, promises to replace conventional fax systems during the next decade, at least in fax-intensive operations. Also referred to as Unified Fax Messaging, the technology has been standardized by the International Computer Facsimile Association (ICFA), an affiliate member of the Electronic Messaging Association. Numerous ICFA members have developed systems based on ITU-T Recommendations T.434 and T.30 [4-12].

T.434

T.434 is an industry standard for *Binary File Transfer* (*BFT*) that permits compliant facsimile devices to send any file type, reproducing the original quality at the receiving end. Additionally, the received document is in the form of an editable file, if allowed by the sender. T.434 provides for interoperability among BFT products from disparate manufacturers, allowing data files to be sent much as e-mail messages — *Fax-On-Demand* essentially becomes *File-On-Demand*. The standard works with fax PCs, fax servers, and Group IV fax machines. Benefits of T.434 include increased throughput and reduced document storage requirements through data compression. Additionally, the specific file attributes (e.g., image format as in .EPS, .PCX, or .BMP files) are maintained. You can also edit and annotate received documents. In addition to working with computer-based facsimile systems, some standalone fax machines support the standard. The standard also has potential for linking fax systems with photocopiers, scanners, e-mail gateways, and PCs; it may also invite integration with PBXs and voicemail systems.

T.30

T.30, a Group III/IV-compatible standard, describes the handshaking-protocol used between two fax devices for establishing and maintaining communications. T.30 provides for routing faxes to users via subaddresses or fax mailboxes. Message security is included; only those responsible for certain manual routing processes can view the cover page. The routing can be accomplished in several ways, including DTMF, DID, OCR, and manual. *Dual Tone MultiFrequency* (*DTMF*) routing requires the sender to enter the appropriate fax extension via a telephone tonepad.

Direct Inward Dialing (*DID*) routing requires a PBX or fax server which is so equipped; each fax extension must have a separate DID number. *Optical Character Recognition* (*OCR*) software permits the server to recognize the name or special identification of the intended recipient; OCR currently is more expensive and less reliable than the other options. Manual routing is the most common approach, with an individual viewing only the cover page and then routing the fax as appropriate.

In a client/server computing environment, each LAN-connected client workstation is assigned a fax extension number. Inbound fax messages received by the fax server are automatically routed to the specific workstation associated with the intended recipient. Through entry of the appropriate security password, the recipient then accesses the facsimile message. Assuming that the message is T.434-compliant, the recipient can edit and annotate it prior to either fax response or forwarding to a user-definable distribution list. Several companies (e.g., Brooktrout) have developed software that allows the server to recognize the dialed telephone number with the trailing subaddress; the fax then can be routed to a fax machine, another client workstation, or an e-mail address. Server software developed by various companies enables the server automatically to determine whether to send the message via the PSTN, or the Internet, or another IP-based network as an e-mail attachment [4-13].

IP FAX

Fax over IP is a very recent development. This offers significant cost savings compared with the traditional method of transmission over the circuit-switched PSTN. You could easily accomplish the traditional method developed as fax transmission over the PSTN through the use of low-cost Group III terminal equipment which incorporated fax modems for transmission of the fax data over the ubiquitous analog network. Group IV devices simply extended that capability to digital circuits, adding a significant level of intelligence in the process. The contemporary fax document almost always originates as a data file that increasingly is sent from computer to computer, rather than printed out and manually fed into a conventional fax machine. You cannot argue the logic behind sending a fax data file over a packet optimized for data, rather than over the highly inefficient circuit-switched network optimized for voice. The trick is to somehow provide a mechanism for interfacing the huge installed base of contemporary fax machines with a transmission network for which they clearly were not designed.

The Internet and emerging, special-purpose IP networks are built on the concepts of packet switching and the underlying TCP/IP (Transmission Control Protocol/Internet Protocol) protocol suite for packet data. Without getting too deep into the specifics of packet switching and the TCP/IP protocol suite — presented in several subsequent chapters — suffice it to say that the two concepts work together very nicely to support reliable fax transmission over a highly shared packet data network. Packet networks require that a file of data be fragmented into multiple, discrete units (known as packets) of data which then flow independently over the network from the originating edge to the terminating edge, where they are linked together and where the original file of data is reconstituted. Packet networks are the major freeways of the Information Superhighway. That is, the packets flow into, across, and out of a network which may support thousands or even millions of simultaneous transmissions, each in packet form, and all of which contend for limited resources in the form of switches and transmission facilities. Under load, this packet-by-packet contention for limited network resources results in congestion, which imposes variable and unpredictable levels of delay on the individual packets. Contemporary fax machines rely on an internal timing mechanism between the transmitting and receiving terminals. The carefully timed PSTN supports this approach beautifully. Because packet networks violate this timing mechanism, however, the devices simply cannot transmit effectively over such a network.

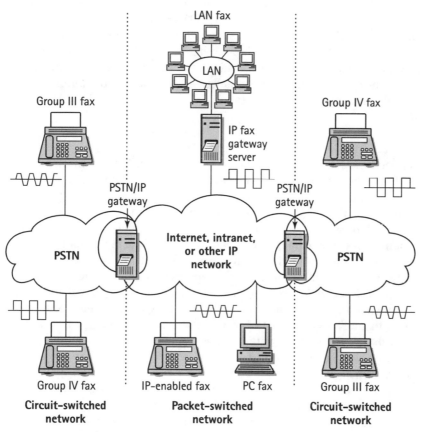

Figure 4-2 IP Fax, with alternative methods of network access

In order to send a fax document over a packet network (Figure 4-2), the terminal equipment must adapt to the inherent nature of that network. You can typically accomplish this adaptation process through a fax *gateway*, which serves as a physical gate between the circuit-switched and the packet-switched networks. Just as importantly, the gateway runs gateway protocols that convert from the carefully timed PSTN to the TCP/IP-based packet network. IP-enabled fax devices (e.g., fax machines, PCs, and servers) do not require the services of such a gateway. Relevant IP fax standards include T.37 and T.38.

T.37 T.37 is an ITU-T Recommendation (June 1998) for store-and-forward fax via e-mail through the incorporation of *SMTP* (*Simple Mail Transfer Protocol*) and *MIME* (*Multipurpose Internet Mail Extension*). SMTP is an application-layer extension of TCP/IP that governs electronic mail transmissions and receptions. MIME is a SMTP extension that supports compound mail; in this context, MIME provides for the attachment of a compressed fax image to an e-mail. Fax image documents are attached to e-mail headers and encoded in the *TIFF-F* (*Tagged Image File Format-Fax*) compressed data format. In *simple-mode*, T.37 restricts fax transmission to the most popular fax machine formats (e.g., standard or fine resolution, and standard page size); this restriction is effected through limitation of TIFF-F encoding to the S-profile. Simple mode provides no confirmation of delivery. *Full-mode* extensions include mechanisms for ensuring call completion through negotiation of capabilities between the transmit and receive devices. Full-mode also provides for delivery confirmation.

T.38 T.38 is an ITU-T Recommendation (June 1998) for store-and-forward fax via e-mail. Derived from X.25 packet standards, T.38 addresses IP fax transmissions for IP-enabled fax devices and fax gateways, defining the translation of T.30 fax signals and *Internet Fax Protocol* (*IFP*) packets. The specific methods for various T.38 implementations include fax relay and fax spoofing. *Fax relay*, also known as *demod/remod*, addresses the demodulation of standard analog fax transmissions from originating machines equipped with modems, and their remodulation for presentation to a matching destination device. Fax relay depends on a low latency IP network (i.e., one second or less) in order that the session between the fax machines does not *time out. Fax spoofing* is used for fax transmissions over IP networks characterized by longer and less predictable levels of packet latency which could cause the session with the conventional fax machines to time out. Packet transmission over such a network can result in variable levels of delay of packet receipt, packet-by-packet, or a timing phenomenon known as *jitter*. You can compensate for both the longer level of delay and the jitter by padding the line with occasional *keep-alive packets* to keep the session active, rather than allowing it to time out. You spoof, or fool, the receiving device into thinking that the incoming transmission is over a realtime, carefully timed voice network. Delays up to 5 seconds can be tolerated in this manner.

T.38 provides for two transport protocols, *User Datagram Protocol* (*UDP*) and *Transmission Control Protocol* (*TCP*). UDP is the faster of the two, but the less reliable, due to lack of error detection and correction mechanisms at the network level. T.38 overcomes this shortcoming either through redundant transmission of the image data packets – inherently inefficient at the network level – or through a *Forward Error Correction* (*FEC*) technique – inherently inefficient at the device level. TCP includes an error correction mechanism employed at the router level, with the routers typically positioned only at the edges of the network. Switches typically are positioned in the core of the network. Although T.38 strips this process from consideration for the IP fax packets, the level of delay nonetheless is increased; thereby, spoofing techniques are required to maintain fax sessions.

The inherent efficiencies of fax transmission over packet-based IP networks can lead to lower network costs. Within the mass-used IP network, the cost of the packet transmission is negligible, and not distance-sensitive; this compares favorably with a relatively expensive fax call over the PSTN. IP-enabled fax devices essentially incur no usage-sensitive transmission costs other than those possibly imposed by an IP fax service provider; the costs of so enabling a device vary widely, but generally can be justified for fax-intensive environments. Devices that are not so enabled must make use of an IP gateway provided by a service provider – the costs to the end user of transmission in this environment vary widely, and do not necessarily compare favorably with the traditional approach. In either case, access to the packet network is on the basis of a local call, which does not carry a per-minute charge. Carriers supporting IP fax include a number of domestic U.S. Local Exchange Carriers (LECs) and IntereXchange Carriers (IXCs), Internet Service Providers (ISPs), and foreign telephone companies (PTTs), in addition to the emerging next generation providers of IP-based networks. A number of fax service bureaus also have announced support, as have manufacturers of fax machines, and fax servers and server components. IP fax-capable routers have the ability to transmit a fax over an IP network assuming that the level of delay is acceptable, and to default to the more conventional means of transmission over the PSTN when delays are unacceptable [4-14], [4-15], and [4-16]. Such routers also have the ability to secure the fax document during transmission via the IPSEC (IP Security) encryption mechanism, thereby providing a substantial level of security over the inherently insecure Internet and other IP networks.

The Future of Fax

Rather than being totally replaced by e-mail and other forms of messaging technology, facsimile appears to have a long and prosperous, although diminished, remaining life. Dependable, inexpensive, standardized, and virtually ubiquitous, fax promises to continue its role as a valuable communications tool. While e-mail offers a number of advantages over fax, it is not widely available in developing countries. Further, facsimile is an inexpensive and highly effective complement to other messaging systems. Traditional, standalone fax machines continue to grow in numbers even as e-mail replaces fax as the preferred method of communications for the technically privileged with access to the Internet. As a highly effective, lowest common denominator, traditional fax transmission will survive well into the future.

As costs continue to drop and as PCs equipped with fax boards and software become more common, fax will penetrate virtually every small business and household. Fax servers will become commonplace in medium and large businesses; according to IDC, 720,000 fax server ports shipped worldwide in 1998 [4-1]. The ability of fax servers to convert incoming fax messages into an e-mail format, and deliver them to an e-mail mailbox, adds significant value for the technically privileged.

IP Fax will grow at very significant levels over the next decade. IP-enabled CPE (Customer Premise Equipment) will become commonplace in medium- to large-sized organizations. Packet-based IP networking likely will become the transport method of choice, offering the same quality as conventional fax, but at significantly lower cost to the user organization.

Fax-On-Demand (FOD) will continue to challenge direct mail, and will become used extensively in fulfillment of information requests generated by various, more traditional, forms of advertising, as well as those generated by access to the World Wide Web. Mobile fax will become commonplace, as more laptop computers are equipped with fax modems in the form of *PCMCIA (Personal Computer Memory Card Industry Association)* cards, also known as PC cards. The trend toward *PDAs (Personal Digital Assistants)* may encourage mobile fax, as well [4-17] and [4-18].

Either standalone color fax machines, special fax compression techniques, or computer fax techniques can accomplish color fax. Color fax machines, which began to appear commercially in 1995, will increase in popularity as dependable and affordable multifunction devices are developed. Such devices will take the form of combined faxes/printers/scanners/copiers. The technology exists today through interfaces between computers and color copiers, but is relatively expensive and non-standard; as a result, its application is unusual.

Fax compression technology, through the use of special software, will become more common. InfoImaging Technologies (U.S.), for instance, has developed 3D Fax Software which will compress any file at 100:1. The proprietary software, which must reside on both transmitter and receiver at a cost of approximately U.S. $100-$200, can transmit up to 1 GByte (1GB) of data in 99 pages of dot patterns which are decompressed by the receiving system to yield the image in its original form. You can also send the faxed information (text, image, video, or multimedia files or computer programs) to a standard fax machine and then scan it into a computer where the software will act on it to restore the information to its native form. In this manner, you can send a color photograph via a standard black & white fax machine, scan it into the computer, and restore it to its original color form [4-19]. Fax compression is becoming increasingly important as the average Fortune 500 company spends an average of U.S. $14 million on fax-related network usage — 37% of the total long distance bill (Gallup/Pitney Bowes Fax Usage and Application Study, 1997). Due to differences in time zones, that figure rises to as much as 75% for many companies doing business in Asia [4-20].

Major international carriers (e.g., AT&T, MCI Worldcom, and Sprint) have developed various fax network offerings, all of which operate over high-quality digital circuits in the United States and to a select number of other countries with similarly developed infrastructures. Quality is improved and transmission time is reduced, small set-up charges and monthly minimum billings apply; special rates apply in recognition of short-duration calls – typical of much fax traffic. The major IntereXchange Carriers all have developed network-based FOD and fax store-and-forward offerings. A large number of independent fax service bureaus offer highly competitive fax services, both domestically and internationally [4-20].

Voice Processing Systems

Voice processing systems were developed and deployed on a closed trial (*alpha test*) basis in the early 1970s, as a replacement for answering machines. In the United States, the AT&T Bell Operating Companies (BOCs) trialed CO-based systems. However, the impending MFJ forestalled their commercial deployment, as voicemail was considered an *enhanced service*, which the RBOCs initially were prohibited from offering.

VMX (subsequently merged with Octel, and currently a division of Lucent) developed and marketed the first commercial system around 1978. That system was a standalone voicemail system with an interface to the PBX, from which the call was forwarded in the event of a busy or no-answer condition at the user station. Since that time, a number of manufacturers have entered the voice processing business, changing the nature of the systems considerably to include increased feature content, integrated messaging, PC platforms, application development toolkits, and networking.

The Technology

Voice processing systems are specialized computer systems consisting of ports, processors, an operating system, codecs, and storage. Although typically special-purpose, the computer platform may be a general-purpose computer with special application software. The operating system typically is UNIX, MS-DOS, or Windows NT, although it may be proprietary. Similarly, the processors may be Intel or another industry standard, or they may be incorporated into proprietary *ASICs* (*Application-Specific Integrated Circuits*) which are under the skin (i.e., contained within) of a multifunction box that tightly integrates the functions of a small PBX and voice processor. The codecs serve to convert incoming analog signals to digital format, compressing the data in the process in order to conserve system storage capacity. Disk drives or ASICs may contain application programs and provide for storage of data – including digitized voice greetings and incoming messages that store in individual mailboxes in the form of memory partitions. The amount of storage is sensitive to factors such as the number of mailboxes, the number of messages to be stored, the average message length, the nature of the analog-to-digital conversion process and compression algorithm, and the number of messages to be archived.

A customized voice greeting provides the calling party with menu options that are exercised through either DTMF selection or speech recognition. The latter option, unusual at this time, may become commonplace as the logic shifts to the host computer, rather than the current approach of using special-purpose DSP (Digital Signal Processor) interface boards. The speech input can be either analog or digital, depending on the nature of the connecting circuit. The voice processing system digitizes the signal, as required, and compresses the voice data, employing a proprietary code format and compression scheme.

You must have an interface between the voice processor and a KTS, PBX, ACD, or Central Office. In a PBX or Central Office application, you generally can access the voice processing system from the switch in the event of a busy or no-answer condition at the target station. Alternatively, the voice processing system can act as an *automated attendant*. The switch answers the call and forwards it to the voice processor, which enables the caller to access a department or station directly, through interaction with a menu of options. In the event that the caller does not know the desired station number, an automated directory provides that information on the basis of a name search conducted through the caller's tonepad commands. Once the station number is identified, the voice processor signals the switch, instructing it to connect the call. Interfaces into general-purpose computer systems also are becoming commonplace. In such an application, the system provides access to a database or perhaps an e-mail mailbox, with the data being converted from text to synthesized speech.

Networking of voice processing systems (Figure 4-3) is fairly routine in large user organizations, although generally limited to systems of the same origin (manufacturer) and generic software load. In a networked environment, multiple systems are connected via dedicated system ports. On a scheduled basis, the various systems will engage in a computer-to-computer dialogue, transferring messages to the systems on which reside the destination mailboxes. The nature of the network can vary widely, although digital networks are preferred because the information is in a data format. This non-realtime transfer of voice data can be accomplished very cost-effectively over packet data networks such as Frame Relay. *AMIS (Audio Messaging Interface Specification)* enables the internetworking of unlike systems, although few manufacturers support it.

Platforms for voice processing no longer are limited to proprietary hardware, except in cases of larger systems for intensive applications. Many smaller organizations and those with certain, specific applications currently make use of special software and voice cards (printed circuit boards) which reside on PC platforms in a client/server environment. A number of manufacturers offer client/server application software suites that include an automated attendant, voicemail, customized mailboxes, and audiotex. Such a CT approach is highly functional and very cost-effective, although concerns remain relative to reliability and database integrity. Additionally, the voice message requires substantial amounts of memory, even when highly compressed [4-21].

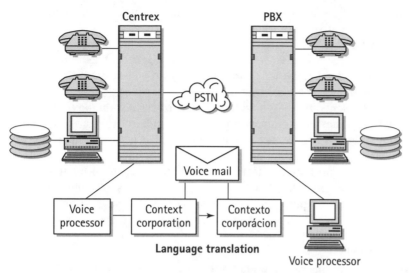

Figure 4-3 Networked voice-processing systems, with PBX, Centrex, and host interfaces

The Applications

The applications for voice processing have increased dramatically; with penetration having reached the point that it is virtually ubiquitous. You can categorize typical applications as voicemail, audiotex, call processing, and Interactive Voice Response (IVR) [4-22] and [4-23].

AUDIOTEX

Audiotex, a simple technology, enables callers to select prerecorded messages from a menu. Essentially a voice bulletin board, audiotex generally is incorporated into a more substantial suite of voice-processing applications such as call processing. The audiotex feature may enable callers to select options to gain information. For instance, for hours of operation (Press 1), to get directions to the company location (Press 2),to gain access to recent press releases (Press 3), or to determine the price of the stock at the close of the last trading day (Press 4).

VOICEMAIL

Voicemail, the most common application, involves the direction of the incoming call to a voice mailbox associated with a particular user or application. Voicemail stores the incoming message in the mailbox then advises the user – using one of several techniques (e.g., message-waiting lamp indication and stuttered dial tone) – of the fact that a message is waiting. When the user accesses the system and enters the proper command and password, the message is re-synthesized and played back, ultimately in analog audio form. Features may include personalized greeting, message broadcasting using a user-definable distribution list, message archiving, message forwarding, message annotation, automated call return, and access to a console attendant or alternative answering point.

In addition to what might be described as more legitimate applications, the future portends increased use of voice junk mail. Advertisers such as radio stations have built voicemail databases that enable them to broadcast advertisements to thousands of current and potential customers. While such use is aggravating to many voicemail recipients, they do have the option of calling the advertisers and requesting that they remove their names from such a database. The carriers are particularly unhappy about such use, because it not only places great demands on the involved voicemail systems and the network, but also threatens to yield en masse cancellations of highly profitable voicemail subscriptions. A more legitimate and common application is for school districts to notify parents of their children's absence from school, mail report cards, schedule sporting events and practice sessions, or announce school closings or delays due to inclement weather [4-24].

CALL PROCESSING

Call processing applications position the voice processing system as a front-end call processor to a PBX or ACD. The *automated attendant* feature of the system will answer the call and provide menu options that can be invoked through either DTMF input or voice recognition software. Features may include automated call routing, Automatic Number Identification (ANI), and Fax-On-Demand (FOD) access. Once the caller selects a menu option, the call can be directed to the appropriate agent, extension, or computer resource. Should the system be unable to connect the call immediately, the call either can be placed in queue or the caller can leave a call-back message in a general system mailbox, rather than simply abandoning the call.

American Airlines provides toll-free access to its reservations centers, with the ACD front-ended by a voice processor which prompts the caller through options including domestic vs. international reservations, and AAdvantage Frequent Flyer Program status. Based on the called number and DTMF input, this processor directs the caller to the appropriate agent group or to an automated database access system.

DATABASE ACCESS: INTERACTIVE VOICE RESPONSE (IVR)

In a *database access* application, the voice processing system is positioned as a front-end, although to general-purpose computers on which reside appropriate databases (Figure 4-3). As a means of imposing a level of security to the transaction, various means of caller authentication can be employed. For instance, you can require DTMF input of a PIN for access. Or you can use more unusual and expensive techniques such as *speech recognition* (recognition of voice commands) and *voice print matching* (verification of the caller's identification by matching the characteristics of the voice input to a stored sample) before the caller can access textual computer information. That information (e.g., bank or credit card account information) then either is played back from pre-recorded "sound bites" or is voice-synthesized for the benefit of the caller, yielding what is commonly known as *Interactive Voice Response* (*IVR*). Access to multiple databases often is provided across a LAN. Features may include voice recognition, voice print matching, and text-to-speech capability. Reservations centers and financial institutions make heavy use of such capabilities in support of routine transactions, thereby reducing staffing levels and providing enhanced customer service on a 24/7 basis. Telephone companies increasingly use voice recognition technology to provide automated access to local directory databases [4-25], [4-26], and [4-27].

Major banks, for instance, commonly provide automated access to account information without human intervention. Callers are prompted to enter their account numbers, followed by user-definable PINs (Personal Identification Number), social security numbers, or federal tax ID numbers. At that point, menu options include the account balance, last five checks posted, and last three deposits posted. Airline reservations centers make use of IVR for automated flight status information. The caller dials a special number set aside for that purpose, enters a series of commands (e.g., date and flight number) via tonepad signaling, and is provided the required information without the costly involvement of an agent.

Voice Processing Developments and Futures

The future of voice processing is very bright, indeed. While such systems initially were a North American phenomenon, they now are commonplace in Europe and are gaining greater acceptance in Asia and other regions. Specific technology futures include archival, multimedia/unified messaging, voice-to-text, voice-to-fax, and language translation.

Computer Telephony (*CT*) has impacted voice processing to a very considerable extent, with the application software residing on a LAN-attached server in the form of an industrial-strength Pentium PC running UNIX, DOS, or the Windows NT operating system. The server runs at high clock speed, has a high-speed internal bus, and includes substantial RAM and hard drive memory. CT systems may allow the front-end voice processor to actually process the call, connecting the caller to the target station without the involvement of the switch. Typical of the evolution of program logic, some manufacturers of smaller CT-based telephone systems have reduced much of the voice processing software to the chip level. Embedding the core voice processing functions in ASICs, this firmware approach enables much faster system operation than a software approach, although sacrificing some level of programmability at the user level. In order to overcome this limitation and to permit the user organization to customize the application, a combination of firmware and software is what drives system operation.

Archival technology has been developed to allow voice messages to be saved on an external archival system in the form of digitized audio files. This technology, still in its early stages, is not widely available. Currently, voice-processing systems generally enable the user to archive a message within the system, although internal memory limitations restrict the number and length of stored messages.

MultiMedia messaging, also known as *unified* or *integrated messaging*, enables multiple messages in multiple formats to be developed, coordinated, and networked.

A voice message can, thereby, be associated with a text or image document. For instance, a voice processor acting as a front-end might recognize a fax tone and store the fax along with the voice message; subsequently, the target user can listen to the voice message while viewing the fax document. The ability to store voice, textual (e-mail), image (fax), and even video messages in a single mailbox and to access them from a single point of interface has obvious advantages. Unfortunately, the underlying technologies required are complex and generally remain unaffordable at this time. Although CT systems provide the user with the ability to accomplish this feat relatively easily through coordinated access to multiple media from both a telephone set and a computer monitor, such systems currently are not widely implemented. Additionally, remote or mobile users do not have access to such system capabilities across a Wide Area Network. While text-to-speech and speech-to-text systems enable the remote worker to access a wide range of message formats from a single device (e.g., telephone set or laptop computer), the messages typically must be presented sequentially, rather than simultaneously. Advanced pager technology, while impressive, is even more limited. While the emerging IP-based Wide Area Networks promise to overcome some of these limitations at the network level, the underlying technologies and architectures at the system level currently are proprietary in nature [4-28].

Voice-to-text and *voice-to-fax* technologies have been developed which will convert voice messages to text or fax messages, and vice versa. While the technology remains fairly immature at this time, a number of commercially available products will convert text to speech for applications such as remote e-mail access from a telephone.

Speech Recognition software enables the caller to speak commands to the voice processing system, rather than entering commands via the telephone tonepad. Such systems are speaker-independent, although the speaker must speak clearly and the network connection must be relatively free of noise. While all but the most expensive systems currently are limited in vocabulary, such technology will become increasingly affordable and, therefore, prevalent in the foreseeable future. IBM, for instance, has developed speech recognition technology to the point that computer system vocabularies exceed 50,000 words [4-22] and [4-29].

Language Translation systems will accomplish language conversion, as well. The technology, which also is in the developmental stages, is planned for implementation by AT&T and other IXCs, replacing human translators currently providing such services.

Voice processing systems are destined to become even more commonplace – to the chagrin of many who bemoan the fact that they no longer can talk to a live human being. While users often hide behind voicemail in order to be more productive in the workplace, callers understandably get frustrated at their inability to reach them. Additionally, many systems are set up intentionally to defeat the caller's attempts to reach any live person – this phenomenon is known as *voicemail jail*.

Electronic Mail (E-Mail)

Once upon a time, we communicated by talking over the fence or the dinner table. Over longer distances we wrote letters, which were sent through the highly reliable, but very slow, U.S. postal system. The Pony Express, which arrived in April 1860, could deliver a letter from St. Louis, Missouri to Sacramento, California in 10 days or less. Eighteen months later, the completion of the transcontinental telegraph network doomed the Pony Express. The telegraph was used sparingly – telegrams were expensive and rarely bore good news. Shortly thereafter, the telephone arrived, replacing mail and telegraphy as the primary means of communications. Federal Express and other courier services have since become a routine means of sending written documents, to the point that we wonder how we ever got along with *snail mail*. Fax machines then became affordable and popular, enabling instantaneous transmission of documents. Then came *electronic mail (e-mail)*, an application software system originally intended for textual messaging. E-mail now permits the attachment of other forms of information, including binary files, images, graphics, and even digitized voice. Nonetheless, its primary use remains for textual messaging.

Source: Lou Harris Survey 505 Chief Information Officers, 1995

Figure 4-4 Electronic mail growth

According to a 1995 Lou Harris survey of 505 chief information officers and senior executives, 62% of corporate employees and 83% of government employees used e-mail (Figure 4-4). In 1995, BIS Strategic Decisions, Inc. estimated that the worldwide messaging market would grow from 45 million mailboxes in 1995 to 67 million in 1998 [4-30]. About the same time, it was estimated that over 100 million e-mail addresses existed and that well over 1 billion e-mail messages were sent monthly across the Internet, alone. Current estimates indicate that more than 100 million e-mail users send over 7 trillion messages per year, compared with about 1 billion letters sent by *snail mail* (postal service). Even these estimates likely fall short of the truth. For many of us, e-mail is the first thing we check at the start of the business day and the last tool we touch at day's end. It has, indeed, become a fundamental mode of communications for the electronically privileged.

E-mail provides the ability to distribute information to large numbers of people, virtually instantaneously and very inexpensively. For instance, a 50-page document can be transmitted coast-to-coast in approximately 30 seconds using a high-speed modem. The cost of such a transmission is in the range of pennies rather than tens of pennies for facsimile, or tens of dollars for overnight delivery via Federal Express or a similar courier service [4-31]. The dark side of e-mail, however, includes the fact that once you click the mouse, the message is sent and virtually irretrievable. Gone are the days when you dictated a sensitive letter and let it rest overnight in a desk drawer while emotions cooled so you could reread and edit it in the light of a brighter day. Getting darker, still, e-mail is an easy way for reckless or malicious employees to instantaneously expose company secrets, damage reputations, offend coworkers, spread computer viruses, and otherwise create a host of legal and technical problems [4-32].

The Technology

E-mail involves application software that resides on a computer platform of some description. E-mail was popularized as early as the 1970s, as part of the office automation concept designed to lead us toward the paperless office – about as successful as the personal helicopter. Typically residing on a midrange computer, early systems included IBM PROFS (PRofessional OFfice System), DEC DECmail (included in the All-in-One applications suite), and the Wang Office. The proliferation of PCs and PC LANs in the 1980s and 1990s stimulated the growth of e-mail, which then became affordable and, therefore, accessible by a much larger community of potential users.

The contemporary e-mail network often is in the form of a *client/server* configuration involving a dedicated *server* to which *client* workstations gain access for messaging purposes. Clients, or user *agents*, are the workstations that create, transmit, and receive the messages. They include software that effects compatibility with the server. Servers provide message store, transport, and directory services to the client. Various clients can be linked to a server through Application Programming Interfaces (APIs), messaging *middleware* (software which logically sits between client and server), and a driver package. Examples include Microsoft Messaging Application Programming Interface (MAPI) and Apple Computer, Inc.'s Open Collaboration Environment (AOCE). Such APIs permit client applications such as word processing and spreadsheets to communicate with an e-mail server. In other cases, special drivers must access servers running proprietary access protocols.

A server may be in the form of a mainframe (logically partitioned), mid-range, or PC computer platform. The server and the clients generally are LAN-attached. The server also may be provided on a service bureau basis, such as with specialized carriers and online services including America Online, AT&T EasyLink, Australia Online, CompuServe, MCI Mail, and Prodigy. Many client/server e-mail systems run equally effectively in several operating system environments, such as Windows, Macintosh, OS/2, and UNIX.

NETWORKING

Although some e-mail networks are closed, these messaging islands are increasingly rare. E-mail servers typically support multiple protocols, with internetworking between disparate e-mail systems adding great value to messaging technologies. Most provide for Wide Area Networking over a *backbone*, or centralized high-capacity network, in order to provide for both outbound and inbound message communications with the outside world. Remote access to the internal e-mail resources generally is provided to employees, vendors, clients, and others within the inner circle.

PROTOCOLS

Each e-mail network is governed by a set of *protocols* – the rules and conventions by which the network, and its various component elements, operates. Such protocols are embedded in the application software and the specific Operating System (OS) or Network Operating System (NOS) which governs how the computer or computer network functions. An element of the software that achieves compatibility between the client workstation and the server over the network generally resides on the client, as well as on the server (Figure 4-5). E-mail protocols govern such characteristics as addressing conventions, routing instructions, message structure, and message transfer. Protocol examples include ITU-T Recommendations X.400 and X.500, and various proprietary protocols [4-33].

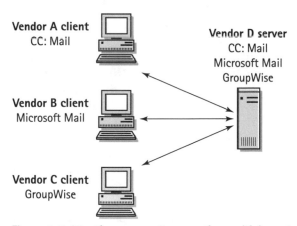

Vendor A client
CC: Mail

Vendor D server
CC: Mail
Microsoft Mail
GroupWise

Vendor B client
Microsoft Mail

Vendor C client
GroupWise

Figure 4-5 Client/server e-mail, supporting multiple protocols

X.400 *X.400* is an ITU-T international standard protocol for e-mail document exchange. X.400 is compatible with the International Organization for Standardization (ISO) Open Systems Interconnection (OSI) model, functioning at Layer 7, the Application Layer. As depicted in Figure 4-6, X.400 permits disparate e-mail systems to interoperate at a minimal level, over either X.25 packet networks or asynchronous dial-up circuits [4-34].

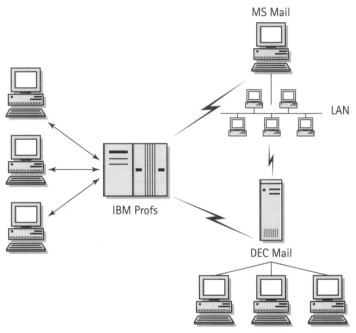

Figure 4-6 Networked e-mail (X.400)

X.500 AND LDAP *X.500* is an international standard developed jointly by the International Organization for Standardization (ISO) and the ITU-T. X.500 provides for global directory services that theoretically enable network managers to store information about all users, machines, and applications in a distributed fashion. The current version of X.500 provides for directory replication functions, which permit multiple copies of the directory information to be stored throughout the network, rather than reside on a centralized server. The current version also provides improved security through authentication access controls. Although X.500 has yet to be fully embraced by software developers, a number of proprietary e-mail products have incorporated X.500. A move currently is underway to place a X.500 directory on the Internet; functioning much like a telephone white pages, it would enable telephone and e-mail users to quickly find the addresses of other users, with certain security-oriented limitations [4-35] through [4-39]. While X.500 is a very robust global directory standard, it requires significant computational resources to implement, and often receives criticism for being over-engineered.

Lightweight Directory Access Protocol (*LDAP*), was developed to simplify the demands of the X.500 DAP. Developed at the University of Michigan and described in the IETF's RFC 1777, LDAP is a lean subset of X.500 that can run over TCP/IP networks. LDAP can run as a standalone directory system, or can be used as a means of accessing a X.500 directory.

PROPRIETARY PROTOCOLS Proprietary protocols include cc:Mail (Lotus Development Corp.), Lotus Notes (Lotus Development Corp.), Microsoft Mail (Microsoft Corp.), StreetTalk (Banyan Systems Inc.), BeyondMail (Banyan Systems, Inc.), and GroupWise (Novell Inc.). At the end of 1994, more than 12 million users of the two most popular desktop e-mail systems, cc:Mail and Microsoft Mail, an increase of 7 million over the previous year [4-40].

Through *gateway* technology, such as is in place on the Internet, unlike mail systems can interoperate. Gateway software acts as a protocol translator, or interpreter, converting from one native environment to another [4-41]. In this manner, cc:Mail and Microsoft Mail software, for instance, can pass messages. For instance, several editors, the publisher, and I were able to accomplish much of the editing process for this book via e-mail. From my home office, using a desktop computer running Eudora e-mail software, and with Internet access through a local ISP (Internet Service Provider), I sent electronic drafts as e-mail attachments. The editing process continued on the road via a laptop running AOL software through hotel PBXs. The recipients of this mail were able to respond with edits until the document was deemed satisfactory. Incompatibility wasn't even an issue, although my command of the English language (or lack thereof) was a constant concern.

Features

E-mail systems offer a growing number of features that commonly include time and date stamping, and the ability to read, write, reply, and archive messages. Archived messages can be sorted by criteria such as status, priority, sender, date, size, and subject. A variety of file types (e.g., text, binary, audio, video, and image) and file formats can be attached or appended. Features also can include encryption for additional security, receipt confirmation, automated response, and automated forwarding. The ability to build customized distribution lists enables a user to send a single message to large numbers of user mailboxes with the click of a mouse.

The Applications

While e-mail traditionally has been text-oriented, it is now often appended with binary, audio, video, and image files. The process of doing so, however, remains somewhat cumbersome and is system-specific. Further, the compression algorithms associated with attached files require that both the sender and the receiver have matching software for compression and decompression. While much of that software is available at no charge, it is non-standard and can be cumbersome (read aggravating) to use. Nonetheless, e-mail has become essential for the conduct of business. Indeed, it is virtually universal, having found its way into personal use through online information services, connected via the Internet and mail *gateways*, which serve as protocol converters [4-42].

The Future: Unified Messaging

Especially since the commercialization of The Internet, e-mail has become an indispensable tool in our professional and even in our personal lives. My daughter can attest to this fact — she regularly sends e-mail requests for money from her apartment at Texas Tech University, where she should be (but is not) majoring in fundraising. Future enhancements to, and issues surrounding, e-mail include unified messaging, remote access, and connectivity.

Unified messaging (Figure 4-7) extends across e-mail, voicemail, and fax technologies. E-mail messaging increasingly includes binary computer files, graphics files, image files, video files, and even voice and audio files. While such attachments can be very bandwidth-intensive, they clearly enhance the effectiveness of the communication. As an admitted abuser of the Internet, I must confess to regularly sending multi-MB PowerPoint graphic files as e-mail attachments. While the ideal unified messaging system (i.e., providing a single mailbox for fax mail, e-mail, and voicemail) does not exist, the technology exists; the costs are just too high. Currently more realistic is integrated messaging, which provides a single user interface in the form of a computer keyboard or telephone tonepad for accessing the various mailboxes simultaneously in order to access multiple media on a coordinated basis [4-23], [4-43], and [4-44].

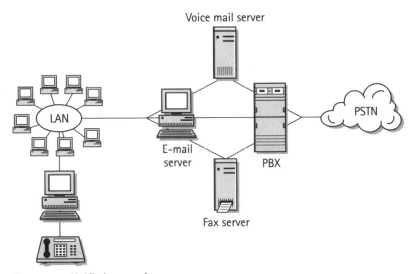

Figure 4–7 Unified messaging

SIMPLE MAIL TRANSFER PROTOCOL (SMTP)

Connectivity likely will remain an issue for some time. A minimum set of agreements must be reached within the e-mail development community. Issues include commonality of header fields, end-to-end messaging services (e.g., priority transfer, confirmation notification, and security), addressing schemes, and management standards. For example, most systems use *SMTP* (*Simple Mail Transfer Protocol*), defined by the IETF in RFC 821 to pass e-mail to and through the Internet. Yet each SMTP gateway may deal with addressing schemes in a different way, causing conflicts during the process of message routing. Additionally, each e-mail system places different limitations on the size of file attachments, and neither delivery confirmation nor user authentication are supported between such systems through SMTP. Further, binary files typically get converted to text and then converted back to binary files on the receiving end, resulting in a complete loss of formatting.

Notably, SMTP was developed to support the 7-bit ASCII (American Standard Code for Information Interchange) code for simple text. This coding works just fine for relatively simple alphabets (e.g., 26-character English), supporting uppercase and lowercase characters. ASCII also supports numbers 0-9, punctuation marks, and a reasonable set of control characters (e.g., paragraph break and page break). ASCII, however, does not support the rich text formatting (e.g., *italics*, **bold**, and color, other than the default black in which this document is printed) supported by most contemporary word processing programs. This 7-bit format also prevents the transmission of 8-bit binary data found in executable files.

MULTIPURPOSE INTERNET MAIL EXTENSION (MIME) *Multipurpose Internet Mail Extension* (*MIME*) was developed to overcome SMTP's ASCII-based limitation. MIME standards, as defined in the IETF's RFC 2045, include a number of *types* and *subtypes* that support a range of data formats. Those types include the following:

- *Text type* for textual messages. Subtypes include *plain text* for 7-bit ASCII, and *rich text* for enhanced text formatting.

- *Image type* for image files. Subtypes include *GIF* (*Graphics Interchange Format*) and *JPEG* (*Joint Photographic Experts Group*).

- *Video type* for time-varying picture images. The *MPEG* (*Moving Pictures Experts Group*) subtype is defined.

- *Audio type* for basic audio data at 8 KHz.

- *Application type* for executable code and any data that doesn't fit neatly into any of the other types. Subtypes include *octet-stream* for binary data and *postscript* for PostScript files.

- *Message type* for encapsulated messages within e-mail. *Partial* subtype permits a long e-mail message to be fragmented at the transmitter and re-assembled at the receiver.

◆ *Multipart type* supports the combination of multiple types into a single e-mail message [4-45].

SPAM AND FREEDOM OF SPEECH

Junk mail plagues the e-mail community, just as it does the worlds of facsimile, voicemail, and snail mail. Advertisements, once considered a breach of e-mail etiquette, have become a fact of life on the Internet. Those of us who subscribe to technology magazines almost always are requested or even required to include our e-mail addresses so vendors can deluge us with junk mail. Perhaps the master of bulk e-mail advertising is Cyber Promotions (previously Promo Enterprises), which regularly sends unsolicited electronic ads to millions of e-mailboxes; the company reportedly expects to earn $1 million in 1999, up from $30,000 in 1997. Junk e-mail has justifiably earned the nickname *spam*, reportedly named after Hormel's ever-popular (?) canned meat product made of leftovers from the processing of pork, plus lots of additives. The analogy supposedly is that junk e-mail is broadcast all over, just as the Hormel meat product spatters when hurled against a solid object with sufficient force. The U.S. federal government and a number of states have attempted to either limit or eliminate spam, but always run up against arguments of the Constitution's guaranteed freedom of speech. Most recently (February 1999), the State of Virginia has taken steps to become the first state to outlaw spam, although the ACLU (American Civil Liberties Union) is challenging the proposed law.

References

[4-1]   Kauffman, Maury. "Fax Stats to the Max." *Computer Telephony,* December 1998.

[4-2]   Green, James Harry. *The Irwin Handbook of Telecommunications, 2ⁿᵈ edition.* Irwin Professional Publishing, 1992.

[4-3]   Glossbrenner, Alfred and Emily. *The Complete Modem Handbook.* MIS:Press, 1995.

[4-4]   Grigonis, Richard. "Beyond Fax and Beyond." *Computer Telephony,* August 1995.

[4-5]   "How Network Fax Systems Work." *Datapro Communications Analyst.* Datapro Information Services Group, November 1995.

[4-6]   Coleman, Ken and Meley, Mimi. "Implementing Network Facsimile Successfully." *Datapro Communications Analyst.* Datapro Information Services Group, February 1995.

[4-7]   Sullivan, Kristina B. "Faxing Still Alive and Well." *PC Week*, March 16, 1998.

[4-8]   "Network Fax: Solving The Productivity Puzzle." *CTI*, June 1998.

[4-9]   Warren, Stuart. "Fax Card Roundup." *Computer Telephony*, August 1995.

[4-10]   Lazar, Jerry. "The Truth About Fax." *Information Week*, February 19, 1996.

[4-11]   Bort, Julie. "Serve It Up with Fax On Demand." *InfoWorld*, November 7, 1994.

[4-12]   Cohen, Jodi. "New Standards Help Bridge Gap Between Fax, Messaging Worlds." *Network World*, November 14, 1994.

[4-13]   "Evolution of the Fax." *Information Week*, April 3, 1995.

[4-14]   Adelson, Josh. "Beyond Cost Savings: IP Fax Benefits Today." *CTI*, October 1998.

[4-15]   Arnum, Eric. "Fax Via The 'Net'." *Business Communications Review*, October 1998.

[4-16]   "Fax Over IP – Opportunities and Options." Natural Microsystems. http//:www.naturalmicrosystems.com.

[4-17]   Hedtke, John. "Keep in Touch With Mobile Faxing." *Mobile Office*, April 1995.

[4-18]   Resnick, Rosalind. "Faxing From the Fast Lane." *Mobile Office*, June 1995.

[4-19]   Abate, Tom. "Fit to Fax." *San Francisco Examiner*, May 19, 1995.

[4-20]   Brennan, Tom. "Beware the Fax Beast." *Network World*, November 27, 1995.

[4-21]   Kalman, Steve. "Beyond Voice Mail." *Network World*, August 7, 1995.

[4-22]   Wolf, Robert. "A Primer to Using Voice Technologies." *TeleProfessional*, March 1996.

[4-23]   Radisich, Barbara Noble and Outlaw, Joe. "Voice Processing Systems: Overview." *Datapro Communications Analyst*. Datapro Information Services Group, July 1995.

[4-24]   Flash, Cynthia. "Press One for Voice Junk Mail." *San Francisco Examiner*, November 19, 1995.

[4-25]   Kinsey, Graeme. "How Interactive Voice Response (IVR) Systems Can Boost Business Efficiency." *Telecommunications,* April 1995.

[4-26]   Lenz, Mary. "IVR's Role in The Help Desk." *Call Center Magazine*, February 1995.

[4-27]   Grigonis, Richard. "IVR – Complicated but Beautiful." *Computer Telephony*, June 1995.

[4-28]   Kopf, David. "The Reincarnation of Unified Messaging." *America's Network*, November 15, 1998.

[4-29]   Foster, Peter and Schalk, Thomas B. *Speech Recognition*. Telecom Library, Inc., 1993.

[4-30]   Stahl, Stephanie. "Pumping Up Corporate E-Mail." *Information Week*, June 12, 1995.

[4-31]   Eager, Bill. "Online and the Bottom Line: E-Mail Is Money." *Data Communications*, March 21, 1996.

[4-32]   McCune, Jenny C. "This Message is For You." *Beyond Computing*, June 1996.

[4-33]   Meier, Edwin E. and Meier, David C. "How to Avoid a Postal Career? Make Sure Your E-Mail Works Well With Your Network." *Communications Week*, January 23, 1995.

[4-34]   Myer, Ted. "Straight Talk about E-mail Connectivity." *Business Communications Review*, July 1995.

[4-35]   Schwartz, Jeffrey. "Is X.500 In Your Future?" *Communications Week*, June 17, 1996.

[4-36]   Burkert, Debbie. "International X.500 Standard Makes Global Directory Searches Possible." *Network World*, May 1, 1995.

[4-37]   Gillooly, Caryn. "Finding the Way." *Information Week*, January 1, 1996.

[4-38]   Davis, Jessica. "X.500 Key to Internet Publishing, Commerce." *InfoWorld*. November 27, 1995.

[4-39]   Johnson, Johna Till. "An X.500 Method to Directory Madness." *Data Communications*, May 21, 1995.

[4-40]   McNamee, Giles W. "The Message Is the Medium." *Internetwork*, October 1995.

[4-41]   Delmonico, Dayna and Rist, Oliver. "It's Not Your Father's E-Mail Anymore." *Communications Week*, June 17, 1996.

[4-42]   Baker, Richard H. *Networking the Enterprise*. McGraw-Hill, Inc., 1994.

[4-43]   Minifie, Tom. "Unified Messaging Is A Key Productivity Aid In The Information Age." *Telemarketing & Call Center Solutions*, May 1996.

[4-44]   Snyder, Joel. "Roadblocks to E-mail Convergence." *Network World*, November/December 1995.

[4-45]   Chae, Lee. "Tutorial. Lesson 110: E-Mail and MIME." *Network Magazine*, October 1997.

Chapter 5

Public Switched Telephone Network (PSTN)

Of the many wonderful scientific discoveries and inventions which have made the nineteenth century remarkable, certainly none is of more popular interest than the simple little piece of apparatus known as Bell's articulating telephone. By this instrument it becomes possible to transmit ideas between far-distant places, not in the form of signs afterwards to be deciphered, but as actual articulations, an echo of those produced by the human voice at the point of transmission. Source: *Wonders of the Universe*, 1899.

The old networks were designed around voice traffic, or *Plain Old Telephone Service (POTS)*. Telegraphy was conducted over a separate, pre-existing network. Since data, image, and video systems didn't exist until many years later, there certainly was no requirement to network them. The characteristics of voice traffic were, and still remain, well known and easily understood. Specifically, voice calls are occasional, short, bidirectional, continuous, stream-oriented, and analog in their native form.

Voice calls typically are occasional, because talking on the telephone is not the focus of most people's personal and professional lives. Clearly there are exceptions, such as agents who work in call center environments, as explored in the discussion of ACDs in Chapter 3. Human-to-human voice calls also tend to be short in duration – three minutes or so, on average. While business calls tend to be short and to the point, purely personal calls, more social in nature, tend to last longer. Additionally, some people (e.g., me) tend to express themselves in very concise terms, while others (e.g., my mother) tend to be very wordy. (I beg you to hold this comment in confidence.) Voice processing generally abbreviates voice communications, as we noted in Chapter 4.

Clearly, voice calls are conversational, or bidirectional, in nature. Further, the usage of the circuit is fairly constant, or potentially so. Regardless of the direction of the conversation (talking vs. listening) and the number and length of pauses in the conversation, the network is required to support the communication when active. Voice communications is characterized as *isochronous*, or stream-oriented. In other words, all elements in the network must be available to accept, switch, transport, and deliver the active communication – this effectively means 100% of the time. Further, each element of the voice communication must be delivered to the receiver in exactly the sequence in which it was presented to the transmitter, and with no significant level of either *latency* (i.e., delay), or *jitter* (i.e., variation in delay). Finally, the native information signal is analog, rather than digital, in nature.

145

Analog transmission over copper twisted pair was quite suitable, and remains so. However, the inherent advantages of other media, as we discussed in Chapter 2, often make them preferable in contemporary applications. Circuit switching also was quite suitable and still is. Manual switchboards eventually gave way to SxS (Step-by-Step), XBar (CrossBar) and, ultimately, ECC (Electronic Common Control) switches. Local switches were interconnected with other local switches through intermediate network switches for longer distance connections. Contemporary networks, of course, are much more sophisticated, supporting huge volumes of voice, as well as data and even some level of video and image transmission. Analog has given way to digital, copper has yielded to fiber, wires have given way to wireless communications in many applications, and so on.

A number of developing next-generation public networks are based on packet-switching concepts and protocols developed for data communications, promising both lower costs and increased functionality. We will explore *Voice over IP* (*VoIP*) later in this chapter. *Voice over Frame Relay* (*VoFR*), discussed in Chapter 10, also is possible, although issues of quality can be significant. While both VoIP and VoFR make use of highly sophisticated compression techniques to deal with quality issues, reliable *toll quality* voice (i.e., the traditional level of quality we have come to expect) is difficult to achieve in such networks.

As more people became comfortable with the new telephone technology, more people subscribed to the service, which made the technology more useful. Businesses came to depend on telephony, and usage increased further. When costs began to drop, the technology became generally affordable and usage increased even further. Long distance usage – highly profitable to the carriers – increased, especially as rates reduced.

Thousands of independent, privately-owned telephone companies sprang up in the United States. Around the turn of the 20th century, the Bell System had approximately 800,000 telephones in service, compared to about 600,000 for the independents [5-1]. In many cities and towns, multiple telephone companies operated in direct competition under franchises granted by the local government. In sparsely populated rural areas and isolated towns and cities (e.g., in Alaska), which were not commercially viable, telephone cooperatives and municipally-owned telcos formed, a number of which still exist. Approximately 1,500 U.S. independents (non-Bell companies) still exist [5-2]. Notably, the telephone was not accepted elsewhere quite so quickly. Reportedly, a group of British experts stated that the telephone "may be appropriate for our American cousins, but not here, because we have an adequate supply of messenger boys."

Initially, these networks were isolated islands of local service; in other words, they were not interconnected. The telephone companies soon interconnected with each other and with the long distance network, usually under government and regulatory pressure. In the United States, the Bell System avoided providing interconnection, preferring to aggressively acquire the independent telcos and even acquiring a large block of stock in Western Union – its chief competitor at the time.

Increasingly pressured by the federal government under antitrust laws, Nathan C. Kingsbury, an AT&T vice-president, wrote a letter to the U.S. Attorney General in December, 1913 to resolve various issues. Known as the *Kingsbury Commitment*, that letter committed AT&T to dispose of its holdings in Western Union, to purchase no more independent telephone companies without the approval of the Interstate Commerce Commission (ICC), and to make interconnection with the independent telephone companies. Eventually, national standards were established to govern the nature and rules of interconnection; the ITU-T governs standards recommendations at the international level.

Many nations acquired, or even confiscated, the telephone networks from the private owners, forming Post, Telegraph, and Telephone (PTT) agencies. The British government on January 12, 1912 assumed full control and ownership of the national telephone system, leaving the United States as the only major nation in which the network was privately owned. Eventually, people viewed access to telephone service as a basic human right in many industrialized nations. In 1935, an Act of Congress defined the concept of *universal service* and created the Federal Communications Commission, which was chartered with accomplishing this goal. The goal (admittedly paraphrased, and based on my best recollection from my days at Southwestern Bell) of the Bell System, for instance, became "universal service of the highest possible quality at the lowest possible cost." In order to ensure that high-quality basic service was available universally, a complex set of cross-subsidies formed to fund the deployment of the network in high-cost areas, with particular emphasis on single-line residential service.

Governments have discovered that they cannot easily fund the capital-intensive upgrades their networks require and they cannot effectively serve the communications needs of their constituents at reasonable cost. They also have come to recognize that the networks are immensely valuable assets, which the governments can sell in order to fund various social programs. Therefore, the networks have been opened to competition in many nations. The networks also rapidly are being *privatized*, either partially, with the government continuing to hold controlling interest for some period of time, or completely. As a result, service has become more universally available around the world, the quality of service has improved, the range of services has increased, and the overall cost to the user has dropped considerably.

Network Characteristics

Each type of network can be described in terms of a number of key characteristics that define its basic nature and application. The Public Switched Telephone Network (PSTN) can be characterized as a network designed for voice communications, primarily on a circuit-switched basis, with full interconnection among individual networks. The network is largely analog at the local loop level, digital at the backbone level, and generally provisioned on a wireline, rather than a wireless, basis.

Voice (Primarily)

The original network was designed to carry voice communications, only. At the time, the only other form of telecommunications was telegraphy – the province of Western Union. The contemporary PSTN still exists primarily to support voice communications. While much data traffic continues to transverse the network, intensive data traffic largely travels special purpose data networks. Image information also can be transported, as another form of data; facsimile is an excellent example of image traffic over the PSTN. Additionally, special videoconferencing equipment and interfaces of various types support video traffic.

Note that much Internet traffic travels over the PSTN, at least through the LEC networks. For example, I access an ISP (Internet Service Provider) over the PSTN through a modem embedded in a desktop or laptop computer. Over an analog local loop, the modem dials the telephone number of the ISP, and the connection is provided through a circuit-switched Central Office. The ISP's local loop is in the form of a channelized T-1 circuit. Should you need a connection to the Internet, it is supported from the ISP to the Internet backbone over an unchannelized T-3 leased from the LEC. This traditional method of Internet access likely will change in the near future, with the advent of new technologies such as *Digital Subscriber Line* (*DSL*). I discuss in detail this Internet access scenario, and the underlying technologies, in later chapters.

Switched (and Dedicated)

Contemporary voice networks are largely circuit switched, thereby providing great flexibility to the end users and significant economies to the carriers. Large user organizations, which communicate intensively between well-defined physical locations (e.g., headquarters, region, and field locations), often employ dedicated circuits in order to mitigate network costs. Such dedicated circuits generally are leased from the carrier(s), making use of existing PSTN transmission facilities. In relatively rare instances, user organizations will deploy their own facilities, often in the form of private microwave. In very rare instances, large end user organizations will purchase from the carrier a set of fiber optic facilities that can be used to connect the user's locations on a dedicated basis. Such optical fibers would be contained within a larger set of facilities deployed for the carrier's own use and sold to the user on an as-available basis.

Analog (and Digital)

The traditional voice network originally was analog in nature. The local loop connection terminating at the residence or small business premise generally is still analog, although ISDN – digital from end-to-end – finally has achieved some level of popularity. Large user organizations often have digital access circuits in the form of T-carrier.

Backbone circuits in the internal telephone-company networks and internetworks largely have converted to digital for reasons that include increased bandwidth, improved bandwidth utilization, superior error performance, and enhanced network management capabilities. This conversion process largely is complete in most major industrialized nations and regions, including Australia, Hong Kong, Japan, New Zealand, North America, Singapore, and Western Europe. Developing nations and regions (e.g., The Philippines, Thailand, and Eastern/Central Europe) either are converting the PSTN to digital, or abandoning obsolete analog facilities in favor of constructing new digital networks.

Interconnected!

Complete interconnection among all local and long distance, and national and regional networks is fundamental to the PSTN. As discussed earlier, islands of telephony were interconnected many years ago in order that any subscriber might have the ability to connect to any other, subject to availability of transmission and switching capacity, and issues of national or regional security. In other words, any-to-any connectivity is fundamental.

Wired (and Wireless)

While the traditional networks largely are wired (i.e., twisted pair and optical fiber), much wireless technology also is employed. Wired networks generally perform better in terms of bandwidth, error rate, security, and other dimensions, as discussed in Chapter 2. Fiber optic transmission systems are particularly notable in these respects. Note that wired networks, and especially those employing optical fiber, are very much under the control of the owner, because they are not so susceptible to environmental interference (e.g., precipitation, sunspots, and static electricity). Further, each wire or fiber is a self-contained world of bandwidth, whereas wireless systems are limited by frequency allocation. While wired networks often are more difficult and costly to deploy and reconfigure, they are advantageous in the long term.

A limited radio spectrum, electromagnetic interference, lack of security, and an assortment of other limitations all plague wireless networks. Therefore, they generally are avoided in the architecture of the PSTNs of developed nations. Microwave, however, is used extensively in many networks, either as a primary means of connection where wired networks are impractical, or as backup in the event of network overload or failure. Satellite communications also is used extensively for certain international communications and in order to provide access to island nations and remote areas. Wireless Local Loop (WLL) technology has gained in popularity in recent years as an effective alternative means of accessing the IXC and even the LEC networks. WLL is an excellent example of a *facilities bypass* technology, that enables the user organization to access the network on a wireless basis, bypassing the facilities of the Incumbent Local Exchange Carrier (ILEC) in the process. WLL often compares quite favorably with ILEC access circuits in terms of both speed of deployment and cost. However, issues of security and interference remain.

Developing nations make extensive use of satellite and microwave systems, and currently deploy WLL aggressively. The advantages of wireless communications, as we noted in Chapter 2, include both the rapidity and low cost of deployment, particularly in difficult terrain (e.g., mountainous) or where nearby islands must be interconnected. The nation of India, for instance, makes extensive use of satellite communications to link thousands of remote villages. Similarly, remote towns in the outback of Australia are linked to the PSTN via satellite. Microwave extensively links cities in island nations such as The Philippines and Malaysia, where WLL also has found considerable application.

Numbering Plan Administration (NPA)

In order for any telephone to connect to any other telephone in the world, you need a carefully developed and administered numbering plan, or *logical addressing* scheme. The ITU-T is responsible for numbering plan administration at the international level, with each nation or region having similar responsibility within its domain. Coincident with the breakup of the Bell System, Bellcore (Bell Communications Research, now Telcordia Technologies) in 1983 assumed responsibility for the *North American Numbering Plan* (*NANP*) — established in 1947 by AT&T and Bell Telephone Laboratories as a means of integrating the *area code* and Central Office exchange codes in the area loosely known as North America. This area, officially known as World Zone 1, excludes Mexico, and includes the Continental United States, Hawaii, Puerto Rico, the Virgin Islands, and parts of the Caribbean. Within each state in the United States, the dominant LEC (read the Bell Operating Company) administered the NANP under the direction of the FCC [5-3]. In Canada, the Ministry of Communications controls the numbering plan; in the Caribbean, the various governments delegate administration. In 1995, the *North American Numbering Council* (*NANC*) was chartered as an impartial body to assume oversight responsibility for the NANP. In January 1998, NANP direct administration was removed from Bellcore and placed in the hands of Lockheed-Martin, thereby enhancing the administrative function with a presumed level of impartiality. Bellcore (now Telcordia Technologies, Inc., a SAIC company) retained a seat on the NANC, and now provides NANP consulting services. The U.S. number format comprises fixed-length, 10-digit national numbers, which fit into the international NPA dialing scheme.

The current international NPA convention specifies a maximum of 15 digits, although the number of digits required for calling within a nation varies. In many cases, numbering schemes vary within the same country; for instance 6- and 7-digit telephone numbers co-exist in Australia during the period of transition to full 7-digit convention.

When dialing a telephone number, the user effectively instructs the network to establish a connection between two physical addresses based on a logical address, which is a series of numbers following a specific pattern. Using an example I am familiar with, the following logical addressing convention functions in establishing a connection originating from a physical address in Australia and terminating at another associated with The Context Corporation at 1500A East College Way, PMB 443, Mount Vernon, Washington 98273, USA:

◆ *0015*: *00* indicates that the call is international; *15* is the *country code* for the United States.

◆ *1+* (usually) indicates that the call is crossing a *Numbering Plan Area* (*NPA*), or *area code*, boundary.

◆ *360* indicates the NPA (Numbering Plan Area), or area code, which is a physical area. Specifically, 360 is the area of western Washington surrounding the Greater Seattle metropolitan area and which happens to be in LATA 674.

◆ *336* indicates a specific Mount Vernon Central Office exchange. These three digits are associated with an exchange that resides in a wire center, which may house several such exchanges.

◆ *3448* indicates the port and circuit ID, which is associated with a local loop, which, in turn, is associated with terminal equipment at the physical address of The Context Corporation.

Through such a series of dialing steps, the logical address of The Context Corporation is translated, in steps and across carrier domains, by the several networks in order to route the call to the target telephone system. Changes in the dialing scheme require changes in switch logic (i.e., PBXs, COs, and Tandems) in order that the switches can recognize the legitimacy of the dialing pattern. The Context Corporation also has an 800 number, that the network translates into 360.336.3448 in order to route domestic calls on a toll-free basis.

Demand for telephone numbers has increased over the past few years as a result of the popularity of cellular telephony, fax machines, pagers, and modems for computer access to the Internet — all of which require telephone numbers. As a result, the numbering plan has come under extreme pressure in the United States and internationally; hence, the expansion of the international dialing convention, and the addition of 640 new area codes approved by the FCC in 1995 for use in the United States. The FCC expects another 88 existing area codes to be exhausted by 2010, or so [5-4], [5-5], [5-6], [5-7], [5-8], [5-9], and [5-10]. The changes in the NPA have impacted the network to a considerable extent, as all network switches must be reprogrammed to recognize and honor dialing instructions under the new conventions.

In order to understand the implications of NPA changes, you must understand the difference between the old and new conventions. Traditionally, the U.S. area code was a three-digit, *NNX number*. In other words, the first and second digits were limited to specific numbers (N), while the third digit consisted of any number (X).

Specifically, the first digit could be any number other than 1 or 0. The use of a 1 or 0 confuses the network, which interprets it as an instruction to provide access to an operator, connect a call across an area code boundary, or connect an international call. The second digit must be a 1 or 0, and the third digit can be any number. As the existing area codes were exhausted, the FCC opened the second position; therefore, NNX became NXX. Consequently, The Context Corporation found itself removed from the Seattle 206 area code and established in the new 360 area code on the basis of a geographic split. In order for callers to reach the company, all involved switching devices had to be reprogrammed to recognize the validity of the new area code and, thereby, process the call, rather than reject it. End users were required to make software changes in their PBX systems, and the carriers had to make software changes to all network switches. Not only were such software enhancements expensive, but some older switches could not be upgraded, thereby either denying access to the new number or requiring additional system replacements or peripheral equipment to effect compatibility.

Notably, both area codes and Central Office prefixes are geographically specific, with the exceptions of 500, 700, 900, and toll-free (i.e., 800, 888, and 877) services. When an existing area code is exhausted and a new one is required, there are two choices. The traditional choice includes a geographical split of an existing area code (e.g., 206 and 360), but this causes considerable disruption. The contemporary choice involves an overlay area code, which requires that the caller always dial a 10-digit telephone number, even to place a local call. Neither solution is particularly attractive. Central Office prefixes (i.e., NXXs) are not only geographically specific, but also typically are parceled out as a single entity, rather than being shared among service providers (i.e., ILECs and CLECs). Therefore, each LEC in need of a NXX gets a block of 10,000 telephone numbers, whether it needs it or not. The end result of this wasteful approach to numbering likely will bring about the expansion of the numbering scheme. In other words and probably soon, we will have to dial 10, 12, or 15 digits to place a local call. Welcome to the Information Age, my friend!

Domains

Let us consider the concept of *domains*, or spheres of influence, as perhaps the most effective, fundamentalmeans of examining the network. Specifically, we can examine the traditional voice network in terms of functional, regulatory, and carrier domains.

Functional Domains

Functional domains address the various functions performed in the PSTN. Customer premises equipment, switches, and transmission facilities all are physical elements of the PSTN, each performing specific functions, and all supported by a signaling and control system. At a higher level, you can view the PSTN in terms of providing the functions of network access, transport, switching, and service delivery.

CUSTOMER PREMISES EQUIPMENT (CPE)

CPE is the term used for transmit and receive equipment in the voice world. Generally, the user owns CPE, rather than renting it from the telephone company, as was the case in the United States until the late 1960s. CPE includes voice terminals (telephone sets), key equipment, PBXs, and ACDs.

INSIDE WIRE AND CABLE

Inside wire and cable includes all wires and cables inside the customer premise. In the voice world, such wires and cables connect the terminal equipment to the common equipment, such as a PBX or a Key Service Unit (KSU). Inside wire and cable extends to the *demarcation point* (*demarc*) — the point of delineation between the customer premise and the carrier network. Generally in physical form, the demarc is the point at which the carrier's responsibility ends and the end user's begins. Such responsibilities include installation, upgrade, maintenance, and security.

SWITCHES

Switches, as we established in Chapter 1, are the devices that establish connectivity between circuits through an internal switching matrix. In a traditional PSTN environment, such switches are circuit switches, which include Central Office Exchanges, tandem exchanges, access tandem exchanges, and International Gateway Facilities. On demand and as available, circuit switches set up such connections between circuits through the establishment of a *talk path*, or *transmission path*. The connection and the associated bandwidth are provided temporarily, continuously, and exclusively for the duration of the *session*, or call.

CENTRAL OFFICES (COs)

The Local Exchange Carriers (LECs) own Central Offices (COs), also known as *exchanges*. COs provide local access services to end users via local loop connections and within a relatively small area of geography known as an exchange area, or *Carrier Serving Area* (*CSA*). In other words, the CO provides the ability for a subscriber within that neighborhood to connect to another subscriber within that neighborhood. COs also provide a number of services, such as custom calling features (e.g., call waiting, call transfer, and three-way calling) and Centrex. Also through the CO a subscriber typically gains access to the LEC metropolitan calling area, which does not involve a long distance (toll) charge. Finally, most subscribers also gain access to the various long distance networks through the CO.

COs, also known as *end offices*, reside at the terminal ends of the network; in other words, they are the first point of entry into the PSTN and the last point of exit. They also are known as *Class 5 offices*, the lowest class in the switching hierarchy. Manufacturers of COs include Lucent (5ESS), which previously was AT&T; Nortel (DMS), which previously was Northern Telecom; Siemens (EWSD); and Ericsson (AXE).

TANDEM SWITCHES *Tandem Switches* are network switches that serve in partnership with lesser switches, linking them together. In other words and in the classic sense, tandem switches serve no end users directly; rather, they serve to interconnect lesser switches. At the lowest level, tandem switches serve to link together CO switches over dedicated interoffice trunks, forming a fully interconnected and toll-free metropolitan calling area in the process. Depending on the design philosophy of the service provider, there may be as many as four levels of tandem switches in the backbone of the network. At each level, the tandem switches serve to interconnect lesser network switches. Contemporary network switches often are multifunctional — with one physical and logical partition serving as a CO, and another serving as a tandem.

ACCESS TANDEM SWITCHES *Access Tandem Switches* serve to connect the Local Exchange Carriers (telcos) to the Interexchange Carriers (long distance carriers) over dedicated interoffice trunks, known as *access trunks*. In this manner, the local service providers originally were interconnected to the long distance providers. As access tandem switches represent an additional point of potential network failure, involve additional costs to the IXC, and impose additional delay on the process of call setup, the larger IXCs often terminate high-capacity trunks directly in the LEC COs or tandem switching centers. Thereby, the access tandem arrangement is bypassed. Where the physical space is available and can be securely partitioned, the LECs must lease space to the IXCs in order that they can colocate termination facilities. The cost to the IXC of such leased space is based on actual costs to the LEC, plus a reasonable profit margin.

INTERNATIONAL GATEWAY FACILITIES (IGFs) *International Gateway Facilities* (*IGFs*) are the switches owned by the international carriers. Located at *landing points* on each end of the international connection, they provide connectivity between the international carriers and the national and local carriers on the originating and terminating ends.

TRANSMISSION FACILITIES

Transmission facilities, which we explored in Chapter 2, are the physical transmission media and associated electronics that provide the circuits in all domains of the PSTN. Oftentimes, a combination of media is employed, including twisted pair, coaxial cable, microwave, satellite, infrared, and optical fiber.

ACCESS *Access,* best expressed as the local loop, functions to provide access to the carrier-provided Wide Area Network (WAN). Access facilities typically extend from the customer premise to the LEC CO exchange, with the *demarcation point*, or *demarc*, serving as the point of separation between the CPE and LEC domains. Generally, the Incumbent LEC (ILEC) provides the access facilities, which terminate in the ILEC CO. A Competitive LEC (CLEC) may provide its own access facilities, typically in the form of optical fiber to areas where there is a significant concentration of high-volume commercial traffic. Access increasingly is provisioned through Wireless Local Loop (WLL) technologies, with microwave systems typically used for this purpose. Alternatively, the CLEC may lease existing facilities from the ILEC in those states that support competition in the local loop.

Access facilities also may provide direct connection from the customer premise to the IXC networks, bypassing the LEC switching systems in the process. The IXCs may provide those access loops themselves, or they may lease them from the ILEC. Alternatively, those facilities may access those loops from Competitive Access Providers (CAPs), also known as Alternative Access Providers (AAVs). An access environment employs transmission facilities, switches, and signaling and control systems.

TRANSPORT *Transport* is information transportation in the backbone of the PSTN, i.e., within the cloud. Transport can be in the LEC domain, or the IXC domain for long-haul applications. Either individually or in concert, and depending on the geographic scope of the communication, both LECs and IXCs may participate in information transport. Also, a third-party carrier, i.e., a *carrier's carrier,* may provide the transport facilities. A transport environment also employs transmission facilities, switches, and signaling and control systems.

SIGNALING AND CONTROL
Signaling and control systems and networks are used to signal within the network and to control its operation. Examples include status indication (i.e., on-hook and off-hook), dial tone provision, call routing control, busy indication, ringing, and performance monitoring.

SERVICES
Services include a wide variety of options provided by LECs, IXCs, and CAPs/AAVs. Such services include various discounted calling plans, custom-calling services, Centrex services, and toll-free (800/888/877) calling.

Regulatory Domains

There exists a complex set of domains that address regulatory and standards areas of responsibility. While it would be much simpler if these domains were discrete, you must contend with overlapping domains.

INTERNATIONAL
Regulation is largely nonexistent at the international level, although it is heavily influenced by the *International Telecommunication Union-Telecommunication Standardization Sector (ITU-T)* — chartered by the United Nations (UN). Previously known as the *Consultative Committee for International Telephone and Telegraph (CCITT)*, the predecessor organizations of the ITU-T date to 1865, at which time the focus was on the interconnectivity of national telegraph networks. The ITU-T

primarily is responsible for setting standards recommendations intended to ensure the interconnectivity of national networks. Specific standards recommendations also address voice, data, fax, and video applications. The *International Telecommunication Union-Radiocommunication* (*ITU-R*), previously known as the *Consultative Committee for International Radio* (*CCIR*), governs over-the-air communications. Intelsat and other consortia are responsible for allocating and managing satellite orbital slots.

The *International Organization for Standardization* (*ISO*) comprises a group of various national standards-setting organizations. The *American National Standards Organization* (*ANSI*) represents the United States. The ISO has great influence over a wide range of international standards; for our purposes, the ISO is best known for the development of the *OSI* (*Open Systems Integration*) *Reference Model*, which we will explore in Chapter 6.

REGIONAL

Regional authorities, although few in number, have the same responsibility within a more compact region. For example, DG XIII (Directorate General XIII) is responsible for such issues within the *European Union* (*EU*), which largely comprises Western Europe. Previously known as the *European Community* (*EC*), the EU has real authority in the areas of regulation and standards, establishing and enforcing policy matters such as network competition within a member nation's network.

NATIONAL

National regulation is critical in most areas of the world, although less so in the case of the EU member nations, which have ceded a good deal of this privilege to the regional authority. Most nations have well-defined and tightly enforced rules, regulations, and standards which serve their requirements. Areas of influence often include such issues as competition, rates and tariffs, radio frequency spectrum allocation, and characteristics of electrical local loops. National authorities also determine the basis on which international carriers can establish a presence at landing points for purposes of interconnection with the national networks. In the United States, the Federal Communications Commission is the national authority. New Zealand is most unusual in that the national network was entirely deregulated, and the regulator abolished. In Australia, AUSTEL recently was disbanded in favor of market self-regulation. Limited legislative and judicial controls remain in place in both countries. Closer to home again, much discussion has evolved around abolishing the FCC.

STATE OR PROVINCE

In the United States, Canada, and many other countries, state or provincial regulation is considered important. Issues of intrastate competition, and rates and tariffs are managed at this level. State *Public Utility Commissions* (*PUCs*), also known as *Public Service Commissions* (*PSCs*), formed in the United States beginning in 1937. In some cases, the state PUCs have taken the lead in terms of deregulation and competition.

Illinois, for instance, for years and well before the federal Telecommunications Act of 1996, permitted some level of competition in the local exchange environment. In Chicago, specifically and for a number of years, CAPs have provided local and Centrex service in competition with the LECs. As the Telecommunications Act of 1996 has been tied up in the courts, the state regulators have assumed a preeminent role in the introduction of competition into the local exchange. Currently, 37 states permit some level of competition.

LOCAL

Local regulation enters the picture relative to local zoning ordinances that might dictate wireless tower placement and allowable height, CATV franchises, and cable right-of-way. In Milpitas, California, for instance, the local regulators demanded the right to levy franchise taxes against Pacific Bell when the LEC sought right-of-way permission to lay fiber optic cables to deliver CATV programming in competition with the incumbent CATV provider. PacBell refused to submit, arguing that state and federal authorities regulated it, not local authorities. As a result, the Information Superhighway ground to a halt in Milpitas in 1994.

In some instances, local regulation predominates; Alaska and certain Scandinavian countries are unusual in that they have many municipally-owned LECs. Commercial carriers had no interest in providing service in such sparsely populated areas, given the high costs of provisioning and the low potential for revenues and profits.

Rates and Tariffs

Carriers traditionally have been required to file a set of *tariffs* with the appropriate regulatory authority, which describe the services the carrier intends to offer in that domain; the rates it proposes to charge for them; and the proposed obligations, rights, and responsibilities of the both the carrier and the customer. The regulatory authority examines the tariff filing, holds public hearings on the proposal, and renders a binding decision, which the carrier can appeal to the regulator or through the judicial system [5-3].

At the state level, the regulatory authority is in the form of a PUC (Public Utilities Commission), which has the authority to regulate all exclusively intrastate matters. National regulation is the domain of the FCC, which has the responsibility to determine all interstate issues, including radio frequency allocation.

Regulators evaluate tariff filings and determine rate schedules based on a complex and varying set of considerations including allowable costs of service provisioning and support, which involves both capital investment and operating costs of the carrier. Particularly at the state level, regulators attempt to restrict rates to reasonable and affordable levels. At the same time, the regulator must permit the carrier a reasonable rate of *Return on Investment (ROI)* that positions the company well to secure necessary funds for expansion and enhancement of its facilities through both the equity (stock) and debt (bond) markets. Additionally, the regulators generally attempt to ensure that residential service is universally available at reasonable cost. As a result, rates for business users traditionally have been set well above the costs of providing service; thereby, a complex set of cross-subsidies supports low residential rates. Basic service rates for access services (local loops) generally are kept at low levels, especially for residential consumers. Enhanced services (e.g., voicemail and custom-calling features) and long distance are considered to be optional and, therefore, are priced to yield more profit in support of basic services.

As the network monopolies were dismantled and the trend toward competition developed, the various regulators focused on the incumbent and dominant carriers in their respective domains. Beginning with the Carterphone decision in 1968, carrying through the MFJ in 1982 and continuing into the Telecommunications Act of 1996, the emphasis, therefore, has been on AT&T, GTE, and the ILECs. The intentions of the FCC—and now the PUCs—are to encourage competition by providing the new entrants with an advantage. Once the incumbent carriers (i.e., AT&T and the ILECs) have demonstrated that they no longer hold dominant positions, the regulators relax restrictions on them in favor of permitting market forces to prevail. This intent has been demonstrated with respect to the IXC market, as the FCC gradually has relaxed its requirements of AT&T. This trend likely will continue as a result of the Telecommunications Act of 1996, which is discussed in detail in Chapter 15.

Regulation hasfocused on voice network services provided in the traditional fashion by the incumbent carriers. Such services certainly are more basic and necessary than data and other services. This posture now can be argued, particularly with the advent of the Internet. In fact, voice communications recently has become possible over the Internet through equipping a PC with a high-speed modem, speakers and microphone, and special software. Considered by many as a threat to the traditional PSTN and the concept of universal service, a number of interested parties have requested that the FCC examine the issue, with the intent to regulate or ban voice over the Internet, altogether. Interestingly, the major IXCs are not parties to this request; AT&T and others have taken strong positions as Internet service providers and intend to encourage its use. *Voice over Frame Relay* (*VoFR*), is possible, and increasingly is used where excess Frame Relay bandwidth is available. Although the cost of implementing voice over either the Internet or Frame Relay networks is a hindrance, and although the quality of the voice communication generally is poor in either case, advances in technology promise to improve quality, lower cost, and therefore, threaten the PSTN. I discuss the Internet and Frame Relay in length in subsequent chapters.

Now, the greatest threat to the PSTN comes from next-generation carriers such as Level 3 and Qwest. These carriers are building high-speed packet data networks running the IP (Internet Protocol) protocol and optimized for voice communications in a highly compressed format. These *Voice over IP* (*VoIP*) networks—inherently enhanced data networks—are exempt from most regulations. Currently, these networks are not fully deployed and their services not widely available. Therefore, the level of voice quality is yet to be determined, especially under heavy load. Yet, these networks are inherently more efficient than the traditional voice networks; therefore, costs to the consumer are likely to be much less.

Local exchange competition, voice over the Internet, Voice over Frame Relay, and Voice over IP all threaten the concept of universal service, which has been a cornerstone of the PSTN since the formation of the FCC in 1934. In order to ensure the universal availability of voice service at affordable cost to the subscriber, a complex structure of *settlements* (cross-subsidies) developed between incumbent IXCs and LECs. Thereby, a subscriber in a high-cost area such as Hackberry, Arizona could gain affordable network access, as could a subscriber in New York, New York, despite the obvious cost differences in the carriers' service. Unless the integrity of the universal service fund is maintained, with all carriers contributing, the concept of universal service may be relegated to a historical footnote.

Carrier Domains and Network Topology

Some years ago, and certainly prior to AT&T's divestiture of the Bell Operating Companies in 1984, the network was relatively simple in terms of its ownership and topology. Each operating telephone company provided service in its franchised serving areas, and gained access to the AT&T long distance network on a fairly straightforward basis. Beginning in the late 1920s, the network organized on a layered basis, with five levels of hierarchy, known as classes [5-3].

Class 5 offices are the *local exchange offices*, or Central Offices (COs), which serve end users through local loop connections. The approximately 19,000 Class 5 offices in the United States are geographically positioned to address a *Carrier Serving Area* (*CSA*), as illustrated in Figure 5-1. The CSA has a radius of approximately 18,000 feet, which is the typical maximum length of a local loop without special conditioning provided by either amplifiers (analog signal boosters) or repeaters (digital signal regenerators). The carrier can extend the radius of the CSA through the deployment of either intelligent remote COs, or unintelligent remote line shelves. The remotes are connected to the centralized CO through high-capacity circuits. Should significant volumes of traffic be exchanged directly between COs, they may be directly interconnected. More commonly, they are interconnected through tandem switches.

Class 4 offices are *tandem toll centers*, which serve to interconnect Class 5 offices not connected directly. As the lowest class of toll center, these also serve as the first point of entry to the long distance, or toll, network. Class 4 offices are interconnected within a relatively local toll network and provide access to higher-order toll centers. In many instances, a Class 4 office also serves as a Class 5 office; in other words, a hybrid switch serving as both a Central Office and a tandem toll office, with the separate functions provided through logical and physical partitioning within the switch. Approximately 1,500 tandem toll centers existed in North America prior to AT&T's divestiture of the BOCs.

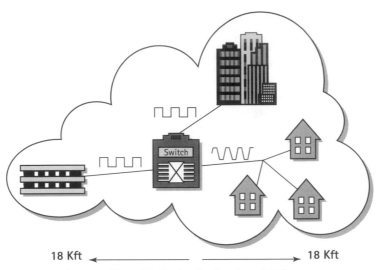

18 Kft ←——————— ———————→ 18 Kft

Figure 5-1 Class 5 office with Carrier Serving Area (CSA)

Class 3 offices, or *primary toll centers*, are higher-order toll centers, generally serving to connect Class 4 offices for intrastate toll calling. Class 4 offices typically serve to interconnect independent telcos and BOCs. Approximately 200 such offices existed prior to divestiture.

Class 2 offices, or *sectional toll centers*, serve to interconnect primary toll centers, largely for interstate calling within a geographic region such as the Northeast or the Southwest. Approximately 67 sectional toll centers existed in the AT&T network prior to divestiture.

Class 1 offices, or *regional toll centers*, serve to interconnect sectional toll centers in support of interregional calling. There were 10 regional toll centers in place in the United States prior to divestiture; seven currently exist in the United States, and two in Canada.

As illustrated in Figure 5-2, the offices traditionally were interconnected on a hierarchical basis, with end offices residing at the bottom of the network food chain. As a user places a long distance call, the Class 5 switch examines and analyzes the destination telephone number in the context of the geographic area it serves. Based on that information and relying on program logic, the CO processes and routes the call. Local long distance calls (e.g., within the San Francisco Bay Area) either are handled by directly connected Class 5 offices, or through a Class 4 tandem toll office which interconnects multiple Class 5 offices. A coast-to-coast call, on the other hand, might involve all 5 classes of the hierarchy. For instance, a call from Turlock, California to New York, New York originates in the Class 5 switch of Evans Telephone Company, an independent telco, and is handed to a nearby AT&T tandem toll center. The call then works its way up the hierarchy until it reaches the Class 1 regional toll center in San Francisco. High-capacity, coast-to-coast tandem toll trunks carry the call to New York City, where it works its way down an abbreviated hierarchy and is delivered to the target number in Manhattan. Note that each switch acts on the call more or less independently. In the above classic scenario, each switch looks at the call, determines whether or not it can serve the connection request, and hands the call off to another switch, either higher or lower in the hierarchy. The sole exception is the terminating Class 5 switch, which finally serves to establish the connection to the target telephone number. While the switches work together to set up the connection, each acts independently and forwards the connection request blindly along, never knowing what will happen end to end. The same set of processes takes place in each switch, the same logic is exercised, and a talk path is set up through each switch and across each interconnecting transmission link.

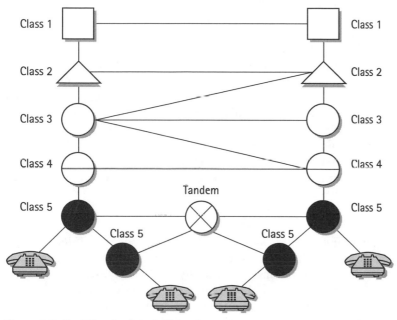

Figure 5–2 Traditional network hierarchy

This approach was quite sensible in the days when AT&T dominated the local and long distance networks. As calls worked their way through the network, ever larger volumes of traffic were aggregated by ever more capable switches, and shipped over trunks of ever greater capacity, taking advantage of the economies of scale.

This network topology has flattened over the years as the cost of transport over fiber optic facilities has dropped, the cost of switches has decreased, and competition has increased. As a result, there exist fewer more intelligent and multifunctional switches, interconnected by higher capacity transmission facilities in a *sparse network configuration*.

Contemporary carrier and service provider domains fall into three categories: local exchange; interexchange or national; and international. Competitive Access Providers (CAPs) are a relatively recent breed of carrier, typically focusing on the provisioning of direct access to the interexchange carrier through bypassing the local exchange carrier. Overlay carriers and wireless carriers also are relatively new entrants. While you can segment the domains cleanly along these lines, changes in regulation are blurring the lines to a significant extent. This is particularly the case in the United States as a result of deregulation, culminating in the Telecommunications Act of 1996, which we will explore in some detail in Chapter 15.

CUSTOMER PREMISE EQUIPMENT (CPE)

CPE, as we noted, is the terminal and switching equipment located on the customer premise. While such equipment traditionally was rented to the subscriber by the LEC, deregulation generally places both the privilege and the responsibility of ownership on the end user. Similarly, inside wire and cable generally is deregulated.

DEMARCATION POINT (DEMARC)

The demarc constitutes the boundary between the end user and carrier domains. In a residential environment, the demarc is in the form of a *Network Interface Unit (NIU)*. A NIU includes a *protector*, which serves to protect the premise wiring and equipment from aberrant voltages possibly induced by carrier power supplies, power utility transformers, or lightning strikes. Contemporary NIUs are intelligent, enabling telco technicians or automatic test systems to regularly test the integrity of the local loop from the Central Office to the customer premise. The NIU is located outside the residence, perhaps on an outside wall or in the garage, because the regulated telco cannot place equipment inside the premise under the terms of the Modified Final Judgement (MFJ), which set the terms for the breakup of the Bell System.

In a business environment, the demarc, or *Minimum Point of Entry (MPOE)*, is defined as the closest logical and practical point within the customer domain. In a high-rise office building, for instance, it typically is defined as a point of the entrance cable 12" from the inside wall. Newer entrance cable facilities involve a physical demarc, while older facilities typically are tagged by telco technicians in order to indicate a logical point of demarcation. From that point inward, the cable and wire system is the responsibility of the user and/or building owner, as appropriate.

LOCAL EXCHANGE CARRIERS (LECs)

LECs provide local telephone service, usually within the boundaries of a metropolitan area, state, or province. Their primary charter is to provide local voice services through a network of local loops and Central Offices (COs), which can be connected either directly or through a tandem switch, as depicted in Figure 5-3. The LECs also provide short-haul, long distance service, Centrex, certain enhanced services such as voicemail, and various data services. In most states in the United States, there exist both *Incumbent LECs* (*ILECs*) and *Competitive LECs* (*CLECs*).

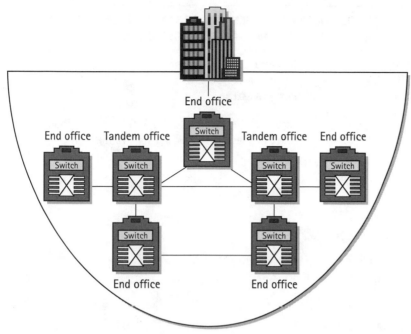

Figure 5-3 ILEC metropolitan serving area, with COs interconnected directly and through a tandem switch

ILECs are the original LECs, each of which was awarded by the regulatory authority a franchise to provide service within a given geographic area. Originally, a municipal or county government awarded those franchises. The *Bell Operating Companies* (*BOCs*), originally were wholly owned by the AT&T Bell System and a reported directlyto AT&T general headquarters, which dominated the ILEC landscape. Effective January 1, 1984, those 22 operating telephone companies were spun off from AT&T as a result of the *Modified Final Judgement* (*MFJ*). Also known as the *Divestiture Decree*, the MFJ was rendered by Judge Harold H. Greene of the Federal District Court in Washington, D.C. on January 8, 1982. The MFJ, in fact, was a negotiated settlement representing the culmination of the U.S. Justice Department's long efforts to break up what it characterized as an oppressive monopoly. As a result, the BOCs were reorganized into seven *Regional Bell Operating Companies* (*RBOCs*), also known as *Regional Holding Companies* (*RHCs*) as noted in Table 5-1. Over time, the RBOCs fully absorbed the individual BOCs, creating a single legal entity with a centralized management structure. Cincinnati Bell and Southern New England Telephone (SNET) were not affected in this manner, because they were not wholly-owned subsidiaries of AT&T.

Table 5-1 BELL SYSTEM OPERATING COMPANY ORGANIZATIONAL STRUCTURE, BEFORE AND AFTER THE MFJ, AND TO THE PRESENT

Bell Operating Companies (BOCs), Pre-divestiture	Regional Bell Operating Companies (RBOCs), Post-divestiture
Illinois Bell	Ameritech (IL). Acquisition by SBC Communications scheduled (estimated second-half 1999)
Indiana Bell	
Michigan Bell	
Ohio Bell	
Wisconsin Telephone	
Bell of Pennsylvania	Bell Atlantic (PA)
Diamond State Telephone	
The Chesapeake and Potomac Companies (DC, MD, VA, & WV)	
New Jersey Bell	
South Central Bell	Bell South (GA)
Southern Bell	
New England Telephone	NYNEX (NY). Acquired by Bell Atlantic (August 14, 1997)
New York Telephone	
Pacific Bell	Pacific Telesis (CA). Acquired by SBC (April 1, 1997)
Nevada Bell	
Southwestern Bell	Southwestern Bell Corporation (TX), now SBC Communications
Mountain Bell	US West (CO)
Northwestern Bell	
Pacific Northwest Bell	

In addition to causing AT&T to divest the BOCs, the MFJ effectively limited the BOCs to providing basic voice and data services within defined geographical areas, known as *Local Access and Transport Areas* (*LATAs*). These services included *intraLATA* toll service, also known as *local long distance*, within the confines of the

196 defined LATAs. Additionally, the BOCs and RBOCs could not engage in certain other activities such as manufacturing communications equipment and providing enhanced services such as voicemail; subsequently, the latter restriction was lifted.

AT&T Long Lines, which became AT&T Communications (now AT&T Corporation), was restricted from providing intraLATA toll, as were MCI (now MCI Worldcom), US Sprint (now Sprint Corporation) and the balance of what were known as the *Other Common Carriers* (*OCCs*). Those companies, which became known as Interexchange Carriers (IXCs, or IECs), were limited to providing long distance service on an interLATA basis (across LATA boundaries). Further, AT&T could not enter the local service business, although the OCCs had no limitations in that respect.

AT&T Technologies (now Lucent Technologies) was formed of Western Electric, the manufacturing arm of AT&T, and AT&T Bell Telephone Laboratories (Bell Labs) — the research and development organization. Of all the AT&T entities, only Bell Labs could retain the Bell name. The RBOCs, in consortium, formed Bell Communications Research (Bellcore) as a R&D entity. Bellcore focused on the needs of its RBOC client/owners in terms of software R&D, standards development, and other requirements; under the terms of the MFJ, it initially was precluded from involvement in the physical sciences [5-11] and [5-12]. The RBOCs divested Bellcore in 1998, when it became clear that they would be competitors, rather than collaborators, in a deregulated environment. SAIC (Science Applications International Corporation) acquired Bellcore, and changed its name to Telcordia Technologies, Inc. in March 1999. Telcordia's stated focus is on next-generation networks.

In the United States, LECs traditionally had the exclusive rights to local and intraLATA markets, although many states either eroded or modified this policy; Connecticut, for instance, has permitted local exchange competition since July 1, 1994. The Telecommunications Act of 1996 has set the stage for complete and open competition for virtually all services. As this act has bogged down in the courts, the various state regulators have taken the initiative in terms of local service competition.

In addition to the RBOCs and their LEC subsidiaries, approximately 1,500 independent telephone companies exist, according to the United States Telephone Association. GTE is the largest independent, although Bell Atlantic is scheduled to acquire it in the second half of 1999. Southern New England Telephone Company (SNET) — partially owned by AT&T prior to the MFJ — was acquired by SBC (October 26, 1998).

At this point, it is worth noting that the Telecommunications Act of 1996 has changed this landscape in a very dramatic way. Casting aside the MFJ, the act permits the IXCs to begin competing immediately with the ILECs for local and intraLATA service. The act also allows the RBOCs to offer interLATA long distance service outside the states in which they operate as ILECs. Once the RBOCs have satisfied certain local competition requirements, they can offer interLATA toll services within their home states, as well. While some provisions of the act remain under legal challenges, the states have taken the initiative within their domains of jurisdiction.

Competitive Local Exchange Carriers (CLECs) can compete for local service in a large number of states. While many CLECs originated as Competitive Access Providers (CAPs), others were Interexchange Carriers (IXCs), and still others were created specifically as CLECs. Metropolitan Fiber Systems (MFS), for instance, originally was a facilities-based CAP. Subsequently, MFS acquired UUNET, a very large Internet access and backbone provider. MFS then was acquired by MCI, which then was acquired by Worldcom, with the combined company assuming the name MCI Worldcom. While MFS has lost its identity, the network that it constructed serves MCI Worldcom well for IXC access, and has positioned it well as a CLEC.

AT&T has constructed fiber optic facilities for direct access to the premise in areas where there exist high concentrations of large user organizations. In Spokane, Washington, AT&T Wireless has trialed a Wireless Local Loop (WLL) solution based on its PCS network technology and licenses. More recently, AT&T has amassed wireless licenses in over 300 markets in order to bypass the ILEC to reach its business customers without the investment and delay of constructing wireline facilities. In July 1998, AT&T also acquired TCGI (Teleport Communications Group, Inc.), a large CAP with both wireline and wireless access facilities. In March 1999, AT&T acquired TCI (Tele-Communications Inc.), a large CATV provider, to gain access to its Hybrid Fiber Coax (HFC) cable network. In combination with – and through some significant investments in – network upgrades, these fiber, coax, and wireless networks will provide access to a very large potential customer base. Further, they will support voice, data, and video communications, and high-speed Internet access. AT&T strategically seeks to become a full-service provider, in both the LEC and IXC domains.

WinStar is a CLEC with its origins in the CAP domain. WinStar uses licensed microwave in the 38-GHz range for access to over 3,500 buildings in the United States; the company holds licenses in 160 markets. Teligent uses a similar approach, holding 24-GHz microwave licenses in approximately 75 markets [5-13].

Nextlink is a CLEC with a very substantial fiber optic network servicing approximately 50 domestic markets. In January 1999, the company acquired WNP Communications, which held Local Multipoint Distribution Services (LMDS) wireless licenses in a large number of markets. Added to the LMDS licenses which it held jointly with Nextel, a sister company, and which licenses it also fully acquired, the company has wireless access to its fiber optic network in most major markets.

INTEREXCHANGE CARRIERS (IXCs OR IECs)

IXCs are responsible for long-haul, long-distance connections across LATA boundaries. The IXC networks are connected to the LECs through a *Point of Presence (POP)* which typically is in the form of a tandem switch. An interLATA call originating in a LEC serving area is recognized as such and is passed to the access tandem switch, which, in turn, passes the call to the IXC POP via dedicated trunks leased from the ILEC (see Figure 5-4). Alternatively, the IXC may collocate network termination equipment in the LEC exchange office, assuming that space is available and that secure physical separation can be established and maintained.

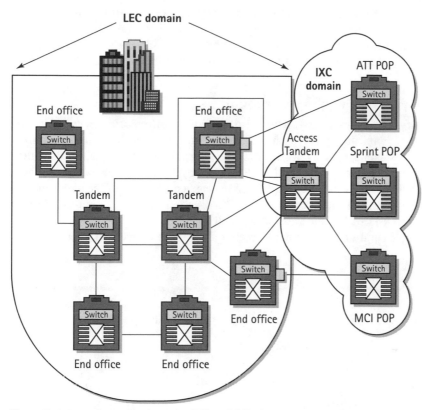

Figure 5-4 Interconnection between LEC and IXC via access tandem switch and via collocated termination equipment

Increasingly, large users seek to gain direct access to the IXC POP, bypassing the LEC switching network in the process. Such a bypass arrangement typically is effected through a leased line provided by the ILEC. Alternatively, the ILEC can be completely bypassed through a direct link, which often is wireless in nature and is provided directly by the IXC. You can also access IXCs through a CAP, which provides either wireless or fiber optic cable connections directly from the customer premise to the IXC POPs, totally bypassing all LEC facilities.

IXCs, by definition, are facilities-based, or *heavy*, carriers. While they prefer to contract directly with large end users, they also often work through non facilities-based carriers *(light carriers)*, including resellers, aggregators, and agents. Of the 400 or so heavy carriers, AT&T, MCI Worldcom, and Sprint dominate the market. Emerging next-generation carriers such as Frontier, IXC, Level 3, The Williams Companies, and Qwest, promise to offer stiff competition. These carriers are in various stages of deploying state-of-the-technology, long-haul, fiber optic networks, often laying hundreds of optical fibers along each route. Through each fiber, each lightwave runs at speeds up to 10 Gbps, thereby supporting up to approximately 130,000 voice channels. With Dense Wavelength Division Multiplexing (DWDM), up to 32 lightwaves are introduced into each fiber. While the cost of deploying these networks is incredible, the ultimate cost-per-bit transmitted will remain close to zero.

COMPETITIVE ACCESS PROVIDERS (CAPs)

Competitive Access Providers (*CAPs*), also known *as Alternative Access Vendors* (*AAVs*), provide an alternative means of connection between large user organizations and IXCs, completely bypassing the LEC network in the process. CAPs generally deploy high-capacity, fiber optic facilities from IXC POPs to areas where there exist a high density of large user organizations (e.g., commercial office parks and urban business areas). In many cases, the CAP will extend the fiber optic connection directly to the user's CPE, such as a PBX, as depicted in Figure 5-5. Wireless CAPs, such as Teligent and Winstar, provide access on the basis of licensed microwave.

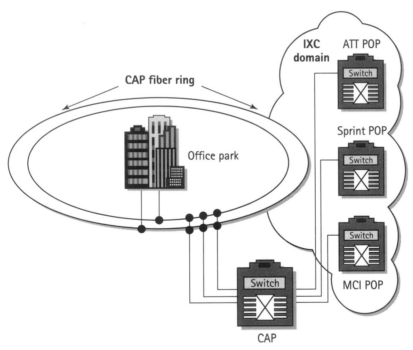

Figure 5-5 End user access to an IXC via a CAP, bypassing the ILEC

An optical fiber approach presents numerous benefits, including the fact that the performance characteristics of the fiber optic facilities are far superior to the traditional LEC copper local loop. Additionally, the CAP network automatically provides a measure of local loop redundancy; the CAP facilities are used for IXC access, while the LEC local loops can still be used for IXC access in the event of a failure in the CAP network. Further, the fiber optic network generally is redundant, thereby minimizing the likelihood of a service-affecting network failure. As the fiber optic network also offers substantial, and even elastic, bandwidth, the user organization typically can increase its level of access to the IXC much more quickly and easily than through a LEC connection. Call setup time (speed of connection) also is improved, as the LEC CO, tandem switch, and access tandem switch all are bypassed. Finally, the costs of IXC access often are much reduced because the CAP's unregulated rates generally are highly competitive.

CAPs operate most especially in the United States, where they now function as voice/data CLECs, providing Centrex service, local calling service, high-speed data services, and certain enhanced services. Independent CAPs operating in the United States include Electric Lightwave, Nextlink, Teligent, and Winstar.

INTERNATIONAL RECORD CARRIERS (IRCs)

IRCs are carriers of record which provide communications transport services across national borders. You can accomplish access to the IRC from the LEC or IXC domain by connection to an International Gateway Facility (IGF) which connects to the IRC's transmission network. Contemporary IRC transmission facilities are largely satellite and submarine fiber optic cables, the latter often jointly owned through consortia. Examples of IRCs include AT&T, Cable & Wireless (C&W), HongKong Telecom International (HKTI), and MCI Worldcom.

OVERLAY CARRIERS

Overlay carriers build networks that overlay the traditional PSTN. While such networks are unusual in highly developed countries, they are common in developing nations. In some countries of Eastern/Central Europe, for example, private carriers have been franchised to build overlay digital microwave networks to provide service to large government, education, and commercial organizations. In such cases, the PSTN simply could not be upgraded quickly to provide satisfactory communications, which are considered vital to economic growth. Overlay carriers generally deploy microwave systems that effectively overlay the outdated wireline facilities of the incumbent carriers.

Signaling and Control: An Expanded View

The two basic types of information transfer are data (content) and control (nondata). Signaling messages fall into the latter category. In order for the network to function properly, the various devices, components, or elements of the network must have the capability to signal each other, indicating their status and condition. Typical status indications include available (dial tone), unavailable (busy), and available (ringing signal). The terminal devices also must pass identification information, as well as certain instructions through the network, perhaps as far as to the receiving terminal. Such information and instructions might include the originating number or circuit and the target number, based on the dialed digits. Within the carrier network, such information includes route preference and route availability [5-3]. Additionally, the network must determine and honor the end user's designated IXC in order that a long distance call can be handed off to the carrier of choice.

Signaling and control systems and networks also handle billing matters, perhaps querying centralized databases in the process. Billing options might include bill to originating number (e.g., DDD and WATS), bill to terminating number (e.g., InWATS or 1800/1888/1877), bill to third number (third party), and bill to calling card with verification of a PIN against a database.

Finally, certain network management information often is passed over signaling and control links. Such information is used for remote monitoring, diagnostics, fault isolation, and network control. In this fashion, a centralized *Network Operations Center* (*NOC*) can monitor the network, and faults or degradations in performance can be determined and isolated. Diagnostic routines can then be invoked in order to determine the specific nature of the difficulty. Finally, you can instruct the network element in difficulty to resolve the problem, perhaps by resetting or reinitializing itself, or by disabling a failed port and activating a standby port.

In-Band Signaling and Control

In-band signaling and control functions take place over the same physical path as the conversation, and occupy the same frequency band (analog) or time slots (digital). The impact of simultaneous conversation and signaling disrupts the data stream and, therefore, can be most unpleasant. As a result, it seldom operates in contemporary networks, with the exception of analog local loops.

By way of example, I frequently call long distance to talk with my son in East Texas. During those conversations, Barrett has a habit of "accidentally" depressing the buttons on the tonepad with his chin. The resulting *DTMF* (*Dual Tone MultiFrequency*) signals are interpreted by the network as a priority instruction set. Since the signaling tones occupy the same range of frequencies at the same moment in time, they override and interfere with the conversation. In contemporary networks, this in-band signaling and control technique actually is disruptive only over the local loops, which extend from the CPE to the edge of the network cloud; internally, the networks make use of out-of-band signaling and control. Nonetheless, Barrett gets a set of tones in his ear and I get a set of tones in my ear — Barrett finds this to be highly amusing, while I find it highly aggravating, which Barrett finds even more amusing, and so on, and so on.

Notably, in-band signaling and control goes wherever the call goes, at least at the edges of the network. You can use this fact to your advantage. For instance, you can signal and control a voice processor. When checking your voicemail, you access the voice processor, which begins to "talk" to you. Since you know exactly what the machine is going to say, you simply send DTMF tones to the machine through the dial pad, overriding the data transmission. You enter your password while the machine "talks" to you. You enter option "1" to play the message, enter "2" to repeat the message, enter "3" to save the message, and so on...all while the machine "talks" to you. In other words, you override the downstream data transmission with higher-priority signaling and control data, saving time and money in the process.

Out-of-Band Signaling and Control

Out-of-band signaling and control, in the simplest analog application, takes place over frequencies separate from those which carry the information. In a contemporary digital network, signaling and control data generally occupies separate, designated time slots. In either case, there is no interference between the two functions; i.e., out-of-band signaling and control is non-disruptive. Out-of-band signaling and control is the standard approach in digital networks and, most certainly, in the internal carrier networks.

Common Channel Signaling and Control (CCS)

The carriers use *Common Channel Signaling & Control* (*CCS*) systems to carry large volumes of signaling and control information in support of high-traffic networks. CCS links are digital in nature, and may be in the form of high-speed optical fiber. Essentially, the CCS network is, in fact, a highly robust subnetwork that supports the operations of the primary communications network. The CCS subnetwork connects the various network switches to centralized computer systems of significant intelligence and on which reside very substantial databases. Through the use of centralized intelligence supported by carefully synchronized databases, you can control the operations of an entire network and monitor its performance, from end to end. While complicated and expensive to design and deploy, CCS networks are more effective and less costly than the alternative of placing lesser levels of intelligence in each of the various network switches — each required to perform redundant processes in complete harmony.

Signaling System 7 (*SS7*), the current version, was developed and deployed based on ITU-T standards recommendations. Thereby, all carriers can achieve and manage interconnection on a standard basis (see Figure 5-6). SS7 significantly speeds call setup and call completion processes. Additionally, SS7 is responsible for the delivery of many enhanced custom-calling features often associated with ISDN. These CLASS (Customer Local Access Signaling Services) services include Caller ID, which has been enhanced as Name ID, providing the name of the calling party as listed in the telephone directory. Other services include Selective Ringing (or Priority Ringing), Selective Call Forwarding, Call Block (or Call Screen), Repeat Dialing, Call Trace, and Automatic Call-Back (Call Return). SS7 is fully deployed in all major IXC networks. While SS7 is largely deployed in the major ILEC networks, older Class 5 switches do not support it.

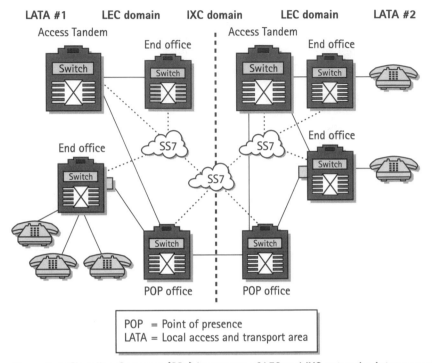

Figure 5-6 Signaling System 7 (SS7) in support of LEC and IXC networks, interconnected

Network Services

You can group network services into several categories that define their basic nature. Those categories include access services, dedicated services, switched services, and virtual services.

Access Services

Access services are those services that provide circuit access to the network, generally to the LEC Central Office. The circuits may be analog or digital, and single-channel or multichannel. Access services include residential and business lines, and PBX trunks.

RESIDENTIAL LINES

Residential lines are local loop connections between the residential premise and the Central Office Exchange. Although generally analog in nature, the market penetration of digital ISDN BRI (Basic Rate Interface) local loops has increased.

BUSINESS LINES

Business lines are local loop connections between the business premise and the Central Office Exchange. Business lines provide access to single-line and multiline terminal sets, as well as to Key Telephone Systems (KTSs). Business lines generally are analog in nature, although digital ISDN BRI has increased in popularity.

PBX TRUNKS

PBX trunks are local loop connections between PBX switches and network switches. As noted in Chapter 3, PBX trunks may be incoming only, outgoing only, or bidirectional (combination) in nature. Trunk connections may be provisioned individually and may be analog in nature. More typically, trunks are provisioned on a high-capacity, digital, multichannel basis (e.g., T-1 and ISDN PRI, or Primary Rate Interface). Trunks that serve a specific, common purpose are grouped into a *trunk group*.

Dedicated Transport Services

Dedicated circuits, in the traditional sense, are leased-line transport circuits that are dedicated to a specific use by a specific user organization. Again, they may be either analog or digital, and either single-channel or multichannel. Typically, the LEC provides dedicated circuits on an intraLATA basis, although CAPs also provide such circuits to the extent that their facilities match user requirements. Currently, an IXC must provide InterLATA leased lines, typically with the ILEC or CAP providing the local loop connection to the IXC POP, and the IXC providing the interLATA portion to the destination POP, where the circuit interfaces with the ILEC local loop serving the target location.

FOREIGN EXCHANGE (FX OR FEX)

Foreign Exchange (*FX* or *FEX*) lines or trunks connect the user premise more or less directly with a foreign exchange (i.e., with an exchange other than the local exchange that normally provides local dial tone). As is the case with all leased lines, FX circuits generally are billed on a distance-sensitive basis, and without any consideration of usage. As described in Chapter 3, a user organization can lease a FX circuit from Dallas, TX to Denton, TX to support outgoing and incoming traffic between those general areas; the circuit terminates in Dallas CPE but has a Denton local telephone number. Neither long distance charges nor any other usage-sensitive charges apply to the traffic.

TIE LINES AND TIE TRUNKS

Tie lines, as described in Chapter 3, are circuits that connect KTS systems together directly and across the PSTN. Tie trunks connect PBXs together. Since they are leased circuits, in neither case are network switches involved. Between two PBX systems, for instance, the carrier(s) provide dedicated circuits which pass through wire centers housing network switches. The circuits bypass the switches – unnecessary in this application – yet take advantage of amplifiers or repeaters, multiplexers, and other systems embedded in the carrier network. Tie trunks generally are in the form of digital T-carrier; tie lines may be either analog or digital.

OFF-PREMISE EXTENSION (OPX)

OPX circuits are dedicated PSTN circuits that connect a PBX or KTS system to an extension voice terminal located off-premise. The terminal appears exactly as would an on-premise extension, providing the user with the same level of functionality. OPXs are unusual, as both the circuit and the special purpose system interface card are expensive. Additionally, and as contemporary users are not office-bound, voicemail, cellular telephony, pagers, and other technologies are adequate alternatives for most situations.

Switched Transport Services

Switched services include all typical local and long distance voice traffic, whether inbound or outbound. Specific services include DDD, WATS, Virtual WATS, In-WATS, 500, and 900/976. Deregulation, divestiture, and resulting competition have for many years reduced the costs of these services, and very significantly. The emergence of specialized VoIP carriers will further intensify the price wars, as many long distance services truly will become commodities, rather than highly differentiated service offerings.

MESSAGE TELECOMMUNICATIONS SERVICE (MTS)

The Bell System introduced *Message Telecommunications Service (MTS)*, also known as *Direct Distance Dialing (DDD)* or *1+ dialing*, in November 1951. MTS enables the user to place long distance calls on a dialed basis, without the intervention of an operator. Such calls traditionally were billed on the basis of a combination of distance, duration, and time of day; contemporary calls generally are billed on the basis of a flat, blended rate based solely on duration. Discounts may apply to long duration and off-peak calls. DDD calls may be short-haul intraLATA (LEC or IXC), long- haul interLATA (IXC), or international in nature.

While the last manual exchange in the United States converted to dial many years ago, there remain a large number of *non-dialable toll points* in remote, rural areas of the United States. These toll points are six-digit numbers in the 88X-NXX format. Operator intervention is required to access these telephone numbers, which terminate in locations that are beyond the reach of cable systems and are too low and sheltered (e.g., in a narrow, deep canyon surrounded by steep cliffs) to be reached via satellite. Operators must still act on long distance calls in some developing countries, particularly in the case of international calling where *International DDD (IDDD)* is not in place.

WIDE AREA TELECOMMUNICATIONS (WATS)

WATS service resembles DDD service, but is billed according to a variety of discount plans for large user organizations. WATS originally required special purpose outgoing trunks that had access to specific areas of the country according to mileage bands 1-5, which were presented as concentric areas of coverage. Band 1, for instance, provided intrastate coverage, while Band 5 provided full national coverage. The greater the area of coverage, of course, the higher the cost of the WATS service. Traditional WATS was provided on a full-time or a measured basis. You could categorize full-time WATS as "all-you-can-eat" WATS because it was billed at a flat rate, with no usage monitoring or billing. Part-time, or measured, WATS was billed on a flat rate for the first 10 or 20 hours of usage, with overtime charges applying to traffic over the threshold. Clearly, the process of analyzing traffic patterns and configuring an optimum WATS network, with overflow to DDD, could be a fairly complex process.

Banded WATS has been abandoned in favor of *1+ WATS*, also known as *Virtual WATS,* – enabled by increased network intelligence, and encouraged by increased competitive pressure. Virtual WATS simply involves a discounted billing arrangement, including a small monthly fee and discounted usage which is sensitive to calling volume and volume commitment. The traditional requirement for special purpose circuits no longer exists, because the originating circuit and responsible user entity are identified by the billing systems, with the appropriate rating algorithm applied at the time the bill is rendered.

IN-WATS

Also known as *800 Service, In-WATS* resembles Virtual WATS, with the charges billed to the called party. Therefore, the call is toll-free, at least to the caller. In-WATS (1800) service became so popular in the United States that the supply of numbers was exhausted several years ago. Therefore, 888 numbers were added, and 877 numbers were added soon afterwards. Future additions will follow this existing convention of 8NN, with the last two numbers being identical. Outside the United States, In-WATS service is known by various terms, including *Freephone* and *Green Number,* and is accessed through various dialing conventions, including 0800 and 0500. The ITU-T implemented in 1997 a *Universal International Freephone Number (UIFN)* convention, which involves dialing 800 + 8 digits. As distributed UIFN databases have to be developed, deployed, and synchronized, and as many national networks have to be adjusted to recognize the UIFN numbering convention, it is unlikely that the service will be truly "universal" for a number of years.

In-WATS is an effective means of encouraging current and prospective customers to call, because they incur no toll charges. Incoming call centers, therefore, are heavy users of In-WATS, often terminating large numbers of In-WATS numbers in a single call center. An ACD in a call center often is equipped to recognize the In-WATS number called, with the called number being delivered to the system through *Dialed Number Identification Service* (*DNIS*), available at additional cost from the carrier. Based on the DNIS and other information, the ACD can route the incoming call to the optimal agent group and agent with greater effectiveness and efficiency, delivering a screen pop in the process.

In-WATS also is a cost-effective means for telecommuters and mobile employees to access various company offices for both voice and data applications. With the billing reversed to the target number, the company is relieved of the cost of processing expense vouchers for telephone charges; further, the cost of the call is far less than if it were charged to a calling card.

In-WATS was the first instance of an *Intelligent Network* (*IN*) service. The In-WATS numbers dialed do not represent real telephone numbers, at least not in the classic sense. In other words, they do not conform to the standard numbering scheme, wherein a telephone number (logical address) relates directly to a physical location (physical address) based on a standard numbering convention. Rather, an In-WATS number can be directed to any location within the carriers' domains. In order to direct the call to the proper physical location, the network must query a database of In-WATS numbers to translate that number into a conventional number associated with a specific physical location. Additionally, the database advises the originating LEC as to how the call should be routed. In the case of an interLATA call, the call routes to the IXC with which the target user has an In-WATS relationship [5-14]. LECs also offer In-WATS services, although the RBOC offerings currently are limited to intraLATA calling.

500 SERVICES

A relatively new phenomenon, *500 services* support *follow-me* personal communications services in the United States. From a remote location, the subscriber may access the network logic in order to program (or reprogram) a priority sequence of numbers to which calls should be forwarded, with such a sequence perhaps including a cellular number. A single number can be used for both voice and fax, with facsimile routing invoked through a special dialing instruction such as * or #, after a voice prompt. Soon, 500 numbers will provide the capability to selectively forward calls received only from those who have knowledge of a Personal Identification Number (PIN). Now, 500 numbers effectively offer the first set of capabilities promised by *Personal Communications Services (PCS)*, whereby one number theoretically can be retained for life — transportable across carriers and carrier domains.

AT&T offered a similar service a few years ago in the form of *700 services*. The service provided follow-me call forwarding, although only AT&T long distance subscribers could access a 700 number. No companies currently market 700 services [5-15], [5-16], and [5-17].

900/976 SERVICES

900/976 services are premium information services that carry either a flat cost per call or the cost per minute that the calling party determines. The revenues are divided among the sponsoring party receiving the call and the various carriers involved. Originally intended for applications such as telethons and informational services, 900/976 services have gained a bad reputation because many providers of telephone sex and other questionable services make extensive use of them.

Virtual Private Network (VPN) Services

Virtual Private Network (*VPN*), or *Software-Defined Network* (*SDN*), services are intended for use by very large user organizations. Classic voice VPNs are circuit-switched in nature, creating the effect of a private, leased-line network, but without the associated issues of design complexity, long deployment time, high recurring cost, and vulnerability to failure. VPN services generally are interexchange in nature because they find their greatest application in large enterprises that transcend LATA boundaries. Each terminating location in the multisite enterprise is identified, and the level of bandwidth required by each is determined. Dedicated access circuits are established between each point of termination and the closest VPN-capable IXC POP. Internal to the carrier network, dedicated circuits do not interconnect the various customer locations (see Figure 5-7). Rather, routing tables are established to route the traffic over specified high-capacity transmission facilities on a priority basis. This ensures that the level of service provided is equivalent to that of a true private network. The carrier realizes the benefit of sharing the involved network with other users, passing on the savings to the VPN customer.

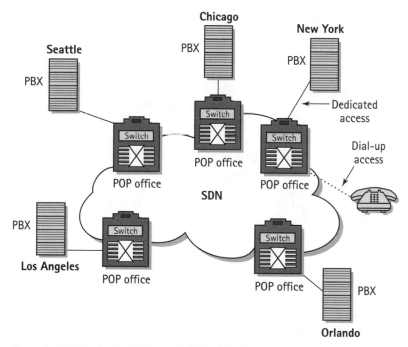

Figure 5-7 Virtual Private Network, United States domestic

VPNs offer the advantage of scalability because new sites can be added and bandwidth to individual locations can be increased, while maintaining a graceful relationship between the incremental cost and the incremental functionality. Additionally, configuration and reconfiguration effort and expense are reduced, as the only significant requirement is that the points and level of access be considered. Clearly, the time frame associated with carrier provisioning or reconfiguring such a network also is reduced, as dedicated circuits need not be provided between the various points of termination. Further, such a network is more resilient than a truly dedicated network, since the carrier network is highly redundant; therefore, the carrier quickly can route traffic around a point of blockage or catastrophic failure [5-12]. While VPNs may be international in scope, they are generally limited to calling on a domestic basis or between two nations.

Value-Added Services

You can define *value-added services*, also known as *enhanced services*, as those that alter the form, content, or nature of the information, thereby adding value to it. Examples include store-and-forward services such as voicemail, e-mail, and fax mail. In the data world, networks that accomplish the process of protocol conversion are considered as providing value-added services. Value-added services increasingly are offered by carriers of substance.

Portability: A Special Issue

Portability of numbers is an issue of real significance, and increasingly so. Traditionally, all numbers have been associated with either a geographic area (e.g., NPA and exchange code), a carrier (e.g., 800, 500, and 900 numbers), or a service offering (e.g., DID). Users prefer to retain the same number (logical address), regardless of physical location, carrier, or service offering. The intensity of the issue increased considerably with the advent of competition in the local exchange domain.

In the United States, 800 numbers (currently 888 and 877, as well) have been portable across carriers since 1992 (although subject to restriction by LATA boundary). For the most part, the ILECs are restricted to offering intraLATA services. Such restrictions are expected to be lifted in the future, once the ILECs satisfy the requisite conditions of the Telecommunications Act of 1996. The IXCs, as we discussed, can provide service on an intraLATA, as well as an interLATA, basis.

Portability of local numbers became an issue of great significance several years ago, when a small number of states began to permit competition in the local exchange. As the CLECs began to provide local service, they attacked the installed base of large ILEC customers. They were forced to require that those customers change their telephone numbers to fit into a block of DID numbers leased by the CLEC from the ILEC. Regardless of the attractiveness of the CLEC service offerings, potential customers were understandably reluctant to undergo a number change, which involved a potentially significant loss of business, potentially considerable costs for reprinting stationary and otherwise advertising the new number, and an obvious disruption in the business of the enterprise. Further, customers would have to change numbers again, if they were unhappy with the new provider and, therefore, choose either to return to the ILEC or to switch to another CLEC. The issue grew exponentially with the drafting of the Telecommunications Act of 1996, and the expectation that the CLEC business would experience dramatic growth.

Therefore, the act mandated the establishment of the *Local Number Portability Administration* (*LNPA*) to oversee the development and deployment of a mechanism for *Local Number Portability* (*LNP*). The first implementation of LNP was in the state of Illinois, which was among the first to permit competition in the local exchange and which has served as the model for the current method. That method involves the use of a *Local Routing Number* (*LRN*) of 10 digits, and makes use of both the SS7 signaling and control network and the Advanced Intelligent Network of which SS7 supports. When a caller dials a telephone number, the originating Central Office consults a *Signaling Control Point* (*SCP*), which dips into a regional database. The database, as appropriate, provides the LRN, as well as the identification code of the CLEC, in order that the call can route to the competitive carrier. *Number Portability Administration Centers* (*NPACs*) serve as clearinghouses for all local operators. Lockheed Martin, which currently is responsible for administration of the North American Numbering Plan (NANP), operates the NPACs. Note that LNP, as the name suggests, is local in nature; in other words, the number is portable between LECs only within the local calling area supported by the serving LEC (i.e., not across ILEC domains and not between calling areas involving toll calls). Currently, LNP is by no means fully implemented. In the meantime, *Interim Number Portability* (*INP*) is provided on the basis of remote call forwarding – a widely available custom calling service provided by the LECs. INP allows calls to the original telephone number to be forwarded to the new telephone number; note that two telephone numbers are required.

As a footnote, 500 numbers and 900 numbers (both of which are geographically independent) currently are not portable across carriers, although the FCC has determined that such portability lies in the public interest [5-2], [5-17], and [5-18].

The ultimate in portability, as we see it today, is the concept of *Personal Communications Services* (*PCS*), which we will explore in Chapter 11. In its full form, PCS involves inexpensive wireless phones that will offer two-way access anywhere and anytime for voice, data, video, and image communications. PCS, at least theoretically, will enable an individual to retain a single number (i.e., logical address) for life. That number will serve many devices (e.g., voice telephones, fax machines, and computer modems), with the caller prompted to make the appropriate selections and with the called party controlling options for the restriction of such privileges. While in the early stages of development and deployment, PCS likely will have great impact early in the 21st century.

Equal Access: Another Special Issue

Equal access is intended to ensure that the end user can access any IXC with equal ease. In other words, a user can dial a long distance call from the residence or business premise simply by dialing the telephone number, without requiring the user to dial special access codes. Equal access is intended to facilitate a competitive environment through removing unnecessary technical barriers. Prior to its implementation in the United States, access to an IXC other than AT&T required dialing a lengthy carrier access number, a lengthy authorization code, and the target telephone number; this requirement clearly placed other carriers at a competitive disadvantage.

The implementation of equal access required that users in a specific geographic area be surveyed and afforded the right to choose a carrier on the basis of preselection. Users who did not respond were assigned a default carrier; such defaults were selected randomly and spread across the available carriers based on their respective local market penetration. All user choices or default selections compiled in a centralized database residing on a database server, which is queried as each call is placed. Based on the originating circuit number, the database is consulted and the call connected through the designated IXC carrier. This same process can apply equally to all outgoing calls, regardless of distance (i.e., local, intraLATA, *inter*LATA, and international), subject to regulatory approval and deployment of the technology. New customers similarly have the right to choose a long distance carrier; if they choose not to do so, they are assigned a carrier based on the same random selection process.

Alternatively, the user can access the carrier through dialing an access number (1010XXX). Such a technique would be used in order to place a call through another carrier in the event of a failure or blockage of the network of the primary carrier. The technique also is used to access a carrier that advertises special rates — generally to their great advantage, not the caller's.

Access charges are intended to compensate the LEC for the costs of connecting the call across expensive local loop facilities, conducting the preselection survey, investing in the database server, and administering the equal access database. While the structure of access charges varies from country to country, they include some combination of Subscriber Line Charges (SLC) and Carrier Access Charges (CACs).

The *Subscriber Line Charge* (*SLC*) is billed to the user by the LEC on a monthly basis. The SLC is a flat-rate, recurring charge that generally varies by type of facility (e.g., residence line, business line, PBX trunk, and FX line). The SLC applies to all users of LEC loops, whether or not they use the LEC network for IXC access. The FCC recently imposed an additional SLC, in the form of a *Digital Port Line Charge* (*DPLC*), for all digital circuits, including ISDN.

The *Carrier Access Charge* (*CAC*) is billed by the LEC to the IXC in two forms. First, flat-rate, recurring charges apply for tandem exchange termination. Second, the *Carrier Common Line Charge* (*CCLC*) is a minutes-of-use charge that applies to each call connected to the IXC.

VoIP: The Next-Generation PSTN?

As I noted earlier in this chapter, a number of next-generation carriers currently are building incredibly capable networks. While some (e.g., Frontier, IXC, and Williams) currently base their networks on conventional circuit-switching technology, others (e.g., Level 3 and Qwest) offer Voice over Internet Protocol (VoIP) in some areas and plan to expand that offering aggressively. VoIP is an incredibly compelling concept, although it has yet to prove itself in the context of a large and complex network such as these carriers are constructing. While I discuss the details of SONET fiber optics, ATM switching, IP, data compression, and other elements of the VoIP mix in other chapters, I find it appropriate to discuss the overall concept now. VoIP may well be the next-generation PSTN. More correctly, IP may well be the dominant protocol in the next generation of networks, which will support a blend of voice, data, fax, video, and multimedia information.

As I noted previously, voice originates as an acoustic signal. In order to transmit voice over a network, it must first be converted to an analog electrical signal format. To send that voice signal over a digital network, it must be encoded into a digital (data) format, and it must be decoded back into an analog signal on the receiving end. The standard encoding technique is Pulse Code Modulation (PCM). PCM requires that the analog signal be sampled 8,000 times per second at precise and regular intervals; in other words, each sample represents exactly 125 microseconds of a voice information stream. Each of the PCM samples comprises 8 data bits, or one data byte (think of it as a *sound byte*). The string of sound bytes in a voice conversation, according to the normal conventions, requires a 64 Kbps channel, also known as a DS0 (Digital Signal level Zero), which is the fundamental building block of all digital telephony. A sound byte might represent an utterance, or it might represent a moment of silence (i.e., a *silence byte*). A voice transmission contains lots of moments of silence. Further, the human conversational convention generally involves only one active direction of the conversation at a given time. In other words, we take turns talking, rather than overtalking each other.

In a conventional PSTN scenario, each of the sound bytes (including silence bytes) associated with one voice transmission is interleaved with those of other transmissions through a process of Time Division Multiplexing (TDM), and flows across the network, from end to end. At every step of the way, every network element must maintain a very tight and highly synchronized timing of the individual sound bytes. Essentially, all of the circuits and switches must ensure that each originating sound byte in a stream of sound bytes is received in exactly the same order and at exactly the same pace as it was created. Only in this fashion will the voice stream retain its fluidity and reasonably natural sound. If a number of voice samples suffer loss or error in network transit, the quality will suffer. If some voice samples arrive in rapid succession and others are delayed, the voice stream will lose its fluidity and will sound "herky-jerky," *if　you k　n o　w wha t　I me　an.* This variability in timing, also known as jitter, is most unpleasant. All of the elements in the network (e.g., access circuits, end offices, multiplexers, transport circuits, repeaters, and tandem switches) must work together in a highly synchronized fashion in order to support *toll quality* voice communications. To ensure that the quality of the voice transmission is preserved, conventional TDM networks commit a time slot for each sampled byte, whether a sound byte or a silence byte. This approach works beautifully, but wastes limited bandwidth resources.

VoIP, like Fax over IP (Chapter 4), involves a totally different type of network. VoIP supports the transmission of voice data over a highly shared packet data network running the IP (Internet Protocol) and involving advanced compression techniques. The first step in VoIP is the collection of a number of PCM voice samples in a temporary memory buffer at the IP gateway. The gateway is a protocol converter, responsible for converting the PCM datastream to a compressed IP packet stream. Physically, the gateway can be under the skin of a PBX or ACD, or can be a standalone CPE device situated between the PBX or ACD switch and the local loop. More likely, the gateway can be in the form of a router situated at the edge of the carrier network, where a CO sits in a conventional PSTN. In either case, the gateway contains a number of *Digital Signal Processors* (*DSPs*), which are silicon chipsets on *Printed Circuit Boards* (*PCBs*) that fit into slots in a cabinet.

Using G.723.1, one of the standard compression algorithms, the buffer in the gateway gathers 160 voice samples, each representing 125 microseconds (1/8000th of a second) of the voice stream. Therefore, the set of 160 samples represents 20 milliseconds (1/50th of a second). The set of 160 samples is evaluated as a discrete set of binary data, and any redundant data (generally quite a lot) is identified. For example, human speech often contains long pauses. Even during a continuous stream of utterances, there are relatively long pauses that are not noticeable to human beings, but which are quite discernable to computer systems. These pauses are noted and compressed out of the data set, with the beginning and the length of the pause being noted. Similarly, an utterance contains a lot of redunnnnnnnnnnnn-dancy. This is noted in a similar fashion. The DSPs are responsible for the process of analog encoding to the digital format through a built-in codec, and for voice compression.

Also, at the gateway, the compressed set of binary data is prepended with an IP control mechanism known as a header, and now is in the form of a data packet. (see Figure 5-8) Each packet, considered a discrete, standalone unit of data or *datagram*, is presented to the network. Each packet independently wends its way through a packet network, comprising various combinations of routers and switches and interconnecting links until it reaches the terminating edge gateway, as identified by the IP address contained in the packet header. (Note that, once again, a logical address is translated into a physical address. In this case, the IP address is a set of bits in the first field of data, and the physical address is a gateway, rather than a local loop.) The key advantage to a packet data network is that all of the resources (i.e., circuits and switches) are highly shared. That is, the packets are presented to the gateway and queued up in a buffer until such time as the packet switch has the available computational resources to process it. In other words, until it can read the address information, consult a routing table, and make a decision as to the specific route across which the packet should be forwarded. Once processed, the packet might queue in a buffer until the selected circuit is available to send it on its way. If there are many switches and links en route, the packet must endure this process many times. At the terminating gateway, the packet is received, the data packet decompressed (reinserting the periods of silence and the redundancies) and decoded, and an approximation of the original acoustic signal is reconstructed.

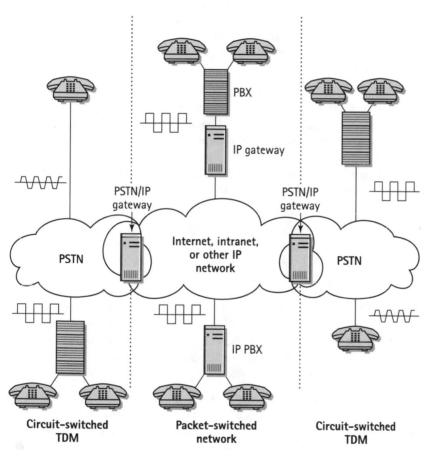

Figure 5-8 VoIP, with alternative methods of network access

This essentially reduces the bandwidth in the network required to support the voice transmission. To the extent that bandwidth demands are reduced, efficiency is increased, more data can be sent over the same circuits and through the same switches in the same period of time, and costs are lowered. If this sounds too good to be true, it's because it is too good to be true...and the reasons are many:

◆ First, the process of compression and decompression takes some time – not much time, but some.

◆ Second, packets encounter variable and unpredictable levels of delay as they wend their way through the network. If the network is under a relatively light load at a particular instant, the routers and switches can fairly instantly process the packet, and the links can become available almost immediately. If the network is under relatively heavy load at a particular instant, the packet might queue up for a much longer period of time. The more routers, switches, and links in a chosen path, the longer the potential level of delay, or *latency*.

◆ Third, the stream of packets might take a relatively short path on one call, and a relatively long path on the next call, all depending on the load on the network at the time. The longer the path, the greater the propagation delay (physical propagation delay is approximately 1 nanosecond per foot of copper-based media, and is greater in optical fiber due to modal dispersion). The more devices (e.g., routers and switches) involved, the more processes involved, and the greater the cumulative delay as the processes are invoked.

◆ Fourth, individual packets in a stream of packets might well take different physical paths. The longer the path, the greater the propagation delay. The more devices (e.g., routers and switches) involved, the more processes involved, and the greater the cumulative delay as the processes are invoked. Note that each packet is treated individually. The final result can be an unacceptable level of jitter, even if the packets arrive in the proper sequence. If the packets arrive out of sequence, they must be resequenced in order to be played in the proper order. If some packets are delayed too long, they may not arrive in time to be played in the proper order, in which case they are rejected.

◆ Fifth, individual packets might suffer errors in transit. Errored data is of no value. In fact, errored data is of decidedly negative value. Once the packet arrives, however, it must either be accepted or rejected. There is no time for a retransmission of an errored voice data packet.

So, the inherent nature of the packet network is problematic. While this approach offers great efficiencies, it also imposes variable and unpredictable levels of delay on the packets. In other words, VoIP is a classic design trade-off between cost and performance. Next-generation VoIP networks propose to optimize this trade-off in several ways:

◆ First, next-generation carriers deploy gateways (i.e., routers) only at the edges of the network, where the most complex decisions must be made and where the most involved (read time-consuming) processes must be invoked. They deploy high-speed ATM switches in the core of the networks, where speed is of the essence. The routers and switches currently can run at speeds of 1 Tbps, at least according to the design specifications.

◆ Second, the carriers define paths from each gateway to every other gateway, thereby ensuring that all packets travel the same route. Therefore, all of the packet voice transmissions from San Francisco to Dallas, for example, likely will suffer reasonably similar levels of delay, at least.

◆ Third, the carriers deploy incredibly high-speed optical fiber transmission systems in the core. Each fiber currently can support as many as 32 lightwaves (light frequencies), with each currently running at a rate of as much as 10 Gbps and supporting approximately 130,000 voice channels at standard PCM rates of 64 Kbps. Hundreds of fibers lay along a given path.

◆ Fourth, the compression algorithms are extreme, and will become more so. Traditional PCM voice requires 64 Kbps, which actually is substantially overstated, as we will explore in Chapter 7. VoIP will require as little as 5.3 Kbps, depending on the specific algorithm selected, plus IP overhead.

To illustrate the concept of compressed, packetized voice, consider the following analogy. You have become concerned about your health. You finally decided to take your grandmother's advice and include a daily bowl of stewed prunes in your diet. (Your grandmother has lived a long and healthy life, but isn't much of a gourmet!) You call your grandmother and ask her to pick some prunes from her orchard and send them to you on a regular basis. Daily, your grandmother picks prune plums (bytes), puts 160 of them (data set) in a bowl (buffer), dehydrates (compresses) them, removing the water (silence) in order to reduce their weight and volume (bandwidth), and lower the cost of postage (network cost). The result is prunes. Every day she sends you a small, numbered box (packet) of prunes through the mail, along with specific instructions that you eat them every day, at exactly the same time of the morning, and in exactly the same order in which she mailed them to you. In that fashion, you always will have fresh prunes for breakfast and you will remain regular (perfectly timed). You follow her instructions precisely for some number of days. Each day you open a box of prunes, put them in a bowl (buffer) and soak the contents in order to reinsert the water (silence), thereby reconstituting (decompressing) them to an approximation of their original form. The disaster strikes. One box (packet) of prunes (sound bytes) arrives in sequence, but crushed (errored). As the contents (compressed voice payload) are inedible (unintelligible), you throw away (discard) the box and its contents. The next day, the postal system fails you, and no box of prunes arrives (latency, or delay). The next day, two boxes arrive (jitter); you eat two bowls of prunes for breakfast, and regret it. You call your grandmother and ask her to send the daily prune ration via Federal

Express (high-speed network). They almost always arrive every day, and at exactly at the same time. Each box (packet) still wends its way through the network independently, but the overbuilt (broadband) network of high-speed access circuits (couriers), high-speed jumbo jets (transport circuits), and high-speed airports and processing centers (routers and switches) provides a good balance of cost and performance. Federal Express does such a good job that they lower their costs. You are such a good customer that Federal Express offers you a discount; the total cost compares favorably to that of growing your own prune plums.

Now, back to the bottom line, so to speak. Circuit switching and TDM are inherently wasteful, but perform well for stream-oriented transmissions, such as voice. Packet networks are inherently efficient, but are not intended to support voice. Next-generation carriers overcome this quandary through a combination of effectively over-engineering the packet network and using complex compression algorithms and buffers to improve performance. While the bottom line is yet to be fully calculated, pro forma analyses suggest that the result may well be pleasant in terms of cost and at least acceptable in terms of performance. Piper Jaffray estimates that the total IP telephony market reached U.S.$83.9 million in 1997, reached U.S.$419.3 million in 1998, and will reach U.S.$14.7 billion in 2003 [5-19].

References

[5-1]   Brooks, John. *Telephone: The First Hundred Years*. Harper & Row, 1976.

[5-2]   *1996 MultiMedia Telecommunications Market Review and Forecast*. MultiMedia Telecommunications Association, 1996.

[5-3]   *Engineering and Operations in the Bell System*. Bell Laboratories, 1977.

[5-4]   Greene, Tim. "Bells Bond to Spread the Word on New Area Codes." *Network World*, May 20, 1996.

[5-5]   Potter, David C. "Cracking the NANP Code." *Telecommunications*, October 1995.

[5-6]   Potter, David C. "Surviving the North American Numbering Plan." *TeleProfessional*, March 1996.

[5-7]   Toth, Victor J. "Winners and Losers in FCC's New NANP System." *Business Communications Review*, October 1995.

[5-8]   Toth, Victor J. "Preparing for a New Universe of Toll-Free Numbers." *Business Communications Review*, November 1995.

[5-9]   Greene, Tim. "Phone Numbers Are Running Out." *Network World*, May 20, 1996.

[5-10]   Rohde, David. "Those #$ (&%*!% Area Codes." *Network World*, September 18, 1996.

[5-11]   Tunstall, W. Brooke. *Disconnecting Parties*. McGraw-Hill, Inc., 1985.

[5-12]   Elbert, Bruce R. *Private Telecommunication Networks*. Artech House, 1989.

[5-13]   Lawyer, Gail. "Out THERE Air Wars?" *X-Change*, January 1999.

[5-14]   Rebber, Roger. "Parade of Carrier Options." *Call Center Magazine*, February 1996.

[5-15]   Taff, Anita. "Follow-Me Phoning." *Mobile Office*, November 1995.

[5-16]   Greene, Tim and Wexler, Joanie. "Follow-Me Phone Numbers Available." *Network World*, February 15, 1995.

[5-17]   Seybold, Andrew M. "Follow-Me Phone Numbers." *Mobile Office*, August 1995.

[5-18]   Toth, Victor J. "The FCC's Complex Plans for Local Number Portability." *Business Communications Review*, September 1995.

[5-19]   Jackson, Edward R. and Schroepper, Andrew M. "IP Telephony. Driving The Open Communications Revolution." Piper Jaffray, February 1999.

General References

Elbert, Bruce R. *Private Telecommunication Networks*. Artech House, 1989.
Engineering and Operations in the Bell System. Bell Laboratories, 1977.

Gasman, Lawrence. *Manager's Guide to the New Telecommunications Network*. Artech House, 1988.

Introduction to Telecommunications. AG Communications Systems, 1990.

Keen, Peter G.W. and Cummins, J. Michael. *Networks in Action*. Wadsworth Publishing Company, 1994.

Sexton, Mike and Reid, Andy. *Transmission Networking: SONET and the Synchronous Digital Hierarchy*. Artech House, 1992.

Sherman, Kenneth. *Data Communications: A Users Guide*. Reston Publishing Company, Inc., 1981.

Chapter 6

Fundamentals of Data Communications

...I submit to the public a small machine by my invention, by means of which you alone may, without any effort, perform all the operations of arithmetic, and may be relieved of the work which has often times fatigued your spirit....Blaise Pascal, 1623-1662.

Little did the humble Pascal understand the complexity of computing systems which would develop over the next 300 or so years, much less the requirement for networking them. Dr. George Stibitz first demonstrated the ability to communicate with a remote calculating machine in 1940. At Dartmouth College in Hanover, New Hampshire, Dr. Stibitz explained and demonstrated the use of a calculator newly developed by Bell Telephone Laboratories. The calculator was located in New York City and communications took place over standard telegraph lines [6-1]. Contemporary computers, even the most lowly personal computers (PCs), ship from factories with communications capabilities that astounded experts of even 10 years past.

Up to this point, we have explored the world of voice communications. During that process, we learned that many of the devices and circuits in the Public Switched Telephone Network are digital in nature. In large part, the contemporary PSTN is a data network, transporting and switching voice data. This chapter introduces the basic concepts of the communications of computer data. Reflecting the reality of contemporary systems and networks, the balance of this book truly focuses on computer data.

In order to comprehend the intricacy of contemporary data communications systems and networks, it is necessary to develop a solid understanding of certain basic concepts. These definitions and concepts extend across all technologies and service offerings, from the historical to the most contemporary. The historical is more than a footnote; it is important for purposes of understanding. Indeed, the contemporary and future networks are built on those fundamental concepts.

This chapter first addresses the concept of functional domains – as in Chapter 5, which dealt with the world of PSTN voice communications. I will explain terminal equipment, communications equipment, and communication software, and provide a detailed discussion of modems and DSUs/CSUs. We will explore the concept of protocols at length, with discussion of basic protocol dimensions and issues. I also will discuss computer network architectures, with emphasis on IBM's *Systems Network Architecture (SNA)* and the *Open Systems Integration (OSI)* reference model. Finally, we will pause to consider the importance of security in data systems and networks.

Functional Domains

Functional domains comprise the spheres of influence exerted by the various network elements that perform specific tasks in a data network. Data terminal equipment, data communications equipment, communications software, switches, and transmission facilities all are physical elements of such a network — each performing specific functions, and all supported by a signaling and control system. Since we explored the general nature of circuit switches in Chapters 1 and 5, we will not repeat that discussion; nor will we reexamine signaling systems, which I discussed in Chapter 5.

Data Terminal Equipment (DTE)

The data equivalent of Customer Premise Equipment (CPE) in the voice world, *Data Terminal Equipment (DTE)* comprises the computer transmit and receive equipment — including a wide variety of *dumb* terminals, or terminals without embedded intelligence in the form of programmed logic. Such terminals are devices that merely provide a user interface to a more capable host computer; examples of dumb terminals include the Hewlett-Packard HP2521P and the Televideo 950. Semi-intelligent terminals (e.g., IBM 317x and 327x) possess a limited amount of intelligence, enabling them to perform certain, limited processes, independent of the intelligence contained in the host. Intelligent terminals generally are in the form of Personal Computers (PCs) that are networked to a host computer. Such devices are highly capable in their own right, although and in this context, they often are linked across a network to an even more capable host. At the top of the terminal food chain are client workstations, highly intelligent and capable devices that access a more capable server in a *client/server* environment. In such an operating environment, clients' requirements for access to files, applications, and network communications software are satisfied by a server which typically is accessed across a LAN (Local Area Network). As a result, the client workstation can perform certain appropriate functions (e.g., screen formatting) related to the specific user task at hand, while the server's memory and processing power is dedicated to the performance of tasks accomplished more effectively on a centralized basis.

DTE also is in the form of *host computers* such as mainframes and midrange (minicomputer) computers. Host computers, also known as *host nodes*, are highly capable devices with substantial processing power and storage memory. Hosts also, at least theoretically, are carefully administered to ensure that they operate successfully and reliably. Hosts also serve as highly effective information repositories, with the data backed up and archived on external storage media such as magnetic tapes.

Data Communications Equipment (DCE)

Also known as *Data Circuit Terminating Equipment* (*DCTE*), *Data Communications Equipment* (*DCE*) is the equipment that interfaces the DTE to the network and resolves any issues of incompatibility between those domains in the process. Incompatibility issues can include digital vs. analog, voltage level, transmission speed, and bit density. DCE includes modems, DSUs and CSUs, and Front-End Processors (FEPs), all of which I discuss in greater detail later in this chapter.

Communications Software

Communications software often is required and generally is embedded in the computer operating system; alternatively, it can take the form of a systems task under the control of the computer's operating system. The role of communications software is to assist the operating system in managing local and remote terminal access to host resources, to manage security, and to perform certain checkpoint activities. The remote terminals interface to the operating system access methods, which contain the specific code required to transfer data across the network channels between the devices. An example of an access method includes IBM's *VTAM (Virtual Telecommunications Access Method)*.

Alternatively, commercial communications management software can control and manage access to the host. IBM's *CICS (Customer Information Control System)* is such a product. This software resolves contention issues between diverse applications without impacting programs or terminals. It handles polling, selection, and program interrupts, thereby ensuring minimum response time. It also resolves error conditions at both the data and line levels. *RAM (Random Access Memory)* maintains CICS and other *TSR (Terminate-and-Stay-Resident)* software.

Networks

Networks provide the connections between computer resources in order to accommodate the flow of information. Networks support the logical transfer of data during a communications session through the establishment of paths, circuits, or channels over a physical medium. The network can be in the form of a Local Area Network (LAN), a Metropolitan Area Network (MAN), or a Wide Area Network (WAN). These networks support communications over areas of increasing geographic scope. Data LANs, MANs, and WANs, which I discuss in later chapters, also can be interconnected.

Switches

Developed in support of voice communications, circuit switches serve for the flexible interconnection of circuits, and in the process provide a communications path that supports a continuous stream of transmission. Traditional circuit switches remain widely used in support of data communications, although they lost much ground to packet switches during the past 30 years. Frame and cell switches, highly evolved forms of packet switches, have appeared in recent years, and represent the switching techniques for data communications far into the future.

Packet switches are highly advanced computerized switching devices that have substantial capacity as well as the ability to share high-capacity transmission systems among large numbers of individual user transmissions. In capsule, such switches read the destination address of each segment (e.g., packet, frame, or cell) of data in a data stream. Each individual packet, frame, or cell then is forwarded through the switch and across the network. As all packet network resources are highly shared, the network operates with much greater efficiency than does a network based on circuit switching. I discuss packet, frame, and cell switching in detail in later chapters.

DCE: An Expanded View

While we have discussed, and will discuss, data networks and switches in great detail in other chapters, this is a convenient and meaningful place to pause and explore the concept and detail of several types of data communications equipment. Specifically, let's examine modems, codecs, terminal adapters, CSUs and DSUs, and Front-End Processors.

Modems

*Modems mo*dulate and *dem*odulate signals. In other words, they change the characteristics of the signal in some way. Modems, as discussed in this chapter, are of several basic types: line drivers, short-haul modems, and conventional modems. The term also is used to describe a wide variety of other devices such as ISDN Terminal Adapters (TAs) and ADSL Splitters, each of which we explore in subsequent chapters.

LINE DRIVERS

Line drivers actually are interface converters, rather than modems in the classic sense. Line drivers extend the distance of a digital connection, within finite limits, by converting the digital signal to a low-voltage, low-impedance signal that can transmitt more effectively and over longer distances over dedicated, specially conditioned twisted pair circuits. For example, the RS-232 specification (more correctly known as EIA-232) generally limits the distance between devices to 50 feet at transmission rates of 56 Kbps; at lower speeds, line drivers can reshape the digital pulses to extend that distance. At speeds of up to 9.6 Kbps, line drivers can extend that limitation to 500-5,000 feet. You can extend the distance farther through the cascading of line drivers in a unidirectional network; bi-directional communications requires separate pairs and separate sets of line drivers.

SHORT-HAUL (LIMITED-DISTANCE) MODEMS

Short-haul modems are used where line drivers fail in terms of either capacity or distance. Short-haul modems can work at distances between 5,000 and 100,000 feet, with speed-dependent distance. Also known as *limited-distance modems*, they usually are used for private line and hardwired links, but can operate over local loop facilities.

CONVENTIONAL MODEMS

Conventional modems provide for digital communication across an analog circuit, accomplishing the digital-to-analog conversion in order to resolve that dimension of incompatibility between the DTE and the network. AT&T set the original de facto standards for modems with the introduction of the DataPhone in 1961 [6-2]. Currently, standards are international in nature, designated as the *V.xx* family of ITU-T Recommendations. The digital input is in the form of varying electrical voltages, which represent binary *1*s and *0*s. The output from the modem is a modulated analog carrier wave, which can be modulated in terms of its amplitude, frequency, or phase, or a combination. Through this process, the *1*s and *0*s of the digital data world can be sent over the POTS (Plain Old Telephone Service) voice network. While we prefer a networks that are digital from end-to-end for reasons that include error performance and bandwidth, this often is not the case. In developed countries, of course, the core of the carrier network generally is fully digital in nature. In consideration of lower costs and greater availability, however, the local loop often is analog in residential and small business applications.

It certainly is worth mentioning, and even emphasizing, that modems are unique in the wired world in terms of their portability. Essentially, modems work virtually anywhere. Indeed, contemporary *road warriors* would be lost without the advantage of modem access to the Internet from hotel rooms, airports, and client sites. While the modem speed may be constrained by the internal processes of an intermediate PBX, the device is absolutely indispensable for remote access to e-mail and other applications through the Internet and World Wide Web, a corporate intranet, or another IP-based network.

Now, let's consider the way conventional modems work using a simplified example. While researching this book through the World Wide Web, sending drafts to various editors and to my publisher, and otherwise fooling around, I used a modem connection. (GTE doesn't offer ADSL in my Carrier Serving Area, and my Internet Service Provider doesn't support ISDN.) To set up the modem connection to my ISP, I click an icon and the modem internal to my desktop computer "goes off-hook," gets a dial tone from the Central Office at the edge of the PSTN, and dials the telephone number of the local ISP. The ISP's modem answers, and the two modems pass a set of data back and forth in a process known as *handshaking*, in order to negotiate the basis on which the communication will be conducted. Specifically, each modem identifies itself and its capabilities to the other through a set of data organized into a frame. The frames are passed simultaneously between the modems, with one using a relatively high range of frequencies and the other a relatively low range. Each modem knows exactly the format of the data bits and fields within the frame, as each is based on standards in the form of ITU-T Recommendations. The data is passed at the rate of 2400 baud — the maximum expected available signaling rate, internationally, over an analog network. (Recall from Chapter 1 that baud rate refers to the number of signal events, or signal transitions; bit rate refers to the rate of information transfer.) Assuming that everything is just right in the network (i.e., the analog local loops are in good condition and there are no issues of interference at the moment), the modems then start to pass data at 2400 baud over the analog local loops by modulating the sine waves. Note that modem networks are balanced and symmetrical; in other words, there are two modems, and they each must be able to communicate on the same basis. Note also that the lowest common denominator always rules — the more capable modem must adapt to the capabilities of the lesser. Now, let's examine the specifics of the modulation techniques, remembering that each baud can be represented by one or more sine waves. Also note that each baud can support one or more bits.

AMPLITUDE MODULATION (AM) *Amplitude Modulation* (*AM*) involves the modulation of the amplitude of the analog sine wave, as depicted in Figure 6-1. Using a (single-bit) AM technique, each *1* bit entering the transmitting modem is expressed as a relatively high-amplitude sine wave or series of sine waves. Each *0* bit is expressed as one or more low-amplitude sine waves, with the high and low levels defined in terms of a reference level. At 2400 baud, this *unibit* technique yields a transmission rate of 2400 bps.

It is possible to express multiple bits by defining four levels of amplitude. In a *dibit* (2-bit) coding scheme, for instance, the lowest level of amplitude represents a *00* bit pattern, the next highest a *01* bit pattern, the next a *10*, and the highest a *11*. In this fashion, the speed of data transmission is doubled at the same analog line speed; i.e., at 2400 baud, the transmission rate is 4800 bps. Thereby, the connection time is halved and the cost of transmission reduces considerably. Amplitude modulation rarely operates individually because it is highly sensitive to the impacts of attenuation and line noise. Note that the appropriate regulatory body (e.g., FCC) sets the maximum allowable amplitude level.

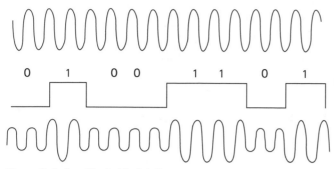

Figure 6-1 Amplitude Modulation

FREQUENCY MODULATION (FM) Also known as *Frequency Shift Keying (FSK)*, *Frequency Modulation (FM)* is the sole technique used in low-speed, Hayes-compatible modems. FSK involves the modulation of the frequency of the analog sine waves (see Figure 6-2). Using a single-bit FM technique, *1* bits are transmitted as relatively low frequency signals, and *0* bits as high-frequency signals, with low and high frequencies related to a reference frequency. Again, the benefits of dibit transmission can be realized by defining four levels of frequency, with each sine wave or set of sine waves representing a 2-bit pattern (*00, 01, 10*, and *11*).

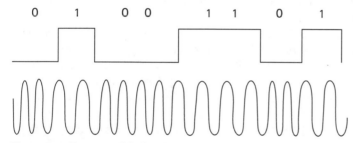

Figure 6-2 Frequency Modulation

PHASE MODULATION (PM) *Phase Modulation (PM)*, or *Phase Shift Keying (PSK)*, involves the carefully synchronized shifting of the position of the sine wave (see Figure 6-3). Using a single-bit technique, the continuous sine wave pattern is interrupted and restarted at the baseline to indicate a change in value (e.g., from a *1* bit to a *0* bit). Once again, the advantages of dibit transmission can be achieved by defining four phase shifts separated by 90 degrees (0, 90, 180, and 270). Through the definition of eight phase shifts separated by 45 degrees (0, 45, 90, 135, and so on), contemporary modems can affect *tribit* transmission, achieving 3 bits of data per signal.

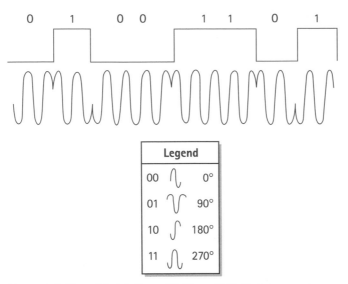

Figure 6-3 Phase Modulation with Phase Shift Keying examples

AMPLITUDE MODULATION AND PHASE SHIFT KEYING AM and PSK often are used in combination. For example, *Quadrature Amplitude Modulation* (*QAM*) combines differential phase and amplitude shifts to achieve 16 distinct states; thereby, 4 bits can be represented with a single signal impulse. At a signaling rate of 2400 baud, a transmission rate of 9600 bps can be achieved. The ITU-T V.29 recommendation specifies two possible amplitude values for each of eight phase angles. The combined use of multiple levels of amplitude and phase shift yield transmission rates of as much as 28.8 Kbps over voice-grade analog circuits, using conventional high-speed V.34 modems. Transmission speed improves to 33.6 Kbps through V.34+ modems.

Conventional modems can be external or internal. They also can take the form of a PCMCIA (Personal Computer Memory Card Industry Association) card, which fits into a slot on a laptop computer. *Multiplexing modems* perform some of the functions of a multiplexer, but at a more limited level. Multiple data streams can be transmitted over a single circuit. *Voice/data modems* permit voice and data transmission over the same circuit, with data transmitting during lulls in the voice conversation. Data rates up to 28.8 Kbps can be achieved, although the quality of the voice signal may suffer considerably with such a high data rate coexisting on the same circuit.

Conventional modems can be characterized along a number of dimensions including asynchronous vs. synchronous, compression, diagnostics, equalization, gain control, and band limitation.

ASYNCHRONOUS VS. SYNCHRONOUS Modems can be either asynchronous or synchronous. Asynchronous modems transmit one character at a time, with the receiving device relying on start and stop bits to separate transmitted characters. Synchronous modems prove much faster, as the signal is *synchronized* (timed) by a *Transmit Clock* (*TC*) in either the transmit modem or the transmit terminal. The paired modems synchronize on that clocking pulse in order to distinguish between blocks of data being transmitted, rather than identifying each individual character in a transmission. When large amounts of data are transmitting, synchronous modems increase the efficiency of data transfer, resulting in increased speed of transfer and lower associated transmission cost [6-3].

DIAGNOSTICS Diagnostics is a characteristic of higher-speed, more expensive modems. Such modems can test their internal clock, transmitter, and receive circuits. Additionally, they may have the capability to monitor their performance and even diagnose certain conditions contributing to performance degradation. Further, they are manageable through higher-level *Element Management Systems* (EMSs) — typically located remotely and capable of managing large numbers of modems and modem pools (groups of modems to which access is shared among multiple users).

ERROR CORRECTION Error correction capabilities are included in some modems; a modem protocol known as *MNP* (*Microcom Networking Protocol*) was among the first. While proprietary error correction software remains embedded in certain modems, the ITU-T V.42 and subsequent generations of modems have standardized this function.

COMPRESSION Compression is a characteristic of high-speed modems, enabling the transmission of multiple bits with a single signal (sine wave) or change in signal. Compression makes use of digital shorthand to represent a large number of bits in a specific sequence through a fewer number of analog signals or signal changes in a specific sequence. Compression rates of 4:1 are routine in many contemporary modems. In addition to numerous proprietary compression schemes, there are standard techniques such as those embedded in modems designed in compliance with ITU-T Recommendation V.42bis. The term *bis* comes from Latin, meaning *second*; in other words, the second and enhanced release of the standard. Third releases are designated *ter*, translated from Latin as *third*.

EQUALIZERS *Equalizers* compensate for channel distortion, thereby improving transmission rate and error performance.

AUTOMATIC GAIN CONTROL (AGC) AMPLIFIERS *AGC* (*Automatic Gain Control*) amplifiers serve to adjust for amplitude variations and to ensure that the incoming signal is of a constant strength.

BAND-LIMITING FILTERS Band-limiting filters improve error performance by managing the frequencies of the incoming signal, filtering out any extraneous frequencies.

56 KBPS MODEMS: THE CONVENTIONAL MODEM BECOMES UNCONVENTIONAL

A relatively new modem technology, 56 Kbps modems are asymmetric in nature, providing a maximum of 56 Kbps downstream and 33.6 Kbps upstream. US Robotics (now 3Com) was the first to develop 56 Kbps technology; Lucent, Rockwell, Motorola, and others soon followed with modems based on a different compression algorithm. The two proprietary (read incompatible) approaches, known respectively as *x2* (28.8 Kbps or so, times 2) and *K56flex* (*Kbps flexible*), were standardized in November, 1998 with the ITU-T Recommendation V.90. Generally, the modems are combined data/fax modems because they have the ability to emulate a fax machine. They also generally consist of a combination of firmware and hardware, although some are entirely software-based. (Note that firmware is faster, but software is more flexible.) Both x2 and K56flex modems are upgradeable to V.90 through a software download, although you can expect some performance degradation when connecting upgraded x2 and K56flex modems.

The actual transmission speed realized in either direction depends on the characteristics of the analog local loop, as is always the case with rate-adaptive modems. The performance of the local loop is sensitive to loop length and such anomalies as mixed wire gauges, poor mechanical splices, *bridged taps* (multiple appearances of the same cable pair, usually as a result of old and unused connections to other customer premises), and poorly insulated splice casings. EMI (ElectroMagnetic Interference) caused by electrical storms, radio transmissions, electric motors, and other sources of electromagnetic energy also clearly impact modem performance. Additionally, high-speed transmissions (e.g., T-1 and ADSL) taking place on twisted pairs in proximity within the same cable may affect transmission speed. As high-speed transmissions involve signals of high frequencies, high amplitude, or both signals, they can interfere with other cable pairs. In other words, 56 Kbps represents the maximum, rather than the norm, over an unconditioned cable pair—just as is the case with 33.6 Kbps through a V.34+ modem. 56 Kbps modems are able to achieve this high theoretical transmission rate by virtue of the fact that the PSTN largely is digital in nature; in fact, the modems depend on it.

A 56 Kbps modem configuration (see Figure 6-4) requires that each end of the connection have installed a compatible modem connected through the circuit-switched PSTN. At the originating user end, the PC connects to the PSTN through a 56 Kbps modem via an analog local loop. The serving Central Office as well as the entire carrier network(s) must be digital, including both the originating and terminating Central Offices, all tandem offices, and all transmission facilities. At the terminating end (e.g., corporate intranet site or ISP), the local loop connection must be digital (e.g., T-carrier or ISDN). Matching 56 Kbps technology must be in place at the terminating device, typically in the form of an access server or switch. As the transmissions need suffer only one D-to-A-to-D (digital-to-analog-to-digital) conversion process, the potential amount of quantizing noise is limited, resulting in higher speed transmission without sacrificing error performance. Since the PSTN in the United States uses PCM (Pulse Code Modulation) for voice-grade, A-to-D conversions, the theoretical transmission speed limit is 64 Kbps, symmetric; intrusive signaling and control is assumed to rob 8 Kbps, thereby limiting the theoretical effective transmission rate to 56 Kbps. While bit-robbing generally is not a problem outside the United States, the international ADPCM (Adaptive Differential PCM) standard reduces usable bandwidth to effectively 32 Kbps, thereby causing the 56 Kbps modem to throttle back. (See Chapter 7 for detailed discussions of T-carrier, PCM, and ADPCM Kbps.)

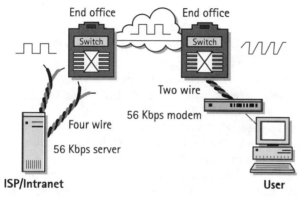

Figure 6-4 56 Kbps modem configuration

The asymmetric nature of these modems is due to several factors. First, the upstream relationship between the modem and the network is not highly precise. In other words, the digital network cannot interpret the modulated sine waves without the introduction of some quantizing noise, which limits the effective throughput. Actually, it can be done, it's just that you need a relatively sophisticated (read expensive) modem. Therefore, asymmetry is less expensive. As the manufacturer makes its profits on end-user modems in volume, the price point is important. If enough end users are attracted to high-speed, inexpensive modems, the lower volume of the much more expensive software for 56 Kbps servers yields profits, as well. Second, the end user generally does not require full 56 Kbps bandwidth on a symmetric basis, as most of the bandwidth is required downstream (i.e., downstream from the network). After all, the bandwidth-intensive graphics generally are downloaded from the World Wide Web of a corporate intranet site; upstream, the user often sends only a few mouse clicks or keyboard commands or, perhaps, a textual e-mail. If users need to send bandwidth-intensive files upstream, they are not worse off than with a V.34+ modem.

Notably, 56 Kbps modems also are V.34+ modems. Assuming that the terminating modem is V.34+ or lesser, the 56 Kbps modem "falls back" to that standard, which supports symmetric transmission at 33.6 Kbps. (Note that the lowest common denominator always determines the maximum level of performance.) Also notably, the fine print on the boxes of the 56 Kbps modems notes that they currently are limited to 53.3 Kbps because they cannot exceed FCC amplitude (signal strength) limitations. (Note, again, the lowest common denominator rule – the network, in this case.) The FCC established this limitation many years ago in order to minimize the likelihood that transmissions on a cable pair might cause interference on adjacent pairs in the same cable sheath. While the FCC is considering relaxing this restriction, it is clear that the modem manufacturers – rather than the FCC – are responsible for the fine print on the modem boxes [6-4] through [6-8].

Codecs

The reverse conversion of analog to digital is necessary in situations where it is advantageous to send analog information across a digital circuit. Certainly, this often is the case in carrier networks where huge volumes of analog voice are digitized and sent across high-capacity, digital circuits. This requirement also exists where high-capacity digital circuits connect premise-based, analog PBX or KTS voice systems to Central Office Exchanges or to other PBXs or KTSs.

The device that accomplishes the A-to-D conversion is known as a *codec*. Codecs *code* an analog input into a digital (data) format on the transmit side of the connection, reversing the process – or *dec*oding the information on the receive side in order to reconstitute the analog signal. Codecs are used widely to convert analog voice and video to digital format, and to reverse the process on the receiving end.

Terminal Adapters (TAs) and NT-Xs

Terminal Adapters (*TAs*) are interface adapters for connecting one or more non-ISDN devices to an ISDN network. TAs, which are ISDN DCE, are equivalent to protocol or interface converters for use with equipment that does not have ISDN capability built in; the TAs must be tuned exactly to the specific terminal equipment. *Network Termination* (*NT*), in ISDN networks, is a function accomplished through the use of Network Termination logic embedded in the carrier network and the user equipment. *NT2* is an interface to an intelligent device responsible for the user's side of the connection to the network, performing such functions as multiplexing and switching; a NT2 is the interface to an ISDN-compatible PABX or router. *NT1* is responsible for interfacing to the carrier's side of the connection, performing such functions as signal conversion and maintenance of the local loop's electrical characteristics. These functions resemble those provided by Data Service Units (DSUs) and Channel Service Units (CSUs).

Channel Service Units (CSUs) and Data Service Units (DSUs)

Channel Service Units (*CSUs*) and *Data Service Units* (*DSUs*) are devices which, in combination, serve to interface the user environment to an electrically based, digital local loop. In contemporary systems, CSUs and DSUs generally combine into a single device known variously as a *CSU/DSU, CDSU,* or *ISU (Integrated Service Unit)*. It typically appears in the form of a chip set on a printed circuit board found under the skin of another device such as a channel bank, multiplexer (MUX), switch, or router. They are used in a wide variety of digital voice and data networks, including DDS and T-carrier, which I discuss in detail in Chapter 7.

CSUs

Channel Service Units provide the customer interface to the circuit. They also permit the isolation of the DTE/CPE from the network, for purposes of network testing. CSU functions include electrical isolation from the circuit for purposes of protection from aberrant voltages, serving the same function as a protector in the voice world. Additionally, the CSU can respond to a command from the carrier to close a contact, temporarily isolating the DTE domain from the carrier domain. This enables the carrier to conduct a *loopback test* in order to test the performance characteristics of the local loop from the serving Central Office to the CSU and back to the Central Office. Many contemporary CSUs also have the ability to perform various line analyses, including monitoring the signal level.

The CSU also serves to interface the DTE domain to the carrier domain in an electrical environment. For instance, within the DTE, *1* bits commonly are represented as positive (+) voltages and *0* bits as null (*0*) voltages. The network requires that *1* bits be alternating + and – voltages and that the *0* bits be *0* voltages. Further, the network requires assurance that *ones density* is achieved. Depending on the carrier network, 15-80 zeros can be transmitted in a row as long the density of ones is at least 12.5 percent (1 in 8) over a specified interval of time. CSUs insert, or *stuff, 1* bits on a periodic basis in order to ensure that the various network elements maintain synchronization.

The CSU also serves to provide signal amplification and generates *keep alive* signals to maintain the circuit in the event of a DTE transmission failure. Finally, the CSU stores in temporary memory data describing its performance in order that it might be considered by an upstream network management system.

Smart CSUs increasingly are positioned as *Integrated Access Devices* (*IADs*). These multiport devices support interfaces to voice, data, and video devices such as PBXs, routers, and videoconferencing units. The programmable IAD supports bandwidth allocation for the various devices, enabling them to share a single T-1 or other digital facility.

DSUs

Data Service Units convert the DTE unipolar signal into a bipolar signal demanded by the network. DSU functions include regeneration of digital signals, insertion of control signals, signal timing, and reformatting.

Front-End Processors (FEPs)

Front-End Processors (*FEPs*) combine the functions of a concentrator and a message switch. In other words, they have the ability to concentrate and switch traffic between multiple terminals and among groups of terminals in order to share a single circuit for access to mainframe resources. They also serve as an interface to *Wide Area Network (WAN)* circuits to serve mainframe resources to remote terminals. Most FEPs are midrange computers which, in turn, connect to the primary host mainframe; FEPs have their own databases. FEPs provide additional functions including error detection and correction, queuing, editing validation, and limited application processing. While the mainframe clearly could perform such tasks, it is more cost-effective to apply a lower order computer to the performance of such mundane and highly repetitive tasks – thereby reserving the power of the mainframe for more difficult and demanding tasks in support of user-oriented applications.

Protocol Basics

Protocols are rules of behavior. In the context of data communications, protocols are the procedures employed to ensure the orderly exchange of information between devices on a data link, data network, or system. Protocols comprise standards which, at a basic level, include the dimensions of line setup, transmission mode, code set, and non-data exchanges of information such as error control (detection and correction). Protocols have two major functions: handshaking and line discipline [6-9].

Handshaking – The sequence that occurs between the devices over the circuit, establishing the fact that the circuit is available and operational. The handshaking process also establishes the level of device compatibility, determines the speed of transmission by mutual agreement, and so on. Devices accomplish the process of handshaking by passing frames of data back and forth in order to negotiate the basis on which they will communicate. Communications always will be in consideration of the least capable device, as the lowest common denominator always prevails.

Line Discipline – The sequence of network operations that actually transmits and receives the data, controls errors in transmission, deals with the sequencing of message sets (e.g., packets, blocks, frames, and cells), and provides for confirmation or validation of data received.

Protocol Converters – Devices that translate from one native protocol into another (e.g., from ASCII to IBM SNA/SDLC).

Gateways – Hardware/software combinations that connect devices running different native protocols. In other words, gateways run gateway protocols for purposes of protocol conversion – perhaps at all layers of the OSI Reference Model (i.e., from the Physical Layer to the Applications Layer). In addition to protocol conversion, gateways provide a gateway connection between incompatible networks; examples include X.25-to-Frame Relay gateways and T-carrier-to-E-carrier International Gateway Facilities (IGFs). In the contemporary data communications domain, gateways commonly are known as routers.

Protocol Analyzers – Diagnostic tools for displaying and analyzing communications protocols. Analyzers enable technicians, engineers, and managers to test the performance of the network to ensure that the systems and the network function according to specifications. LAN managers, for instance, use protocol analyzers to perform network maintenance and troubleshooting and to plan network upgrades and expansions.

Line Set-Up: Connectivity

A very basic protocol issue involves the manner in which the circuit is set up between devices. There are three alternatives: simplex, half-duplex, and full-duplex (see Figure 6-5).

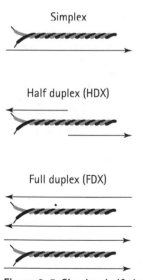

Figure 6-5 Simplex, half-duplex (HDX) and full-duplex (FDX) transmission

Simplex Unidirectional transmission. The information flows in one direction across the circuit, with no capability to support a response in the other direction. Simplex circuits are analogous to escalators, doorbells, fire alarms, and security systems. Contemporary applications for simplex circuits, although rare, include remote station printers, card readers, and alarm systems (e.g., fire, smoke, and intrusion alarms). Generally speaking, simplex transmission is conducted across dedicated circuits of low capacity. An intrusion alarm, for instance, requires very little bandwidth because the only information sent across the circuit indicates that an electrical contact has been broken. The intrusion alarm circuit must be dedicated from end-to-end (e.g., contact to central alarm station) in order to avoid the possibility that either failure or congestion in a switch or other intermediate device prevents the alarm from being registered. The circuit must be simplex to prevent the alarm from being reset remotely, rather than investigated locally. Simplex circuits often are tariffed as burglar alarm circuits.

Half-Duplex (HDX) Transmission operates in both directions, although not simultaneously. HDX generally is used for relatively low-speed transmission, usually involving two-wire, analog circuits provided on a circuit-switched basis through the PSTN. Since the circuit must be turned around in order to support the change in direction of the conversation, it tends to limit the speed of conversational data communications. Line turnaround time is a limiting factor – within the range of 50-500 milliseconds (thousandths of a second), depending on the length of the circuit. In many environments, HDX is the predominant transmission mode, although high-performance networks are becoming increasingly available and cost-effective. Examples of HDX application include line printers, polling of remote buffers, and modem communications (many modems can support FDX, as well). HDX is used extensively in transaction-based communications, such as credit card verification and ATM (Automatic Teller Machine) networks. Such applications are not affected seriously by delays associated with line turnaround.

Full-Duplex (FDX) A fully bidirectional transmission mode in which communications is supported in both directions, simultaneously. FDX traditionally requires two simplex physical circuits, one operating in each direction – although FDX also can be accomplished over a single copper pair or a single optical fiber. FDX circuits generally are characterized as four-wire, high-capacity, dedicated circuits, of which most are multichannel in nature. All wideband and broadband circuits are FDX in nature, as are most multichannel circuits. FDX circuits sometimes are used to connect half-duplex terminals in order to avoid issues of line turnaround. More typical examples of FDX applications include channel links between host processors, channel links between controllers/concentrators and hosts, and other applications involving the interconnection of substantial computing systems. Carrier services that deliver FDX capabilities include DDS, E/T-Carrier, and broadband services such as Frame Relay, SMDS, and ATM. I discuss all of these in later chapters.

Transmission Mode: Transmission Method

There are two basic methods of data transmission: asynchronous and synchronous. Let's also explore the concepts of isochronous and pleisiochronous communications.

ASYNCHRONOUS

Asynchronous, or *character-framed*, transmission, is a method that grew out of telegraphy and teletypewriting. From Latin and Greek, it translates as *not together with time*; in other words, not synchronous. Asynchronous transmission is a start-stop method of transmission in which each computer value (i.e., letter, number, punctuation mark, or control character) is preceded by a *start bit* that alerts the receiving terminal to the transmission across the circuit of something worthy of its attention. A *stop bit* succeeds the transmitted computer value, which advises the receiving terminal that the transmission of that set of information ends; some asynchronous protocols make use of two stop bits.

PCs, teletypes, and other devices that make use of asynchronous transmission *frame*. This means they surround each byte of information with start and stop bits, which are interpreted by the receiving terminal and subsequently stripped away in order to get to the actual data *payload*. The inclusion of start and stop bits adds two or three bits of *overhead* to the transmission of each 8-bit byte. Additionally, asynchronous transmission adds a *parity checking* bit for error control, which is relatively poor. The framing of the data with these three or four bits of control information yields an overhead, or inefficiency, factor of 20-30 percent.

Asynchronous transmission can be characterized as start-stop (not synchronized) transmission of one character at a time at a variable speed. Additionally, overhead is high and error control is poor.

SYNCHRONOUS

From Latin and Greek origins, *synchronous* translates as *together with time*. Such transmission is *message-framed* and overcomes the inefficiencies of asynchronous, start-stop transmission for high-speed data communications applications. Rather than surrounding each character with start and stop bits, a relatively large set of data is *framed,* or *blocked*, with one or more synchronization bits or bit patterns used to synchronize the receiving terminal on the rate of transmission of the data. Through the receipt of the synchronizing bits, or *clocking pulses*, the receiving device can match its speed of data receipt to the rate of data transmission across the circuit. Thereby, each bit and byte of data and control information can be distinguished separately, because the device knows when to expect what information, in which data fields, and in what sequence. Since only a few framing bits and synchronizing bits surround the large block of data, the overhead is much reduced, the efficiency of transmission is much increased, and the effective throughput is much greater.

The Morse printing instrument...is a beautiful, but rather complicated piece of mechanism, for besides the printing and electric arrangements it is furnished with clockwork to keep the paper tape in motion whilst the message is being delivered. But lately these accessories have in many cases been dispensed with, and the operator depends upon his ear for the translation of the message sent. Source: *Wonders of the Universe.* The Werner Company, 1899.

Error control in synchronous communications protocols is quite sophisticated and reliable, involving statistical sampling techniques and mathematical calculations performed on the set of data. You can characterize synchronous transmission as transmission of multiple characters at a time, organized into character sets and presented in blocks or frames. The transmission is synchronized, and takes place at a predetermined and relatively high rate of speed. Further, error control is excellent and overhead relatively low.

ISOCHRONOUS (ISOC)

Isochronous (*Isoc*) data is synchronous data transmitted without a clocking source. From the Greek *isochronos*, translating as *equal in time*, all bits are of equal importance and are anticipated to occur at regular intervals of time. Bits are sent continuously, with no start/stop bits for timing. Rather, timing is recovered from transitions in the data stream, with a whole number of bit-length intervals between characters. Bit integrity is preserved, with no modifications (i.e., bipolar conventions). The transparent isochronous transmission does not recognize control characters. While there are few commercial applications, some T-carrier nodes operate isochronously on the DS-1 links, syncing up with several lines operating at slightly different speeds. Isoc often is used in secure military applications that require encryption. Isochronous voice and video transmission also is supported by several recent LAN standards, such as Isochronous Ethernet (IsoEthernet), which I discuss in Chapter 8.

Real-time, uncompressed voice communication is a type of isochronous data because human conversation is not synchronized and can be presented in a continuous stream. If voice were synchronous, we would all talk at a precise and common rate of speed — not overtalking each other. Similarly, real-time, uncompressed video communication is isochronous, or stream-oriented. The traditional circuit-switched, PCM-based PSTN supports isochronous datastreams beautifully. Through this network, and from end-to-end, time slots commit to the real-time, uncompressed voice transmissions — whether sound or silence is being carried. Further, those time slots appear at regular, precisely timed intervals (i.e., every 125 microseconds, or every 8,000[th] of a second). While this approach is very effective, it also is wasteful — as I discussed in Chapter 5 and will discuss much further in subsequent chapters.

PLEISIOCHRONOUS

From the Greek *pleion*, meaning *more*, *pleisiochronous* communications involves more than one timing source for the integration of networks, perhaps running at different speeds. Such networks require careful synchronization of transmission systems of varying levels of bandwidth through the use of highly accurate clocking devices. The preferred approach involves a master clocking source, a cesium clock; all lower-order devices (e.g., switches and MUXs) *slave* off the master clock. Through such a technique, the T/E carrier hierarchy is developed, with a master clocking source serving to ensure that digital facilities of lesser capacities can aggregate into facilities of higher capacities, with each set of data retaining its individual integrity. For example, multiple T-1 circuits running at 1.544 Mbps can be interfaced with a single T-3 circuit running at 44.736 Mbps.

Code Sets

Analogous to alphabets, *code sets* or *coding schemes*, are employed by all computer systems to create, store, and exchange information. While code sets vary, they all rely on a specific combination of *1s* and *0s* of a specific total length in order to represent something of value, such as a letter, number, punctuation mark, or control character (e.g., carriage return, line feed, space, blank, and delete).

The first widely accepted standard coding scheme was Morse code, invented by Samuel Morse for use in telegraphy. Morse code uses a series of *dots* and *dashes* to represent letters, numbers, and punctuation marks. In order to speed transmission, the fewest number of dots and dashes represent commonly used letters (e.g., *E* is •, *T* is -, *A* is • -). Contemporary standard coding schemes include Baudot, ASCII, EBCDIC, and Unicode.

BAUDOT CODE (ITA #2)

Morse code was the primary communication code for many years, until Emile Baudot invented the Baudot Distributor in the 1870s. That device provided for the transmission of values in a five-bit coding scheme over a line between two synchronized electromechanical devices. The Baudot Distributor soon gave way to the teletype, which also was based on the Baudot coding scheme, subsequently known as International Telegraph Alphabet #2 (ITA #2).

Baudot code (updated in 1930) is limited to 32 (2^5) characters. Considering that each bit has two possible states (*1* or *0*), 5 bits in sequence yield 2^5 (32) possible combinations. Since 32 values is not sufficient to represent all 26 characters in the English alphabet, plus the 10 decimal digits, necessary punctuation marks and the space character, the shift key operates to shift between letters and other characters. An arrow pointing down represents letters (LTRS). Lowercase (LTRS shift) means that all following characters are alpha characters (LTRS). An arrow pointing up represents figures (FIGS). When a FIGS character is recognized, all succeeding characters are recognized as FIGS numbers and special characters [6-9] and [6-10].

Baudot employs asynchronous transmission, as start and stop bits separate characters. Error detection and correction requires human editing. Therefore, Baudot is a human-to-human, rather than a machine-to-machine, communication technique — with detected errors requiring retransmission.

Clearly, Baudot is a highly limited coding scheme. The limited range of expression (32 characters) is barely enough to accommodate the relatively simple English,

French, and Spanish alphabets. For that matter, all letters must be in uppercase. Additionally, the asynchronous requirement for start and stop bits makes Baudot overhead intensive. Finally, the error detection and correction technique is far less than desirable. As a result, Baudot currently is limited to use in teletypewriters and very old telex machines.

As a footnote, limited coding schemes are not necessarily overly limiting. For instance, proprietary 5-bit and 6-bit codes are used in the airline reservations systems (e.g., American Airlines' SABRE System and United Airlines' APOLLO). Such applications involve a limited character set which is easily accommodated by a 5- or 6-bit code; in fact, a 7- or 8-bit coding scheme would be inefficient.

EXTENDED BINARY CODED DECIMAL INTERCHANGE CODE (EBCDIC)

Extended Binary Coded Decimal Interchange Code (*EBCDIC*), developed by IBM in 1962, was the next standardized code used extensively. An improvement over earlier (1950) Binary Coded Decimal (BCD) and (1951) Extended Binary Coded Decimal (Extended BCD), EBCDIC was developed to enable different IBM computer systems to communicate based on a standard coding scheme. Although EBCDIC is standardized today, users have the ability to modify the coding scheme [6-9].

EBCDIC involves an 8-bit coding scheme, yielding 2^8 (256) possible combinations and, thereby, significantly increasing the range of expression. As a result, more complex alphabets can be supported, as can upper- and lowercase letters, a full range of numbers (1-10), and all necessary punctuation marks. Equally importantly, if not more so, the 8-bit coding scheme supports a large number of control characters, which is critical in the coordination of communications between complex mainframe computers.

EBCDIC-based machines communicate on a synchronous basis, thereby improving on the speed of transmission. Since start and stop bits do not surround each character, overhead reduces, efficiency of transmission improves, and more payload bits can move per unit of time. Further, a more complex, machine-to-machine error detection and correction technique yields improved performance in that regard. Detected errors may require retransmission, although *forward error correction* is often employed, with the receiving system identifying, isolating, and correcting the errored bits.

AMERICAN (NATIONAL) STANDARD CODE FOR INFORMATION INTERCHANGE (ANSCII OR ASCII)

Developed in 1963, *American Standard Code for Information Interchange* (*ASCII*) was specifically oriented towards data processing applications. It was modified in 1967 by the American National Standards Institute (ANSI) to address modifications found in contemporary equipment; that version – originally known as ASCII II – is now known simply as ASCII [6-9].

ASCII employs a 7-bit coding scheme (see Figure 6-6), supporting 128 (2^7) characters, which is quite satisfactory for most alphabets, punctuation characters, and so on. As ASCII was designed for use in asynchronous computer systems (non-IBM, in those days), fewer control characters were required, making a 7-bit scheme acceptable.

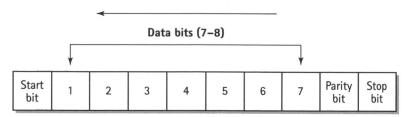

Figure 6-6 ASCII code example, with character framing

As is the case with asynchronous communications, in general, start and stop bits frame each character, without employing synchronization bits. ASCII makes use of a simple error detection and correction scheme known as parity checking. Parity checking is error prone with detected errors often going unnoticed or requiring retransmission, although *forward error correction* currently is employed.

UNIVERSAL CODE (UNICODE)

Universal Code (*Unicode*) attempts to standardize longer and more complex coding schemes used to accommodate more complex alphabets such as Japanese and Chinese. In the Japanese language, for instance, even the abbreviated Kanji writing system contains well over 2,000 characters; Hatakana and Katakana alphabets are also used, further adding to the complexity. As 7- and 8-bit coding schemes cannot accommodate such a complex alphabet, computer manufacturers traditionally have taken proprietary approaches to this problem through the use of two linked 8-bit values.

Unicode supports 65,536 (2^{16}) characters, thereby accommodating the most complex alphabets; in fact, multiple alphabets can be satisfied simultaneously. Further, Unicode standardizes the coding scheme so computers of disparate origin can communicate information on a standard basis. Since the transfer of Unicode data does not require translation of proprietary coding schemes, speed of transfer is improved, errors are reduced and costs are lowered.

Supported by relatively substantial machines, Unicode employs synchronous transmission and sophisticated error detection and correction conventions, as discussed above in connection with EBCDIC.

Data Format

Data formatting is a critical part of a communications protocol. Data formats enable the receiving device to logically determine what is to be done with the data and how to go about doing it. Data formats include code type, message length, and transmission validation techniques. A data format generally involves a header, text, and a trailer (refer to Figure 6-7), with the actual data content contained within the text field. While the header and trailer are overhead, they serve critical functions in support of the successful transfer of the data content. Generally, both a header and trailer frame the data content, or text. In total, the header, text, and trailer comprise what is known variously as a packet, block, frame, or cell; the specific terminology is sensitive to the specific protocol involved.

Figure 6-7 Data format, with header, text, and trailer!

Header A *communications header* precedes the data to be transmitted, establishing the fact that the transmission link exists both physically and logically. The header also includes synchronization bits that provide for synchronization between the devices and the link. Address fields in the header include originating address and destination address. The originating address identifies the originating device so a response can be directed correctly, and so a retransmission can be requested if the data suffers errors during transmission. The destination address enables the receiving device to direct the data correctly, and enables intermediate devices (e.g., switches and routers) to route the data correctly. Certain data protocols also use fields in the header to identify the length of the text field and the type of data, and to indicate its tolerance for delay or loss during network transit. The *user header* includes user-definable information such as system access (*password*), organization or department ID, operator ID, terminal ID, database or application ID, destination address, message sequence number, date/time ID, and message priority.

Text The *text* portion of the data set is the information to be communicated. It may contain either a fixed or a variable amount of information, depending on the specific protocol involved. The text is preceded by Start-of-Text (STX) and succeeded by End-of-Text (ETX) control characters so the receiving device can determine the location of the message data. The *text field* also is known generically as the *data field*, or the *payload.*

Trailer The *trailer, tail,* or *trace* portion of the data set contains information relative to the analysis of the message, including message tracking and diagnostics. Trailing the text, the trailer information may contain the originating ID, the data block number and total number of blocks being transmitted, and identification of system processing points involved in the transmission. The trailer often includes an error detection and correction mechanism to manage the integrity of the transmitted data.

Error Control: Data Transmission Integrity

The integrity of the transmitted data is of prime importance. There are several techniques that you can employ for error detection and, ideally, correction. These three basic modes of error control are recognition and flagging, recognition and retransmission, and recognition and forward error correction.

Recognition and Flagging Provides for no automatic means of correction of errors. Used primarily in networks involving dumb terminals with no means of buffering or retaining information transmitted; retransmission of errored data is not possible. Detected errors simply are flagged (identified) as such by the receiving device; error correction requires a human-to-machine request for retransmission.

Recognition and Retransmission Used in more sophisticated networks where the transmitting device has *buffer memory* and, therefore, can retransmit an errored set of data that has been detected. Serious failures in the devices and/or the circuit can result in repeated errored retransmissions, which lower the throughput of the communication link. In other words, recognition and retransmission is network-intensive.

Recognition and Forward Error Correction (FEC) Involves the addition of enough information that the receiving device can make the required corrections, without requiring retransmission. While the addition of this redundant information automatically increases overhead to the data and, therefore, has a negative effect on the efficiency with which the network resources are used, it enables the receiving device to correct for most errors without requesting a retransmission – which might also be errored. However, FEC places a load on the computational resources of the receiving device. FEC can be characterized as system-intensive, rather than network-intensive.

ECHO CHECKING

Echo checking is one of the earliest means of error detection and correction. The receiving device *echoes* the received data back to the transmitting device. The transmitting operator can view the data as received and echoed, making corrections as appropriate. However, errors also can occur in the transmission of the echoed data, making this approach highly unreliable.

You can characterize echo as very slow and overhead intensive because characters are transmitted one at a time, in asynchronous mode; therefore, the process is bandwidth intensive, as well. Further, the error detection and correction process is manual (human-to-machine) and decidedly unreliable. As a result, contemporary data communications seldom use echo checking.

PARITY CHECKING

Parity checking is by far the most commonly used method for error detection and correction because it is used in asynchronous devices such as PCs. Parity involves the transmitting terminal's appending one or more *parity bits* to the data set to create *odd parity* or *even parity*. In other words, an odd or even value always is created, character-by-character or set-by-set of data. This less than ideal approach is implemented easily and offers reasonable assurance of data integrity. There are two dimensions to parity checking: vertical redundancy checking and longitudinal redundancy checking.

Bit/Value	C	O	N	T	E	X	T	P
1	1	1	0	0	1	0	0	0
2	1	1	1	0	0	0	0	0
3	0	1	1	1	1	0	1	0
4	0	1	1	0	0	1	0	0
5	0	0	0	1	0	1	1	0
6	0	0	0	0	0	0	0	1
7	1	1	1	1	1	1	1	0
P	0	0	1	0	0	0	0	

Figure 6–8 Example ASCII code with VRC and LRC odd parity checking

Vertical Redundancy Checking (VRC) entails the appending of a parity bit at the end of each transmitted character or value to create an odd or even total mathematical bit value. The receiving device executes the same mathematical process to verify that the correct total bit value was received. Speaking in terms of the logical manner in which humans add numbers physically positioned in columns, the two devices sum the bit values vertically, as represented in Figure 6-8. While inexpensive and easily implemented in computers employing asynchronous transmission, this approach is highly unreliable. VRC often is characterized as *send and pray*.

> *There is no greater mistake than to call arithmetic an exact science. There are...hidden laws of numbers, which it requires a mind like mine to perceive. For instance, if you add a sum from the bottom up, and then again from the top down, the result is always different.* Maria Price La Touche, 1824-1906.

Longitudinal Redundancy Checking (LRC), or *Block Checking Character (BCC),* adds another level or reliability because data is viewed in a block or data set.

Again, this approach is characterized in terms of the manner in which human beings add numbers in rows across columns, as though the receiving device were viewing data set in a matrix format. This additional technique of checking the total bit values of the characters on a horizontal basis employs the same parity (odd or even) as does the vertical check (see Figure 6-8). While remaining relatively inexpensive and easily implemented in devices employing asynchronous transmission, LRC/BCC adds a significant measure of reliability. However, it is less than completely reliable, as compensating errors still can occur in non-adjacent characters. Also known as *checksum*, the LRC is sent as an extra character at the end of each data block [6-10].

BLOCK PARITY

The technique of *block parity* improves considerably on simple parity checking. While *Spiral Redundancy Checking (SRC)* and *Interleaving* improved on the detection of errors due to increased transmission speeds and more complex modulation techniques, they gave way to *Cyclic Redundancy Checking (CRC)*, which is commonly employed today.

CRC validates transmission of a set of data, formatted in a block or frame, through the use of a statistical sampling process and a unique mathematical polynomial — both of which are known to the transmitter and receiver. The transmitting device statistically samples the data in the block or frame and applies a 17-bit generator polynomial based on an Euclidean algorithm. The result of that calculation is a description of the text field, which is appended to the block or frame or text as either a 16- or 32-bit value. The receiving device executes the identical process, comparing the results of its process to the CRC value appended to the data block. The result is an integrity factor of 10^{-14}; in other words, the possibility of an undetected error is 1 in 100 trillion. By way of example and at a transmission speed of 1 Mbps, one undetected error is expected approximately every 3 years!

An unerrored block or frame is *ACK*nowledged by the receiving device through the transmission of an *ACK*, whereas an errored block or frame is *N*egatively *A*c*K*nowledged with a *NAK*. A NAK prompts the transmitting device to retransmit that specific block or frame, which has been stored in buffer memory. The transmission of an ACK by the receiving device cues the sending device that the block or frame of data can be erased from buffer memory, and that the next block or frame of data then can be sent.

While CRC is relatively memory- and processor-intensive and therefore expensive to implement, it is easily accommodated in high-order computers that benefit from synchronous transmission techniques. As CRC ensures that data transmission is virtually error-free, it is considered mandatory in most sophisticated computer communications environments.

FORWARD ERROR CORRECTION (FEC)

Forward Error Correction (FEC) involves the addition of redundant information embedded in the data set so the receiving device can detect errors and correct them without requiring a retransmission [6-11]. The two most commonly employed techniques are *Hamming* and *BCH* (Bose, Chaudhuri and Hocquengham).

While even more memory- and processor-intensive than CRC, FEC enables the receiving device to correct for errors in transmission, thereby avoiding most requirement for retransmission of errored blocks or frames of data. As a result, FEC improves the efficiency, or throughput, of the network, reducing transmission costs in the process — without sacrificing data integrity.

Data Compression

As the length of the data sets increases, the distances over which they travel increase, and the likelihood of errors in transmission increases accordingly, *data compression* becomes sensible. Additionally, data compression significantly can reduce the bandwidth required to transmit a set of data. Regardless of the level of bandwidth available in even the most capable networks, bandwidth always has an associated cost. Data compression techniques can include formatting, redundant characters, commonly used characters, and commonly used strings of characters.

Formatting Data formatting need not be transmitted across the network. In a basic example, data compression might involve the removal of formatting from a commonly used form, such as an expense report. Such formatting can involve a large amount of redundant data because the receiving device can reformat the data easily, placing the various fields of data in the appropriate places on the form — which resides in memory. An excellent example is that of access to the Internet and the World Wide Web through client/server software such as America Online, Netscape Navigator, or Microsoft Internet Explorer. In each case, many of the graphic-intensive screens are stored on the client workstation. When accessing the various Internet *portals*, therefore, you do not need to download the full set of graphics. This process is extremely bandwidth-intensive and, therefore, ultimately translates into long delays and higher costs. Rather, only the updated information must be downloaded.

Redundant data This data can be identified easily by the transmitter and communicated to the receiver. This approach is also known as *string coding*, yielding compression factors of as much as 4:1. An excellent example is that of fax modem compression algorithms, which use various methods of *run-length encoding*. As transmitting fax modems scan a document from left to right and from top to bottom, they can quickly sense a run of whitespace. Then, the transmitting modem notes that "nothing" is being transmitted and notes the length of the run of "nothing," all in a very few bits stored in an internal buffer. Once some "real" data appears, the modem notes this fact and begins to send corresponding bits to the internal buffer. Once a specific number of bits are stored in the buffer, the modem packs them into a frame that it transmits. As runs of "nothing" and runs of "real" data reoccur, the modem recognizes that fact and adjusts accordingly. Very quickly, therefore, the transmitting modem can transmit a document with lots of whitespace, with that transmission requiring very little bandwidth through the supporting network. (Try faxing a white sheet of paper. Then try faxing a document of very dense text. You'll immediately see the difference.)

Commonly used characters You can identify and abbreviate these easily through the use of an identifier and a smaller set of bits, similar to the technique used by Samuel Morse in the development of Morse code. *Huffman coding* is commonly used in this instance, yielding *compaction factors* of 2:1 or 4:1.

Commonly used strings of characters Similarly, these characters can be identified and transmitted in abbreviated form. Such an approach relies on the probability of character occurrence following a specific character (e.g., *Q* is generally followed by *U*). *Markov source* and other techniques address this potential.

Asynchronous Data Link Control (DLC) Protocols

Asynchronous Data Link Control (DLC) protocols are used primarily for low-speed data communications between PCs and other very small host computers. *Framing* occurs at the byte level, with each byte surrounded by a start bit (a *0* bit) and a stop bit (a *1* bit). A parity bit often accompanies each character, as well. *Telex* transmission incorporates an additional stop bit.

Kermit and XMODEM are asynchronous protocols, organizing information into 128-byte packets. Kermit also uses CRC error control. The data also can be *blocked* at the application level, and adding the technique of LRC can complement VRC for improved error control.

Bit- vs. Byte-Oriented Synchronous Protocols

Two general types of data communications protocols exist – byte-oriented and bit-oriented. While the performance characteristics of byte-oriented protocols are acceptable for many applications, bit-oriented protocols are much more appropriate for communications-intensive applications in which the integrity of the transmitted data is critical.

Byte-oriented protocols communicate value strings in byte formats, generally of 8 bits per byte. Control characters (e.g., start bit, parity bit, and stop bit) are embedded in the header and trailer of each byte or block of data. As byte-oriented protocols are overhead intensive, they are used exclusively in older computer protocols at the second layer, or *link layer*. Byte-oriented protocols generally are asynchronous and half-duplex (HDX), operating over dial-up, two-wire circuits. One example is that of *Bisynchronous Communications (Bisync, or BSC)*.

Bit-oriented protocols transmit information in a much larger bit stream, with opening and closing flags identifying the separation of the text from the control information – which addresses control issues associated with the entire data set. The much less overhead-intensive, bit-oriented protocols are usually synchronous and full-duplex and operate over dedicated, four-wire circuits. Examples include IBM's *Synchronous Data Link Control (SDLC)* and the ISO's *High-Level Data Link Control (HDLC)*.

BINARY SYNCHRONOUS PROTOCOL (BISYNC OR BSC)

IBM developed *Bisync* in 1966 as a byte-oriented protocol that frames the data with control codes that apply to the entire set of data. Bisync organizes data into *blocks* of up to 512 characters, which are sent over the link sequentially (one at a time). An ACK or NAK is transmitted from the receiving terminal to the transmitting device following the receipt of each block. Error control is based on a Block Checking Character (BCC) that is transmitted along with the data; the receiving device independently calculates the BCC and compares the two calculations.

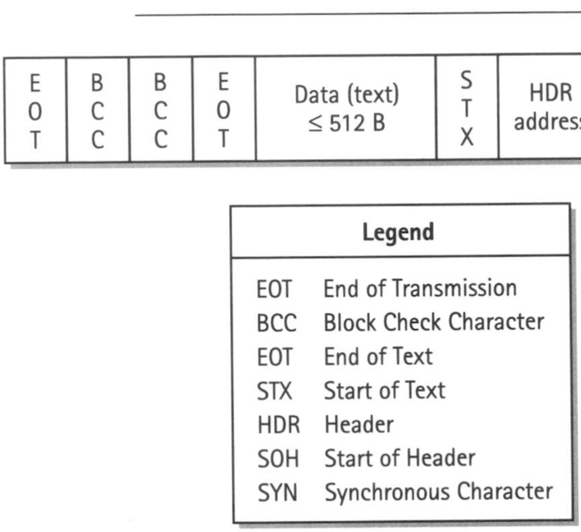

E O T	B C C	B C C	E O T	Data (text) ≤ 512 B	S T X	HDR address	S O H	S Y N	S Y N

Legend	
EOT	End of Transmission
BCC	Block Check Character
EOT	End of Text
STX	Start of Text
HDR	Header
SOH	Start of Header
SYN	Synchronous Character

Figure 6–9 BSC block

The Bisync block consists of synchronizing bits, data, and control characters sent in a continuous data stream, block-by-block. The specific elements of the Bisync block, as illustrated in Figure 6-9, are as follows and in sequence [6-12] and [6-13].

◆ *PAD*: PADding character is sent as the first character to alert the receiving device of the transmission of a block of data and to ensure that the receiving device is in step with the data bits.

◆ *SYN*: SYNchronizing characters (usually two) establish character synchronization between the transmission and receiving devices.

◆ *SOH*: Start of Header precedes the routing information.

◆ *Header*: Header addresses information indicating the address of the transmitting device.

◆ *STX*: A Start of Text control character indicates the beginning of the data.

◆ *Text*: This is the data being transmitted.

- *ETX*: An End of Text control character indicates the end of the data.

- *BCC*: Block Check Characters detect errors.

- *EOT* or *PAD*: An End Of Transmission, or PADding, character, trails the transmission to ensure the receipt of all previous characters and to indicate the end of the block.

SYNCHRONOUS DATA LINK CONTROL (SDLC)

Synchronous Data Link Control (*SDLC*), developed in the mid-1970s, is at the heart of IBM's System Network Architecture (SNA). SDLC is a bit-oriented, point-to-point protocol that uses bit strings to represent characters. SDLC uses CRC error correction techniques—specifically known as *Frame Check Sequence* (*FCS*) here. SDLC supports high-speed transmission and generally employs full-duplex (FDX), dedicated circuits. SDLC can work either in HDX or FDX, supports satellite transmission protocols, and works in point-to-point or multipoint network configurations.

Up to 128 *frames* can be sent in a string, with each frame containing up to 7 blocks—each up to 512 characters. Each block within each frame is checked individually for errors. Errored blocks must be identified as such to the transmitting device within a given time limit, or they are assumed to have been received error-free. As a carefully timed, point-to-point protocol, SDLC depends on high-performance circuits, usually in the form of dedicated leased lines.

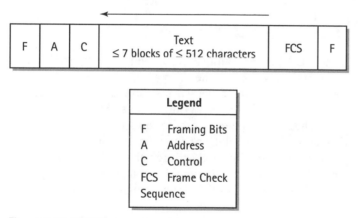

Figure 6–10 SDLC frame

The SDLC frame consists of synchronizing bits, data, and control characters sent in a continuous data stream, frame-by-frame. The specific elements of the SDLC frame (see Figure 6-10) are as follows and in sequence [6-12].

- *Flag* (F): Flag bits, in a specific bit pattern, alert the receiving device to the transmission of the frame.

◆ *Station Address* (A): This address field identifies the specific device transmitting the frame.

◆ *Control* (C): The control field contains commands or responses to control the data link.

◆ *Information* (I): This information (data) is being transmitted.

◆ *Frame Check Sequence* (FCS): This field contains the CRC character sequence used to check the integrity of the transmitted address and control information, as well as the data.

◆ *Flag* (F): Flag bits, in a specific bit pattern, alert the receiving device to the end of transmission of the frame.

HIGH-LEVEL DATA LINK CONTROL (HDLC)

The International Organization for Standardization (ISO) developed HDLC as a superset of IBM's SDLC and the U.S. National Bureau of Standard's (NBS) ADCCP protocols. A version of HDLC is the *Link Access Procedure-Balanced (LAP-B)*, which is used in packet-switched networks conforming to the ITU-T X.25 Recommendation. While HDLC was built on SDLC and is very similar, the two generally are not compatible depending on the framing conventions in the specific HDLC implementation.

Network Architectures

A *network architecture* defines the communications products and services that ensure the various components can work together. Early on, even the various systems of a given manufacturer did not interoperate, let alone afford connectivity with the products of other manufacturers. While IBM's Systems Network Architecture (SNA) and the Digital Equipment Corporation's DECnet architectures solved these internal problems, they still did not interoperate (nor are they ever likely to do so). Truly *open* systems architectures still remain in the distant future, although great strides have been made in this regard through the Open Systems Interconnection (OSI) model fostered by the International Organization for Standardization (ISO).

A number of standard computer network architectures have been defined, many of which segregate various functions into discrete layers of responsibility for ease of development and management. Network architecture examples include Xerox Networking System (XNS), DECnet; Advanced Research Projects Agency network (ARPAnet), the U.S. government-sponsored predecessor to the commercial network we now call the Internet; U.S. Department of Defense Network (DDN); IBM's Systems Network Architecture (SNA); and the Open Systems Interconnection (OSI) model.

Layered Operations Models

Layered models serve to enhance the development and management of a network architecture. While they primarily address issues of data communications, they also include some data processing activities at the upper layers. These upper layers address application software processes, presentation format, and the establishment of user sessions. Each independent layer, or level, of a network architecture addresses different functions and responsibilities. The layers work together, as a whole, to maximize the performance of the process. The various functions address the functions of data transfer, flow control, sequencing, error detection, and notification.

Data transfer enables the transfer of data from one node to another. Included are such issues as normal or expedited data flow; packet, block, or frame sizing; and data assembly and segmentation. *Flow control* controls the flow of packets through the network to reduce congestion and the resulting degradation of network performance. *Sequencing* of the data packets is required where packets may take different routes between nodes. *Error detection* is required to ensure data integrity. *Notification* provides for the advice from receiver to transmitter of the receipt of packets and their condition.

SYSTEMS NETWORK ARCHITECTURE (SNA)

Developed in 1974 by IBM, SNA was a five-level design architecture that has grown into a seven-layer model. SNA comprises software and hardware interfaces that permit various IBM systems and software to communicate. SNA includes *network nodes, physical units,* and *logical units.*

Nodes Physical devices in the SNA network. Nodes can include computers, communications processors (e.g., FEPs), terminal controllers, and terminals.

Physical Units (PUs) These manage the communications hardware and software, participating in the controlling and routing of network communications. All physical devices are assigned a PU Type (1, 2, 3, or 5) that identifies the level of the device (i.e., terminal, controller, communications processor, or host node) and its origin (i.e., IBM/SNA or non-IBM/SNA).

Logical Units (LUs) These units manage communications software for communications with end users. A logical unit *session* is an end-to-end communication between an end-user terminal and the originating application residing in the host. For example, LU 6.2 supports peer-to-peer communications between intelligent devices, without requiring the host to assume responsibility for communications support activities. LU 6.2 is also known as *Advanced Program-to-Program Communications (APPC).*

Although similar, SNA is not compatible with the OSI model.

OPEN SYSTEMS INTERCONNECTION (OSI) MODEL

The *OSI Reference Model* is a layered architecture (see Figure 6-11) consisting of a set of international networking standards known collectively as X.200. Developed by the ISO, the basic process began in 1977 and was completed in 1983. The OSI model defines a set of common rules that computers of disparate origin can use to exchange information (communicate). As is the case with SNA and other such proprietary architectures, the model is layered to segment software responsibilities, with supporting software embedded in each node to provide an interface between layers. Specific levels of service can be negotiated between nodes.

The transmitting device uses the top layer, at which point the data is placed into a packet, prepended by a header. The data and header, known collectively as a *Protocol Data Unit* (*PDU*), are handled by each successively lower layer as the data works its way across the network to the receiving node. At the receiving node, the data works its way up the layered model; successively higher layers strip off the header information.

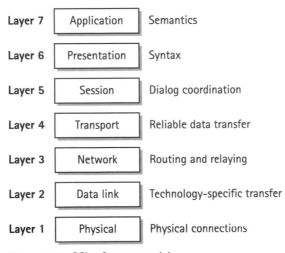

Layer 7	Application	Semantics
Layer 6	Presentation	Syntax
Layer 5	Session	Dialog coordination
Layer 4	Transport	Reliable data transfer
Layer 3	Network	Routing and relaying
Layer 2	Data link	Technology-specific transfer
Layer 1	Physical	Physical connections

Figure 6-11 OSI reference model

Layer Seven (Application Control) provides support services for user and application tasks. File transfer, interpretation of graphic formats and documents, and document processing are supported at this level. For example, X.400 e-mail messaging takes place at Layer Seven. TCP/IP extensions such as *User Datagram Protocol* (*UDP*), *Simple Mail Transfer Protocol* (*SMTP*), *Telnet*, and *File Transfer Protocol* (*FTP*) also take place at Layer Seven.

Layer Six (Presentation Control) performs functions related to the format and display of received data by terminals and printers. Functions herein include data formatting, code set (e.g., Baudot, ASCII, EBCDIC, and Unicode), code set conversion, and text compression and decompression.

Layer Five (Session Control) formats the data for transfer between end nodes, provides session restart and recovery, and general maintenance of the session from end-to-end.

Layer Four (Transport Control) is responsible for maintaining the end-to-end integrity and control of the session. Data is accepted from the Session Control layer and passed through to the Network Control layer. The two protocols that can be used at this layer include Transmission Control Protocol (TCP) and the five levels of the OSI Transport Protocol (TP). These protocols ensure end-to-end integrity of the data in a session. The X.25 packet-switching protocol operates at Layers One, Two, Three, and Four.

Layer Three (Network Control) is comprised of software that addresses the PDUs and transports them to the ultimate destination, setting up the appropriate paths between the various nodes. At this layer, message routing, error detection, and control of internodal traffic are managed. The Internetwork Protocol (IP) operates at this layer. Note that IP provides a mechanism for ensuring the integrity of a datagram, or individual packet of data, from node to node. TCP, which operates at Layer Four, ensures the integrity of a stream of datagrams involved in a data session, from end-to-end across the network.

Layer Two (Data Link Control) establishes the communications link between individual devices over a physical link or channel. At this level, framing, error control, flow control, data sequencing, time-out levels, and data formatting occur. HDLC is used at this level. Local Area Networks (LANs) operate at Layers Two and One, and Network Interface Cards (NICs) cut across portions of these two layers.

Layer One (Physical Control) defines the electrical and mechanical aspects of the interface of the device to a physical transmission medium, such as twisted pair, coax, or fiber. Communications hardware and software drivers are found at this layer, as well as electrical specifications such as EIA-232 (RS-232). Synchronous Optical NETwork (SONET) and T-Carrier are additional examples of Layer One.

Security

Security is an issue of prime importance across all dimensions of communications and networks, but perhaps most importantly in the world of data communications. In the traditional data world of *mainframes in glass houses*, security was controlled very tightly. In the contemporary world of distributed processing and networked computer resources, security is much more difficult to develop and control. Perhaps the greatest strength of networks is that they enable information to be shared; perhaps the greatest weakness of networks is that they enable information to be shared. The trick, of course, is to permit only legitimate users to share. Security encompasses a number of dimensions, including physical security, authentication, authorization, port security, transmission security, and encryption.

Physical Security

Physical security involves access control – i.e., control over the individuals who have access to the facilities in which the systems reside. Clearly, access must be restricted by security guards, locks and keys, electronic combination locks, and/or electronic card key systems which require additional input, such as a Personal Identification Number (PIN). The latter is preferable because the system can maintain a record of specific access. Physical security also entails some decidedly low-tech tools such as document shredders and burn bags, which jointly serve to make paper documents and electronic media unusable after they serve their purposes.

Authentication

Authentication provides a means by which network managers can authenticate the identity of those attempting access to computing resources and the data they house. Authentication consists of *password protection* and *intelligent tokens*. Impose *password protection* to restrict individuals on a site, host, application, screen, and field level. Passwords should consist of a reasonably long length – alphanumeric in nature and changed periodically. There is a current trend toward the use of dedicated password servers for password management. *Intelligent tokens* are one-time passwords generated by hardware devices and verified by a secure server on the receive side of the communication. They often work on a cumbersome *challenge-response* basis.

Remote Authentication Dial-In User Service (*RADIUS*) is a highly popular public network authentication service. Developed by Livingston Enterprises, Inc., and based on a model defined by the IETF, RADIUS comprises an authentication server installed on the user's host computer and client protocols. Remote users are authenticated through a series of encrypted communications between the remote client and the centralized server. RADIUS is an open approach that can be modified easily to work with any security system and virtually any communications device.

Authorization

Authorization provides a means of controlling which legitimate users have access to which resources. Authorization involves complex software that resides on every secured computer on the network; ideally, it provides *single sign-on* capability. Authorization systems include Kerberos, Sesame, and Access Manager.

Kerberos, the best-known authorization software, makes use of private-key authentication and a UNIX-based distributed database. Developed by the Massachusetts Institute of Technology (MIT), Kerberos is available free, although commercial versions exist. Since Kerberos uses DES, it is not easily exportable to other nations [6-14]. IBM's Kryptoknight is a Kerberos variant – weaker, but exportable. Kerberos is named for Cerberus, the three-headed dog that guarded the gates of Hades in Greek mythology.

Sesame (Secure European System for Applications in a Multivendor Environment) was developed by the ECMA (European Computer Manufacturers Association). It is flexible, open, and intended for large, heterogeneous network computing environments. It also is highly complex and not effective for smaller applications.

Access Manager uses an API for applications, employing scripting. *Scripting* involves a process of mimicking the log-on procedures of a program, providing basic levels of security for small networks.

Port Security

Port security is essential to deny unauthorized remote access. Passive devices report on unauthorized access, usage anomalies, etc. Active devices, which are preferable, act to deny access to unauthorized users and disable ports if user-definable parameters are exceeded.

Transmission Security

Transmission security is critical to ensure that unauthorized entities are not permitted to intercept the data as it communicates across the network. Transmission of data is especially insecure over analog links because analog transmission does not lend itself to encryption. Wireless transmission is inherently insecure, although digital wireless system support signal encryption. Transmission security is virtually ensured over coaxial cable and, especially, over fiber optic cable because you cannot tap these media easily. In order to maximize security, however, it is necessary that the data be *encrypted*.

Encryption

Encryption involves scrambling and compressing the data prior to transmission; the receiving device is provided with the necessary logic to decrypt the transmitted information. Encryption logic generally resides in firmware included in standalone devices, although it can be built into virtually any device. For instance, encryption logic often is incorporated into routers, which can encrypt data on a packet-by-packet basis. Encryption comes in two basic flavors: private key and public key. *Private key* is a symmetric encryption method that uses the same key to encrypt and decrypt data, and requires that the key be kept secret. *Public key* is an asymmetric encryption method with two keys – an encryption (encoding) key that can be used by all authorized network users, and a decryption (decoding) key that is kept secret. Data encryption standards include *DPF* (*Data Private Facility*) and *DES* (*Data Encryption Standard*), a 56-bit technique that uses a challenge-response approach and intelligent tokens. *Triple DES* is a more complex version of DES, which encrypts the data three times.

Firewalls

Firewalls comprise application software that can reside in a communication router, server, or some other device. That device physically and/or logically is a first point of access into a networked system. On an active basis, the device can block access to unauthorized entities, effectively acting as a *security firewall*. Firewalls can use one or more basic approaches to access control. A *packet-filtering firewall* examines all data packets, forwarding or dropping individual packets based on predefined rules that specify where a packet is permitted to go, and in consideration of both the authenticated identification of the user and the originating address of the request. *Proxy firewalls* act as intermediaries for user access requests by setting up a second connection to the resource. That second connection can be established at the application layer (Layer 7) by an *application proxy*, or at the session (Layer 5) or transport (Layer 4) layer by a *circuit relay* firewall. A *stateful inspection* firewall examines packets, notes the port numbers that they use for each connection, and shuts down those ports once the connection is terminated. Firewalls are the subject of much continuing interest, especially as organizations seek to protect their data from the ravages of hackers and other less-than-honorable creatures that prowl the Internet [6-15] and [6-16].

References

[6-1]   Shelly, Gary B. and Cashman, Thomas J. *Introduction to Computers and Data Processing.* Anaheim Publishing Company, 1980.

[6-2]   Brooks, John. *Telephone: The First Hundred Years.* Harper & Row, 1976.

[6-3]   Keen, Peter G.W. and Cummins, J. Michael. *Networks in Action.* Wadsworth Publishing Company, 1994.

[6-4]   English, David. "V.90 Modems: The end of the Line." *PC World,* January 1999.

[6-5]   Cray, Andrew. "New Juice for analog Modems?" *Data Communications,* December 1998.

[6-6]   Fratto, Mike. "V.90 Modems Burn Up the Wires With Standards-Based 56-Kbps Access." *Network Computing,* November 15, 1998.

[6-7]   Wexler, Joanie. "56k Modems: A Bandwidth Bird in the Hand." *Business Communications Review,* October 1998.

[6-8]   Shah, Deval and Holzbaur, Helen. "56K? No Way." *Data Communications,* August 1997.

[6-9]   Sherman, Kenneth. *Data Communications: A Users Guide.* Reston
           Publishing Company, Inc., 1981.

[6-10]   Held, Gilbert. *Understanding Data Communications.* SAMS Publishing,
           1994.

[6-11]   Doll, Dixon R. *Data Communications: Facilities, Networks and Systems
           Design.* John Wiley & Sons, 1978.

[6-12]   *Data Communications Concepts.* IBM (GC21-5169-5), September 1985.

[6-13]   Gelber, Stan. *Introduction to Data Communications: A Practical
           Approach.* Professional Press Books, 1991.

[6-14]   Voydock, Victor L. and Kent, Stephen T. *Security Mechanisms in High-
           Level Network Protocols.* ACM, 1983. Reprinted: Partridge, Craig.
           Innovations in Internetworking. Artech House, 1988.

[6-15]   Schultz, Keith. "Taming the Flames." *Communications Week*, March 10,
           1997.

[6-16]   Newman, David, Holzbaur, Helen and Bishop, Kathleen. "Firewalls:
           Don't Get Burned." *Data Communications*, March 21, 1997.

Chapter 7

Conventional Digital and Data Networks

...in 1816, Mr. Ronalds (afterwards Sir Francis Ronalds) showed that an electric telegraph was possible, and endeavoured to persuade the Government of the importance of his system. The official reply to his appeal was as follows "Mr. Barrow presents his compliments to Mr. Ronalds, and acquaints him, with reference to his note of the third instant, that telegraphs of any kind are now wholly unnecessary, and that no other but the one now in use will be adopted. Admiralty Office, Aug. 5, 1816." The "one in use," here indicated, was the semaphore, . . . which, it may be mentioned, was quite useless during the night, or when fog prevented the signals being seen. Source: *Wonders of the Universe*, The Werner Company, 1899.

Data communications began in 1835 with the invention of the first practical telegraph by Samuel F.B. Morse and with his first long-distance message, *What hath God wrought!*, sent from Baltimore, Maryland to Washington, D.C. in 1846. This simplex (in this context, *simplex* means one-way, single channel) device used start and stop signals of varying lengths over uninsulated iron, and later copper, wire. Subsequently, the technology improved to *diplex* (one-way, two-channel) and *quatraplex* (one-way, four-channel). Western Union, the first commercial data communications carrier, was founded in 1856 to provide telegraph services [7-1].

Modern data communications beyond the boundaries of the data processing center originally involved the physical transfer of punch cards or magnetic tapes via mail or courier. While this approach is still used in some cases (more than you might think) as a primary means of data transfer, it is generally a last resort. *Sneakernet* is slow and expensive. The traditional voice network, despite its severe limitations, became a common means of electronic data transfer for short, low-speed communications. As the demand for data networking developed, and as the enabling technology evolved, a number of alternatives emerged. Data communications currently is growing at an incredible rate, while voice is growing at about 5-6 percent — roughly the rate of population growth.

Evolution of Data Networking

It is worth noting that all Wide Area Network (WAN) communications initially consisted of voice, with the exception of the separate telegraph networks; that largely remained the case for over 100 years. As a result, the networks evolved in a manner that best supported voice communications.

The Voice Model

The voice Public Switched Telecommunications Network (PSTN) was designed to support voice-only communications. As a result, you can characterize it in terms such as analog, two-wire, two-way, narrowband, circuit-switched, and ubiquitous.

ANALOG

The network is presumed to be analog. The local loop is always analog, unless digital circuits are ordered specifically (e.g., ISDN and T-carrier). The carrier networks largely are digital, for reasons which include increased traffic capacity and improved error performance.

TWO-WIRE

Two-wire local loops predominate, and are quite satisfactory for narrowband voice and low-speed data. Four-wire local loop circuits are used only when required in support of more demanding applications such as ISDN BRI (Basic Rate Interface), T-1, and ISDN PRI (Primary Rate Interface), and emerging broadband services. The internal carrier networks are four-wire — in support of high-capacity, wideband and broadband communications.

COPPER

Copper twisted pair remains the predominant medium in the local loop, although fiber optic cable deploys to business premises on a selective basis. Hybrid fiber/copper networks increasingly are deployed, with fiber to the neighborhood and copper to the premises. In the traditional LEC (Local Exchange Carrier) environment, these hybrid networks generally support some version of DSL (Digital Subscriber Line), which I discuss in Chapter 9. In the traditional CATV (Community Antenna TeleVision) domain, hybrid networks are deployed to increase the performance quality of entertainment TV, although many CATV providers now operate as CLECs (Competitive LECs), as discussed in Chapter 14. Also, the increased use of some form of radio technology (e.g., microwave and PCS) reduces the cost, delay, and general aggravation of deploying wired facilities to the customer premises. Generally speaking, the internal networks of the service providers have upgraded to optical fiber. Microwave and satellite have continuing application in certain areas due to issues of climate, terrain, and population density. They also are used for backup purposes in the event of a catastrophic failure of the primary facilities, and as the primary means of access to sparsely populated areas and island nations.

TWO-WAY

Two-way, or duplex, communications is conversational in nature. Such a mode of communications is absolutely fundamental to the PSTN because the parties in a voice conversation require the ability to communicate in both directions.

CIRCUIT-SWITCHED

Circuit-switched networks traditionally have been considered appropriate for voice PBXs and various types of network exchanges because they provide a continuous talk path for the duration of the conversation. Dedicated, leased-line circuits are provided for very large organizations that communicate intensively between fixed locations (e.g., PBX tie trunks).

NARROWBAND

Narrowband (low-capacity) facilities are quite satisfactory for most voice communications. Wideband (DS-1 and DS-3) access applies to high-capacity local loops for PBX applications. Broadband (DS-3+) communications currently is limited, for the most part, to backbone carrier networks.

UBIQUITOUS AND AFFORDABLE

"Ubiquitous" and "affordable" are key terms in the voice world, at least in developed countries. Since the Federal Communications Act of 1934, the PSTN in the United States has cross-subsidized to ensure that basic telephone service is available almost universally (ubiquitous) and at reasonable cost, even in remote, rural, and *high-cost* areas. In fact, universal access to high-quality, affordable service now is viewed as a basic human right in many countries.

INTERCONNECTION

Interconnection is fundamental to the PSTN, which provides for connection between voice terminals, virtually regardless of location. LECs, IXCs, and international carriers all are interconnected.

HIERARCHICAL

The hierarchical structure of PSTNs is traditional; it has multiple levels of carriers and switches, including Local Exchange Carriers (LECs), IntereXchange Carriers (IXCs) and International Record Carriers (IRCs). As noted in Chapter 5, hierarchical switch structures dominated carrier network design for many years. Contemporary configurations tend to be flatter, with many switches serving multiple purposes. Increasingly, the network intelligence centralizes; a small number of databases serve to provide multiple switches with routing instructions, for instance.

Data over Voice Networks

The next step in the evolution of networking was that of data transmission over voice networks. In the late 1950s, large organizations (initially in North America) desired the ability to move data over telephone lines. This first was accomplished with a variation of the IBM 729 tape drive, which interfaced with the analog PSTN through a matched pair of *Bell datasets* (1957) [7-2], or *DataPhones* (1961) [7-1], via acoustic couplers and telephone sets. Datasets quickly spread around the world, rented by the telcos and PTTs to end users until deregulation afforded users the option of acquiring and interconnecting such equipment. The original datasets connected to the PSTN through a *Direct Access Arrangement (DAA)* device that served as a coupler, or protector, to protect the network from high signal levels, out-of-band frequencies, and aberrant voltages. This protection is incorporated into contemporary modems and other devices, which are standardized and regulated by the ITU-T on an international basis and by the FCC (United States) and other national regulatory bodies.

The telcos began to digitize their networks in the 1960s, as digital technology became reliable and inexpensive enough to support telecommunications applications, and as the requirement surfaced for increased bandwidth in the carrier networks. Digital transmission facilities, in the form of T-carrier (North America) and E-carrier (Europe), increased the traffic capacity of existing facilities. In the 1970s, analog Electronic Common Control (ECC) switches began to be replaced with fully digital switches. Data transmission at relatively high speeds and over fully digital networks became a reality, although a number of years passed until such capability became widely available.

Dataphone Digital Service (DDS) was the first publicly available service that was digital from end to end. Although still in use, it now competes with E/T-carrier, X.25, ISDN, Frame Relay, and ATM for data communications applications.

Data Networking over the WAN (and MAN): Digital Data Networking

The evolution of data communications progressed at a snail's pace for over a hundred years. For much of that time, neither the applications nor the enabling technologies existed. DDS and X.25 represented major steps forward in the 1960s. T-carrier added to the solutions suite in the 1970s. ISDN began to appear in the 1980s, but generally did not develop into a viable service offering. Only very recently, in the United States, has ISDN emerged from 25 years of obscurity to offer cost-effective solutions in certain applications.

In very recent years, however, the evolution of digital data networking over the Wide Area Network (WAN) and Metropolitan Area Network (MAN) has progressed with truly blinding speed. Frame Relay is widely deployed both domestically and internationally. ATM, while currently deployed on a limited basis, is viewed by most industry experts as the backbone network technology of choice far into the future. Broadband ISDN (B-ISDN), the ultimate service offering of ATM, is touted as the culmination of network technologies in a broadband service scenario.

Clearly, digital transmission offers significant advantages, especially for data transmission. Those advantages include increased bandwidth and bandwidth utilization, improved error performance and increased throughput, and enhanced management and control. This chapter focuses on conventional digital data networking options, which include dedicated leased lines, circuit switching, and packet switching. Specifically, those technologies and service offerings include Dataphone Digital Service (DDS), Switched 56, classic Virtual Private Networks (VPNs), T-carrier, X.25 and Packet Switching, and ISDN. I provide a detailed introduction into emerging data networking options in a later section. Those technologies include Frame Relay and Cell Relay (SMDS, ATM, and B-ISDN).

Dataphone Digital Service (DDS)

AT&T introduced *Dataphone Digital Service* (*DDS*), also known as *Digital Data System* and *SubRate Digital Loop* (*SRDL*), in 1974 [7-2]. The term now is used generically to describe an end-to-end, fully digital, dedicated service provided by most carriers. DDS is widely deployed in the United States and Canada and many other developed countries, and is intended for relatively high-speed data transport applications between purely digital devices (i.e., computers). Employing specially conditioned, dedicated, leased-line circuits provided to user organizations by the carriers, a DDS configuration may be either point-to-point or multipoint. In either event, all network control is the responsibility of a designated *head-end* system. The head-end, usually in the form of a Front-End Processor (FEP), controls all access to the network through a process of polling the remote devices. Additionally, all communications must pass through the head-end; in other words, devices cannot communicate directly like a *mesh* network, where all locations are interconnected directly.

DDS is intended for full-duplex (FDX) synchronous communication – provided over four-wire circuits, between devices of significance, and which communicate intensively (i.e., frequently, and passing significant volumes of data). The DDS network provides network timing and synchronization through a master clock, which ensures that all clocks in all slaved network nodes operate at the same rate, or clock speed, and at the same clock phase, or sinusoidal wave phase. Those same timing signals are provided to end user Data Communications Equipment (DCE) for transmission synchronization. DCE is in the form of a DSU/CSU, as described in previous chapters. The DSU/CSU generally operates at the full line rate, or on a subrate basis (lower speed), as required. While transmission generally is full-duplex (FDX), half-duplex (HDX) and simplex transmission also is served.

Transmission rates vary, within limits, according to the user organization's requirements. Bandwidth generally is available at line rates of 2400 bps, 4800 bps, 9600 bps, 19.2 Kbps, and 56 Kbps (64 Kbps service is available in some areas). Note here that the DDS signals actually are carried inside T–Carrier channels in the internal carrier networks. (I discuss T-carrier later in this chapter.)

While the cost of DDS circuits varies according to specific carrier tariffs and pricing strategies, cost is sensitive to distance between the points of termination and the level of bandwidth. Such is the case with all dedicated leased-line services. A traditional rule of thumb is that DDS generally is cost-effective in applications that require communications between two locations, for a total of equal to or greater than one hour per day, at a rate of 56 Kbps.

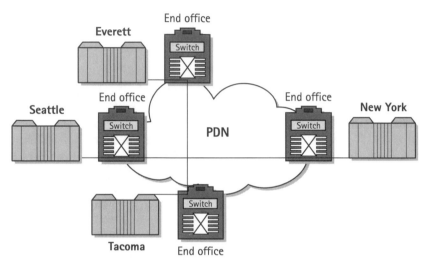

Figure 7-1 DDS leased lines connecting data centers in New York and Seattle, with drops to Everett and Tacoma

The cost equation changes, of course, where multiple locations connect in a multipoint network configuration. A *multipoint circuit* also is known as a *multi-drop circuit* in telco parlance because local-loop connections historically are dropped from poles where they connect to larger cables. Multipoint circuits also are referred to as *fantail circuits* because they fan out like the tail of a fish on the distant end. As noted in Figure 7-1, a headquarters data center in New York might be connected to a regional data center in Seattle. Field offices in Everett and Tacoma can cost-effectively take advantage of the same coast-to-coast circuit, since the incremental circuit mileage is short and the associated cost of those additional drops, therefore, is low.

In such a multipoint network, the head-end addresses each remote system connected to the circuit on the basis of a unique logical address, and in a user-definable and variable polling sequence. The target device recognizes its address and responds across the network, while all other devices remain silent. Then, the two computer systems conduct a dialogue until such time as either the data transfer is complete, or the head-end truncates the communication in order to address other devices according to its programmed polling schedule. ATMs (Automatic Teller Machines) commonly are connected to the central bank in such a manner. In a typical scenario, the central computer polls the individual ATMs, downloads the user's request for a cash withdrawal, and matches the account number and PIN for authentication purposes. It then queries the centralized database to determine the assigned level of withdrawal privileges and the current account balance, and authorizes or denies the cash withdrawal.

DDS provides excellent reliability – generally in the range of 99.99 percent (the famous four 9's). You should note, however, that all dedicated services are susceptible to catastrophic failure from such causes as *cable-seeking backhoes*. Therefore, network redundancy must be considered in the form of either back-up DDS circuits or some alternative network service.

From an applications perspective, DDS is used for relatively intensive data-only communications applications between fixed physical addresses. In such an environment, it can be highly cost-effective since usage charges do not apply to network traffic. Typical applications include connecting data centers for purposes of file transfer or data backup. Image transfer and other bandwidth-intensive applications such as CAD (Computer-Aided Design) can make cost-effective use of DDS circuits, also benefiting from the bandwidth and excellent error performance offered by the dedicated digital circuit. DDS also serves to connect e-mail and Group IV facsimile servers in a messaging network. Perhaps most commonly, DDS is used in intensive transaction-processing environments, as in the ATM example stated earlier. Department store chains often put into place extensive DDS networks to support transaction-processing applications between the centralized data processing center and the retail stores. Similarly, oil companies traditionally had large and complex DDS networks in place, with the tail circuits connecting large numbers of retail outlets to a long-haul circuit that terminated in the data center. The oil companies still make use of short-haul, multidrop circuits to connect multiple outlets to a central retail outlet that is equipped with a satellite dish. The long-haul portion of the connection to the data center is provided over satellite facilities.

Switched 56

Switched 56 (Kbps service) is the popular term for *Digital Switched Access* (*DSA*), although 64 Kbps service is available in some areas. Switched 56 is a circuit-switched digital service intended generally for the same applications as is DDS, although it is more cost-effective for less intensive communications. Although the service is switched, rather than dedicated, most of the general characteristics and all of the components closely resemble DDS, with the sole exception that digital carrier exchanges are involved in setting up the DSA connections. DTE is in the form of computer systems, which connect to digital local loops through DCE in the form of a DSU/CSU. Digital exchanges serve to switch the connection (see Figure 7-2), which is provided through digital carrier transmission facilities on the basis of special routing logic.

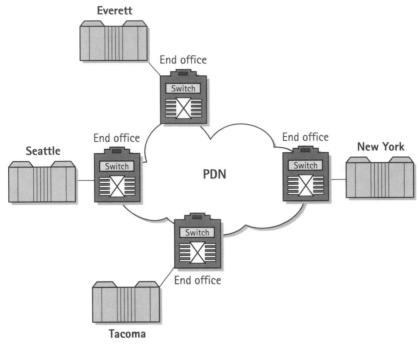

Figure 7-2 Switched 56 Kbps service

The key difference between DDS and Switched 56 is that the calls are switched between physical locations on the basis of a logical address the computer equivalent of a voice telephone number. In fact, Switched 56 is the digital data equivalent of a circuit-switched voice call through the PSTN. Based on specific routing instructions contained in program logic, the digital network switches establish the end-to-end connection over entirely digital circuits. The call is set up, maintained, and torn down much like a voice call. Further, the call is priced similarly. In other words and depending on the pricing strategy of the carrier, the cost of the call either is priced on a blended, flat-rate basis, or is priced sensitive to distance, duration, time of day, and day of year. As the carriers' Switched 56 service networks typically are not interconnected, generally calling is limited to each specific carrier domain unless the user has made arrangements otherwise.

While DDS is more cost-effective for applications in which communications are intensive between specific physical locations, Switched 56 Kbps service is more cost-effective for communications between locations that communicate less frequently or communicate less data. As Switched 56 calls are switched through the highly redundant carrier networks, rather than relying on vulnerable dedicated circuits as with DDS, Switched 56 services often are employed as backup to DDS facilities.

Virtual Private Networks (VPNs): In the Classic Sense

Virtual Private Networks (VPNs), also known as Software Defined Networks (SDNs) grew out of the voice world, as did the majority of network technologies. In a purely data context, VPNs are IXC offerings (AT&T, MCI Worldcom, and Sprint) that operate much like Switched 56, although the level of bandwidth provided can be much greater. Depending on the carrier, VPNs support the following bandwidth levels on a circuit-switched basis:

- ◆ 56/64 Kbps
- ◆ N x 64 Kbps
- ◆ 384 Kbps (Video)
- ◆ 768 Kbps (Video)
- ◆ 1.536 Mbps (Video)

A number of access technologies can provide access to a VPN, including LEC- and IXC-dedicated digital loops, Switched 56, and ISDN. The IXC VPN service provides priority access and data transport between privileged sites. A wide variety of features are supported, including managed security at the network level. A VPN provides performance similar to that of a dedicated leased-line network, with the additional advantages of flexibility and redundancy.

Digital Carrier Systems and Networks: T-carrier

Carrier systems are defined as systems that derive multiple logical channels from a single physical communications path, thereby supporting multiple communications. Initially developed for use within public carrier (i.e., LEC and IXC) networks, the systems provided increased traffic capacity between exchanges without requiring additional transmission facilities. As voice traffic grew dramatically in the post-war (WWII) period, the Central Office (CO) exchanges were strained, as were the transmission facilities connecting them – carrier systems solved that problem [7-1].

The original *N-carrier* (*N* = *N*umber of channels) system, introduced in 1950, employed twisted pair cable for connecting CO exchanges on an analog basis. A two-wire or four-wire analog connection employed multiplexers to deliver *groups* of 12 and, later, 24 Frequency Division Multiplexed (FDM) voice-grade channels. Technology developed to provide *supergroups* of 60 channels and *master-groups* of 600 channels [7-2], [7-3], and [7-4].

L-carrier (*L* = Larger) was quite an improvement, employing coaxial cable and an analog transmission scheme. L5E, the last L-carrier system, used 22 coaxial pairs (*tubes*) to carry a total of 132,000 simultaneous voice grade conversations. Although this was an impressive improvement over N-carrier, the inherent problems of analog transmission were still present. Additionally, the coax cables were expensive and bulky, and the analog Radio Frequency (RF) amplifiers were expensive and prone to failure [7-2] and [7-3].

The U.S. Bell System first introduced digital carrier in 1957 in Newark, New Jersey. Designated *T-carrier* (*T* = *T*runk, relating to the *trunk side* , or carrier side, of the network), it refers to a specific set of cable pairs and digital repeaters spaced every 6,000 feet or so [7-5]. T-carrier was rapidly and extensively deployed throughout the carrier networks, initially for short-haul interexchange trunking [7-2]. T-1, also known as *digroup* (*digital group*), was offered commercially to end users by AT&T in 1977 on the basis of a *special assembly* tariff, and was added to the interstate DDS Tariff #267 in December 1981 [7-6]. In 1983, AT&T tariffed T-1 under the name *Accunet 1.5*. T-1 provides 24 channels, based on a convenient multiple of 2 x 12 channels, which formed the basis for the original analog N-carrier [7-2]. Currently, there are about 200,000 private and public T-1 links in service, and about 1,200 private networks based on T-3 use [7-7].

T-Carrier Concept

T-carrier is a dedicated, digital, leased-line service offering that employs time division multiplexing (TDM) in order to derive multiple channels from a single four-wire circuit operating in full-duplex (FDX) transmission mode. In capsule, T-carrier offers the advantages of digital error performance, increased bandwidth, and improved bandwidth utilization. As is the case with digital services, in general, it also delivers increased management and control capabilities to the carriers and end users, alike. Additionally, T-carrier is medium-independent. In other words, it can be provisioned over any of the transmission media discussed in Chapter 2 (i.e., twisted pair, coax, microwave, satellite, infrared, or fiber optic cable), at least at the lower transmission rates of DS-0 (64 Kbps) and T-1 (1.544 Mbps). At the higher rate of T-3 (44.736 Mbps), twisted pair transmission is not suitable due to issues of signal attenuation.

As is the case with any dedicated service offering, T-carrier cost is sensitive to distance and bandwidth. While T-carrier initially was deployed in support of voice transmission, it supports data, image, and video, as well. Further, T-carrier supports any and all such information streams on an unbiased basis; essentially, it offers the advantage of supporting integrated communications. As noted in Figure 7-3, T-carrier can obviate the need for multiple voice, facsimile, data, video, and image networks [7-3] and [7-4].

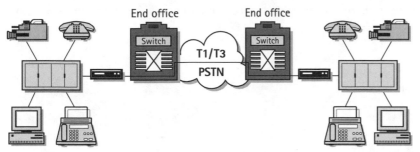

Figure 7-3 T-carrier as a replacement for multiple dedicated, leased-line networks

The significance of T-carrier extends well beyond its practical advantages. Specifically, as the first digital carrier system, it set the standards for digital transmission and switching, including the use of Pulse Code Modulation (PCM) for digitizing analog voice signals. T-carrier not only set the basis for the North American digital hierarchy (see Table 7-1), but it led to the development of similar standards, such as E-carrier in Europe (see Table 7-2) and J-carrier in Japan. Ultimately, the CCITT (now ITU-T) developed international standards recommendations to ensure interconnectivity of national networks. Although T-carrier, E-carrier, and J-carrier are very different in terms of certain specifics of the protocols employed (e.g., transmission rates, encoding techniques, and signaling and control methods), their basic characteristics are much the same.

Channelized T-Carrier

The fundamental building block of T-carrier is a 64 Kbps channel, referred to as *DS-0 (Digital Signal level Zero)*. Digital carrier is a channelized service, at least in a standard voice implementation. In other words, a single, high-capacity digital circuit supports multiple logical channels, with each channel supporting a separate conversation. A T-1 circuit, for instance, operates at a total signaling rate of 1.544 Mbps, supporting the standard 24 Time Division Multiplexed (TDM) information-bearing channels, each with a channel width of 64 Kbps (refer to Figure 7-4). E-1 supports 30 TDM channels of 64 Kbps, plus two separate signaling and control channels; J-1 supports 24 channels as does T-1.

The American National Standards Institute (ANSI) set the T-carrier hierarchy standards (see Table 7-1) in its T1.107 specifications. Beginning at the T-1 level, the hierarchy progresses up to T-3, which provides bandwidth of approximately 45 Mbps in support of 672 channels. Most end users subscribe to T-1 services since one or more T-1s generally satisfy their bandwidth requirements. Generally, the next step is T-3; the intermediate levels are unusual in end-user implementation, although the carrier networks employ them extensively. As expected, while the data rate increases, the carrier reference frequency increases, and issues of signal attenuation and crosstalk increase; this fact creates special engineering problems [7-6] which can be resolved by various means including spacing repeaters ever more closely together [7-5].

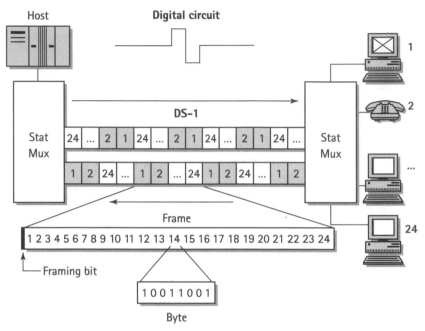

Figure 7-4 Channelized T-1

Table 7-1 NORTH AMERICAN DIGITAL CARRIER HIERARCHY (T-CARRIER)

Digital Signal (DS) Level	Data Rate (Mbps)	Number of 64-Kbps Channels (DS-0s)	Equivalent # T-x's
DS-0	64Kbps	1	Not applicable
DS-1 (T-1)	1.544	24	1 T-1
DS-1C (T-1C)	3.152	48	2 T-1
DS-2 (T-2)	6.312	96	4 T-1, 2 T-1C
DS-3 (T-3)	44.736	672	28 T-1, 14 T-1C, 7 T-2
DS-4 (T-4)	274.176	4,032	168 T-1, 84 T-1C, 42 T-2, 6 T-3

The process of transmitting data (voice, data, video, or image) in given and consistently repeated channels, or time slots, is know as *byte interleaving*. Each byte of a given conversation to be transmitted is accepted by the MUX (assuming capacity is available) and is assigned one or more time slots. In total, those time slots comprise a channel, which traditionally is 64 Kbps, derived from 8,000 time slots per second (and each of these time slots comprises an 8-bit byte). In a baseline example, those time slots are reserved for that conversation, with the MUX providing the transmitting device with regular and repeated access to them for the duration of the communication.

Unchannelized T-Carrier

Unchannelized T-carrier can support bandwidth-intensive services that do not lend themselves to 64-Kbps channelization and standard framing conventions [7-8]. In other words, the traditional convention of 64 Kbps channels can be abandoned in favor of carving the T-1 pipe into any combination of segments of bandwidth of any usable size or increment. Additionally, any combination of bits can be transmitted, including an infinite number of zeros, without concern for the violation of the 1s density rules (discussed later in this chapter) — in other words, a *clear channel* of 64 Kbps or more, rather than a 56 Kbps channel [7-5] and [7-6]. For instance, a very high-speed data communication or a full motion videoconference might require a full T-1 pipe. A less intensive communication might require 512 Kbps; i.e., 8 channels, or one-third of a T-1 facility. Such services are supported through customer equipment in the form of highly intelligent Time Division Multiplexers (TDM MUXs), routers, or data switches (refer to Figure 7-5). In a private, dedicated, leased-line network, this is easily accomplished. However, the carrier must be aware that such use will be made of the facility, so the entire facility can be allocated and managed properly.

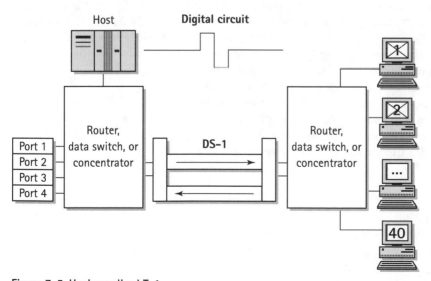

Figure 7-5 Unchannelized T-1

Unchannelized T-carrier commonly is used for access to a packet-based network such as Frame Relay or ATM. Chapter 10 discusses how these services switch data in packet format, specifically in the form of frames or cells. The switches employed in such networks multiplex frames or cells over an unchannelized T-carrier circuit. Carving the packets or cells into 8-bit samples for transmission over 64-Kbps channels serves no purpose; in fact, it introduces additional levels of difficulty.

Encoding

While T-1 is a digital service, it also supports the transmission of analog data. Voice and video, analog in their native forms, must be digitized through the use of codecs prior to transmitting over a T-1 circuit. The standard digitizing technique for voice, known as *Pulse Code Modulation (PCM)*, was developed as an integral part of T-carrier. It also became the standard technique for digitizing voice in PBXs and other devices, for the obvious reason of providing seamless transmission between such devices and the network. The quantizing techniques typically employed include PCM and ADPCM; non-standard approaches included CVSD, VQL, VQC, and HCV.

PULSE CODE MODULATION (PCM)

Pulse Code Modulation (PCM) is based on the *Nyquist theorem* developed by Harry Nyquist in 1928. Nyquist established the fact that the maximum signaling rate achievable over a circuit is twice the number of signal elements [7-9]. In consideration of the Nyquist theorem, PCM specifies that the analog voice signal be sampled at twice the highest frequency on the line. A voice-grade analog line that provides bandwidth of 4,000 Hz requires the signal to be sampled 8,000 times per second. Each sample is a measurement of the amplitude of the sine wave; the frequency of signal change is automatically taken into account. The individual samples are encoded (*quantized*, or quantified) into 8-bit binary (digital) approximate values, based on a table of 255 standard values of amplitude. The individual samples then are transmitted in regular time slots over the T-carrier circuit; the process reverses on the receiving end of the connection to reconstitute an approximation of the original analog voice signal (see Figure 7-6). The sampling rate and the 8-bit coding scheme — although the subject of much debate — yield very high quality voice, despite the excessive bandwidth requirement. You should note that sampling that is too infrequent results in a reconstructed analog voice signal that is less than smooth and accurate and, therefore, displeasing. The phenomenon of *quantizing noise* yields unacceptable levels of voice quality [7-2] and [7-5].

4,000 Hz

  × 2

8,000 Samples/Second

  × 8 Bits per Sample

64 Kbps

The above calculation shows that 8,000 8-bit samples per second yields a bandwidth requirement of 64 Kbps for a PCM-encoded digital voice signal. As PCM was the first standard technique widely used in digital carrier systems, the channel width of 64 Kbps became the worldwide standard for all forms of digital networking.

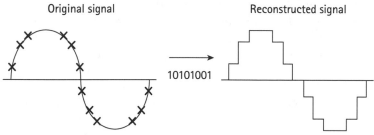

Original signal   Reconstructed signal

10101001

Figure 7-6 PCM encoding of analog voice signal, with reconstruction of
           approximate analog voice

This standard approach of channelized T-1, as noted previously, was developed and optimized for voice communications using PCM and TDM. Notably, T-carrier was developed for use in the carrier networks, and subsequently was made available to end users. As a carrier-provided service, T-1 must conform to the expectations of the carrier network, unless special arrangements are made. This is true of leased-line T-carrier networks, as depicted in Figure 7-3. It is particularly true of T-carrier when applied as an access service for purposes of access to, rather than through, the carrier network. For example, an end user organization that employs a T-1 local loop from a PBX to a circuit-switched PSTN must conform to the requirements of the carrier, which typically specifies 24 channels of 64 Kbps, and which specifies PCM-encoded voice. Conversely, large end-user organizations with large carrier-provided Virtual Private Networks (VPNs) may take advantage of more efficient encoding techniques such as ADPCM, assuming that the carrier supports them. The following discussion explains how ADPCM supports toll-quality voice at 32 Kbps, thereby yielding more efficient use of available bandwidth.

DIFFERENTIAL PULSE CODE MODULATION (DPCM)

Differential Pulse Code Modulation (DPCM) is more bandwidth efficient than PCM, as only the changes in signal level are encoded and transmitted. Based on the logical assumption that the change, or differential, in the voice signal occurs relatively slowly, fewer bits can be used to represent each sample. Specifically, 4 bits generally are used in this form of compression, which yields a 2:1 *compression ratio*. This level of compression enables a T-1 circuit to support 48 channels of 32 Kbps, rather than the PCM standard of 24 channels of 64 Kbps. DPCM generally provides voice quality comparable to that of PCM. However, noise (distortion) may result on occasion when the signal varies significantly from one sample to another (e.g., modem transmission over a T-carrier circuit).

4,000Hz × 2 = 8,000 Samples/Second × 4 Bits Per Sample = 32Kbps

ADAPTIVE DIFFERENTIAL PULSE CODE MODULATION (ADPCM)

Adaptive Differential Pulse Code Modulation (*ADPCM*) can improve the quality of DCPM further, without increasing the number of bits required. Through increasing the range of signal changes that can be represented by a 4-bit value, DPCM adapts to provide higher quality for voice transmission. Since ADPCM does not interface with a CO exchange based on PCM, it is necessary that special equipment be used to insert two compressed voice conversations into a single PCM channel. A *Bit Compression Multiplexer (BCM)* generally is in the form of a printed circuit board that fits into the T-1 MUX [7-5].

Notably, ADPCM overcomes the deficiency of DPCM with respect to support of modem transmissions over T-1. As you undoubtedly notice when dialing into the Internet, modem tones are very different from voice tones in that both the amplitude and frequency shifts are extreme. As noted previously, DPCM cannot accommodate these shifts. ADPCM, conversely, can distinguish a modem tone. Once the presence of a modem transmission is distinguished, ADPCM adapts by reverting to a channel width of 64 Kbps.

DIGITAL SPEED INTERPOLATION (DSI)

Digital Speed Interpolation (*DSI*) is rooted in a voice compression algorithm known as *Time Assigned Speech Interpolation* (*TASI*) developed by Bell Labs in the 1950s for transatlantic telephone cable systems [7-10]. DSI makes the legitimate assumption that there are predictable pauses in normal human speech. During those pauses, additional voice signals are inserted through a technique known as *silence suppression*. Since DSI works on the basis of statistical probabilities, you can employ it effectively only when there are a significant number of voice conversations supported. For instance, 72 channels yield additional compression of 1.5:1, and 96 channels yield an additional 2:1, for a total compression ratio of 8:1 (8 Kbps per voice conversation). Newer implementations can provide as much as 16:1 (4 Kbps), although voice quality is compromised at this level.

DSI suffers the disadvantage of degradation of the signal quality during periods of heavy use. If the parties speak rapidly, with few pauses, the voice signal can be *clipped*, or truncated, to make room for another signal. The more conversations supported, however, the lower the statistical probability of such degradation. DSI also suffers from high overhead; regardless of the number of channels supported, as much as 96 Kbps of overhead is required.

QUANTIZING VARIATIONS

Variations in the quantizing method are sometimes employed, although they are neither generally accepted nor widely deployed. Those variations include the following [7-5]:

Variable Quantizing Level (*VQL*): Compression Ratio = 2:1 (32 Kbps)

Continuously Variable Slope Delta (*CVSD*): Compression Ratio = 4:1 (16 Kbps), or 8:1 (9.6 Kbps)

Vector Quantizing Code (*VQC*): Compression Ratio = 4:1 (16 Kbps)

High Capacity Voice (*HCV*): Compression Ratio = 8:1 (8 Kbps)

Framing

T-carrier employs a very specific set of conventions to transmit information. Framing is one example. Using T-1 as an illustration, each channel of input is Time Division Multiplexed into a T-1 *frame*, or set of data. In other words, conversation 1 might be allocated time slot 1 (channel 1), conversation 2 might be allocated time slot 2 (channel 2), and so on through conversation 24 and channel 24. That set of sampled data is inserted into frame 1, which is prepended by a framing bit to distinguish it from subsequent frames of data. The process then repeats for frame 2, and so on.

The combined processes of voice encoding and framing yield a total T-1 bandwidth of 1.544 Mbps. Of that total, 1.536 Mbps is available for information transfer, as noted in the following calculation; the remaining 8 Kbps is required for framing.

4,000 Hz = 8,000 Samples/Second × 8 Bits Per Sample = 64Kbps = DS-0 × 24 Channels

× 2

8,000 Samples/Second

  × 8 Bits per Sample

64 Kbps = DS-0

 × 24 Channels

1.536 Mbps

+ 8 Kbps Framing

1.544 Mbps = T-1

There exist several generations of framing conventions, which are designated as D1, D2, D3, D4, and Extended SuperFrame (ESF). Additionally, the ITU-T has developed an international set of recommendations for framing digital carrier signals.

D1 FRAMING

Developed in 1962, D1 Framing *robbed* the *Least Significant Bit (LSB)* – the 8th bit – in order to insert a signaling bit in each channel of each frame. The signaling bits were in the form of alternating *1s* and *0s*. The quality of digitized voice conversation was not affected because 7 bits are satisfactory for reconstructing a high-quality approximation of the analog voice input. However, by truncating an 8-bit value, data is seriously impacted; the integrity of the data stream is violated in the process. (Imagine the impact of a bit change that converts a decimal point to a comma during the transmission of a financial transaction. Now, take a look at the balance of your checkbook. Get the idea?) As a result, data transmission was limited to 56 Kbps. While D1 framing no longer is used, the least significant bit still is robbed, even in the contemporary D4 framing technique. Therefore, data transmission remains constrained to 56 Kbps in many carrier networks.

D2 FRAMING

D2 Framing was used to create a superframe, a 12-bit pattern for framing locators. Information was transmitted in a 12-frame sequence or *superframe*.

D3 FRAMING

Still in use, *D3 Framing* assumes that all inputs – whether voice or data – are analog. It uses a *superframe* format and sequence bits.

D4 FRAMING

D4 Framing, also known as *M24 Superframe* uses a 12-bit sequence (1000 1101 1100), repeated every 12 frames, to enable robbing of the least significant bits of the 6th and 12th frames, only. Voice and data are accommodated; data is treated as a digital input. This approach improves available signal capacity and yields better voice transmission. However, data transmission remains limited to 56 Kbps, as even the slightest level of bit robbing negatively affects the integrity of the data stream. Additionally, *one's density* must be maintained through the insertion of *stuff bits*. Considered together, the 12 frames are designated a superframe.

EXTENDED SUPERFRAME (ESF)

Extended SuperFrame (*ESF*), originally tariffed by AT&T in 1985, is now widely available. ESF superframes are 24 frames in length; signaling is performed in frames 6, 12, 18, and 24. ESF offers the advantages of non-disruptive error detection (6-bit CRC) and network management, using only 8 Kbps of overhead [7-2], [7-3],and [7-4]. This is accomplished since the highly intelligent ESF channel banks require only 2 Kbps for purposes of synchronization. Thereby, the remaining 6 Kbps of the framing bits are liberated for other signaling and control purposes.

ITU-T FRAMING CONVENTIONS

ITU-T framing conventions differ greatly from those described above, which are used in North America and Japan (modified). ITU conventions call for Level 1 (E-1) to employ 32 DS-0 channels, 30 for information and 2 specifically designated for signaling and control. The first such DS-0 channel carries the functional equivalent of framing bits, while the second carries signaling bits [7-5].

Transmission

T-carrier transmission facilities can include unshielded twisted pair (22 or 24 gauge), shielded copper, coaxial cable, microwave, satellite, infrared, or fiber optic cable. Therefore, digital carrier is said to be medium-independent. Regenerative repeaters reshape and boost the signal at regular intervals. For example, repeaters are spaced at intervals of approximately 6,000 ft. in a twisted pair T-1 circuit, also known as a *T-span* or *T-1 pipe*. The repeaters are powered by the CO exchange at levels up to 100 volts. The repeaters maintain their synchronization through the transmission bit stream; therefore, bipolar transmission is critical, as is the 1s density rule.

Note that twisted pair is not used at transmission rates above T-1. At higher speeds, the native carrier frequency is so high as to make twisted pair unusable due to issues of signal attenuation — at least in a WAN environment. Note that twisted pair performs well at very high frequencies in the LAN domain (see Chapter 8). As the UTP (Cat 3, 4, or 5) is specifically designed for that such frequencies, the cable runs are short (100 meters or less), and the environment can be controlled to minimize issues of ambient interference. For reasons discussed in Chapter 2, optical fiber is the preferred medium, although infrared and microwave offer significant benefits where cabled systems are not practical.

Hardware

DS-1 equipment is required both for end-user organizations and for carriers; that equipment must be of the same generation in order to effect compatibility. Ideally, within the user organization, DS-1 equipment should be of the same origin and software generic as is the carrier side in order to deliver the same functionality and feature set. Hardware includes channel banks, channel service units and digital service units, multiplexers, and digital cross-connect systems.

CHANNEL BANKS

Channel banks were among the first DS-1 devices. Designed for voice-only service in analog applications, channel banks interface analog switches (PBXs and COs) to DS-1 circuits. Channel banks perform two functions, in sequence. First, they multiplex up to 24 (in a T-1 application) analog signals on a common *Pulse Amplitude Modulation (PAM)* electrical bus. Second, they encode the individual PAM channels into a digital format, using PCM, for transmission over a DS-1 circuit [7-3] and [7-4].

Channel banks also accommodate digital data. As relatively unintelligent devices, channel banks place each conversation on a separate channel; for instance, a 9.6 Kbps data conversation occupies a 64 Kbps channel, just as does a 56 Kbps data transmission or a digitized voice conversation. Therefore, channel banks do not make efficient use of available bandwidth. Combined channel banks and CSUs often are in the form of printed circuit boards that fit into PBX card slots for seamless interface to a network T-1 circuit.

CHANNEL SERVICE UNITS (CSUs) AND DIGITAL SERVICE UNITS (DSUs)

Developed circa 1974, Channel Service Units (CSUs) and Digital Service Units (DSUs) were discussed at length in Chapters 1 and 6. Here I briefly recap their functions. They are devices which, in combination, interface the user environment to the digital network at the physical (mechanical) and electrical level, corresponding with Layer 1 of the OSI model. In contemporary systems, they generally combine into a single device, known as a *CDSU* or an *ISU (Integrated Service Unit)*, which may reside under the skin of another device, such as a multiplexer (MUX). They are used in a wide variety of digital data networks, including DDS and T-carrier.

MULTIPLEXERS (MUXs)

Multiplexers (MUXs) are a significant step up from channel banks in terms of intelligence, capability, and cost. Originally based on channel banks and containing CSUs and DSUs, contemporary Statistical Time Division Multiplexers (Stat MUXs) offer a tremendous range of flexibility and capability. MUXs typically offer capabilities that include support for both channelized and non-channelized service, support for multiple medium interfaces (e.g., twisted pair, coax, and fiber), support for multiple trunk types (e.g., DID and combination), support for superrate transmission (i.e., channels of a width greater than 64 Kbps), and support for subrate transmission (i.e., channels of a width less than 64 Kbps). Additionally, they offer the advantages of user-definable configuration, internal diagnostics capability, voice compression, and T-carrier to E-carrier protocol conversion. Intelligent MUXs also have the ability to allocate bandwidth on a priority basis for specified users and applications, and even to reserve bandwidth, perhaps for a scheduled videoconference. Intelligent MUXs can allocate bandwidth on a dynamic basis, assigning channel capacity as required to meet the demands of traffic. For instance, a videoconference may require superrate capacity for a short period of time; multiple, low-speed data communications may require subrate channels for a brief moment; and, at other times, the entire capacity of the circuit may be in support of 32 Kbps voice conversations. Finally, contemporary multiplexers commonly are capable of being remotely configured and managed.

Recently, a new breed of multiplexers has emerged in the form of *Integrated Access Devices (IADs)*. These devices, which can be quite small and very low in cost, support multiple interfaces – perhaps to a small PBX for voice and a router for Frame Relay. Substantial economies can be realized through an IAD, which enables a single T-1 circuit to be shared by multiple data types in support of multiple applications and services.

NODAL MULTIPLEXERS

Nodal MUXs, a further step up the MUX food chain, are true network nodes acting as T-carrier network switches. In addition to serving as traditional MUXs for the resident site, they also serve as true networking devices – much like a combined CO/Tandem switch in the voice carrier world. Nodal MUXs provide the additional function of dynamic alternate routing (see Figure 7-7), which enables them to switch traffic over an alternate path in the event of a condition of blockage or failure in the primary circuit.

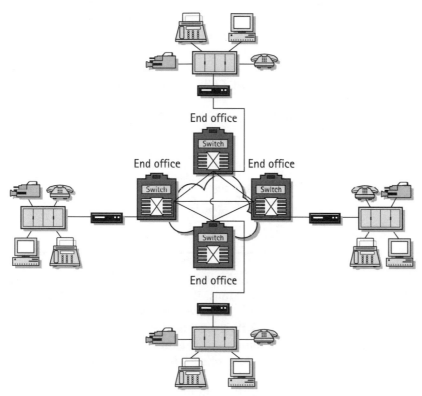

Figure 7-7 Private T-carrier network with nodal multiplexers to provide dynamic alternate routing in a fully meshed network configuration

DIGITAL ACCESS CROSS-CONNECT SYSTEM (DACS OR DCCS)

Digital Access Cross-Connect Systems (*DACS* or *DCCS*) are non-blocking, electronic common control switches that serve to cross-connect digital carrier bit streams on a buffered basis by redirecting individual channels or frames from one circuit to another. Effectively, they provide an electronic common control means of cross-connection that replaces the traditional manual method of physical cross-connection of wires. A DACS can redirect traffic to better manage the capacity and performance of the T-carrier network [7-10]. Although originally developed for carrier use, DACS also are deployed in large user organizations to support private digital carrier networks. Smaller versions, residing on a PC, are available for less communications-intensive environments. Typically of significant port capacity, DACS provide support for DS-0, DS-1, and DS-3 [7-3].

Variations on the Theme: E-Carrier and J-Carrier

While the United States set the theme for digital carrier, the concept was quickly adopted by the CEPT (Committee on European Post & Telegraph). The resulting E-carrier standard differs greatly in its implementation. The Japanese version, J-carrier, resembles T-carrier, but with differences sufficient to cause incompatibility.

Table 7-2 INTERNATIONAL (ITU-T) DIGITAL CARRIER HIERARCHY (E-CARRIER)

DS-x Level	Data Rate (Mbps)	Number of 64 Kbps Channels (DS-0's)
1	2.048	30
2	8.448	120
3	34.368	480
4	139.264	1920
5	565.148	7680

E-carrier is characterized by an entirely different digital hierarchy, (refer to Table 7-2) beginning with E-1, at 2.048 Mbps. E-1 supports 30 clear information channels, with two channels set aside for non-intrusive signaling and control. This signaling and control convention, plus the fact that there are no 1s density rules that apply, results in E-carrier's providing clear channel communications of a full 64 Kbps per channel. The E-carrier *multiframe* (16 frames) corresponds to the T-carrier superframe (12-24 frames).

J-carrier closely resembles T-carrier, although the hierarchy is slightly different. Line coding and framing also varies from the ANSI approach developed in the United States. The advantages of these differences are questionable; not surprisingly, incompatibility is assured. The J-carrier digital hierarchy begins at 1.544 Mbps, and proceeds to 6.313 Mbps, 32.064 Mbps (J-1), 97.728 Mbps (J-3), and 397.20 Mbps [7-3] and [7-6]. Table 7-3 provides a clear comparison of the various DS Levels.

Table 7-3 DIGITAL HIERARCHY: T-CARRIER, E-CARRIER AND J-CARRIER
BASED ON CCITT G.702

DS Level	Number of Data Channels	Total Signaling Rate (Mbps)		
		T-Carrier (North America)	E-Carrier (International)	J-Carrier (Japan)
DS-0	1	0.064	0.064	0.064
DS-1	24	1.544		1.544
	30		2.048	
DS-1C	48	3.152		3.152
DS-2	96	6.132		6.132
	120		8.448	
DS-3	480		34.368	32.064
	672	44.37		
DS-3C	1,344	91.053		
	1,440			97.728
DS-4	1,920		139.264	
	4,032	274.176		
	5,760			397.200
DS-5	7,680		565.148	

Fractional T-1

Fractional T-1 (FT-1), originally offered in Canada, first was tariffed in the United States in 1987 by Cable and Wireless. Now offered by many LECs and IXCs, FT-1 provides T-1 functions and features, but involves fewer DS-0s. It is offered in fractions of T-1 channel capacity, generally at 1, 2, 4, 6, 8, or 12 DS-0 channels. Subrate transmission also is available at speeds including 9.6 Kbps. FT-1 is particularly applicable where remote locations connect to a more significant location such as a regional office. There, they connect to a full T-1 MUX or nodal processor, which aggregates the traffic with that of the larger site over a full T-1/T-3 backbone network. Additionally and clearly, FT-1 also serves videoconferencing, data communications, and other applications that require more than 56/64 Kbps — but less than a full T-1 [7-4].

T-Carrier Applications

The applications for digital carrier are many. Large user organizations find digital carrier services to be highly cost-effective for local loop access, typically replacing multiple, individual PBX trunks. Large corporations find T-carrier effective for private, leased-line networks or access to virtual private networks (VPNs). The ability of T-carrier to accommodate voice, facsimile, data, video, and image information on an unbiased basis and, therefore, to eliminate or reduce the number and variety of specialized circuits, offers great advantage.

Internet service providers (ISPs) commonly use channelized T-1 to provide modem-based access to small users requiring channel width of no more than 64 Kbps. This channel width is perfect for even the highest speed conventional modems (V.90 at 56 Kbps), which gain access to the ISP on a dial-up basis through the circuit-switched PSTN. ISPs commonly make use of unchannelized T-carrier (T-1 or T-3) for access to an Internet backbone provider. The unchannelized approach is preferred for this application because data typically moves between the ISP and the Internet backbone provider using the packet-based Frame Relay protocol, which I discuss in Chapter 10.

Given current tariffs, a T-1 in the United States generally becomes cost-effective in replacement of 7-10 or more individual circuits; a T-3 generally becomes cost-effective at a level of 3-4 T-1s. Notably, the relationship is far different in Europe and parts of Asia, where leased-line costs are considerably higher.

Even in comparison to newer LAN internetworking technologies such as Frame Relay, T-carrier often holds it own. For instance, a large bank in Missouri several years ago tripled the size of its private T-carrier network to 30 nodes in conjunction with a recent merger; plans exist to increase the network by another 20 nodes by 1997. The primary application is the transport of data from ATM machines and remote bank branches to IBM mainframes located at the central site in St. Louis. The T-spans are leased from a combination of IXCs [7-11]. Incidentally, Frame Relay and T-carrier naturally coexist. A large number of user organizations now run Frame Relay data over the dedicated, leased-line networks they put in place years ago for PCM-based voice traffic. Also, and as discussed above, access to a packet-based Frame Relay network often is accomplished over unchannelized T-carrier circuits.

T-Carrier Developments and Futures

The most significant recent and emerging developments of digital carrier relate to equipment and applications. Many manufacturers of CSUs/DSUs have incorporated intelligence into their products, in effect turning them into commodity-level MUXs. MUX manufacturers have developed adapter cards that enable the transmission of SNA, ISDN, Frame Relay, and ATM over T-carrier. Manufacturers of Frame Relay routers and ATM routers and switches rely on direct T-1, and often T-3, interfaces.

Direct connection of Ethernet and Token Ring LANs is sometimes supported, with the MUX effectively acting as a bridge or router. Some manufacturers have also released direct SONET fiber optic interfaces at speeds up to of 155 Mbps. Contemporary MUXs are addressable devices that can be managed and controlled remotely. Additionally, several manufacturers of traditional MUXs have incorporated inverse multiplexing capabilities. Inverse multiplexing spreads a high-bandwidth transmission (e.g., a videoconference or file transfer) across multiple DS-0 channels or across multiple DS-1 circuits.

T-carrier certainly offers cost and performance advantages when compared to individual trunking. Additionally, it is attractive due to its ability to integrate voice, data, video, and other forms of information. Additionally, competition and deregulation have caused T-carrier costs to drop dramatically during the past 10 years or so, although they recently have crept up a bit. Yet, in a private, leased-line network application, T-carrier suffers from the same flexibility and vulnerability issues that affect alternative leased-line technologies. As a result, VPNs have replaced T-carrier networks in many large, voice-intensive user applications. Additionally, ISDN competes effectively with T-carrier in PBX-CO trunking applications. In data-intensive applications, leased-line T-carrier networks are losing ground to emerging broadband VPN network technologies such as Frame Relay and ATM, which ultimately are likely to replace T-carrier networks, altogether.

X.25 and Packet Switching

Paul Baran and his research associates for the RAND Corporation invented packet switching in the early 1960s. Interestingly enough, the concept first was published in 1964 as a means of transmitting secure voice for military application. In the late 1960s, the U.S. General Accounting Office (GAO) issued a report suggesting that there existed a large number of data centers supported, at least in part, by the federal government. Further, the report indicated that many of those data centers were underutilized, and others were severely stressed. The imbalance was due largely to the lack of a WAN technology that would permit the sharing of those resources on a cost-effective basis.

As a result of that study, the Advanced Research Project Agency NETwork (ARPANET) was developed. ARPANET, the first sophisticated packet-switched network architecture, was born in 1971. ARPANET was intended to link computers on a time-share basis in order to share computer resources on a cost-effective basis [7-12]. Specifically, ARPANET was designed to support various defense, higher education, and research and development organizations [7-13]. In 1983, the majority of ARPANET users spun off to form the Defense Data Network (DDN), also called MILNET (MILitary NETwork), that included European and Pacific Rim continents. Locations in the United States and Europe that remained with ARPANET, then merged with the Defense Advanced Research Project Agency Network to become DARPA Internet, or DARPANET [7-14].

Packet switching soon was commercialized and made widely available by Telenet, Graphnet (a facsimile-like service), and others. Packet switching was utilized very early on and most extensively in Europe. In fact, packet switching quickly became available in most countries, and currently is virtually ubiquitous. The CCITT (now the ITU-T) in 1976, internationally standardized X.25 as the interface into a packet-switched network. Note that there is no such thing as a X.25 network; rather, there are packet-switched networks which employ the X.25 protocol.

The wide availability of packet switching has made it consistently popular over the last 20 years or so. Additionally, packet networks are highly cost-effective for applications that require many-to-many connectivity, and involve relatively low data volumes. That popularity is growing and is ensured well into the future, largely through its historical deployment as the network technology of the Internet. You should note that X.25 is an interface specification, and does not define the internal operations characteristics of the data network.

The Concept of Packet Switching

The basic concept of packet switching is one of a highly flexible, shared network in support of interactive computer communications across a WAN. Previously, large numbers of users spread across a wide area – and with only occasional communications requirements – had no cost-effective means of sharing access to computer resources (read *time-share*) from their remote terminals. Specifically, the issue revolved around the fact that asynchronous communications are *bursty* in nature. In other words, data transmission occurs in bursts of keystrokes or data file transfers. Further, there is lots of idle time on the circuit between transmissions of relatively small amounts of data in one direction or the other. Additionally, those early networks consisted of analog, twisted pair facilities, which offered very poor error performance and relatively little bandwidth.

Existing circuit-switched networks certainly offered the required flexibility, as users could dial up the various host computers on which the desired database resided. Through a low-speed modem – which was quite expensive at the time –data could be passed over the analog network, although error performance was less than desirable. However, the cost of the connection was significant because the calls were billed based on the entire duration of the connection, even though the circuit remained idle much of the time. Dedicated circuits could address the imbalance between cost and usage, since costs are not usage-sensitive and dedicated circuits can be shared among multiple users through a concentrator. However, dedicated circuits were expensive, especially in long-haul applications, and involved long implementation delays. Further, users tended not to be concentrated in locations where they could make effective use of dedicated circuits on a shared basis. Finally, large numbers of dedicated circuits were required to establish connectivity to the various hosts.

Packet switching solved many of those problems in the context of the limitations of the existing networks – namely, their analog, twisted pair nature. Packet-switched networks support low-speed, asynchronous, conversational, and bursty communications between computer systems. Since packet-switched network usage can be billed to the user on the basis of the number of packets transmitted, such networks are very cost-effective for low-volume, interactive data communications. This cost advantage comes from the fact that the bursty nature of such interactive applications enables large volumes of data transmissions from multiple users to be aggregated in order to share network facilities and bandwidth [7-14]. Further, packet-switched networks perform the process of error detection and correction at each of the packet switches, or nodes; thereby, the integrity of the transmitted data improves considerably.

Understanding the concept and nature of packet switching requires the examination of a number of dimensions and characteristics of such networks. Specifically, let's explore packet structure, switching and transmission, error control, connectionless service, latency, permanent virtual circuits vs. switched virtual circuits, protocol conversion, and access techniques.

PACKET STRUCTURE

Information transports and switches through the network on the basis of *packets* (see Figure 7-8). Each packet is of a fixed maximum size, typically containing 128B (B=byte or octet) or 256B of *payload* (user data); some networks can accommodate packet sizes of up to 4,096B. The typical upper limit of a packet is 512B or 1,024B [7-15] – the latter packet size is used in many airline reservation networks.

Flag	Address	Control	Payload	CRC
(8 bits)	(8 bits)	(8–16 bits)	(128B/256B)	(16 bits)

Figure 7-8 Packet structure

A beginning flag (8 bits) and an ending flag (8 bits) encapsulate the payload data, and serve to distinguish each packet from other packets traveling the same path. The beginning flag also serves as synchronizing bits in order that the packet *nodes* (intelligent switches) and the receiving terminal equipment might synchronize on the rate of transmission. As discussed in Chapter 6, this approach reduces overhead in data transmission, thereby improving the efficiency of transmission. A packet address field of 8 bits (4 bits for the calling DTE and 4 bits for the called DTE) is prepended to the data so the various packet nodes can route each packet on its way over an appropriate path, ultimately to the target device. Control data (8-16 bits) includes the packet sequence number so the target node and terminal equipment can identify errored, corrupt, or lost packets, and to resequence the packets should they arrive out of order. Additionally, the control data includes the number of the virtual circuit (4 bits) and virtual channel (8 bits) over which the data will travel, if a path is preordained. Finally, error control data is included in the form of a CRC check (16 bits), as discussed in Chapter 6; this level of error control offers a high degree of reliability [7-14].

PACKET SWITCHING & TRANSMISSION

In a typical scenario, the transmitting terminal, equipped with a modem, dials a telephone number to gain access to a local packet node on a circuit-switched basis through the LEC Central Office Exchange. Alternatively, a short-haul, dedicated circuit might connect the user location directly to the packet node. Once the connection to the packet node is established, the transmitting device sends a control packet across the network to establish a data session with the target host computer. The originating node receives that packet, checks for transmission errors, reads the address, and forwards the packet toward the destination, across the most direct and available link. The process repeats at each node until the data reaches the packet node serving the target host. That node sends the packet to the target device, which acknowledges its receipt and establishes a session by responding with a control packet to the originating device.

Then, the originating device begins sending a stream of data, segmented into packets, with each packet numbered sequentially. Each packet routes through the network independently, from node to node, in the direction of the target device — based on the most direct and available path at that instant. Should a reasonable route or the computational resources of the node not be available immediately, the packet will hold in queue in buffer storage at a node for a defined length of time, until a link becomes available. Once the communication session is complete, a control packet is sent across the network to terminate the data call.

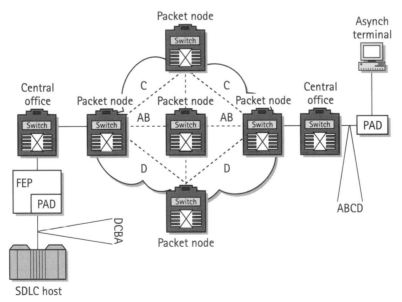

Figure 7-9 Packet switched network, supporting transmission in datagram mode

In the above scenario (see Figure 7-9), each packet may take a different route from transmitter to receiver, in as a *datagram* mode of transmission — which is *connectionless*, rather than *connection-oriented*, in nature. The datagram mode deals with each packet individually, without any consideration that each packet is one of a stream of packets involved in a session. This mode, therefore, requires that the packets resequence before transmitting from the final node to the receiving device. ARPANET pioneered the concepts of *locally adaptive routing, network message segmentation,* and datagram transmission mode.

The internodal links originally were dedicated analog trunks, which later were replaced by digital circuits — usually 56 Kbps DDS circuits. Over time, many of those circuits were replaced with T-carrier facilities. Currently, the facilities generally are high-speed and fiber optic in nature, although a variety of analog and digital media are employed in consideration of specific network economics.

ERROR CONTROL

X.25 also provides for error control through the use of a Cyclic Redundancy Check (CRC). Should an error occur in transmission, the node receiving that packet will recognize the error and correct for it by requesting a retransmission of the corrupted packet. Each node acting on the packet repeats that process. Additionally, lost packets are discovered at the destination node through examination of packet sequence numbers. Then, retransmissions of lost packets are requested.

Error control was extremely important in early packet networks because the facilities consisted of analog twisted pair. Through a cascading error control process, the integrity of the individual packets and of the packet stream could improve considerably. However, this process is demanding of the computational resources of the nodes, thereby adding to their cost. Additionally, the process is time-consuming because each packet must be checked for errors prior to being forwarded to the next node. The time consumed during the error-checking process imposes some level of latency on each packet; the more nodes involved, the greater the level of latency. As you will discover in Chapter 10, Frame Relay is a packet service that has shifted the error control process to the end user domain in order to improve network speed and reduce cost. Notably, the process of retransmission used in packet networks has a negative effect on overall throughput because errored packets that require retransmission consume bandwidth.

CONNECTION-ORIENTED

I should note that X.25 packet switching is a *connection-oriented* service. That is to say that a call is set up over a shared path (virtual circuit), over which all packets may travel in support of a logical connection. Conversely, each packet may travel over a different path, depending on the availability of the various network links at any given moment in time. Each packet of data is addressed separately and, therefore, is capable of working its way through the network independently of the other packets in a stream of packetized data. This characteristic of packet networks is a critical advantage because the network and all of its elements are shared among a large number of users. Hence, the cost of transmission across such a network is very low in the context of an appropriate application. Again, note that X.25 is an interface standard; as such, it does not address the internal operation of the network.

PERMANENT VIRTUAL CIRCUITS (PVCs) AND SWITCHED VIRTUAL CIRCUITS (SVCs)

Packet switching supports a large number of conversations over virtual circuits riding over the same, previously designated circuit or path. While the individual packets of the typical user may travel different paths, *Permanent Virtual Circuits* (*PVCs*) may support large users. In this scenario, all packets travel the same path between two computers; which path is established by routing instructions programmed in the involved nodes. The circuits involved in the route are defined on a *permanent* basis, until such time as they are permanently redefined, perhaps as the service provider rebalances the network to improve overall performance in consideration of changing usage patterns. As the circuits are shared by large numbers of users and large numbers of packets and packet streams, rather than being committed to a single data stream, they are *virtual* in nature. The definition of the virtual circuits comprising the path mitigates improves the level of service that a user organization might expect. While latency always is an issue in packet networks, a virtual circuit at least provides some assurance that the level of latency will remain fairly consistent, from packet to packet. As all packets travel the same path, they are much more likely to arrive in sequence – barring retransmissions associated with errored packets. Further, a virtual circuit that creates significant levels of packet error can be identified more easily, and the problem can be corrected more readily than if packets whizzed around the network over multiple changing paths and circuits. Since PVCs are permanently defined, however, they are subject to catastrophic failure. Should an individual switch or circuit in a PVC fail, the network provider either must correct the problem or redefine the PVC. In the meantime, the user organization cannot use the network, unless a backup PVC is provided at additional cost.

Alternatively, the network may select the most available and appropriate path on a call-by-call basis using *Switched Virtual Circuits* (*SVCs*); again, all packets in a given session travel the same path [7-16]. SVCs are advantageous because the path is set up in consideration of both the condition and the load at the instant the connection is required. Therefore, failed and congested switches and circuits are bypassed, and overall performance is improved. This process of automatic load balancing offers benefits to both the user organization and the carrier. However, PVCs demand a greater level of network intelligence that adds to total network cost; this translates into higher cost to the end-user organization. The establishment of a SVC also involves some level of delay since the network nodes must examine multiple paths in order to make a proper selection.

PROTOCOL CONVERSION

As an option, packet-switched networks accomplish protocol conversion (refer to Figure 7-8). Protocol conversion can include any protocol that is well established, well understood, widely deployed and, therefore, supported by the carrier. As this process of protocol conversion adds value, packet networks (X.25) are widely recognized as the first *Value-Added Networks (VANs)* [7-20]. This capability certainly added great value at one time — when protocol conversion was quite demanding of limited and expensive computational resources. In many cases, the carriers accomplished the process more cost-effectively than the end user organizations. The limited number of supported protocols included asynchronous, IBM Bisync (BSC), and IBM SDLC.

In this contemporary world, however, the cost of protocol conversion is relatively minor and the number of protocols requiring support is considerable. Further, protocol conversion adds to the overall packet latency, affecting all users of a shared packet network. Therefore, and in a contemporary setting, protocol conversion generally is best accomplished by intelligent devices in the end user, rather than the carrier, domain. As I note in Chapter 10, Frame Relay is a packet service that shifts from the protocol conversion process to the end-user domain to improve network speed and reduce cost.

LATENCY

Latency, or delay, is a troublesome and limiting characteristic of packet networks. As each packet may take a different route though the network, each may travel a route of a different length; therefore, propagation delay may vary from packet to packet. Additionally, each packet may travel through a different number of packet nodes, each of which must act on the packet to read its address, check for errors, request retransmissions of errored packets, and so on. Each of these processes compounds the issue of packet delay. Further, each packet may encounter different levels of congestion in the network, which may add to packet delays. Finally, additional delay is imposed on each packet if protocol conversion is required; while this process adds value, it also adds to the latency factor. The end result reveals some level of latency not only is assured, but also is variable and uncertain in magnitude [7-6].

While this characteristic of packet switching does not affect many applications, it renders others ineffective. For instance, e-mail communications over the Internet is not seriously impacted, although you may experience aggravating delays. Conversely, the quality of isochronous (stream-oriented) communications such as real-time audio, voice, or video suffers considerably from latency. Such stream-oriented communications suffer especially from jitter, or variable levels of latency. Therefore, audio, voice, and video are not supported effectively over a packet network, such as the Internet — at least not in contemporary terms. The technical challenges of transmitting isochronous data over the latency-ridden Internet, however, are the subject of intense research interest, with many organizations developing products that they hope will meet the quality of the PSTN that users expect. In the nearer term, emerging special-purpose, packet-based IP (Internet Protocol) networks promise to overcome these limitations through broadband switching, broadband transmission systems, and sophisticated compression algorithms. I discussed such networks briefly in Chapter 5, and I will discuss them in greater detail in several following chapters.

ACCESS

X.25 actually is the ITU-T Recommendation for a standard describing the physical, link, and packet-level protocols between the user DTE/DCE and the network [7-14] and [7-15]. Devices capable of packetizing the data connect over a X.25 link. In a true X.25 environment, the user accomplishes the packetizing process through DCE in the form of a *PAD* (*Packet Assembler/Disassembler*), for which *X.3* is the standard. The PAD also may contain intelligence for password protection and performance reporting [7-8].

Occasional or casual users typically access a packet network on a dial-up basis, from asynchronous PCs through modems, as described above. In such a scenario, the actual packetizing of the data is performed at the originating network node. For example, individuals accessing the Internet through an online information service often use this approach.

Large user organizations often access the network via a dedicated, leased-line link to the closest network node. Such access often is in the form of an unchannelized T-1 facility, perhaps supporting Frame Relay. Large users connecting substantial hosts to an X.25 network present data to the node under the terms of a protocol known as subscriber *Link Access Procedure Balanced (LAPB)*, which ensures error-free local access and egress on a full-duplex (FDX) basis. The PAD segments the user data into a packet, and encapsulates it in a LAP-B frame before presentation to the network [7-16] and [7-17]. The frame level procedure described in X.25 can be either the ISO *High Level Data Link Control Procedure (HDLC)* or IBM Bisync (BSC) [7-17]. *Internet Service Providers* (*ISPs*), for instance, make heavy use of such dedicated facilities.

NETWORK INTERCONNECTION

X.25 networks are widely available as a Public Data Network (PDN) service offering, generally using packets of 128B or 256B. However, certain applications are supported more effectively by transmission of larger packets. For example, the airline reservation systems (e.g., American Airlines' SABRE and United Airlines' APOLLO) deploy custom packet networks which use packet payloads of 1,024B. As this application involves the frequent transmission of relatively large sets of data (e.g., flight schedules, fares, and seating availability), a larger packet size is more appropriate. The larger packet size improves efficiency because the payload is very large, while the overhead information is roughly the same in a smaller packet. A larger packet is more likely to contain an errored bit, require retransmission and, therefore, reduce throughput; the custom reservation networks employ digital facilities to minimize this exposure. In the United States and other highly developed countries, the reservation networks largely have shifted to Frame Relay, although X.25 remains heavily used elsewhere.

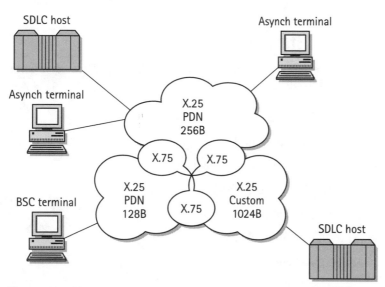

Figure 7-10 Disparate packet networks interconnected via X.75, with protocol conversion

The interconnection of such disparate networks is accomplished through the ITU-T Recommendation X.75. Through an X.75 network-to-network interface, as depicted in Figure 7-10, issues of packet size are resolved so information flow is not affected. This relatively simple level of protocol conversion occurs at a network node that examines the packet for errors, and either segments the payload of a large packet into multiple smaller packets, or combines the payloads of multiple smaller packets into a single larger one. Once the resulting packet payload(s) have formed, the node encapsulates each with the necessary control data in the form of a header and trailer, and presents each to the target network.

Packet-Switching Hardware

The user of a X.25 packet network may require no hardware other than a PC and modem. Occasional and casual users of the Internet through an online information service (e.g., America Online, Australia Online, CompuServe, and Prodigy) fall into this category. The packetizing of the asynchronous data is performed at the local X.25 node. Larger users install DCE in the form of a Packet Assembler/Disassembler (PAD), which is specified by the ITU-T as X.3. The PAD performs the packet assembly (segmentation) of the data for the transmitting device, disassembling the packet for the receiving device to reconstitute the data in its native format.

Packet carriers, of course, must invest in packet nodes rather than circuit switches. Such packet nodes are intelligent devices capable of supporting complex routing tables, buffering packets in temporary memory, resolving packet errors, and accomplishing protocol conversions.

Packet–Switching Standards

The ITU-T sets standards recommendations for packet switching. Those standards include the following [7-6], [7-8], and [7-17]:

- ◆ X.3: Packet Assembly/Disassembly functions

- ◆ X.25: Interface between DCE and DTE for public packet networks

- ◆ X.28: Terminal-to-PAD communications formats

- ◆ X.29: Host-to-PAD communications formats

- ◆ X.31: Packet-mode services over ISDN

- ◆ X.32: Defines X.25 synchronous dial-up mode

- ◆ X.75: Internetwork call control procedures

Packet–Switching Applications and Futures

X.25 packet switching originally was intended for interactive time-sharing, which involves long connect times and low data volumes. While X.25 still supports such applications effectively, contemporary applications include online interactive processing (e.g., reservations systems), messaging (e.g., e-mail), batch file transfer (e.g., data backup), information service access (e.g., America Online, CompuServe, and Prodigy), and Internet access.

Packet switching offers the advantage of being a highly mature, if limited, network technology. Therefore, it is relatively inexpensive to deploy and is highly cost-effective in support of applications that require many-to-many connectivity and involve relatively low volumes of data transport. Additionally, it is virtually ubiquitous, having been deployed in every corner of the globe. However, it proves limited in terms of speed and is characterized by significant levels of latency. As a result, many applications and service providers are moving toward newer network technologies. For example, the airline reservations systems are rapidly moving to Frame Relay, at least for the domestic U.S. networks. Internet Service Providers prefer Frame Relay or ISDN. The Internet backbone network largely has shifted to Frame Relay or ATM, operating at minimum speeds of T-1 or T-3. Much of the Internet backbone has been upgraded to fiber optic facilities operating at speeds of 155 Mbps, or much more. The future of packet switching is assured, however. Its low cost and high availability certainly work in its favor. Additionally, low-intensity users outside the United States will continue to access the Internet on a dial-up basis through X.25 packet switches.

X.25 continues to experience growth in Africa, Central Europe, Latin America, and other developing regions. In such areas, the poor quality of the networks makes X.25's error-correction capabilities a must for data communications. Demand has slackened in Western Europe and North America, where some Internet access remains X.25-based, at least at the edges of the networks [7-18].

Integrated Services Digital Network (ISDN)

A CCITT study group first explored *ISDN* (*Integrated Services Digital Network*) as a concept from 1968 to 1971. A more focused conceptual study took place during the 1981-1984 CCITT study period. The first set of published standards recommendations appeared in 1984 in the form of a CCITT *Red Book*, which provided the basic framework for the concept, network architecture, UNI (User Network Interface) protocols, and common channel signaling protocols. As a result of the 1985-1988 study period, a *Blue Book* was published that provided descriptions of supplementary services, rate adaptation, ISDN frame relay, and the initial set of B-ISDN (Broadband ISDN) recommendations. (The color of the books has no significance, other than the fact that a different color represents each study period.)

ISDN, rather than a technology, is described as a suite of services based on a set of technologies, including transmission, switching, and signaling and control. ISDN is a set of international standards recommendations that permits the provisioning of a wide range of services intended to be available on an ubiquitous basis. Additionally, the ISDN network is accessible through a standard set of interfaces — one for low-bandwidth applications and another for high-bandwidth.

The specific characteristics of ISDN include its entirely digital nature; CPE, transmission facilities, and switching systems all are fully digital. The three identified channel types include B-channels (Bearer channels) that bear the information, D-channels (Data channels) for signaling and control, and H-channels (High-speed channels) for channel aggregation to accommodate bandwidth-intensive applications. The User Network Interface (UNI) protocols include Basic Rate Interface (BRI) for low-speed termination, and Primary Rate Interface (PRI) for high-speed access. Common Channel Signaling System #7 (SS7) is a fundamental requirement of ISDN.

Announced to the world amidst great fanfare, ISDN quickly captured the imagination of carriers, manufacturers, and user organizations worldwide. ISDN offered the compelling advantages of improved bandwidth, flexibility, error performance, reliability, availability, and interconnection to a wide range of services. Unfortunately, it stalled. For the past 25 years, ISDN has progressed at a legendary slow pace. Among the many reasons for its slow development are long delays in standards development, lack of adherence to standards, lack of availability, regulatory hurdles, circuit and equipment costs, and poor marketing.

Standards development at the ITU-T is infamously slow. Standards traditionally were released every four years, in monsoon fashion and with total droughts in the interim. Over time, the various committees attained the privilege of developing and releasing certain standards recommendations on an intermediate basis; standards then came in showers. Currently, ITU-T standards sprinkle over the network landscape as they become available.

Standards from the ITU-T actually are in the form of standards recommendations. Individual member nations can implement ISDN options as they see fit – or deviate from the standards, as long as international interconnectivity is accomplished at some reasonable level. The most notable international difference is that of the basic ISDN hierarchy. The North American version follows the T-1 hierarchy, with PRI including 24 B channels; the European (ITU-T) version is based on E-1, providing 30 B channels. While this difference is understandable in the context of maintaining backward compatibility with existing networks, it also perpetuates issues of basic protocol incompatibility.

Systems manufacturers of COEs and PBXs have a strong interest in maintaining the proprietary nature of their systems architectures. Therefore, they implement ISDN in distinctly different ways. *ISDN compatibility* became *ISDN compliance*, a decidedly lower level of conformance.

Additionally, carriers have implemented non-standard versions of ISDN. Pacific Bell, for instance and until very recently, offered ISDN at a rate of 56 Kbps per channel – rather than the standard 64 Kbps. This limitation was due to the fact that SS7 was not deployed fully in the ISDN carrier network; as a result, in-band signaling and control consumed 8 Kbps of channel bandwidth. Actually, the limitation remains in some areas of the Pacific Bell network and some other carriers.

Islands of ISDN resulted from these various implementations. A given carrier, using the hardware and software of a given manufacturer, could not easily achieve full connectivity with another carrier deploying another version of ISDN. Weary of delays in the standards process, some carriers (e.g., Southwestern Bell) developed and implemented proprietary versions of ISDN, further contributing to the problem. In recent years, this problem has been mitigated through cooperation of the manufacturers and carriers, with the active involvement of Bellcore (now Telcordia) [7-19] and [7-20].

Availability of ISDN was slow to develop because the carriers were reluctant to invest in the technology unless they were convinced that a market existed for the services and/or the technology offered internal cost savings. ISDN is not inexpensive to deploy – a fact that unfortunately has been reflected in relatively high installation charges, recurring circuit charges, and equipment costs. Availability recently has increased to a significant extent because of the RBOC's and GTE's considerable commitments to its deployment. The independent telcos also increasingly have made ISDN a priority, although they understandably lag far behind the RBOCs due to cost-of-service factors [7-21].

Regulators generally have required that the LECs pass on the cost of ISDN infrastructure to ISDN users, rather than averaging those costs across the entire rate base. In other words, they have viewed ISDN as an optional service that must pay its own way, or the carriers must absorb any associated losses. Since the carriers were unwilling to do so, ISDN rates remained high. Coincident with the development of competition in the local exchange, and encouraged by the regulators, the ILECs (Incumbent Local Exchange Carriers) have exercised more freedom in pricing ISDN attractively. Each ILEC, of course, has its own pricing strategy involving installation charges, monthly rates, and usage charges. The CLECs (Competitive LECs) are free to price ISDN (and any other service offering) as they see fit, and generally price it at very attractive levels.

Rates for ISDN access historically were not tariffed at attractive levels, compared with the cost of basic services. Again, the regulators were, and remain, largely responsible. The ILECs bear responsibility, as well, because they have not been willing to absorb initial losses in order to stimulate the growth of the service offering. Ameritech, for instance, currently charges $145 for installation and up to $44.66 per month for a low-speed ISDN BRI circuit in Illinois, assuming that the full ISDN circuit is intended for both voice and data capabilities. In Ohio, the installation charges and monthly are somewhat less, but Ameritech imposes an additional charge of $26 per month for a line extender (repeater) if the premise is more than three miles from an ISDN Central Office. In Missouri, Southwestern Bell currently charges as much as $250 for installation, plus a link extension (repeater) charge of $44.80 if required, and $88.14 per month, depending on the package selected. In California, Pacific Bell charges $28.82 per month, plus FCC surcharges of $6.07 Subscriber Line Charge (SLC), $0.97 Digital Port Line Charge (DPLC), and $.012 Presubscribed Interexchange Carrier Charge (PICC). Pacific Bell's installation charges total $195.75. Rates for PRI also vary considerably; in some cases based on a per-channel charge, and in other cases on a flat rate per PRI. Some carriers charge for usage, generally at a rate of $0.01-$0.015 per minute per channel, sometimes charging packet traffic based on packet volume. Some carriers charge monthly rates as high as $500, which pales by comparison to the British Telecom rate of around U.S. $600 per month in the U.K., but is high compared to the rates of about U.S. $45 in Germany [Minoli and Mettern]. Generally speaking, the various rate plans and configuration options are extraordinarily confusing.

Equipment costs were high because the manufacturers constantly were investing in R&D to maintain ISDN compliance with developing standards. Additionally, the limited demand for ISDN caused the manufacturing runs to be small — lower costs are achieved through increased volume. For example, Terminal Adapters, which provide the interface to an ISDN circuit for non-ISDN equipment, have lowered in price from about $1,000 in 1993 to an average of less than $250 today, depending on configuration and complexity.

Marketing by the ILECs proved ineffective. Not only were costs maintained at unattractive levels, but advertising and promotion were minimal, and availability was highly limited. Further, meaningful and cost-effective applications were not identified and stressed. With typical lack of foresight, the LECs placed heavy emphasis on the low-speed BRI version — which is suitable only for residence, small business, and SOHO (Small Office/Home Office) application. High-speed PRI was not emphasized heavily as a replacement of T-1 trunking. ISDN Centrex was touted heavily, but with limited success. Centrex ISDN marketing was heavily slanted toward CO-based Local Area Networking, which proved as successful as the paperless office.

While ISDN has frustrated the industry, in general, over 200,000 ISDN access lines currently exist worldwide. Some industry pundits forecast that more than 750 million will be installed by the year 2000. I do not share that level of enthusiasm, as V.90 modems, DSL (Digital Subscriber Line), cable modems, and other technologies have stolen much of ISDN's thunder. ISDN is much more mature in Europe and certain parts of the Pacific Rim than it is in the United States. In those regions, the regulators encouraged deployment. Additionally, marketing was much more effective, focusing on PRI, rather than BRI [7-20] and [7-22].

Standard Interfaces and Channel Types

The current version of ISDN is Narrowband ISDN (N-ISDN); I discuss Broadband ISDN (B-ISDN), which is still on the drawing boards, in Chapter 10. ISDN currently is available in essentially two interface varieties (see Figure 7-11): BRI (2B+D) and PRI (23B+D) in North America, and 30B+D in Europe and many other countries). In each case, the ITU specifies the electrical characteristics, signaling, coding, and frame formatting. There is one variation on the theme; H-channel, designed for high-bandwidth applications, *bonds* multiple B channels. Regardless of the specifics of the interface and channel type, ISDN offers the advantage of symmetric bandwidth; essentially, each channel provides 64 Kbps in each direction, simultaneously.

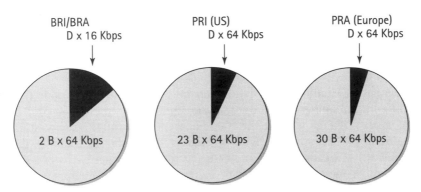

Figure 7-11 ISDN BRI and PRI interfaces

BASIC RATE INTERFACE (BRI)

Basic Rate Interface (*BRI*), also known as *Basic Rate Access* (*BRA*) and *2B+D*, provides 2 *B* (*Bearer,* or information-bearing) channels, each operating at the clear-channel rate of 64 Kbps by virtue of SS7 non-intrusive signaling. Each B channel can carry digital data, digitized voice (PCM-encoded at 64 Kbps or a lower rate), or a mixture of low-speed (subrate) data as long as it all is intended for the same destination. BRI also provides a *D* (*Delta*, or *Data*) channel at 16 Kbps, which is intended primarily for purposes of signaling and control, messaging, and network management. The D channel also generally is made available for packet data transmission and low-speed telemetry when not in use for signaling purposes; cost-effective applications include credit card authorization, which involves very small bursts of data [7-23]. BRI is used primarily for residential, small business, Centrex, and telecommuting applications, which are not particularly bandwidth-intensive. The B channels can be *aggregated,* or *bonded,* to provide up to 128 Kbps to a given conversation, such as a videoconference; additionally, multiple BRIs can be bonded for even greater capacity. Whether bonded or not, ISDN BRI provides multiple channels over a single physical loop, which is a great advantage.

A single BRI line can support up to 16 devices that contend for access to the BRI channels through a Terminal Adapter. The devices can be in the form of telephones, facsimile machines, or computers. Additionally, up to 64 individual telephone numbers can be supported [7-24]. While BRI supports as many as three simultaneous calls, the specifics of the carrier offering determine how you can use them. Some carriers (e.g., Ameritech) offer a confusing array of ISDN BRI packages that either restrict particular B channels to voice or data application, or enable them both to be used for voice or data. Ameritech and others also offer BRI variations that include only a single B channel.

BRI uses an 8-pin connector as defined by the International Organization for Standardization (ISO) in ISO 8877 and which uses a RJ-45 jack. Full-duplex (FDX) connectivity is accomplished over a digital twisted pair local loop through the application of special carrier electronics; four-wire connectivity is accomplished over two or one physical pairs, depending on the specifics of the carrier's implementation. A NT1 (Network Termination 1) device provides for compatibility with network protocols.

PRIMARY RATE INTERFACE (PRI)

Primary Rate Interface (*PRI*) also is known as *23B+D* in the United States and Japan; the European or ITU version is known as *Primary Rate Access* (*PRA*) or *30B+D*. PRI offers 23 B (*Bearer*) channels, plus 1 D (*Delta*, or *Data*) channel. Both the B and D channels operate at 64 Kbps. The individual B channels can be used as discussed in the case of BRI, but the D channel is reserved exclusively for signaling. As the standards provide for a D channel to support up to 5 PRI connections, numerous carriers have recently embraced this concept, thereby yielding additional usable bandwidth for user application. For example, the first PRI in a PBX trunking application would be provided at 23B+D; the next 4 PRIs would be delivered at 24B+0D.

PRI provides a full-duplex (FDX) point-to-point connection through a NT2-type intelligent CPE switching device (e.g., a PBX or router) device for protocol interface with the carrier COE switch.

While designed for transmission over a standard T-1 trunk, PRI is a significant improvement over T-1, because the channels can be allocated dynamically. In other words, each channel can act as an incoming, outgoing, combination or DID trunk, as the need arises. The nature of the channel can be determined as required or as specified — based on user-definable parameters. Additionally, multiple B channels can be aggregated to serve bandwidth-intensive applications, such as videoconferencing.

H CHANNELS

H channels (*H*igh-speed *channels*), are functionally equivalent to B channels, but provide greater aggregate bandwidth in PRI applications. H_0 channel signals have an aggregate bit rate of 384 Kbps, while H_1 channels operate at an aggregate of 1.536 Mbps for the North American version (H_{11}) and 1.920 Mbps for the European version (H_{12}). This capability of channel aggregation enables multirate communications on a dynamic basis through inverse multiplexing over multiple B channels. It does have a drawback, however, when compared to traditional inverse MUXs because the connection must be torn down and reinitiated when channels are added or dropped. The feature is known variously as *Multirate ISDN*, *Nx64*, *Channel Aggregation,* and *bonding.* H channels find application in fast faxing (Group IV), videoconferencing, high-speed data transfer, and high-quality audio transmission.

ISDN Equipment

ISDN hardware, at the end user side of the connection, includes Terminal Equipment (TE), Terminal Adapters (TAs), and Network Terminations (NTs) as depicted in Figure 7-12. The carrier requires digital COs that are equipped with ISDN and SS7 software.

TERMINAL EQUIPMENT (TE)

Terminal Equipment (*TE*) is the term for a functional device that connects a customer site to ISDN services; examples include computers, telephones, facsimile machines, and videoconferencing units. *TE1* has a built-in ISDN interface, while *TE2* devices do not enjoy native ISDN compatibility.

TERMINAL ADAPTERS (TAS)

Terminal Adapters (*TAs*), also known as *ISDN modems*, are interface adapters for connecting one or more TE2 (non-ISDN) devices to an ISDN network. TAs act as ISDN DCE, serving a function equivalent to protocol or interface converters. Applied to equipment that does not have ISDN capability built in; the TAs must be tuned exactly to the specific CPE/DTE. TAs can be in the form of either standalone units or printed circuit boards fitting into an expansion slot of a PC.

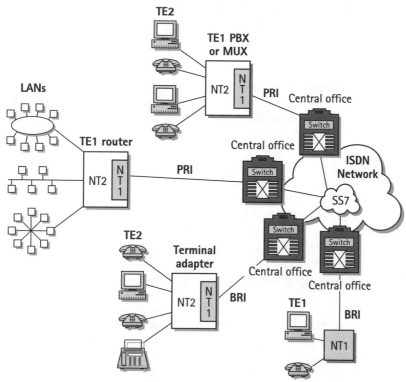

Figure 7-12 ISDN terminations in TE1 and TE2 CPE

A key function of the TA is that of *rate adaption*, which effectively throttles down the transmission rate from 64 Kbps to the rate at which the non-ISDN device is capable [7-25]. For example, a non-ISDN PC might be capable of only 19.2 Kbps through the serial port. Another example involves a connection supported at only 56 Kbps (non-ISDN or Pacific Bell "ISDN") on the receiving end; the device throttles down to that rate, rather than 64 Kbps. Rate adaptation is accomplished in North America through the ITU-T V.120 protocol; the European standard is V.110.

NETWORK TERMINATIONS (NTS)

Network Terminations (*NTs*) are Network Termination devices – NT1s and NT2s. *NT2s* (*Network Termination type 2*) are intelligent devices responsible for the user's side of the connection to the network, performing such functions as multiplexing, switching, or ISDN concentration. A NT2 device likely would be in the form of a PABX, LAN router, or switching hub. *NT1s* (*Network Termination type 1*) physically connect the customer site to the carrier side of the connection, performing such functions as signal conversion and maintenance of the local loop's electrical characteristics. In a PRI environment, these functions resemble those provided by Data Service Units (DSUs) and Channel Service Units (CSUs). In a BRI environment, these devices are TE1 devices.

INVERSE MUXS

Offered by some manufacturers, Inverse MUXs enable multiple BRIs to *bond*, or link, for greater aggregate transmission over a BRI circuit(s). For example, four BRIs can be linked to support a 512 Kbps data transmission. Such an approach competes effectively with Fractional T-1 (FT-1).

D-CHANNEL CONTENTION DEVICES

D-Channel Contention Devices, also known as *ISDN routers* and offered by some manufacturers, permit as many as eight devices to share a BRI circuit, contending for access to the B channel. The individual devices identify themselves to the network through contention for the D channel. The ISDN router also serves traditional switch functions within the context of the small-user domain.

ISDN Characteristics and Benefits

ISDN is unusual, if not unique; it is undoubtedly the most carefully planned, well coordinated and best documented network technology in history. Despite this fact, its popularity has lagged due to the previously mentioned issues of cost, availability, and applications. The key characteristics of ISDN include its end-to-end digital nature – unusual for a circuit-switched network. Through a small family of interfaces, a wide range of services can be accessed through the LEC, IXC, or CAP. Rate adaption and channel aggregation permit bandwidth-intensive applications to be supported on a dynamic basis.

ISDN's reliance on SS7, as discussed in Chapter 5, offers a number of advantages that include faster call set-up and non-intrusive signaling and control. Additionally, SS7 (either with or without ISDN) makes possible a number of interesting CLASS services, including Caller ID, Name ID, call trace, selective call forwarding, and selective call blocking.

ISDN also is interoperable with X.25, Frame Relay, SMDS, and ATM. In fact, ISDN standards were developed specifically with these services in mind. Frame Relay, in particular, closely aligns with ISDN link-level protocols. Broadband ISDN (B-ISDN), although years in the future, is dependent on ATM network technology.

ISDN Characteristics and Drawbacks

ISDN does have some drawbacks. These include limited availability, standards variations, channel application, and high cost. As discussed earlier, availability is limited in most nations because ISDN and SS7 software is costly for the carriers to deploy; while ISDN capability can be extended to non-ISDN CO exchanges, that incremental cost is not trivial. As we also discussed, standards vary by carrier and manufacturer and BRI offerings often limit the user to a single voice channel.

Not surprisingly, cost/benefit considerations dictate the success or failure of technologies, regardless of how compelling they appear at first glance. The cost of an ISDN BRI circuit often is more than twice that of an analog line, and installation costs can range considerably. These costs tend to discourage ISDN to some extent, particularly in voice-intensive environments where ISDN BRI may limit voice to a single channel.

Additionally, many carrier tariffs impose a usage surcharge in the form of a flat rate per minute (which ranges from $0.01 to $0.015 per minute) and a packet surcharge for packet data. The usage charge applies to local, as well as long-distance, calls. While these additional usage charges tend to discourage ISDN usage, the faster speed of data transfer may serve to reduce call connect time significantly. Pacific Bell [7-24] suggests that a 20MB file can be transmitted from California to Japan via a 90 Kbps ISDN connection in 3.7 minutes at a cost of $6.32. This compares quite favorably with an analog modem transfer at 14.4 Kbps, which takes 23.1 minutes and costs $29.85. Group IV facsimile transmission over ISDN lines also offers significant long-distance cost savings when compared to Group III analog transmission.

Hardware costs are additional in support of ISDN. In a BRI environment, such additional equipment might include Terminal Adapters (TAs), Inverse MUXs, and BRI contention devices. In a PRI application, ISDN software for PBXs and routers represents an additional cost; older systems might require replacement to effect ISDN compatibility.

A final cost issue centers on equal access charges, or Subscriber Line Charges (SLCs). In 1995, the FCC considered the application of the SLC to ISDN on a per-channel basis, rather than the standard per-circuit approach. Although the FCC relented under pressure from carriers and users, a Digital Port Line Charge (DPLC) subsequently was imposed; that charge currently is $0.97 per port, and is intended to increase over time.

Notably, required ISDN hardware depends on local power. In other words, the phones don't work when the power goes out. While large end-user organizations are accustomed to providing power backup in the form of an *Uninterruptible Power Supply* (*UPS*) for host voice (e.g., PBX, ACS, and KTS) and data (e.g., mainframes, LANs, and routers) systems, residential and SOHO users are not. Therefore, ISDN BRI is not recommended as a full replacement for analog telephones; rather, it should be considered a supplemental service to support a mixture of voice and data applications. Also, note that ISDN adds no value to voice communications, other than enhanced voice quality and extending functionality from an ISDN-based PBX system.

Also note that ISDN is required on both ends of the connection in order to provide any benefit. For example, an ISDN BRI is of no value, whatsoever, for access to the Internet or World Wide Web (WWW) unless ISDN is in place at the Internet Service Provider (ISP) site. Similarly, ISDN BRI is of no value to the telecommuter for corporate intranet access unless the host location also supports ISDN, in the form of either BRI or PRI.

It also is worth noting that ISDN is horribly wasteful of network resources in an Internet, WWW, or intranet application. Remember that ISDN is a circuit-switched service. Also remember from Chapter 1 that circuit switching provides temporary, continuous, and exclusive connectivity. Now, consider that interactive data applications such as the Internet, WWW, and intranet are best served by packet-based networks—as discussed earlier in this chapter. Several carriers, including Pacific Bell and US West, recently stimulated IDSN through tariffs that negated usage charges during off-peak hours. Those pricing plans proved highly successful because they encouraged the use of ISDN for purposes of access to the WWW. However, the increased usage of the PSTN, which we noted is highly inefficient for packet data application, caused substantial network congestion. Since then, manufacturers of carrier-class equipment have developed devices that recognize the telephone number of an ISP and shunt that traffic around the circuit switch to a packet-switched network, thereby eliminating this issue in equipped Central Offices.

ISDN Standards

As mentioned earlier in this chapter, ISDN standards are voluminous. While still under development in some respects, current ITU-T standards for ISDN include the following:

◆ I.441/4511: ISDN Primary Rate Interface (PRI)

◆ I.515: Parameters for ISDN internetworking

◆ Q.700: Signaling System Number 7 (SS7) specifications

◆ Q.921: Layer 2 specification for D channel; Link Access Protocol-D (LAP-D)

◆ Q.931: Layer 3 User Network Interface (UNI) specifications

◆ V.110: B-channel procedures (Europe) for Terminal Adapters (TAs)

◆ V.120: B-channel procedures (North America) for TAs

In addition to the ITU-T, other organizations are actively developing and promoting ISDN standards. For example, ANSI (United States) and ETSI (Europe) each lobby the ITU for the acceptance of their parochial ISDN variations.

ISDN Applications

The applications for ISDN are broad in range. While ISDN was long phrased *a technology in search of an application*, it recently has opened to applications developers, and aggressively so. There is no *killer ap* for ISDN; rather, there are a number of applications which, in total, promise to ensure the future of ISDN. A host of applications that benefit from the improved quality of digital networking and are bandwidth-intensive are well served by ISDN. Further, ISDN offers an affordable circuit-switched alternative to DDS, Switched 56, and T-carrier, which simply cannot be cost-justified in many cases.

Personal office internetworking, remote office internetworking, and *telecommuting* (or *Telework*) all are facilitated by the increased bandwidth and error performance offered by ISDN BRI. In such applications, file transfers and facsimile transmission is accomplished much more quickly and with much greater clarity; the improved quality of the voice communications presents an added benefit [7-26].

ISDN also is used for access to packet data networks, including X.25, Frame Relay, and ATM, with users benefiting from the faster call set-up and tear-down time made available by virtue of SS7. Since either the B channels or D channels can be used for packet data transfer in a BRI implementation, ISDN offers additional flexibility and bandwidth utilization. Additionally, some manufacturers of Terminal Adapters offer built-in X.25 PADs and Frame Relay FRADs (Frame Relay Access Devices) for end-to-end error correction [7-27].

As a replacement or backup for dedicated digital services, ISDN performs well for data and image networking, whether in a host-to-host, LAN-to-LAN, or remote LAN access application. Intensive users of the Internet and World Wide Web find ISDN bandwidth to be of great advantage because the speed of call set-up and file transfer increase a lot compared to dial-up analog connections. For instance, a typical WWW page takes 1.5 minutes to load over an analog line with a 28.8 Kbps modem, but less than 20 seconds at BRI speed of 128 Kbps [7-28]. As discussed in Chapter 3, incoming call centers can take advantage of ISDN to increase productivity, as well as make use of remote agents working from home.

At least one example merits further discussion, for purposes of illustration. A remote worker might desire to access an application residing on a LAN-connected server. An ISDN call to a local LAN site saves on long-distance charges; that LAN site connects the user to a remote site through another ISDN link. When the remote client workstation is idle, ISDN disconnects the LAN-to-LAN link to save on long-distance charges. Through a process known as *spoofing*, the application remains alive, as it continues to see a logical link over the B channel. The interactive data conversation can quickly be reinitiated due to the fast call set-up time of SS7 — which is an integral element of ISDN. The remote worker in this scenario might be a telecommuter working from home several days a week.

In terms of vertical markets, ISDN is of particular interest in the Health Care and Education sectors, largely because of its ability to support imaging and video through rate adaption. For example, TeleMedicine enables specialists to diagnose and treat patients in remote areas based on video examination and transmission of X-ray images across error-free and high-speed ISDN links.

The applications for ISDN are virtually unlimited, at least in terms of the network services that you can access. Through a single ISDN local loop, voice, facsimile, data, video, and image information can be accommodated. Additionally, simultaneous access to multiple networks and network services can be accomplished, perhaps including circuit-switched voice, X.25 packet, and Frame Relay. From a user's perspective, ISDN is highly flexible. From a carrier's perspective,

ISDN offers the advantage of consolidating access to multiple networks, thereby relieving the strain on local loop, switching, and transport facilities. Additionally, ISDN offers LECs the promise of putting the telco world back together much like it was before deregulation, divestiture, and competition. In other words, the LECs can market ISDN as a single network access solution – sort of a *one-stop shop*.

Notably, ISDN PRI often is used as a backup to Frame Relay. In the event of a Frame Relay network failure, such as the total failure experienced in the AT&T network in 1998, the ISDN PRI circuits respond immediately without dropping the data session. This approach offers diversity of both networks and services, offering greater protection than a backup Frame Relay PVC (Permanent Virtual Circuit) – which also would be affected by a total network outage.

Variations on the Theme

ISDN has experienced differing levels of success around the world due to various marketing approaches, pricing strategies and, in some cases, aggressive government support. For instance, the Japanese government has lent strong support to the development and deployment of high-technology networks and network services.

Telecom Australia achieved much success in marketing PRI to large user organizations, in part as an alternative to leased lines. An unusual offering is that of semi-permanent circuits within PRI, priced at approximately 50 percent of the cost of a dedicated circuit. In the competitive Australian telecom environment, this approach was successful in countering leased-line networks offered by alternative carriers such as Optus.

Deutsche Bundespost Telekom offers ISDN on a widely available and low-cost basis. In excess of 80 percent of Germany's population has access to ISDN within six weeks. Pricing is very attractive compared to leased lines. For application development, CAPI (Common Application Programming Interface) is supported.

Europe, for years, has offered a service known as *0B+D*. This offering provides access to a solo 16 Kbps D-channel for low-speed data transmission. Packet data is supported at speeds up to 9.6 Kbps, with signaling and control consuming the balance of the capacity; no B channels are involved. This service effectively challenges X.25 packet networking for transaction-oriented applications such as credit card authorization.

A number of Local Exchange Carriers in the United States now offer ISDN BRI variations such as 1B+D and 0B+D for applications where only a single B channel or a single D channel is required.

ALWAYS ON DYNAMIC ISDN (AO/DI)

In recent years, a number of U.S. carriers and hardware manufacturers have announced the limited availability of Always On Dynamic ISDN (AO/DI). This variation on the ISDN theme enables the user to establish an always on ISDN BRI connection to an ISP, corporate intranet site, or corporate video server; for example, through special equipment and using only the D channel. The D channel maintains the *always on* logical link between the client and the server systems, enabling the transfer of data (e.g., e-mail, stock quotes, or news bulletins) at rates of up to 9.6 Kbps, and without the call set-up time required for a circuit-switched connection (see Figure 7-13). A portion of the D channel operates as a link to a X.25 packet network, with the Multilink Point-to-Point Protocol (MPPP) used for access to the network from the Terminal Adapter. The D-channel AO/DI service employs the X.25 packet protocol that is used for signaling and control purposes in the SS7 network. The TCP/IP protocol is encapsulated within the X.25 logical channel carried by the D channel, in support of connectionless data transfer. *Packet handlers* route the data packets around the circuit-switched network, and over the X.25 packet-switched network, thereby maximizing efficiency and avoiding the unnecessary use of the circuit-switched PSTN for such an inappropriate application. Should the need arise to activate one or both B channels for transfer of large sets of data or to es-tablish a videoconference, the equipment automatically activates one or both B channels. Once the need for the B channel(s) has ceased, the equipment automat-ically terminates those channel connections, the cost of which typically is usage-sensitive. The cost of D-channel usage in an AO/DI application generally is based on a flat rate per month, with surcharges for kilopackets or megapackets applying above a defined threshold[7-29 and 7-30].

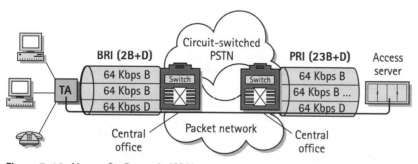

Figure 7-13 Always On Dynamic ISDN

Broadband Data Networking

Although Broadband Data Networking will be discussed in detail in Chapter 10, it is worth a quick overview of certain key technologies and service offerings, including Frame Relay and Cell Relay.

Frame Relay, a relative newcomer, was deployed first in the early 1990s. Much like packet switching, each frame is individually addressed. Frame Relay also makes use of special switches and a shared network of very high speed. Unlike packet switching, Frame Relay supports the transmission of virtually any computer data stream. Frame Relay frames can vary in length (up to 4,096 bytes), although Implementation Agreements such as those from the Frame Relay Forum suggest a fixed length (such as 1,600 bytes) in order to ensure multivendor and carrier inter-operability. Rapidly gaining in popularity, Frame Relay is widely available in many highly developed nations; international Frame Relay service also is becoming widely available. A primarily data-oriented service, Frame Relay generally does not support voice or video effectively. As is the case with X.25 packet switching, Frame Relay overhead is relatively high, delays (latency) in transmission are expected, and network congestion can result in lost data; the responsibility for error detection and correction shifts to the user in a Frame Relay environment.

Cell Switching, in the form of Asynchronous Transfer Mode (ATM), clearly is the future of communications networking — at least in backbone implementations. ATM organizes data into cells of fixed length (48 octets of payload, plus 5 octets of overhead), shipped across very high-speed facilities and switched through very high-speed, specialized switches. Further, ATM will be the platform for Broadband ISDN (B-ISDN). ATM is primarily data-oriented, although it is ultimately intended also to support voice and video. Standards are still developing and availability is limited. Current disadvantages of ATM include its relatively high cost, high over-head, and technical complexity.

References

[7-1]   Brooks, John. *Telephone: The First Hundred Years*. Harper & Row, 1976.

[7-2]   *Engineering and Operations in the Bell System*. Bell Telephone Laboratories, Incorporated, 1977.

[7-3]   Bates, Regis J. *Introduction to T1/T3 Networking*. Artech House, 1992.

[7-4]   Trulove, James E. *A Guide to Fractional T1*. Artech House, 1992.

[7-5]   Flanagan, William A. *The Guide to T-1 Networking*. Telecom Library Inc., 1990.

[7-6]   Minoli, Daniel. *Enterprise Networking: Fractional T1 to SONET, Frame Relay to BISDN*. Artech House, 1993.

[7-7]   Nolle, Tom. "Don't Bury Traditional T1 Just Yet." *Business Communications Review*, September 1995.

[7-8]   Gelber, Stan. *Introduction to Data Communications: A Practical Approach*. Professional Press Books, 1991.

[7-9]   Doll, Dixon R. *Data Communications: Facilities, Networks, and Systems Design*. John Wiley & Sons, Inc., 1978.

[7-10]   Elbert, Bruce R. *Private Telecommunication Networks*. Artech House, 1989.

[7-11]   Korzeniowski, Paul. "T1 Continues to Grow in Private Networks."
         Business Communications Review, February 1996.

[7-12]   Kleinrock, Leonard. *Principles and Lessons in Packet Communications*.
         Partridge, Craig. *Innovations in Internetworking*. Artech House, 1988.

[7-13]   Heart, F.E.; Kahn, R.E.; Ornstein, S.M.; Crowther, W.R. and Walden,
         D.C. *The interface message processor for the ARPA computer network*.
         Partridge, Craig. *Innovations in Internetworking*. Artech House, 1988.

[7-14]   Spohn, Darren L. *Data Network Design*. McGraw-Hill, Inc., 1993.

[7-15]   Stallings, William. *ISDN and Broadband ISDN with Frame Relay and
         ATM, Third Edition*. Prentice-Hall, 1995.

[7-16]   Rybczynski, Antony. *X.25 Interface and End-to-End Virtual Circuit
         Service Characteristics*. Partridge, Craig. *Innovations in
         Internetworking*. Artech House, 1988.

[7-17]   Held, Gilbert. *Understanding Data Communications*. SAMS Publishing,
         1994.

[7-18]   Burch, Bill. *X.25* "Protocol Proves to Have Enduring Appeal." *Network
         World*, October 31, 1995.

[7-19]   Levitt, Jason. "Hold The Phone!" *Information Week*, May 15, 1995.

[7-20]   Horak, Ray. "ISDN: To Be Delivered as Promised?" *Datapro
         Communications Analyst*, Datapro Information Services, January 1995.

[7-21]   Greene, Tim. "Sprint/United, Other Small Carriers Get Into ISDN
         Game." *Network World*, August 7, 1995.

[7-22]   Skvarla, Carol A. "ISDN Services in the U.S.: Overview." *IT Continuous
         Services*. Datapro Information Services, April 14, 1998.

[7-23]   Stargess, James. "ISDN D Channel Packet Service: Coming Soon To a
         Store Near You." *Network World*, March 11, 1996.

[7-24]   *ISDN: A User's Guide to Services, Applications & Resources in
         California*. Pacific Bell, 1994.

[7-25]   "ISDN and Data Networking." *Datapro Communications Analyst*,
         Datapro Information Services, May 1995.

[7-26]   Case, Linda and Mulligan, John. *ISDN As a Telecommuting Solution*.
         Bellcore, 1996.

[7-27]   Tredinnick, Ian. *X.25:* "A New Lease on Life with ISDN."
         Telecommunications, June 1995.

[7-28]   Kalman, Steve. "So You Want to Use ISDN...." *Network World*,
         December 4, 1995.

[7-29]   LeFevre, Jim. "Intel Taps NetManage for Always On/Dynamic ISDN." *ENT*, May 6, 1998.

[7-30]   Minoli, Daniel and Mattern, Peggy. "Integrated Services Digital Network (ISDN) Standards and Implementations." *IT Continuous Services*. Datapro Information Services, March 10, 1999.

Chapter 8

Local Area Networks: Connectivity and Internetworking

Just as computer networks have grown across continents and oceans to interconnect major computing facilities around the world, they are now growing down corridors and between buildings to interconnect minicomputers in offices and laboratories. Source: Robert M. Metcalfe and David R. Boggs. Xerox Palo Alto Research Center. *Ethernet: Distributed Packet Switching for Local Computer Networks.* Association for Computing Machinery, Inc., 1976.

Once upon a time, computer networks consisted of mainframes in *glass houses*; input was in the form of punch cards read by card readers and output was in the form of printed results via local printers. A few local terminals existed for input purposes, mostly control and programming. All processing occurred on a *batch* basis, rather than interactive. In other words, the input transmitted in a batch from a card reader over a short circuit to the processor, the processor processed the program in a batch, and the printer received the output in a batch. The first true mainframe was the IBM 360, introduced in 1964 [8-1]. As the first computer capable of both scientific and business computing, it went full circle – hence the designation *360* (degrees) [8-2]. During my pursuit of several degrees (academic) at The University of Texas at Austin, my programs, which seldom ran successfully, were processed in batch mode on a CDC 6600 mainframe computer. That "heavy metal" machine cost roughly $6 million, occupied a huge room, was water cooled, required tons of air conditioning to keep the ambient temperature low, and had enough large cabinets to house the population of a small nation.

Over time, input to the mainframe extended to multiple users at dumb terminals that connected to ports on the mainframe through *terminal controllers*, or *cluster controllers*. Controllers essentially act as traffic *concentrators* to enable multiple inputs from clusters of slow terminals to share one of a limited number of very expensive ports on the host computer. As time ticked away, *Remote Job Entry (RJE)* was developed to enable the remote entry of data over the WAN, with the clusters of dumb terminals and terminal controllers residing at remote locations.

Parallel to the development of data networking, the computers themselves began to change. Computers became more powerful as processor speeds increased with the development of ever-faster microprocessors on silicon chips. Memory became more available as chip technology and hard drive technology both improved. Additionally, computers became ever smaller and less expensive, to the point that the current typical desktop PC is equivalent to an early mainframe that would have filled a moderate-size office building. (That PC, by the way, also is more powerful and infinitely easier to use.) The PC was legitimized by the introduction of the IBM PC in 1983. By 1993, an estimated 75 percent of professionals had a PC or work-station on the desktop. In this day and age of the mobile professional, of course, many of those PCs are laptops, which often are just as powerful as a true desktop machine.

It was logical that all of this computing power and storage capability on all of these desktops would lead to a need to network those devices within the workplace. An estimated 80 percent of data transfer is confined to the workplace, while only 20 percent travels across the WAN. Whether or not that figure is accurate, PC users clearly have a requirement to share access to hosts, applications, databases, and printers. They also require a means to share access to WANs. LANs provide a solu-tion to those requirements.

Robert M. Metcalfe and his associates at the Xerox Palo Alto Research Center (Xerox PARC) first conceived LAN technology. That concept originally was known as the Altos Aloha Network because it connected Altos computers through a con-cept based on the University of Hawaii's AlohaNet packet radio system technology. In a memo written May 22, 1973 it became known as *Ethernet*, from *luminiferous ether*, [8-3] the nonexistent omnipresent passive medium once thought to support the transmission of electromagnetic energy through a vacuum. This highly experi-mental technology supported a transmission rate of 2.94 Mbps over thick coaxial cable. Xerox commercialized the technology, renaming it *The Xerox Wire*. Gordon Bell, vice president of engineering at Digital Equipment Corporation (DEC), hired Metcalfe as a consultant in 1979 for the expressed purpose of developing a LAN network technology that would not conflict with the Xerox patent. Metcalfe then facilitated a joint venture of Digital, Intel, and Xerox. Known as DIX [8-4], the ven-ture standardized the technology in 1979 at 10 Mbps, reverting to the name *Ethernet*; it quickly became a *de facto* standard. LANs were recognized officially in February 1980, when the IEEE established Project 802 at the request of members. In December 1982, the first standard was published and circulated. While IEEE 802.3, to which we commonly refer as *Ethernet*, actually is a variation on the Ethernet standard, we will adopt the conversational reference throughout this book, and not dwell on that technical distinction. Essentially, and for our purposes, 802.3 is Ethernet.

Ethernet clearly remains the most popular LAN standard. In part, that popularity is due to the fact that 802.3 was the first standard. In part, it also is due to the inherent simplicity of Ethernet, as compared to other standards such as Token Ring. Also, Digital's chip design team sourced chip manufacturing to Intel, Advanced Micro Devices Inc., and Mostek — thereby creating a highly competitive environ-ment that quickly led to low chip prices. Token Ring, conversely, is more complex and costly. Developed by IBM, Token Ring chips were sourced exclusively to Texas

Instruments. The impact of this decision was that of higher prices due to the lack of competition[8-4]. According to Metcalfe's estimates [8-5], in 1994 there were 50 million Ethernet-Connected Computers, 5 million of which were on 10 Mbps networks. Further, 500,000 Ethernet networks were TCP/IP registered and 50,000 were connected to the Internet. No doubt those numbers have increased considerably in the past few years, as have the speeds at which Ethernet runs.

This discussion of the basic concepts of LANs and LAN internetworking serves as the launching pad for discussion of the network technologies of the future. In this chapter, I will address the definition, origin, and evolution of LANs and their application. Dimensions of LANs to be explored include media alternatives, physical and logical topology, baseband vs. broadband, media access control, and standards and standards bodies. I will define and illustrate bridges, routers, hubs, switches, and gateways, as well as LAN operating systems. This chapter will conclude with a discussion of LAN internetworking, remote LAN access, and recent developments in the realm of high-speed LANs.

LANs Defined

A LAN is a form of local (limited-distance) shared packet network for computer communications. LANs interconnect computers and peripherals over a common medium so users might share access to host computers, databases, files, applications, and peripherals. LANs offer raw bandwidth of 1 Mbps to 100 Mbps or more, although actual throughput often is much less. LANs are limited to a maximum distance of only a few miles or kilometers, but they may be extended through the use of bridges, routers, and other devices. Data transmits in packet format, with packets varying in size and ranging up to 1500B+. Generally, LAN specifications are the province of the IEEE, although ANSI and other standards bodies increasingly are involved.

LAN Applications and Benefits

LANs are used almost exclusively for data communications over relatively short distances such as within an office, office building, or campus environment. LANs enable multiple workstations to share access to multiple host computers, other workstations, printers and other peripherals, and WAN connections. LANs increasingly are used for imaging applications, as well. Additionally, they are employed for video and voice communications, although currently on a limited and generally unsatisfactory basis.

LAN applications include communications among the workstation and host computers, other workstations, and servers. The servers may serve to provide the client workstation with access to text files, image files, applications, printers, or communications software for access to the WAN.

LAN benefits include the fact that a high-speed transmission system is shared among multiple devices in support of large numbers of active terminals and large numbers of active applications — sort of a multi-user, multitasking computer network. LAN-connected workstations realize the benefit of decentralized access to very substantial centralized processors, perhaps in the form of a mainframe host computer, and storage capabilities (information repositories). Additionally, current technology enables multiple LANs to internetwork through the use of LAN switches and routers.

LAN Dimensions

LANs can be characterized along a number of common dimensions, for ease of understanding. Those dimensions include transmission medium, physical and logical topology, baseband vs. broadband, and media access control method.

Media Alternatives

The shared medium for LANs can include most of the transmission media discussed in Chapter 2. Although coaxial cable was the original medium and still is used widely in various configurations, unshielded twisted pair (UTP) recently has become the medium of choice in many environments. Fiber optic cable is used widely as a backbone technology, although it seldom is deployed to the desktop. Wireless LANs generally are limited to special radio technologies, but infrared technology is used in certain applications; microwave and infrared systems connect LANs and LAN segments in a campus environment. Satellite rarely is used in any way because propagation delay renders it unsatisfactory for interactive communications.

COAXIAL CABLE
Coaxial cable was the transmission medium first employed in LANs. Although it is expensive to acquire and costly to deploy and reconfigure, its performance characteristics are excellent. Additionally, DP/MIS managers are comfortable with coax; it traditionally was specified in the mainframe and midrange computer world. In fact, the technology initially didn't exist until very recently to make effective use of other options such as twisted pair, fiber optics, and radio systems.

In retrospect, perhaps the use of coaxial cable lessened the resistance of DP/MIS managers to the concept of LANs. Those who lived in the mainframe world (most did), regarded (many still do) PCs with disdain. They also sneered (many still do) at twisted pair, which they referred to as *telephone wire.*

The advantages of coaxial cable include high bandwidth (500+ MHz), exceptional error performance, and lack of severe distance limitation. Additionally, security is high and durability is excellent. Conversely, the costs of acquisition, deployment, and reconfiguration are high. The disadvantages of coaxial cable have been mitigated to a large extent through the development of new coax designs. Those designs also affect the performance of the system, however. By way of example, I offer three variations on the theme: ThickNet, ThinNet, and Twinax.

ThickNet   Thick Ethernet, also known as 10Base5, uses traditional thick coax, often referred to as *goldenrod* (undoubtedly referring to its high cost and high value). 10Base5 translates to 10 Mbps, Baseband (one transmission at a time over a single, shared channel), and 500 meters maximum segment length. While individual devices can be separated by much greater distances over the medium in a data communication, each segment (link) in the network can be no more than 500 meters; you can use a maximum of two repeaters to extend each individual segment.

ThinNet   Thin Ethernet, also known as 10Base2, uses coax of thinner gauge. The thinner cable is less costly to acquire and deploy, although its performance is less in terms of transmission distance. 10Base2 translates to 10 Mbps, Baseband, and 200 meters maximum segment length (actually 185 meters, rounded up).

Twinax   Twinaxial cable, resembles ThinNet coax, but with two conductors, rather than one. Twinax is used in older IBM midrange systems such as Systems 34, 36, and 38, as well as the younger IBM AS/400 and RS/6000.

TWISTED PAIR

Recently, twisted pair has become very popular as a LAN medium. Although its performance characteristics are less appealing, its low cost and high availability certainly are attractive. *Unshielded Twisted Pair (UTP)* performs nicely at low data rates, often using the same cable plant for LANs as is used for telephone terminals. Hence, note the current tendency to pull multiple Category 5 UTP pairs to each jack — voice and data terminals can share a common wiring system. Additionally, UTP proves to perform at very high data rates (100 Mbps) over short distances (up to 100 meters).

The advantages of UTP include its low costs of acquisition, deployment, and reconfiguration; its durability is moderate. The disadvantages of UTP include its relatively low bandwidth and poor error performance over long distances. Since the carrier frequency must be high to support a data rate of 10 Mbps or more, and as high-frequency signals attenuate relatively significantly, error performance suffers considerably over a distance. Additionally, UTP offers little security as the radiated electromagnetic field is considerable at high speeds (frequencies).

The disadvantages of UTP have been mitigated to some extent, and the LAN applications have increased through the development and use of Category (Cat) or Level 3, 4, and 5 UTP. Since Cat 5 is by far the most capable of these standard options, it currently is deployed almost exclusively. The following discussions of 10Base-T, 10Base5, and CDDI serve to illustrate the application of UTP in the LAN domain.

10Base-T   or twisted-pair Ethernet, uses Cat 3, 4, or 5 UTP. 10Base-T trans-
                lates to 10 Mbps; Baseband; Twisted pair. The maximum segment
                length between the 10Base-T hub and the attached device (e.g.,
                workstation or printer) is 100 meters or less. The 10Base-T hub is a
                wire hub that serves as a multiport repeater, as well as a central
                point of interconnection. 100Base-T is a similar Ethernet hub tech-
                nology, running at 100 Mbps and requiring Cat 5 UTP or better.

1Base5   a variation on the theme of 10Base-T, uses Cat 3, 4, or 5 UTP.
                1BaseT translates to 1 Mbps; Baseband; 500 meters or less.

CDDI   or Cable Distributed Data Interface, also is known as TPDDI
                (Twisted Pair Distributed Data Interface). CDDI employs Cat 5
                UTP as an inexpensive means of connecting workstations and
                peripherals to FDDI fiber optic backbone LANs. Transmission
                rates up to 100 Mbps are supported; distance is not specified,
                but is generally less than 20 meters. CDDI is rarely used, and
                FDDI generally is deployed only as a backbone technology for
                the interconnection of major computing resources (e.g., hubs,
                switches, routers, and host computers), rather than workstations
                and peripherals. While CDDI represents an unusual predecessor
                technology, it does provide us with another useful example of
                the use of UTP in a high-speed LAN environment.

Additionally, Category 3 (Cat 3) UTP often is used for 4 Mbps Token Ring LANs;
Category 4 (Cat 4) UTP has a bandwidth of 20 MHz and commonly is used for 16
Mbps Token Ring LANs.

Shielded Twisted Pair (STP) sometimes is used in LAN applications, although it
traditionally is unusual outside of Token Ring LANs. STP might be used in a high-
noise environment in which UTP data transmission is especially susceptible to
ElectroMagnetic Interference (EMI) or Radio Frequency Interference (RFI). Examples
include manufacturing environments where there are large numbers of powerful
machines, power plants, and old buildings where it might be impossible to avoid
placing wires close to electric motors or flourescent lights in wiring a LAN. STP,
however, generally was avoided in favor of either ThinNet or Twinax in such environments. As noted in Chapter 2, Category 6 (Cat 6) is a developing cabling specification for SFTP (Shielded Foil Twisted Pair) or ScTP (Screened Twisted Pair)
intended to support signaling rates up to 200 MHz. Cat 6 applications include
100BaseT, ATM, and Gigabit Ethernet — all of which involve very high carrier frequencies. In such applications, the primary consideration typically is not ambient
noise. Rather, it is the potential that, at such high frequencies, each copper circuit
in a multi-pair cable between a hub or switch and a terminal has significant potential to interfere with another, adjacent circuit.

FIBER OPTIC CABLE

Because of its outstanding performance characteristics, optical fiber also is used extensively in contemporary LAN applications. However, its cost and fragility generally relegate it to use as a backbone technology. FDDI (Fiber Distributed Data Interface) is the current LAN standard (IEEE and ANSI) for such a network. FDDI can be extended to the desktop, either directly or through the use of twisted pair in a CDDI application.

The advantages of fiber include its high bandwidth – which is 100+ Mbps in the LAN world – and its excellent error performance (Bit Error Rate (BER) (10^{-14}). Additionally, fiber can transmit data over very long distances and with excellent security. The disadvantages of fiber include its high costs of acquisition, deployment, and reconfiguration. As fiber is very fragile; it must be protected carefully. Additionally, few users truly require 100 Mbps at the desktop – at least for the moment – and the cost of an optical fiber Network Interface Card (NIC) is considerably more than that of a UTP NIC.

As LAN speeds have increased by orders of magnitude during the past several years, however, optical fiber has enjoyed great popularity for the interconnection of hubs, switches, and routers – many of which currently feature direct optical fiber interfaces. As noted in Table 8-1, the interconnection of 100 Mbps Ethernet hubs and switches is supported over much longer distances with fiber than with Cat 5 UTP. Therefore, Cat 5 UTP is relegated to terminal connections and fiber generally is used only for backbone applications. While the specifics of the optical fiber system vary widely, light emitting diodes (LEDs) traditionally have been used in conjunction with MultiMode Fiber (MMF). As discussed in Chapter 2, this combination works well at speeds up to 400 Mbps or so over short distances, and is relatively inexpensive. With higher speeds, and longer distances, laser diodes and Single-Mode Fiber (SMF) are the choice.

Table 8-1 FAST ETHERNET (100 MBPS) DISTANCE RESTRICTIONS [CONOVER]

Cable Type	Duplex	Maximum Distance
Cat 5 UTP	Full or Half	100 m
MultiMode Fiber (MMF)	Full	2 km
MultiMode Fiber (MMF)	Half	400 m
Single-Mode Fiber (SMF)	Full	32 km

The advent of Gigabit Ethernet (GE) standards in 1998 definitely speaks to optical fiber, as no other medium supports such high data rates, even over the short characteristic of Local Area Networks. In support of the interconnection of GE switches, and in order to deal with issues of *modal dispersion* and *pulse dispersion*, which I detailed in Chapter 2, several optical fiber standards were developed. 1000Base-SX uses *shortwave* lasers that operate at wavelengths of approximately 850 nm (nanometers). These shortwave lasers are relatively inexpensive and couple efficiently to low-cost MMF for transmission over relatively short distances. 1000Base-LX uses *longwave* lasers that operate at wavelengths of approximately 1,300 nm. 1000Base-LX offers improved performance over longer distances, although the cost of the technology is considerably greater than that of 1000Base-SX [8-6], [8-7], and [8-8]. Table 8-2 provides a brief comparison of these two standards.

Table 8-2 [8-6] and [8-7] GIGABIT ETHERNET (IEEE 802.3Z) MEDIA SPECIFICATIONS

Standard	Fiber Type	Core Diameter (microns)	Modal Bandwidth (MHz per km)	Distance Limitations (minimum to maximum in meters)
1000BaseSX	MultiMode	62.5	160	2-220
1000BaseSX	MultiMode	62.5	200	2-275
1000BaseSX	MultiMode	50.0	400	2-500
1000BaseSX	MultiMode	50.0	500	2-550
1000BaseLX	MultiMode	62.5	500	2-550
1000BaseLX	MultiMode	50.0	400	2-550
1000BaseLX	MultiMode	50.0	500	2-550
1000BaseLX	Single-Mode	9	Not applicable	2-5,000

There are developing specifications for GE over copper, although none are standardized currently. The developing specification for 1000Base-CX involves an electrically balanced copper cable in the form of shielded 150-ohm Twinaxial cable, and will interconnect clustered GE switches over distances of no more than 25 meters (50 meters with a single repeater). Developing Cat 6 and Cat 7 standards are intended to support gigabit speeds between terminals and switches.

WIRELESS

Wireless LANs (*WLANs*) offer the obvious advantage of avoiding cabling costs — important especially in a dynamic environment where there is frequent reconfiguration of the workplace. Additionally, WLANs have found acceptance in providing LAN capabilities in temporary quarters, where costly cabling soon would have to be abandoned, and in older buildings where wires are difficult or impossible to run. Radio Frequency (RF) and Infrared (Ir) technologies support WLAN communications.

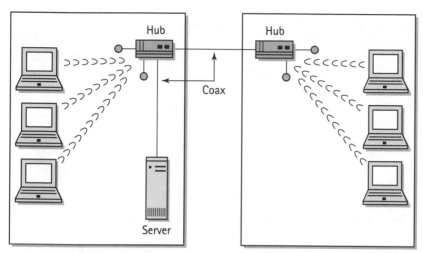

Figure 8-1 Wireless LAN configuration

The most common approach is the RF approach, which involves fitting each workstation with a low-power transmit/receive radio antenna (generally in the form of a PC card). Frequency assignments for commercial applications can be in the 900 MHz, 2 GHz, and 5 GHz bands. A hub antenna is located at a central point (see Figure 8-1), such as the center or a corner of the ceiling, where line-of-sight can be established with the various terminal antennae. While line-of-sight is not strictly required, it is desirable — particularly at higher frequencies. The hub antenna then connects to other hub antennae and to the servers, peripherals, and hosts via cabled connections, which also connect together multiple hub antennae for transmission between rooms, floors, buildings, etc. In order to serve multiple workstations, *spread spectrum* radio technology often is employed to maximize the effective use of limited bandwidth. Spread spectrum involves scattering packets of a data stream across a range of frequencies, rather than using a single transmission frequency. A side benefit of spread spectrum is that of increased security, since the signal is virtually impossible to intercept [8-9]. While the raw aggregate bandwidth of a wireless radio LAN generally is described as 2-4 Mbps, the effective throughput falls more in the range of 1-2 Mbps per hub [8-10]. Some wireless LANs also use direct sequence transmission, in which the signal is sent simultaneously over several frequencies; thereby, there is a stronger likelihood that the signal will get through to the access hub [8-11]. Regardless of the frequency range employed, contemporary buildings are full of metal and electronic interference, which combine to reduce the effectiveness of RF-based wireless LANs.

Some WLANs use unlicensed frequencies (902 MHz, 2.4 GHz, and 5.7 GHz). This approach avoids expensive and lengthy licensing by the regulatory authorities such as the FCC. However, there exists significant potential for interference from other such systems in proximity. Additionally, a wide variety of other devices (e.g., garage door openers, bar code scanners, and industrial microwave ovens) use the same frequencies, which are in the ISM (Industrial/Scientific/Medical) bands. The systems that use licensed frequencies in the 2 GHz and 5 GHz ranges avoid the potential for interference, but require that the manufacturer carefully police the deployment of such systems on a site-specific basis and under the terms of an omni-license.

A final option for RF-based WLANs is an approach dubbed 100BaseRadio. This approach takes advantage of multiple range channels in the bands at 5.2 GHz, 5.3 GHz, and 5.775 GHz. Those bands recently were allocated as Unlicensed National Information Infrastructure (U-NII) for high data rate communications. Operating at aggregate rates theoretically as high as 100 Mbps, 100BaseRadio allocates that bandwidth across multiple users through 10-12 independent channels, each running at 10-20 Mbps spread across the three bands [8-12].

The IEEE 802.11 standard begins at theoretical maximum transmission rates of 2 Mbps, with optional fallback to 1 Mbps in noisy environments. The limited number of products supporting that specification generally deliver actual throughput of less, sensitive to factors such as background noise and distance [8-13]. 802.11 uses both direct sequence and frequency-hopping techniques in the unlicensed 2.4 GHz range, with future plans to run at 10 Mbps in the 5 GHz range, and over infrared. The 802.11 standard uses the same collision-based access protocol as is optional with Ethernet, which comprises the vast majority of LANs [8-14] and [8-15].

Although somewhat unusual, infrared light can be used as the transmission medium, rather than radio. As described in Chapter 2, an infrared LAN system generally requires line-of-sight between the light source and receiver. Within a room, however, the light signal can bounce off walls, ceilings, and other surfaces until it reaches the receiver; since the light signal cannot penetrate solid objects, it bounces around until it loses power. This infrared transmission technique is known as *diffused propagation* [8-5]. PDAs (Personal Digital Assistants) make widespread use of infrared to establish links with workstations and other PDAs for data transfer. Infrared printer ports are fairly common. Infrared technology is commercially available at speeds of 1.5, 4, 155 Mbps, and even 622 Mbps [8-16]. Microsoft's announcement (April 1999) of infrared support for Windows 2000 likely will provide a boost to the use of infrared in the LAN domain.

Whether using radio or infrared light frequencies, wireless LANs are a relatively immature technology that is yet to be accepted widely. Acquisition costs are not low particularly when compared to wired LANs, although configuration and reconfiguration costs are virtually nonexistent. Additionally, wireless offers the advantage of portability, particularly in the case of the unlicensed frequencies. On the negative side, bandwidth and throughput are limited, and error performance and security are issues of some significance. [8-10], [8-17], and [8-17]

Topology: Physical and Logical Configurations

The physical topology (layout) of a LAN is in the form of a Bus, Ring, or Star. As Trains, Ovals, Planets, and Constellations are not defined, you should avoid vendors promoting such topologies at all costs!

BUS TOPOLOGIES

As shown in Figure 8-2, *bus* topologies are multipoint electrical circuits. The original bus topology employed coaxial cable, although contemporary bus systems also can make use of UTP or STP. Data transmission is bi-directional, with the attached devices transmitting in both directions. While generally operating at a theoretical raw data rate of 10 Mbps, actual throughput is much less. Bus networks employ a decentralized method of media access control known as CSMA (Carrier Sense Multiple Access), which enables the attached devices to make independent decisions relative to media access and initiation of transmission. This approach results in data collisions, from which the transmitting device must recover through retransmission. As bus networks are not carefully controlled from a centralized point, a given device cannot determine when, if ever, it will be afforded access to the shared bus. Therefore, such networks can be characterized as non-deterministic in nature. Bus networks are specified in the IEEE 802.3 standard, and generally have a maximum specified length of 2.5 km (1.55 miles).

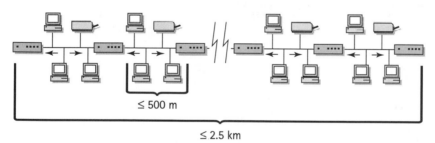

Figure 8-2 Ethernet bus topology

The original, classic Ethernet was based on a bus topology comprising coaxial cable segments that could be a maximum of 500 meters in length. Each segment could support as many as 1,024 network addresses, each of which were associated with an attached device. The maximum segment length was due to issues of attenuation at the relatively high carrier frequency. Ethernet segments could connect through *bridges*, which function as signal repeaters. The total route length of the entire Ethernet was limited to 2.5 km — a function of both signal propagation time and Media Access Control (MAC) mechanisms. I discuss CSMA/CD and CSMA/CA, the Ethernet MAC standards, later in this chapter.

A *tree* topology is a variation on the bus theme, with multiple *branches* off the *trunk* of the central bus. Bus networks also suffer from the vulnerability of the bus

– should the bus be compromised, the entire network is compromised. Similarly, tree networks are dependent on the integrity of the *root* bus [8-2].

RING TOPOLOGIES

Ring networks (refer to Figure 8-3) are laid out in a physical ring, or closed loop, configuration. Information travels around the ring in only one direction, with each attached station or node serving as a repeater [8-2]. Rings generally are coax or fiber (FDDI) in nature, operating at raw transmission rates of 4, 16, 20, or 100+ Mbps. Rings are deterministic in nature. They employ token passing as the method of Media Access Control to ensure all nodes can access the network within a prede-termined time interval. Priority access is recognized. A master control station con-trols access to the transmission medium, with backup control stations assuming responsibility in the event of a master failure. Throughput is very close to raw bandwidth, as data collisions do not occur in such a carefully controlled environ-ment. On the negative side, the failure of a single node can compromise the entire network. Electrical ring networks are specified in the IEEE 802.5 standard; FDDI is an ANSI specification. Token-Passing Ring, IBM Token Ring, and FDDI all are based on ring topologies.

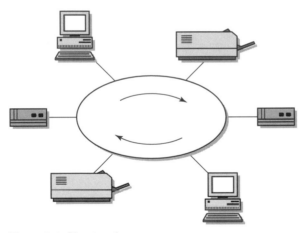

Figure 8–3 Ring topology

STAR

Star topologies (refer to Figure 8-4) consist of a central node, or point of intercon-nection, to which all other devices are attached directly, generally via UTP or STP. The central node is in the form of a hub, switch, or router. Transmission rates vary, with 10Base-T operating at 10 Mbps, AT&T's StarLAN operating at 1-10 Mbps, and both 100Base-T and 100VG-AnyLAN at 100 Mbps. Perhaps the greatest advantage of a star is that individual devices can connect to the node via UTP or STP. Another key advantage of a star is that a disruptive or failed station can be isolated, thereby eliminating any negative affect it may have on LAN performance. Additionally, multiple attached devices simultaneously can share the full bandwidth of the LAN, at least in a switched environment. The primary disadvantage is that a hub failure is catastrophic; as all connectivity is provided through the central hub, its failure affects the entire LAN. Examples of star configurations include 10 Base-T, 100Base-T, 100VG-AnyLAN, AT&T's StarLAN and DataKit, and ATM.

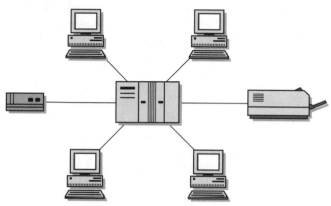

Figure 8-4 100Base-T Star topology

Physical versus Logical Topology

A network may be laid out physically in one fashion, but operate logically in an entirely different manner. For example, 100Base-T (see Figure 8-4) physically appears as a star configuration because the devices are arrayed around a central node in the form of a hub. However, 100Base-T operates as an *Ethernet bus*. The bus still exists, but under the skin of the central *hub* to which all stations in the workgroup connect via UTP. The classic Ethernet coax bus collapses and resides under the protection of the hub chassis, taking the form of a *collapsed backbone*. In this fashion, the network gains the logical advantages of the Ethernet protocol, as well as the physical advantages of a UTP-based star. Similarly, a ring network might operate logically as a ring, but be supported physically by a collapsed backbone bus.

Baseband versus Broadband

There exist two LAN transmission options: *baseband* and *broadband*. Baseband LANs, the most prevalent by far, are single-channel systems that support a single transmission at any given time. Broadband LANs support multiple transmissions via multiple frequency channels, with the channels derived through frequency division multiplexing (FDM), as discussed in Chapter 1. While broadband LANs were quite common in the 1980s, they are unusual in contemporary applications. Note that the term *broadband* has an entirely different meaning in the LAN and WAN domains. In the wide area network (WAN) domain, broadband means capacity equal to or greater than 45 Mbps (T-3).

BROADBAND LANS

Broadband LANs are multichannel, analog LANs (see Figure 8-5) typically based on coaxial cable as the transmission medium, although fiber optic cable also is used on occasion [8-2]. Aggregate bandwidth is as much as 500 MHz, and individual channels offer bandwidth of 1-5 Mbps, with 20-30 channels typically supported. The various channels are multiplexed onto the carrier through Frequency Division Multiplexing (FDM). Radio modems accomplish the digital-to-analog conversion process, providing the digital device with access to an analog channel. The modems, which must be tuned and managed carefully, may be fixed-frequency or frequency-agile. *Fixed-frequency* modems are tuned to a specific frequency channel, while *frequency-agile* modems can search for an available channel. Although frequency-agile modems are more expensive to acquire and administer, they offer improved communications and bandwidth utilization. Since the LAN is analog in nature, it can accommodate voice and video easily. The IEEE standard for broadband LANs is *10Broadband36*, translated as *10* Mbps, *Broadband* (multichannel), with *36*00 meters maximum separation between devices.

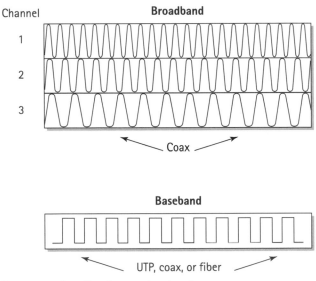

Figure 8-5 Broadband versus baseband

The characteristics of broadband LANs, generally speaking, are not endearing. However, their unique properties do have application. For example, Sea World, the chain of ocean theme parks, uses broadband LANs extensively to support analog paging (audio voice), closed circuit analog TV (video), as well as data. As the LAN is analog, it supports audio and TV easily. Further, the application is static, rather than dynamic because the paging zones and closed-circuit TV channels require fixed amounts of bandwidth, and the associated frequency channel assignments need to be changed infrequently, if ever. Further, the locations of the terminal equipment (paging source and horns, and VCRs and TV monitors) are fixed, or seldom change. The data transmissions typically are low speed in nature and in support of transaction processing applications such as cash and credit card transactions initiated from the ticket counters, restaurants, and gift shops. Since the transaction processing applications are low speed, the requisite channels are narrowband. As the coax-based broadband LAN is entirely on Sea World property, it can be deployed and controlled carefully for maximum performance. CATV providers are making extensive use of broadband LAN technology as they introduce two-way Internet access and two-way voice communications over coaxial cable systems originally deployed in support of one-way entertainment TV.

BASEBAND LANS

Baseband LANs are single channel, supporting a single communication at a time (see Figure 8-5). They are digital in nature, varying the bit state through *voltage on/off* or *light pulse on/off*. Total bandwidth of 1-100 Mbps is provided over coax, UTP, STP, or fiber optic cable. Interconnection of Gigabit Ethernet switches requires fiber optic cable in support of speeds of 1 Gbps. Distance limitations depend on the medium employed and the specifics of the LAN protocol. Baseband LAN physical topologies include Ring, Bus, Tree, and Star.

Baseband LANs are by far are the most popular and, therefore, by far the most highly standardized. Ethernet, Token Passing, Token Ring, and FDDI are all baseband in nature. While they are intended only for data, data communications is, after all, the primary reason for the existence of LANs. Recently, Ethernet, FDDI, and other LANs have announced versions that support voice, video, and videoconferencing. While the support of such isochronous traffic offers clear advantages in support of workgroup communications, the LAN data traffic can be impacted to a considerable extent.

Media Access Control

Media Access Control (MAC), at the physical and electrical level, is accomplished at the *Network Interface Unit (NIU)*, or *Network Interface Card (NIC)*. A NIU or NIC is at the board level, with the boards typically fitting into an expansion slot of an attached device (e.g., workstation, printer, or server). Alternatively, multiple cards may be contained within a multiport device that supports multiple workstations on a pooled basis. Each NIU/NIC has a unique logical address for purposes of identification, with the address hard-coded on a silicon chip at the time of manufacture.

Media Access Control describes the process that is employed to control the basis on which devices can access the shared network. Some level of control is required to ensure the ability of all devices to access the network within a reasonable period of time, thereby resulting in acceptable *access times* and *response times*. It also is important that some method exist to either detect or avoid data collisions, which are caused by multiple transmissions placed on the shared medium simultaneously. Media Access Control can be accomplished on either a centralized or decentralized basis, and can be characterized as either deterministic or non-deterministic in nature.

CENTRALIZED CONTROL

A centralized controller polls devices to determine when access and transmission by each station can occur. Stations transmit when requested, or when a station transmission request is acknowledged and granted. This process of polling requires the passing of control packets, which entail overhead and which, therefore, reduce the amount of throughput relative to the raw bandwidth available. Additionally, the failure of the central controller disrupts the entire network; in such an event, the controller is taken off-line and a back-up controller assumes responsibility. Centrally controlled networks generally employ deterministic access control, whereby each device can determine either the specific point in time at which it is provided access, or the maximum interval of time that transpires between access opportunities. The primary advantage of centralized control is that access to the shared network is accomplished on an orderly (controlled) basis. Access can be provided in consideration of several levels of priority, with the most critical transmissions gaining privileged levels of access. Alternatively, all devices can be of equal priority and, therefore, can share equally in access privileges. Token Ring and FDDI networks are examples of central control.

DECENTRALIZED CONTROL

Decentralized control is somewhat anarchistic, as each station assumes responsibility for controlling its access to the shared network. Additionally, each station must assume responsibility for detecting and resolving any data collisions that might occur in the likely event that its access and transmission to the shared medium overlaps with that of other devices. Decentralized control networks generally use non-deterministic, or contentious, media access control. For instance, Ethernet LAN control is decentralized.

DETERMINISTIC ACCESS

Deterministic access is a media access control convention that enables both the centralized master station, which commonly is in the form of a server, and each slaved station to determine the maximum length of time that passes before access is provided the network. In other words, each station can be guaranteed the right to communicate within a certain time frame. Additionally, the system administrator can assign access priorities. Deterministic access is also known as *non-contentious* because the devices do not contend for access; rather, access is controlled on a centralized basis.

Deterministic access employs *token passing*. The *token*, which consists of a specific bit pattern, indicates the status of the network — *available* or *unavailable*. The token is generated by a centralized master control station, as described previously, and transmitted across the network. The station in possession of the token controls the access to the network. That station either may transmit or require other stations to respond. Transmission is in the form of a data packet of a predetermined maximum size, determined by the number of nodes on the ring and the traffic to be supported; oversized transmissions are segmented, or fragmented. After transmitting, the station passes the token to a successor station, in a predetermined sequence. While the process is complex and overhead-intensive, it yields careful control over the network — thereby avoiding data collisions.

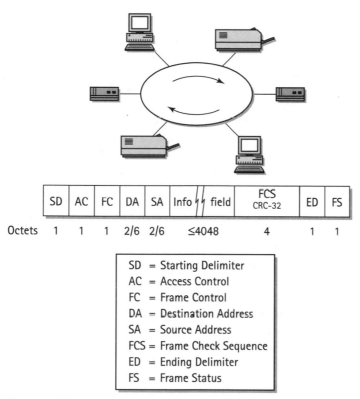

Figure 8-6 Token passing, with 4 Mbps token ring frame format

Deterministic access is especially effective in high-traffic environments where a lack of control causes chaos in the form of frequent data collisions. It also finds application in environments such as process control, where it is critical that each station can access the network on a periodic basis. For example, oil refineries employ deterministic media access control through proprietary token-passing

LANs. The refining process requires that the nature of the specifics of the crude oil (raw material) be considered in terms of a number of characteristics, including sulfur content, paraffin content, and viscosity. With those factors in mind, the refining process is tailored to act on the raw material in such a way as to ensure that the end product (e.g., 92 octane, unleaded gasoline) remains consistent from one batch to another. In a hypothetical scenario, the master control station addresses tokens to individual devices in the form of various sensors. The individual sensors monitor pressure and temperature conditions, as well as the rate of flow of various chemicals through valves throughout the entire process. In order to control the process effectively, each sensor must be addressed on a regular basis so that it can transmit data to the master controller. Additionally, some devices at certain times during the process may require more frequent priority access. In consideration of that data, the master controller commands other devices to increase or decrease temperature, open or close valves, and so on. Such a network also is highly redundant so a network or device failure does not compromise the integrity of the process.

CATV (Community Antenna TV) providers in a convergence scenario are applying an extension of this concept in field trials. Internet access is provided to large numbers of residences, businesses, and schools over a two-way coaxial cable system terminating in cable modems at each premise. As much as 500 Mbps is reserved for such applications, with as much as 10 Mbps available to an individual user. In order to manage contention over such a network, which extends over fairly significant distances, a token-passing media access control technique might be employed, with the master station located at the CATV provider's head-end.

General characteristics of token-based networks include a high level of access control, which is centralized. Access delay is measured and assured, with supported priority access. Throughput is very close to raw bandwidth, as data collisions are avoided; throughput also improves under load, although absolute overhead is higher than with non-deterministic access techniques. Deterministic access standards include Token-Passing Ring, IBM Token Ring (refer to Figure 8-6), and Token-Passing Bus.

Token-based LAN technologies are somewhat overhead intensive, due to the token passing and management processes. However, they can more than compensate for that fact by avoiding data collisions. Token Ring, for instance comes in 4, 16, and 20 Mbps flavors; in each case, bandwidth utilization is virtually 100 percent under full load [8-18].

NON-DETERMINISTIC ACCESS

Non-deterministic access, or *contentious* media access control, places access control responsibilities on the individual stations. Also known as Carrier Sense Multiple Access (CSMA), this approach is most effective in low-traffic environments. There are two variations on the theme: CSMA/CD and CSMA/CA.

Carrier Sense Multiple Access (CSMA) is a decentralized, contentious media access control method used in Ethernet and other bus-oriented LANs. Each of *multiple* stations, or nodes, must *sense* the *carrier* frequency to determine network availability before *accessing* the medium to transmit data. Further, each station must monitor the network to determine if a collision has occurred because collisions render the transmission invalid and require a retransmission. In the event of a busy condition or a collision, the subject station backs off the network for a calculated random time interval before attempting subsequent access.

CSMA works much like an old telephone *party line*, where there are multiple subscribers with individual logical addresses (in the form of telephone numbers) connected to a single physical circuit. When placing an outgoing call, the subscriber must pick up the telephone to monitor the line for a short while to sense the level of activity. If there is no activity, a call can be placed. If there already is a call in progress, another call attempt cannot be made without causing interference (and hard feelings). Rather, the telephone must be hung up; subsequent random monitoring of the circuit can take place in order to determine its availability. Incoming calls are addressed to each party on the party line by varying the number of rings, indicating the unique logical address of each party sharing the circuit; only the target party can answer the call without creating ill will. In other words, media access control protocols govern the manner in which the circuit is managed to the satisfaction of all parties.

The above CSMA approach is known as *Nonpersistent CSMA*; variations include *1-Persistent CSMA* and *P-Persistent CSMA*. CSMA is implemented in two standard means: CSMA/CD and CSMA/CA. In either case, latency and throughput degrade under heavy loads of traffic; for example, a classic Ethernet network running at the theoretical speed of 10 Mbps typically provides no more than 4-6 Mbps throughput. While it is less costly than Token Ring networking, it also delivers less efficient use of bandwidth [8-18].

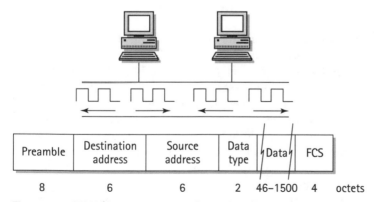

Preamble	Destination address	Source address	Data type	Data	FCS
8	6	6	2	46–1500	4	octets

Figure 8-7 CSMA/CD, with Ethernet frame format

Carrier Sense Multiple Access with Collision Detection (CSMA/CD) is the most common media access control method used in bus networks (see Figure 8-7). In an Ethernet environment, for example (Figure 8-6), the transmitting station sends a data packet in both directions of the bus. This is appended with a *preamble* (8 octets) for purposes of synchronization, destination (6 octets), and source (6 octets) addresses, as well as a type field (2 octets) identifying the higher layer protocol used in the data field (46-1500 octets). A Frame Check Sequence (FCS) consisting of a 32-bit CRC serves for error control [8-19]. Each *transceiver* (*trans*mitter/re*ceiver*) of each station along the way reads the address prepended to the data packet. If the address matches, the transceiver provides the packet to the target device. If the address does not match, the transceiver forwards the packet to the next transceiver. If a node detects a data collision, that station sends a brief *jamming signal* over a subcarrier frequency of the network to advise all stations of the collision. Then, all devices back off the network, with each calculating a random time interval before attempting a retransmission. CSMA/CD is designed to work with packets of specific minimum and maximum sizes. In the Ethernet environment, for example, note that the frame (packet) size varies in length from 64 to 1,518 bytes.

Several factors help to determine the maximum packet size. First, and as the Ethernet is shared, a file transfer fragments into subsets of data so one transmission does not speak to the entire level of bandwidth available across the network for a long period of time. Second, the maximum frame size is a trade-off between raw efficiency and throughput. In other words, a stream of unfragmented, unframed data is most efficient because it requires little overhead. However, a single bit error in a data stream associated with a bulk file transfer requires that the entire file be retransmitted. This process might have to repeat an infinite number of times, with the file never making it from transmitter to receiver without error. By fragmenting the file into subsets of data in the form of frames, the level of overhead increases, as each frame requires 18 octets of overhead, plus 1 octet of preamble. However, an errored bit is confined to a single frame — which easily can be retransmitted without significant likelihood of error, and without serious degradation of overall throughput across the LAN.

The minimum packet (frame) size is a direct function of the design of the classic Ethernet, and the CSMA/CD control mechanism. In the most extreme case, an Ethernet comprises a great number of segments — each is up to 500 meters in length, supports as many as 1,024 addresses, involves a great number of transceivers, and connects to one or more other segments through a bridge. The total route length of the classic Ethernet is up to 2.5 kilometers. Given issues of propagation delays across the segments and through the bridges, it takes a given amount of time for a frame to traverse the network from the originating device to the target device — which is 2.5 kilometers away, in the worst possible case. If that frame of data encounters a data collision at the extreme distant end just before it reaches the target device, it takes an identical amount of time for a collision notification to be received across the subcarrier channel by the transmitting device. Then, a retransmission is used to adjust to that fact. If such notification is not received in time, the originating device assumes that the data was received in good form, when that is not the case. Therefore, the minimum frame size in classic Ethernet is 64 octets, which includes 46 octets of payload and 18 octets of overhead.

Carrier Sense Multiple Access/Collision Avoid (CSMA/CA) includes a priority scheme to guarantee the transmission privileges of high-priority stations. CSMA/CA requires a delay in network activity after each completed transmission. That delay is proportionate to the priority level of each device, with high-priority nodes programmed for short delays and low-priority nodes programmed for relatively long delays. As collisions may occur still, they are managed either through *Collision Detect* or through retransmission after receipt of a *Negative Acknowledgment (NAK)*. CSMA/CA is more expensive to implement because it requires that additional programmed logic be embedded in each device or NIC. CSMA/CA does, however, offer the advantage of improved access control, which serves to reduce collisions and, thereby, improve the overall performance of the network.

Wireless LANs (WLANs), as standardized in IEEE 802.11 and as discussed earlier in this chapter, employ CSMA/CA. The 802.11 standard uses a *Positive Acknowledgement (ACK)* mechanism, which requires that the transmitting station first check the medium to determine its availability. The transmitter sends a short *Request To Send (RTS)* packet, which contains the source and destination network addresses, as well as the duration of the subject transmission. If the shared medium is available, the destination station responds with a *Clear To Send (CTS)* packet. All devices on the network recognize and honor this acknowledged claim to the shared network resources. If the source station does not receive an ACK packet from the destination station, it retransmits RTS packets until access is granted.

LAN Equipment

In addition to the attached devices (also referred to as nodes or stations), LANs may make use of other devices to control physical access to the shared medium, extend the maximum reach of the LAN, switch traffic, etc. Such hardware is in the form of NICs/NIUs, transceivers, MAUs, bridges, hubs, routers, and gateways. As with much of the technology addresses in this book, the lines blur between these devices and their individual functions. Therefore, I focus on the classic definitions, expanding on those concepts and illustrating multifunctional devices as appropriate.

Network Interface Cards (NICs)

Also known *as Network Interface Units (NIUs)*, *Network Interface Cards (NICs)* are printed circuit boards that provide physical access from the node to the LAN medium. The NIC (refer to Figure 8-8) is responsible for fragmenting the data transmission, as previously discussed, and formatting the data packets with the necessary header and trailer. A standard IEEE NIC contains a unique, hard-coded logical address, which it prepends to each data packet in the header. The NIC typically has some amount of buffer memory, which enables it to absorb some number of bits transmitted by the associated device, form the packets, and hold them until such time as the network is available. In the context of the OSI Reference Model, NICs function at the bottom two layers — the Physical and Data Link layers. The NIC also may contain a microprocessor that can relieve the attached device of some routine computational functions.

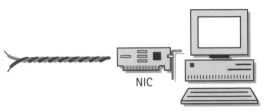

Figure 8-8 Ethernet-attached workstation with Network Interface Card (NIC)

The NIC can be fitted into the expansion slot of a PC, or can exist as a separate box. A standalone, multiport NIC can serve a number of devices, thereby providing an additional level of contention control. *Transceivers* (*transmitter/receivers*) are used in LANs to receive a carrier signal and then transmit it on its way. They are embedded in NICs/NIUs and MAUs. *MAUs* (Media Access Units, or *Multistation Access Units*) are standalone devices that contain NICs in support of one or more nodes.

Bridges

Bridges are relatively simple devices that connect LANs of the same architecture (e.g., Ethernet-to-Ethernet). Bridges operate at the bottom two layers of the OSI Reference Model, providing Physical Layer and Data Link Layer connectivity. Bridges, at the most basic level, act simply to extend the physical reach of a LAN, passing traffic from one LAN segment to another based on the destination address of the packet. In other words, they act as LAN repeaters where specified distance limitations are exceeded (see Figure 8-9). Bridges have buffers so they can store and forward packets in the event that the destination link is congested with traffic.

A key advantage of bridges is their inherent simplicity. As protocol-independent devices, they do not perform complex processes on the data packets traveling through them; neither do they attempt to evaluate the network as a whole to make end-to-end routing decisions. Rather, they simply read the destination address of the incoming data packet and forward it along its way to the next link; cascading bridges accomplish the same process, link-by-link. As a result, bridges are inexpensive and fast. Such bridges can support multiple LANs and LAN segments connected by multiple media. Essentially, multiple ports are provided with interfaces to an appropriate combination of coax, UTP, STP, RF, infrared, and fiber optic transmission systems. Additionally, the same bridge can support multiple LANs of disparate origin. For instance, Ethernet-to-Ethernet and Token Ring-to-Token Ring connectivity can be provided [8-13]. It also is possible to interconnect disparate LANs such as Ethernet-to-Token Ring, through the use of an *encapsulating bridge*;

such a bridge encapsulates the native LAN data, surrounding it with control information appropriate to the LAN of which the target device is attached (refer to Figure 8-10).

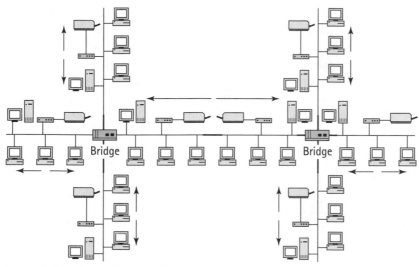

Figure 8-9 Bridged LAN network

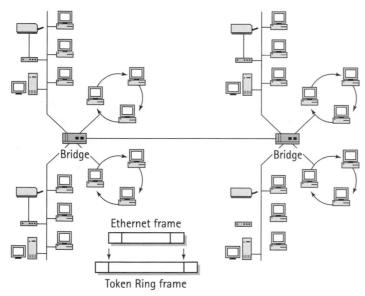

Figure 8-10 Encapsulating bridge, supporting Ethernet-to-Token Ring

More sophisticated bridges add more functionality, although they are more expensive and slower. Such bridges also can *route* traffic at a simple level between LANs based on the destination address. The system administrator can enter the routing table into program logic or it can be *learned* by the bridge as it views the originating addresses of traffic passing through it over a period of time [8-21]. When initialized, *self-learning bridges* typically broadcast a query to all attached devices. When the devices respond to the query, the bridges associate the originating addresses of the data packets with the port over which the incoming data was presented. In this fashion, they build address tables on a port-by-port basis. Subsequently, the bridges view the destination addresses of transmitted data packets, consult the address table, and forward the packets only over the link connected to the proper port. Since the packets are not forwarded across other links, such *filtering bridges* do a great deal — at very low cost — to relieve overall congestion on a segment-by-segment basis. As a result, they thereby improve overall access and throughput. Over time, the bridges add new addresses to their routing tables and delete old addresses that have not viewed in some definable period of time. From time to time, the bridges may repeat the broadcast query process in order to rebuild and resynchronize their address tables.

Media Access Control (MAC) bridges are more sophisticated, still. MAC bridges have the ability to connect unlike, or disparate, LANs (e.g., Ethernet-to-Token Ring). This is accomplished through the process of *encapsulation*, or *translation*, as depicted in Figure 8-10. When operating in this mode, the bridge alters the packet/frame format by encapsulating, or enveloping, the original packet with control data specific to the protocol of the destination LAN supporting the target device. Such an approach might be used to connect an Ethernet LAN to a Token Ring LAN, or where two Ethernet LANs are connected via a FDDI backbone [8-20].

Specific bridge protocols include Spanning Tree, Source Routing Protocol, and Source Routing Transparent.

Spanning Tree Protocol (STP) Bridges, also known as *learning bridges*, are defined in IEEE 802.1 standards. Spanning tree bridges are self-learning, filtering bridges for use in connecting LANs on a point-to-point basis. The bridge is programmed or teaches itself the addresses of all devices on the network; subsequently, the network *tree* of the bridge provides only one *span* (link) for each LAN-to-LAN connection. Some spanning tree bridges also have the capability to provide security by denying access to certain resources based on user and terminal ID. Bridges that support the spanning tree algorithm have the ability to automatically reconfigure themselves for alternate paths if a network segment fails, thereby improving overall reliability [8-22].

IBM Source Routing Protocol (SRP) bridges are programmed with specific routes for each packet, based on considerations such as the physical location of the nodes and the number of bridges involved. The maximum number of bridges *hopped* is 13.

Source Routing Transparent (SRT) is defined in the IEEE 802.1 standard. It is effectively a combination of STP and SRP. The SRT router can connect LANs by either method, as programmed [8-2].

Hubs

Hubs reflect the trend toward star, and away from bus, configurations. Hubs can be either active or passive. *Passive* hubs act simply as cable-connecting devices, while *active* hubs also serve as signal repeaters [8-2]. The first generation of hubs (1984) acted as LAN concentrators and repeaters, with a single internal collapsed backbone bus for connecting like LANs. The second generation accommodated multiple LAN architectures (e.g., Ethernet and Token-Passing Ring) over separate ports; rudimentary network management and configuration capabilities were included, as well [8-20].

A *collapsed backbone* is a fairly simple concept, and one worth exploring in some detail. LANs traditionally work on the basis of a common electrical bus (i.e., shared cable medium) to which each device or group of devices is directly connected. While this approach works effectively, it requires that the cable be deployed through the entire workplace. The traditional coax medium is expensive to acquire and deploy — as is fiber optic cable. Additionally, the cable is susceptible to physical damage unless conduits, armoring or some other means protects it. All of these involve additional cost. Alternatively, the high-speed backbone bus can be collapsed and placed within a hub, to which the devices are connected by means of a less expensive medium such as UTP. In this manner, the backbone bus is protected and the cost of cabling is reduced. Should an individual device (e.g., workstation, NIC, or MAU) create difficulty, disabling the port attached to the hub can isolate it. Should a UTP cable suffer damage, the connection can be similarly disabled and the problem corrected at relatively low cost. While the UTP cable is inherently less capable than coax or fiber, equivalent bandwidth can be provided as long as the distances between the devices and the hub are within tolerable limits. This is an accurate description of a 10Base-T configuration, as illustrated in Figure 8-11. Multiple hubs can be interconnected with various media, depending on bandwidth requirements and distances involved.

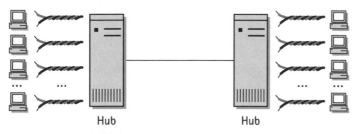
Hub   Hub

Figure 8-11 10-Base-T Hubs, interconnected

In the context of the OSI Reference Model, hubs operate at LLayers 1 and 2, providing Physical Layer and Data Link Layer connectivity. Since a hub is protocol-specific, like a bridge, it works quickly. Actually, a hub is very much like a bridge, except that it provides terminal connectivity on a twisted-pair basis. A hub inherently does nothing internally to control congestion, except for filtering inter-hub traffic. A 10Base-T hub, for instance, runs the Ethernet CSMA/CD protocol over the collapsed backbone bus, and the attached devices do the same through UTP NICs. Hubs do serve to control congestion, however, because they are positioned as workgroup solutions that serve to confine traffic to the users connected to the hub — much as filtering bridges serve to confine traffic to a coax segment in a classic Ethernet implementation.

Intelligent Hubs, the third generation, provide multiple buses for multiple LANs either of the same or disparate architectures (see Figure 8-8). They support multiple media (e.g., coax, UTP, and fiber), multiple speeds, and multiple LAN protocols. As addressable devices, they can be managed centrally via *SNMP* (*Simple Network Management Protocol*) or another appropriate network management protocol. Intelligent hubs also provide bridging and basic routing capabilities [8-20].

Regardless of the generation of the hubs, they serve, at minimum, as central points of interconnection for LAN-attached devices. Additionally, they serve as concentrators of LAN traffic and as repeaters, with multiple hubs interconnected through high-speed media [8-21]. A number of hub manufacturers offer stackable hubs, which offer the advantage of scalability; in other words, the hubs can be stacked and interconnected to increase port and traffic capacity [8-23].

Switches

Intelligent hubs with basic routing capabilities also are known as *LAN switches*. They have the ability to read the target address of the packets and forward them directly to the appropriate port associated with the target LAN segment or LAN-attached device. In the process, the switch avoids contributing to congestion on other LAN segments. The LAN switch also offers the advantage of a high-capacity, multi-bus switching matrix that can provide full LAN bandwidth to multiple, simultaneous communications on a point-to-point basis. For instance, one workstation can access another over a connection of 10 Mbps, while another has connection to a database server at a full 10 Mbps, and while still another is passing a file to a print server at high speed [8-24].

LAN switches (see Figure 8-12) are more sophisticated intelligent hubs that also possess basic routing capabilities. Such devices may contain one or multiple high-speed internal busses. Each bus can support multiple logical links by subdividing its capacity through a process akin to time division multiplexing. In order to accomplish this minor miracle, the native data packet may be stored in buffer memory, examined for errors, and fragmented into smaller subsets of data. The packet fragments then flow across the shared bus, directed only to the designated output port of the switch. At the receiving port, the data fragments eventually gather in buffer memory, and are reformed into a reconstituted packet. For instance and depending on the switch manufacturer, a Token Ring frame of up to 18,000 bytes may fragment into units of 28, 64, or 4,096 bytes. The trade-off in size of data fragment is that of performance — small fragments enable more users to share the bus at any given time, while larger fragments improve switching speed because the switch must analyze and act on fewer packet headers.

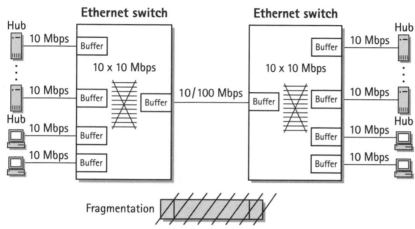

Figure 8–12 Interconnected LAN switches, with buffers and fragmentation

Switches can read the destination address of the packets, filtering and forwarding as appropriate. Filtering options may include MAC address (Layer 2) and IP address (Layer 3). Switches operate at the Physical and Data Link Layers of the OSI Reference Model — Layers 1 and 2, respectively. Layer 3 and Layer 4 switching (admittedly arguable terms) involve a combination of switches and routers, with routers making network and transport-level decisions relative to establishment of a network path, and with the switches executing that path based on router instructions. I discuss all of these variations on the switching theme later in this chapter.

Switches may operate on either a cut-through or a store-and-forward basis. In a cut-through scenario, the address of the data packet is read quickly, and the packet is flowed through the switching matrix quickly, bit by bit. Store-and-forward switches buffer the packet as it is presented to the incoming switch port, permitting the entire packet to be examined for errors before it is propagated through the switching matrix to the output port. While cut-through switching is faster and less expensive, it carries with it the risk of the propagation of errored data and the resulting potential for negative impact on overall throughput.

LAN switches may be positioned at the workgroup level, where they can support a number of simultaneous transmissions. Switches also may be positioned in the backbone, in order to relieve congestion between workgroup-level hubs and switches. The cost of switches has dropped dramatically in recent years to the point that they often compete effectively against hubs. However, switch costs are sensitive to factors such as the type and speed of the transmission media interfaces, the number and speed of the ports, the number and size of the buffers, the number and speed of the internal busses, and the complexity of the internal switching matrix.

Routers

Routers are highly intelligent devices that support connectivity between like and disparate LANs, as noted in Figure 8-13. Additionally, routers can provide access to various WANs, such as X.25, ISDN, and Frame Relay. Router interfaces to ATM also are possible, although other approaches such as LAN Emulation (LANE) and Multiprotocol over ATM (MPOA) also may be employed — as I will discuss in Chapter 10. Routers are protocol-sensitive; they typically support multiple protocols, and large and varying packet sizes such as might be involved in supporting both Ethernet and Token Ring. Routers typically operate at the bottom three layers of the OSI model, using the Physical Layer, Link Layer, and Network Layer to provide connectivity, addressing, and switching [8-21].

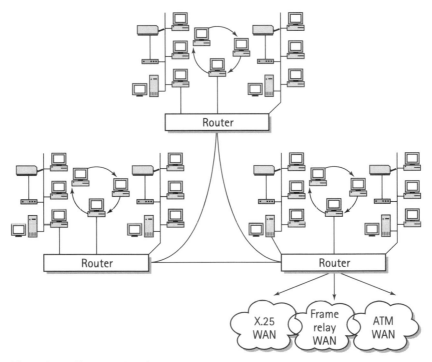

Figure 8-13 Router network

Server-based routers also are available in the form of router software embedded in a server. As they perform more slowly than their hardware-based relatives do, they generally are not considered up to the task of serving an enterprise-wide application. They do have application, however, in support of smaller, remote sites [8-25].

In addition to supporting filtering and encapsulation, routers route traffic based on a high level of intelligence that enables them to consider the network as a whole. Conversely, bridges, hubs, and switches simply view the network on a link-by-link basis. Routing considerations might include destination address, payload type, packet priority level, least-cost route, minimum route delay, minimum route distance, and route congestion level. Routers also are self-learning, as they can communicate their existence to other devices and can learn of the existence of new routers, nodes, and LAN segments. Routers constantly monitor the condition of the network, as a whole, to dynamically adapt to changes in the condition of the network, from edge to edge. Routers are multiport devices with high-speed backbones that can be on the order of 1 Gbps+. Additionally, they typically provide some level of redundancy so they are less susceptible to catastrophic failure [8-20].

Routers are unique in their ability to route data based on network policy. Policy-based routers can provide various levels of service based on factors such as the identification of the user, the terminal, and the type of payload. From one edge of the enterprise network to the other, an edge router can select the most appropriate path through the switches or routers positioned in the core. An important part of this process often is that of dividing the enterprise network into multiple *subnets*. Users associated with a subnet may be afforded access to only a limited subset of network resources in the form of sites, links, hosts, files, databases, and applications. In addition to being limited in terms of access to such resources, users on such a subnet may be prevented from receiving data from them. In effect, even the very existence of those resources is *masked* from view. Creation of such isolated subnets may serve for reasons of security, or simply as a means of avoiding unnecessary congestion.

Routers commonly are capable of alternate routing and inverse multiplexing. As noted by Charles Darling [8-26], what dedicated WAN links lack in cost-efficiency they make up for in terms of lack of reliability (e.g., backhoe-fade). Select manufacturers now offer routers that sense that network failure and re-establish the connection via an alternate connection; while a back-up ISDN BRI link may be painfully slow compared with a T-1 connection, Darling suggests that *slow* is better than *stop*. Additionally, some routers offer inverse multiplexing capabilities over ISDN and T-carrier facilities.

Router protocols include both bridging and routing protocols because they perform both functions. Those protocols fall into three categories: gateway protocols, serial line protocols, and protocol stack routing and bridging.

Inter-router protocols are router-to-router protocols that can operate over heterogeneous networks. The protocol passes routing information and *keep-alive* packets during periods of idleness. Examples include *RIP* (*Routing Information*

Protocol) from Novell and *OSPF* (*Open Shortest Path First*) from the Internet Engineering Task Force (IETF).

Serial Line Protocols provide for communications over serial or dial-up links connecting unlike routers. Examples include HDLC, SLIP (Serial Line Interface Protocol), and PPP (Point-to-Point Protocol). in Chapter 12, which deals with the Internet, I provide more discussion of these specific protocols.

Protocol Stack Routing and *Bridging Protocols* advise the router as to which packets should be routed and which should be bridged.

Gateways

A term originally applied to what we now call routers [8-27], *gateways* are at the top of the LAN food chain. Gateway routers can perform all of the functions of bridges and routers, as well as accomplish protocol conversion at all seven Layers of the OSI Reference Model. Generally consisting of software residing in a host computer equivalent in processing power to a midrange or mainframe, gateway technology is expensive but highly functional.

Protocol conversion, rather than encapsulation, can serve to fully convert from Ethernet to Token Ring, to FDDI or any other standard or proprietary LAN protocol. Additionally, protocol conversion can address higher layers of the OSI model, perhaps through Layer 7, the Application Layer. IBM SNA, DECnet, Internet TCP/IP, and other protocols can convert from network-to-network. As the process of protocol conversion is complex, gateways tend to operate rather slowly as compared to bridges and routers. As a result, they impose additional latency on packet traffic and may create bottlenecks of congestion during periods of peak usage. Once again, routers tend to position at the edge of the complex enterprise network, where they can be used to full advantage. Therefore, they make complex and time-consuming decisions and invoke complex and time-consuming processes only where required. Switches tend to be positioned within the core of the network because they can operate with greater speed, perhaps on the instructions of the routers.

LAN Segmentation

LAN segmentation is a concept that simply involves dividing a single LAN into two or more physical segments. A typical LAN segment might involve a workgroup that communicates intensively on the bases of stations-to-stations, stations-to-specific servers, or stations-to-specific peripherals such as local printers. As the usage is intensive, the traffic patterns are well understood, and the traffic is highly localized, a LAN segment can be effected through the use of a filtering bridge (this function may be included in a router or intelligent hub). The physical LAN still exists in its physical and logical entirety — it is just segmented.

The advantage of segmentation is that the relatively intensive traffic within the workgroup is confined to a physical and logical segment (domain) of that LAN.

Therefore, that traffic does not affect the users on the balance of the LAN. When a LAN divides into many, relatively small segments, the concept is known as *microsegmentation*. While the cost of the bridges may be of concern, the performance advantages often outweigh cost considerations.

LAN Operating Systems

A *LAN Operating System*, or *Network Operating System* (*NOS*), is software that provides the network with multiuser, multitasking capabilities across the network. The operating system facilitates communications and resource sharing, thereby providing the basic framework for the operation of the LAN. The operating system consists of modules that are distributed throughout the LAN environment; some NOS modules reside in *servers* and other modules reside in the *clients*.

Digressing for just a moment, the *client/server* model originated with the development of the U.S. Department of Defense ARPANET in the 1960s. As the cost and size of computer systems decreased and as the capabilities of those systems and the networks increased, the embodiment of client/server changed. A contemporary *client* is an application that generally resides on a microcomputer. Example applications include word processing, and spreadsheet and database software. The client runs against a *server* – which is a multiport computer containing large amounts of memory and enables multiple clients to share its resources – while performing certain functions independently. Servers are database engines capable of processing client requests for information, and managing the resident data. For example, client/server continues to be used extensively in the Internet. When accessing America Online, Prodigy, CompuServe, or another service provider, you make use of a Graphic User Interface (GUI) and browser software that resides on the PC. When initiating an Internet session, that software runs against software installed in the service provider's communications server. Through this approach, the two devices communicate most effectively without requiring that the software be downloaded from the server as a part of every Internet session; since the graphic files are huge, a great deal of time and bandwidth would be wasted. Once connected to the communications server, you subsequently can access a large number of database servers on a point-and-click basis, courtesy of the GUI, and with only the target data being transmitted across the Internet.

In addition to supporting multitasking and multiuser access, LAN operating systems provide for recognition of users based on passwords, user IDs, and terminal IDs; on the basis of such information, they can manage security by monitoring access privileges. Additionally, LAN operating systems provide multiprotocol routing, as well as directory services and message services. DOS-based LAN operating systems include Novell NetWare, Sun Microsystems' TOPS/DOS, and Microsoft's Windows NT Server. OS/2 and UNIX-based LAN operating systems include Banyan VINES, Hewlett-Packard HP-UX, IBM LAN Server, Linux, Microsoft LAN Manager, Novell NetWare, and Sun SunSoft Solaris. According to International Data Group,

4.3 million servers existed in 1998, and the market share (refer to Figure 8-14) showed Windows NT Server at 35.8 percent, Novell NetWare at 24.2 percent, Unix at 17.4 percent, Linux at 17.2 percent, and all others at 5.4 percent [8-28].

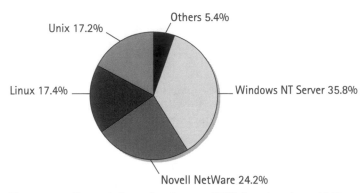

Figure 8-14 Network Operating Systems (NOSs) market share, 1998

LAN Internetworking

LAN internetworking simply networks two or more LANs, of similar or dissimilar nature. The LANs may be in proximity, or they may be separated by continents and connected by international WANs. Equipment used for LAN internetworking includes that discussed above, plus a few other options. Specifically, the range includes bridges, hubs, switches, routers, gateways, PADs (X.25), TAs (ISDN), and FRADs (Frame Relay Access Devices).

WANs

Wide Area Network (WAN) options for internetworking geographically distant LANs include dial-up options such as X.25 Packet Switching, ISDN, and Switched 56/64 Kbps. Dedicated leased-line options include DDS, T-carrier, and Fractional T1. Recent and developing fast packet network services include Frame Relay, SMDS (Switched Multimegabit Data Service), and ATM (Asynchronous Transfer Mode). These services are available from a wide variety of vendors, including LECs, IXCs, and specialized data carriers.

High-Level Internetworking Protocols

These provide the means by which the LANs can interconnect, at some level — including dealing with issues of data formatting, addressing, and sequencing, as well as flow control and error control. The internetworking protocols that I will address briefly include TCP/IP, XNS, SPX/IPX, and APPN.

TCP/IP (Transmission Control Protocol/Internet Protocol) integrates dissimilar systems and networks, operating at OSI Layers 3 and 4. TCP/IP initially was developed for the U.S. Department of Defense for use in ARPANET, which became standardized as X.25. In response to the fact that early ARPANET protocols were subject to frequent network crashes, Vinton G. Cerf and Robert E. Kahn proposed a new set of core protocols in 1974. That set of design protocols were the foundation for the development of the TCP/IP protocol suite. The U.S. Department of Defense stimulated development by funding Bolt, Beranek, and Newman (BBN) to implement TCP/IP for UNIX operating systems and the University of California at Berkeley to incorporate the BBN code into the Berkeley UNIX variation [8-27].

The TCP/IP protocol suite was intended as a means of gluing together disparate networks, independent of host hardware, operating systems, transmission media, and data link technologies. The resulting Internet is transparent to the user, appearing as a single network. Additionally, TCP/IP can support internetworking in the face of high error rates, as well as node or link failures [8-27].

TCP/IP has become widely popular as an internetworking protocol because it is effective, inexpensive, and well understood. TCP/IP remains a foundation of the Internet, and enjoys wide usage in a variety of networks and internetworking applications. The TCP/IP code resides in the public domain, thereby encouraging its use and further development — which continues to this day. The TCP/IP protocol suite is divided into two distinct protocol layers: TCP and IP.

Transmission Control Protocol (TCP) is a virtual circuit protocol, managing the flow of user application data and providing translations of application names to lower-level addresses. TCP supports reliable, peer-to-peer communications on a *connection-oriented* basis. TCP accepts the data stream, segments it, and passes it to IP for routing. On the receiving end of the data transfer, TCP accepts the segmented data from IP, resolves error conditions, resequences the data segments, and passes them to the target device [8-20] and [8-21]. TCP is datastream-oriented. In other words, TCP views packets of data as elements of a stream of data, the integrity for which it assumes end-to-end responsibility.

Internet Protocol (IP) is the protocol layer that defines the nature of the format of the data packets and the routing of the data by IP address. The IP element of the TCP/IP protocol suite accepts the segmented data from TCP, routes it, resolves error conditions, and presents the data to TCP for resequencing. IP is a *best effort* protocol, meaning that it provides no assurance of delivery — it is the responsibility of TCP to detect errored or lost packets and to effect resolution of such conditions [8-27] and [8-29]. IP is datagram-oriented and *connectionless* in nature. In other words, IP deals with each packet as a separate, disconnected entity — regardless of whether it is an element of a stream of packets.

XNS (Xerox Networking System) originally was developed for integrating Xerox office systems. Each packet is routed like a datagram in an X.25 network — independently and over the best available link.

SPX/IPX (*Sequenced Packet Exchange/Internet Packet Exchange*) Novell's derivative of XNS, using echo protocol and error protocol. SPX/IPX is the defined interface for Novell NetWare.

APPN (*Advanced Peer-to-Peer Networking*) is an IBM protocol that permits routing of LAN traffic, independent of a Front-End Processor (FEP). Supporting X.25, Token Ring, and other network protocols, APPN is an integral part of SNA and SAA and provides a transition toward routers, rather than IBM's traditional approach.

Virtual LANs (VLANs)

Virtual LANs are software-defined LANs that group users by logical addresses into a virtual, rather than physical, LAN through a switch or router (refer to Figure 8-15). The LAN switch can support many virtual LANs, which operate as subnets [8-30]. Users within a virtual LAN traditionally are grouped by port address, MAC (Media Access Control) address, or IP address. Each node is attached to the switch via a dedicated circuit. More recently introduced are policy-based VLANs, which can base VLAN membership on such factors as protocol, location, user name, and workstation address [8-31]. Users also can be assigned to more than one virtual LAN, should their responsibilities cross workgroup domains.

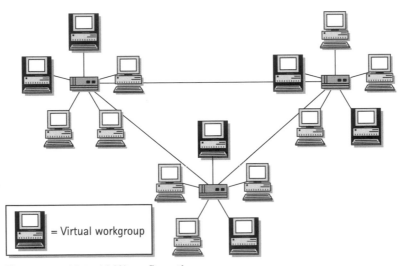

□ = Virtual workgroup

Figure 8-15 Virtual LAN configuration

The LAN switches can be networked, thereby extending the reach of the virtual LAN. The networking is generally provided through FDDI, 100Base-T, Gigabit Ethernet, or ATM over optical fiber links. VLANs also can be extended across the WAN through routers and via dedicated leased lines or ATM. Remote LAN access currently cannot be accommodated on a true VLAN basis. VLANs are proprietary; standards are not likely in the near future.

The advantages of switched virtual LANs include the fact that bridge and router networks can be flattened and simplified, including the elimination of source-routing, bridge hop restrictions. You can reduce congestion through intelligent microsegmentation, yielding increased throughput, increased access, and reduced response time. Workstations can be provided with full bandwidth at each port. Particularly in the case of Layer 3 (e.g., IP-based) VLANs, physical Move, Add, & Change (MAC) activity reduces, as much of these requirements can be resolved through software changes [8-32] and [8-33]. Since the estimated cost of a MAC varies from $300-$1,000, this approach can offer significant savings in a highly dynamic environment. Additionally, security is much improved, through the association in software of users and terminals with subnetworks and hosts. Additionally, a measure of security is provided through software firewalls within the confines of each domain [8-34] and [8-35].

On the downside, VLANs are not easily implemented or managed. It takes a good deal of effort to develop the switch database and identify the various logical subnets. Further, VLANs typically require a complete replacement of the typical switch or router network; software upgrades just aren't available.

Remote LAN Access

Remote LAN access is the ability to access a LAN from a remote location. The need for remote LAN access is increasing, worldwide — especially in the United States and Western Europe. *Telecommuting* is growing at a fast pace, as predicted a decade or more ago. Various market research firms suggest that 4-9 million employees worked at least eight hours from home in 1992. In 1998, it was estimated 20 million people worked from home, and an additional 9 million work at home after normal business hours [8-36].

The concept is one of providing access from remote locations to one or more host computers, which typically are LAN-attached. In support of telecommuters, contractors, remote offices, and the Small Office/Home Office (SOHO), remote LAN access often is essential to the operation of the enterprise. Additionally, remote access often is provided to customers, suppliers, trading partners, etc. The yield is that remote users are provided access to resources with the same level of privilege as though they were on-site [8-21]. Key components to be examined are the network, the equipment, and the applications supported. Other issues include security management and network management.

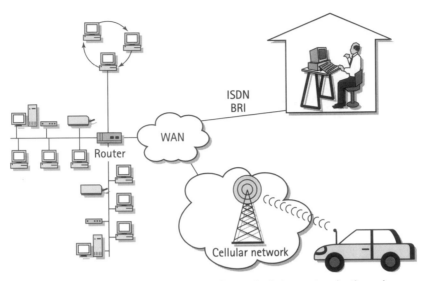

Figure 8-16 Remote LAN access from wireline and wireless networks through an access router with firewall

The network is clearly a developing enabler. The network can assume a variety of forms, depending on issues such as availability, cost, and bandwidth (as illustrated in Figure 8-16). Network options literally run the full range of conventional data networks, including the analog PSTN, ISDN, Switched 56, and Frame Relay. Finally, and in order to support truly mobile remote LAN access, cellular radio and packet radio data networks commonly are employed [8-37] and [8-38].

Equipment required varies according to the nature of the network employed. Improvements in equipment, as well as improvements in network technologies, have enabled cost-effective, remote LAN access. That equipment can include high-performance workstations and high-speed modems for access to the PSTN. Access to X.25 networks requires PADs (Packet Assemblers/Disassemblers), ISDN requires TAs (Terminal Adapters), and Frame Relay requires FRADs (Frame Relay Access Devices). Access via a cellular network or a wireless packet data network requires the use of wireless modems. Clearly, the LAN side of the connection requires the installation of modem pools, routers, and various other devices in order to support remote user access.

Applications most often supported include e-mail, file transfer, and database access. Additional applications include scheduling, printing, access to on-line services, client support, and Internet access.

LAN Standards and Standards Bodies

Standards developed by the IEEE (Institute of Electrical and Electronics Engineers) largely have governed the world of LANs since the formation of Project 802 in February 1980. Project 802, working within the scope of the OSI reference model, was chartered to deal with the two bottom layers. Notably Layer 2, the Data Link Layer, was divided into two subgroups: Media Access Control (MAC) and Logical Link Control (LLC) [8-2]. The initial focus was on Ethernet, and the first recommendation was finalized in December 1982. The IEEE membership, the U.S. National Bureau of Standards, and the ECMA (European Computer Manufacturers Association) accepted that first release of three standards. The ISO (International Organization for Standardization) issued correlating international standards — known as 8802 LAN Standards. Since then, the IEEE has continued to develop a broad range of LAN and MAN standards. IEEE standards include the following:

802.1:	Architecture and Internetworking (High-Level Interface). Defines architecture layers and rules for interconnection of disparate LAN protocols. Includes data formatting, network management, and internetworking.
802.2:	Defines equivalent of Logical Link Control services, including protocol for data transfer. Largely addresses bridges.
802.3:	Defines CSMA/CD Access Method and Physical Layer Specifications. Commonly referred to as the *Ethernet* standard.
802.4:	Token-Passing Bus Access Method and Physical Layer Specifications.
802.5:	Token-Passing Ring Access Method and Physical Layer Specifications. Includes Token Ring.
802.6:	Metropolitan Area Network (MAN) Access Method and Physical Layer Specifications. DQDB (Distributed Queue Dual Bus) is defined. SMDS (Switched Multimegabit Data Service), discussed in Chapter 10, was derived from 802.6.
802.7:	Broadband Technical Advisory Group. Standards for definition of a broadband cable plant design. Established guidelines for LAN construction within a physical facility such as a building.
802.8:	Fiber Optic Technical Advisory Group. Established to assess impact of fiber optics and to recommend standards. Note that this standard is distinct from that of ANSI's FDDI.

802.9:   *Integrated Services LAN* (*ISLAN*). Designed for the integration of voice and data networks, both within the LAN domain and interfacing to publicly and privately administered networks running protocols such as FDDI and ISDN.

802.10: *Standard for Interoperable LAN Security* (*SILS*) for internetworking.

802.11: Wireless, initially focusing on the 2.4-GHz band.

802.12: 100VG-AnyLAN.

In addition to the IEEE, other standards bodies are involved in the establishment and promotion of certain LAN and computer networking standards. ANSI (American National Standards Institute), for instance, developed the following standards:

X.3T9-3: HPPI (High Performance Parallel Interface)

X3T9-5:   FDDI (Fiber Distributed Data Interface)

Table 8-3 DIMENSIONS OF POPULAR LAN STANDARDS

LAN Dimension	Ethernet	IBM Token Ring	Fiber Distributed Data Interface (FDDI)
Standard	IEEE 802.3	IEEE 802.5	ANSI X3T9-5
Logical Topology	Bus	Ring	Ring
Physical Topology	Bus, Star	Ring, Star	Dual Ring, Dual Bus
Media	Coax, UTP, STP	Coax, UTP, STP	Fiber
Transmission Mode	Baseband	Baseband	Baseband
Bandwidth	10, 100 Mbps; 1 Gbps	4, 16, 20 Mbps	100 Mbps
Media Access Control	Non-Deterministic: CSMA/CD, CSMA/CA	Deterministic: Token-Passing	Deterministic: Token-Passing
Payload Size	Up to 1,500 Bytes	Up to 4,048 Bytes (4 Mbps)	Up to 36,000 Bytes
Traffic Type	Data	Data	Data, Video, Voice

Life in the Fast LAN: The Need for Speed

During the past few years, traditional LANs have been pushed to their limits as end user organizations connect more workstations and users become more active, resulting in more LAN traffic. Increased use of graphics and other more bandwidth-intensive applications have developed, also increasing the strain. Collaborative computing increases the demands on existing LAN technologies; especially as voice and videoconferencing are employed to enhance the collaborative experience. Users also have become increasingly impatient, demanding faster response times. In general, LAN users mirror the times in which we live — more is better, bigger is better, and faster is better, yet. Bandwidth of 10 Mbps, 16 Mbps, and even 20 Mbps just doesn't cut the mustard anymore! In response to this requirement, Fast LANs began to develop offering bandwidth of 100 Mbps, and now an incredible 1 Gpbs. Fast LAN options currently include 100Base-T (Fast Ethernet), 100VG-AnyLAN, and Gigabit Ethernet (GE).

100Base-T, or Fast Ethernet

A variation of 10Base-T and standardized as IEEE 802.3u (June 14, 1995), *100BASE-T* is a high-speed LAN standard; it uses CSMA/CD and operates at 100 Mbps through an Ethernet switching hub. Contemporary 100Base-T hubs and switches can support both 10-Mbps users and 100-Mbps "power users." Cat 3, 4, or 5 UTP can be used in four-pair configuration, with Cat 5 UTP required for transmission at 100 Mbps and supporting a maximum LAN diameter of 500 meters. Three pairs are used for transmission; the fourth pair is used for signaling and control (CSMA/CD)in half-duplex mode [8-39]. Connections to nodes, servers, and other switching hubs can be provided at 100 Mbps. The 100 Mbps media include fiber (up to 30 miles, or 50 km without repeaters) and Cat 5 UTP at 100 meters. Some manufacturers support full-duplex transmission, yielding a theoretical total bandwidth of 200 Mbps [8-40]. Remember, however, that Ethernet is collision-prone — 100 Mbps of theoretical bandwidth may yield only 58 Mbps throughput for a hub technology. Switches supporting 100Base-T, however, yield much improved performance through the support of multiple simultaneous transmissions. 100Base-T quickly overpowered most competing technologies, given the huge installed Ethernet Base.

IsoEthernet (Isochronous Ethernet Integrated Services)

Ratified by the IEEE in the Fall of 1995, *IsoEthernet* added a little speed to traditional 10Base-T Ethernet. Providing aggregate bandwidth of 16.144 Mbps, IsoEthernet was intended to support isochronous (stream-oriented) traffic such as real-time voice and videoconferencing through an Ethernet switching hub. The 809-2a standard provides 10 Mbps for data traffic and sets aside an additional 6.144 Mbps for voice and video through 96 64-Kbps ISDN B channels and 1 ISDN D channel at 64 Kbps. Multiple B channels can be linked — most typically required in support of videoconferencing. In fact, the entire network can function in isochronous mode at 16.144 Mbps, providing 248 B channels at 64 Kbps. IsoEthernet is limited to a single hub. Advances in LAN switching, including Gigabit Ethernet and ATM, basically have relegated IsoEthernet to an interesting historical footnote.

100V G-AnyLAN

100VG-AnyLAN (*VG*=*V*oice *G*rade) is a joint development of AT&T Microelectronics, Hewlett-Packard, and IBM. Standardized by the IEEE 802.12 committee, 100VG-AnyLAN supports Ethernet, Token Ring, and other LAN standards, incorporating a collisionless polling technique. However, it's not quite as simple as it appears on the surface — a router upgrade is required to connect 100VG Ethernet and 100VG Token Ring [8-41].

Distances are 100 meters for Cat 3 UTP (four pairs), 150 meters for Cat 5 UTP (two pairs) and Type 1 STP (two pairs), and 2000 meters for fiber; the specifications suggest higher possible speeds [8-41]. All pairs are used for transmission in half-duplex mode at 25 MHz. Priority access is provided through the DPMA (Demand Priority Media Access) technique. 100VG-AnyLAN can be deployed in a scaleable star topology [8-39]. Since 100VG-AnyLAN has the ability to support priority access and collisionless transmission, some view it as superior to 100BASE-T for multimedia LAN communications. However, the huge embedded base of Ethernet, as well as manufacturer support for it, makes 100BASE-T a natural choice for most organizations [8-40].

Not surprisingly, an exception to this judgement deals with linking non-Ethernet LANs. 100VG-AnyLAN does a much better of linking Token Ring LANs, for instance. While Ethernet sends data in frames with a maximum payload of 1,500 bytes, Token Ring can accommodate data fields up to 16,000 bytes. 100VG-AnyLAN handles this well, while 100BASE-T doesn't [8-42] and [8-39]. 100VG-AnyLAN represents another of those interesting historical footnotes. While it works beautifully, it is underpowered by today's standards, and this world is almost exclusively Ethernet. Further, routers can translate protocols between unlike LANs, and much more.

High-Speed Token Ring (HSTR)

High-Speed Token Ring (*HSTR*) is proposed to run at speeds of 100 Mbps initially. Plans are to increase the speed to 155 Mbps and 1 Gbps, over time, to compete with ATM and Gigabit Ethernet, respectively. In order to achieve these speeds between Token Ring switches, the specification is expected to borrow the Physical Layer specifications from FDDI and ATM. The maximum frame size will increase to approximately 18,000 bytes for HSTR in order to increase efficiency and improve throughput. While the initial set of specifications for High-Speed Token Ring (HSTR) currently remain under final consideration, HSTR certainly will offer a bandwidth boost for Token Ring environments. Given the existence of ATM LAN switches running at 155/622 and Gigabit Ethernet at 1 Gbps, however, HSTR seems woefully underpowered. Given the fact that Ethernet dominates the LAN domain, it appears that HSTR will receive relatively little support. In fact, several products have been developed to support HSTR over Ethernet for smooth integration of the two specifications in a mixed environment. Additionally, a number of key manufacturers (e.g., Cisco and Texas Instruments) have withdrawn from the High-Speed Token Ring Alliance (HSTRA).

FDDI (Fiber Distributed Data Interface)

FDDI is the standard (ANSI X3T9-5; IEEE 802.2) for a fiber optic, token-passing ring LAN. Bandwidth is at 100 Mbps, although several manufacturers offer 200 Mbps, full-duplex interfaces. The excellent performance characteristics of fiber optics, in general, apply well to the LAN world. Error performance is in the range of 10^{-14}, and devices can be separated by as much as 1.2 miles (2 kilometers) over multimode fiber and 37.2 miles (62 kilometers) over single-mode fiber [8-43] and [8-44]. The maximum frame size is 9000 *symbols* (1 symbol = 4 bytes), which easily accommodates the native frame sizes of all standard LAN networks [8-45].

FDDI largely is deployed as a backbone technology for the interconnection of major computing resources such as hubs, switches, routers, and servers. While FDDI can be extended to the device levels, the cost of opto-electric termination is high. A direct fiber interface to a PC workstation can be accomplished at an average cost of around $500, although that cost can reach as much as $1,500. The advantages of FDDI, however, can be extended to the workstation through a concentrator that accomplishes the opto-electric conversion process for multiple attached devices. The connection from the concentrator to the workstations is accomplished via UTP over distances of 100 meters or less, based on a standard known variously as *CDDI* (*Cable Distributed Data Interface*) and *TPDDI* (*Twisted Pair Distributed Data Interface*).

The fragility of the fiber is a deterrent to the application of FDDI, as well. The FDDI specifications provide for a dual counter-rotating ring, which provides a measure of redundancy. Should the primary ring fail, a *Dual Attached Station (DAS)* or *Dual Attached Concentrator (DAC)* can communicate with any other device by transmitting in the opposite direction through the secondary ring, which typically is collocated in the same cable sheath as the primary ring (see Figure 8-17). If there is more than one physical failure in the cable plant, however, the ring segments and the network fails. There are dual-homing solutions to this dilemma, although they involve considerable additional expense, with the designated stations connected via fiber to multiple servers to provide redundancy [8-46].

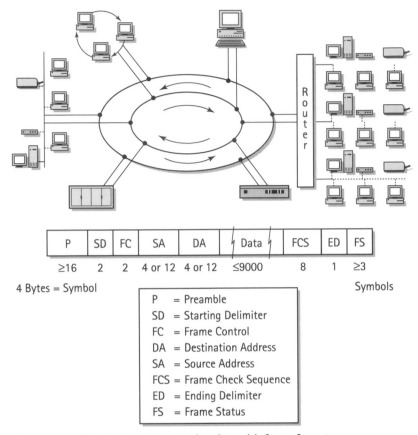

Figure 8-17 FDDI dual counter-rotating ring, with frame format

Despite its reliability and throughput characteristics, sales of FDDI hubs and switches peaked at $220 million in 1997, and are expected to drop to $40 million in 2001, according to the Dell'Oro Group [8 47]. Not only is FDDI's high cost a detriment, but optical fiber backbones currently can be deployed at much higher speeds for the interconnection of hubs, switches, routers, and the like. Further, FDDI is underpowered by today standards – Gigabit Ethernet puts 100 Mbps to shame. ATM runs at speeds of 155 Mbps and 622 Mbps in the LAN environment, and supports not only LAN data but also any form of data, including voice and video.

Gigabit Ethernet (GE)

The standard for *Gigabit Ethernet* (*GE*) was finalized and formally approved on June 29, 1998, as IEEE 802.3z. Although fully compatible with both 10 Mbps and 100 Mbps Ethernet, most equipment has to be upgraded to support the higher transmission level. Gigabit Ethernet addresses the bandwidth problem in 10/100 Mbps

Ethernet networks, which are beginning to feel the stress of bandwidth-intensive, multimedia-based Internet and intranet applications, as well as scientific modeling and data warehousing and data backup. As a backbone LAN technology, however, Gigabit Ethernet faces strong opposition from ATM.

GE is available in two flavors: shared and switched (see Figure 8-18), both of which support multiple ports that run at 1 Gbps in full-duplex. Shared GE essentially is a much higher speed of 10BaseT and 100BaseT. Shared GE is a high-speed hub that uses CSMA/CD for Media Access Control over the shared bus. Therefore, you can characterize Shared GE as a brute force attack on congestion. Switched GE addresses the congestion problem through buffering incoming Ethernet frames, and passing them to the output port when the shared bus becomes available. The shared bus can run at a speed of several Gbps. The more substantial Switched GE products offer non-blocking switching through a crossbar switching matrix, which may run at a total of tens of Gbps [8-48]. The cost of a GE switch is greater than that of a GE hub, and is sensitive to such factors as port density, buffer placement and capacity, switch matrix complexity, and throughput.

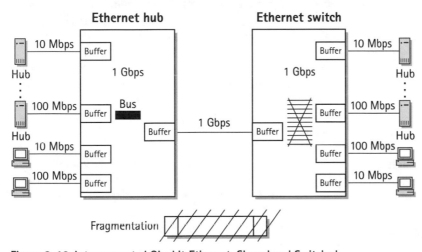

Figure 8-18 Interconnected Gigabit Ethernet, Shared and Switched

While GE resembles traditional Ethernet, differences include frame size. As the clock speed of GE is one or two orders of magnitude greater than its predecessors (10/100 Mbps), issues of roundtrip propagation delay affect error detection. To avoid potentially incredible collision rates, the minimum frame size has increased from 64 bytes to 512 bytes, which generally is equivalent to transmitting a 64-byte frame at 100 Mbps in terms of propagation delay. This larger minimum frame size provides more time for the transmitting device to receive a collision notification in the event of a congestion condition. Although non-standard, some manufacturers have increased the maximum frame size from 1,518 bytes to a *jumbo frame* size of

9,000 bytes, which improves the frame throughput of a GE switch. Since each frame requires switch processing of header information, the fewer frames presented to the switch, the more data the switch can process, switch, and deliver in a given period of time. Where multiple GE switches are networked, jumbo frames may be passed between them. Where the GE hub or switch interfaces with lesser, standards-based Ethernet devices, the jumbo frame must be fragmented to effect compatibility [8-49], [8-50], [8-7], and [8-51].

Physical transmission media currently is limited to fiber optics, as detailed earlier in this chapter. MultiMode Fiber (MMF) supports gigabit transmission at distances up to 550 meters, and Single Mode Fiber up to 5 km. In either case, there is a minimum distance of 2 meters because of issues of signal reflection (echo). While UTP, STP, and other electrically based media are anticipated in the near future, distances will be highly limited. Cat 5 UTP is anticipated to support full-duplex transmission over distances up to 25 meters, with each of four-pair carrying a 125-MHz signal.

Clearly, the application for Gigabit Ethernet largely will be in the backbone, for interconnecting lesser Ethernet hubs, Ethernet switches, and high-performance servers — rather than connecting individual nodes. GE hubs and switches, however, commonly offer 10/100/1000 Mbps ports. Both half-duplex and full-duplex interfaces will be supported, with full-duplex offering the advantage of virtual elimination of issues of data collisions. Half- and full-duplex declarations will be made on a port-by-port basis.

As a practical matter, GE involves a backbone upgrade at the level of the wiring closet/data center switch. Early Gigabit Ethernet products range from $6,000-$160,000, depending on factors such as the number of and speed (10/100/1000 Mbps) of ports supported and the level of scalability. Costs dropped rapidly, however, and are expected to continue to drop. Chassis-based systems, as opposed to standalone systems, offer advantages including hot-swappable power supplies, switching matrixes, and switching modules. The market for GE is anticipated to increase from approximately 200,000 ports in 1998 to 1.8 million ports in 1999, and 18 million ports and over $1 billion by the year 2002 [8-52].

Asynchronous Transfer Mode (ATM)

Developed originally for broadband WAN application and therefore discussed in detail in Chapter 10, *Asynchronous Transfer Mode (ATM)* has increasingly significant application as a backbone LAN technology, as well. ATM is based on cell switching technology that accommodates any form of information. ATM switches deal with data cells of 53 octets, 48 of which are data payload and five of which are control overhead. Isochronous voice and video can be supported as effectively as asynchronous or synchronous data. The fixed size of the cell enables ATM to support very high throughput speeds, as the switch always knows what packet size to expect. ATM LAN switches originally were specified at 155/622 Mbps, although the ATM forum approved a 25.6 Mbps standard. While the cost of ATM in LAN application currently is expensive, it does offer great advantage in terms of its flexibility.

ATM is an excellent backbone solution, offering very high switching speeds at 155/622 Mbps, with throughput coming very close to those theoretical maximums. A version operating at 25.6 Mbps was developed several years ago as a desktop solution, but never gained a following because of its relatively high cost and lack of speed in the face of Ethernet solutions running at 100 Mbps and more. Currently, ATM is the only standard switching solution to support Quality of Service (QoS) guarantees, although there are a number of initiatives designed to support QoS for IP-based networks. In fact, ATM is well positioned as the ultimate solution, given its ability to support multiple levels of QoS for various types of data, such as uncompressed and compressed voice and video, and connection-oriented and connectionless data protocols. ATM offers excellent access and congestion control, as well. Also, ATM is a standards-based solution, which permits the deployment of multivendor LANs, although care must be exercised in this regard.

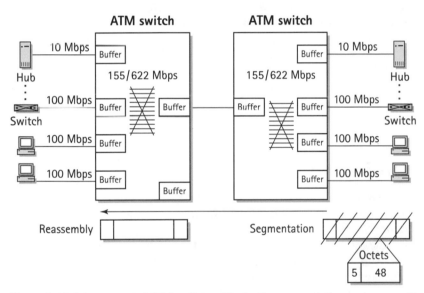

Figure 8-19 Interconnected ATM switches, illustrating segmentation and reassembly

In the LAN domain, ATM operates much like other switching technologies, at least at a fundamental, conceptual level. Using an Ethernet example, an originating ATM-attached device (e.g., workstation, hub, or switch) interfaces to a backbone ATM switch or ATM-capable router at a port speed of 10/100 Mbps. At the input port, the Ethernet frames are buffered and segmented into payloads of 48 octets. Each cell is prepended with a header of five octets, and is flowed through the complex ATM switching matrix, which has an internal speed of 155/622 Mbps. In a two-switch backbone environment (see Figure 8-19), the cells flow to the output port and over an optical fiber link to the next switch, where they flow through that switching matrix to the buffer associated with the designated output port. At the buffer, the cells are gathered, the headers are stripped away, the frame is reassembled in its native format, and the reconstituted frame is presented to the destination device. While ATM's *cell tax* (i.e., overhead) of better than 10 percent has subjected it to a good deal of criticism, that shortcoming is at least partially counterbalanced by its excellent access and congestion control mechanisms, which combine to yield excellent throughput.

Assuming that ATM fulfills its promise as the ultimate WAN backbone solution, the deployment of ATM on the premise offers seamless access to an ATM-based WAN. All of the incumbent domestic IXCs (Interexchange Carriers), in fact, have announced plans to migrate their voice networks from circuit-switching to ATM. ATM's unique ability to support all forms of data offers the potential for an single network solution to voice, video, and data communications applications over an integrated access link. These factors have led a number of PBX, data switch, and router manufacturers to develop a wide variety of ATM-based or ATM-capable switches. Such switches are positioned either as multimedia communications controllers within the CPE domain, or as *Integrated Access Devices* (*IADs*) for WAN access. ATM's current drawbacks include its relatively high cost and its high level of complexity. Ethernet switches operating at 100 Mbps and 1 Gbps certainly challenge ATM in the LAN backbone. In fact, Ethernet switches increasingly are being touted for voice and video, as well as data, applications. While Ethernet inherently does not offer QoS, mechanisms have been developed to support differential levels of treatment for various native data types.

Layer 3 Switching

Switches run at Layer 2, the Data Link Layer of the OSI Reference Model. Switches make blind decisions about forwarding data on a hop-by-hop basis, and without consideration of the network as a whole. *Layer 3 Switching* (see Figure 8-20) relies on decisions made by routers in consideration of the levels of availability and performance of network links and nodes. Layer 3 switching is datagram-oriented; each packet is considered independently. Packet-by-packet, data is sent across a route predetermined in consideration of these factors. This approach is not session-oriented because it does not consider each packet to be associated with a stream of packets in a data session. In other words, the Layer 3 switches have no idea and have no concern as to the existence or nature of a preceding or a succeeding packet in a data communications session.

Layer 3 switching is exemplified by *tag switching*, a Layer 3 (Network Layer) switching technique developed by Cisco Systems for high-performance packet forwarding through a router. A label or *tag* is assigned to destination networks, subnetworks, or hosts. As a packet stream is presented to the tag edge router, the router analyzes the network-layer header prepended to each packet, selects a route for the

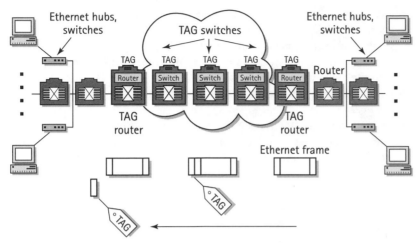

Figure 8-20 Tag switching

packet from its internal routing tables, and prepends the *Protocol Data Unit* (*PDU*) with a tag from its *Tag Information Base* (*TIB*). It then forwards the packet to the next-hop tag switch — typically a core tag switch. The core switch(es) then forward the packet solely on the basis of the short tag, eliminating the need to reanalyze the full header. When the packet reaches the tag edge router at the egress point of the network, the tag is stripped off and the packet is delivered to the target device. While this approach adds a small amount of overhead to each packet, the speed of packet processing is improved considerably, particularly in a complex network in which multiple routers or switches must act on each packet.

Consider the following analogy. When you send a personal letter through the mail, you fill out the complete address longhand. That full address contains the name of the intended recipient, the street address and apartment or suite number, the city, the state, and the ZIP code or other postal code. As the letter is first processed at the edge of the system, a computer system scans the ZIP code through the use of Optical Character Recognition (OCR) or Optical Mark Recognition (OMR), and a postal code is added in the form of a bar code. In the event that the OCR or OMR software cannot translate the handwritten ZIP code, a postal worker adds the bar code on a manual basis. As the letter works its way through the core of the system, electronic devices rely solely on the bar-coded ZIP code to forward the letter to the destination edge of the postal processing network. All mail destined for the same local post office is batched and delivered there. At that office, the street address is read in full and the mail is sorted for individual routes and carriers. The carrier verifies the address before depositing the mail in your mailbox. Consider the bar-coded ZIP code as analogous to a tag — it adds additional overhead, but speeds up the process or sorting and forwarding in the network of mail centers. Such is the case with Tag switching.

You can apply tag switching to IPX and other network protocols, as well as IP. Tag switching also enables Layer 2 switches to participate in Layer 3 routing, reducing the number of routing peers with which each edge router must deal. This enhances the scalability of the network. The first application of tag switching likely will be in the Internet, where scalability is of great importance. Additionally, tag switching's improved speed of packet processing promises to enhance overall Internet performance.

Note that this scenario also illustrates a common approach to complex networking – route at the edge and switch in the core. This approach applies the greatest level of intelligence (and cost and processing and delay) to the edges of the network, making all significant decisions as the data is presented to the network ... and removed from it. This approach also achieves the greatest speed in the network core, where speed is critical. Overall, this approach optimizes performance of the complex network and internetwork [8-53].

Cisco has submitted the tag switching specification to the IETF for consideration as an Internet standard. At the IETF level, tag switching has been redefined as *MultiProtocol Label Switching* (*MPLS*). MPLS labels can define either hop-by-hop routes or explicit end-to-end routes, and indicate Grade of Service (GoS), VPN, and other types of information that affect the manner in which the traffic is to be carried through the network [8-54].

Layer 4 Switching

Layer 4 Switching is content-smart and application-aware. Layer 4 switching is session-oriented in nature, considering the nature of the traffic and the expectations of that traffic in terms of factors such as delay and loss. In consideration of those factors, the network route is selected, including the selection of the server most appropriate and available where multiple server options exist. The Layer 4 switch also considers each data packet as an element of a stream of packets in a data session, which session might be connection-oriented or connectionless in nature, and which session might involve asynchronous, synchronous, or isochronous data [8-55].

Ipsilon Networks coined the term *IP Switching* to describe a class of switch that combines intelligent IP routing with high-speed ATM switching hardware in a single, scalable platform. The IP switch implements the IP protocol stack on ATM hardware, enabling the device to dynamically shift between store-and-forward and cut-through switching based on the flow requirements of the traffic as defined in the packet header. Data flows of long duration, thereby, can be optimized by cut-through switching, with the balance of the traffic afforded the default ATM treatment – which is hop-by-hop, store-and-forward routing. Ipsilon suggests that first-generation IP switches can achieve rates of up to 5.3 million PPS (packets per second) by avoiding ATM cell segmentation and reassembly, ATM overhead, and ATM switch processing of each cell header. Clearly, one of the advantages of IP switching is the use of IP (Internet Protocol), a protocol that is mature, well understood, and widely deployed across a wide range of networks.

Layer 4 switching goes beyond IP, to include IP extensions such as FTP (File Transfer Protocol), which is connection-oriented, and UDP (User Datagram Protocol), which is connectionless in nature. Layer 4 switching services can exploit this information contained in the header to determine the nature of the transmission path that must be established in order to satisfy the requirements of each traffic type. Thereby, different classes of traffic can be afforded differential levels of service. Contemporary routers can exercise this level of intelligence at wire speeds through logic embedded at the chip level – in *ASICs (Application-Specific Integrated Circuits)* [8-56].

Minding Your Ps and Qs

The IEEE recently has taken steps to enable Layer 2 switches to support Quality of Service (QoS), which actually is more in the form of Grade of Service (GoS). In September 1998, the IEEE adopted the 802.1p specification. That specification, in conjunction with the previously adopted 802.1q specification for VLAN tagging, paved the way for standards-based multivendor GoS. The 802.1 specification enables switches and other devices (e.g., bridges and hubs) to prioritize (*P*) traffic into one of eight classes which affect the manner in which the buffer queues (*Q*) are managed. Class 7, the highest priority, is reserved for network control data such as Open Shortest Path First (OSPF) and Routing Information Protocol (RIP) table updates. Classes 6 and 5 can be used for voice, video, and other delay-sensitive traffic. Classes 4 through 1 address streaming data applications through loss-tolerant traffic such as File Transfer Protocol. Class 0 is a "best effort" class. Since Ethernet does not provide a mechanism for priority identification in the frame header, 802.1q is employed. That specification defines a 32-bit tag for such purposes. Desktop systems, servers, routers, or Layer 3 switches can set the 802.1q tag [8-57] and [8-58].

Ps and Qs are the mechanisms by which Layer 2 switches support voice and video, as well as LAN traffic in the converged LAN domain. Within the customer premises, these specifications encourage the development of the convergence scenario via such relatively inexpensive technologies as switched Ethernet.

FireWire

Based on the IEEE 1394 standard, *FireWire* is designed to eliminate the bottleneck at the serial port of the LAN-attached PC. While 100-Mbps LANs address the bottleneck of the shared medium, they overwhelm the attached workstation (sort of like drinking out of a firehose). As videoconferencing and multimedia applications increase in popularity, it is necessary to increase the speed of the SCSI (Small Computer Serial Interface) to support them and take full advantage of the speed provided by the LAN. FireWire addresses that requirement through standards for 100, 200, and 400 Mbps.

Non-Standard LANs

In addition to standard LANs, there exist a number of nonstandard options. Some are proprietary standards that serve certain applications and vertical markets, such as the oil refining industry described earlier. Others are more widely accepted, such as *ARCnet* (*A*ttached *R*esource *C*omputer *net*work). Developed in 1977 by Datapoint Corporation, ARCnet is a highly reliable, low-cost token bus system based on a physical star and logical ring, and a character-oriented protocol. Delivering 2.5 Mbps on a standard basis, a new version delivers 20 Mbps [8-21]. The ARCnet standard resembles the IEEE 802.4 specification, although it employs a baseband network [8-2].

References

[8-1]   Shelly, Gary B and Cashman, Thomas J. *Introduction to Computers and Data Processing*. Anaheim Publishing Company, 1980.

[8-2]   Nunemacher, Greg. *LAN Primer, Third Edition*. M&T Books, 1995.

[8-3]   Metcalfe, Robert M. and Boggs, David R. *Ethernet: Distributed Packet Switching for Local Computer Networks*. Association for Computing Machinery, Inc., 1976.

[8-4]   Allocca, Lisa. "Networking for the Masses." *Internet Week*, May 4, 1998.

[8-5]   Metcalfe, Bob. "From the Ether." *InfoWorld*, October 31, 1994.

[8-6]   Conover, Joel. "Building a Better Infrastructure." *Network Computing*, October 1, 1998.

[8-7]   Henderson, Tom. "Gigabit Ethernet Blueprint." *Network Magazine*, September 1998.

[8-8]   "Technology Overview: Gigabit Ethernet" Cisco Systems. www.sms.ee/kkk/giga.html.

[8-9]   Williams, Veronica A. *Wireless Computing Primer*. M&T Books, 1996.

[8-10]   Ketchersid, John and Ferguson, Jerry. "Freedom!" *Network World*, November 13, 1995.

[8-11]   Larsen, Amy K. "Wireless LANs: Worth a Second Look." *Data Communications*, November 1995.

[8-12]   Langley, John. "Moving wireless LANs into fast lane." *Network World*, February 8, 1999.

[8-13]   Null, Christopher. "Unplugging the LAN." *Network World*, February 8, 1999.

[8-14]   Surkan, Michael. "Standardization Is Now in the Air." *PC Week*, July 28, 1997.

[8-15]   Weinbaum, Barry. "The Benefits of IEEE 802.11 for Wireless Local Area Networks." *Wireless and Mobility. 1998 Buyers Guide.*

[8-16]   Lee, Yvonne L. "Notebooks Connect to Network via Infrared." *InfoWorld*, April 8, 1996.

[8-17]   "Wireless LANs Get Throughput Boost." *Information Week*, January 22, 1996.

[8-18]   Tolly, Kevin. "Token Ring vs. Ethernet: The Real Cost Story." *Data Communications*, May 21, 1995.

[8-19]   Miller, Mark A. *Internetworking: A Guide to Network Communications LAN to LAN; LAN to WAN, Second Edition.* M&T Books, 1995.

[8-20]   Spohn, Darren L. *Data Network Design.* McGraw-Hill, Inc., 1993.

[8-21]   Levy, Joseph R. and Hartwig, Glenn. *Networking Fundamentals: From Installation to Application.* MIS: Press, 1995.

[8-22]   *Ethernet Tutorial & Product Guide.* LANTRONIX, 1995.

[8-23]   Petrosky, Mary. "Hub Shopping Spree." *Network World*, May 29, 1995.

[8-24]   Lopez, Steve. "Why Switch?" *Internetwork*, March 1995.

[8-25]   Roberts, Erica. "Server-Based Routing Reconsidered." *Data Communications*, March 1996.

[8-26]   Darling, Charles B. "Routers Can Save Your WAN Dollars." *Datamation*, July 1, 1995.

[8-27]   Feit. Sidnie. *TCP/IP: Architecture, Protocols and Implementation.* McGraw-Hill, Inc., 1993.

[8-28]   Bruno, Lee. "Power to the People?" *Data Communications*, April 1999.

[8-29]   Comer, Douglas E. *Internetworking with TCP/IP, Second Edition.* Prentice-Hall, 1991.

[8-30]   Jacobs, Paula. "Virtual LANs: Too Good to Be True?" *Network World*, March 27, 1995.

[8-31]   Conover, Joel. "Minding Your Virtual Ps and Qs." *Network Computing*, October 15, 1997.

[8-32]   Held, Gilbert. "Virtual LANs Become Reality." *LAN Magazine*, April 1997.

[8-33]   Mandeville, Robert and Newman, David. "VLANs: Real Virtues." *Data Communications*, May 1997.

[8-34]   Morency, John P. "Do VLANs Really Deliver?" *Business Communications Review*, July 1995.

[8-35]   King, Steven S. "VLANs Raise Delicate Design Issues." *Network World*, April 17, 1995.

[8-36]   Minoli, Daniel. "Telecommuting Demand Characteristics." *Datapro Information Services*, November 4, 1998.

[8-37]   Allard, Hank. "Remote LAN Access: Strategies & Solutions." *Network World* Technical Seminars, 1995.

[8-38]   Gangler, Barbara. "Remote Possibilities." *Internetwork*, June 1995.

[8-39]   Finneran, Michael. "Life in the Fast LAN." *Business Communications Review*, May 1995.

[8-40]   Rosen, Ron. "User's Guide to 100Base-T and 100VG-AnyLAN." *Handbook of Local Area Networks*. John P. Slone, editor. Auerbach Publications, 1995.

[8-41]   Rauch, Peter and Lawrence, Scott. "100VG-AnyLAN: The Other Fast Ethernet." *Data Communications*, March 1995.

[8-42]   Newman, David and Levy, Bruce. "100Base-T vs. 100VG: The Real Fast Ethernet." *Data Communications*, March 1996.

[8-43]   Peri, Ron. "Life in the Fast Lane." *Communications Week*, January 23, 1995.

[8-44]   Sullivan, Kristina B. "Promise of FDDI Holds True." *PC Week*, January 15, 1996.

[8-45]   *Implementing FDDI in Enterprise LANs*. SysKonnect, Inc., 1995.

[8-46]   Heneghan, Hank. "New Configurations Make FDDI More Survivable." *Network World*, November 20, 1995.

[8-47]   Korzeniowski, Paul. "Sun Setting on FDDI." *Business Communications Review*, April 1999.

[8-48]   Axner, David. "Going Gigabit." *Network World*, July 20, 1998.

[8-49]   Fontana, John. "Gig Ethernet Juices Up NT." *InternetWeek*, September 7, 1998.

[8-50]   Fontana, John. "Jumbo Frames Support Reaches Critical Mass." *InternetWeek*, October 26, 1998.

[8-51]   Lounsbury, Al. "Gigabit Ethernet: The Difference Is In The Details" *Data Communications*, May 1997.

[8-52]   Clark, Elizabeth. "The Gigabit Gamble." *Network Magazine*, September 1998.

[8-53]   Landau, Jack V. "Clearing Up the Confusion About Multilayer Switching." *Telecommunications*, April 1999.

[8-54]   Petrosky, Mary. "MPLS Group Should Unite on Routing Approach." *Network World*, April 5, 1999.

[8-55]   Bellman, Bob. "Adding Smarts to the Network Cloud." *Business Communications Review*, December 1998.

[8-56]   "Cutting Through Layer 4 Hype." www.foundrynet.com.

[8-57]   Bruno, Charles and Tolly, Kevin. "Minding Your QoS p's and q's." *Network World*, April 19, 1999.

[8-58]   Sherman, Doug. "Tackling the p's and q's of LAN traffic." *Network World*, September 7, 1998.

Chapter 9

Broadband Network Infrastructure

Et loquor et scribo, magis est quod fulmine iungo. I speak and I write . . . but more, it's with light(ning) that I connect. The poet Giovanni Pascoli, describing his views of the telegraph, 1911. Translated from Latin by Daniel Minoli, Enterprise Networking: Fractional T-1 to SONET, Frame Relay to BISDN. Artech House, 1993.

The future of wide area networking involves technologies that are only now being refined, indeed, only now being defined in many instances. Broadband networking addresses the near and distant future of telecommunications — *the need for speed*! As I noted in previous chapters, the PSTN set the stage, remains in place and highly available, works beautifully for voice and quite well for many non-voice applications, is highly reliable, and is cost-effective. However, it offers limited bandwidth, is assumed to be analog twisted-pair at the local loop level, introduces errors in transmission, is relatively slow in establishing connections, and is expensive for communications-intensive applications.

Conventional public data networks (PDNs) introduced significant improvements over the PSTN. Although designed specifically for data communications, the PDNs still relied, at least in part, on the PSTN model for basic connectivity (e.g., local loops, data nodes collocated with voice switches, and common transport facilities). The traditional data model included both dedicated and circuit-switched options, as well as the X.25 packet-switched alternative. Conventional PDNs provided improved performance in terms of speed, error control, throughput, and network management.

The broadband network model is emerging still. Although some broadband network technologies are quite immature, they are rapidly being deployed in backbone networks in developed countries. They also now are being extended directly to large end users for purposes of network access. Broadband networks also rely on the voice model to some extent, often using the same, although upgraded, local loops; equipment collocated in PSTN end offices; and common, although upgraded, backbone transmission facilities. Some broadband technologies are intended specifically for data transmission, although others are designed to support a full range of voice, data, video, and image traffic. In this chapter, you will discover broadband access and transport technologies.

Broadband networking is defined, in the classic sense, as DS-3 (T-3) or greater, providing bandwidth of 45 Mbps or more. This classic definition certainly applies to the long-haul transport facilities in the backbone of the carrier network. Short-

331

haul access, or local loop, facilities also may fit this definition, at least in the case of optical fiber. Generally speaking, access technologies are not broadband truly, but certainly are much more capable than conventional local loops.

Broadband access and transport technologies often provide bandwidth on demand in order to address the dynamic bandwidth requirements of applications such as videoconferencing and multimedia conferencing, and bursty LAN-to-LAN and Internet traffic. As expected of high-speed networks, error performance is excellent and network management generally is robust. Broadband optical fiber systems are highly redundant and, therefore, highly resilient. While these networks are highly cost-effective for bandwidth-intensive applications and in support of large volumes of traffic, the absolute cost of acquisition and deployment is quite high. As a result, the necessary infrastructure is deployed cautiously.

In previous chapters, I discussed the fundamentals of transmission systems (Chapter 2), and the nature and specifics of both the PSTN (Chapter 5) and conventional digital and data networks (Chapter 7). Those discussions set the stage for an in-depth presentation of the latest in access and transport technologies. This chapter deals with a number of developing local loop technologies. It also details SONET, the standard for optical fiber transmission in backbone networks.

Access Technologies

Regardless of the sophistication and elegance of the backbone network technology, you still need to gain access to it to share in its capabilities. Despite the hyperbole about fiber optic cable or hybrid fiber/coax connections to the premise, little investment has been made in such access technologies. Some large user organizations in commercial office parks or high-rise buildings have direct fiber connections from LECs, IXCs, or CAPs. A privileged few residential and small business customers have such access in areas where various field trials are underway. The rest of us must contend with the limitations of the twisted pair local loop. However, significant advances have been made in the use of UTP. Additionally, fiber and wireless technologies have been developed to extend broadband capabilities to the premise. Specifically, let's explore wireline local loop access technologies grouped into the xDSL family, developing CATV options, and the wireless technologies grouped into what is known variously as Wireless Local Loop (WLL) and fixed wireless.

Before progressing with the discussion of the individual technologies, let's pause to take note of the fact that only meaningful (read revenue-producing, profit-producing, or cost-saving) applications can justify their implementation. Some of the technologies are incremental in nature. In other words, they are enhancements of existing copper local loop (i.e., UTP or coax) technologies. The incremental approaches substantially improve the performance of the underlying transmission media, within the limitations imposed by the regulators and the basic laws of physics. Wireless local loops often overlay the traditional copper network, bypassing it for a variety of reasons that include cost and performance. Optical fiber loops involve either a complete replacement of trunk facilities in the loop, or an overlay. Regardless of whether the access technology is characterized as an enhancement, an overlay, or a replacement, the absolute cost of its deployment is fairly significant. Yet, you can overcome that cost through the revenues it yields in terms of supporting profitable applications that are resource-intensive.

xDSL (Generic Digital Subscriber Line)

xDSL (*generic Digital Subscriber Line*) encompasses a group of digital network access technologies largely intended for the residential, Small Office/Home Office (SOHO) and small business markets. DSL is provisioned over conventional Unshielded Twisted Pair (UTP) local loop facilities, which comprise the vast majority of network access facilities owned by the Incumbent Local Exchange Carriers (ILECs). Beginning in 1880 and continuing through much of the 20th century, UTP was the only option, or the only viable option, for most applications. As you learned in previous chapters, UTP inherently is the most limited of all transmission media in terms of the dimensions of bandwidth, error performance, and distance. However, a two-wire UTP circuit is quite sufficient in support of analog voice, and analog voice-grade data through modems. It also is quite sufficient in support of ISDN BRI, a digital service offering running at a total signaling rate of 144 Mbps. UTP even supports Fractional T-1, T-1, and ISDN PRI at signaling speeds up to 1.544 Mbps. The main reason that we continue to use UTP, quite simply, is that it is there. The main reason that we continue to deploy UTP is that it is relatively inexpensive to acquire and deploy, especially as an extension of a legacy UTP-based network.

Very recently, however, the embedded twisted-pair local loop has become strained under the pressure of increased demand for improved speed of information transfer and improved error performance. In large part, this is due to the growth of data communications — especially the popularity of the Internet and World Wide Web (WWW). As a result of these factors and competition from CATV providers and others, the ILECs have aggressively sought to develop technologies to extend the life of the embedded UTP local loop through improving its general performance characteristics.

xDSL is a group of technologies including ADSL, G.lite, HDSL, HDSL2, IDSL, RADSL, SDSL, and VDSL. Some of these are proprietary, some are standardized, and others are in the process of standardization. All of these technologies are digital in nature, and make use of sophisticated compression algorithms and multiplexing techniques to squeeze as much performance as possible from the inherently limited, UTP-based local loop. Each technology is loop-specific, requiring special equipment on each end of the point-to-point local loop circuit. Most xDSL technologies support both voice and data; voice is afforded preferential treatment and data is supported at relatively high speed. One option supports video, as well, and one supports data only. Most of the technologies involve centralized *splitters*, also called modems or filters, into which the customer side of the loop connects. Voice signals, which run at frequencies up to 4 kHz, "cut through" the locally-powered splitter in the event of a power failure; therefore, and very much unlike ISDN, the phones still work if the lights go off. A key advantage of all xDSL technologies is that they support "always-on" data access because the circuit is always available from the PC through the on-premises splitter to the centralized splitter and *DSLAM* (*DSL Access Multiplexer*) in the Central Office, or other centralized location, and to the Internet. Unlike ISDN and conventional modems, xDSL imposes no delays through the establishment of a circuit-switched connection over the PSTN.

All xDSL technologies are fairly demanding of the local loop — some are absolutely unforgiving and some are adaptive to local loop anomalies. Before we examine the specific technologies, let's examine the problems with the electrically-based, local loop, each of which has definite impact on xDSL performance.

- ◆ **Loop Length** has a significant effect on signal strength and, therefore, on error performance. This is particularly true at high frequencies that attenuate (i.e., lose strength) much more quickly (i.e., over a shorter distance) than do low frequencies. Further, attenuation especially is an issue given the narrow gauge (usually 24- or 26-gauge) of voice-grade, twisted-pair outside cable plant. As all of the xDSL technologies are designed to support relatively high-speed data, they run at relatively high frequencies, at least in comparison to the 4 kHz range over which voice is supported. Many of the xDSL technologies are designed to work over local loops of as much as 18 kft., which describes the vast majority of those in the domestic ILEC franchised market areas. Other xDSL technologies require shorter loop lengths due to the higher frequencies utilized.

- ◆ **Splices and Mixed Gauges** can cause echo, or signal reflection, which is a source of noise, or signal distortion. It is not at all uncommon to find mixed 24- and 26-gauge cable in a given local loop. The ILEC craftspeople just didn't close their eyes and reached into the warehouse for a reel of cable, but the effect is the same as if they had. Telcordia Technologies estimates that the average residential local loop involves 22 splices, each of which contributes to the problem [9-1]. Some of those splices may not be mechanically sound, and some of the splice casings may not be well insulated. The problem is likely to be worse with longer subject loops. Echo cancellers and error detection and correction algorithms can compensate for much of this noise, but this always causes difficulty.

- ◆ **Bridged Taps** are sections of a cable pair not on the direct electrical path between the Central Office and the customer premises. They generally are in place because a previous customer between the Central Office and the subject building was connected to the Central Office through the same pair. When that customer disconnected service, the splice was not removed. Since high-frequency signals require a point-to-point local loop for maximum performance and as a bridged tap increases the electrical loss on the pair, they must be removed for xDSL services to work, or at least to work optimally.

- **Load Coils** are passive devices that filter frequencies above 4 kHz. Load coils must be removed for xDSL services to function. In other words, xDSL performs best over a *dry copper pair* (i.e., a pair with no electronics), also known as a *burglar alarm circuit*.

- **Interference** is an inherent problem with UTP, as discussed in Chapter 2. UTP is susceptible to ambient noise from a variety of sources, such as static electricity, radio and TV stations, and electric motors in proximity. Also, and in a multi-pair distribution cable, a high-frequency xDSL service on one cable pair can adversely affect POTS service, T-1 service, or other xDSL services on adjacent pairs. A high frequency signal, such as xDSL, radiates from the center of the copper core, with the phenomenon of *crosstalk* increasing over distance. *Far-End CrossTalk* (*FEXT*), which is crosstalk at the customer-premises end of the loop, generally is not a significant problem. This is because the circuit is point-to-point, and individually terminates in a Network Interface Unit (NIU) absent of other pairs (at least absent of a great number of other pairs carrying high-frequency signals). *Near-End CrossTalk* (*NEXT*), which is crosstalk at the telco end of the loop is much more of a problem because multiple high-frequency signals may be presented through the same multi-pair cable, and can interfere with each other to a considerable extent. Note that interference is a particular issue where adjacent loops transmit at the same range of frequencies; this phenomenon tends to limit the number of T-1s in a single cable, and similarly limits the number of DSL circuits in a given cable.

- **Inside Wire** systems are of uncertain quality in residential, SOHO, and small business environments. In many cases, the inside wire has been in place for many years, and has been spliced over and over again as buildings were remodeled and as new jacks were added for analog telephones, fax machines, and computer modems. Professionals completed some of this work; amateurs did the rest. My home office, for instance, is in the remodeled basement of a house built in 1927. It's a great place to write a book, but it hardly boasts a state-of-the-technology wiring system. My lovely wife, Margaret, telecommutes in connection with her consulting practice, so we share the space. We have three lines coming into our SOHO, are adding a fourth, and I can't even count the number of jacks for our analog telephone sets, fax machine, and computer modems. Margaret installed some of the jacks, so I have to be careful what I put in print, but suffice it to say that our wiring system is somewhat unusual in nature. In any event, running high-speed data to our workstations would be an interesting, and uncertain, experience.

- **Voice Instrument Signaling States** can impact data communications in a xDSL environment. While analog voice circuits and instruments are standardized, the wide variety of devices vary enough in their electrical characteristics to cause unpredictable problems when integrating voice and data over a common inside wiring plan. xDSL data communications sessions can be dropped when analog telephones ring, when they go off-hook, and when they go back on-hook. The ultimate solution is an adaptive splitter or modem. The interim solution, at least for some versions of xDSL, involves equipping the offending telephone sets with inexpensive add-on filters that plug in between the set and the jack.

◆ Digital Loop Carrier (DLC) systems are voice-grade multiplexers embedded in a local loop distribution plant to increase its efficiency. SLC 96 (Subscriber Line Carrier 96), for instance, involves a four-wire copper circuit that runs from the Central Office to a remote node, and provides four T-1 logical circuits in support of 96 voice-grade channels of 64 Kbps. At the remote node are concentrated and multiplexed individual voice-grade local loops (as many as 96) that terminate at customers' premises (see Figure 9-1). SLC 96 and other much more advanced DLC systems are highly cost-effective in the support of voice-grade communications services to areas that are far removed from the Central Office. DLC systems, however, filter high-frequency signals such as xDSL, shaping and grooming them to fit into 64 Kbps channels – one per telephone number. Traditional DLCs, therefore, render xDSL inoperable. The only viable solution is to split the voice channels off, and run them through a *Next-Generation DLC* (*NGDLC*). The video and data channels must split off and run through a remote *DSL Access Multiplexer* (*DSLAM*), a packet multiplexing device designed specifically for that purpose. An estimated 30 percent of all local loops in the United States are served through DLCs. In densely-packed urban areas, relatively few DLCs are required, while sparsely populated rural areas make extensive use of DLCs. Bell Atlantic, for example, serves only 15 percent of its customers through DLCs, while BellSouth serves approximately 40 percent of its customers in this fashion. DLCs exist in about 74 percent of Southwestern Bell loops [9-2], [9-3], and [9-4].

Also, before we explore the specifics of the xDSL technology options, let's pause to examine the network elements that generally are involved. Those elements include splitters or modems, local loops, and DSLAMs.

◆ *Splitters* or *modems* are interface units that must be installed in matching pairs – one at the customer premises and one at the edge of the network. Centralized *splitters* may be in the form of enhanced *Network Interface Units* (*NIUs*), which are the point of termination and demarcation between the carrier-provided local loop and the inside wire and cable system. The NIUs generally are attached to the outside of the building, or are positioned just inside the basement wall, garage wall, or other point of entry.

Alternatively, splitters may be in the form of a *set-top box*, much as a CATV converter. The splitter functions as a Frequency Division Multiplexer (FDM) and/or Time Division Multiplexer (TDM), depending on the specific xDSL technology involved. Additionally, the splitter compresses the data transmissions. The splitter also may function as a codec, digitizing analog voice and fax transmissions as required. G.lite and other xDSL technologies sometimes use decentralized modems, rather than centralized splitters. Such modems are positioned functionally between the PC or LAN, and the inside wire and cable system, using frequencies above 4 kHz for high-speed data transmission.

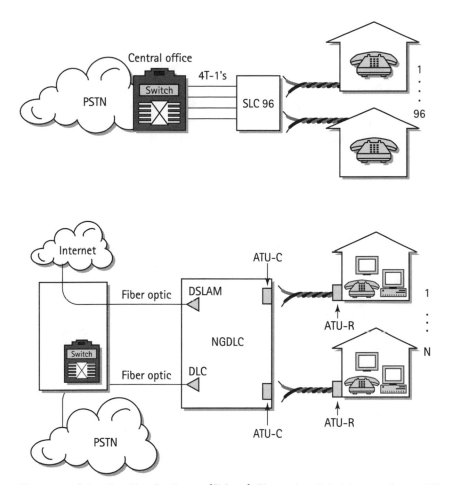

Figure 9-1 Subscriber Line Carrier-96 (SLC-96), illustrating digital loop carrier; and Next-Generation DLC (NGCLC) with built-in DSL Access Multiplexer (DSLAM)

- ◆ The *local loop* is the point-to-point circuit between the customer premises and the edge of the network. Functionally, the local loop terminates first in a NIU at the customer premises, with the splitter or modem functionally positioned between the NIU and the terminal equipment. At the edge of the network is positioned a matching splitter/modem technology. If the service provider is an ILEC, that point of interface may be in the form of a xDSL line card associated with a Central Office switch. In the upstream direction, the ILEC splitter splits off the low-frequency voice signals for presentation to the PSTN (Public Switched Telephone Network), and the high-frequency data signals for presentation to the PDN (Public Data Network) through the DSLAM.

- ◆ The *DSL Access Multiplexer* (*DSLAM*) interfaces the xDSL local loop to the PDN, such as the Internet, perhaps through the aforementioned ILEC splitter. The DSLAM is a packet multiplexer, usually connected to the PDN over an unchannelized T-1, T-3, or SONET circuit.

- ◆ A *Single Point Of Termination* (*SPOT*) frame typically is used where a CLEC or ISP is leasing dry copper pairs from the ILEC for purposes of provisioning xDSL data services. The SPOT frame, and other hardware, is collocated in the ILEC Central Office, generally in separately secured leased space. The ILEC cross-connects the individual leased circuits at the Main Distribution Frame (MDF), and terminates them in the SPOT frame, where the CLEC or ISP connects them to the DSLAM.

In total, xDSL deployment is expected to grow very quickly, and to be very substantial in the near future. International Data Corp. estimates that there will be as many as 2.5 million lines installed by year-end 2001 [9-5]. Datamonitor estimates that xDSL will serve as many as 5.5 million European households by the year 2002 [9-6]. While these estimates may well be on the aggressive side, there seems little question that xDSL will make a significant impact during the next decade. The xDSL technologies discussed first are those intended largely for the residential, SOHO, and small business markets: ADSL, RADSL, IDSL, and G.lite. The technologies discussed last are those intended primarily for the larger business market: HDSL, HDSL2, and SDSL.

ASYMMETRIC DIGITAL SUBSCRIBER LINE (ADSL)

Asymmetric Digital Subscriber Line (*ADSL*) is an advanced, high-bandwidth local loop technology designed to extend the life of existing UTP loops for the transmission of broadband signals. Developed by Bellcore (now Telcordia) at the request of the RBOCs, and standardized by ANSI as T-1.413, ADSL provides for very high-capacity transmission over relatively short local loops in the *Carrier Serving Area* (*CSA*). ADSL makes use of *DMT* (*Discrete MultiTone*) signaling, which is used in T-1, to accomplish this feat. The ADSL Forum, dedicated to the promotion of xDSL technologies, promotes this technology [9-7].

The term "asymmetric" comes from the fact that bandwidth is provided on an asymmetric basis, with more bandwidth in the downstream direction than in the upstream direction. In addition to supporting POTS voice over a separate analog channel running at 4 kHz and below, ADSL supports high-speed data at frequencies of 26 kHz and above. A high-speed downstream channel is provided in increments of 1.536 Mbps up to 6.144 Mbps, based on T-1 specifications. Additionally, a bidirectional channel is provided in increments of 64 Kbps, up to 640 Kbps.

The individual channels are derived either by frequency division multiplexing (FDM), or by echo cancellation. With FDM, one frequency band is designated for downstream data and another for upstream data. Then, Time Division Multiplexing (TDM) divides each directional frequency into one or more high-speed and low-speed channels. Echo cancellation overlaps the upstream and downstream channels, and separates the two by local echo cancellation at each end of the circuit. In either case, a 4 kHz channel is split off for POTS at the DC (Direct Current) end of the band [9-8]. Table 9-1 displays several standards-based ADSL options. The higher-speed versions (up to 51.84 Mbps) also are known as *Very High Data Rate Subscriber Line* (*VDSL*).

Table 9-1 ADSL VARIATIONS

Downstream Channel (Simplex)	BiDirectional Channel (HDX)	Maximum Distance
6.144 Mbps (US)*	640 Kbps	2 miles (3 Km)
51.84 Mbps (US)	5 Mbps	0.6-1.2 miles (1-2 Km)
155 Mbps (US)	15 Mbps	500 meters
8 Mbps (European)	608 Kbps	3-4 Km

*4 bearer channels @ 1.536 data rate yields a data rate of 6.144 Mbps; overhead is additional. Further variations exist as specified in ANSI T-1E1.4/94-007 Revision 8.

The original inputs of voice, data, and image information are anticipated to be carried across the WAN via an ATM backbone network — ideally based on fiber optics. The video signals also may travel across the broadband ATM WAN, may be received at the Central Office *head-end* via broadcast satellite or microwave, or the programming may be stored on tape or disk in a video server at the CO. The voice input is handled at each end of the connection through a frequency splitter that ensures it is unaffected by the presence or absence of digital data. At the network side of the loop, the video and data inputs are time division multiplexed into an ADSL signal that originates in an *ATU-C* (*ADSL Transmission Unit-Centralized*). The signal then travels the local loop cable plant, terminating in a matching *ATU-R* (*ADSL Transmission Unit-Remote*) located on the customer's premises (refer to Figure 9-2).

The ATU-R acts as a modem, splitting the total bandwidth into three channels: the downstream channel, the bidirectional channel, and a voice channel. The ATU-R can be in the form of a standalone unit, or a printed circuit board in a PC or other host computer. Alternatively, the ATU-R can be contained within a set-top box in a video or TV application. The bit error rate (BER) of ADSL is 10^{-9}, which compares favorably even with traditional T-1 at 10^{-7}.

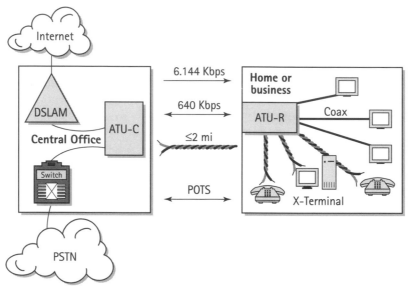

Figure 9-2 Asymmetric Digital Subscriber Line (ADSL) configuration in example residential application, illustrating bandwidth, ADSL Terminating Units (ATUs), and DSL Access Multiplexer (DSLAM)

ADSL is intended for applications requiring a high-speed downstream channel and a relatively low-speed upstream channel. While the technology is not appropriate for many bandwidth-intensive, conversational data communications applications, it seems ideal for entertainment TV (CATV), business TV, and educational TV. Telecommuters also can be well served by ADSL for remote LAN access. In a SOHO (Small Office/Home Office) environment, ADSL provides plenty of bandwidth for most applications, including Internet access, and file and image transfer. Into the future, ADSL promises to serve Video-On-Demand (VOD) applications, providing sufficient bandwidth for multiple downstream video channels, as well as the upstream video selection.

The primary interest in ADSL has resided with the incumbent telcos, which are facing competition from CATV companies for the residential voice and data market. As the CATV providers prepare to compete for that business, they are upgrading existing coaxial cable plant to add bidirectional, switched voice and data capabilities.

The CAPs and IXCs have similar plans, although they either must build new local loop facilities to reach that market on a wired or wireless basis, acquire incumbents with local loop facilities of one form or another, or lease loops from the incumbents. In the face of that pressure, the telcos must find a means to increase bandwidth in the local loop to compete effectively. Their options include laying new cable plant (fiber optic or coax), making use of wireless technology, or increasing the capacity of existing twisted pair plant. ADSL offers a relatively inexpensive solution, accommodating entertainment TV, videoconferencing, and higher-speed data transfer over existing cable plant of varying gauges. Most carriers view ADSL as a short-term access solution, filling the bandwidth gap until more substantial cable plant is deployed.

While ADSL has performed well under laboratory conditions, it has yet to prove itself in the field. Standards-based ADSL is completely unforgiving of anomalies in the UTP-based local loop cable plant, as detailed above. Loop lengths must fall within limits defined in Table 9-1, and the number of splices must be kept to a minimum. Mixed gauges, bridged taps, and loading coils cannot be tolerated. Clearly, only a very small percentage of local loops meet these criteria. Where these anomalies exist, they must be removed. Where the insulation of the cable pair or splice casing is old, cracked or otherwise compromised, the cable plant must be rehabilitated or replaced. Once the cable plant is deemed acceptable, a splitter must be installed at the customer premise, and the circuit must be tested in order to meet the very tight tolerances. The local loop demands and the installation of a splitter require an ILEC "truck roll," which makes the provisioning process fairly labor-intensive and, therefore, expensive.

Bell Atlantic was a primary force behind ADSL development, and continues to champion the technology. All major ILECs in the United States have trialed full-rate ADSL at the lowest speed levels. Those trials have been limited to areas characterized by excellent cable plant serving affluent neighborhoods with reasonably high densities of users receptive to a bundled suite of voice, data, and video services.

In addition to the strong interest of U.S. LECs, ADSL has gained the attention of foreign carriers. British Telecom (UK) began a field trial in February 1994, and Telefonica de Espana followed a month later. Trials also are being conducted by Mercury Communications (UK) and Telecom Australia, and are planned for the networks of Italy, France, Korea, The Netherlands, Hong Kong, Brazil, Finland, Norway, and Germany. The costs of implementing ADSL technology are high in absolute terms, but can be quite reasonable when compared to the alternative of laying new cable plant, such as hybrid fiber/coax. There also exist non-standard versions trialed by GTE and other carriers.

RATE-ADAPTIVE DIGITAL SUBSCRIBER LINE (RADSL)

Rate-Adaptive Digital Subscriber Line (RADSL) is a non-standard ADSL variation. Much like a conventional modem, RADSL modems adapt the downstream transmission speed in consideration of the capability of the circuit. Since ADSL assumes a high-quality local loop and as such loops are unusual, the adaptive nature of RADSL clearly makes the technology widely relevant.

Nortel's 1-Mbps modem (see Figure 9-3) is an excellent example of RADSL. Nortel's solution supports data speeds up to 1.3 Mbps (actually 960 Kbps) downstream and 120 Kbps upstream over 24-gauge UTP loops up to 18,000 feet miles in length, 26-gauge loops up to 15,000 feet, and mixed-gauge loops of shorter length. The bit error rate (BER) of 10^{-7}, consistent with T-1 standards, is ensured even over longer loop lengths, despite the presence of some reasonable number of bridge taps, and even in consideration of electromagnetic interference (EMI). If the length of the loop, the number of bridge taps, or the level of EMI cause difficulty, the matching modems on each end of the circuit adapt dynamically to the maximum allowable speed, given the requirement to maintain the defined BER. Much like the handshaking process defined for conventional modems in Chapter 6, the modems negotiate and renegotiate that speed level (baud rate). The carrier also can set maximum data rates manually.

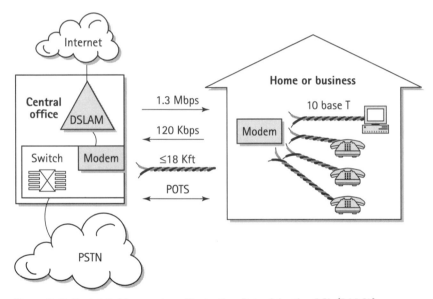

Figure 9-3 Nortel 1-Meg modem, illustrating Rate-Adaptive DSL (RADSL)

The modem uses advanced 64 QAM (Quadrature Amplitude Modulation) and adaptive equalization. The premises-based modem connects to the local loop via a standard RJ11 telephone jack, and connects to computers and LANs via a 10BaseT port. The modem also supports a RJ11 jack interface for connection to an analog telephone set, fax machine, or conventional computer modem. Voice and data communications are supported simultaneously over the same local loop through frequency division multiplexing, with the voice channel running at 4 kHz and below. The premises-based modem is locally powered, but provides cut-through connectivity for Central-Office powered voice-grade communications in the event of a local power failure. At the network side of the loop is a matching modem in the form of a ASIC (Application-Specific Integrated Circuit) embedded in a digital line card in a Nortel Central Office circuit switch, or in a remote node [9-9], [9-10], and [9-11].

G.LITE

Also known as *ADSL Lite, Universal ADSL,* and *Splitterless ADSL, G.lite* is a proposal of the Universal ADSL Working Group (UAWG) for a simplified version of RADSL. G.lite has been standardized as an interoperable extension of the ADSL specification ANSI T-1.413, and has been accepted by the ITU-T for international standards development as G.992.2. Final ITU-T standards are expected in 1999. Three deployment options are under review, all of which are intended to support simultaneous voice and data communications over a single UTP local loop of one physical pair.

◆ *Splittered ADSL* resembles the current standardized version of ADSL, in that a single, professionally installed splitter would be installed at the point of termination of the local loop at the customer premises. This approach ensures the highest level of data performance, while ensuring that other signals in a multi-pair cable are not affected by high-frequency ADSL data signals. However, this approach also involves an expensive "truck roll."

◆ *Distributed Splitter ADSL* involves a number of ADSL splitters, some that front-end PCs and others that front-end analog telephone sets. This approach ensures that the voice and data channels do not interfere with each other, and avoids the costs and delays associated with the professional installation of a single splitter, as described in the Splittered ADSL option.

◆ *Splitterless ADSL* (see Figure 9-4), which is the most attractive of the G.lite options, is intended to support simultaneous voice and data without the requirement for either a centralized splitter, or multiple distributed splitters. Rather, high-frequency data communications are supported over a single ADSL modem that front-ends each PC. While the standards process is still in progress, early versions of such modems are available now. Compaq, Dell, and other manufacturers currently offer computers with early versions of built-in G.lite modems.

Regardless of the approach(es) ultimately adopted as standards recommendations, G.lite is anticipated to operate on an asymmetric basis over loops up to 18,000 feet, at speeds of up to 1.544 Mbps downstream, and up to 512 Kbps upstream. Internal wiring undoubtedly will be an issue. Maximum performance can be achieved by upgrading the internal wire to Category 5, at least for the PC connection, and by home-run cabling the jacks to the Network Interface Unit (NIU) [9-12], [9-13], and [9-14].

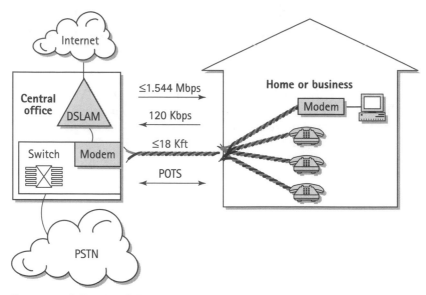

Figure 9–4 Splitterless G.lite

ISDN DIGITAL SUBSCRIBER LINE (IDSL)

ISDN DSL is a xDSL technology that uses ISDN BRI (Basic Rate Interface) technology to deliver symmetrical transmission speeds of 128 Kbps or 144 Kbps on digital copper loops as long as 18,000 feet. Like ISDN BRI, discussed in Chapter 7, IDSL terminates at the user premise on a standard ISDN TA (Terminal Adapter). At this point, the two concepts diverge. ISDN is a circuit-switched service that connects to a Central Office at the edge of the carrier domain. Conversely, IDSL is an always-on data access service that terminates, more or less directly, in a DSLAM. ISDN supports voice, data, video, and any other form of traffic through one or more Bearer (B) channels – each with a width of 64 Kbps. ISDN also can support X.25 packet data over a Data (D) channel at speeds of 9.6 Kbps. IDSL supports data access through a contiguous slice of bandwidth with a width 128 or 144 Kbps. ISDN can support multiple transmissions, each over a separate channel. IDSL supports a single data transmission at a time, over a single, wider channel.

IDSL (refer to Figure 9-5) is a dedicated access service for data communications applications, only. At the LEC CO, the loop terminates in collocated electronics in the form of either an IDSL access switch or an IDSL modem bank connected to a router or DSLAM. In the event that the LEC is not serving as the ISP (Internet Service Provider), the connection is made to the third-party ISP POP via a high-bandwidth dedicated circuit, such as unchannelized T-1 or T-3.

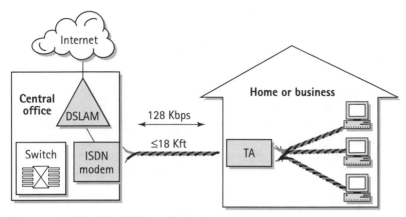

Figure 9-5 ISDN DSL (ISDL) configuration

IDSL offers several advantages over competing technologies. IDSL is based on ISDN network technologies, which are standardized, well understood, and widely implemented. IDSL operates at frequencies that do not interfere with other signals riding over adjacent pairs in a multi-pair copper cable. IDSL makes use of standard, off-the-shelf DCE (Data Communications Equipment) at the customer premises in the form of a Terminal Adapter. IDSL offers fully symmetric bandwidth, although it admittedly is less than that offered by competing DSL technologies, at least in the downstream direction. IDSL does not require a "truck roll" for CPE purposes, although one may be required to condition the circuit. On the negative side, IDSL is application-specific, supporting data only and, therefore, requiring an additional local loop. While a number of ISPs have announced their intentions to provide IDSL service, the current status of those plans is unclear. UUNET, for example, began offering IDSL nationwide in March 1997, but since has announced its future support for G.lite. The relatively little bandwidth supported by IDSL clearly places it at a disadvantage compared to technologies such as G.lite [9-15].

VERY-HIGH-DATA-RATE DIGITAL SUBSCRIBER LINE (VDSL)

Very-high-data-rate Digital Subscriber Line is a high-speed (up to 51.84 Mbps) ADSL technology in the very early stages of definition. Initial VDSL implementation likely will be in asymmetric form, essentially being very high-speed variations on the ADSL theme. Goals are stated in terms of submultiples of the SONET/SDH principal speed of 155 Mbps. (I discuss SONET/SDH later in this chapter.) Specifically, target downstream performance is 51.84-55.2 Mbps over UTP local loops of 1,000 feet (300 meters), 25.92-27.6 Mbps at 3,000 feet (1,000 meters), and 12.96-13.8 Mbps at 4,500 feet (1,500 meters). Upstream data rates are anticipated to fall into three ranges: 1.6–2.3 Mbps, 19.2 Mbps, and a rate equal to the upstream rate. The line coding technique for VDSL has not been chosen. Frequency Division Multiplexing (FDM) will separate downstream and upstream channels, and separate them both from POTS voice channels.

The application for VDSL is in a hybrid local loop scenario, with FTTN (Fiber-To-The-Neighborhood) providing distribution from the CO to the neighborhood, and with VDSL over UTP (Unshielded Twisted Pair) carrying the signal the last leg to the residential premise. Clearly, the specific application is for highly bandwidth-intensive information streams such as are required for support of HDTV and Video-on-Demand. Early work on VDSL has begun in standards bodies including ANSI T1E1.4, ETSI, DAVIC, The ATM Forum, and The ADSL Forum [9-16] and [9-17].

HIGH BIT-RATE DIGITAL SUBSCRIBER LINE (HDSL)

Bellcore (now Telecordia Technologies) also developed *High Bit-Rate Digital Subscriber Line* (*HDSL*) at the request of the RBOCs as a more cost-effective means of providing T-1 local loop circuits over existing UTP. HDSL eliminates repeaters in the T-1 local loop for distances up to 12,000 feet, which can be extended another 12,000 feet through the use of a *line doubler*, which essentially is a HDSL repeater. Conventional T-1 uses two pairs, each of which operates in a simplex mode (one upstream and one downstream) at the full T-1 transmission rate of 1.544 Mbps (see Figure 9-6). At such a high transmission rate, the native carrier frequencies are relatively high (in the range of 1.5 MHz), and issues of attenuation are significant. As a result, it is necessary that repeaters be spaced at approximately 6,000 feet, in order to adjust for distortion and signal loss. Also, the radiated electromagnetic field is significant at T-1 frequencies. Therefore, interference between the T-1 pairs and other pairs in the cable system is an issue.

HDSL, while it also uses two pairs of UTP, splits the pairs into full-duplex (FDX) channels. Each pair operates at 784 Kbps, which is half the T-1 rate, plus additional overhead. As the transmission rate, per pair, is halved, the frequency level is roughly halved. Therefore, the signal loss is much less and the strength of the radiated electromagnetic field is much less. The yield is that of longer transmission distances without repeaters, and with less distortion. In order to achieve this efficiency, HDSL uses the same 2B1Q (2 Binary, 1 Quaternary) coding scheme used in ISDN. On each end of the HDSL circuit, termination gear is installed. These convert the HDSL signal back into conventional T-1 format. The demarcation point (demarc) on the customer premise, for example, is in the form of a HDSL modem, which presents the user's Digital Signal Unit (DSU) with a standard T-1 signal. For HDSL to function properly, as one might expect, the UTP cable plant must be in good condition, although HDSL is reasonably tolerant of mixed gauges and bridged taps. Note that HDSL's limitation of circuit length confines it to use in an access environment – HDSL is not a technology to be used in long-haul, private-line, T-1 applications.

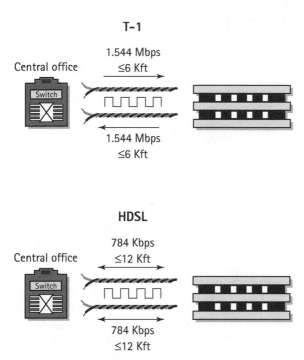

Figure 9-6 Comparison of T-1 and HDSL

The real advantage of HDSL is that a T-1 access circuit can be provisioned at much lower cost and in a much shorter interval of time. As repeaters are eliminated or reduced in number, the incremental cost of HDSL is mitigated to some extent. Additionally, the cable plant supporting HDSL does not require special conditioning or engineering, further reducing costs, as well as enabling service to be provisioned much more quickly. Finally, HDSL offers error performance of approximately 10^{-10}, as compared to the 10^{-7} level offered by repeatered T-1 over twisted pair [9-18]. The bottom line is that T-1 network access can be provisioned much more quickly and much less expensively with HDSL – and error performance is better than with traditional T-1. The carriers, therefore, realize T-1 revenues more quickly, and at such reduced costs that many pass on those cost savings to end users in the form of lower installation charges and reduced monthly rates for the service. An estimated 500,000 or more HDSL loops are installed in the United States [9-15]. The international version of HDSL supports E-1 at a total signaling speed of 2.048 Mbps, with the signal split over three pairs.

HDSL2, the second generation of HDSL, is expected to be standardized in 1999. HDSL2 supports T-1 over a single twisted pair, and over the same loop lengths (up to 12,100 feet). Development is under way also to provision HDSL2 over two copper loops in order to extend the maximum transmission span to as much as 16,500 feet. HDSL2's level of performance is achieved through an advanced 16-pulse PAM 2B1Q line coding technique [9-19]. *Symmetric DSL (SDSL)*, also known as *Single-line HDSL*, is a variation on HDSL, running at speeds of 384 and 768 Kbps for loop lengths of 18,000 feet and 12,000 feet.

Community Antenna TeleVision (CATV)

During the past several years, *Community Antenna TeleVision (CATV)* networks have been the subject of much attention as an alternative means of providing an integrated suite of services. CATV networks were developed for the delivery of TV signals from a single, shared antenna to communities and other areas where TV reception was poor. For maximum signal strength, the tall community antenna was positioned on a hilltop or other highest point in the area to achieve maximum line-of-sight. From the antenna, multiple analog TV signals were interwoven through a Frequency Division Multiplexer (FDM) and carried over a coaxial cable system to the community or neighborhood to be served. Each analog TV signal requires a 6 MHz channel, approximately 4.5 MHz of which is required for the signal, with the balance serving as *transition bands*, or *guard bands*. Contemporary coax-based CATV systems support a raw bandwidth total of 500-750 MHz, thereby supporting a great number of TV channels, all of which reside on the system simultaneously. At the residential premises, the coax cable drops terminate in *converter boxes*, or *set-top boxes*, which serve as frequency division demultiplexers. As each individual channel is selected, the set-top box selects the appropriate frequency range. Traditionally, these networks have been analog, coax-based, one-way networks for the downstream delivery of analog entertainment TV. CATV networks are deployed in a *tree and branch* architecture, with multiple drops off each branch – one drop per residence. Aside from the fact that the antenna now includes microwave and satellite antenna for national broadcast TV and radio feeds, few changes occurred in the CATV network for a great many years (refer to Figure 9-7).

Beginning in the mid-1990s, a few large CATV providers began to upgrade their aging coaxial cable systems. As many of those networks were installed in the late 1960s and early 1970s, they were in awful shape. Further, those networks were strained for capacity as the CATV providers sought to increase revenues and profits through the introduction of premium movie channels and *Pay Per-View (PPV)*. The upgrades, in some cases, went beyond simple coax upgrade and replacement, and included optical fiber in the trunk facilities from the head-end to the neighborhood, where they terminated in an opto-electric conversion box, which interfaced with the existing coax for ultimate termination at the premises.

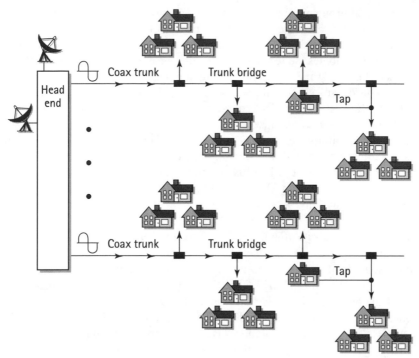

Figure 9-7 Traditional Community Antenna TeleVision (CATV) network, with tree
and branch architecture

Since the telecommunications domain was deregulated with the Telecommunications Act of 1996, the CATV providers began to consider operating as CLECs, as well. The technology exists to upgrade the coaxial cable system to support two-way communications through frequency splitting, much as is done over twisted-pair in xDSL technologies. The coax amplifiers and set-top boxes could be upgraded, as well. Further, the system could be converted to digital by replacing the amplifiers with repeaters, and TDM channels could run inside the FDM channels, much like xDSL. The coax cable certainly offers much more in the way of bandwidth and distance than the twisted-pair, and with an upgrade, error performance could be improved to levels that would make twisted-pair pale by comparison. With optical fiber in the long-haul portion of the network (i.e., from the head-end to the neighborhood), it became clear that CATV system could compete very effectively with the ILEC local loop. Further, the largely unregulated CATV providers could not be forced to wholesale their local loops to competitors, unlike the requirements placed on the ILECs by federal and state regulators.

There were several problems with this scenario. Most of the CATV operators were overburdened with debt, and, therefore, could not afford to make the necessary capital investments in network upgrades. The requisite investment in the necessary circuit and packet switches added greatly to the problem. Further, the CATV providers lacked the necessary skills and management and billing systems to support transaction-based voice and data services. Also, no standards existed for the set-top boxes. As the CATV networks generally were not interconnected, the CATV domain simply was not standards-based.

Major telecommunications companies, as they have begun to acquire the CATV providers, are addressing the cash and management problems associated with this scenario. Most notably, AT&T in early 1999 acquired TCI (TeleCommunications, Inc.) and is in the process of acquiring MediaOne, two of the largest CATV providers in the United States; they will invest billions of dollars in system upgrades. The lack of standards for set-top boxes was resolved in March 1997 by the *DOCSIS* (*Data Over Cable Service Interface Specification*), developed by the limited partnership known as the *Multimedia Cable Network Systems Partners Ltd.* (*MCNS*). Through matching DOCSIS cable modems at the head-end and the customer premises, two-way cable paths are provided over a *HFC* (*Hybrid Fiber-Coax*) system. The head-end portion of the network is in the form of a *Cable Modem Termination System* (*CMTS*), which supports a packet data connection to an IEEE 802.3 10/100-Mbps Ethernet port on a router. The modem on the customer premises is in the form of a TV/data set-top box, which supports traditional coax connections to multiple TV sets and a 10/100BaseT Ethernet connection to a PC or to a hub serving multiple PCs.

DOCSIS is asymmetric in nature, like most xDSL technologies. DOCSIS modems carve a downstream channel from the coax cable in the form of a 6-MHz channel between 91 MHz and a system-dependent upper limit of 857 MHz. The upstream path is supported between 5 MHz and 42 MHz. Downstream transmissions are broadcast to all premises on the shared point-to-multipoint network. Upstream transmissions from the user premises to the head-end are supported either through the contentious CSMA/CD access protocol used in Ethernet LANs or through TDM, depending on the specifics of the CATV provider's implementation [9-20] and [9-21]. The current version of DOCSIS defines a 64-point QAM (Quadrature Amplitude Modulation) compression scheme for the downstream channels, yielding 6 bits per Hertz and yielding a potential of 36 Mbps per 6 MHz channel. Overhead for framing and Forward Error Correction (FEC) reduces that level to about 27 Mbps of shared bandwidth per 6 MHz channel. Traffic in the upstream direction is supported over 1.8 MHz channels, each of which can operate at 3.6 Mbps through use of the QPSK (Quadrature Phase Shift Keying) compression technique, which yields 2 bits per Hertz. Again, framing and FEC overhead reduces the level of usable bandwidth, in this case to about 1.8 Mbps [9-22]. Unfortunately, only modems from three manufacturers have received DOCSIS certification as of April 1999.

There also are *telco-return* modems that use the circuit-switched PSTN for the upstream path, although this approach generally proves less than totally satisfactory. The telco-return approach requires the use of a telco-provided local loop, which adds costs to the equation. Also, the mismatched speeds on the upstream and downstream paths cause the downstream server to slow down, therefore running at less than optimum efficiency.

The CATV networks remain troubled by several inherent limitations. First, CATV is a consumer-oriented network. CATV networks primarily serve residential neighborhoods, and do not extend to most businesses. (After all, you are supposed to work at work, not watch TV.) While this is not a limitation in the context of xDSL, it is an overall limiting factor. Second, CATV networks are multipoint bus networks, much like a classic Ethernet 10Base5 LAN (covered in Chapter 8). Since your voice and data transmissions pass every other house connected to the coax cable, security is a major concern in the absence of an effective encryption mechanism. Third, and again much like 10Base5, the local loop network is shared. Therefore, the more active users on the network, the worse the performance. While the CATV providers speak of total bandwidth as much as 500 Mbps and user access at rates of as much as 10 Mbps, those are "best case" figures; they are quoted on the assumption that the load on the shared medium is light enough to support transmission rates of 10 Mbps for all active users. DOCSIS cable modems work on an asymmetric basis, as do most xDSL options. Specifically, the maximum speed of the downstream channel is 10 Mbps, and the maximum upstream speed ranges from 200 Kbps to 2 Mbps, depending on the specifics of the CATV network. The compression technique employed is either 64 QAM (Quadrature Amplitude Modulation) or QPSK (Quadrature Phase Shift Keying). Currently, QAM is preferred for the downstream channel, delivering up to 27 Mbps per 6-MHz channel, and QPSK is preferred for the upstream channel [9-23] and [9-24].

Especially with the strength of AT&T behind it, CATV has an excellent chance of securing a large segment of the market for high-speed Internet access. Of the 105 million (approximately 95 percent) of U.S. homes passed by CATV and the 75 million or so CATV subscribers, Kinetic Strategies estimates that cable modem service was commercially available to more than 11 million homes as of May 1998. Kinetic Strategies also predicts that total subscriber count will reach 1 million by the end of 1999 [9-23]. While that estimate seems unrealistic, even a fraction of 1 million is a lot. In favor of the CATV option is cost – high-speed Internet access over CATV networks generally is a fraction of the cost of xDSL and ISDN.

Wireless Local Loop (WLL)

Wireless Local Loop (WLL) technologies, which I discuss in more detail in Chapter 11, involve a relatively low-power digital radio transmitter capable of supporting bidirectional communications. A number of manufacturers have released such products for voice applications; AT&T, Ericsson, and Motorola particularly are notable in this regard. Such a system is designed to support voice and low-speed data in a relatively small geographic area, with a radio transceiver located at the customer premise and serving multiple terminal devices. Spread spectrum radio provides improved security, as well as improved bandwidth utilization.

While its Quality of Service (QoS) generally does not compare favorably with wired alternatives, WLL does offer the advantages of rapid deployment and immunity to many issues of topography. WLL is not limited to narrowband voice, by the way; broadband WLL operates much like ADSL, although on a wireless basis. Bellcore standard systems for broadband WLL include ADML and LMDS. *Asymmetric Digital Microcell Link* (*ADML*) provides up to 1 Gpbs aggregate bandwidth at each radio site; (1 Mbps can be provided to each premise. *Local Multipoint Distribution Services* (*LMDS*) resembles ADML, but with a greater area of coverage.

Hybrid Local Loops

Hybrid local-loop technologies include some combination of media and transmission technologies. Generally discussed in the context of a *convergence* scenario (refer to Chapter 14), hybrid local loops typically involve Fiber-To-The-Neighborhood (FTTN), terminating in a remote shelf comprising a TDM MUX and an opto-electric conversion device. The signal is carried the last few hundred meters or so over coax in a CATV environment, UTP-based xDSL in a ILEC environment, or radio (WLL). This approach provides maximum bandwidth and signal quality to a remote unit, which contains all of the expensive opto-electric conversion equipment so the conversion process can be accomplished on a centralized basis for large numbers of user premises. The relatively short connection from the remote unit to the premise can be supported easily at high speeds by either conventional wireline or wireless local-loop systems.

SONET/SDH

SONET/SDH is a set of international standards for broadband communications over SingleMode Fiber (SMF) optic transmission systems, thereby enabling manufacturers to build equipment that supports full interconnectivity and interoperability. SONET/SDH uses a transfer mode that defines switching and multiplexing aspects of a transmission protocol, supporting both asynchronous and synchronous traffic in any form. Intended primarily for the carrier networks, SONET/SDH also can be deployed to the user premise, although such implementation currently is unusual. The *Network-to-Network Interface* (*NNI*), also known as *Network Node Interface*, was specified by the CCITT (now ITU-T) in order that national and regional networks can be blended into a cohesive global network. The *User Network Interface* (*UNI*) also was specified so users can connect to SONET/SDH on a standard basis.

SONET/SDH describes the characteristics of a fiber optic physical infrastructure (OSI Layer 1), rather than a set of services. However, a number of recently developed services depend on the bandwidth, error performance, flexibility, and scalability that can be provided best over a SONET infrastructure. Examples of such services certainly include Frame Relay, SMDS, ATM, and B-ISDN, all of which are discussed in Chapter 12. Additionally, T-carrier, DDS, N-ISDN, and X.25 network traffic benefits from the performance characteristics of the SONET infrastructure. For that matter, even voice traffic gains advantage in terms of improved performance and lower cost of transport.

According to The Insight Research Corporation, the SDH/SONET transmission equipment market is expected to grow from US$6.3 billion in 1998 to US$14.9 billion in 2003. The SDH/SONET market is strongest in the United States, China, Germany, India, Mexico, the United Kingdom, and Canada [9-25]. With the exception of definition and initial discussion of SDH, this chapter focuses on SONET, the original and U.S. standard.

SONET (Synchronous Optical NETwork) was the first attempt to develop a set of fiber optic system standards. As each manufacturer's products were designed according to proprietary specifications, they were incompatible – they simply did not interconnect, much less interoperate. Therefore, each fiber optic link (e.g., from CO-to-CO) absolutely was required to have equipment of the same origin at both ends. This limitation effectively forced the carriers to select a single equipment vendor, thereby limiting the ability of other manufacturers to compete, and stifling technical creativity. Additionally, the interconnecting carriers limited fiber optic systems either to a single vendor, or to opto-electric interfaces that limited the capacity to far less than that actually supported by the individual systems. (The lowest common denominator always rules.) Therefore, the economic and technical benefits of a multi-vendor market were limited, and largely unrealized.

Initial standardization efforts began in 1984, when MCI proposed the development of connectivity standards, or *mid-span fiber meets*, to the *Interexchange Carrier Compatibility Forum (ICCF)*. The ICCF then requested that the *Exchange Carriers Standards Association (ECSA)* develop those standards [9-26]. In 1985, Bellcore proposed SONET to the ANSI T-1X1 committee, and the process continued until final approval for a much-revised SONET was gained in June 1988. The resulting ANSI specification for SONET Phase 1, was released in T-1.105-1988 and T-1.106-1988, specifying a basic transmission level of 51.84 Mbps, which carries a signal originating as the electrically-based T-3 of 45 Mbps, plus additional overhead for optical processing.

SDH (Synchronous Digital Hierarchy) is the international version of SONET standards. The CCITT (now ITU-T) began the initial SDH efforts, driven by the SONET impetus, in 1986. In 1988, the SONET standards were accepted by the CCITT, with modifications that were mostly at the lower multiplexing levels. These differences largely are due to the requirement to accommodate the complexities of internetworking the disparate national and regional networks. The ITU-T Recommendations referenced are G.707, G.708, and G.709.

Standards work continues on SONET/SDH, with the involvement of standards bodies and associations including ANSI, EIA, ECSA, IEEE, ITU-T (previously CCITT), and Telcordia Technologies (previously Bellcore) [9-27]:

◆ ANSI (*American National Standards Institute*), founded in 1918, coordinates and harmonizes private sector standards development. ANSI also serves as the U.S. representative to the International Organization for Standardization (ISO), the originator of the Open Systems Interconnection (OSI) Reference Model.

◆ EIA (*Electronic Industries Alliance,* previously *Electronic Industries Association*) was founded in 1924 as the Radio Manufacturers Association. A trade organization representing the interests of U.S. electronics manufacturers, the EIA assists in the development of Physical Layer (Layer 1) interfaces, including opto-electric interfaces and test procedures for SONET.

◆ ECSA (*Exchange Carriers Standards Association*), formed in 1984, represents the interests of the U.S. IXCs. The ECSA T-1 committee addresses issues of functionality and characteristics of interconnection and interoperability. The T-1X1 committee addresses issues of digital hierarchy and synchronization.

◆ IEEE (*Institute of Electronic and Electrical Engineers*) is a worldwide professional association dealing with SONET only peripherally. The IEEE has significant responsibility for the development of LAN standards, including FDDI, which has great impact on SONET.

◆ ISO (*International Organization for Standardization*) is an organization comprised of the national standards organizations (e.g., ANSI)of the various nations. The ISO heavily influences international standards set by the ITU-T, and in our context, is known best for its involvement in the OSI (Open Systems Interconnection) Reference Model.

◆ ITU-R (*International Telecommunications Union-Radiocommunications Sector*). The ITU sector that deals with issues of radio standards, the ITU-R parallels the ITU-T, in the wireline domain.

◆ ITU-T (*International Telecommunications Union-Telecommunications Standardization Sector*), previously the CCITT (Consultative Committee for International Telegraphy and Telecommunications), is an agency of the United Nations. The ITU-T develops international standards in order to promote a world order of interconnectivity and interoperability. ITU-T sometimes also is abbreviated as ITU-TS or ITU-TSS. ITU-T predecessor organizations date to 1865.

◆ **Telcordia Technologies**, previously *Bellcore* (*Bell Communications Research*), was formed in 1984 under the terms of the Modified Final Judgement (MFJ) which forced the divestiture by AT&T of the Bell Operating Companies (BOCs). Bellcore was the research and development arm of the RBOCs, its client/owners. Bellcore originally focused on standards development, test procedures, and Operations Support System (OSS) development, rather than the physical sciences. Bellcore was privatized and acquired by SAIC in 1998, as the interests of the RBOCs were no longer common in a deregulated, competitive environment. The name was changed to Telcordia Technologies in April 1999, with the stated focus of emerging technologies.

SONET Standards Development

SONET standards were developed in three phases. Phase I (1988) defines transmission rates and characteristics, signal formats, and optical interfaces. Phase I also defines *Optical Carrier* (*OC*) levels and *Data Communications Channels* (*DCC*), used for network management purposes in support of mid-span meet at the payload level. While Phase I does not support network management from end-to-end, neither does it preclude that potential. Phase II refines the physical portion of the standards and defines protocols used on data communications channels DS-1 to DS-3. Phase II also defines interoperability parameters for mid-span meet, network management, OSI *CMISE* (*Common Management Information Service Elements*), and add/drop multiplexer capabilities. Phase II further defines *OAM&P* (*Operations, Administration, Management & Provisioning*) procedures and connectivity to B-ISDN. Phase III provides all network management (OAM&P) requirements for mid-span meet. Phase III also defines all network management standard message sets (e.g., alarm state, circuit-pack failure, and intermittent failure) and addressing schemes for interconnection. Finally, Phase III provides for ring and nested protection switching standards [9-26] and [9-27].

SONET/SDH Transmission Hierarchy

SONET defines the Synchronous Transport Signal Level-N (STS-N) as the electrical signal. When converted to an optical signal for transport over a standard fiber optic medium, the term *Optical Carrier-N* (*OC-N*) is applied. As noted in Table 9-2, the basic building block of the digital hierarchy is OC-1 at 51.84 Mbps – SONET begins at broadband levels. Notably, the various STS levels are considerate of the existing digital signal hierarchy, thereby achieving backward compatibility with legacy systems. In other words and by way of example, a T-3 frame maps comfortably into an STS-1 signal that becomes an OC-1 frame. Similarly, multiple T-1 frames can be aggregated to form and map into an STS-1 signal, which then becomes an OC-1 frame.

Table 9-2 SONET/SDH SIGNAL HIERARCHY

Optical Carrier (OC) Level	SONET STS Level	SDH STM Level	Signal Level	Equivalent DS-3 (45 Mbps) Channels	Equivalent DS0 (64 Kbps) Channels
OC-1	STS-1		51.84 Mbps	1	672
OC-2	STS-2		103.68 Mbps	2	1,344
OC-3*	STS-3	STM-1	155.52 Mbps	3	2,016
OC-4	STS-4	STM-3	207.36 Mbps	4	2,688
OC-9	STS-9	STM-3	466.56 Mbps	9	6,048
OC-12	STS-12	STM-4	622.08 Mbps	12	8,064
OC-18	STS-18	STM-6	933.12 Mbps	18	12,096
OC-24	STS-24	STM-8	1.24416 Gbps	24	16,128
OC-36	STS-36	STM-12	1.86624 Gbps	36	24,192
OC-48	STS-48	STM-16	2.48832 Gbps	48	32,256
OC-96	STS-96	STM-32	4.976 Gbps	96	64,512
OC-192	STS-192	STM-64	9.953 Gbps	192	129,024
OC-256**	STS-256		13.219 Gbps	256	171,360
OC-768**	STS-768		52.877 Gbps	768	516,096

* OC-3 was defined by the CCITT as the basic transport rate for B-ISDN [9-28].
**OC-256 and OC-768 have not been defined fully.

At OC-1, for instance, a T-1 bit stream of 45 Mbps is presented as a STS-1 signal of 51.84 Mbps, with an actual maximum payload rate of 49.54 Mbps [9-29]. When converted from an electrical signal to a fiber optic photonic signal, the bit stream is known as OC-1. The OC-1 comprises 810-byte frames transmitted at a rate of 8,000 frames per second, or every 125 microseconds. SONET speeds range from OC-1 (51.84 Mbps) to OC-96 (4.976 Gbps), as currently defined in full. OC-255 (13.2192 Gbps) and OC-768 (52.8768 Gbps) have yet to be defined fully. Fractional speeds are achievable at virtually any level—multiplexing subrate transmissions below OC-1 to form an OC-1 channel.

SONET terms of significance include the following:

- **Optical Carrier (OC)** is the definition of the SONET optical signal. The fully defined OC levels begin at OC-1 (51.84 Mbps) and culminate in OC-192 (9.953 Gbps).

- **Synchronous Transport Signal (STS)** is the electrical equivalent of the SONET optical signal; it is known as *Synchronous Transport Module* (*STM*) in SDH. The signal begins as electrical and converts to optical for transmission over the SONET optical fiber facilities. Each STS-1 frame is transmitted each 125(s (125 microseconds, or 125 millionths of a second, or 8000 times per second), yielding raw bandwidth of 51.84 Mbps. The STS frame includes five elements, Synchronous Payload Envelope, Section Overhead, Line Overhead, Path Overhead, and Payload.

- **Synchronous Payload Envelope (SPE)** is the envelope that carries the user payload data. It is analogous to the payload envelope of a X.25 packet. The SPE consists of 783 octets (87 columns and nine rows of data octets).

- **Transport Overhead (TO)** consists of Section Overhead and Line Overhead.

- **Section Overhead (SOH)** of nine octets is dedicated to the transport of status, messages, and alarm indications for the maintenance of SONET links.

- **Line Overhead (LOH)** of 18 bytes controls the reliable transport of payload data between network elements.

- **Path Overhead (PO)**, contained within the SPE, comprises nine octets for the relay of OAM&P information in support of end-to-end network management.

- **Payload** is the actual data content of the SONET frame and rides within the SPE. Total usable payload at the OC-1 level consists of up to 49.54 Mbps, into which a T3 frame fits quite nicely. The balance of the 51.84 Mbps is consumed by Transport Overhead and Path Overhead.

- **Multiplexing** is on the basis of direct Time Division Multiplexing (TDM). Either full SONET speeds or lesser asynchronous and synchronous data streams can be multiplexed into the STS-N payload, which then converts into an OC-N payload. In other words, an appropriate combination of FDS-1, DS-1, DS-2, and DS-3 signals can be multiplexed directly into an electrical STS-1 payload, which then converts into an optical OC-1 payload. The multiplexing process involves byte interleaving, much as described for traditional TDMs.

SONET/SDH Topology

SONET networks are highly redundant, with dual fibers providing backup. Although they can be laid out in a linear, star, ring, or hybrid fashion, the optimum physical topology is that of a dual, counter-rotating ring. In a SONET dual-ring topology, one fiber transmits in one direction, and the other transmits in the other direction. Through this layout, it is highly unlikely that any device on the network can be isolated through a catastrophic failure, such as a *cable-seeking backhoe*. Should such a failure occur, the *Automatic Protection Switching* (*APS*) feature of SONET permits the *self-healing* network to recover. There are two primary implementations of the SONET physical topology: path-switched and line-switched rings.

Path-switched rings employ two fibers. As illustrated in Figure 9-8, all traffic moves in both directions, thereby providing protection from network failure. A path-switched approach also improves error performance because the receiving stations examine both data streams, selecting the better signal.

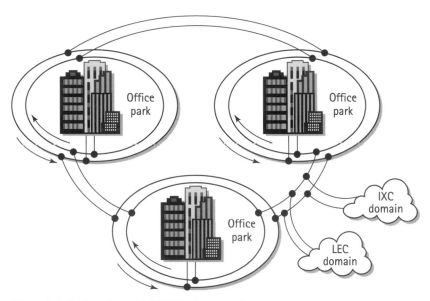

Figure 9-8 Path-switched SONET implementation

Line-switched rings involve either two or four fibers. In the single-ring implementation, traffic moves in one direction, with the other fiber acting as backup. In the event of a network failure, the backup ring is activated to enable transmission in the reverse direction. A four-fiber implementation, which is preferred and typical in carrier-class networks, supports transmission in one direction over one fiber in each of the two rings. By way of example, Fibers #1 in Rings #1 and #2 might transmit in a clockwise direction, while Fibers #2 in Rings #1 and #2 transmit in a counterclockwise direction. The second fiber in each ring acts to support transmission in the reverse direction in the event of a failure in the primary ring. Line-switched rings smaller than 1,200 kilometers offer standard restoral intervals of 50 milliseconds or less [9-30]. Larger rings, such as long-haul transport rings in IXC networks, involve longer restoral intervals due to the increased time of signal propagation.

Paths, Tributaries, and Channels

The SONET pipe has the ability to carry information at Gbps speeds with excellent performance characteristics, including error performance and network management. The pipe also can carry any variety of asynchronous and synchronous information (e.g., voice, data, video, and image) and present it in a number of frame sizes. While the STS-1 frame is the basic building block, multiple STS-1 frames can be linked together in a process known as *concatenation*. Concatenated STS-Nc (N = Number; c = concatenated), signals are multiplexed, switched, and transported over the network as a single entity. This approach, which currently is defined for STS-3c and STS-12c, offers clear advantages where larger increments of bandwidth are required, as the overall level of overhead is reduced, thereby increasing the payload size. The SONET pipe consists of Virtual Paths, Tributaries, and Channels, as reflected in Figure 9-9.

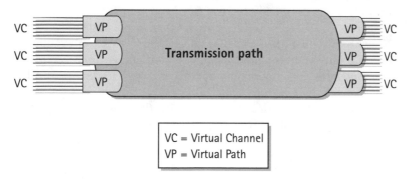

Figure 9-9 Relationship of Path, Virtual Path, and Virtual Channel

Virtual Paths, or *Virtual Containers,* are simply end-to-end communications paths, or routes or circuits, which carry traffic from one end point to another. The path is not fixed or dedicated, neither is it dedicated to a particular conversation or user. A Virtual Path consists of many Virtual Tributaries.

Virtual Tributaries carry one form of signal, such as a DS-1, DS-2, or DS-3 signal within a byte-interleaved frame. Virtual Tributaries can be mapped into a single Virtual Path. A Virtual Tributary may be channelized (e.g., a 48-channel T-1 for voice) or unchannelized (e.g., a clear channel DS-1 for full motion video). Virtual Tributaries are sized to accommodate the originating signal and in consideration of the legacy digital hierarchy. For instance, VT-1.5 operates at 1.544 Mbps (T-1), VT2 at 2.048 Mbps (E-1), VT3 at 3.152 Mbps (T-1c), and VT6 at 6.312 Mbps (T-2). Individual VTs are distinguished by the use of a *pointer,* which identifies the position of the VT within the STS frame; the pointer also provides synchronization in a SONET environment.

Virtual Channels, or *Tributary Units,* exist within Virtual Tributaries. For example, a Virtual Tributary might carry a T-1 frame. Within that tributary, there might exist 24 channels with each channel carrying a single voice or data communication in multiple time slots.

SONET Frame Format

The STS-1 frame (see Figure 9-10) is the basic building block for SONET, much like the DS-1 frame in a T/E-carrier environment. The STS-1 frame can be considered logically as a matrix of 9 rows of 90 octets, yielding 810 octets in total. The data is transmitted from top to bottom, one row at a time and from left to right. SONET accommodates payloads (data content) in increments of 765 octets, logically organized in matrixes of 9 rows x 85 columns. The payload is contained within a Synchronous Payload Envelope in increments of 774 bytes (9 rows x 86 columns), with the additional column attributable to Path Overhead (POH). Where superrate services require more than a single STS-1, they are mapped into a higher level, concatenated STS-Nc, with the constituent STS-1s kept together [9-31]. For example, a 135 Mbps B-ISDN H4 frame requires a huge amount of contiguous, unbroken bandwidth. SONET accommodates this requirement by linking three STS-1s into an STS-3c; the c indicates *concatenation* [9-32].

The SPE, which contains the payload data, actually *floats* within the SONET frame. While SONET is a synchronized network, with all devices relying on a common clocking signal, variations in clocking can occur. Those clocking variations can result from different master clocks in different national networks, thermal expansion and contraction in individual fiber optic cables, and other phenomena. Rather than buffering individual frames to effect synchronization, floating mode operation enables the network to adjust to frame float with the SPE identified by the pointer. The floating mode reduces cost and delay that would be caused by the use of buffers to synchronize each frame and SPE exactly [9-32].

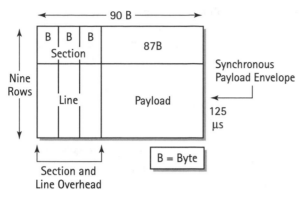

Figure 9-10 SONET frame structure

The SONET overhead structure mirrors that of the existing digital carrier network for purposes of non-intrusive, end-to-end network management. Overhead layers include Path Overhead, which is further divided into Section Overhead, Line Overhead, and Path Overhead.

SECTION OVERHEAD

Section Overhead (*SOH*) of nine (9) bytes provides for management of optical network segments between *Section Terminating Equipment* (*STE*) in the form of repeaters. The repeaters can be standalone or built into switches, such as Digital Cross Connect Systems (DCCSs or DXCs). At the Section Layer, every repeater in the network performs the section overhead functions. These include framing, span performance and error monitoring, and STS ID numbering. These functions resemble those performed by traditional point-to-point protocols such as SDLC and LAP-D. The 9 bytes of Section Overhead include 1 byte STS-1 signal ID, 2 bytes *Bit Interleaved Parity* (*BIP*) for error monitoring, 1 byte *Orderwire* (connection request), and 3 bytes *DCC* (*Data Communication Channel*).

LINE OVERHEAD

Line Overhead (*LOH*) of eighteen (18) bytes controls the reliable transport of payload data between network elements. A DXC (Digital Cross-Connect System) performs Line Layer functions, including error control, switching and multiplexing, order-wire, express orderwire (priority connection request), automatic protection switching to back-up circuits, insertion of payload pointers, and synchronization control. The 18 bytes of Line Overhead comprise 3 bytes STS-1 pointer, 1 byte BIP (error monitoring), 2 bytes APS (Automatic Protection Switching), 9 bytes DCC, 1 byte orderwire, and 2 bytes reserved for future use.

PATH OVERHEAD

Path Overhead (*POH*), (not to be confused with *Pooh,* the bear) of nine (9) bytes, comprises all aspects of end-to-end performance monitoring and statistical reporting.

Path management is an essential responsibility of the Add/Drop Multiplexers (ADMs). Functions performed at the Path Layer include end-to-end performance monitoring, statistical reporting, STS Mapping, and DS-to-OC mapping. The 9 bytes of Path Overhead comprise 1 byte trace, 1 byte BIP, 1 byte Payload ID, 1 byte maintenance status, 1 byte user ID, 1 byte frame alignment, and 3 bytes reserved for future use.

SONET/SDH Hardware

The hardware aspects of SONET are difficult to describe in discrete terms because many of the functional elements overlap. Just as manufacturers of traditional voice and data equipment often build multiple functional elements under the skin of a single box, so do SONET/SDH equipment manufacturers. Given that caveat, the following is a description of the discrete functional aspects of hardware devices.

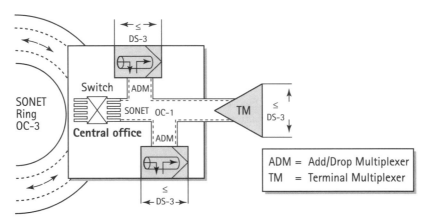

Figure 9–11 Terminal Multiplexer (TM) and Add/Drop Multiplexer (ADM) in SONET application

Terminating Multiplexers are *Path Terminating Equipment (PTE)* that provide user access to the SONET network (see Figure 9-11), operating in a manner similar to a T-3/E-3 Time Division Multiplexer. Multiple DS-0s and DS-1s can be multiplexed to form an STS-1 or STS-3 frame, for instance. Terminal multiplexers also accomplish the conversion from electrical STS-N signals into Optical Carrier (OC-N) signals.

Concentrators perform the equivalent functions as traditional electrical concentrators and hubs. SONET concentrators combine multiple OC-3 and OC-12 interfaces into higher OC-N levels of transmission [9-26].

Add/Drop Multiplexers do not have exact equivalents in the electrical (DS) world, although they perform roughly the same functions as traditional T-carrier TDMs.

Generally found in the Central Office Exchange, they provide the capability to insert or drop individual DS-1, DS-2, or DS-3 channels into a SONET transmission pipe (see Figure 9-11). ADMs accomplish the process electrically, with the OC-N channel being converted prior to the process and reconverted subsequently. ADMs offer great advantage over traditional DS-N MUXs. The T-carrier approach, for instance, requires that a DS-3 frame be de-multiplexed into its 28 component DS-1 frames, which must be broken down into 24 DS0 channels in order to extract and route an individual channel. Once that is accomplished, the process must be reversed to reconstitute the DS-3, minus the extracted DS0, and send it on its way. ADMs perform the additional functions of dynamic bandwidth allocation, providing operation and protection channels, optical hubbing, and ring protection.

Digital Loop Carrier (DLC) systems typically are located at the Local Exchange Carrier (LEC) office and are used to concentrate traffic in multiple DS0s into a single DS-3 signal. Once they perform this intermediate step, they hand off the STS-1 signal to a Terminating MUX that performs the OC-N conversion.

Digital-Cross-Connects (DXCs) perform approximately the same functions as their electrical equivalents (DACs/DCCSs), providing switching and circuit grooming down to the DS-1 level. They provide a means of cross-connecting SONET/SDH channels through a software-driven, electronic common control cross-connect panel with a PC user interface. The routing of traffic through a DXC is accomplished through the use of *payload pointers*, which point to the payload in the OC-N frame and provide synchronization. Importantly, DXCs also serve to connect the fiber rings. DXCs perform the additional functions of monitoring and testing, network provisioning, maintenance, and network restoral.

Regenerators perform the same function as their traditional electrical equivalents. Often found under the skin of other SONET equipment, they are opto-electric devices that adjust the amplitude, timing, and shape of the signal.

Advantages of SONET

SONET offers a number of advantages, in addition to the inherent advantages of fiber optic transmission systems, in general. Certainly, the fact that SONET is highly standardized offers the benefits of interconnectivity and interoperability between equipment of different manufacturers. That standardization translates into freedom of vendor choice and yields lower costs through competition. Additionally, SONET/SDH is extendible to the premise on a fully interoperable basis. The increasing availability of SONET local loops provides end-to-end advantages of enhanced bandwidth, error performance, dynamic bandwidth allocation, and network management. In an end-to-end deployment scenario, SONET is particularly attractive in support of broadband services such as Frame Relay, ATM, and ultimately, B-ISDN.

In bandwidth-intensive applications, the high absolute cost of SONET can be offset by virtue of its extraordinarily high capacity. Whether deployed in a carrier network or extended to the user premise, SONET supports the aggregation of all forms of traffic, including voice, data, video, image, and facsimile. As a result, a SONET infrastructure can obviate the need for multiple transmission facilities in support of individual services. The simplicity of multiplexing and de-multiplexing via ADMs serves to reduce costs, delay, and error. Clearly, SONET/SDH offers the considerable advantage of network resiliency through its inherent redundancy and self-healing capabilities.

Finally, SONET offers tremendous security, as with fiber optic transmission systems, in general. Fiber is difficult, if not impossible, to physically tap without detection. More to the point is the fact that it is difficult to identify the one channel for detection out of the thousands of information channels supported in a SONET mode. As Francis Bacon said in 1625, "There is no secrecy comparable to celerity." (Of Delay, *Essays*) – celerity, or speed, is a hallmark of SONET.

Applications of SONET/SDH

SONET primarily is deployed in backbone carrier networks, where its many advantages can be put to full use. Particularly in a convergence scenario, the carriers have the potential to realize considerable cost savings by using a single fiber infrastructure in support of bandwidth-intensive video and image streams – in addition to voice, data, and facsimile traffic. That scenario increasingly delivers SONET fiber to the premises of large end user organizations and ultimately, perhaps, to the residential premises. In fact, a number of xDSL technologies discussed earlier in this chapter are proposed to make effective use of SONET in a hybrid network configuration.

It's interesting to track the developments in SONET speeds over the past few years, using a few select examples. In 1994, Sprint announced the completion of the Silicon Valley Test Track, linking seven companies and several learning institutions to test ATM switching technologies. The initial OC-1 ring was planned to be upgraded to OC-3 in early 1995 and to OC-12 later in the year [9-33]. Shortly thereafter, Sprint deployed the first international SONET ring, linking four cities in New York, USA and three in Canada. The capacity of that OC-48 (2.5 Gbps) SONET ring increased to 10 Gbps through the use of Wave Division Multiplexing (WDM) equipment in order to derive four OC-48 channels [9-34]. AT&T announced in May 1996 plans to beef up its network with WDM equipment to realize 20 Gbps over OC-48 SONET fiber – an eight-fold increase [9-35]. While these are excellent examples of the deployment of SONET operating at incredible speeds for their time, they no longer serve as effective examples of what can be accomplished in the domain of optical networking.

A wide variety of carriers currently deploy fresh SONET networks, and upgrade existing networks, to operate at OC-192 speeds of 10 Gbps. These carriers include not only the incumbent voice and data IXCs (IntereXchange Carriers), but also the ILECs (Incumbent Local Exchange Carriers), CLECs (Competitive LECs), and CAPs (Competitive Access Providers). Most impressive, perhaps, is the rate at which some of the next-generation carriers deploy SONET. Literally from the ground up, these carriers deploy SONET at speeds up to OC-192 (where justified by anticipated traffic) in their long-haul networks. Their overall costs range up to US$10 billion and more, in anticipation of huge volumes of voice, data, and video traffic, using various combinations of circuit-switching, Frame Relay, ATM, and IP. Nextlink, Level 3, and Qwest are excellent examples. Nextlink, for example, lays optical pipe along its rights-of-way at a rate of as many as 688 fibers per route; each fiber runs at a speed of as much as 10 Gbps (OC-192), currently runs WDM (Wavelength Division Multiplexing) through as many as four windows, and each of which windows supports a 10-Gbps data stream. While this currently is a *dim fiber* network (i.e., a network in which some fibers are *lit* only partially, and some are left *dark* for future use), the potential is incredible. If all fibers were lit at OC-192, with the full 32 optical wavelengths currently specified by the ITU-T, that portion of the network would run at an aggregate rate of approximately 220,160 Gbps, or 220.160 Tbps. At that rate, the cost of billing a customer for the transport of a 1-MB (one-megabyte) file would far exceed the cost of actually providing the service. The ultimate issue, of course, involves getting the bandwidth where it's needed. That's where access technologies are just as important as transport technologies, and that's where SONET in the local loop becomes very important.

End user organizations can gain the advantage of SONET local loops with increasing ease through a number of the ILECs, CLECs, and CAPs. Particularly where data traffic requirements are significant, SONET offers the advantage of direct and seamless high-speed access to the carriers' SONET backbone. For high-speed T-3 (45 Mbps) access to Frame Relay networks, SONET local loops have become increasingly advantageous. For ATM at speeds of 155 Mbps and 622 Mbps, SONET access is virtually a requirement, as T-1 and even T-3 do not address these levels of bandwidth.

SONET also finds application in campus environments, including not only institutions of higher learning, but also business campuses. In such an environment, significant volumes of data and image information often are transmitted between buildings, perhaps between mainframes, Gbps Ethernet switches, ATM switches, or routers. In such applications, optical fiber makes sense (in fact, it may be the only viable solution) and SONET makes even more sense. Mission-critical environments, such as airports, find the redundancy and resulting resiliency of a SONET infrastructure particularly attractive.

An interesting and fairly recent application of SONET technology is that of the 1996 Summer Olympics in Atlanta, GA. BellSouth, the incumbent LEC, deployed 40 OC-48 SONET rings to transport CD-quality voice, broadcast-quality video, and data simultaneously to nine cities in the Greater Atlanta area where the 26 various competitions took place. All information flowed through the SONET pipes, including competition results, accreditation, data, voice, and video. The uncompressed digital video signals traveled to the International Broadcast Center, where the signals were sold to other broadcasters and to produce 40 worldwide video satellite feeds for approximately 3,000 hours of Olympic coverage [9-36].

SONET and/or Wavelength Division Multiplexing (WDM)

Currently, something of a debate rages around the subject of SONET versus *Wavelength Division Multiplexing* (*WDM*) and, particularly, *Dense Wavelength Division Multiplexing* (*DWDM*). The debate centers on issues of cost and complexity; SONET is relatively expensive, overhead intensive, and complex.

As discussed in Chapter 2, WDM enables multiple wavelengths to be introduced into a single fiber through a process of Frequency Division Multiplexing (FDM) at the optical level. In order to accomplish this feat, multiple diode lasers are transmitted at a given speed and at a given light frequency, or visible color of light, over a SingleMode Fiber (SMF). As each frequency *window* is added, the bandwidth of the system is increased by a factor of one. For example, a system operating at 10 Gbps enjoys a bandwidth increase of 10 Gbps as each frequency is added. DWDM, loosely defined as WDM supporting eight or more wavelengths, currently supports as many as 32 wavelengths defined by the ITU-T. Several manufacturers have announced non-standard versions, supporting as many as 80 wavelengths at OC-192 [9-32]. As is the case with FDM in general, the optical signals do not interfere with each, as they are separated by frequency. In terms of bandwidth, therefore, WDM and DWDM offer significant cost advantages over SONET, which requires that the laser diode light sources and the Avalanche Photo Diode (APD) light detectors be upgraded to run at higher speeds. Currently, 10 Gbps (OC-192) is the maximum speed fully defined for SONET/SDH. Further, there are technical limits to the speed at which the laser diodes and APDs can operate. There also are finite speed limitations to optical transmission, at least based on our current understanding of the laws of physics.

The nature of the repeating devices in the optical network also yield cost advantages for WDM. *Erbium-Doped Fiber Amplifiers* (*EDFAs*), or *light pumps*, are used to maximum effect in conjunction with WDM systems because they simultaneously can amplify multiple light frequencies – which must be in the range of 1550 nanometers. SONET, conversely, specifies optical repeaters, which essentially are back-to-back opto-electric conversion devices tuned to a specific optical wavelength, or *lambda*. At the inbound port, the repeater accepts the optical signal, converts it to an electrical signal, boosts and filters the signal, converts it back to an optical signal, and sends it over the outbound port. While EDFAs currently are more expensive than repeaters, fewer of them are required. EDFAs can be spaced at intervals of 80-120 kilometers, while optical repeaters often must be spaced at intervals of 50-100 kilometers [9-37] and [9-38]. Further, an EDM EDFA can simultaneously amplify multiple wavelengths in both directions. A SONET repeater can act only on a single wavelength in a single direction. The exact spacing of the repeaters or amplifiers is sensitive to a number of design factors.

Finally, the nature of the multiplexers differs greatly in WDM and SONET. SONET makes use of very sophisticated and expensive Add/Drop Multiplexers (ADMs), which can deal with SONET frames, or even individual channels within a frame. WDM, on the other hand, makes use of *Optical Add/Drop Multiplexers* (*OADMs*), which multiplex at the lambda level (refer to Figure 9-12). The OADMs also effectively perform a process of optical switching, or *photonic switching*, at the lambda level, thereby obviating the requirement for complex and expensive SONET Digital Cross Connects (DXCs).

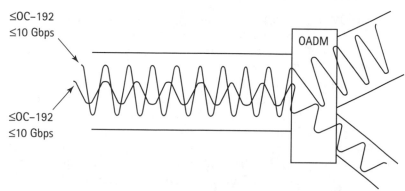

Figure 9-12 Optical Add/Drop Multiplexer (OADM), switching optical signals at
the lambda level

All of these factors cause many to suggest that DWDM, rather than SONET, is the future of optical transmission. Others, including myself, feel that nothing could be further from the truth. Rather, SONET and DWDM will coexist quite nicely in the future. Those promoting DWDM at the expense of SONET assume that a user or carrier can make effective use of a full lambda. Certainly, a large user organization may be able make effective use of an OC-1 (52 Mbps), OC-3 (155 Mbps), or even OC-12 (622 Mbps) lightstream for access or transport purposes, perhaps in support of integrated voice, data, and video over ATM. However, carriers cannot cost-effectively dedicate a full lightstream for that purpose, when they can run it at OC-192 rates of 10 Mbps in support of a large number of end users and a great variety of native data types. Since SONET is TDM-based, it can handle any type of data; in fact and as previously discussed, SONET can support multiple data types over the same facility. Rather, the long-haul carriers typically will use SONET at the access level. For long-haul transport, they will run SONET transparently inside each DWDM wavelength, thereby realizing the advantages of each. The SONET frame format will be supported inside DWDM, EDFAs will be used for signal amplification, and OADMs will switch signals at the optical level. An additional argument in support of this approach centers on the robust nature of SONET OA&M features, on which the carriers rely greatly to manage and maintain their networks. Further, WDM is purely a point-to-point technology, with no provisions for recovery in the event of a network failure; the self-healing feature of SONET is of great value in optical networking.

As I noted earlier, The Insight Research Corporation estimates that the SDH/SONET transmission equipment market is expected to grow from US$6.3 billion in 1998 to US$14.9 billion in 2003 [9-25]. Insight also estimates that the WDM market will grow from US$980 million in 1998 to $US5.2 billion in 2003 [9-39].

Packet over SONET (POS)

Packet over SONET (*POS*) is a MAN/WAN technology touted as the latest threat to ATM. POS offers the advantage of supporting packet data such as IP through either a direct optical interface to a router, or through a SONET demarc in the form of a Terminating Multiplexer (TE). POS uses SONET as the Layer 1 protocol, encapsulating packet traffic in HDLC (High Level Data Link Control) frames and using PPP (Point-to-Point Protocol) for Layer 2 link control, with the IP packet traffic running at Layer 3. The result is that the combined overhead factor (SONET + PPP + IP) is only approximately 5 percent for a 1,500-byte IP datagram. This level of efficiency compares very favorably with ATM, which boasts an overhead factor of about 11 percent for the same IP datagram. This level of performance can be achieved only if packet data is to be transmitted, and only if the service is provided over the equivalent of a SONET-based, point-to-point private line, provisioned in the form of a Virtual Channel (VC). Thereby, POS traffic bypasses any ATM switches that might be in place in the carrier network. If multiple data types (e.g., voice, packet data traffic, SDLC data traffic, video, and fax) require support, and if multiple Quality of Service (QoS) guarantees are required, ATM remains the solution [9-40] and [9-41].

References

[9-1]   "General Introduction to Copper Access Technologies." ADSL Forum. www.adsl.com

[9-2]   Woloszynski, Charles. "Gearing Up for ADSL." *Bellcore Exchange*, Summer 1998.

[9-3]   Lindstrom, Annie. "The DLC Dilemma." *America's Network*, October 15, 1998.

[9-4]   Rodey, Bill. "Penalty for Interference?" *America's Network*, May 1, 1998.

[9-5]   "To Data in Dash to Erase Cable's Lead." *New York Times*, January 20, 1998.

[9-6]   "Europe Will Close Broadband Gap." *TechWeb News*, April 11, 1998.

[9-7]   Paone, Joe. *ADSL: "The New Kid on the Block". Internetwork*, June 1996.

[9-8]   "ADSL Tutorial." ADSL Forum. www.adsl.com

[9-9]   "1 Mbps modem challenges ADSL." *Communications News*, January 1988.

[9-10]   Kopf, David. "Copper-Based Alternatives Vie for Attention." *American's Network*, October 1998.

[9-11]   "Nortel 1-meg Modem: Next Generation Data Access." Northern Telecom. www.nortel.com

[9-12]   "About the UAWG and UADSL." Universal ADSL Working Group. www.uawg.org

[9-13]   Cavanaugh, Ken. "Splitting Out the Issues of the ADSL G.lite Initiative." *Telecommunications*, October 1998.

[9-14]   Lindstrom, Annie. "G.Lite gets into the starting blocks." *America's Network*. March 1, 1999.

[9-15]   Babaie, Sassan. "IDSL Accelerates xDSL Entry." *X-Change*, February 1998.

[9-16]   "VDSL-Frequently Asked Questions." ADSL Forum, www.adsl.com

[9-17]   "VDSL Tutorial. Fiber-Copper Access to the Information Highway." ADSL Forum. www.adsl.com

[9-18]   "CopperOtics Enhancing the Performance and Application of Copper Cable with HDSL." PairGain Technologies, Inc., 1995.

[9-19]   "Second-Gen HDSL Ready to Roll as One-Pair Solution to T1 Line Shortage." *Telecommunications*, April 1999.

[9-20]   "Data Over Cable Service Interface Specifications FAQ." Cable Television Laboratories, Inc., www.cablemodem.com

[9-21]   Nikolich, Paul. "Cable modems deliver fast 'Net access." *Network World*, March 1, 1999.

[9-22]   Finneran, Michael. "The Cable Modem Picture Comes into Focus." *Business Communications Review*, March 1999.

[9-23]   Mason, Charles. "CATV's answer to ADSL." *America's Network*, August 1, 1998.

[9-24]   "Cable Modem FAQ." *Cable Datacom News*. www.cabledatacomnews.com

[9-25]   "Data Demands Drive SONET/SDH, WDM." *Telecommunications*, December 1998.

[9-26]   Spohn, Darren L. *Data Network Design*. McGraw-Hill, Inc., 1993.

[9-27]   Davidson, Robert P. and Muller, Nathan J. *The Guide to SONET: Planning, Installing & Maintaining Broadband Networks*. Telecom Library, 1991.

[9-28]   Sexton, Mike and Reid, Andy. *Transmission Networking: SONET and the Synchronous Digital Hierarchy*. Artech House, 1992.

[9-29]   Miller, Mark A. *Analyzing Broadband Networks: Frame Relay, SMDS, & ATM*. M&T Books, 1994.

[9-30]   Hines, I.J. *ATM: The Key to High-Speed Broadband Networking*. M&T Books, 1996.

[9-31]   Minoli, Daniel. *Enterprise Networking: Fractional T-1 to SONET, Frame Relay to BISDN*. Artech House, 1993.

[9-32]   Kingsley, M. Scott and Amoss, John J. "Synchronous Optical Network (SONET): Overview." *IT Continuous Services*. Datapro Information Services, July 22, 1998.

[9-33]   "Sprint's SONET Ring Links Silicon Valley." *New Media*, December 1994.

[9-34]   Rendleman, John. "Sprint Readies International Fiber Ring." *Communications Week*, June 10, 1996.

[9-35]   Schroeder, Erica. "AT&T's Fiber Network to Get Eightfold Boost." *PC Week*, May 13, 1996.

[9-36]   Dziatkiewicz, Mark. "Network of the Olympians." *Convergence*, March 1996.

[9-37]   Finneran, Michael. "DWDM and New Switching Architectures". *Business Communications Review*, July 1998.

[9-38]   Bellman, Bob. "Riding the Wave to an Optical Infrastructure." *Business Communications Review*, April 1999.

[9-39]   Rosenberg, Robert. "Backbone's Big Boy." *America's Network*, November 15, 1998.

[9-40]   Shok, Glen. "Here's Packet over SONET in a nutshell." *LAN Times*, April 27, 1998.

[9-41]   Parente, Victor R. "Packet Over Sonet: Ringing Up Speed." *Data Communications*, March 1998.

Chapter 10

Broadband Network Services: Frame Relay, SMDS, ATM, B-ISDN, and AINs

To be great is to be misunderstood. Source: Ralph Waldo Emerson. *Self Reliance,* First Series, 1941.

Broadband networks offer great potential. As emerging technologies, they also are greatly misunderstood, for which fact we authors, consultants, and lecturers are eternally grateful. (Hopefully, we foster understanding – rather than confusion.)

The concept of broadband networking has its roots in the early 1970s when the CCITT (now ITU-T) first defined Broadband ISDN. Anticipating the development of highly bandwidth-intensive applications, and the demand for them, B-ISDN was defined on a preliminary basis – the result of those continuing efforts remain in the distant future. In the meantime, however, a number of developments have taken place. First, the demand for computer internetworking grew at rates that astounded even the most astute computer and data network pundits. Second, imaging systems developed and increasingly required networking. Third, the potential for videoconferencing applications became apparent. Fourth, the development and commercialization of the Internet and World Wide Web truly has been mind-boggling. Finally, entertainment networking now captures the attention of telcos and others as they compete to develop networks that will carry TV content, as well as voice, data, video, image, facsimile, and all other forms of data over a single, integrated network. By the way, all of the above applications, which address real user demands in a cost-effective manner, truly are the drivers of technology.

Chapter 9 addressed broadband infrastructure technologies. This chapter addresses the services offered that frame the applications. The focus here is on three network service offerings, which are technology-based. Those services are Frame Relay, Synchronous Multimegabit Data Service (SMDS), and Asynchronous Transfer Mode (ATM). Together, they fall under the umbrella term *Fast Packet Services* (see Figure 10-1). *Fast,* of course, refers to the fact that they rely on a broadband (45 Mbps or more) transmission infrastructure, in the form of SONET/SDH, and on very fast and capable switching systems. *Packet* is a generic term referring to the manner in which data is segmented ... into packets, frames, blocks, cells, etc ... and handled separately, yet generally linked in some way through the network. *Services* is the operative word here. From the Latin *servitium*, it refers to the condition of a slave, whose function is to give good by providing usefulness to others. No matter how elegant the underlying technologies, their ultimate value is in enabling the creation and delivery of services of value. At the bottom of Figure 10-1, note the access standards defined by the ITU-T.

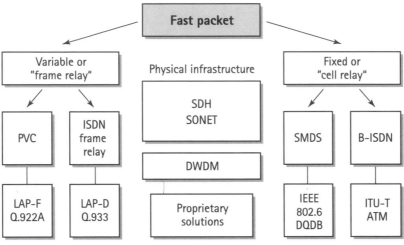

Figure 10-1 Fast Packet Services networking
(Source: Frame Relay Forum)

This chapter concludes with a brief exploration of Advanced Intelligent Networks (AINs) and B-ISDN. AINs reflect the marriage of computer, database, and network technologies, offering tremendous potential in the creation and delivery of services. B-ISDN is the ultimate concept in network service delivery, at least now.

Do not despise the bottom rungs in the ascent to greatness, wrote Pulilius Syrus (*Moral Sayings*) in the 1st Century, B.C. So it is with Fast Packet networking, which has its roots in relatively slow X.25 packet networking, which has its roots in the AlohaNET packet radio network. (It seems as though good ideas never die.)

Frame Relay

Frame Relay has experienced unprecedented growth since its commercial introduction by Wiltel (since acquired by LDDS Worldcom – now MCI Worldcom) in 1992. According to various sources the, U.S. domestic market for Frame Relay services reached approximately $1 billion in 1996, has grown steadily to a projected $5 billion in 1999, and will reach approximately $11 billion in 2002. Total worldwide Frame Relay service revenues are expected to be in the range of $15 billion in 2002.

Clearly, U.S. users have the greatest appetite for Frame Relay, although it also enjoys great popularity in the region of the European Union (EU), and increasingly is available for international networking.

Frame Relay Defined

Frame Relay is a network interface, or access, standard that was defined in 1988 by the ITU-T in its I.122 Recommendation, *Framework for Providing Additional Packet Mode Bearer Services*. Access to a Frame Relay network is accomplished using the *LAP-D* (*Link Access Procedure-D channel*) signaling protocol developed for ISDN; it originally was intended as an ISDN framing convention for a bearer (information-bearing) service. Frame Relay standards say nothing about they manner in which the internal network operates. As with X.25 packet networks, such issues of packet switching and transport are left to manufacturers that develop proprietary switching technologies [10-1]. The vast majority of Frame Relay access is at rates of Fractional T-1, DS-0 (64 Kbps) [10-2] and below because the vast majority of connected sites are small, remote locations in a larger enterprise network. Access speeds of T-1 are common for connection of centralized data centers, with multiple T-1s often aggregated for higher-speed access. Most Frame Relay service providers of significance also support T-3 and Fractional T-3, at least in the major metropolitan serving areas. Notably, Frame Relay is backward-compatible, as it considers the characteristics of the embedded networks and the standards on which they are based. Electrical and optical interfaces are not rigidly defined for Frame Relay.

Very much analogous to a streamlined and supercharged form of X.25 packet switching, Frame Relay sets up and tears down calls with control packets. Frame Relay also forwards packets of data, in the form of frames. Similar to X.25, Frame Relay multiplexes frames of data over a shared network of virtual circuits for maximum network efficiency. The interface is in a FRAD (Frame Relay Access Device) that can be implemented on the customer premise, and which is analogous to a X.25 PAD (Packet Assembler/Disassembler). Like X.25, Frame Relay is intended for bursty data traffic. While both X.25 and Frame Relay can support voice, video, and audio, the inherently unpredictable levels of packet delay and packet loss over such a highly shared network can yield results that are less than totally satisfactory.

Beyond the basic conceptual levels, the two technologies diverge, as reflected in Table 10-1. Frame Relay is a connection-oriented service working under the assumption of error-free transmission facilities for both network access and transport. It is based on the generally fiber optic nature of the transport facilities in the network core. Frame Relay assumes no responsibility for error detection and correction in the user information field because there are assumed to be no errors in transmission or switching as the frames transverse the network; rather, error control is the responsibility of the end user. In other words, Frame Relay operates at Layers 1 and 2 of the OSI Reference Model. This ceding of responsibility to the end user reduces the load on the computational resources of the network, thereby reducing latency (delay) significantly, and yielding faster processing and relaying of each frame of data. However, Frame Relay does check for errors in the control field, which is used for frame routing, queuing, and other network purposes. As errors in this control field cause frames to be discarded even if the integrity of the payload is maintained, this relatively simple and, therefore, easily and quickly accomplished level of error control is significant. Unlike X.25, Frame Relay is protocol-independent and provides no protocol conversion services. Protocol conversion was a key advantage of X.25 since the computational resources involved were expensive and not widely available 30 years ago; that certainly is not the case today. Additionally, there were relatively few protocols to be supported 30 years ago. In fact, I probably could count them on my fingers and toes. The number of protocols in use today far exceeds the number of fingers and toes of my entire family, including Max, the brave and fierce canine companion who has remained by my side during the process of writing this Second Edition. Whether accomplished in the network domain (X.25) or in the user domain (Frame Relay), both error control and protocol conversion involve processes that require computational resources. As processes always cost money and take time, they add to the cost of the network service, impose additional latency on each packet processed, and contribute to overall network congestion. In order to minimize cost, latency, and congestion, Frame Relay, therefore, does not support either error control (except in the packet header) or protocol conversion. It's a very fair tradeoff.

TABLE 10-1 X.25/FRAME RELAY COMPARISON

Attribute	X.25	Frame Relay
Facilities	Analog Assumed	Digital Assumed
Payload	128B/256B/512B/ 1024B, Fixed	(4,096B, Variable
Access Speed	(56 Kbps-DS1	(56 Kbps-DS1, DS3
Link Layer Protocol	LAP-B	LAP-D/LAP-F
Latency	High	Moderate
Orientation	Connection-Oriented	Connection-Oriented
Error Control	Network	User
Protocol Conversion	Yes	No
Primary Application	Interactive Data	LAN-to-LAN

Stripping these processes out of the Frame Relay network is counterbalanced, to some extent, by the variable size of the packet. Recall that packet-switched networks based on the X.25 protocol insist on fixed-length packets of 128, 256, 512, or 1,024 bytes. This fixed length has the advantage of predictability, which yields improved congestion management as the size of the network buffers can be engineered more precisely and as each packet takes the same time to work its way through the switching matrix of each network node. Conversely, Frame Relay standards specify a frame payload that is variable in length up to 4,096 octets; this payload supports a payload as large as that of 4-Mbps Token Ring. Subsequently, the Frame Relay Forum developed an Implementation Agreement (IA) that limits the maximum size to 1,600 octets for purposes of interconnectivity and interoperability of Frame Relay networks, and the switches, routers, and other devices that form the heart of the networks. This smaller frame easily supports the largest standard 802.3 Ethernet frame. As Ethernet clearly is the dominant LAN standard and as Frame Relay was designed for LAN-to-LAN internetworking, this frame size generally is adequate. Regardless of the maximum frame size, the frames are variable in length. This variability yields unpredictability, which contributes to congestion.

Frame Relay Standards

A wide range of manufacturers and carriers, both domestic and international, support Frame Relay. Standards bodies include ANSI, ETSI, and the ITU-T. The Frame Relay Forum, a voluntary group of manufacturers and other interested parties, develops and promotes Implementation Agreements (IAs), which address manufacturer interoperability issues based on the standards. Table 10-2 notes select relevant standards.

Table 10–2 FRAME RELAY STANDARDS*

Subject Area	ITU–T	ANSI
Architecture & Service Description	I.233	T1.606
Data Link Layer Core Aspects	Q.922 Annex A	T1.618
PVC Management	Q.933 Annex A	T1.617 Annex D
Congestion Management	I.370	T1.606a
SVC Signaling	Q.933	T1.617

*Source: DigiNet Corp.

Frame Relay Access

Frame Relay access is provided on the basis of a dedicated digital link into a Frame Relay node. The typical speed of the access link can range up to 44.736 Mbps and can be in the form of DDS (56/64 Kbps), Switched 56/64 Kbps, ISDN BRI (64/128

Kbps) or PRI (1.544 Mbps), FT1 (N x 64 Kbps), T-1 (1.544 Mbps), and T-3 (44.736). Several carriers also offer Frame Relay service at speeds of 6 Mbps, which comprises the equivalent of four T-1s, and 10 Mbps – equivalent to traditional Ethernet 802.3.

Customer DCE is the form of a FRAD (Frame Relay Access Device). The FRAD may be a standalone device that performs the sole function of assembling and disassembling frames, although it generally is embedded under the skin of another device, such as a router. From the FRAD, access is gained to the link and, subsequently, to the Frame Relay network node at the edge of the carrier network. At the node resides the FRND (Frame Relay Network Device). The UNI (User Network Interface), as defined by ANSI and ITU-T, defines the nature of this access interface.

Frame Relay Network

The Frame Relay network (refer to Figure 10-2) consists of specified network interfaces in the form of the User Network Interface (UNI) and Network-to-Network Interface (NNI). The specifics of the internal carrier network are based on ISDN, generally making use of Permanent Virtual Circuits (PVCs). While most of the major carriers currently do not support Switched Virtual Circuits (SVCs), both MCI and Qwest do offer them domestically. Frame Relay networks can be public, private, or hybrid.

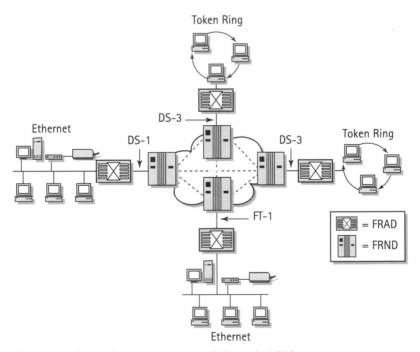

Figure 10-2 Frame Relay network, with fully meshed PVCs

User Network Interface (UNI) is the demarcation point between the user DTE and the network, and is in the form of a FRAD (Frame Relay Access Device) and a FRND (Frame Relay Network Device). The FRAD, which is a DCE (Data Communications Equipment) device, may be either standalone, or contained under the skin of another device, such as a router. The FRAD typically is on the customer premises, although it may be included in the FRND for use on a dial-up basis. The FRND is the point of interface to the carrier network, and generally is embedded in an edge network switch, which typically is in the form of a router.

Network-to-Network Interface (NNI) is defined as the interface between Frame Relay networks and is based on multinetwork PVCs. Most network-to-network connections are provided over digital SONET optical fiber trunks and through ATM switches. This current method of internetwork connection has implications relative to Implicit Congestion Notification and Network Management. A NNI is required, for example, if a user organization wishes to connect from an intraLATA Frame Relay network provided by a RBOC to an interLATA network provided by a long-haul carrier. The NNI is provided at additional cost.

ISDN is the basis of the internal Frame Relay network, although the user links generally are not ISDN. Additionally, the ISDN LAP-D protocol governs the user links, although they generally are not ISDN for reasons that include lack of availability and additional cost.

Permanent Virtual Circuits (PVCs) define fixed paths through the network for each source-destination pair, based on programmed logic. Such path (i.e., circuit) definitions are "permanently" fixed in network routing tables, until such time as they are "permanently" changed. As bandwidth is made available only when required, the circuit is virtual in nature. Regardless of the levels of network traffic, the PVC always is used to serve a given source-destination pair. In the event of a catastrophic failure that affects an element (e.g., link or switch) of a PVC, a backup PVC can be invoked – assuming that one has been defined. Backup PVCs are at additional cost. Frame Relay networks generally are based on PVCs, as depicted in Figure 10-2. PVCs may be fully symmetric, with equal bandwidth in each direction, or they may be asymmetric, with more bandwidth in one direction than in the other.

Switched Virtual Circuits (SVCs) are set up call-by-call, based on programmed network routing options. These options are triggered by a unique E.164 address, which is the equivalent of a Frame Relay telephone number. A SVC call is established as the originating FRAD sends a request to the network node, including a E.164 destination address and bandwidth parameters for the call. The network node responds with a DLCI designation, the originating FRAD responds with an acceptance message, and the data transfer ensues. At the end of the call, the SVCs are torn down. The next SVC provided for the same source-destination pair could differ greatly, depending on network availability. SVCs offer the advantage of improved performance through automatic load-balancing, as they are defined on a call-by-call basis. SVCs also offer any-to-any flexibility (much like a dial-up call of any type), and resiliency, as the VCs are selected and set up in consideration of the overall performance of the network from-end to end. Carriers that support SVCs typically offer the option of defining a *Closed User Group* (*CUG*), for purposes of security. The CUG prevents both the initiation of a call to, and the reception of a call from, any site not defined in the CUG.

Mesh Networking is easily accomplished with Frame Relay, and on a scalable basis. In other words, the cost of Frame Relay implementation is relatively proportionate to the task at hand. As more sites are added to the network, more FRADs, access links, and FRNDs are added. As the bandwidth requirement increases at any given site, the capacity of the access link increases. The costs grow relatively gracefully as the network expands to provide access to additional sites, and as bandwidth increases on a site-by-site basis. While full mesh networking is unusual, it can be accomplished at significantly lower cost than with a private, leased-line network. Frame Relay networks can be classified as Virtual Private Networks (VPNs).

Network Processing is not performed in Frame Relay – at least not to the extent experienced in X.25 networks. A Frame Relay network assumes that the frame is error free. As the link is digital (ideally SONET) and based on ISDN, there is no compelling requirement to check for errors. Once the frame is identified as valid and once the address is recognized, the frame is relayed through the core of the network to the next node and, ultimately, to the end user. Frame Relay also assumes that all frames pass through the network successfully, and are received in the order transmitted. This is the equivalent of removing OSI Layer 3 functions from the X.25 model. Further, Frame Relay assumes no responsibility for protocol conversion. When compared with X.25 and traditional packet switching, this reduction in network processing yields lower cost and reduced packet latency, somewhat counterbalancing the effect of the variable-size frame to reduce issues of overall network congestion.

Frame Relay Equipment

Frame Relay, as a service offering, depends on certain hardware and firmware in order to accomplish the interface. That equipment includes the Frame Relay Assembler/Disassembler (FRAD), the Frame Relay Network Device (FRND), and the Frame Relay switch.

Frame Relay Assembler/Disassemblers (*FRADs*) also known as *Frame Relay Access Devices*, are CPE – which is analogous to Packet Assembler/Disassemblers (PADs) in a X.25 packet-switched network. The FRAD essentially organizes the user data into a Protocol Data Unit (PDU), which can vary in size up to 4,096 octets. The FRAD then encapsulates the PDU into a Frame Relay frame, placing the necessary control information around it. FRADs can be standalone units, serving multiple hardwired devices, or they can be in the form of a printed circuit board that fits into the expansion slot of a workstation. Additionally, FRADs can be incorporated into X.25

PADs, T-carrier MUXs, or even PBXs for dedicated networks. More likely, they are incorporated into a high-end bridge or router serving a LAN. In early 1996, several vendors announced CO-based FRADs, which offer the potential to eliminate the end user investment in such equipment. Although they are limited in functionality, intended largely to support conversion of SDLC traffic to frame format, they offer advantages to user organization seeking to migrate from dedicated networks connecting large data centers [10-3], [10-4], and [10-5].

Frame Relay Network Devices (*FRNDs*) are the link-terminating equipment in the Central Office. The FRND serves to terminate the digital local loop in the Frame Relay switch. The service providers own the FRNDs.

Frame Relay Switches are nodal processors capable of switching frames at very high speed. They contain buffers that, within limits, can absorb incoming frames until the switch can act on them, as well as buffers that can absorb outgoing frames until the forward link becomes available. In combination, these incoming and outgoing buffers are used to exercise flow control. The switches contain very high-speed switching matrixes and internal busses. They have sufficient intelligence, in the form of routing tables, to read the control information embedded in the frames. This enables the switches to route the frames correctly over the PVC — identified previously in the call set-up process. The nodal processors also have intelligence sufficient to check for errors in the frame, although error-correction processes are performed at the end-user level. Additionally, the nodal processors may have the intelligence to prioritize certain types of traffic that are delay-sensitive, such as SDLC, voice, and video. Since the switches perform no error correction or protocol conversion functions, they act on the frames very quickly, thereby minimizing latency. Frame Relay nodal processors can be managed from a centralized Network Operations Center, thereby enhancing the scalability of the network [10-6]. The Frame Relay switch also may contain a voice compressor module, where voice is communicated over Frame Relay using a version of the ACELP (Algebraic Code-Excited Linear Prediction) compression algorithm. While Frame Relay is not intended for voice, it can be accommodated with varying degrees of quality. Frame switches are owned by the service provider in a public network scenario, and by the end user in a private network scenario.

Frame Relay Protocol: Frame Structure

The Frame Relay Protocol involves the relaying of frames of user data across the network. In an appropriate WAN data application, the preponderance of the frame is payload in the form of user data; relatively little control information is included. As illustrated in Figure 10-3, the five data fields in the ANSI T1.618 frame format comprise beginning and ending flags, an address field, an information field, and a frame check sequence (FCS). Although the Frame Relay Protocol is a subset of the HDLC (High Level Data Link Control) protocol used in other data communications environments, it lacks control information such as frame sequence number. In the Frame Relay environment, it is the responsibility of the user to identify and correct for frame sequence errors or missing frames, as well as corrupted or truncated frames.

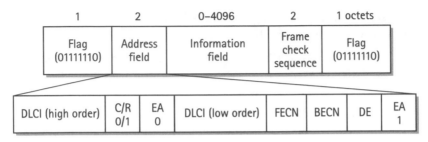

Address field format – 2 octets (default)

> DLCI: Data Link Connection Identifier
> C/R: Command/Response Field
> FECN: Forward Explicit Congestion Notification
> BECN: Backward Explicit Congestion Notification
> DE: Discard Eligibility
> EA: Address Field Extension

Figure 10-3 Frame Relay frame

◆ **Flag Field:** 1 octet, fixed binary sequence (01111110) is employed to identify and separate frames. Flag fields appear at the beginning and end of the frame.

◆ **Address Field:** 2 octets are used as a default length. Address fields include the necessary control information in the Data Link Connection Identifier (DLCI). The address field also contains a Command/Response field, Address Field Extension, Forward and Backward Explicit Congestion Notification fields, and Discard Eligibility data.

◆ **Data Link Connection Identifier (DLCI):** 10 bits that identify the data link, the virtual circuit (i.e., PVC or SVC), and its service parameters to the network. Those service parameters include frame size, Committed Information Rate (CIR), Committed Burst Size (B_c), Burst Excess Size (B_e), and Committed Rate Measurement Interval (T_c). I discuss the significance of these service parameters later in this chapter.

◆ **Command/Response (C/R):** 1 bit reserved for use of the FRADs, rather than the Frame Relay network. C/R is defined to facilitate the transport of polled protocols such as SNA, which require a Command/Response for signaling and control purposes.

◆ **Address Field Extension (EA):** 2 bits that signal the extension of the addressing structure beyond the 2-octet default. The use of EA must be negotiated with the carrier when the service is established. As the popularity of Frame Relay grows and as large public and private Frame Relay networks develop, provisions are in place to expand the EA field to as many as 60 bits.

◆ **Forward Explicit Congestion Notification (FECN):** 1-bit field available to the network to advise upstream devices of congestion. The FRAD clearly recognizes when the frame carrying the FECN survives. It also is advised that subsequent frames may not be so fortunate. Should subsequent frames be discarded or corrupted in transmission, the receiving device is advised that recovery may be required in the form of requests for retransmission. If the upstream device controls the rate of data transfer, it has the opportunity to throttle back.

◆ **Backward Explicit Congestion Notification (BECN):** 1-bit field used by the network to advise devices of congestion in the direction opposite of the primary traffic flow. If the target FRAD responds to the originating FRAD in the backward direction, the BECN bit is set in a backward frame. If there is no data flowing in the backward direction, the Frame Relay network creates a frame in that direction, setting the BECN bit. If the originating FRAD is capable of reducing the frame rate, it is well advised to do so, as the network may discard frames once the notification is posted.

◆ **Discard Eligibility (DE):** 1-bit field indicating the eligibility of the frame for discard under conditions of network congestion. Theoretically, the user equipment sets the DE, in consideration of the acceptability of the application to packet loss. Should the user equipment not set the DE, the network switches may do so on a random basis, with results that may be less than totally pleasing. SDLC, voice, and video traffic, for instance, do not tolerate loss.

◆ **Information Field:** Contains user information, either in the form of payload data or internetwork control information passed between devices such as routers. Although the Information Field may be 4,096 octets in length, ANSI recommendations dictate that the maximum size be 1,600 octets. This payload size is consistent with 802.3 Ethernet LAN traffic, which comprises the vast majority of LAN traffic. This frame size of 1,600 octets also is addressed in Implementation Agreements from the Frame Relay Forum, which were developed to ensure the interconnectivity and interoperability of Frame Relay networks.

◆ **Frame Check Sequence (FCS):** 2-octet CRC (Cyclic Redundancy Check) supporting header error control in frames with information fields up to 4,096 octets in length. Note that no error control is provided for the user payload data contained in the Information Field. Rather, error control for payload data generally is accomplished by running the TCP/IP protocol within the Information Field as part of the payload.

Local Management Interface (LMI) Protocol

The LMI protocol provides operational support for the User Network Interface (UNI). Originally defined by the Frame Relay Forum in 1990, it since has been adopted by ANSI and the ITU-T. The LMI is a polling protocol between the FRAD and the network, which verifies the existence and availability of the PVC, as well as the integrity of the UNI link.

Congestion Management

Frame Relay, as a highly-shared network, is extremely efficient. Since all the links and all the switches that comprise the network are shared among large numbers of users and user organizations, the network is subject to variable and unpredictable levels of congestion. Indeed, it is designed for congestion as a natural occurrence and in support of bursty LAN-to-LAN internetworking applications – which are tolerant of delay and loss, and which have the time and ability to adjust and recover. This fact serves to reduce the overall cost of the network service, although it compromises the level of performance – a classic network optimization scenario in which an appropriate balance is struck between cost and performance. Congestion management is addressed through the following parameters, specified in an addendum to ANSI T1.606 [10-6], [10-7], and [10-8]:

◆ **Access Rate:** Maximum data rate of the access channel, as defined by the bandwidth of the access link available for data transmission (e.g., a DS-0 of 64 Kbps, a Fractional T-1 of 768 Kbps, or a full T-1 of 1.536 Mbps). Data can be transmitted or received over the access link at lesser rates, of course.

◆ **Committed Information Rate (CIR):** The data rate that the network guarantees to handle across the Virtual Circuit (VC, which can be either a PVC or a SVC) under normal conditions over a period of time. The CIR typically is an average data rate over a period of a month. The CIR is based on mutual agreement between the carrier and the customer, and should be based on the average maximum amount of traffic required to be supported reliably over the VC during the busiest hour of the day. The VC is defined as a matched source-destination pair, which can be either symmetric (i.e., equal in both directions) or asymmetric (i.e., more in one direction than in another) in terms of bandwidth. In the event that the CIR is exceeded, the network reserves the option to mark excess frames as DE (Discard Eligible) if the DCE has not already done so. The discard function typically takes place in the entry node at the edge of the network, in order to obviate any issues of unnecessary congestion in the network core. There is no model for the relationship between CIR and Access Rate. Some carriers permit *zero CIR*, meaning that CIR is set at 0 percent. At *zero CIR*, all Offered Load is handled on a *best effort* basis, with absolutely no commitments or guarantees. Some carriers permit, or even require, the CIR to be set at 100 percent, meaning that all Offered Load will be guaranteed, with the maximum Offered Load determined by the Access Rate and Port Speed. Some carriers require that the CIR for a VC be set at no less than 50 percent of the Access Rate and Port Speed, with that relationship capped at T-1 speeds – at T-3 levels of 44.736 Mbps, the bursts are too wildly variable to be managed effectively. Significantly, multiple VCs can be supported over a single access line.

- **Offered Load:** The data rate offered to the network for delivery measured in bps. The aggregate offered load can be less than the Access Rate supported by the access link and/or the Port Speed of the FRND, but can never exceed whichever is less. As is always the case, the lowest common denominator defines the maximum level of performance.

- **Committed Burst Size (B_c):** Maximum amount of data that the carrier agrees to handle under normal conditions. The B_c cannot exceed the CIR for a VC.

- **Excess Burst Size (B_e):** Maximum amount of data that the network attempts to deliver over a specified time (T), as required by the user. In recognition of the bursty nature of LAN-to-LAN communications, the transmitting device may burst above the CIR for a brief period of time; the network attempts to accommodate such bursts within limits of burst size and burst interval. The network reserves the option to mark the excess data DE (Discard Eligible), should the user CPE hasn't done so already.

- **Measurement Interval (T):** Time interval measuring burst rates above the CIR and the length of such bursts.

- **Discard Eligibility (DE):** Indicates the eligibility of the frame for discard, in the event of congestion. Either the FRAD or the FRND may set DE. Theoretically, at least, the FRAD is programmed to recognize when the CIR is exceeded and to volunteer frames for discard should the network suffer unreasonable levels of congestion. The FRAD must make DE decisions in consideration of the user-layer application's tolerance for frame loss. For example, SDLC data, and voice and video, are not tolerant of loss; such data must be confined to the CIR and must not be marked DE. Ethernet LAN data, on the other hand, is tolerant of loss; such data can exceed the CIR for the VC and can be marked DE without compromising the *best effort* expectations of the user-layer application.

◆ **Explicit Congestion Notification (ECN):** The means by which the network advises devices of network congestion. *Forward Explicit Congestion Notification (FECN)* advises the target device of network congestion so it can adjust its expectations. *Backward Explicit Congestion Notification (BECN)* advises the transmitting device of network congestion so it can reduce its rate of transmission accordingly. Theoretically, it is the responsibility of the various devices on the originating end of the data communication to adjust in some way. However, not all FRADs have the ability to adjust; high-end routers can impose a certain amount of flow control through buffering. The switches and hubs behind the FRAD have no ability to adjust other than filling their buffers, which typically are highly limited in capacity, if they exist at all. The originating terminal devices and peripherals have no ability to adjust, other than filling their very limited buffers, if any, and then simply stopping.

◆ **Implicit Congestion Notification:** Inference by user equipment that congestion has occurred. Such inference is triggered by realization of the user device (e.g., FRAD, mainframe, or server) that one or more frames have been lost. Based on control mechanisms at the upper protocol layers of the end devices, the frames are resent to recover from such loss.

Aside from the congestion mechanisms specified in the frame standards, there are two types of congestion control algorithms. *Closed-loop algorithms* prevent frames from entering the network unless there is an extremely high probability of their being accepted, transported, and delivered without discard. *Open-loop algorithms* permit the acceptance of the frames with no prior knowledge of the likelihood of their successful delivery. The closed-loop algorithm fairly allocates backbone trunk bandwidth among all the PVCs configured on a particular trunk, and in proportion to the CIRs [10-9].

How Frame Relay Networks Work

Frame Relay networks typically are configured on a star, or *hub and spoke*, configuration, as illustrated in Figure 10-4. In this example, 96 remote sites connect to a centralized data center. The access links serving the remote sites are defined as DS-0 at 64 Kbps, and the access link serving the centralized data center is unchannelized T-1 at a signaling rate of 1.544 Mbps, of which 1.536 Mbps is available for data transmission and .008 Mbps is used for signaling and control purposes. Each of the PVCs between the remote sites and the centralized data center is set at a CIR of 32 Kbps, which is 50 percent of the Access Rate for each remote site. The aggregate rate of the CIRs for the 96 PVCs is double the Access Rate of the link serving the centralized data center; this relationship is a common maximum for Frame Relay service providers.

In this example, 48 of the remote sites can initiate a data session to the central-ized data center at a rate of 32 Kbps, which is within the CIR of each of the PVCs, and is exactly the Access Rate of the T-1 link to the data center. On the average, at least, the carrier supports the CIR rate without frame loss. Should any of the 48 active remote sites burst above the CIR, the excess frames are marked as DE (Discard Eligible) and are subject to discard if the network suffers congestion. Frames are marked DE by the transmitting FRAD in consideration of the tolerance of the user layer application for loss. Should the excess frames not be subject to im-mediate discard, the carrier nodes buffer the excess frames, since the Access Rate of the T-1 is *oversubscribed*. As the level of data destined for the data center dimin-ishes, the excess frames are accommodated, assuming that the buffers in the carrier nodes have not filled and the excess frames, therefore, subsequently have been dis-carded. In a closed-loop scenario, should any other of the 48 remaining sites initi-ate a call to the centralized data center, that call is denied because the access link to the data center is oversubscribed. If the public Frame Relay suffers congestion, overall, FECN and BECN bits are set in frames flowing in both directions so both originating and destination FRADs are advised of the condition and have the option of adjusting accordingly – if capable of doing so. As the PVCs are suscepti-ble to catastrophic failure, backup PVCs (not shown) also typically are in place. Should both SNA traffic and LAN traffic be supported over the subject network, either the demanding and well-behaved SNA traffic is designed to the CIR, or a separate PVC is provided in its support.

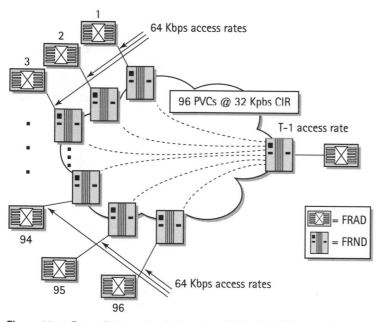

Figure 10-4 Frame Relay network, based on PVCs with CIRs set at 32 Kbps between a centralized data center and remote sites in a star configuration

In addition to public, carrier-based Frame Relay services, a number of end-user organizations run the Frame Relay protocol over their legacy T-carrier, leased-line private networks. This approach takes advantage of both the performance characteristics of the legacy network, and the protocol independence of Frame Relay, thereby enabling the sharing of the existing infrastructure for a wide variety of data traffic (e.g., SDLC, LAN-to-LAN, and IP-based traffic). As the leased-line network is private, rather than public and shared, issues of congestion management are entirely under the control of the user organization. Therefore, desired performance levels are easily established and controlled. In such an environment, issues of congestion that might affect voice and video in a negative way are eliminated. Virtually all the major manufacturers of T-carrier nodal MUXs support Frame Relay through special interface cards.

Voice over Frame Relay (VoFR)

The very concept of transmitting voice over any sort of data network, much less a packet data network, would have been viewed as completely bizarre before 1995 (at the very earliest). Currently, the concept is firmly entrenched, although the specifics have yet to be proven fully. Voice over data networks includes *Voice over Frame Relay* (*VoFR*), *Voice over Internet Protocol* (*VoIP*), and *Voice Telephony over Asynchronous Transfer Mode* (*VTOA*). Frame Relay certainly was not designed for voice traffic, and neither was IP; although ATM was designed from the ground up for all types of traffic. I reveal, in some depth, VoIP and VTOA in later chapters. For the moment, let's focus on VoFR.

While Frame Relay is intended as a data networking service, specifically and originally for LAN-to-LAN internetworking, it also can be used in support of isochronous voice and voice-band data (i.e., fax and analog modems). However, you must consider the fact that issues of delay can affect the quality of the voice transmission over time. Even within the constraints of the CIR, the level of bandwidth is measured and ensured only as an average over a period of time, rather than on a constant basis. Since Frame Relay is a packet-switching, rather than a circuit-switching network service technology, there is no provision for temporary, continuous, and exclusive bandwidth through a Frame Relay network. As a result, voice frames suffer from delay, loss, and error at levels that are variable and unpredictable in nature. The voice frames that make it to the egress side of the network are delivered to the receiving device in order as they are received. Any voice frames received out of order are discarded, as are any errored ones. The result can be less than aesthetically pleasing. In the event that the received voice stream becomes unintelligible, the listener always can resort to the *Huh?* protocol, as in "Huh? What did you say?"

Assuming, however, that the end-user organization is prepared to yield some unpredictable level of quality, Frame Relay supports voice and other voice-band data, and at very reasonable cost. Generally speaking, you should use the Frame Relay network predominantly for data networking. Assuming, however, that excess capacity exists at the CIR level, and assuming that the network is not experiencing congestion at the moment (i.e., no explicit congestion notifications have been delivered and no implicit congestion notifications have occurred), near toll-quality voice is possible over a Frame Relay network. Why would you even consider Voice over Frame Relay (VoFR)? There really is only one answer: It's FREE...or at least very inexpensive, especially over flat-rate PVCs or SVCs.

Actually, it turns out that there might be another reason, or at least an additional reason. AT&T pre-announced (May 1999) its MultiMedia Networking Service (MMNS), which includes VoFR. While MMNS is a working name for the service, it is an integrated voice and data Frame Relay service that has been in intensive beta test for some months. While the service will cannibalize AT&T's traditional TDM-based toll network, it will help feed the AT&T Solutions Inc. group, the managed-services and outsourcing arm. Sprint announced a similar offering in 1997, but never released it. MCI Worldcom announced a VoFR option in 1998, although it does not run over the principal Frame Relay network [10-10]. If you are interested in a managed service option, therefore, VoFR has taken on new meaning. Ultimately, however, the only reason to consider VoFR is that it can ride free within the CIR limits of a Frame Relay intended for LAN-to-LAN communications.

VOFR THEORY: COMPRESSION IS THE KEY

In consideration of the fact that the voice information stream is not constant, and certainly is not constantly changing at a high rate of speed, VoFR can take advantage of various compression techniques to relax the amount of bandwidth required for the voice stream. Specifically, only the changes in speech patterns from one set of samples to another need to transmit across the network. For instance, the natural and predictable pauses in human speech can be noted, eliminated on the transmit side, and reinserted on the receive side through a process known as *silence supression.* Similarly, redundant or repetitive speech sounds can be removed on the transmit side and reinserted on the receive side. Once the silence is suppressed and the redundancy noted, the remainder of the set of voice samples can be further compressed and inserted into relatively small frames. The small frame size is provided so that a large number of *sound bytes* can be presented to and carried through the network on a frequent basis, with minimal jitter. While this approach is somewhat overhead-intensive, it provides for a relatively normal flow of speech information. There exist a number of low bit-rate compression algorithms, both standard and proprietary, that are implemented by various router manufacturers. The most popular are those in the ACELP (Algebraic Code-Excited Linear Prediction) family. ACELP and other compression algorithms support very reasonable voice quality (under conditions of low network congestion) at bit rates as low as 8 Kbps. Additionally, the Frame Relay Forum adopted Conjugate Structure-Algebraic Code Excited Linear Prediction (CS-ACELP) as FRF.11. According to the Frame Relay Forum, only 22 percent of normal speech comprises essential components, with the balance comprising either pauses, or repetitive speech patterns [10-11].

◆ **CELP (Code Excited Linear Prediction):** Key to CELP and its derivatives is the creation and maintenance of a code book, which is a binary description of a set of voice samples. Specifically, CELP involves the binary description of a set of 80 PCM voice samples, representing 10 ms (10 milliseconds, or 1/100th of a second) of a voice stream, and gathered in a buffer. Then, the data set is compressed to remove silence and redundancy, the volume level is normalized, and the resulting data set is compared to a set of candidate shapes in the code book. The data transmitted across the network includes the index number of the selected code description and the average loudness level of the set of samples. Every 10 ms, the code is sent across the network in a block of 160 bits, yielding a data rate of 16 Kbps, which compares very favorably with PCM voice over circuit-switched TDM networks at 64 Kbps. The compression rate is 4:1. At the receiving end of the transmission, the transmitted code is compared to the code book, the PCM signal is reconstructed and, eventually, the analog signal is reconstructed. The reproduction is not perfect, but generally is close enough to yield good perceived quality through this process of voice synthesis. The devices that perform these processes of compression and decompression are *DSPs* (*Digital Signal Processors*), which include the basic codec function. Figure 10-5 illustrates this compression process.

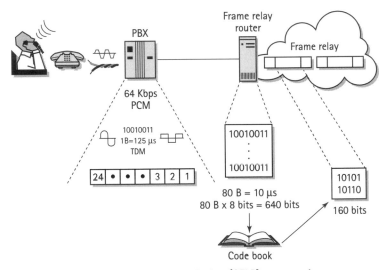

Figure 10-5 Code Excited Linear Prediction (CELP) compression

◆ **LD-CELP (Low Delay-Code Excited Linear Prediction):** As defined in ITU-T G.728, LD-CELP also is geared to a rate of 16 Kbps, although bit rates as low as 12.8 Kbps can be achieved. The lower level of delay suggested by the designation is due to the fact that only five PCM samples, representing 0.625 ms of the voice stream, are accumulated in a block. Considering that each sample is expressed as a 2-bit value, and that five samples equal a pattern of 10 adjacent bits, 10^5 yields 1,024 possible combinations, each of which describes a section or shape from the code book, and each of which is part of an overall voice stream. The more frequent transmission of the shorter data blocks yields lower levels of delay through faster processing by the DSPs, and the compression technique yields more efficient use of bandwidth. LD-CELP yields quality that generally is considered to be on a par with ADPCM (Adaptive Differential Pulse Code Modulation), discussed in Chapter 7.

CS-ACELP (Conjugate Structure-Algebraic Code Excited Linear Prediction): As defined in ITU-T G.729, ACELP improves on the CELP concept through the algebraic expression, rather than the numeric description, of each entry in the code book. ACELP yields quality that is considered to be as good as ADPCM, but requiring bandwidth of only 8 Kbps. Proprietary versions of ACELP exist, as well [10-12].

Other, non-standard compression algorithms take the bit rate as low as 4.8 Kbps (or lower), but with considerable loss of quality. Current ITU-T standard recommendations for voice compression used in various VoFR codecs include those presented in Table 10-3, all of which begin with PCM voice. In addition to the base compression algorithms, various *continuity algorithms* are employed to intelligently fill the void of missing or errored compressed voice frames by stretching the previous voice frames or blending several frames together.

The perceived quality of the voice signal is based on exhaustive tests conducted with panels of *expert listeners*. The results of those tests are expressed in terms of the *Mean Opinion Score* (*MOS*). In addition to considering the raw quality of the resulting speech signal, the MOS is affected by the level of delay associated with the processes of compression and decompression.

Table 10-3 ITU-T STANDARD VOICE COMPRESSION ALGORITHMS*

ITU-T Standard	Compression Algorithm, Year	Bit Rate	Mean Opinion Score (MOS)	Compression Delay (milliseconds)
G.711	Pulse Code Modulation (PCM), 1988	64 Kbps	4.4	0.75
G.723, (H.324 G.723.1 umbrella)	Dual Rate Speech Coder for Multimedia Communication, 1996	6.3 & 5.3 Kbps	3.5–3.98	30.0
G.726 (FRF.11)	Adaptive Differential Pulse Code Modulation (ADPCM), 1991	40, 32, 24, & 16 Kbps	4.2	1.0
G.728	LowDelay-Code Excited Linear Prediction (LD-CELP), 1994	16 Kbps	4.2	3.0–5.0
G.729 (FRF.11)	Conjugate Structure-Algebraic Code Excited Linear Prediction (CS-ACELP), 1996	8 Kbps	4.2	10.0

Source: [10-13] and [10-14]

Regardless of the compression technique employed, VoFR suffers from some additional loss of quality due to issues of echo, delay, delay variability (i.e., jitter), and loss. Through network buffering and voice frame prioritization, these factors can at least be mitigated, but never entirely overcome. Additionally, some FRAD manufacturers support the definition of a separate PVC for delay-sensitive traffic such as voice, while others support multiplexing of voice data frames only over the same PVC as that used in support of data. Some manufacturers support both small frame sizes for voice and large frame sizes for data, while others force all data into the smaller frame size more appropriate for voice; the latter approach forces all data into the less-efficient (more overhead-intensive) frame size. Notably, VoFR FRADs are proprietary in nature, thereby requiring that a single-vendor VoFR network [10-13] through [10-20].

In order to mitigate the inherent difficulties of transmitting delay-sensitive voice traffic over Frame Relay, some manufacturers and carriers offer various priority management techniques. Several manufacturers of multifunction FRADs and routers, for instance, support the identification of high-priority traffic in the frame header. Some carriers also offer PVCs of varying levels of delay/priority. Infonet, for example, offers three PVC levels:

◆ VC/Interactive: Top priority; suited to delay-sensitive applications such as voice and SNA; premium pricing

◆ VC/lan2lan: No-priority designation; suited to LAN traffic, which can tolerate some level of delay

◆ VC/Access: Low-priority designation; suited to Internet access, e-mail, monitoring, and other low-priority applications that can tolerate relatively significant levels of delay

Frame Relay Costs

The costs of Frame Relay vary widely amongst equipment manufacturers and carriers. It is clear, however, that Frame Relay is highly cost-effective for internetworking large numbers of sites at rates up to 44.736 Mbps (T-3). Such networks can be configured as a full mesh, a partial mesh, or a star.

The end user's equipment cost is for the FRAD, which can be standalone, or built under the skin of a bridge or router; a DSU/CSU also is included in the device for interface to an electrically-based digital access link. In addition to the cost of the FRAD, the carriers' charges typically include some combination of port charge (bandwidth-sensitive), access link (bandwidth- and distance-sensitive), Committed Information Rate (CIR) per VC (Virtual Circuit), and burst size (B_c) – the B_c is sensitive to the time interval (T).

Frame Relay networks originally were priced on a case-by-case basis. In consideration of the widespread popularity of the service, however, the FCC in October 1995 classified Frame Relay as a *basic service*. This reclassification requires that the RBOCs, AT&T, MCI Worldcom, and Sprint file tariffs. The publishing of Frame Relay rates enables smaller users to comparison-shop, simplifying the process and likely reducing their costs. Larger users, on the other hand, lose some bargaining power. Significantly, the FCC has taken a position that likely will extend to other fast packet services in the future [10-21] and [10-22].

Prices have varied considerably since the FCC decision, as the ILECs (Incumbent Local Exchange Carriers), the incumbent IXCs (IntereXchange Carriers), and their competitors seek to develop and hone their individual strategies. In the highly competitive Frame Relay market, mesh networking can be accomplished at costs as little as 50 percent of the cost of a comparable FT-1 network. Costs can be mitigated to some extent through the use of compression devices, which permit transmission at a lower Port Speed and CIR through the recognition of patterns within data frames intended for multicasting, or transmission to multiple addresses.

Bell Atlantic, for instance, offers both "Local Frame Relay" for intraLATA networking, and "FCC Frame Relay" for interfacing to interLATA carriers. The intraLATA service is available at Access Rates of 56/64 Kbps ($175 per month on a month-to-month basis, plus a non-recurring charge of $800) and 1.536 Mbps ($435 on a month-to-month basis, plus a non-recurring charge of $1,000); 3-year and 5-year options are available at lower monthly rates. The monthly charge for each additional PVC (Bell Atlantic does not offer SVCs) over an access link is $1.25 per month, plus a $5 non-recurring charge. The cost of the CIR associated with each PVC over a 56/64 Kbps access link is $5 per month, with CIRs offered at 8, 16, and 32 Kbps. Bell Atlantic's "FCC Frame Relay" offering for interLATA access specifies charges for each UNI (User Network Interface), mirroring the charges for 56/64 Kbps and 1.536 Mbps "Local Frame Relay" Access Rates. The charge for a 1.536 Mbps NNI (Network-to-Network Interface), which is the only option, is $220 per month. Again, additional PVCs are $1.25 per month, and the monthly CIR charge is $5 per month, per PVC, for a 56/64 Kbps access link. Access links of 1.536 Mbps can support CIRs of 56/64 Kbps ($2 per month), 128 Kbps ($4), 192 Kbps ($7), 256 Kbps ($9), 384 Kbps ($12), 512 Kbps ($25), and 768 Kbps ($28) [10-23]. While Bell Atlantic's prices and options are not typical necessarily, they are representative of the overall philosophy of the ILECs. Note that the charges for the Access Rate include the charge for the port, the speed of which exactly matches that of the access link; no usage charges are specified. Also, note that costs are distance-insensitive, with the exception of the fact that a NNI must be provisioned for access to an interLATA carrier in a long-haul application; the charges for that long-haul network are additional, of course.

IntraLATA Frame Relay is the province of the IXCs, including the incumbents (e.g., AT&T, MCI Worldcom, and Sprint) and their competitors (e.g., Level 3, Nextlink, and Qwest). Some of these carriers (e.g., AT&T and MCI Worldcom) also offer "Local Frame Relay." AT&Ts price for this local service is $255 per month for 56 Kbps and $1,100 for 1.536 Mbps, regardless of whether the access link is provided by AT&T, or leased from an ILEC and resold. MCI Worldcom's 56 Kbps service is priced at $216 for the port and access line, if resold, and $116 on its own access lines; 1.536 Mbps service is priced at $696 and $546, respectively [10-24].

In terms of interLATA Frame Relay, a representative cost comparison of AT&T, MCI Worldcom, and Qwest is interesting. On the basis of port-only charges (refer to Table 10-4), and notwithstanding other considerations, Qwest looks very appealing.

Table 10-4 COMPARISON OF PORT-ONLY CHARGES FOR INTERLATA FRAME RELAY*

Port Speed	AT&T	MCI Worldcom	Qwest
56 Kbps	$295	$268	$190
1.536 Mbps (T-1)	$2,690	$2,327	$1,595

Source: [10-24] and [10-25]

Although SVCs are unusual at this time, the carriers typically charge on a usage-sensitive basis, with no minimum monthly charge for usage. Qwest, for example, currently charges $0.04 per megabyte for SVC traffic. At that rate, 800 megabytes per month over a usage-sensitive SVC equal the cost of a 32-Kbps CIR over a Qwest PVC. While Qwest and MCI Worldcom currently offer price caps on SVCs, the costs can get out of hand if traffic volumes are high. MCI Worldcom and others also offer usage-based PVCs with price caps, typically with no minimum monthly charge for usage [10-26]. MCI Worldcom, for example, also offers fixed-rate SVCs, with specified maximum usage levels.

Frame Relay Advantages and Disadvantages

Frame Relay's unique characteristics offer some advantages over its predecessor technologies of X.25, Switched 56/64 Kbps, and DDS. Additionally, Frame Relay is widely available both domestically and internationally. The market is highly competitive, which puts it in an advantageous position relative to other fast packet technologies, such as SMDS and ATM.

FRAME RELAY ADVANTAGES

Advantages of Frame Relay include its excellent support for bandwidth-intensive data and image traffic. Even stream-oriented traffic such as real-time voice and video can be supported, although issues of frame latency and loss always impact the quality of such traffic over Frame Relay networks. The absolute speed of Frame Relay, its improved congestion control, and reduced latency certainly are improvements over X.25 networks. Since Frame Relay is protocol-insensitive, it can carry virtually any form of data in variable-size frames. Bandwidth-on-demand, within the limit of the access line, is provided, generally with reasonable costs for high-speed bursts. Additionally, the network is highly redundant, thereby providing improved network resiliency — especially in the case of Switched Virtual Circuits, which are increasingly being supported by the major carriers.

As a Virtual Private Network (VPN) service technology, the elimination of dedicated circuits makes Frame Relay highly cost-effective when compared to services such as DDS and T-carrier. Frame Relay is reasonably priced due to both its highly shared VPN nature and the fact that the service is widely and, therefore, highly competitive. In fact, savings of 30-40 percent over leased lines are commonly reported. Frame Relay costs also are scalable, maintaining a graceful relationship with the needs of the user organization in terms of bandwidth and number of terminating locations. Full-mesh, partial-mesh, and hub-and-spoke networking, therefore, all can be accomplished at reasonable cost, on either a symmetric or an asymmetric basis.

FRAME RELAY DISADVANTAGES

Disadvantages of Frame Relay include its latency, which is inherent in a highly shared VPN. Although Frame Relay's latency level is an improvement over X.25, it does not compare well with SMDS and ATM. The latency issue can be significant when Frame Relay is used in support of SNA traffic, and generally renders it largely unsuitable for voice and video, at least when measured in terms of traditional "toll quality."

Frame Relay also offers no inherent mechanisms for frame sequencing and error control for the user payload, unlike its predecessor X.25, which performed these on a hop-by-hop basis at the network nodes. As Frame Relay assumes that these functions are accomplished at higher layers in the end-user domain, Frame Relay is relieved of these responsibilities. Stripping out these functions offers the advantage of reduced processing at the network nodes and, therefore, reduced latency, congestion, and cost. However, the elimination of these functions also compromises the reliability of the data stream. In order to compensate for this shortcoming, data applications typically involve running TCP/IP inside the Information Field as part of the user payload. As a result, the error control is performed on an end-to-end basis in the CPE domain. Since TCP/IP commonly is used in support of LAN communications, this additional step and the additional overhead associated with TCP/IP is not considered particularly burdensome — after all, Frame Relay is intended for LAN-to-LAN internetworking. Where realtime voice and video applications are supported over Frame Relay, TCP/IP is not part of the protocol mix because there is no time to recover from loss or error, in any event.

Note that Frame Relay generally is provisioned on the basis of PVCs (Permanent Virtual Circuits), which are preordained source-destination paths. Like private, leased-line networks, such paths are susceptible to catastrophic failure and require backup. Backup PVCs can satisfy this requirement because they are invoked virtually immediately if the primary PVC fails. SVCs (Switched Virtual Circuits) are more reliable, as they automatically seek a reliable path on a call-by-call basis. If the entire network fails, however, neither option is satisfactory. For example, the entire AT&T Frame Relay network failed in April 1998 for a period of up to 23 hours, depending on which press releases you believe. The problem apparently had to do with bugs in some software upgrades on a Cascade (now Cisco) switch, again depending on which press releases you believe [10-27-10-30]. A more effective backup strategy in the event of such a catastrophic failure is carrier redundancy, rather than PVC redundancy, or even SVCs. MCI Worldcom suffered a similarly catastrophic failure in the summer of 1999. The most effective backup is in the form of both carrier and service redundancy, such as ISDN, which is a common backup strategy for Frame Relay in environments where data connectivity is both mission-critical and time-sensitive.

Frame Relay Applications

Frame Relay was designed to fill the gap between packet-switched networks (X.25), circuit-switched networks (Switched 56/64 Kbps), and dedicated data networks (DDS, T/E-carrier). It is intended for intensive data communications involving block-level communications of data and image information. Frame Relay supports voice and low-speed video, although the quality generally is spotty due to intrinsic issues of frame latency, jitter, and loss.

Frame Relay applications primarily, therefore, are data or image in nature. LAN internetworking is the driving force behind Frame Relay, although controller-to-host, terminal-to-host, and host-to-host applications abound. The recent availability of dial-up access also makes the service cost-effective for bandwidth-intensive telecommuting application. Internet Service Providers (ISPs) and Internet Backbone Providers make significant use of Frame Relay, both for user access to the ISP and for backbone network application. In Internet applications (indeed, a great many data applications), TCP/IP runs inside Frame Relay in order to ensure the reliability of the data stream.

An excellent example of the application of Frame Relay is that of the airline reservation networks, all of which are transitioning from X.25. Apollo Travel Services is converting its reservations network to Frame Relay to connect approximately 15,000 travel agency workstations at 1,000 sites. Owned by United Airlines, USAir, and Air Canada, Apollo expects response time to improve to two seconds from the current four seconds. The network will run at 56 Kbps, as opposed to current speeds of 2,400 bps to 4,800 bps. Using AT&T's InterSpan Frame Relay Service, running over a TCP/IP network platform, the service also will offer mesh networking between travel agencies, without having to go through the Apollo head-end for e-mail and other purposes [10-31].

Voice over Frame Relay, over both private and public networks, is an option that recently has created a lot of interest. Although the voice stream is subject to intrinsic Frame Relay delays and although the service is overhead-intensive for such an application, it does enable the user organization to take advantage of occasional excess bandwidth to connect voice for *free*. Advanced compression techniques such as standards-based ACELP (Algebraic Code-Excited Linear Prediction) and LD-CELP (Low Delay-Code Excited Linear Prediction) appear to offer the best quality voice at 16 Kbps, 8 Kbps, and even 4.8 Kbps [10-28].

Switched Multimegabit Data Service (SMDS)

Switched Multimegabit Data Service (*SMDS*) is an offshoot of the *Distributed Queue Dual Bus* (*DQDB*) technology defined by the IEEE 802.6 standard for *Metropolitan Area Networks* (*MANs*), as a means of extending the reach of the LAN across a metropolitan area. The original work on the DQDB concept was done at the University of Western Australia where it was known as *Queued Packet Synchronous Exchange* (*QPSX*). Subsequently, the original technology was licensed to QPSX Ltd., formed by the University of Western Australia and Telecom Australia [10-6]. The commercial success of SMDS is attributable to further development work by Bellcore, at the request of the RBOCs. Bell Atlantic introduced the first commercial offering in 1992 at 45 Mbps, based on a test implementation at Temple University [10-32].

Since then, SMDS enjoyed limited, short-lived success in the United States through deployment by most of the RBOCs and GTE. As the RBOCs and their subsidiary BOCs primarily are LECs (Local Exchange Carriers) limited to providing service within the confines of the LATA, they have exhibited particular interest in network technologies that are appropriate for providing service in confined geographic areas. This geographical limitation of SMDS, therefore, does not pose a practical limitation for the LECs. Additionally, SMDS is extendible across the WAN.

While the RBOCs deployed SMDS fairly aggressively in the past, their ardor cooled noticeably, beginning in 1996. Clearly, the popularity of Frame Relay affected SMDS adversely. Further, and as the Telecommunications Act of 1996 promises eventually to release them from the artificial LATA constraints, they also increasingly are deploying ATM, which is not geographically restrained and which is much more flexible. By way of example, US West pulled the plug on SMDS on April 1, 1996, citing its long-term interest in ATM and the relative popularity of its competing Transparent LAN Service. Despite its having actively promoting SMDS, US West peaked at three customers – all in the Minneapolis-St. Paul area [10-33]. NYNEX (now Bell Atlantic), by the way, decided early on to skip over SMDS in favor of ATM [10-34]. While other RBOCs have remained loyal to SMDS, they also likely have similar plans. Ameritech, for instance, peaked at about 80 in its five-state region. MCI Communications (now MCI Worldcom) peaked at approximately 130 SMDS customers [10-35], and although they still support those remaining, they no longer offer the service to new customers. Pacific Bell (now part of SBC) also no longer offers the service, but Bell South continues to offer SMDS at access speeds of 56/64 Kbps and 1.544 Mbps. If the above sounds negative, it's because SMDS by no means is the ultimate answer for all networking requirements – the ultimate solution appears to be ATM, upon which B-ISDN is founded. SMDS really has little future, outside of niche domestic markets. For data communications, Frame Relay and native LAN services have received a much better, and much longer-lasting reception.

A notable departure from the gloom and doom scenario surrounding SMDS is the continuing commitment of Bell Atlantic. In its original territory (i.e., not including the acquisition of NYNEX), SMDS has continued to enjoy a level of acceptance that is more than modest. In fact, Bell Atlantic had a customer base of approximately 2,000 SMDS customers in May 1999. Given the emphasis on the college and university, health care, and governments markets – which are well-served by the service and which vertical markets are well-represented in Bell Atlantic's franchised serving areas – this anomaly really isn't that surprising. Temple University, the original test site, has expanded its SMDS network considerably over the past few years, serving 30 sites at speeds up to 34 Mbps (the E-3 version of DS-3). Notably, however, this continuing commitment and expansion of SMDS runs over ATM in the carrier backbone, thereby protecting Temple University's investment in SMDS while providing a smooth, gradual transition path to ATM [10-36].

SMDS also has enjoyed moderate success in Western Europe, where the nations tend to be small in geographic terms and where the population density of large businesses is high in the major metropolitan areas. The European version of SMDS is known as *CBDS (Connectionless Broadband Data Service)*. CBDS is available in Australia (Telecom Australia), Germany (DBP), and England (BT). In something of a last-gasp marketing effort, several U.S. carriers have renamed SMDS along European lines. Bell South renamed its service *Connectionless Data Service* (*CDS*), while Ameritech chose *Connectionless Broadband Data Service* (*CBDS*).

The history of the SMDS Interest Group (SIG) underscores the overall failure of SMDS. The SIG was a consortium of vendors and consultants that worked to advance SMDS as a standards-based, interoperable solution for high-performance data connectivity. On June 17, 1997, the Board of Trustees announced that its mission of advancing the cause of SMDS was fulfilled and the group was disbanded, turning all its responsibilities over to unnamed regional organizations. Essentially, the SIG lost the battle, declared victory, and went home. Despite all of this negativity, SMDS remains an excellent service technology that performs well in serving the needs of niche markets, both vertical and geographic. SMDS is more than a historical footnote that promoted the cause of high-performance data communications. It is worth exploring further.

SMDS Defined

According to Bellcore (now Telcordia Technologies), SMDS is a high-speed, connectionless, public, packet-switching service that extends Local Area Network-like performance beyond the subscriber's premises, across a metropolitan or wide area. SMDS is a MAN network service based on cell-switching technology. Generally delivered over a SONET ring, SMDS has a maximum effective serving radius of approximately 30 miles (50 Km). SMDS is a connectionless service that accepts user data in the form of a Protocol Data Unit (PDU) up to 9,188 octets in length over access lines of up to 45 Mbps (T-3). The user data is segmented into 53-octet cells, 48 octets of which are payload and 5 octets of which are overhead. The segmentation process can occur either at the network node or in the user equipment.

SMDS is designed to support LAN-to-LAN traffic under the IEEE 802.6 standards, although other data applications are supported effectively. SMDS offers excellent performance characteristics, including a guaranteed rate of access, transport, and delivery. SMDS also provides a smooth migration path to ATM. In fact, the 53-octet cell format was chosen specifically for this reason.

SMDS Standards

The IEEE developed the original MAN standard, 802.6. That standard was intended for the interconnection of DQDB subnetworks within metropolitan areas. The DQDB subnetworks can provide data concentration, routing, or switching functions; or can interconnect workstations, hosts, and LANs over a metropolitan area [10-8]. According to the IEEE, the 802.6 DQDB standard is intended to provide "a high-speed shared medium access protocol for use of a dual, counter-flowing, unidirectional bus subnetwork." Bellcore then modified that standard to develop SMDS, a carrier service based on the 802.6 concept and intent. The scope of the standard includes two layers: DQDB and Physical. The two layers contain the defined functions of Medium Access Control (MAC), connection-oriented service, and isochronous service.

Medium Access Control (MAC) is defined in support of Logical Link Control (LLC) for purposes of establishing network compatibility at the link level with other networks, such as Ethernet, FDDI, and Token Ring. Connectionless service is supported at this level.

Connection-Oriented Service is defined for asynchronous communications such as signaling functions. Signaling requires a guaranteed and consistent path through the network.

Isochronous Service is defined for applications that are stream-oriented and particularly delay-sensitive. Real-time, digitized voice and video are common and realistic examples.

Bellcore issued a number of standards in the form of Technical References (TRs). The TRs cover Generic System Requirements, Access Requirements, Networking Requirements, Operations Interfaces, Frame Relay Access to SMDS, and a host of other issues relative to access, network management, billing, and operations. Bellcore also issues Technical Advisories (TAs), which are preliminary documents that ultimately become TRs.

The *SMDS Interest Group* (*SIG*), formed in 1991, released a number of technical implementation specifications that address specifics such as AppleTalk and DECnet over SMDS networks. The European SIG has developed a similar set of specifications. Rather than standards bodies, the SMDS Interest Groups were voluntary organizations of manufacturers, carriers, consultants, and other interested parties. *European Telecommunications Standards Institute* (*ETSI*) adopted most 802.6 standards elements, including many SMDS features, for the European market.

SMDS Access

Access to a SMDS network is via a dedicated digital facility up to 45 Mbps (T-3) from the *Subscriber Access Terminal* (*SAT*) through a generic interface known as the Subscriber Network Interface (SNI). Access typically is on the basis of a dedicated T-1 facility at 1.544 Mbps, or T-3 at 44.736 Mbps, although access also is provided at 56/64 Kbps. Where direct access to a SMDS network is not available, access can be accomplished via Frame Relay Network-to-Network Interface (NNI).

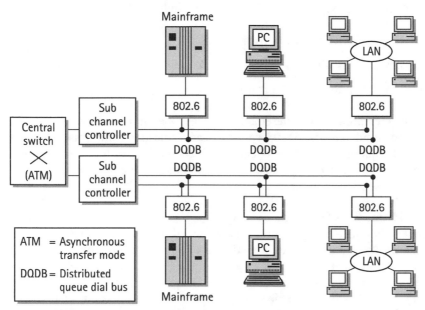

Figure 10-6 Distributed Queue Dual Bus (DQDB)

DISTRIBUTED QUEUE DUAL BUS (DQDB)

Distributed Queue Dual Bus (*DQDB*) is the IEEE 802.6 standard that Bellcore adapted for SMDS access purposes. DQDB is based on a dual-bus architecture as illustrated in Figure 10-6. Each bus is unidirectional, carrying data in 53-octet cells. As the two busses act in concert, full-duplex (FDX) transmission is supported. In order to access the SMDS network, a reservation is placed on the upstream bus. As the reserved time slots are presented on the downstream bus, the access unit, or DQDB engine, places data on those allocated time slots, which appear at intervals. The intervals of presentation are regular for delay-sensitive isochronous data (e.g., voice and video), and irregular for data applications that are tolerant of delay (e.g., LAN-to-LAN traffic). The access network is implemented in a star topology, with each loop connected to a SMDS cell switch.

SUBSCRIBER NETWORK INTERFACE (SNI)

Subscriber Network Interface (*SNI*) is generic access over a dedicated link that can be DS-0 (56/64 Kbps), DS-1 (1.544/2.048 Mbps), or DS-3 (45/34 Mbps). The access configuration on the customer premise can support either a single CPE device, or multiple devices.

SMDS INTERFACE PROTOCOL (SIP)

SMDS Interface Protocol (*SIP*) is a three-layer network access protocol, based on 802.6 and operating on the generic Subscriber Network Interface (SNI). SIP layers, which do not conform exactly to the OSI model, include the following:

- ◆ SIP Level 1: Physical & Electrical Transport
- ◆ SIP Level 2: Framing & Error Detection
- ◆ SIP Level 3: Addressing & Error Detection

The SIP segmentation process resembles that described in the case of DQDB. The user PDU is encapsulated with SMDS-specific header and trailer information and is segmented subsequently into 53-octet cells. Each cell comprises 5 octets of control information and 48 octets of payload. At the receiving end, the process of reassembly reverses the segmentation process.

DATA EXCHANGE INTERFACE (DXI)

Data Exchange Interface (*DXI*) is a protocol developed by the SMDS Interest Group, dividing the SIP functions between a DSU and a host, bridge, or router. In a DXI implementation, SIP Levels 1 and 2 are based on the ISO HDLC protocol and operate on the bridge or router and the host. SIP Level 3 operates only on the DSU and the network, across the generic SNI. This approach speeds the acceptance of SMDS because SIP can be added to a bridge or router via a software upgrade [10-34].

SIP RELAY

SIP Relay provides for Frame Relay Access, as defined by the SMDS Interest Group. Where SMDS is not available, this approach enables SMDS connectivity via Frame Relay. SIP Relay provides for the encapsulation of the SMDS Level 3 PDU, its transmission across a Frame Relay network, connection to an SMDS network, and delivery to a SMDS address. The process of final segmentation occurs at the point of Frame Relay/SMDS network interconnection.

SMDS Network

As illustrated in Figure 10-7, and as previously discussed, customer DTE gains access to the SMDS network over a dedicated digital link, which usually is in the form of a FT-1, T-1, or T-3 circuit. The DTE can connect through a Subscriber Network Interface (SNI) defined as residing in an intelligent device capable of accommodating SIP Levels 1, 2, and 3 in collaboration with the network-based Switching System (SS). Alternatively, a DXI interface might support multiple DTE; the DXI interface splits SIP functionality between the host, bridge, or router and the DSU. Dual connections are made to the Distributed Queue Dual Bus (DQDB), consisting of an upstream and a downstream bus. The busses provide connection to a cell-based Switching System that resides in the LEC network. The various SSs are interconnected by Inter-Switching System Interfaces (ISSIs) in the form of high-capacity digital trunks. Those trunks are intended to be SONET in nature, operating at OC-3 (155 Mbps) and above.

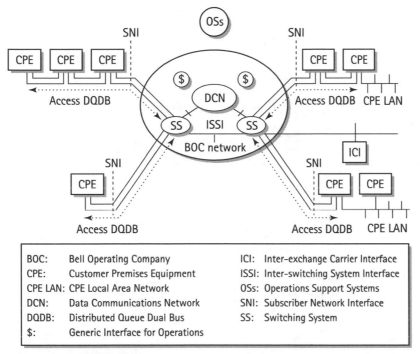

BOC:	Bell Operating Company	ICI:	Inter-exchange Carrier Interface
CPE:	Customer Premises Equipment	ISSI:	Inter-switching System Interface
CPE LAN:	CPE Local Area Network	OSs:	Operations Support Systems
DCN:	Data Communications Network	SNI:	Subscriber Network Interface
DQDB:	Distributed Queue Dual Bus	SS:	Switching System
$:	Generic Interface for Operations		

Figure 10-7 SMDS network
(Source: TR-TSV-000772, Copyright 1991, Bellcore)

The LEC Switching Systems are highly capable devices, with the ability to switch cells of data at very high speed on a connectionless basis. They contain buffers for flow control and can make alternate routing decisions in the event that inter-switch trunks are congested. The SSs contain very high-speed internal busses, in the Gbps range, to accommodate multiple users operating at speeds up to 45 Mbps.

SMDS Protocols: Segmentation and Reassembly, and Cell Structure

The user data is presented to the network in the form of a Protocol Data Unit (PDU) — up to 9,188 octets in length (see Figure 10-8). Such a PDU range accommodates virtually any native protocol, including SDLC. The DQDB protocol layer adds a header and trailer to the PDU, identifying the PDU as a data unit and providing an error control mechanism in the form of a 32-bit CRC. This initial *MAC PDU* (*Medium Access Control PDU*) then divides into 53-octet cells, known as *Segmentation Units*, which travel over time slots through the network.

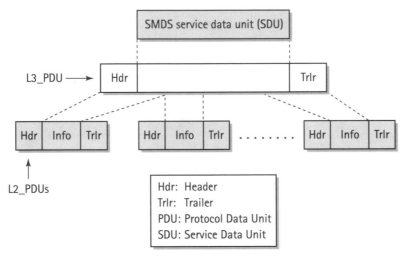

Figure 10-8 SMDS segmentation and cell structure
(Source: TR-TSV-000772, Copyright 1991, Bellcore.)

The structure of the SMDS slot is that of 53 octets, 48 octets of which are reserved for payload and the other 5 of which are overhead. The DQDB slot is divided into two segments, the Access Control field and the Segment field. The *Access Control field* (1 octet) controls access to the bus. The *Segment field* (52 octets) contains the *Segment Header* (4 octets) and the *Segment Payload* (48 octets), or user data.

Two types of SMDS slots are identified. *Queued Arbitrated* (*QA*) slots support asynchronous (non time-sensitive) data traffic. *Pre-Arbitrated* (*PA*) slots support isochronous traffic (e.g., voice and compressed video), which is delay-sensitive.

SMDS Costs

Equipment costs include some combination of SIP-capable hosts, bridges, routers, and DSUs. The DSU, also known as a *SMDSU*, typically is contained under the skin of a DS-1 or DS-3 MUX.

Network access costs include a dedicated access line to a SMDS network node. The dedicated circuit may be FT-1 (N x 64 Kbps), DS-1 (T-1 at 1.544 Mbps or E-1 at 2.048 Mbps), or DS-3 (T-3 at 45 Mbps or E-3 at 34 Mbps). Network costs also typically include a port charge and monthly usage charges, per address.

SMDS Advantages

SMDS has considerable advantages. Intended for LAN-to-LAN internetworking over the MAN, it is extendible to the WAN and has a broad range of data communications applications. Where available, an SMDS network is relatively simple to implement and reconfigure. Unlike Frame Relay, there is no requirement to establish PVCs or SVCs with a connectionless service. Rather, any-to-any connectivity can be established based on SMDS addresses. The avoidance of VCs and the scalability of SMDS make networking highly cost-effective compared with either a leased-line mesh network or a PVC-based Frame Relay network.

Further, SMDS offers excellent access control and congestion control, thereby avoiding the latency issues and exposure to data loss that are characteristic of X.25 and Frame Relay networks. These characteristics also make SMDS an excellent alternative for isochronous communications, which is intolerant of latency and loss. Finally, SMDS provides a smooth migration path to ATM via software upgrades; in fact, it was designed with ATM in mind.

SMDS Disadvantages

SMDS suffers from limited availability. Not all of the RBOCs and CAPs offer SMDS, and that support is dwindling. Primarily intended as a MAN network technology, it can be extended to the WAN, although performance becomes something of an issue as distance increases. In any event, MCI stands alone in the IXC world as supporting SMDS. Unlike Frame Relay and ATM, SMDS is limited to a public offering and doesn't make sense as a private network technology. The limited carrier support for SMDS also translates into limited manufacturer support. While large numbers of manufacturers build Frame Relay and ATM gear, you can count SMDS equipment vendors on your fingers and toes...with digits to spare. This lack of vendor support also translates into a less competitive market with small manufacturing runs and, therefore, higher equipment costs that are not likely to come down [10-32].

While SMDS performs beautifully, is cost-effective and available, it just doesn't have the horsepower (bandwidth) to compete with ATM – and it certainly isn't as flexible. Further, SMDS isn't as cost-effective as Frame Relay.

SMDS Applications

SMDS applications primarily are data in nature. Although intended for LAN internetworking in a Metropolitan Area Networking scenario, SMDS also serves to connect LAN-to-host, controller-to-host, terminal-to-host, host-to-host, and for host channel extension. SMDS also supports image networking beautifully, as well as point-of-sale networking, distributed process control, and desktop publishing. The service also can support isochronous data such as real-time digitized voice and video, although such application is unusual.

Bell Atlantic in March 1996 announced an interesting application for SMDS involving Internet Service Providers (ISPs). While still restricted to intraLATA service provisioning, Bell Atlantic's IP Routing Service (IPRS) offers a means of providing large numbers of dial-up users with analog or ISDN access. In each LATA, a single CO switch is equipped with the capability to accept that IP-addressed traffic and concentrate it through 34 Mbps SMDS pipes, accomplishing the cell segmentation process in the CO switch. At the receiving end, the ISP or intranet managers place a high-capacity switch or router with a SMDS interface. The advantage lies in the high-capacity network access, and elimination of ISDN termination equipment and banks of modems [10-37].

Calgon installed (1996) a multisite SMDS network from MCI to link a number of systems, including IBM mainframes and Token Ring LANs. Applications supported include e-mail, order processing, and inventory updates. The 56-Kbps lines connect to Cisco routers, MultiTech DSU/CSUs, a Cabletron hub, and TCP/IP and IPX network protocols. At the time, ATM was rejected for lack of standards and Frame Relay because of the high cost of multiple PVCs [10-38].

Asynchronous Transfer Mode (ATM)

Asynchronous Transfer Mode (ATM) was developed in concept by the ITU-T as an outgrowth of ISDN standards that developed in the early 1980s. While the concept of Narrowband ISDN (N-ISDN) was intriguing, it soon became clear that the demand would emerge for a wide range of bandwidth-intensive services that would go beyond the scope of narrowband (Nx64 Kbps) or even wideband (1.5 Mbps-45 Mbps) transmission facilities and circuit-switched connections. Given that assumption, which has since proven correct, the ITU-T cast an eye toward the future of broadband (45 Mbps, or more) networking. Broadband ISDN (B-ISDN) was the conceptual result. Although B-ISDN remains very much in the future (N-ISDN has yet to reach its potential, and may never do so), its ATM network technology foundation is beginning to make a mark in the market.

The first ATM network in the United States was a testbed gigabit network known as the *National Research and Education Network* (*NREN*). Sponsored by the U.S. government Advanced Research Project Agency (ARPA) and the *National Science Foundation* (*NSF*), the project began in 1990. Currently, there are a number of such testbed networks in the United States. In Europe, the *Research for Advanced Communications in Europe* (*RACE*) project 1022 was initialized in 1987 to demonstrate the feasibility of ATM. RACE is sponsored by a consortium of carriers, end users, and universities. The *R1022 ATM Technology Testbed* (*RATT*) has exceeded expectations. RACE project 2061, also known as *EXPLOIT*, is a more recent RACE project intended to prove the viability of *Integrated Broadband Communications* (*IBC*) in the European Community (EC). In Japan, Nippon Telephone and Telegraph (NTT) has embarked on a project with the cooperation of manufacturers to replace the existing network trunk structure with ATM by 2005 [10-39].

Since the early 1990s, at the very least, ATM has been highly touted as the ultimate network switching solution, given its high speed, its ability to serve all information types, and its ability to guarantee each information type an appropriate Quality of Service (QoS). While ATM has been accepted more slowly than many expected, it clearly is on the rise. Toward the end of 1998, Datapro Information Services, a subsidiary of Gartner Group Inc., conducted a global networking services user survey. Of the survey respondents, 63 percent of U.S. users used Frame Relay, and 31 percent used ATM. Two years into the future, the 68 percent of the respondents indicated that they would be using Frame Relay, and 50 percent would be using ATM. Internationally, 42 percent used Frame Relay, and 9 percent, ATM. The international forecasts two years hence were 46 percent for Frame Relay, and 23 percent for ATM. While ATM clearly will experience the greater growth, it started from a much smaller base. Frame Relay will remain the service of choice, and the two will coexist. In terms of service revenues, Gartner Group figures that ATM increased from $50-60 million in 1996, to $210-$230 million in 1998, and is projected to exceed $600 million by 2000. These estimates are impressive for ATM, but pale in comparison to Frame Relay, which reached $1.1-$1.3 billion in 1996 and $3.7-$4.1 billion in 1998, and are estimated to reach as much as $7.5 billion by 2000 [10-40]. While ATM ultimately may replace all of the circuit- and packet- and frame-switching technologies currently in place, that day is a long time away. The separate voice and data networks currently offer good price performance, and they can overlap from an applications perspective, although with limitations. ATM is a *fork-lift upgrade*, for which there currently exists no broad-based compelling justification, except in the backbone. When backbones come under pressure, performance becomes more a consideration than raw cost. The pressure currently is in the data backbones, which are growing at incredible rates, and which demand immediate solutions. Placing ATM in the data backbones provides that solution, bringing with it the flexibility to support voice and other information streams as needs arise.

ATM Defined

Asynchronous Transfer Mode (ATM) is a fast-packet, connection-oriented, cell-switching technology for broadband signals. ATM is designed, from concept up, to accommodate any form of information — voice, facsimile, data, video, and image — whether compressed or uncompressed, at broadband speeds and on an unbiased basis. Further, all such data can be supported with a very small set of network protocols, regardless of whether the network is local, metropolitan, or wide area in nature. In terms of user access rates, ATM generally operates at minimum access speeds of DS-1 and DS-3; OC-1 (51.84 Mbps) and OC-3 (155 Mbps) are not uncommon. The backbone transmission rates are DS-3 and OC-1 at a minimum, and generally at OC-3 or better. The ATM Forum more recently and reluctantly approved a

25.6 Mbps ATM LAN standard , with strong encouragement from the *ATM 25 Alliance* [10-41]. While contemporary standards (e.g., 100BaseT and Gigabit Ethernet) overpower this LAN version, and as the ATM Alliance has disbanded, ATM increasingly is finding its way into the LAN domain as a backbone technology running at 155/622 Mbps. ATM is highly scalable in terms of both bandwidth and geographic reach.

ATM can be distinguished from Frame Relay in that ATM is a backbone network technology, whereas Frame Relay is an access technology. ATM also has application on-premise through LAN switches, hubs, routers, and the like; many PBXs now are equipped with ATM switching matrixes, as well.

ATM data consists of three basic types. *Constant Bit Rate* (*CBR*) traffic, such as uncompressed voice based on PCM (Pulse Code Modulation) and TDM (Time Division Multiplexing), requires the presentation of time slots on a regular and unswerving basis. (See the discussion of channelized T-carrier in Chapter 8.) *Variable Bit Rate* (*VBR*) traffic, such as compressed voice and video, and bursty data traffic, requires access to time slots at a rate that can vary dramatically from time to time. *Available Bit Rate* (*ABR*) traffic, such as bursty LAN traffic, can deal with time slot access on an as-available basis. ABR traffic also is known as *best-effort ATM*. As discussed later in this chapter, all earlier classes of service are now specified as CBR, VBR, and ABR in the ATM world; in each case, with specifically defined Quality of Service (QoS) parameters.

In any case, the data is presented to and accepted by the network on an *asynchronous* (start/stop) basis, and the ATM switches *transfer* the data from switch to switch in a hop-by-hop *mode* — hence the term *Asynchronous Transfer Mode*. The optical fiber transmission facilities, of course, are highly synchronized. The ATM switch and all other network elements are synchronized with the pipe, as well.

The user data is sent to the network over a digital facility. At the workstation, router, or ATM switch, data is organized into 48-octet cells. Each cell is prepended with a header of 5 octets and multiplexed, contending for access to a broadband facility — ideally SONET in nature. As the ATM cell is 53 octets in length, with 48 octets of payload and 5 octets of overhead, it is reminiscent of SMDS. SMDS, as discussed earlier in this chapter, actually is a variation of the ATM theme. While SMDS initially provided an immediate solution for certain applications, it since has been relegated to niche applications, and largely has faded away in favor of Frame Relay and ATM. ATM is intended to be the ultimate and complete network transport solution, supporting a theoretically infinite range of services via B-ISDN.

The small cell size reaps several advantages. First, it can accommodate any form of data — digital voice, facsimile, data, video, and so on. Second, the fixed length of the cell offers the network switches the advantage of predictability, as compared to a variable length frame. Third, the fixed cell size facilitates the implementation of switching functions in firmware (i.e., silicon); this enables processes to be accomplished at significantly greater speed than does software. These two considerations yield decreased delay, as data moves through the switching systems and across the transmission links in frequent little blasts. Long, and especially variable, frames occupy the attention of the network for relatively long periods of time, causing delay as other data waits its turn.

ATM is the first network technology to offer true *Bandwidth-on-Demand*, as the bandwidth can vary during the course of the call [10-7]. True enough, other services offer bandwidth that can vary with each call, but none can offer the ability to adjust the amount of bandwidth required to support a call once the call is established. For example, a high-quality videoconference might require 1.544 Mbps (T-1) capacity as a rule. Yet, with the sophistication of contemporary compression techniques, that call might require much less bandwidth much of the time. Once that call is set up, a full T-1 is dedicated to it, regardless of the actual bandwidth requirement moment by moment. ATM is not so rigid; it can adapt dynamically to the bandwidth actually required.

As is the case with Frame Relay and SMDS, ATM networks do not provide for error detection or correction. Neither do they provide for protocol conversion. Rather, these responsibilities shift to the end user. The advantages are increased speed of switching, elimination of associated delay, and reduced cost as the ATM switches require less memory and processing power.

ATM Standards

The ITU-T sets ATM standards. The first set of B-ISDN standards recommendations began in 1988, inexorably linking ATM and B-ISDN. In 1992, the ATM Forum formed as a voluntary organization of manufacturers, consultants, and interested parties; that forum develops interoperability specifications based on member consensus. The Internet Engineering TaskForce (IETF) also has gotten involved because ATM has significant implications relative to the Internet, as least at a backbone level. The Frame Relay Forum (FRF) also works with the ATM Forum in the development and publishing of joint Implementation Agreements (IAs) that specify the protocol interworking functions between Frame Relay and ATM networks. While a lot of work remains to be done in the arena of ATM standards, the following provides a view of some of the more important standards — as well as standards under development and review.

ITU-T Standards Recommendations of significance include:

- ◆ I.113: B-ISDN Vocabulary
- ◆ I.121: Broadband Aspects of ISDN
- ◆ I.150: B-ISDN ATM Functional Characteristics
- ◆ I.211: B-ISDN Service Aspects
- ◆ I.311: B-ISDN General Network Aspects
- ◆ I.321: B-ISDN Protocol Reference Model

- I.327: B-ISDN Functional Architecture Aspects
- I.361: B-ISDN ATM Layer Specification
- I.362: B-ISDN ATM Adaptation Layer Functional Description
- I.363: B-ISDN ATM Adaptation Layer Specification
- I.413: B-ISDN User-Network Interface
- I.432: B-ISDN User-Network Interface-Physical Layer Specification
- I.555: Frame Relay and ATM Internetworking
- I.610: B-ISDN Operations and Maintenance Principles and Functions

Significant ATM Forum Implementation Documents include the following:

- ATM User-Network Interface (UNI) Specification for PVCs
- ATM Broadband InterCarrier Interface (B-UNI) Specification
- ATM Data Exchange Interface (DXI) Specification

Internet Engineering TaskForce (IETF) RFCs (Requests for Comment) include:

- RFC 1483: Definition of Multiprotocol Encapsulation over AAL 5
- RFC 1577: Definition of Classical IP and ARP (Address Resolution Protocol) over ATM
- RFC 1821: Integration of Real-Time Services in an IP-ATM Network Architecture

In 1996, the ATM Forum realized that the plethora of ATM standards were creating confusion in the manufacturer community, and that issues of backward compatibility were developing as the newer standards leapfrogged the widespread implementations of earlier standards. To alleviate this situation, the Anchorage Accord, a milestone ATM Forum document (April 12, 1998) so named because of the meeting location, outlined which versions of ATM Forum specifications vendors should implement. ATM Forum specifications comprise approximately 60 baseline specifications for successful market entry of ATM products and services. Included are Broadband InterCarrier Interface (BICI), Interim Local Management Interface (ILMI), LAN Emulation (LANE), network management, Private Network Node Interface (PNNI), signaling, SMDS (Switched Multimegabit Data Service), and IP (Internet Protocol) over ATM, traffic management, and a number of physical interfaces. The accord also limits the conditions under which specifications are revised in order to reduce the potential for future confusion [10-42] and [10-43].

ATM Access

Access to an ATM backbone network occurs at rates of DS-1 or greater. Whether access is from an end-user CPE environment, or from a Frame Relay, X.25, or SMDS network switch, the access rate is DS-1, DS-3, or a higher rate such as OC-3 (155 Mbps) or OC-12 (622 Mbps). Access is provided through a *User Network Interface (UNI)* specified by the ATM Forum; in each case, the interface address is 20 octets in length.

User Network Interface (UNI) specifically refers to a UNI between a user device and an ATM network. A *Private UNI* is employed in a private ATM network (e.g., LAN domain), and for access to a public network. A *Public UNI* is used between switches in a public ATM network. At the UNI level, the ATM network assumes all responsibility for conversion of the user Protocol Data Unit (PDU) into ATM PDUs and cells. A variation of the UNI concept also is employed by ATM users to access a SMDS network, with the SIP Connectionless Service Protocol provided via ATM Adaption Layer (AAL) 3/4. More commonly in contemporary application, the user interface is through a DS-3 or SDH/SONET connection, although FDDI and Fibre Channel connectivity is supported, as well.

Data Exchange Interface (DXI) is a private UNI for end-user access to an ATM Network from DTE/DCE such as a bridge, router, or ATM DSU. The DXI concept enables the sharing of protocol responsibility between the user and the network provider. At the Physical Layer, the DXI permits connection via V.35, EIA 449/530, or EIA 612/613 HSSI connection. A variation of the HDLC protocol is used at the Data Link layer. The user information is encapsulated within a DXI (HDLC) frame and converted to the appropriate, class-specific ATM protocol at the DCE. The DCE assumes responsibility for functions through Segmentation and Reassembly (SAR), presenting the data to the ATM network switch in ATM cells. Several DXI modes exist that correspond to AAL 3/4 and AAL 5.

Network-to-Network Interface (NNI) also known *as B-ICI (B-ISDN InterCarrier Interface),* is a public UNI for interconnection of public networks via PVCs. NNIs exist for interconnection of ATM networks, and for interconnection of ATM networks and Frame Relay networks. Interoperability issues that need to be addressed include protocol conversion, mapping between virtual circuits, alignment of traffic management parameters, and mapping of local network management information.

Frame UNI (FUNI) is a derivative of the DXI standard. The ATM Forum developed FUNI in early 1995 to extend ATM access to smaller sites at rates from 56 Kbps to 1.544 Mbps (T1). Low-speed data enters a router, which forwards the data to the ATM switch as frames similar to Frame Relay frames. Those frames then are converted to cells.

ATM Network and Equipment

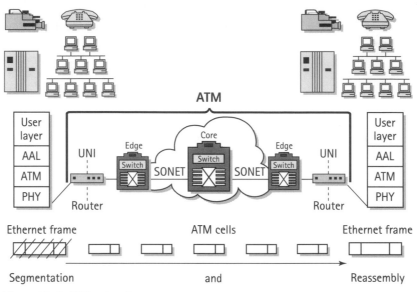

Figure 10-9 ATM network

The ATM network consists of Customer Premise Equipment (CPE), Broadband Switching Systems (BSSs) and interconnecting transmission facilities (see Figure 10-9) [10-8] and [10-44]:

- ◆ **CPE (Customer Premise Equipment)** comprises Data Terminal Equipment (DTE), Data Communications Equipment (DCE), and *true* CPE.

- ◆ **DTE** includes mainframe, mid-range, and PC-server host computers connected through the UNI.

- ◆ **DCE** comprises ATM-equipped bridges, routers, Brouters, and gateways connected through the DXI UNI. A number of vendors offer ATM-premise switches. Such switches are used for LAN interconnection, employing a highly redundant cell-switching fabric capable of switching speeds that can reach as high as OC-12 (622 Mbps).

- ◆ **CPE** includes ATM-based PBXs and video servers. While these devices currently are somewhat unusual, they are gaining market momentum, primarily in the Computer Telephony (CT) space. Such devices are connected via the UNI or the DXI.

BROADBAND SWITCHING SYSTEMS (BSSs)

BSSs (Broadband Switching Systems) are carrier exchange switches capable of broadband switching and transport. They employ highly redundant cell-switching fabrics that currently can operate in a range up to 1 Tbps. ATM switches also are highly intelligent, providing buffering, routing, and flow control, as well as segmentation and reassembly. The switches are highly redundant and fault-tolerant. They fall into two categories: core switches and edge switches:

◆ **Edge Switches** also are known as *access nodes* or *service nodes*. They are distributed in proximity to ATM users and connect to the core switches via fiber facilities, much like a CO in the voice world. In fact, they often are collocated with a CO switch. Edge switches involve cell-switching fabrics that generally operate at aggregate rates of 5 Gbps or more.

◆ **Core Switches** also are known as *backbone switches*. They generally are housed in a wire center, along with a traditional CO circuit switch or Tandem. Core switches involve cell-switching fabrics that generally operate at aggregate rates of up to 1 Tbps.

TRANSMISSION FACILITIES

Transmission facilities at the Network-to-Network (NNI) level and between network nodes are SDH/SONET fiber optic in nature; other media can be supported, but are not ideal. Local loop facilities (UNI and DXI) can be any medium capable of supporting transmission speeds of DS-1 (T-1 at 1.544, and E-1 at 2.048 Mbps) or better, although fiber always is preferable. For very short distances in a premise-based ATM environment, Category 5 UTP supports ATM speeds up to 155 Mbps; Cat 3 UTP has been proven at 25.6 Mbps for distances up to 90 meters. The developing Cat 6 standard supports ATM at greater distances and/or over longer distances because of its improved shielded configuration.

As discussed briefly in Chapter 2, Inverse Multiplexing over ATM (IMA) commonly is used for high-speed access to a public ATM network when there is a requirement for speeds above T-1, and when T-3 or Fractional T-3 (FT-3) services are not available. IMA also is used when a T-3 or FT-3 is not cost-effective, with the crossover point generally in the range of 12 Mbps or 8 T-1s. With that crossover point in mind, IMA permits as many as 8 T-1s to link together to support aggregate bandwidth of up to 12.288 Mbps (1.536 Mbps x 8). The ATM cell stream is spread across the separate T-1s in a round robin fashion, and is resynchronized and reconstituted at the edge switch. While the preferred communications link is in the form of SONET optical fiber, it's not always available. Significantly, IMA actually provides some benefit (at this bandwidth level) in the form of redundancy. As an integrated network service, ATM can support all information types, but typically requires an optical fiber link, which is susceptible to catastrophic failure. Multiple T-1 links provide some level of redundancy in an IMA scenario, as all are unlikely to fail at the same time, unless one very powerful backhoe manages to rip an entire copper cable out of the ground. And, assuming that the T-1 circuits travel different physical routes, even backhoes pose manageable threats [10-45].

ATM Protocols and Cell Structure

ATM is based on a 53-octet cell structure, comprising 48 octets of payload and 5 octets of overhead (see Figure 10-10). Unlike the SMDS cell, all 5 octets of overhead precede the payload. (In certain forms of ATM, such as AAL3/4, there are elements of overhead contained within the payload, as well.) The choice of 48 octets was a compromise between the U.S. ECSA (Exchange Carriers Standards Association) T1S1 committee and the ETSI (European Telecommunications Standards Institute). The ECSA promoted a cell size of 64 octets, while ETSI favored 32 octets, each reflecting the bandwidth required for the parochial PCM voice encoding technique. The decision to use 48 octets was a perfect mathematical compromise [10-46]. It is worth noting that the cell size and composition is very overhead intensive, at about 10 percent. Standard PCM-encoded voice, at 8 bits per sample, can deal effectively with a small cell payload. Data, on the other hand, generally is presented in much larger packets, blocks, frames, and so on. Hence, the data world would have preferred a much larger cell, while many in the voice world actually would have preferred a smaller cell. As Nikita Khrushchev is reported to have said: *If you cannot catch a bird of paradise, better take a wet hen.*

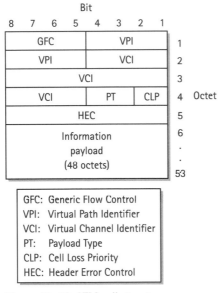

Figure 10-10 ATM cell structure
(Source: TA–NWT-00113, Copyright 1993, Bellcore.)

While this level of overhead, commonly known as the *cell tax*, might seem wasteful of bandwidth, the advantages far outweigh the drawbacks — a classic tradeoff between effectiveness and efficiency. The small cell size offers the advantage of supporting any type of data, including voice, fax, text, image, video, and multimedia — whether compressed or uncompressed. The fixed cell size offers the advantage of predictability, very unlike the variable-length frames of Frame Relay; this level of predictability yields much improved access control and congestion control. Bandwidth is cheap over SONET pipes, especially given the recent development of DWDM (Dense Wavelength Division Multiplexing). ATM switches are geared to process ATM cells at very high speeds. Finally, ATM switches currently operate in the range of 1 Tbps, or more, which makes bandwidth cheap in the switch, as well. In any event, the 48-octet payload was set as a standard for the ATM cell.

The cell comprises a header of 5 octets and a payload of 48 octets (refer to Figure 10-10). The header provides limited Data Link Layer (Layer 2) functionality, managing the allocation of the resources of the underlying Physical Layer (Layer 1) of the transmission facility, which ideally is SDH/SONET in nature. The ATM cell switches also perform Layer 1 functions such as clocking, bit encoding, and physical-medium connection. The header also is used for channel identification, thereby ensuring that all cells travel the same physical path and, therefore, arrive in sequence [10-47]. The header is structured as follows:

◆ **Generic Flow Control (GFC):** 4 bits that provide local flow control, but which field has no significance on an end-to-end basis. The 4-bit field supports 16 (2^4) GFC states. Intermediate ATM switches overwrite this field with additional VPI information [10-8]. In other words and for example, GFC is significant in order to control data flow across a UNI, but is unnecessary at a NNI (Network-to-Network Interface) level. Flow control is a congestion control mechanism, which requires that the various ATM switches and other equipment in both the network core and at the edges communicate with each other to determine the level of congestion along a defined path. If the network suffers congestion in the path, the ATM switches can buffer finite amounts of data; if the limits of the buffers are exceeded, data will be lost. To avoid that potential loss, the network must communicate with end-user devices to constrain the amount of data entering the network so as not to invite further congestion. A *rate-based* mechanism is an end-to-end, flow-control scheme that considers resources edge to edge, communicating the level of available resources through a feedback loop. This approach requires that the transmitting end-user device adjust its rate of transmission downward across the UNI in consideration of congestion. A *credit-based* approach either allows or disallows the end-user device to transmit data across the UNI, based on end-to-end consideration of whether sufficient buffer space is available on each link of the network.

◆ **Virtual Path Identifier (VPI):** 8 bits identifying the virtual path. The path is determined at the input port and is fixed for each call, but is shared among multiple calls. The path is from switch input port, through the switching matrix, to the output port, and, then across a link between any two consecutive ATM entities. The VPI and VCI jointly can be considered as a label for the allocation of resources across an end-to-end path, realizing that the label may require translation (change in value) from link to –link; this translation process would take place at the ATM switching nodes or cross-connect points. As ATM switches, like all switches, work at Layers 1 (Physical Layer) and 2 (Data Link Layer) of the OSI Reference Model, they work on a link-by-link basis.

◆ **Virtual Channel Identifier (VCI):** 16 bits identifying the virtual channel, which is established each time a call is set up in the ATM network. A VC is a unidirectional channel for transporting cells between two consecutive ATM entities (e.g., switches) across a link.

◆ **Payload Type Indicator (PTI):** 3 bits distinguishing between cells carrying user information and cells carrying service information.

◆ **Cell Loss Priority (CLP):** 1 bit identifying the priority level of the cell to determine the eligibility of that cell for discard in the event of network congestion. Clearly, some applications, such as LAN-to-LAN traffic, are tolerant of loss. Other applications, such as voice, are highly intolerant of loss.

◆ **Header Error Control (HEC):** 8 bits providing error checking of the header.

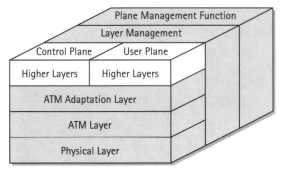

Figure 10–11 ATM protocol reference model (Source: Network VAR.)

The ATM reference model is multidimensional, with three planes and four layers, as illustrated in Figure 10-11. The bottom 2 layers of this reference model loosely compare to the Physical Layer of the OSI Reference Model. As in the OSI model, each layer of the ATM model functions independently to perform its designated functions, all layers are tightly linked, and the functions are highly coordinated. The layers of the ATM reference model are the Physical Layer, the ATM Layer, ATM Adaptation Layer, and higher layers and functions. The planes include the Control Plane, User Plane, and Management Plane.

PHYSICAL LAYER (PHY)

Physical Layer (*PHY*) functions are addressed through two sublayers: the Physical Medium and Transmission Convergence. The ATM Forum's specifications for various User Network Interfaces (UNIs) address the implementation of the Physical Layer. The *B-UNI*, or *Public UNI*, is the specification for carrier internetworks. The

UNI and DXI are Private UNIs, describing the implementation specifics for user access to the ATM network:

♦ **Physical Medium (PM)** sublayer specifies the physical and electro-optical interfaces with the transmission media, on both the transmit and receive side. Timing functions are provided at this level. SDH/SONET optical fiber is the preferred physical medium.

♦ **Transmission Convergence (TC)** sublayer handles frame generation, frame adaption, cell delineation, header error control, and cell rate decoupling. The frame generation function takes the frame of data presented by the transmitting device across the PM sublayer, for presentation to the ATM Layer and subsequent segmentation into cells. On the receive side, the TC sublayer receives data in cells and decouples it to reconstitute the frame of data, checking all the while for header errors before presenting the data to the PM sublayer — which passes the data to the end-user device across the UNI.

ATM LAYER (ATM)

ATM Layer (ATM) functions include multiplexing of cells, selection of appropriate VPIs and VCIs, generation of headers, and flow control. At this layer, all multiplexing, switching, and routing takes place for presentation to the appropriate Virtual Paths and Virtual Channels of the SONET fiber optic transport system, which interfaces through the Physical Layer.

ATM ADAPTATION LAYER (AAL)

ATM Adaptation Layer (AAL) functions are divided into two sublayers: the Convergence Sublayer (CS) and the Segmentation and Reassembly (SAR) sublayer:

♦ **Convergence Sublayer (CS)** functions are determined by the specifics of the service supported by that particular AAL. Service classes are designated as Class A, B, C, and D.

♦ **Segmentation and Reassembly (SAR)** sublayer functions segment the user data into payloads for insertion into cells, on the transmit side. On the receive side, the SAR extracts the payload from the cells and reassembles the data into the information stream as originally transmitted. In other words, the process of segmentation takes place at the ingress edge of the ATM domain. Across the entire ATM network, from switch to switch and from edge to edge, data flows in a cell stream. The cells are decoupled and the data reassembles (reconstitutes to original form) at the egress edge of the ATM domain.

♦ **AAL Types** are supported by the functions of the Convergence Sublayer (CS). There exist defined AAL Types 1, 2, 3/4 and 5, each of which supports a specific class of traffic (see Table 10-5). AAL information is nested within the payload of user information cells.

Table 10-5 ATM ADAPTATION LAYER (AAL) SERVICE CLASSES/CATEGORIES

ITU-T Service Class	Class A	Class B	Class C	Class D	Class X
AAL Type	1	2	3/4; 5 in Message Mode, only	3/4	5
ATM Forum Service Category	CBR	Real-Time VBR (rt-VBR)	Non Real-Time VBR (nrt-VBR)	UBR	ABR
Bit Rate	Constant Bit Rate (CBR)	Variable Bit Rate (VBR)	Unspecified Bit Rate (UBR)	Available Bit Rate (ABR)	
Timing Relationship, Source-Destination Pair	Required	Not Required			
Connection Mode	Connection-Oriented	Connectionless	Connection-Oriented or Connectionless		
Traffic Contract Parameters	Peak Cell Rate (PCR), Cell Delay Variation Tolerance (CDVT)	Peak Cell Rate (PCR), Cell Delay Variation Tolerance (CDVT), Sustainable Cell Rate (SCR), Maximum Burst Size (MBS), Burst Tolerance (BT)	Peak Cell Rate (PCR), Cell Delay Variation Tolerance (CDVT)	Peak Cell Rate (PCR), Cell Delay Variation Tolerance (CDVT), Minimum Cell Rate (MCR)	
Quality of Service (QoS) Parameters	Cell Delay Variation (CDV), Cell Transfer Delay (CTD), Cell Loss Ratio (CLR)	Cell Loss Ratio (CLR)	Not Specified		

ITU-T Service Class	Class A	Class B	Class C	Class D	Class X
Example Applications	Uncompressed Voice, Audio, and Video; Circuit Emulation Service (CES)	Compressed Voice, Audio, and Video; SNA	X.25; Frame Relay; Transaction Processing	SMDS; LAN Traffic; Non Real-Time Buffered Video	Signaling and Control; Network Management; E-mail; File TransferProtocol (FTP); World Wide Web (WWW); Remote LAN Access and Telecommuting; LAN internetworking; LAN Emulation (LANE); IP Traffic including VoIP (Voice over IP)

◆ AAL Type 1 supports Class A traffic, which is connection-oriented *Constant Bit Rate* (*CBR*) traffic timed between source and sink. Such traffic is stream-oriented and intolerant of delay. Isochronous traffic such as digitized, uncompressed voice are supported via Class 1 AAL, which essentially permits the emulation of a T/E-carrier circuit. All such traffic is carefully timed and must depend on a guaranteed rate of network access, transport, and delivery. Such traffic is marked as high-priority in the cell header, so it isn't delayed in transmission; such delay could considerably impact presentation quality. Class A traffic is transmitted over a Virtual Path (VP) and in a Virtual Channel (VC) appropriate for such high-priority traffic.

◆ AAL Type 2 supports Class B traffic, which is connection-oriented, Real-Time Variable Bit Rate (rt-VBR), isochronous traffic timed between source and sink. Compressed audio and video are Class B. For example, Class B traffic includes compressed voice using the relatively simple DSI (Digital Speech Interpolation) technique for silence suppression, as discussed in Chapter 8. Compressed video using the MPEG (Moving Pictures Experts Group) compression algorithms (refer to Chapter 14) also are Class B. Class B traffic is marked as high priority in the cell header and transmitted over an appropriate VP and VC.

◆ AAL Type 3/4 supports Class C or Class D traffic, which is Non Real-Time Variable Bit Rate (nrt-VBR) data traffic with no timing relationship between source and sink. Class C traffic, such as X.25 packet data and Frame Relay data, is connection-oriented VBR traffic with no timing relationship between source and sink. Class D traffic, such as LAN and SMDS data, is connectionless VBR traffic that is sensitive to loss, but not highly sensitive to delay [10-8]. AAL Type 3/4 supports Message Mode and Streaming Mode Service. **Message Mode Service** is used for framed data in which only one Interface Data Unit (IDU) is passed. In other words, it is a single-frame message of up to 65,535 octets($2^{16} - 1$). **Streaming Mode Service** is used for framed data in which more than one IDU is passed. The IDUs can be separated in time; in other words, a stream of IDUs are sent in an asynchronous mode. The IDUs can be up to 65,535 octets, with a 10-bit CRC part of the trailer added at the SAR Layer. As SMDS disappears, this AAL is all but disappearing, in favor of AAL 5.

◆ AAL Type 5 supports Class C traffic in Message Mode, only. Such traffic is Variable Bit Rate (VBR) traffic with no timing relationship between source and sink and consisting of only 1 IDU (see Figure 10-12). AAL Type 5 also is known as *SEAL* (*Simple and Efficient AAL*), as some of the overhead has been stripped out of the Convergence Layer. AAL Type 5 initially was intended solely for use in signaling and control (e.g., NNI applications) and network management (e.g., Local Management Interface, or LMI). The IDUs can vary in length, up to 65,535 octets. A 32-bit CRC check is appended to the IDU at the Convergence Layer, as part of the *trailer.* AAL 5 also supports *Class X* traffic, which is either Unspecified Bit Rate (UBR) or Available Bit Rate (ABR). Such traffic is VBR and either connection-oriented or connectionless [10-48]. AAL 5 currently is used for a wide variety of data traffic, including LAN Emulation (LANE) and IP.

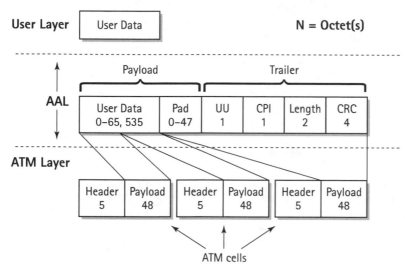

Figure 10-12 AAL Type 5 operation

ATM SERVICE CATEGORIES

ATM defined Service Categories, which relate back to AAL Types and are reflected in Table 10-5, include CBR, rt-VBR, nrt-VBR, UBR, and ABR:

♦ **CBR (Constant Bit Rate)** is a class of service that supports uncompressed voice and video, and circuit emulation. CBR traffic is characterized by a continuous rate of data flow, which is intolerant of loss and delay. Traffic parameters include *Peak Cell Rate* (*PCR*) and *Cell Delay Variation Tolerance* (*CDVT*). QoS parameters include *Cell Delay Variation* (*CDV*), *Cell Transfer Delay* (*CTD*), and *Cell Loss Ratio* (*CLR*). Uncompressed voice, audio, and video are examples of CBR traffic.

♦ **rt-VBR (Real-Time Variable Bit Rate)** traffic is bursty in nature, but depends on timing and control information to ensure the integrity of the data stream. Traffic parameters include *Peak Cell Rate* (*PCR*), *Cell Delay Variation Tolerance* (*CDVT*), *Sustainable Cell Rate* (*SCR*), *Maximum Burst Size* (*MBS*), and *Burst Tolerance* (*BT*). The QoS parameter is *Cell Loss Ratio* (*CLR*). Compressed voice, audio, and video are examples of rt-VBR traffic.

- ◆ **nrtVBR (Non Real-Time Variable Bit Rate)** traffic is bursty, but its non real-time nature is not dependent on loss or delay because there is time to recover. Traffic parameters include *Peak Cell Rate* (*PCR*), *Cell Delay Variation Tolerance* (*CDVT*), *Sustainable Cell Rate* (*SCR*), *Maximum Burst Size* (*MBS*), and *Burst Tolerance* (*BT*). The QoS parameter is *Cell Loss Ratio* (*CLR*). Examples include data traffic such as X.25, Frame Relay, transaction processing, SMDS, LAN-to-LAN, and non real-time buffered voice and video.

- ◆ **UBR (Unspecified Bit Rate)** traffic is a *best-effort* type. Traffic parameters include *Peak Cell Rate* (*PCR*) and *Cell Delay Variation Tolerance* (*CDVT*). No Quality of Service (QoS) commitment is made. Traditional computer applications, such as file transfer and e-mail, fall into this category.

- ◆ **ABR (Available Bit Rate)** is a best-effort category in which the network attempts to pass the maximum number of cells, but with no absolute guarantees. Subsequent to the establishment of the connection, the network may change the transfer characteristics through a flow control mechanism that communicates to the originating end-user device. This flow control feedback mechanism is in the form of *Resource Management Cells* (*RM-cells*). ABR supports VBR (Variable Bit Rate) traffic with flow control, a minimum transmission rate, and specified performance parameters. Traffic parameters include *Peak Cell Rate* (*PCR*), *Cell Delay Variation Tolerance* (*CDVT*), and *Minimum Cell Rate* (*MCR*). No Quality of Service (QoS) commitment is made. ABR service is not intended to support real-time applications.

ATM QUALITY OF SERVICE (QOS) PARAMETERS

The aforementioned references to AAL Service Classes and Service Categories would be incomplete without defining the key QoS parameters just mentioned. ATM network performance parameters are defined in ITU-T Recommendation I.356. Those parameters are used to measure B-ISDN performance of an end-to-end user-oriented connection in terms of *Quality of Service* (*QoS*), specific to each service class and category. The ATM Forum extended this standard through the definition of QoS parameters and reference configurations for the User Network Interface (UNI). The relevant ATM Forum document is Traffic Management Specification Version 4.0 (af-tm-0056.000), April 1996. QoS objectives are not strictly defined.

Performance Parameters defined by the ITU-T address accuracy, dependability, and speed. Accuracy parameters include Cell Delay Variation (CDV), Cell Error Ratio (CER), Cell Loss Ratio (CLR), Cell Misinsertion Rate (CMR), Cell Transfer Delay (CTD), and Severely Errored Cell Block Ratio (SECBR):

◆ **Cell Delay Variation (CDV)** is the variation in an individual cell's *Cell Transfer Delay* (*CTD*) and its expected transfer delay. CTD is a form of *jitter*, which, as you learned previously, can seriously degrade the quality of voice and video payloads. If cells arrive sooner than expected, the clumping can cause the *PCR* (*Peak Cell Rate*) to be exceeded, and the excess cells to be discarded. If some cells arrive too late, the result may be gaps in the received information stream. *Cell Delay Variation Tolerance* (*CDVT*) is a measurement of the maximum allowable CDV tolerance between two end stations. *Peak-to-peak CDV* is negotiated between the end station and the network; *peak-to-peak* refers to the best case compared with the worst case.

◆ **Cell Error Ratio (CER)** is a dependability parameter expressed as the ratio of the number of errored cells to the total number of transmitted cells sent over a measurement interval. CER is not negotiated.

◆ **Cell Loss Ratio (CLR)** is a dependability parameter expressed as the ratio of the number of lost cells to the number of transmitted cells. Cell loss can occur for reasons that include misdirection of cells by a switch, a congestion problem causing a discard in consideration of buffer capacity, a station exceeding its PCR resulting in cell discard, or a cell that exceeds the maximum CTD and arrives too late for consideration and processing. CLR is negotiated between the end stations and the network, and applies to the lifetime of the connection. CLR applies to all service categories except UBR.

◆ **Cell Misinsertion Rate (CMR)** is a dependability parameter expressed as the number of cells received over a time interval at a destination endpoint that were not transmitted originally by the source endpoint. CMR is expressed as a rate, rather than a ratio because the number of misinserted cells is beyond the control of the both the originating and destination endpoints. CMR can result from the corruption of a cell header, which would cause a cell to be misinserted into the cell stream of another source-destination pair of end points; in other words, the cell would be misdirected. CMR is not a negotiated parameter.

◆ **Cell Transfer Delay (CTD)** is the average time it takes a cell to transverse the network, from source to destination across a UNI. CTD is the sum of all delays imposed by coding and decoding, segmentation and reassembly, propagation across transmission media, cell processing at the nodes, queuing of the cell in input and output buffers, and loss and recovery. If a cell arrives too late at the receiving station, it may be considered lost or late, and may be disregarded. If the subject cell is a segment of a larger data packet, the entire packet must be discarded and forgotten, or retransmitted. *Maximum CTD* (*maxCTD*) is negotiated between the end stations and the network.

◆ **Severely Errored Cell Block Ratio (SECBR)** refers to a sequence of some number (*n*) of cells transmitted consecutively (sent in a block) on a given connection – perhaps between OA&M cells. SECBR is a dependability parameter expressed as the number of severely errored cell blocks compared with the total number of cell blocks sent over a period of time, or measurement interval. A severely errored cell block outcome is realized when more than some number of cells in a block are errored, lost, or misinserted. SECBR is not a negotiated parameter.

ATM TRAFFIC CONTRACT

An ATM traffic contract specifies all characteristics of a connection negotiated between a source endpoint and an ATM network. *Traffic parameters* are descriptions of the traffic characteristics of a source endpoint; they may be quantitative or qualitative in nature. Traffic parameters include Peak Cell Rate (PCR), Sustainable Cell Rate (SCR), Maximum Burst Size (MBS), and Minimum Cell Rate (MCR). A *traffic descriptor* is the entire set of traffic parameters associated with a source endpoint. The traffic descriptor is used during connection establishment:

◆ **Peak Cell Rate (PCR)** is the maximum number of cells per second, in a burst, that the network agrees to accept and transfer for a given UNI. Excess cells may be discarded by the ingress switch, or marked as eligible for discard. For CBR service, the PCR is the guaranteed Constant Bit Rate for the virtual circuit. Enforcement of the PCR enables the network to allocate sufficient resources to ensure that the QoS parameters (e.g., Cell Loss Ratio and Cell Transfer Delay) are met. PCR can apply to all service categories.

◆ **Sustainable Cell Rate (SCR)** is the maximum average rate at which the network agrees to accept cells and support their transfer from end to end for each UNI. In other words, SCR is the average throughput. Enforcement of the SCR enables the network to allocate sufficient resources to ensure that the QoS parameters (e.g., Cell Loss Ratio and Cell Transfer Delay) are met over a period of time. SCR applies to VBR services.

◆ **Maximum Burst Size (MBS)** is the maximum size of a burst of traffic that can transmit within the PCR, given the *Burst Tolerance* (*BT*) of the network. MBS is expressed as a number of cells.

◆ **Minimum Cell Rate (MCR)** is the minimum number of cells per second that the network agrees to support for a given originating endpoint across a UNI. This ABR service descriptor, expressed in cells per second, is that rate at which the originating endpoint always transmits during the course of the connection.

HIGHER LAYER PROTOCOLS AND FUNCTIONS

These relate to the specifics of the user Protocol Data Unit (PDU), such as a SDLC frame.

Control Plane functions include all aspects of network signaling and control, such as call control and connection control.

User Plane functions deal with issues of user-to-user information transfer and associated controls (e.g., flow control and error control mechanisms).

Management Plane functions involve the management of the ATM switch or hub. The Management Plane is divided into Plane Management and Layer Management. *Plane Management* acts on the management of the switch as a whole, with no layered approach. Management of and coordination between the various planes is accomplished in Plane Management. *Layer Management* acts on the management of the resources at each specific layer of the model; e.g., Operation, Administration, and Maintenance (OA&M) information.

LAN Emulation (LANE)

LAN Emulation (*LANE*) is a specification (LANE 1.0, January 1995)from the ATM Forum for an ATM service in support of native Ethernet (802.3) and Token Ring (802.5) LAN communications over an ATM network. Supported by software in the end systems (e.g., an ATM-based host, a router, or a LAN bridge – known as a *proxy* in LANE terminology), the ATM network emulates a native LAN environment. LANE acts as Layer 2 bridge in support of connectionless LAN traffic; the connection-oriented ATM service is transparent to the user application. In the LANE environment, the end system is known as a *LAN Emulation Client* (*LEC*), which connects to the ATM network over a *LAN Emulation User-to-Network Interface* (*LUNI*). The network-based *LAN Emulation Server* (*LES*) registers the LAN MAC (Medium Access Control) addresses, and resolves them against (i.e., translates them into) ATM addresses. The LES maps between MAC and ATM addresses through the *Address Resolution Protocol* (*ARP*). Each LEC (LAN Emulation Client) is assigned to an *Emulated LAN* (*ELAN*) by a network-based *LAN Emulation Configuration Server* (*LECS*), which is an optional component of LANE. Each LEC also is associated with a *Broadcast and Unknown Server* (*BUS*) that handles broadcast and multicast traffic, as well as initial unicast frames before address resolution. The BUS broadcasts queries to all stations on an ELAN in order to identify the MAC and ATM addresses of unknown edge devices; that information then is passed to the LES. Referring back to Table 10-5, LANE traffic generally is Class C Variable Bit Rate (VBR) traffic in Message Mode, and is supported over AAL 5. LANE 2.0 (July 1997) supports up to eight sets of QoS parameters, over different VCs (Virtual Channels), with different priority levels set for LANE traffic as CBR, VBR, ABR, or UBR traffic. LANE can be supported over either PVCs or SVCs. A key advantage of LANE is that it obviates the short-term requirement for wholesale changes to either applications or infrastructure. Rather, it positions the user organization for a relatively smooth future transition to true ATM WAN services.

Note, however, that LANE cannot resolve translational problems between disparate LANs (i.e., Ethernet and Token Ring); rather, a router must accomplish protocol conversion. LANE also supports only Ethernet and Token Ring; FDDI, for example, cannot be supported without the intervention of a router. Also, a router or router function is required to support communications between ELANs, which operate as closed user groups, much like a Virtual LAN (VLAN) [10-42] and [10-49] through [10-51].

MultiProtocol over ATM (MPOA)

MultiProtocol over ATM (MPOA) is a specification from the ATM Forum designed to enhance LANE by enabling interELAN communications without the intervention of a router, and the associated packet delay. MPOA provides high-performance, scalable routing functionality over an ATM platform. MPOA expands on LANE, Classical IP over ATM (RFC 1577), and the IETF's NHRP (Next Hop Resolution Protocol) in order to create a standardized notion of a virtual router within an ATM network. Between any two MPOA-capable end devices (e.g., MPOA-enhanced LANE hosts, bridges, or switches), MPOA maps routed and bridged flows of connectionless LAN traffic over cut-through ATM SVCs (Switched Virtual Channels), offloading the packet-by-packet processing steps performed by traditional routers. A route server in the ATM network contains the core intelligence to dynamically track the network topology and performance, thereby providing guaranteed bandwidth, reduced latency, and QoS. Since the routing intelligence is divorced from the packet-forwarding function, MPOA offers a scalable and flexible solution for LAN interconnectivity, corporate intranets, and multimedia applications such as distance learning, desktop videoconferencing, and collaborative work sessions. MPOA supports protocols such as Ethernet, Fast Ethernet, Token Ring, FDDI, and IP. Through the NHRP protocol from the IETF, routing entities within the MPOA network can intercommunicate to determine the most appropriate path for a communication between edge devices, on an inter-ELAN basis. MPOA essentially synthesizes bridging and routing of connectionless interLAN traffic over a connection-oriented ATM network [10-42], [10-49], and [10-51].

ATM Advantages

ATM clearly offers the great advantage of lots of bandwidth, with access rates usually at a minimum of T-1, NxT-1, FT-3, or T-3. SONET access at OC-3 (155 Mbps) and OC-12 (622 Mbps) increasingly are in demand. The backbone generally operates at a minimum of OC-3 (155 Mbps) or better, with ATM switches now supporting direct OC-192 (10 Gbps) interfaces. The advantages of SONET optical fiber, for both access and transport, include bandwidth, error performance, and fault tolerance. ATM is linked closely to SONET, which is not to say that ATM is not medium-independent. While the backbone ATM networks are designed around a SONET fiber optic transmission system, UTP and STP can attach workstations to an ATM LAN switch. The local access facilities generally are copper or microwave at the T-1 and T-3 levels, but fiber is required at higher speeds. Recently, ATM over VSATs was made available internationally to leapfrog national wireline networks that do not support ATM; rates are 8 Mbps or below, and 34/45 Mbps.

Further, ATM is the first service to offer true bandwidth-on-demand. In combination, ATM's strong error performance, access control, and congestion control yield outstanding levels of throughput. ATM also is highly flexible. It is the only technology that can operate equally well in LAN, MAN, and WAN environments. ATM also handles any form of data — voice, facsimile, data, image, video, and multimedia — and with Quality of Service levels geared to match traffic requirements. Further, the traffic can be asynchronous, synchronous, or isochronous in nature, and in any combination. Although some standards have yet to be fully defined, ATM offers interconnection with Frame Relay, SMDS, and X.25 networks. In fact, ATM increasingly is at the core of those networks, whether or not it is apparent to the end user.

Much as I discussed relative to SMDS, ATM offers mesh networking without the need for complex and expensive leased lines. As a result, network configuration and reconfiguration are much simplified. Finally, ATM networks and associated costs are highly scalable, as is the case with any VPN (Virtual Private Network) technology. In other words, the cost of the network is very much in proportion to the scale of the network in terms of attached devices, networked locations, and bandwidth requirements.

ATM Disadvantages

ATM suffers from limited availability, which is not surprising given its youth and inexperience. The incumbent LECs and IXCs all increasingly are placing ATM in the core of their data networks, due to ATM's speed, flexibility, and overall performance characteristics. The emerging competitive long-haul carriers (e.g., Qwest and Level 3) place ATM in the core of their networks, as well, primarily in support of data traffic, including VoIP (Voice over Internet Protocol). The Tier 1 Internet Access Providers (IAPs) such as MCI Worldcom also place ATM in the cores of their networks. The circuit-switched voice networks are slower to adopt ATM, as those legacy TDM-based networks do not feel the strain of growth as do the data networks; in other words, there is no compelling justification for the cost of a forklift upgrade to ATM. Despite the presence of ATM in the cores of the carrier networks, ATM generally is transparent to the end-user organization, aside from the fact that an overall improvement in performance might be noticeable.

In terms of availability to the end-user organization, ATM services remain highly limited. TDM-based networks do a fine job for voice, and at increasingly reasonable cost, given the competitive nature of the contemporary climate of deregulation. (In part, that level of competition, admittedly, is due to the low cost of VoIP over ATM in the core of carriers such as Qwest). Notably, however, the major incumbent IXCs all have announced their intentions to move away from

TDM-based, circuit-switched networks, and towards ATM-based solutions that extend directly to the end-user premises and from edge to edge, at least to those of very large end-user organizations. Sprint was the first to make such an announcement (June 1998), in the form of ION (Integrated On-Demand Network), although AT&T, with its INC (Integrated Network Connection), and MCI Worldcom, with its HyperStream ATM, soon followed suit. Each of these represents a *managed service* offering, involving carrier-owned termination equipment on the customer premises. ILECs such as GTE, Pacific Bell (SBC), and US West have made similar announcements. It is worth noting that some of these announcements were made as far back as mid-1998, yet none of these services were available commercially at the time of this writing in mid-1999. Sprint, the first company to make such an aggressive ATM service announcement, initially indicated that ION would be available to all businesses by mid-1999, and to consumers in late 1999 [10-52]. By the time I begin work on the third edition of this book, however, I do expect to see such *brochureware* translate into real services. The promise, of course, is that a single, integrated solution in the form of ATM will yield savings of 20 percent or so, in comparison to the costs of separate voice, data, and video networks. Notably, Sprint pared those cost-savings estimates down considerably from the original 70 percent, which was based on usage-based SVC costs, rather than on the current and more predictable flat-rate PVCs that it intends to deploy.

ATM is particularly limited with respect to international availability, although Western Europe clearly is an exception. Connecting from the United States even to Europe is most unusual. However, as far back as 1996, Tandem Computer and several client organizations completed an 18-month trial of ATM as a replacement for Frame Relay connections between the United States and Europe. Through the PTAT submarine fiber optic cable, they established a T3 link leased from Cable & Wireless, using Stratacom switches. The test included ABR, VBR, and CBR services, including compressed voice over VBR. Results were reported to be highly positive [10-53].

Aside from issues of availability, it should be noted that ATM is not an inexpensive technology. Complete equipment upgrade generally is required in the form of LAN switches, routers, DSUs, and so on. As noted below, the cost of carriers services is not trivial, either. It also is worth noting that much work remains to be done on ATM standards. Standards for voice and video over ATM are not solidified yet, and network-to-network interfaces have yet to be defined fully. Network management standards are a long way from complete, as you might expect with such a new technology. Finally, ATM is technically challenging, and good technicians are hard to find.

ATM Applications

ATM is intended to support any application that the contemporary mind can conceive. The driving force behind ATM development and deployment currently is that of data applications. ATM does a beautiful job of supporting point-to-point data communications, as well as point-to-multipoint data conferencing. In a high-speed, multimedia, collaborative computing environment, ATM really shines as a workgroup solution.

As a backbone technology, ATM is a true solution to bandwidth bottlenecks. For instance, a number of carriers have deployed ATM to address capacity problems in the cores of their data networks. While traditional voice carriers have not embraced ATM, they likely will do so as their legacy circuit-switched, TDM-based networks age – unless, of course, the cost of the legacy technologies can compete effectively with VoIP running over ATM backbones.

Broadband ISDN (B-ISDN)

Broadband ISDN (B-ISDN) was addressed formally in 1988 through the first set of B-ISDN standards from the ITU-T (I.121). Those standards were revised formally in 1990, and continue to experience revision and augmentation. The ATM Forum, formed in 1992, builds on those standards through the development and promotion of specifications for equipment interfaces in the ATM network. As noted previously, B-ISDN builds on the services foundation of Narrowband ISDN (N-ISDN). However, B-ISDN is based on cell-switching technology, whereas N-ISDN is a circuit-switched standard. B-ISDN makes use of ATM as the backbone network switching and transport technology, with SDH/SONET as the backbone transmission medium.

N-ISDN, as discussed in Chapter 8, generally has been less than a stunning success. Deployment of N-ISDN varies from country to country, and within each nation on a state, province, and metropolitan area basis. Generally speaking, it is not widely available now. Even where available, it generally has not enjoyed great market penetration because of high cost and lack of meaningful applications.

Opinions differ widely relative to the likely success of B-ISDN. Some analysts suggest that B-ISDN is dependent on the success of N-ISDN, while others suggest that it will leapfrog N-ISDN, becoming pervasive in the future world of the converged network. As B-ISDN prototype switches have been built and tested by all major switch manufacturers, the technology certainly exists. The uncertainty revolves around the value of the likely services to be offered, as well as the costs of deploying such a network.

Broadband ISDN (B-ISDN) Defined

B-ISDN is defined by the ITU-T as a service requiring transmission channels capable of supporting rates greater than the primary rate. The *primary rate*, of course, is defined in Primary Rate Interface/Primary Rate Access (PRI/PRA) as DS-1. In other words, B-ISDN is a set of services requiring broadband facilities at 45 Mbps (T-3) or 34 Mbps (E-3).

There are three underlying sets of technologies and standards that are absolutely critical to B-ISDN. First, SS7 is viewed as the signaling and control that supports B-ISDN, as it supports N-ISDN. Second, Asynchronous Transfer Mode (ATM) is the backbone network switching and transport technology. Third, SDH/SONET is the physical backbone network transmission technology.

B-ISDN Access

B-ISDN user access is broadband in nature, relying on SDH/SONET fiber optic transmission standards. Currently, there are two access interfaces specified. *User Network Interface A (UNI A)* operates at OC-3 rates of 155 Mbps, while *User Network Interface B (UNI B)* operates at OC-12 rates of 622 Mbps. Network-to-Network Interfaces (NNIs) will be provided for network access to B-ISDN from Frame Relay, SMDS, and N-ISDN networks.

B-ISDN Services

The ITU-T defines two types of B-ISDN services: interactive and distribution.

Interactive Services involve bidirectional transmission and include three classes of service: conversational, messaging. and retrieval. Conversational services include voice, interactive data, and interactive video. *Messaging services* include compound document mail and video mail. Retrieval services include text retrieval, data retrieval, image retrieval, video retrieval, and compound document retrieval.

Distribution Services may or may not involve user presentation control. By way of example, interactive TV is a service requiring presentation control. Interactive TV actually enables the viewer to interact with the program – perhaps to select a product marketed over TV, to influence the ending of a movie, or to change the camera angle to view a football play from a different perspective. Conventional broadcast TV exemplifies a service requiring no presentation control.

B-ISDN Equipment

B-ISDN user equipment is an extension of those explored in Chapter 8. *Broadband Terminal Equipment 1 (B-TE1)* is defined as B-ISDN-compatible CPE. While the exact nature of the B-TE1 is yet to be determined, it is likely that it will take the form of ATM-compatible B-ISDN communications servers. Those servers will combine the functions of a PBX, data switch, and video switch. At the extreme, they will take the form of ATM-based multimedia communications servers.

Broadband Terminal Equipment Type 2 (B-TE2) is defined as terminal equipment that supports a broadband interface other than B-ISDN. Terminal Equipment Type 2 (TE2) continues to be defined as terminal equipment that supports an interface other than ISDN. Both B-TE2 and TE2 equipment will interface with the network through a *Broadband Terminal Adapter (B-TA)*.

B-ISDN Costs

B-ISDN implementation costs cannot be determined now, although they will be very high. Carrier network costs will include investments in ATM switches and SDH/SONET fiber optic transmission facilities. User investments in totally new hardware and software will be non-trivial, to say the least.

B-ISDN Advantages

B-ISDN will have the clear advantage of being standards-based. As previously noted, ISDN is based on probably the most carefully thought out and documented set of standards in the history of the planet. Unfortunately, the standards actually are standards recommendations, which have not been applied universally on the same basis. Whether or not B-ISDN standards recommendations will suffer the same remains to be seen.

N-ISDN was intended to be available universally. This hasn't happened, of course. We also will have to wait and see if B-ISDN also suffers from lack of availability. In all likelihood, the high cost of implementing B-ISDN will restrict its availability and use to areas where there exist large concentrations of customers with pockets deep enough to afford the service. Where there is sufficient density of demand, their carriers certainly will deploy the underlying technologies.

B-ISDN will support connections that are switched, permanent, semi-permanent, point-to-point, and multipoint. It will support services that are on-demand, reserved, and permanent – and either connection-oriented or connectionless in nature.

Based on the foundation technologies of SS7, ATM, and SONET, B-ISDN will offer significant advantages. Those advantages include broadband switching and transmission, bandwidth-on-demand, and the ability to accommodate all forms of data on a highly flexible basis. Finally, B-ISDN is *future-proof* – there are no understudy service technologies waiting in the wings to supersede B-ISDN.

B-ISDN Disadvantages

If all this seems too good to be true, it's because it is! As Aesop noted in the 6th century B.C., *Every truth has two sides; it is well to look at both, before we commit ourselves to either.* (*The Mule* from *Aesop's Fables*, translated by Thomas James). So it is with Broadband ISDN.

B-ISDN standards are in their developmental infancy. True enough, the underlying technologies are well on their way, but B-ISDN really hasn't been well-defined at this point. When those standards recommendations are set over the next few decades, they likely will remain open to interpretation, as has been the case with N-ISDN. Additionally, the cost of implementing B-ISDN will be very high – and certainly not for everyone.

B-ISDN Applications

B-ISDN applications are all futures, including virtually anything you can imagine, short of teleportation, which likely will be reserved for *Star Trek* reruns. B-ISDN certainly will support any form of data communications we can imagine; connectivity will be supported among any imaginable combination of hosts, workstations, LANs, and servers ... and across any distance. Voice, data, video, and image communications will be supported in the ultimate form of high-resolution multimedia.

High-Definition TV (HDTV) will be supported along with the rest, and on an interactive basis. Large, high-resolution, digital display technologies will replace the TV set and computer monitor, enabling future generations to experience the unbridled joy of interacting with their favorite talk show host on a multimedia basis ... and live (in real time).

Advanced Intelligent Networks (AINs)

Once upon a time, the networks were truly *dumb*. Through the 1960s, and even into the 1970s, they remained fairly dumb. In other words, the networks were composed largely of switches and pipes that could do little more than connect calls as directed, based on a hierarchical order of limited switching intelligence. That intelligence was in the form of very limited programmed logic, housed in databases that interacted at a minimal level. In other words, each switch performed its own job, with little thought of the network as a whole.

Intelligent Network, Version 1 (IN/1) was born in 1976, with the introduction of IN-WATS (800) services and the first Common Channel Signaling (CCS) system. IN/1 provided for the switches to consult centralized, service- and customer-specific databases (see Figure 10-13) for routing instructions and authorization code verification. NI/1 services include INWATS, calling card verification, and Virtual Private Networks (VPNs).

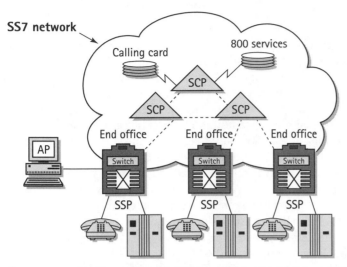

Figure 10-13 Intelligent Network (IN) supporting 800 Services and credit card verification

The linchpin of the intelligent network is the *Service Creation Element* (*SCE*), which is a set of modular programming tools permitting services to be developed independently of the switch – the nature and capability of which can vary by manufacturer and generic. The SCE divorces the service-specific programmed logic from the switch logic, thereby enabling the independent development of the service. The service, therefore, is available to all switches in the network. The concept of a *sparse network* is one of dumb switches supported by centralized intelligence with connectivity between distributed switches and centralized logic provided over high-speed digital circuits. In the context of a complex network, this concept is highly viable in terms of both performance and economics.

The IN/1 approach was lacking in that it still required substantial programming work at both the SCE and the switch level. Bellcore (now Telcordia Technologies) research led to the development of IN/2, which required substantial investment in the end offices. IN/2 was dropped in favor of IN/1+, the current version of AIN [10-54].

AIN Defined

Bellcore defined AIN in the early 1980s as AIN Software Release 1.0. This release is intended to provide a generic and modular set of tools that enable the creation, deployment, and management of services on a flexible basis. The software tools yield a suite of service offerings that are accessible to all network switches, but which operate independently from the switch logic. The services, therefore, can be defined, developed, and deployed quickly, and in a multivendor environment.

The depth and complexity of AIN Software Release 1 caused the telcos to move forward with their own various AIN releases, known as Releases 0.X. All Releases 0.X are fully compatible with Bellcore's Release 1.0, which may never be implemented in its original and defined form. AIN Release 0.0 addresses basic call modeling functions for Service Switching Points (SSPs) and database functions for Service Control Points (SCPs). AIN Release 0.1 defines generic call model for interaction between SSPs and SCPs; it includes features in support of N-ISDN services. AIN Release 0.2 adds Intelligent Peripherals (IPs) [10-54].

Characteristics of AINs include service creation toolkits, which enable the creation of centralized logic residing in centralized databases for the development and delivery of features across the network. AINs support all ISDN Features, including Caller ID, Selective Call Blocking, and Distinctive Ringing. Finally, AINs are intended to provide support for *Personal Communications Services* (*PCS*), which permit subscribed features to be supported across networks of all types. PCS, not to be confused with the "PCS" cellular service, currently is conceptual.

Service Creation Environment (SCE)

The *Service Creation Environment* (*SCE*) is the key distinction of an AIN. The SCE offers the carrier a toolkit for the development of service offerings, which can be provided on a network basis. The services can be generic or customer-specific. Often, you can create the customer-specific services through the linking of generic services and the varying of the available options and parameters. Additionally, the SCE can be opened to the user organization that then can customize the service offering as desired.

AIN Architecture

The architecture of the AIN differs greatly from that of the traditional network, and even from that of IN/1. Those differences largely deal with the nature and location of the programmed logic and the databases, which drive the service offerings. The AIN architecture (refer to Figure 10-14) includes SS7, Service Switching Points, Signal Transfer Points, Service Management Systems, Adjunct Processors, and Intelligent Peripherals.

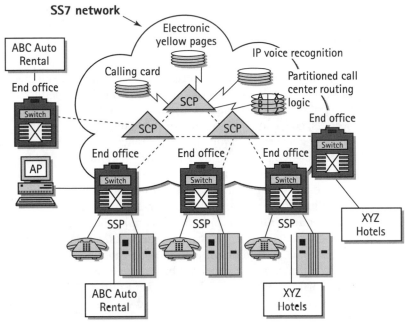

Figure 10-14 Advanced Intelligent Network (AIN) configuration supporting networked
        call centers

Common Channel Signaling System 7 (SS7) as previously discussed, is an out-
of-band signaling system for communication between devices in the carrier networks. SS7 is an absolute requirement for both ISDN and AIN. SS7 is deployed
throughout networks worldwide, and in support of all advanced networks and
network services.

Service Switching Points (SSPs) are PSTN switches that act on the instructions
dictated by AIN centralized databases. SSPs can be end offices or tandem
switches, as defined in the discussion of the PSTN (see Chapter 5).

Signal Transfer Points (STPs) are packet switches that route signaling and control
messages between SSPs and SCPs, and between STPs.

Signal Control Points (SCPs) contain all customer information in databases that
reside on centralized network servers. SCPs provide routing and other instructions
to SSPs, as requested and required.

Service Management Systems (SMSs) are network control interfaces that enable
the service provider to vary the parameters of the AIN services. Under certain circumstances, the user organization may be provided access to a partition of the SMS.

Adjunct Processors (APs) are decentralized SCPs that support service offerings limited either to a single SSP or to a regional subset of SSPs. APs might support routing tables or authorization schemes specific to a single switch or regional subset of switches.

Intelligent Peripherals (IPs) provide intelligent peripheral capabilities to enhance the delivery of certain services by offloading processing demands from the SCPs and providing a basic set of services to the SCPs. The role of the IP typically includes collection of digits, collection and playing of voice prompts, collection of voice responses and their conversion to digits, menu services, and database lookups [Grimes]. For example, voice processing and voice recognition might be implemented in support of the processing of "collect" calls. Services such as MCI's 1-800-COLLECT enable the processing of a collect or third-party, billed call without operator intervention. Voice recognition also can be used for *voice printing*, which permits user authentication in highly secure applications. A number of LECs provide automated directory assistance services, accomplishing database lookups based on voice recognition inputs through Intelligent Peripherals. As the term "IP" (Intelligent Peripheral) has become confusing with the advent of services and networks based on "IP" (Internet Protocol), the term *SRF (Special Resource Function)* often is used to describe these peripherals and the functions they perform.

AIN Services

AIN services truly are open to the imagination. However, the availability of AINs is very uneven within the United States and, certainly, around the world. AIN services are of wide variety, including the following:

- ◆ *Find-Me Service* provides flexible and selective call forwarding. The numbers to which the calls are to be forwarded can be programmed and reprogrammed from any location. Caller priority access can be subject to entry of proper passwords provided by the called party. Such capabilities have appeared in the commercial market, based on Intelligent Peripherals (IPs) known as Personal Assistants. Such systems also provide for scheduling of follow-up calls, provide scheduled reminder messages, and maintain contact lists [10-55].

- ◆ *Follow-Me Service* provides for call forwarding on a predetermined schedule. A telecommuter, for instance, might have the network forward calls to the home office three days a week during normal business hours. Calls would be directed to the traditional office two days a week. Calls clearly outside of normal business hours automatically would be directed to a voicemail system.

◆ *Computer Security Service* automatically would serve to provide secure access to networked hosts based on Calling Line ID (CLID), and supplemented by authorization codes. Additionally, the network automatically would keep a log of all access and access attempts, thereby providing an audit trail.

◆ *Call Pickup Service*, also known as *Call Notification Service*, provides for calls to be answered automatically by a voice processor. The called party can be notified of a deposited voice message by pager, fax, e-mail, or other means. The caller can enter a *privilege code* provided by the called party to distinguish the priority of the calling party. To pick up the call, the called party dials a DISA (Direct Inward System Access) port on the network switch and enters password codes in a manner similar to that used to accesses contemporary voicemail systems.

◆ *Store Locator Service,* also known as *Single Number Dialing*, provides the ability to advertise a single number. The network routes the call to the closest store location in terms of either geography or time zone, based on the originating address (telephone number) of the caller. This service is deployed widely in the United States in support of pizza parlors and other businesses offering delivery services. It also is used widely for directing calls to networked incoming call centers such as reservations centers (e.g., airlines, auto rental agencies, and hotel chains).

◆ *Multilocation Extension Dialing* provides for network routing of calls based on abbreviated numbers. This VPN (Virtual Private Network) service resembles a coordinated dialing plan in a networked PBX environment.

◆ *Call Blocking* typically supports the blocking of calls to international destinations, either in total or to specific country codes. *Content Blocking* supports the blocking of calls to specific numbers, such as *900/976* numbers. This capability is deployed fairly commonly in many foreign networks, but is not widely available in the U.S. PSTN. Cellular radio providers have made extensive use of such capability to avoid cellular fraud involving certain countries in the Middle East, The Bahamas, and South and Central America. Ameritech began offering Call Control Service on a trial basis (1994), enabling residential customers to block calls to specific numbers or to all numbers except those on an allowed list. Widespread deployment of such capabilities are unlikely in the near future.

◆ *Caller Name* is a variation of Caller ID, more correctly known as Calling Line ID (CLID), with linkage to directory services. The incoming call is identified on a *Visual Display Unit* (*VDU*) by originating number and associated directory listing. The VDU can be built into the telephone or can be in the form of an adjunct unit that sits between the telephone and the circuit. In a CTI (Computer Telephony Integration) scenario, the VDU can be in the form of a PC or computer workstation.

◆ *Enhanced Call Return* enables the subscriber to access what is, in effect, a highly sophisticated, network-based voicemail system. Bell Atlantic's trial offering enables the user to call the system and enter security codes to again access to the switch and data stores. A voice announcement identifies the date, time, and phone number of the last incoming call, at which point the return call can be launched by pressing a number on the telephone keypad [10-56].

◆ *Enhanced Call Routing* is a network-based enhancement to 800 calling. The callers are presented with options that enable them to specify their needs and then be connected with the offices or individuals best able to satisfy them. MCI (now MCI Worldcom) and Stentor (Canada) began trials on such a system in early 1995, providing seamless interconnection between the U.S. and Canadian networks [10-57].

◆ *Call Completion Service* enables the Directory Assistance operator to extend the call automatically, perhaps at an additional charge. This capability is offered by cellular providers, such as US West Cellular (at no additional charge), to avoid accidents caused by "driving and dialing."

◆ *Number Portability* serves to provide portability of telephone numbers such as INWATS and *900* numbers. This function is utilized increasingly as the regulators insist on portability of local numbers between LECs (Local Exchange Carriers). *Local Number Portability* (*LNP*) is essential to facilitate local competition, as decreed by the Telecommunications Act of 1996.

AIN Futures

The future of the AIN, as defined by Bellcore, is a bit uncertain. GTE and each of the RBOCs and IXCs have developed their own versions of IN in support of 800 services, calling card verification, and various other services. Whether they will move toward the standard version is not clear, although it appears unlikely. AINs will be implemented across the major carriers; in fact, they already have been deployed in part. As AIN capabilities roll out on a gradual basis, we likely never will see headlines announcing the arrival of AIN. Rather, it has crept into the networks and will continue to do so. Driving forces for the continuing rollout of such capabilities include FCC (May 4, 1995) and state PUC decisions in support of Caller ID and Name ID, which require SS7 and some level of AIN. A number of carriers have offered automated Directory Assistance; that trend is likely to continue. The Telecommunications Act of 1996 introduced local competition and the states have taken the initiative of requiring local number portability and equal access at a local exchange level — AINs are key to implementing such flexibility.

More exotic AIN functionality, as illustrated in Figure 10-14, involves a reservation system taking advantage of processing power embedded in the network; indeed, the following approximate scenario has been followed in several cases. A hotel reservation network might involve incoming call centers in New York, Chicago, and San Francisco. Those call centers are networked through AT&T so callers might be directed to the closest call center that can handle the call based on criteria such as queue length, average holding time, and priority level of the caller as determined by Caller ID or PIN number. In cooperation with a third-party vendor, the hotel company might write a generic software program to accomplish the routing of calls. That program would enable inquiries against a relational database in which resides customer profiles so calls can be handled in the most appropriate way. The program and database might reside on a centralized computer platform located in the Chicago call center, in the data center of the third-party vendor, or perhaps even in the carrier's wire center. The centralized network control and routing system would make frequent status checks against the individual ACDs in the call centers to determine traffic load and make performance comparisons against Quality of Service parameters, which are user-definable. Based on this process, each call would be routed in the most effective manner. Once this system is deployed and performing effectively, it could be made available on a licensed basis to other hotel chains, rental car agencies, and other reservation networks. Each licensed user then might have similar capabilities, with system administrators remotely accessing physical and logical partitions of the programmed logic and databases to support their own reservation network supported by MCI Worldcom or Sprint. Through the development of such a scenario, multiple users take advantage of computer and database technologies embedded in the carrier network, and supporting multiple reservation networks. The interaction between the carriers takes place over SS7 links.

These types of services don't necessarily require broadband networks to support them, although broadband is always good. For that matter and in this world oriented toward instant gratification, more is always better and faster is better, still. Broadband networks certainly fill that need with more bandwidth that supports faster communications. Into the future, the true potential of AINs will be realized only over broadband networks that will be ATM-based, SS7-supported, and multimedia-ready.

References

[10-1]   Flanagan, William A. *Frames, Packets and Cells in Broadband Networking*. Telecom Library, Inc., 1991.

[10-2]   "Frame relay on the rise." *Network World*, May 17, 1999.

[10-3]   Cooney, Michael. "Hypercom Ups Brand Office Ante with New Central FRAD." *Network World*, February 26, 1996.

[10-4]   Cooney, Michael. "Trio Targets Central Office FRAD Market." *Network World*, April 1, 1996.

[10-5]   Ball, David. "CO FRADs: A New Service Model." *Telecommunications*, April 1998.

[10-6]   Minoli, Daniel. *Enterprise Networking: Fractional T1 to SONET, Frame Relay to BISDN*. Artech House, 1993.

[10-7]   Spohn, Darren L. *Data Network Design*. McGraw-Hill, Inc., 1993.

[10-8]   Miller, Mark A. *Analyzing Broadband Networks: Frame Relay, SMDS, & ATM, Second Edition*. M&T Books, 1997.

[10-9]   Hindman, Steve. "SNA over Frame Relay." *Telecommunications*, February 1999.

[10-10]   Rohde, David. "AT&T serves up voice on frame." *Network World*, May 17, 1999.

[10-11]   "A Discussion of Voice over Frame Relay." www.frforum.com. October 1996.

[10-12]   Flanagan, William A. *Voice Over Frame Relay*. Flatiron Publishing, 1997.

[10-13]   Minoli, Dan and English, Michelle. "Voice Over Frame Relay: Overview" *IT Continuous* Services, March 26, 1999.

[10-14]   Packet Voice Primer. Cisco Systems. http://cio.cisco.com/warp/public/cc/sol/mkt/ent/gen/packv_in.html.

[10-15]   Matusow, David. "Giving voice a boost in frame relay nets." *Network World*, May 4, 1998.

[10-16]   Greene, Tim. "Talk is cheap with frame relay." *Network World*, January 18, 1999.

[10-17]   Willis, David. "Listen Up! Cisco Now Does Voice." *Network Computing*, April 1, 1998.

[10-18]   Newman, David, Melson, Brent, and Kuman, Siva S. "Imperfect Pitch." *Data Communications*, September 1996.

[10-19]   Lindstrom, Annie. "Speaking in frames." *America's Network*, June 15, 1998.

[10-20]   Krautkremer, Todd. "Answering the call." *Communications News*, October 1998.

[10-21]   Riggs, Brian. "Frame-Relay Tariffs Spook Users." *LAN Times*, November 20, 1995.

[10-22]   Liebermann, Robert and Szoke, Peter. "How to Size Frame Relay Access for Interconnecting Local Nets." *Network World*, May 6, 1996.

[10-23]   www.cicat.com

[10-24]   Rohde, David. "AT&T, MCI Worldcom heat up local frame relay."
           Network World, December 7, 1998.

[10-25]   Rohde, David. "Qwest throws down pricing gauntlet." *Network World*,
           December 14, 1998.

[10-26]   Willis, David. "Switching On Frame Relay SVCs." *Network Computing*,
           February 22, 1999.

[10-27]   Rohde, David and Gittlen, Sandra. "AT&T frame relay service goes
           down for the count." *Network World*, April 20, 1998.

[10-28]   Rohde, David and Gittlen, Sandra. "AT&T offers facts about frame
           fiasco." *Network World*, April 20, 1998.

[10-29]   Reardon, Marguerite. "Frame Relay." *Data Communications*, June 1998.

[10-30]   Riggs, Brian. "AT&T frame debacle shines light on SLAs." *LAN Times*,
           May 11, 1998.

[10-31]   Thyfault, Mary E. "Frame Relay Travel Net Set." *Information Week*,
           December 25, 1995.

[10-32]   Anderson, Patricia. "Switched Multi-megabit Data Service (SMDS)."
           Datapro Communications Analyst. Datapro Information Services
           Group, August 1995.

[10-33]   Rendleman, John. "Hitting the Wall." *Communications Week*,
           July 22, 1996.

[10-34]   Miller, Mark A. *Internetworking: A Guide to Network Communications
           LAN to LAN; LAN to WAN, Second Edition*. M&T Books, 1995.

[10-35]   Greene, Tim. "US WEST pulls out of SMDS Mart." *Network World*,
           March 11, 1996.

[10-36]   Hill, Stefan K. "SMDS/ATM: Best of both?" *America's Network*,
           May 15, 1999.

[10-37]   Rohde, David. "Bell Atlantic Breathes Internet Life into SMDS."
           Network World, April 1, 1996.

[10-38]   "Calgon Integrates Chemical Plants with SMDS".
           Communications News, February 1996.

[10-39]   "Future Directions Involving ATM." *Datapro Communications Analyst*.
           Datapro Information Services Group, November 1995.

[10-40]   Stuart, Donald. "Frame Relay and ATM Services: Progress Report." *IT
           Continuous Services*. Datapro Information Services, March 2, 1999.

[10-41]   Schatt, Dr. Stan. "Asynchronous Transfer Mode." Computer Intelligence
           InfoCorp., 1996.

[10-42]   Minoli, Daniel. "Asynchronous Transfer Mode (ATM): Technology Overview." *IT Continuous Services*. Datapro Information Services, April 15, 1998.

[10-43]   Newton, Harry. *Newton's Telecom Dictionary, 15th Edition*. Miller Freeman, Inc., February 1999.

[10-44]   Minoli, Daniel. "ATM Public Network Switching Technology." *Datapro Communications Analyst*. Datapro Information Services Group, November 1994.

[10-45]   Hurwicz, Mike. "ATM for the Rest of Us." *Network Magazine*, November 1997.

[10-46]   Minoli, Daniel. *Telecommunications Technology Handbook*. Artech House, 1991.

[10-47]   Minoli, Dan. "ATM-Based Voice: An Overview." *IT Continuous Services*. Datapro Information Group, March 25, 1999.

[10-48]   Minoli, Daniel updated by Raymond, Mark. "ATM and Cell Relay Concepts." *Datapro Communications Analyst*. Datapro Information Services Group, September 1995.

[10-49]   Amoss, John J. "ATM Standards and Status." *IT Continuous Services*. Datapro Information Group, July 14, 1998.

[10-50]   "An Overview of ATM LAN Emulation." Interphase Corporation. www.iphase.com. June 3, 1999.

[10-51]   "LAN Emulation and Multi-Protocol Over ATM." Cabletron Systems. www.cabletron.com. April 29, 1998.

[10-52]   "Bandwidth on Demand: Sprint's New Integrated Network Raises the Stakes." *Telecommunications*, August 1998.

[10-53]   Tanzille, Kevin. "ATM Swims to Strong Showing in Trans-Atlantic Trial." *Communications News*, May 1996.

[10-54]   Briere, Daniel D. and Langner, Mark. "Advanced Intelligent Networks." *Datapro Communications Analyst*. Datapro Information Services Group, November 1994.

[10-55]   Briere, Daniel and Heckert, Christine. "Watching The Demise of Calling Cards." *Network World*, March 25, 1996.

[10-56]   "Bell Atlantic Enhances Return Call." *Advanced Intelligent Network News*, May 17, 1995.

[10-57]   "MCI & Stentor Connect 800 Services as Canadian Telecom Market Heats Up." *Advanced Intelligent Network News*, May 3, 1995.

Chapter 11

Wireless Networking: Voice and Data

Hello, Shreeve! Hello, Shreeve! And now, Shreeve, good night. The first (October 21, 1915) wireless transatlantic telephone call, between H.R. Shreeve, a Bell Telephone engineer at the Eiffel Tower in Paris, France and B.B. Webb in Arlington, Virginia. Source: *Telephone: The First Hundred Years*; John Brooks.

In 1876, Alexander Graham Bell demonstrated the telephone at the Centennial Exposition of the United States in Philadelphia, Pennsylvania. From that simple demonstration of one-way transmission over a distance of several hundred feet, the copper-based telephone network grew at an astounding rate. In 1880, Bell invented the first wireless communications system, using reflected sunlight and photoelectric selenium receivers. Using this technique – however impractical – he was able to transmit intelligible speech a distance of up to 700 feet! Bell named this invention the *photophone*, later renaming it the *radiophone*, which he described as his greatest invention [11-1] and [11-2]. AT&T continued work on the technology, extending its reach to several miles. The German Naval Command made limited use of advanced devices of this sort during World War II [11-2].

Towards the end of the 19th century and not long after Bell's demonstration, a young German scientist named Heinrich Rudolf Hertz discovered the phenomenon of invisible force waves emanating for several meters around an electric spark of sufficient intensity. Classical physicists, at a loss to explain the phenomenon, theorized the existence of an unknown medium, *luminiferous ether*, which conducted that signal. Shortly thereafter, Guglielmo Marconi transmitted these *Hertzian* waves over several kilometers; he named the new technology *radio* because the waves appeared to radiate from the transmitter [11-2]. In 1886, Marconi was granted a patent for the first practical wireless telegraph, for which he shared in the 1909 Nobel Prize in physics. In the meantime (1890), Reginald Fessenden developed wireless voice communications [11-3].

The first commercial application of radio technology was that of broadcast radio, introduced in the United States in 1920. The first radio station, the Westinghouse station KDKA in Pittsburgh, Pennsylvania, inaugurated service by broadcasting returns of the Harding-Cox presidential election. On July 25, 1922, the first commercial station, WBAY owned by AT&T, began broadcasting from the Long Lines building in New York City. Its first paying customer, two months later, was the Queensborough Corporation, advertising its Hawthorne Court real estate development in Jackson Heights. In the meantime, AT&T employees supplied the programming, which consisted of vocal selections, piano recitals, poetry recitations, and other content that seems fairly tame by today's standards. Among the performances was a recitation of James Whitcomb Riley's poem "An Old Sweetheart of Mine" by Miss Edna Cunningham; there is no record of the audience reaction [11-1]. While not an immediate commercial success, radio enjoyed U.S. market penetration of 50 percent of households in 1930, 90 percent in 1940 and essentially 100 percent by 1995.

Television, while first demonstrated in 1926 by John Logie Baier – a Scottish inventor, was refined by yet other Bell Labs employees, Messrs. Frederick Eugene Ives and Frank Gray. The first public demonstration in the United States of color TV took place in 1927, between Bell Labs in Whippany, New Jersey, and Washington, D.C., where the audience included Secretary of Commerce Herbert Hoover. Vaudeville acts were included. Again, there is no record of the reaction of the audience. Delayed by the Great Depression and then World War II, commercial broadcast TV was introduced in 1946 and enjoyed success similar to that of radio [11-1]. Market penetration was estimated at 50 percent in 1955, 90 percent in 1960 and 99 percent in 1995. Wireless radio technology also was deployed early on in maritime communications, or ship-to-shore telephony and telegraphy. The first terrestrial mobile application was a one-way system employed in police radio dispatch trials in 1921 at the Detroit, Michigan Police Department [11-2] and [11-4].

The wireless industry has experienced exponential growth over the last decade – growth that is expected to continue at a pace unprecedented in the history of communications. Recent estimates from Allied Business Intelligence place the total number of wireless users worldwide at between 429 million and 777 million by 2002 [11-5].

While cellular voice telephony accounts for the vast majority of this market, a plethora of new technologies recently have emerged, with a broad set of new applications. The technologies discussed in this section include Trunk Mobile Radio (TMR), paging, cordless telephony, Wireless Office Telecommunications Systems (WOTS), cellular, Wireless LANs, Wireless Local Loop (WLL), Low Earth Orbiting Satellites (LEOs), Personal Communications Services (PCS), and Personal Digital Assistants (PDAs). Within each of these technology/application categories, there exist a number of specific technologies for discussion. Additionally, each technology can support some combination of voice, data, facsimile, video, and image applications.

Wireless is about more than being unplugged or untethered. Wireless, in full form, speaks to a fundamentally different way of working and living. Wireless communications adds the element of mobility, thereby removing the constraints of constant attachments to a physical space such as an office building, school, hospital, or home. Yet, wireless communications technologies are relegated to niche applications and likely will be for quite some time. For many applications, wireless just can't compete with wired networks. I discuss the limitations of wireless and the underlying reasons in this chapter. Theodore Vail, twice president of AT&T (1880s and early 1900s), summed it up when he said, *The difficulties of the wireless telegraph are as nothing compared with the difficulties in the way of the wireless telephone* [11-2]. While wireless telephony may have been quite a trick in those days, it is nothing compared with wireless data communications.

Wireless Defined

Wireless, quite simply, refers to communications without wires. While microwave and satellite communications are without wires, those technologies generally are considered to be high-speed, network backbone or access technologies that are point-to-point, point-to-multipoint, or broadcast in nature. (See Chapter 2 for discussion of the principles and characteristics of radio transmission.) In the context of this discussion, most of the wireless technologies are local loop or local in nature, rather than transport-oriented. The technologies discussed here also are application- and service-oriented.

Standards and Regulations

Standards are very important in telecommunications, and wireless is no exception. Wireless technologies have the dubious distinction of lots of standards most that are incompatible and conflicting. Existing standards include U.S. (FCC), European (CEPT/ETSI), international (ITU-R), and Japanese. There are formal standards, de facto standards, and proprietary specifications, which often are characterized as "standards." Ultimately, you might like to think that the standards wars will yield winners and losers, but that is unlikely in the immediate future.

Regulation is extremely important in the wireless world, since there is a high potential of interference between transmissions. In order to avoid this problem, radio must be managed along several dimensions, including frequency allocation and power level. Regulatory authorities and standards bodies of significance include the ITU-R, IEEE, ETSI, and FCC. The ITU-R (International Telecommunications Union-Radiocommunications Sector) originally was known as the CCIR (Consultative Committee on International Radio). A branch of the ITU-T (nee CCITT), The ITU-R sets international radiocommunications standards. The IEEE (Institute of Electrical and Electronics Engineers) is in the continuing process of developing standards for Wireless LANs, through the 802.11 Working Group. ETSI (European Telecommunications Standards Institute) sets standards within the EC (European Commission) countries of Western Europe. The *RACE* (*Research for Advanced Communications in Europe*) program, which is directed at the promotion of *Integrated Broadband Communications* (*IBC*), addresses wireless in its R1043 recommendation document. The Federal Communications Commission (FCC) has handled regulation of the wireless, as well as the wired, world in the United States since 1934. On a periodic basis, the various national regulatory authorities meet to sort out national and international spectrum allocation issues at *WARC* (*World Administrative Radio Conferences*), which is sponsored by the ITU-R.

Frequency allocation, or *spectrum management,* involves the designation of certain frequencies in the electromagnetic spectrum in support of certain applications. Examples include AM and FM broadcast radio, UHF and VHF broadcast TV, Trunk

Mobile Radio (TMR), cellular radio, and microwave radio. This requirement is essential to avoid interference between various applications using the same, or overlapping, frequency ranges. In limiting each application to a specific range of frequencies, the manufacturers, carriers, and end users of such systems can better be monitored and controlled, as well.

The issue of Radio Frequency Interference (RFI), as discussed in Chapter 2, is tied to the specific frequencies employed, the proxmity of the transmit/receive antennae, and the power levels involved. As I noted, lower frequency signals naturally propagate farther than higher frequency signals, suffering less from attenuation (i.e., loss of signal strength). In consideration of the specific frequency range employed, therefore, the same frequencies cannot be used by multiple antennae within a certain range of proximity without running the risk of mutual signal interference. The power levels of the various transmitters also must be regulated, as stronger signals propagate farther at any given frequency.

ADVANTAGES AND DISADVANTAGES OF WIRELESS

Before dealing with technology and applications specifics, let's pause to address the advantages and disadvantages of wireless, at least in a general way. The deployment and management of networks without wires offers clear benefits, but also suffers from severe limitations.

Deployment of wireless networks certainly can offer advantages of reduced cost of installation and reconfiguration. Tremendous costs can be saved by eliminating requirements to secure terrestrial rights of way, dig trenches and plant poles, place conduits and hang cross-arms, splice cables, place repeaters, and so on. For that matter, wired networks may not be a viable option in rocky or soggy terrain, especially in remote areas of low user density. Additionally, wireless offers greatly improved speed of deployment and reconfiguration. Wireless networks also offer great portability. In other words, the antennae quite easily can be disassembled and reassembled at another location, whereas wired networks must be abandoned, or removed and sold as scrap metal. Finally, wireless networks even can offer the great advantage of mobility, as is the case with cordless telephony, cellular radio, and packet radio data networks.

Wireless also suffers from certain limitations, the most significant of which is that of spectrum availability — radio spectrum is a finite resource. The laws of physics and Mother Nature (not to mention Table 2.1), state that radio operates between 3 kHz and 30 GHz. While that may seem like a lot of spectrum, there also are a lot of applications and users competing for it. This limited radio spectrum divides into even more limited ranges of spectrum allocated in support of specific applications (e.g., microwave and cellular radio). Within each slice of allocated spectrum there clearly exists only so much bandwidth; regardless of how cleverly we design compression algorithms to maximize its use, there remains only so much bandwidth available. As discussed in connection with microwave and satellite radio, in Chapter 2, error performance and security always are issues with airwave transmission.

There are other problems with wireless communications, by the way. Similar to the effect of echo (i.e., reflected energy) in the wired world, wireless communications suffers from *MultiPath Interference*, or *MPI*. As radio signals propagate from the transmitter, they naturally diffuse, or spread out – no matter how tightly they are shaped, or focused. If the communication involves a cell phone and a cell site, for instance, there really is no shaping. Rather, the signal from the cell site to the terminal either is broadcast on an omni-directional basis, or, more commonly, on a vectored basis. The signal from the terminal back to the cell site always is broadcast on an omni-directional basis. Assuming that direct line-of-sight is achievable, some signal elements travel a straight line from transmitter to receiver, while other signal elements bounce off mountains, buildings, cars, trees, your neighbor's dog, and other dense physical objects. This can result in confusion at the receiver. *MPI specter* refers to the *ghosting effect,* which occurs when the path of the echo is relatively long and when some reflected signals, therefore, arrive on a significantly delayed basis. (This ghosting effect is particularly evident in poorly installed coax-based CATV systems, and in traditional antenna-based TV reception in mountainous areas.) In order to overcome the effects of MPI, the receiver must make comparisons between signals to determine and lock onto the signals of greatest strength, earliest arrival, or both.

The Cell Concept: Frequency Reuse

Radio systems are designed for a certain area of coverage, or *footprint*. Even early radio and TV broadcast systems used the concept of coverage areas to provide service to a defined service area. Therefore, you could reuse the same frequencies to support service in metropolitan areas some distance away. For instance, 98.1 (MHz) on your FM dial might be WXYZ in New York and KFRC in San Francisco, California. Similarly, Channel 7 on your TV might be WFAA in Dallas, Texas and KGO in San Francisco; broadcast TV stations in the United States can reuse frequencies if separated by at least 150 miles [11-6]. The size of the cells, of course, is sensitive to frequency and power level, as well as the height of the antennae, the topography, the time of day or night, solar activity, weather conditions, and other factors.

Now, let's digress to my youth. Actually, it's not a complete digression, as it illustrates the points I just made. Some of you may remember Bob Smith. Actually, you may remember him as "Wolfman Jack," a famous rock 'n roll disk jockey of the '60s generation (If you don't remember, just ask your parents.), and later a successful star in movies such as *American Graffiti*. In any event, as a young man in the 1960s, I would drive hundreds of miles over country roads in Texas to see my girlfriend (which tells you something about the size of the Great State of Texas, as well as my difficulty in finding a girlfriend). At 9:00 p.m. on Sunday nights, "The Wolfman" broadcasted from XERF, the AM radio station in Ciudad Acuna, Coahuila, Mexico, and he came through as "clear as a bell" through the little transistor radio that hung from the rearview mirror of my 1962 Volkswagen beetle. It wasn't much of a radio (I couldn't afford the kind that fit in the dashboard), but it was a heck of a radio show, and a heck of a radio station. XERF, you see, blasted "The Wolfman" (and a whole host of radio preachers earlier on a Sunday evening) at 250,000 watts—five times the allowable power for radio stations just across the border in Del Rio, Texas, U.S.A. At that power level, given the right weather conditions, "The Wolfman" could be heard just about as clearly in New York City as I heard him in Corpus Christi. In fact, he overpowered every radio station in North America operating on the same frequency. "The Wolfman" became famous all over North America, at the expense of the poor DJs who tried to make a living on the same frequency band. Having shared that with you, let's get back to serious business.

The formal concept of radio *cells* dates back to 1947, when Bell Telephone engineers developed a radio system concept that included numerous, low-power transmit/receive antennae [11-1]. Scattered throughout a metropolitan area, this sort of architecture served to increase the effective subscriber capacity of radio systems by breaking the area of coverage into *cells*, or smaller areas of coverage. Thereby, each frequency could be reused in non-adjacent cells. Additionally, the cells can be split, or subdivided, further as the traffic demands of the system increase. In other words, cellular radio networks are highly scalable.

Frequency reuse is sensitive to factors that should now be familiar to us as a result of the discussion of microwave and satellite systems in Chapter 2, and our "Wolfman Jack" example. Specifically, those factors include frequency, power level, antenna design, and topography. Higher frequency signals always attenuate to a greater extent over distance, given the same power level. Antenna design is sensitive to wavelength and other factors. Topography is always an issue, as line-of-sight is always preferable.

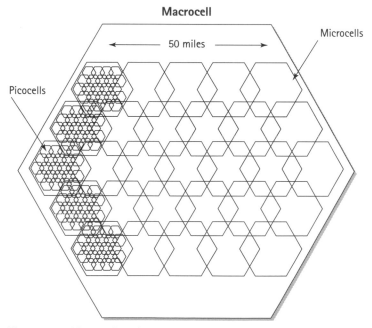

Figure 11-1 Macrocells, microcells, and picocells

Cells generally fall into three categories: *macrocells, microcells,* and *picocells* (see Figure 11-1). As the cells shrink, the advantages of frequency reuse increase significantly. However, the costs of network deployment increase dramatically, and the difficulty of switching traffic from moving transmitters between cells increases considerably. Nonetheless, the increase in traffic-handling capacity can be remarkable, with associated increases in revenue potential. Assuming that 12 channels are available for use in a metropolitan area of a 60-mile radius, consider the following theoretical scenario:

Macrocells cover a relatively large area. One macrocell might support 12 channels and only 12 simultaneous conversations. In a 7-cell reuse pattern (which is typical) with each cell covering a radius of about 11 miles, no improvement is realized; only 12 conversations can be supported. This lack of improvement is due to the fact that the cells must overlap; therefore, conversations on the same frequency channels in adjacent cells interfere with each other.

Microcells cover a smaller area. If a macrocell were divided into 7 microcells, in a 7-cell reuse pattern (refer to Figure 11-2), a reuse factor of 128 is realized. In other words, the same 12 channels could support 1,536 simultaneous conversations.

Picocells are quite small, covering only a few blocks of an urban area or, perhaps, a tunnel, walkway, or parking garage. In a 7-cell reuse pattern, with each cell covering a radius of approximately 1/2 mile, the reuse factor climbs to 514. In other words, the same 12 channels could theoretically support up to 6,168 simultaneous conversations [11-2].

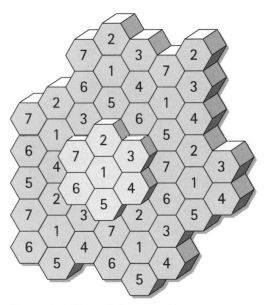

Figure 11-2 Seven-Cell reuse pattern

VECTORS IN CELLS, AND BEAMS IN VECTORS: ANTENNAE DESIGN

Within a given cell, the antenna may operate in either an omni-directional or a vectored mode. The omni-directional approach involves signal transmission from and signal receipt by the centralized base station antenna in all directions. This approach uses all frequency channels in a 360(beam, and all at the same power level. A vectored antenna, which is commonly used in cellular telephony applications, can subdivide the coverage area of the cell into multiple vectors of coverage. Cellular antennae, for example, commonly carve a cell into three vectors, each of 120(. This vectoring approach enables the carrier frequencies within each vector to be managed independently from those within the other vectors in terms of dimensions such as channel allocation and signal strength.

Smart antennae can improve significantly on this concept of vectoring. Such antennae can operate within a given cell and its constituent vectors, further subdividing the coverage through the use of as many as 12 beams, each with a 30(-beam width. Thereby, the footprint of the cell can be sculpted to optimize coverage, channel allocation, and interference. The individual beams can rotate from one vector to another, even remotely and on a dynamic basis in order to adjust to traffic patterns [11-7].

While I have only a limited amount of space to discuss antennae design and while the details of antennae design are the subject for an electrical engineering text, there certainly is at least one other design issue of significance. CDMA systems, which are discussed next, posses the ability to deal with issues of multipath interference (MPI) in a very effective way. CDMA subscriber units (e.g., cell phones) use *rake receivers*, which comprise a set of four receivers, or *fingers*, that work in a coordinated way— much like the tines of a garden rake. One of the fingers constantly searches the multipath signals, and communicates its findings to the other three fingers. Each finger then locks in on a strong signal, and the results of all four fingers combine for even greater signal strength.

Digital versus Analog

Clearly, communications is going digital. Nonetheless, analog does have a place, if for no other reason than it is the incumbent technology. Complete transition from analog is expensive and disruptive, and will take some time to complete. This scenario holds true in the wireless, as well as the wired, world. Just like in the wired world, digital wireless offers the advantages of more efficient use of bandwidth (spectrum) through compression, improved quality of transmission through enhanced error performance, increased throughput (a logical extension of diminished transmission errors), and improved security through encryption. There exist no less than 16 different means of modulating a radio signal, most of which relate to digital radio. Generally speaking, Amplitude Modulation (AM) alone is ineffective, due to the phenomenon of *fading*, or signal attenuation. For the most part, a combination of Phase Shift Keying (PSK) and Amplitude Modulation (AM) yields compression of up to 16:1.

Multiplexing and Access Techniques

Communications networks take great advantage of the concept of *DAMA* (*Demand-Assigned Multiple Access*). DAMA enables multiple devices to share access to the same network on a demand basis; i.e., *first come, first served*. There exist a number of ways in which multiple access (i.e., access to multiple users) can be provided in a wireless network; those techniques largely are mutually exclusive.

Frequency Division Multiple Access (FDMA)

At the most basic level, frequency division is the starting point for all wireless communications because all communications within a given cell must be separated by frequency to avoid their mutual interference. *Frequency Division Multiple Access* (*FDMA*) divides the assigned frequency range into multiple carrier frequencies to support multiple conversations, as depicted in Figure 11-3. In other words, multiple narrowband frequency channels are derived from a wider band of assigned radio spectrum, much as Frequency Division Multiplexers (FDMs) operate in the wired world (Chapter 1). Essentially, transmission #1 takes place on one frequency, while transmission #2 takes place on another, with guard bands separating the channels so the potential for inadvertent overlapping is reduced. The station equipment must be *frequency agile*, in order to search and seize an available frequency channel, especially as the mobile transmitter/receiver moves from one cell to another in a cellular network.

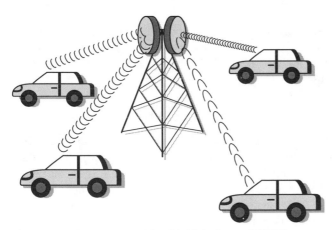

Figure 11-3 Frequency Division Multiple Access (FDMA)

Analog cellular systems employ FDMA exclusively, which also is, at least, the starting point for digital systems. In either scenario, a single channel supports each conversation. A single base station or cell site can support multiple channels, which are subsets of a wider band of radio spectrum. For instance, the U.S. *AMPS*

(*Advanced Mobile Phone System*) system provides for a total allocation of 40 MHz, which is divided into 666 (832 in some areas) frequency pairs. In each of the 734 serving areas defined by the FCC, the available 666 (or 832) channels split equally between *wireline* (incumbent Local Exchange Carrier) and *non-wireline* operators, with the carrier in each category initially determined on a lottery basis. Each of the frequency pairs provides bandwidth of 60 kHz (30 kHz for the forward channel and 30 kHz for the reverse channel). The two channels supporting a single conversation are separated widely to avoid confusion on the part of the terminal equipment. For example, the AMPS system provides for separation of 45 MHz. At maximum, based on a 7-cell reuse pattern, U.S. AMPS cell sites support about 56 frequency channels, considering that 21 of the available 416 channels are reserved for signaling and control purposes [11-6]. On average, the AMPS cell site has a radius of approximately one mile. Table 11-1 provides a comparison of AMPS and GSM (Global System for Mobile Communications), a digital standard discussed later in this chapter.

Table 11-1 COMPARISON OF AMPS (FDMA) AND GSM (TDMA)

	Transmission Mode	Multiplexing Technique	Duplexing Technique	Frequency Band
AMPS	Analog	FDMA	FDD	800 MHz
GSM	Duplex	FDMA/TDMA	TDD	800 MHz & 900 MHz

Frequency Division Duplex (*FDD*) is a means of providing duplex (bi-directional) communications. Forward and backward channels make use of separate frequencies. FDD is used with both analog and digital wireless technologies, including cordless telephony and cellular.

Time Division Multiple Access (TDMA)

Time Division Multiple Access (*TDMA*) is a digital technique that divides each frequency channel into multiple time slots, each of which supports an individual conversation (see Figure 11-4). This concept is exactly the same as in the wired world, where TDMs perform the same function in a T-carrier environment (refer to Chapter 7). The total available bandwidth, the bandwidth of the individual channels, and the number of time slots per channel vary according to the particular standard in place, as well as the specific coding technique employed. For instance, GSM involves a carrier channel of 200 kHz, with a channel rate of approximately 200 Kbps. The channel is divided into eight time slots of 25 Kbps each, easily supporting low-bit-rate digitized voice of 9.6 Kbps, plus overhead for framing and signaling. Each set of eight time slots is organized into a logical frame, and the frames are repeated frequently. Each conversation makes use of two time slots, one for the forward channel and one for the reverse channel. Services based on TDMA offer roughly three times the traffic capacity of FDMA services [11-1]. TDMA was specified first in EIA/TIA Interim Standard 54 (IS-54), and later was included in IS-136 — which is an evolved version of IS-54 for use in cellular and PCS systems. TDMA is used in systems based on the D-AMPS, GSM, and DECT standards. Table 11-1 provides a comparison of GSM and AMPS.

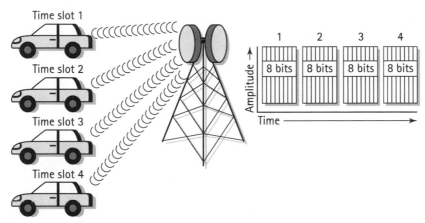

Figure 11-4 Time Division Multiple Access (TDMA)

TDMA terminal equipment is simpler and, therefore, less expensive. This largely is because the transmit and receive functions are not operative at the same point in time, thereby eliminating the full-duplex (FDX) requirement. A typical TDMA system, such as GSM, actually is both FDMA and TDMA. Multiple carrier channels are supported on the basis of frequency separation. Within each carrier frequency channel, multiple time slots (digital channels) are supported.

E-TDMA (*Enhanced TDMA*), developed by Hughes Network Systems, is an improvement over TDMA, employing Digital Speech Interpolation (DSI) compression and half rate *vocoders* (voice coders) operating at 4.8 Kbps in order to improve on bandwidth utilization. E-TDMA reportedly provides 16:1 improvement over analog technology.

Time Division Duplex (*TDD*) is a digital means of providing bidirectional communications. TDD can be employed with both channels using the same frequency; but this *ping-pong* transmission approach can yield poor quality, as it actually is a half-duplex transmission mode. More commonly, TDD is used in conjunction with FDD, with the forward and backward TDM channels riding over separate frequency channels. Further, the time slots are staggered so the frequency-specific transceivers are not asked to transmit and receive at the same exact points in time. For example, time slot #1 might be used on the forward channel, or *uplink*, from the user terminal to the centralized cell antenna, while time slot #3 is used on the backward channel, or *downlink*, from the cell site to the user terminal.

Code Division Multiple Access (CDMA)

Code Division Multiple Access (*CDMA*) is a relatively new technology that has its roots in spread spectrum (SS) radio. Before we go any further, let's explore the fascinating origins of spread spectrum. Hedy Lamarr, the famous actress and dancer of pre-war (WWII) fame, created the concept of spread spectrum in 1940. As the story goes, Lamarr developed spread spectrum to enable multiple player pianos to be synchronized remotely by radio – droves of people supposedly paid good money to go to the resulting radio-controlled piano concerts. In any event, in 1942, a U.S. patent was issued to Ms. Lamarr and George Antheil, a film-score composer to whom Ms. Lamarr had turned for help in perfecting her idea. The patent was for a *secret communication system* that was, in effect, a spread spectrum radio. The Allies used that patented technology extensively during the World War II in the Pacific Theater, where it solved the problem of Japanese jamming of radio-controlled torpedoes. This primitive system used a mechanical switching system, like a piano roll, to shift frequencies faster than the Nazis or the Japanese could follow them. Subsequently, spread spectrum has combined with digital technology, for spy-proof and noise-resistant battlefield communications. In 1962, for example, Sylvania installed it on ships sent to blockade Cuba, where the technology provided improved security, as well as prevented signal jamming. Ms. Lamarr never asked for, and never received, any royalties from the use of her invention. Ms. Lamarr was quite an innovator, by the way, and across multiple disciplines. She delighted and shocked audiences in the 1930s by dancing in the nude in the movie *Ecstacy*, which is not available on videotape, as best I can determine. [11-8].

As spread spectrum radio spreads the bandwidth of the transmitted signal over a spectrum of radio frequencies that is much wider than that required to support the narrowband transmission, it commonly is known as a wideband radio technology. Spread spectrum uses two techniques: Direct Sequence (DS) and Frequency Hopping (FH).

Direct Sequence Spread Spectrum (*DSSS*) is a packet radio technique in which the narrowband signal is spread across a wider carrier frequency band. In other words, the information stream is organized into packets, each of which transmits across the wideband carrier frequency in a redundant manner. Multiple transmissions can be supported in the same manner using the same wideband, with the transmissions from each terminal identified by a unique 10-bit code that is prepended (i.e., added to the front of) to each data packet. That code sequence, or *PseudoNoise* (*PN*) sequence, which is known in advance by both the transmitter and the receiver, enables each transmission to be identified from the inherent background noise, as well as from the interference created by all of the other transmissions sharing the same wideband. Thereby, each receiver can recognize each data transmission intended for it, rejecting all other signals [11-3]. As each signal is spread across the entire available spectrum in a redundant fashion, the likelihood reduces that a given transmission could be blocked entirely by interference from other narrowband signals occupying the same wideband at the same time (see Figure 11-4). *Rake receivers*, so called because they rake in multiple copies of the same transmission like the tines of a garden rake act together to rake up a pile of leaves, lock in on the strongest signal.

Frequency Hopping Spread Spectrum (*FHSS*) which generally is preferred over DHSS, more closely resembles Ms. Lamarr's original concept. FHSS involves the transmission of short bursts of packets over a range of frequency channels within the wideband carrier, with the transmitter and receiver hopping from one frequency to another in a carefully choreographed *hop sequence*. This hop sequence generally is under the control of the centralized base station antenna. Each transmission dwells on a particular frequency for a very short period of time (e.g., no more than 400 milliseconds for FCC-controlled applications), which may be only the time interval required to transmit a data packet or even a single bit. A large number of other transmissions also may share the same range of frequencies simultaneously – each using a different hop sequence. The potential remains, however, for the overlapping of packets. The receiving device can distinguish each packet in a packet stream by reading the various codes prepended to the packet data transmissions, and treating competing signals as noise. In a wireless LAN environment, DSSS typically operates in the 2.4 GHz frequency band, which is one of the ISM (Industrial Scientific Medical) bands defined by the FCC for unlicensed use.

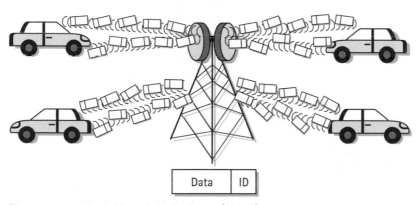

Figure 11-5 Code Division Multiple Access (CDMA)

CDMA improves bandwidth utilization because a great number of users can share the same wideband radio frequency channel (see Figure 11-5). While improvements of up to 2,000 percent (20:1) initially were predicted for CDMA, compared to AMPS, practical results are more in the 3:1 or 4:1 range in cellular telephony applications. Particularly through the use of the FHSS approach, CDMA also provides excellent security, as it is virtually impossible to intercept more than a small portion of a transmission. Encryption, or course, can provide additional security [11-9]. FHSS also offers the advantage of overall improved transmission, since no individual transmission gets stuck with the assignment of a poor quality channel.

Qualcomm – which develops, manufactures, markets, and licenses CDMA products – perfected and commercialized CDMA. The first commercial CDMA system was placed in service in Hong Kong, where cellular phones are considered almost a necessity and where the networks have suffered terrible congestion. Since then, a great number of manufacturers and providers of cellular, PCS, wireless LANs, and other systems and networks have licensed CDMA.

FDMA, TDMA, AND CDMA COMPARED: IT'S PARTY TIME!

The best commonsense means of comparing FDMA, TDMA, and CDMA is to use the *cocktail party* analogy, which has been used by acoustical engineers for many years. Let's make this an international cocktail party – with a great number of people, all wanting to talk at the same time. The cocktail party is being held in a large ballroom (frequency band).

In a FDMA environment, each conversation takes place in its own space (channel). Therefore, the ballroom must be subdivided into smaller rooms (channels) of suitable size (bandwidth) so there is no interference between the pairs of people engaged in each conversation. Each pair occupies a room for the entire duration of the conversation. The pairs can move from room to room (cell to cell) as they make their way from the entrance to the buffet; although they must interrupt their conversations when they leave one room and must enter another room before resuming conversation (*hard handoff,* or *break and make*). The number of simultaneous conversations that can be supported depends on the number of rooms of suitable size that can be derived from the space available in the ballroom. The speakers also must control their volume and frequency levels in consideration of the thickness of the walls (guard bands, or frequency separations) so they do not interfere with others.

In a TDMA environment, multiple pairs of speakers may share an even smaller room, although they have to squeeze (compression) into the physical space. Six people, for example, can hold three separate conversations if they all take turns. The order of the conversations will be carefully controlled, as each pair will get a time slice (time slot) of 20 seconds each minute (frame).

In a CDMA environment, the entire ballroom is open. A larger number of people can fit into the room, because the walls have been removed. A larger number of pairs of people can engage in simultaneous conversations, with the conversations overlapping in frequency, volume, and time. Volume and frequency levels still must be controlled, of course. As highly intelligent receivers, the listening parties can distinguish the transmission of their paired speakers by locking on the language (PN code) spoken, even given the high level of background noise (interference) from other conversations. Since the walls have been removed, the pairs can move from one area to another without losing conversational connectivity (*soft handoff,* or *make and break*).

Switched Mobile Radio (SMR)/ Trunk Mobile Radio (TMR)

The Detroit, Michigan Police Department placed the first experimental two-way mobile radio system into service in 1921, operating in the 2-MHz band. The Bayonne, New Jersey Police Department followed suit in the early 1930s. While this AM (Amplitude Modulation) radio application grew quickly, even as late as 1937 only 40 channels allocated by the FCC to this application. In the late 1930s, FM (Frequency Modulation) replaced AM as the method of choice because of its improved quality of reception and lower power requirements. (FM receivers tend to lock in on the stronger competing signal, whereas AM recognizes all competing signals.) In 1949, the FCC recognized two-way mobile radio as a new class of service, and began to allocate spectrum and regulate its use [11-2] and [11-10].

Commercial applications were offered first in 1946, when AT&T was granted the first license for two-way, mobile FM service in St. Louis, Missouri. In addition to the 50-mile range of the centralized antenna, this service offered the advantage of connection to the PSTN. As the costs were reasonable, the service grew in popularity and the systems soon were oversubscribed. In fact, it was not uncommon for a provider to load as many as 100 subscribers per channel; as a result, service was horrible. In 1976, for example, service in the New York metropolitan area consisted of 20 channels supporting 543 subscribers out of a total population of approximately 20 million. Not surprisingly, there was a waiting list of approximately 3,700 [11-10].

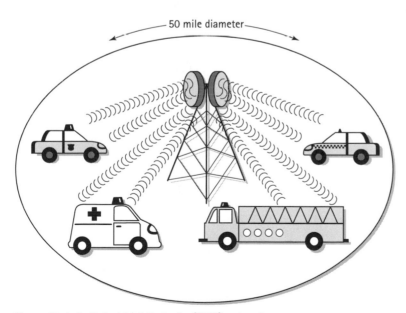

Figure 11-6 Switched Mobile Radio (SMR) network

Switched Mobile Radio (SMR), also known as *Trunk Mobile Radio (TMR)*, entered the scene in the 1960s, marketed as *Improved Mobile Telephone Service (IMTS)*. This commercially available service made better use of FM bandwidth through narrowband communications involving smaller frequency channels. IMTS also enabled users to search multiple frequencies on a manual basis. Shortly thereafter, intelligent mobile sets were developed that searched channels automatically. The concept of SMR/TMR remains much as it was originally. The provider places a radio tower and omni-directional transmit/receive antennae on the highest possible point in the area and blasts the signal at the maximum allowable power level. As illustrated in Figure 11-6, this approach provides a coverage area of 50 miles or more, depending on topography. While some SMR systems support full-duplex communications, many are only half-duplex. This half-duplex communications mode requires the use of the *push-to-talk* protocol, also known as the *over-and-out* and the *CB-radio* protocol. You copy, good buddy?

SMR/TMR largely has been supplanted by cellular service offerings, although it remains widely used in dispatch and fleet applications such as police, fire, and emergency vehicles; as well as taxi fleets, utility fleets (e.g., telephone companies, electric utilities, and CATV providers), and courier services. In the United States, 80 MHz has been allocated for SMR.

Enhanced Switched Mobile Radio (ESMR) is a technique developed by Nextel Communications and Geotek Communications (now bankrupt) for the development of a voice and data, cellular-like network using legacy SMR networks operating in the 800 MHz and 900 MHz. For instance, Nextel acquired and linked a large number of SMR networks throughout the United States. Through the use of TDMA, each frequency channel is divided into multiple time slots to support multiple conversations. ESMR also supports call hand-off so mobile users can maintain connectivity as they travel from cell to cell. The Nextel network, which offers data throughput of 7.2 Kbps, is yet to be fully deployed, although coverage includes most major metropolitan areas in the United States. Nextel terminal equipment supports integrated voice, data, and paging.

Paging

The concept of a paging system to cover a local or metropolitan area was introduced first in 1950 in New York. That first system provided a means by which a centralized antenna could broadcast alerts to small, inexpensive pagers, or beepers. Each page simply represented an identification number, which was recognized only by the pager being addressed. A pager in range beeped, hence the term *beeper*. Response to the page was in the form of a telephone call to the paging company to retrieve a message. The first systems involved proprietary protocols including the *GOLAY* standard from Motorola [11-10].

During the 1970s, an international team of radio engineers developed a standard set of code and signaling formats. That effort evolved into the *POCSAG (Post Office Code Standardization Advisory Group)* code. So known as the British Post Office

(BPO), which was the PTT for the United Kingdom at the time, chaired the effort. The POCSAG standard, which is in the public domain, provides for transmission speed of up to 2400 bps, using channels of 25 kHz in the 150-170 MHz band. The CCIR (now ITU-R) in 1981 standardized that code internationally, and most nations quickly adopted it. POCSAG can support as many as 2 million individual pager addresses. Tone-only, numeric, and alphanumeric pagers are supported on a one-way basis.

Paging in Europe is constrained somewhat by the lack of agreement on common standards, although the POCSAG standard generally is recognized. A digital paging system known as *ERMES* (*European Radio MEssage System*), supported by ETSI and the EC, is making progress. In 1990, 26 system operators from 16 countries signed a Memorandum of Understanding (MoU) to create a pan-European system based on this standard. ERMES operates at 6,250 bps in the 169.4-169.8 MHz band and uses FSK as a modulation method.

Motorola more recently has floated the *FLEX* set of proprietary solutions, which it hopes to see officially accepted as industry standards and which largely have replaced POCSAG in the United States. Those solutions provide two-way messaging, support data transmission, and provide greater bandwidth. FLEX also supports as many as 5 billion addresses, with up to 600,000 supported per channel. The FLEX family of protocols includes the following:

◆ FLEX: 1600 bps; 25 kHz channels; one-way

◆ ReFLEX: 1600, 3200, 6400, or 9600 bps, 25 or 50 kHz channels downstream, and 12.5 kHz channel upstream; two-way

◆ InFLEXion: up to 112 Kbps, 50 kHz channels in the N-PCS (Narrowband PCS range); two-way; supports compressed voice downstream [11-11] through [11-14]

According to estimates from the Personal Communications Industry Association, at year-end 1995 there were well over 34 million pager subscribers worldwide[11-15] and [11-16]. Various other current estimates place the number of paging customers in the range of 50 million, in the United States, alone.

Paging Networks

Pagers generally operate over 25 KHz channels in the 900 MHz band. In 1984, the FCC (U.S.) dedicated 1 MHz of 40 channels in this band for nationwide paging purposes. *RCCs* (*Radio Common Carriers*) and *PPOs* (*Private Paging Operators*) provide paging services. Regulated by the FCC and the state PUCs, RCCs make use of FCC-designated frequencies. PPOs are unregulated, but must share spectrum with other users in the VHF and UHF bands.

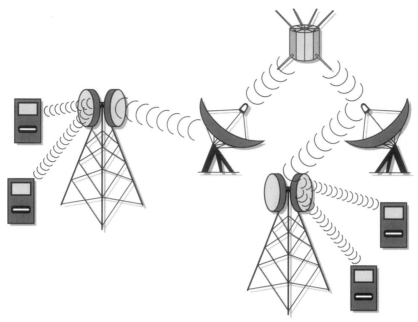

Figure 11-7 Terrestrial paging network with satellite interconnectivity

At the local level, pagers connect to centralized antennae on a wireless basis. The centralized antennae are interconnected, at the terrestrial level, through various means, including private microwave, leased lines, packet-switched, and Frame Relay networks. SkyTel and other paging network service providers provide VSAT satellite links to terrestrial paging networks, as depicted in Figure 11-7. (Note that MCI WorldCom and SkyTel announced on May 28, 1999 a *merger*, read *acquisition* by MCI WorldCom.) In this fashion, the local paging systems are networked so a page can be delivered across a wide area and even globally, rather than only locally. Generally speaking, these satellite links are highly beneficial and highly reliable. The May 1998 failure of the Galaxy IV satellite, however, underscored the vulnerability of even the most sophisticated networks. When the satellite lost its orientation, hundreds of terrestrial paging antennae had to be reprogrammed by hand in a process that took over a week. In addition to the 40 million or so pagers that lost service during this outage, 5,400 of 7,700 Chevron gas stations lost their pay-at-the-pump capabilities, and music-on-hold systems went down causing callers to hang up when they thought they had been disconnected. Additionally, the results of the multistate Powerball lottery drawing could not be broadcast to the 88 TV stations that regularly carry that programming [11-17].

The downstream data to the pager originates in several ways. The most common approach involves the paging party's dialing a telephone number, which often is toll-free. That number may be dedicated to that one pager (which helps explain the pressure on the telephone numbering plan). Alternatively, that number may be one of many associated with the service provider. The telephone number terminates in a voice processor at the central location of the service provider. The voice processor prompts the paging party to use the touchtone keypad of the telephone set to enter a return number. If the telephone number is not dedicated to that one pager, the paging party first is prompted to enter a *PID* (*Pager Identification Number*), more generically known as a PIN (Personal Identification Number), assigned to that one pager. If a textual message is to be sent, the paging service provider provides the option of accessing a human attendant who will answer the call and enter the message (generally limited to 500 characters) for transmission to the alphanumeric pager. Alternatively, many service providers now support Web-based messaging. This approach enables any paging party to access the service provider's Web site via the Internet, and to enter a message of limited length without the intervention of an attendant. Additionally, large organizations with great numbers of employees equipped with pagers may have direct access to the paging system to send alphanumeric messages to their employees. Such access may be on either a dedicated or a dial-up basis, and typically involves proprietary software, which turns a PC into a paging dispatch terminal. These direct links from the user organization to the service provider also may permit the redirection of e-mail and facsimile transmission from corporate servers, once those message formats are converted. As not to overwhelm both the paging network and the terminal equipment, filters must be used to limit the size of the transmitted file.

Paging Equipment

Pagers can be classified as tone-only, numeric, alphanumeric, and voice-enabled. *Tone-only* pagers cause the device to emit an audible tone, and/or to vibrate or blink so it's not disruptive. *Numeric* pagers permit the receipt of numbers, only, on a display. The vast majority of contemporary pagers are *alphanumeric*, capable of receiving and displaying both alpha and numeric characters. Relatively few pagers currently can support the storage of voice messages, which are extremely memory-intensive. This voice capability is accomplished through the downloading of compressed voicemail from a centralized voice processor to the pager over a packet network.

Two-way paging systems have been available abroad for years, but were not introduced in the United States until roughly 1995. The simplest and most common version is known as 1.5-way paging. This approach supports *guaranteed message delivery*, as the network does not attempt to download messages until such time as the pager is within range, turned on, and has enough memory to support the download. The general location of the pager is communicated upstream, so the messages can be downloaded to the antennae supporting that particular geographic area, rather than broadcasting across the entire paging network. (This is much like the way that cellular networks work.) Once downloaded successfully, the pager acknowledges to the network the receipt of the page. Such pagers are alphanumeric, supporting the display of a text message and return telephone number, typically for a telephone or pager.

Full two-way paging enables the recipient of the page to select and transmit a return message, which most commonly is selected from a small set of predetermined messages. Those return messages can also be user-definable, through an RS-232 serial link between the pager and a PC, in support of messages of limited length [11-18] and [11-19]. Although, according to IDC-Link, only 400,00 or so two-way pagers currently are in use, as many as 6 million will be in use by 2001 [11-20].

Pagers also have been incorporated into other devices, such as cellular telephones, watches (e.g., Seiko and Swatch), and, even, keychains – although memory tends to severely limit the number of stored messages. The Seiko pager/watches use the FM radio band, rather than standard pager frequencies. An extra advantage to the Seiko system is that the time automatically can be synchronized up to 36 times a day with the Official Atomic Clock, even adjusting to Daylight Savings Time. Seiko service coverage, however, is highly limited [11-21]. Increasingly, paging capabilities also are merging into Personal Communicators, also known as Personal Digital Assistants (PDAs). These devices are well equipped for two-way messaging, as they incorporate small keypads and even support pen-based (actually stylus-based) data entry. Therefore, ad hoc textual replies can be created with relative ease.

Whether standalone or merged into another device, contemporary pager capabilities include some combination of alphanumeric display, two-way communications, message storage, audible and vibration alert, fax receipt (very unusual), and abbreviated e-mail forwarding (very unusual). Many paging service providers also offer information such as weather reports, sports scores, traffic reports, and stock quotes, all of which are provided through a feature known as *SMS* (*Short Message Service*); SMS currently is limited to 160 characters [11-22]. Limited Web content also may be available. Incoming messages generally may be reviewed, erased, and archived. Both incoming and outgoing messages may be date and time-stamped.

Additionally, several manufacturers offer *PC Pagers* – the cards that fit into the *PCMCIA* (*Personal Computer Memory Card Industry Association*) slot of laptop PCs and PDAs (Personal Digital Assistants) – also known as Personal Communicators. All such cards are PCMCIA Type II and do not require external power supplies. This approach effectively merges the wireless applications of two-way alphanumeric paging, computing, and e-mail. The ability to receive an alphanumeric page through a wireless, laptop PC and to then respond with an e-mail message is truly extraordinary. Although these developments are recent and not widely available, they clearly will achieve some significant level of acceptance in the future, as the workforce increasingly becomes both mobile and information-dependent.

Paging Applications: Contemporary and Developing

At the extreme, pagers currently support applications including message notification, message acknowledgement, information services, stock quotes, and event information (e.g., 1996 Olympics). Even fax, e-mail, and Web content can be received. Video can't be far behind, especially now that it is available over cell phones in Japan.

CreataLink paging service from Motorola takes paging to the contemporary extreme. Through dialing a toll-free number, you can access a menu of eight functions that include turning your car lights off and on, starting or disabling the car engine (a handy trick if your car is stolen), locking or unlocking the car doors, and opening or closing the car trunk. Similarly, into the future, you'll be able to unlock the house so that your children have access to the home after school when you're at work. If your car is equipped with a simple pager built in at the time of manufacture, you automatically could be advised of recalls for safety and maintenance purposes. If your PDA or laptop computer is stolen, you could page it to automatically disable it. Two-way pagers could send information from patients with medical emergencies, and receive authorization to automatically increase the dosage of medication from an implanted drug-release system. Two-way pagers also could be used in telemetry applications for network-based remote utility meter reading. All of these applications would make use of existing paging networks to connect to special-purpose paging units [11-20].

Paging costs generally involve a flat monthly fee, which includes some number of pages. The cost of pages above the threshold generally is sensitive to their nature (e.g., numeric, alphanumeric, or voice). A few paging service providers offer the option of *paging party pays*, which charges the paging party, rather than the paged party, for the page.

Cordless Telephony and Wireless Office Telecommunications Systems (WOTS)

Wireless Office Telecommunications Systems (*WOTS*) generally are in the form of adjuncts that provide cordless telephony communications capabilities behind PBXs, Electronic Key Systems, Hybrids, or Centrex systems. They generally are limited to voice applications, although some also support low-speed data, typically using CDPD technology. WOTS systems involve a wireless master controller, which is hard-wired to special ports on the PBX, KTS, Hybrid, or Centrex. As illustrated in Figure 11-8, the master controller, in turn, is hard-wired to subcontrollers and antennae; these are distributed throughout the office complex or campus in a pico-cell configuration. The terminal equipment is in the form of wireless handsets, which are generally low in cost and limited in range. Some multifunction handsets exist, which can function as traditional cellular phones when the user is out of range of the WOTS system or when otherwise desired [11-10].

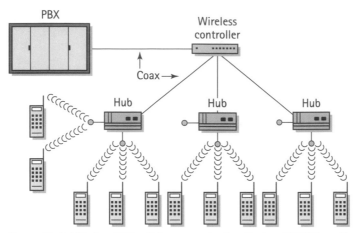

Figure 11-8 Wireless Office Telecommunication System (WOTS) configuration

Generally an extension and application of common cordless telephony, WOTS provides the advantage of mobility for a small group of select employees who must have the freedom to wander around the complex, but must have communications capability at all times. WOTS falls into the general category of *low-tier* systems, which are intended for pedestrian, in building, and Wireless Local Loop (WLL) application. In comparison to traditional wired PBX technologies, WOTS capacities are highly limited. Further, costs are relatively high – in the range of $500-$2,000 per terminal, which easily is double the total cost of a wired PBX terminal. Conversely, the more expensive systems and terminals support paging and e-mail, as well as voice.

Cordless Telephony Standards

There exist multiple cordless telephony standards used to provide WOTS service. Those standards include CT1, CT1+, CT2, CT2+, CT3, DECT, Part 15, AMPS, and PCS [11-14] and [11-15].

CT1 (*Cordless Telephony Generation 1*) was developed in Europe, where it was known as *CEPT-1*. CT1 operates in the 900 MHz range over 40 channels. FDMA and FDD derive two separate channels, one for transmission and one for reception. CT1 is analog and low-cost, but limited in range to 150 meters or so. A variation on this standard is *CT0* – primarily used in the United Kingdom.

CT1+ a variation on CT1, was developed in concert by Belgium, Germany, and Switzerland. CT1+ was intended as the basis for a public wireless service, along the lines of *Telepoint*. Although CT1+ was not successful, it did originate the concept of a *Common Air Interface (CAI)*, which enables multiple manufacturers to develop products in support of a public cordless telephony service offering.

CT2 was developed in the United Kingdom, where it formed the technology basis for the ill-fated *Telepoint* service. CT2 is a digital technology using FDMA and FDD, and is deployed in Europe, Canada, and the Asia-Pacific. While it originally supported only outgoing calling, contemporary implementations support two-way calling. CT2 uses FDMA and does not support hand-off; therefore, the user must remain within range of the antenna used to set up the call. CT2 uses 4 MHz of bandwidth divided into 40 channels – 20 upstream and 20 downstream. Dynamic channel allocation requires a frequency-agile handset. CT2 was the first international standard providing a *Common Air Interface* (*CAI*) for systems operating in the 800 MHz and 900 MHz bands; it is used in Canada and enjoys wide acceptance in Asia. Nortel's Companion System is based on CT2.

CT2+ is an improvement on CT2, supporting two-way calling and call hand-off. CT2+ uses 8 MHz of bandwidth in the 900 MHz range. CT2+ is based on dynamic channel allocation, requiring frequency-agile handsets. Encryption is supported for improved security. A common signaling and control channel offers improved call set-up times, increased traffic capacity, and longer battery life because the handset must monitor only the signaling channel. CT2+ has been used in applications such as the *Walkabout* trial in Canberra, Australia.

CT3 was developed by Ericsson in 1990 as a proprietary solution designed for high-density office environments. CT3 is based on TDMA and TDD, and uses the same frequency bands as CT2+, supporting roaming and seamless hand-off. CT3 has application in a telepoint application (PCS), as well as in office applications (WOTS).

DECT (*Digital European Cordless Telecommunications*) is the pan-European standard for digital cordless telephony, using TDMA and TDD. Ratified by ETSI in 1992, DECT operates in the 1.88-1.90 GHz frequency band, which was set aside for that purpose in all EC member nations. Designed for high-density environments, DECT supports hand-off; therefore, the user can roam from cell to cell within the range of the WOTS system. Functionally, DECT is much like CT3, as it is based on TDMA and TDD. In addition to public cordless telephony, DECT supports WOTS, WLAN (wireless LAN), and WLL (Wireless Local Loop) applications. Ericsson manufacture several systems based on *PWT* (*Personal Wireless Telecommunications*) and *PWT-E* (*PWT-Enhanced*), which are ANSI standards derived from DECT for North American usage and using speech coding at 32 Kbps [11-22].

Part 15 FCC frequencies are used in the United States by AT&T and others for the provisioning of WOTS. These unlicensed frequencies are in the 902-928 MHz range, also known as the *ISM* (*Industrial, Scientific, and Medical*) band. They, therefore, are subject to interference from industrial microwave ovens, bar code scanners, security systems, and other devices. The FCC set aside the 1.910-1.930 MHz spectrum for in-building communications; currently, the spectrum remains to be cleared of existing microwave users.

AMPS (*Advanced Mobile Phone System*) analog cellular frequencies are used in some U.S. WOTS systems, including those offered by Bell Atlantic Mobile (*Office Direct*) and Southwestern Bell Mobile Systems (*FreedomLink*). Since these frequencies are in the licensed AMPS spectrum, they must be offered jointly with the licensee.

PCS (*Personal Communications Services*) frequencies, in the frequency band between 1.92 GHz and 1.93 GHz, are used by some manufacturers. Those frequencies were set aside by the FCC for use in private PCS applications, and do not require licensing [11-16]. The public version of PCS offers an alternative to traditional cellular, and runs in the licensed spectrum between 1.85 GHz and 1.99 GHz. This version must be offered jointly with the licensee.

Cellular Radio

The basic concept of cellular radio dates back to 1947, when numerous, low-power transmit/receive antennae were scattered throughout a metropolitan area to increase the effective subscriber capacity of SMR/TMR radio systems. This architecture broke the macrocell area of coverage into smaller cells. Thereby, non-adjacent cells could reuse each frequency, as discussed earlier in this chapter. Additionally, the resulting cells could split, or subdivide, further as the traffic demands of the system increased. This cellular concept is highly scalable. Traditional cellular radio, I should note, involves a circuit-switching mode.

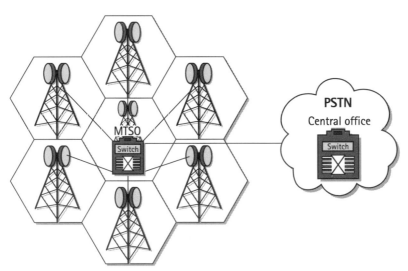

Figure 11-9 Cellular network with Mobile Traffic Switching Office (MTSO) connected to PSTN

This original concept is the basis of cellular radio, which first appeared in Chicago on October 13, 1983. AT&T operated that network for exactly 79 days, when the MFJ took effect. Then, a subsidiary of Ameritech assumed ownership [11-2]. By 1984, the Chicago network already was saturated in some cells and cellular telephones were in the hands of 91,600 people, growing to 19 million by 1994 [11-3] and [11-2]. A cellular telephony network comprises multiple low-power transmit/receive antennae distributed throughout a geographic area, with each cell site having a relatively small, circular area of coverage (see Figure 11-9). The coverage area of each individual cell overlaps those of neighboring cells, with the cell diameter generally a minimum of about 1 mile and a maximum of about 5 miles, sensitive to factors such as topography and traffic density [11-9]. As the terminal device moves out of the effective range of one cell, the call switches from one cell antenna to another through a process known as *hand-off*, in order to maintain connectivity at acceptable signal strength. The hand-off is controlled through a *MTSO (Mobile Traffic Switching Office)* or *MTSX (Mobile Traffic Switching Exchange)*, which is the functional equivalent of the PSTN Central Office. The MTSOs are interconnected and connected to the PSTN through either private microwave or leased-line facilities.

The process of *hand-off* can be accomplished in several ways. The *break and make* approach, also known as a *hard hand-off*, breaks the connection with one cell site antenna before connection is reestablished with another preselected cell site. As the duration of the break is very short, it is not noticeable in voice communication. However, it renders data communications difficult, at best. *Make-and-break*, also called *soft hand-off*, makes the new connection before breaking the old. This gentler approach offers considerable advantages in the transmission of data, particularly when supporting high-speed vehicular traffic, which may move between many cells in a relatively short period of time. Cellular systems, which support high-speed traffic, generally are known as *high-tier* systems. *Low-tier* systems include those intended for pedestrian traffic, or for in-building or Wireless Local Loop (WLL) applications.

Each cell site supports a limited number of frequency channels in order to take advantage of frequency reuse. For instance, U.S. analog AMPS networks divide 333 frequencies (416 in certain areas) among cell sites; the average cell site supports 56 channels. To improve the performance of the network by reducing crosstalk, the original omni-directional antennae were replaced with a vectored version. Vectoring generally involves three vectors, each with coverage of 120 degrees. Splitting the frequencies into three vectors had the unfortunate effect of reducing by two-thirds the number of channels available to any given user in the cell site. As a result, more cell sites of smaller size were required, which entailed additional cost in the range of $500,00 to $1 million per site. Additionally, and for aesthetic reasons, many cities and towns place moratoria on the construction of new antennae sites. Metawave Communications Corp. and others have developed a solution in the form of antenna that divides the area of coverage into multibeam antennae that support all 333 channels on the basis of 12 beams, each with a 360 degree sweep. The *smart* antennae communicate continuously with the MTSO so channel allocation is managed cell by cell and on the basis of the network as a whole, based on shifts in traffic patterns [11-17].

Cellular Standards

Cellular standards are numerous and incompatible. Standards include both analog and digital solutions, with the clear trend toward digital. Digital systems offer the advantages of improved error performance and improved bandwidth utilization through compression. Digital systems also support data communications much more effectively.

ANALOG CELLULAR

Analog cellular was the first approach and remains widely deployed, given its widespread implementation in the early years. Analog standards include AMPS, N-AMPS, TACS, and NMT [11-23]. Collectively, these analog solutions are categorized as G1 (Generation 1) systems.

AMPS (Advanced Mobile Phone System) was developed by Motorola and AT&T and largely is used in the United States. It is an analog technology operating on 50 MHz in the 800 MHz band and supporting 666 (832 in some areas) channels. In the United States, 25 MHz and 333 channels each are provided to the *A Carrier*, or *non-wireline carrier*, and the *B Carrier*, or *wireline carrier* (incumbent telco or telco consortium). Of the total number of channels awarded to each carrier, 21 channels are non-conversational channels dedicated to call setup, call hand-off, and call tear-down. The remaining communications channels are split into 30-kHz voice channels, with separation of 45 MHz between the forward and reverse channels. Based on FDMA and FDD transmission, AMPS does not handle data well, with transmission generally limited to 6,800 bps. Although widely deployed in the United States, Australia, The Philippines, and other countries, AMPS is rapidly giving way to digital technology. In fact, Australian regulators chose to mandate a cutover from analogue (That's Australian for analog, mate.) AMPS to digital GSM and CDMA, beginning December 31, 1999 in Melbourne. This gradually will extend throughout the country during 2000.

N-AMPS (Narrowband AMPS) also developed by Motorola, enhances the performance of an analog AMPS system. System capacity is improved by splitting each 30-kHz channel into three 10-kHz channels, thereby tripling AMPS capacity. Very few U.S. carriers deploy N-AMPS. Motorola equipment is required.

TACS (Total Access Communications System) is a derivative of AMPS, developed for use in the United Kingdom in the 900 MHz band. At this higher frequency, more native bandwidth is available; therefore, TACS supports up to 1,000 channels, each of 25 kHz, compared with the 666/832 channels supported by AMPS. TACS has found acceptance in very few nations, and it is not considered a long-term technology solution. *JTAC (Japanese Total Access Communications System)* is a TACS variation, operating in the 800-900 MHz ranges.

NMT (*Nordic Mobile Telephone*) was developed and placed into service in the early 1980s in Scandinavian countries, including Denmark, Finland, Norway, and Sweden. *NMT 450* operates in the 450 MHz range, which yields excellent signal propagation. Therefore, it is especially appropriate for sparsely populated areas supported by few cell sites. NMT 450 has found little acceptance outside of the Scandinavian countries. *NMT 900* operates in the 900 MHz range, and is appropriate for more densely populated areas. NMT 900 has found acceptance in certain countries in Asia, as well as the Nordic countries, although it is not considered a long-term technology.

DIGITAL CELLULAR

Digital cellular clearly will dominate the cellular radio world into the future. There are a great number of standards, and a number of standards-based solutions, none of which are compatible. Current digital standards include JDC, D-AMPS, GSM, and PCS. Worldwide, GSM clearly dominates. Collectively, these systems are grouped into the G2 (Generation 2) category.

PDC (Personal Digital Cellular) previously known as *JDC* (*Japanese Digital Cellular*), operates in various frequency bands in the 800 MHz, 900 MHz, 1400 MHz, and 1500 MHz ranges. It has not found acceptance outside Japan, with the exception of a few Asian countries under Japanese economic influence.

D-AMPS (Digital-AMPS) also known as *US TDMA*, was specified in IS-54 and later evolved into IS-136. D-AMPS is a North American digital cellular standard that operates in the same 800 MHz band as the earlier analog AMPS. In fact, the two can coexist in the same network. D-AMPS uses the same 30 kHz bands as AMPS, and supports up to 416 frequency channels per carrier. Through Time Division Multiplexing (TDD), each frequency channel is subdivided into six time slots, each of which operates at 8 Kbps. Each call initially uses two time slots (e.g., 1 and 4, 2 and 5, and 3 and 6) in each direction, for a total of 16 Kbps — which supports the data transfer, plus overhead for call processing. While the standard recommends speech compression at 8 Kbps (actually 7.95 Kbps), that is an average because each call can burst up to 48 Kbps. D-AMPS yields a 3:1 advantage over AMPS in terms of bandwidth utilization. IS-136 is known as a *dual-mode* standard because both D-AMPS and AMPS can coexist on the same network, with both using the same 21 control channels for call setup, call hand-off, and call tear-down. Thereby, IS-136 offers carriers the advantage of a graceful transition from analog to digital. IS-136 also includes a non-intrusive *Digital Control Channel* (*DCCH*), which is used for SMS (Short Message Service) and Caller ID. Data communications is supported at up to 9.6 Kbps per channel (paired time slots), and as many as three channels can be aggregated for speeds up to 28.8 Kbps. Group 3 facsimile also can be supported. The speech compression technique is *VSELP* (*Vector Sum Excited Linear Prediction*) and the RF modulation technique is *DQPSK* (*Differential Quaternary Phase Shift Keying*). McCaw

Wireless, which became AT&T Wireless, chose D-AMPS based on TDMA because it needed the capacity in certain systems before CDMA was available. BellSouth Cellular and Southwestern Bell Mobile Systems also use D-AMPS [11-24].

GSM (Global System for Mobile Communications) was adopted by the CEPT in 1987 as the standard for pan-European cellular systems. GSM operates in the 800 MHz and 900 MHz frequency ranges and is ISDN-compatible. GSM carves each 200 kHz band into eight TDMA channels of 33.8 Kbps – each of which supports a voice call at 13 Kbps, plus overhead of 9.8 Kbps. GSM commonly employs a 4-cell reuse plan, rather than the 7-cell plan used in AMPS, and divides each cell into 12 sectors. GSM commonly uses a frequency hopping and time-slot hopping, which also is used in CDMA systems. GSM offers additional security in the form of a *Subscriber Identification Module (SIM),* which plugs into a card slot in the handset, much as a PCMCIA card fits into a laptop computer. The SIM contains user-profile data, a description of access privileges and features, and identification of the cellular carrier in the area of home registry. The SIM can be used with any GSM set, thereby providing complete mobility across nations and carriers supporting GSM – assuming cross-billing relationships. GSM clearly developed to be the international standard of choice. GSM is in place in over 100 countries, and predominates throughout Europe and much of Asia, supporting full roaming privileges from country to country. With minor modifications, GSM is the basis for *DCS 1800*, also known as *PCN (Personal Communications Network)*, in Europe. DCS 1800, in large part, is an upbanded (i.e., operating in a higher frequency band) version of GSM, operating in the 1800 MHz (1.8 GHz) range. Also with minor modifications, it is the basis for *PCS 1900* in the United States, where it also is known as GSM. PCS 1900 is the ANSI standard (J-STD-007, 1995) for PCS at 1900 MHz (1.9 GHz). Unfortunately, PCS 1900 is not compatible with true GSM, which is to the decided disadvantage of its users. Sprint has deployed PCS 1900.

PCS (Personal Communications System) also known as *CDMA Digital Cellular*, is a U.S. term for cellular systems based on EIA/TIA IS-95. PCS uses one or more frequency bands of 1.25 MHz converted from the existing AMPS spectrum of each carrier deploying the service. Since CDMA is employed, no guard bands are required. IS-95 can support dual mode communications, operating in the same network as AMPS. As previously noted, CDMA offers the advantages of improved bandwidth utilization as compared to AMPS (as much as 7:1 or even 15:1), soft hand-off, variable-rate speech encoding, and support for both voice and data. The basic user channel rate is 9.6 Kbps, although various channel rates can be achieved depending on the carrier implementation. The variable-rate speech encoding algorithm runs at maximum rates of 8 Kbps (CELP) or 13 Kbps (*EVRC, or Enhanced Variable Rate Vocoder*), and varies the rate downward to as low as $1/8^{th}$ rate if the level of speech activity permits. The IS-95-B specification supports symmetric data rates up to 14.4 Kbps per channel and the aggregation of as many as eight channels for total bandwidth of 1.152 Mbps. CDMA offers additional advantages in terms of maximum cell size due to improved antennae sensitivity, and battery time due to precise power control mechanisms. IS-95 has been deployed by Airtouch, Ameritech Cellular, AT&T Wireless, Bell Atlantic Mobile, GTE MobilNet, 360(Communications, and others [11-25-11-28].

The Future of Cellular Radio

In 1994, Global Telecoms Business estimated that there were approximately 35 million cellular subscribers in more than 150 countries, and that cumulative growth rates were more than 30 percent per year. The U.S. market grew by almost 50 percent in 1993, and by 325 percent in Pakistan. They went on to say that wireless accounted for nearly 50 percent of Ericsson's sales, compared to a mere 6 percent in 1984. Lehman Brothers estimated cellular penetration of 9.4 percent by the year 2000, equating to 105 million users of a total accessible population of 1.1 billion [11-29]. Those estimates turned out to be very conservative. In the United States alone, the FCC estimated that there were 33.786 million cellular subscribers on January 1, 1996 [11-30]. The Cellular Telecommunications Industry Association estimates that there were over 60 million U.S. users as of June 30, 1998 [11-31]. Analysis Publications estimates that the Western European market will exceed 140 million users by 2003 [11-32]. One thing is certain – cellular radio will continue to grow at incredible rates in the foreseeable future.

We certainly are an increasingly mobile society and we clearly insist on remaining in touch. Cellular radio systems satisfy those requirements. And cellular service increasingly is affordable. While average rates were $0.45 per minute for airtime in the early 1990s (plus toll charges), they have dropped as low as $0.10 per minute in 1999 (with no domestic toll charges). If you travel as much as I do, you know that this compares very favorably with the cost of a long-distance call from an airport pay phone or hotel room – especially when you add the hotel surcharge.

In terms of technological futures, a number of G3 (Generation 3) proposals are under consideration. The ITU has defined a concept known as *IMT* (*International Mobile Telecommunications*) that calls for wireless data rates of 144 Kbps at mobile speeds, 384 Kbps at pedestrian speeds, and 2 Mbps in stationary environments. While the *IMT-2000* (IMT by the year 2000) proposal stalled, work continues. A variety of *W-CDMA* (*Wideband-CDMA*) proposals are under development, although they generally are proprietary and incompatible. The European contingent of the world community proposes something called *UMTS (Universal Mobile Telecommunications System)*, which would support global roaming through a combination of terrestrial and satellite platforms [11-33] through [11-35].

Cellular Data Communications

Cellular data communications is difficult at best because the analog FM networks are not designed to support data, certainly not at speeds above 9.6 Kbps or so. Given the high error rates typical in cellular networks, the data protocol must allow for repeated transmissions of errored and lost data packets, thereby often lowering throughput to the range of 1200 bps. Additionally, radio modems must be used to interface the computer to the cellular CPE and, in turn, to the network. While a number of manufacturers have developed PCMCIA cellular modems that operate at speeds up to 28.8 Kbps [11-36], throughput is much less. Digital cellular systems improve on the analog approach, offering all of data communications advantages enjoyed in the wired world. Those advantages include more usable bandwidth, improved error performance and, therefore, enhanced throughput.

In either event, data-over-cellular networks suffers from the same issues that affect cellular voice, only much more so. For instance, the *break and make* connection technique used in most cellular networks has a very deleterious impact on data communications. Additionally, *signal fade* affects communications as the terminal moves farther from the cell site, especially at high speed. To compensate for these factors, cellular modems must employ the most robust error-correction protocols.

In support of data communications over AMPS cellular networks, several manufacturers unveiled data-ready cellular phones as early as January 1995. Some of the devices have their own keypads, while others connect to a laptop PC for data entry. Display screens vary in size from 16 to 160 characters. In addition to support for voice and short message service, they support Internet access, facsimile, and e-mail [11-37].

CELLULAR DIGITAL PACKET DATA (CDPD)

Cellular Digital Packet Data (*CDPD*) is the data communications technique most commonly trialed and deployed in U.S. cellular networks, although it has not taken hold outside U.S. borders. Based on TCP/IP, CDPD operates over existing AMPS networks in the 800 MHz band, although substantial additional carrier investment is required to implement the technology. CDPD originally was intended to take advantage of the natural idleness in cellular networks in between disconnections and connections and during the *break and make* process — even heavily used cellular networks are said to be idle approximately 20-30 percent of the time. CDPD can use these periods of idleness to transmit packetized data at rates up to 19.2 Kbps, uncompressed, using connectionless protocols including either the Internet Protocol (IP) or OSI *Connectionless Network Protocol* (*CLNP*) [11-38] and [11-39]. CDPD modems, which may be either PCMCIA or external, are frequency-agile. They search for available channels over which to send encrypted packets during the periods of channel idleness. As this approach proved expensive, however, the carriers ultimately deployed CDPD over AMPS channels removed from voice service. WAN connectivity is through the traditional AMPS cellular networks, as well as through the separate CDPD internetworks [11-40] and [11-41].

The 128-byte encrypted packets each contain a destination address, source address, sequence number, and payload [11-3]. The contention method is *DSMA/CD* (*Digital Sense Multiple Access/Collision Detect*), which is much like CSMA/CD used in Ethernet LANs. CDPD operates at Layers 1 & 2 of the OSI Reference Model, providing access to Layer 3 protocols IP or ISO Connectionless Network Protocol (CLNP). As a result of its IP-based design, applications such as Netscape and Mosaic can run on top of CDPD to provide access to the Internet and World Wide Web.

CDPD was formalized in July 1993 by the Cellular Digital Packet Data consortium, which comprises Ameritech Cellular, Bell Atlantic Mobile (BAM), CONTEL Cellular (now GTE Mobilnet), GTE Mobilnet, McCaw Cellular Communications (now AT&T Wireless), NYNEX Mobile Communications, PacTel Cellular (now AirTouch), and Southwestern Bell Mobile Systems. The CDPD Forum, established in June 1994, acts to promote the commercialization of CDPD products and services that are available now in most major U.S. markets.

Third-party application developers have announced the availability of a number of CDPD applications, including LAN access, host access, internet access, call management and voice processing, credit card verification, check verification, and vehicle tracking and dispatch [11-42]. In a cellular radio application, costs for CDPD include activation charges, monthly charges, and usage charges based on some combination of minutes of usage, packets, and kilobytes — whether calls are incoming or outgoing [11-43] through [11-45]. In native mode, CDPD costs can add up quickly due to airtime charges. These costs can be reduced considerably through the use of *middleware*, such as software offered by Wireless Telecom, Inc. Such middleware uses various compression techniques to shorten connect time for data transfers. Additionally, protocol reduction techniques can eliminate both the *Remote Procedure Calls* (*RPCs*) between the mobile client and the Intranet server, and the end-to-end TCP/IP sessions typically established.

MOBILE DATA: THE ORIGINS

Now, I'll take the author's privilege of digressing a bit to discuss the origins of mobile data communications — at least to the best of my ability. It seems that the United States Cavalry faced a major problem in 1907. When a cavalry troop was on patrol, it required some means of communicating back to a command and control center. Therefore, a single mounted soldier trailed behind the troop, unreeling copper wire as he rode along. When it was necessary to send a message, the troop stopped until the communications specialist caught up, or sent a rider back to meet him. Then, the communications specialist reined in his mount, hopped off, planted a metal stake in the ground to complete the circuit, and sent a telegraph message via Morse code. As this approach clearly slowed the movement of the troop, some brilliant engineers sought and found another solution. The solution was to shave a spot on the horse's rump, and attach a copper patch. Since a horse always has at least one foot on the ground, even at a full run, the circuit remained complete and the scouts could send a message while riding. So, that's the true story of the beginning of mobile data communications — and it had nothing to do with wireless. In closing, no mention is made of the attitude of the horse toward this technological breakthrough, although it must have been a humiliating experience which the other horses in the stable undoubtedly found to be highly amusing. Neither is any mention made of the bit error rate (double-entendre intended) [11-46].

Wireless Data Networks: Packet Radio

Data-specific wireless networks have been deployed in the United States during the last several years, with coverage of virtually all major metropolitan areas using the 800-900-MHz radio bands [11-3]. Such networks offer data communications to data-intensive users using proprietary packet protocols; integrated messaging service is supported, as well. Applications include sales agents, maintenance fleets, and truck fleets. Providers include BellSouth Wireless Data, Ardis, and Metricom. Those companies face competition especially from Nextel Communications (Geotek Communications, a previous competitor, filed bankruptcy in February 1999. Currently, Nextel is awaiting final approvals to acquire Geotek's spectrum licenses in the 900 MHz band), and CDPD offerings from the AMPS cellular providers. Charges generally include a set-up charge and a cost per packet, which can vary by packet size; package plans also are available.

BellSouth Wireless Data, previously RAM Mobile Data, was formed in 1988 by RAM Broadcasting Corporation. BellSouth acquired a 49 percent stake in 1992 and acquired the remaining 51 percent in March 1998. BellSouth operates its nation-wide Mobitex service using 200 channels in the 900 MHz band, each channel offering throughput of 8 Kbps. At year-end 1994, RAM claimed to have a presence in 266 metropolitan areas and approximately 7,500 U.S. cities, covering 93 percent of the population. The metropolitan networks are interconnected through the RAM packet data backbone, with WAN access through X.25 and other options. Major users include Kodak, Unisys, Sears, and General Electric [11-3].

ARDIS Co., formerly known as Advanced Radio Data Information Services, was formed in 1990 as a subsidiary of Motorola, merging the IBM Network and Motorola Data Radio Network. In March 1998, American Mobile Satellite Corporation acquired ARDIS. ARDIS builds on the foundation of a network originally designed for IBM in 1983. ARDISnet operates over 600 channels in the 800 MHz band and of-fers throughput from 4.8 Kbps (nationwide) to 19.2 Kbps in selected cities. While the 4.8 Kbps service makes use of a proprietary protocol (*Motorola Data Protocol*, or *MDP*), 19.2 Kbps service is based on *RD-LAP* (*Radio Data-Link Access Protocol*). ARDIS claims to have reached over 11,000 cities in over 427 U.S. metropolitan areas. WAN access is provided through PDNs (Public Data Networks), as well as the ARDIS packet data backbone network [11-47].

Metricom Inc. offers Ricochet, which provides data transmission at 77 Kbps in the unlicensed 902-928 MHz band, and uses spread spectrum technology. Ricochet uses a mesh of low-power, microcellular radio sites in the San Francisco Bay Area, Seattle, and Washington, D.C. WAN connections are provided through asynchronous modems or via the Internet. Despite the low cost of the service, Metricom currently has a subscriber base of only 25,000, and has been unable to open new markets. The company, however, does intend to introduce (in late 1999) an ISDN mobile service operating in unlicensed spectrum in the 902-928 MHz and 2.4 GHz bands, and in the licensed 2.3 HGz band [11-48].

Wireless LANs (WLANs)

As discussed in some detail in Chapter 8, *wireless LAN* (*WLAN*) technology has enjoyed modest success in the LAN world during the last few years. Offering the obvious advantage of no wiring costs, wireless LANs can be deployed to great benefit in a dynamic environment where there is frequent reconfiguration of the workplace. They also offer clear advantages in providing LAN connectivity in temporary quarters, where cabling soon would have to be abandoned. Wireless LANs largely are based on spread-spectrum technology refined in World War II for use in radio-controlled torpedoes. This approach offers significantly increased security and throughput, as discussed earlier in this chapter.

In a typical RF-based WLAN environment, each workstation is fitted with a transmit/receive radio antenna, which can be in the form of a PCMCIA card. A hub antenna is located at a central point, such as the center or corner of the ceiling. Then, that antenna is connected to other hub antennae and to the servers, peripherals, and hosts via cabled connections, which also connect together multiple hub antennae for transmission between rooms, floors, buildings, etc. In order to serve multiple workstations, spread-spectrum radio technology is employed to maximize the effective use of limited bandwidth. A side benefit of spread spectrum is that of increased security. While the raw aggregate bandwidth generally is described as 4 Mbps, the effective throughput is more in the range of 2 Mbps per hub. Some non-standard RF-based systems offer bandwidth up to 11 Mbps, generally in the form of wireless bridges for inter-building applications. Infrared-based bridges run at speeds as high as 622 Mbps, which supports full-speed ATM backbone LAN connectivity.

Although a number of non-standard wireless LANs exist, standards were finalized in 1997 by the IEEE 802.11 Working Group, which began its efforts in 1989. Those standards specify Layers 1 (Physical) and 2 (Data Link). With respect to transmission media, WLANs operate on infrared (Ir), as well as radio frequency (RF) in the 2.4 GHz to 2.4835 GHz range, which is the unlicensed ISM (Industrial, Scientific and Medical) band, and run at speeds of 1 Mbps and 2 Mbps. The RF specifications include both DSSS (Direct Sequence Spread Spectrum) and FHSS (Frequency Hopping Spread Spectrum), and the Ethernet CSMA/CA (Carrier Sense Multiple Access/Collision Avoid) protocol. This Ethernet MAC (Media Access Control) protocol involves the establishment of (what amounts to) a virtual circuit through the positive acknowledgement of the availability of the receiving station through the network. The transmitting station sends a *RTS* (*Request To Send*) packet over the airwaves. If the target device is available, it responds with a *CTS* (*Clear To Send*) packet, which prompts the originating device to begin transmission. Other WLAN-attached devices honor this virtual circuit agreement, thereby avoiding issues of congestion, collision, and packet data loss. This MAC-level protocol works well with the CSMA/CD protocol more typically used in conventional wired Ethernets, thereby supporting physical interconnectivity between the wired and wireless LANs on a logically indistinguishable basis. While 802.11 is specific to the 2.4 GHz range and infrared, WLANs operate in several distinct radio frequency ranges, as well as on an infrared basis.

902 MHz-928 MHz are unlicensed frequencies in the ISM (Industrial, Scientific and Medical) band. That approach avoids expensive and lengthy licensing by the regulatory authorities, but carries with it the potential for interference from other such systems in proximity. As this frequency range was set aside by the FCC for unlicensed in-building communications, such systems are susceptible to interference from other systems that might include cordless telephones, microwave ovens, garage door openers, and RF-based barcode scanning systems. Spread-spectrum technology generally is used at these frequencies to mitigate issues of interference. As power levels are low, distances generally are limited to 500-800 feet. (It's comforting to know, therefore, that your usage of a WLAN in the ISM band likely won't cause garage doors to pop up and down all over the neighborhood. Better yet, garage door openers are unlikely to cause your systems to crash.)

2.4 GHz-2.5 GHz and 5.8 GHz-5.9 GHz microwave systems using spread-spectrum technology also are permitted to operate without licensing. At these high frequencies and at low power levels, signal propagation is highly distance-limited. Many of the systems that use licensed frequencies in this range avoid the potential for interference, but do require that the manufacturer carefully police the deployment of such systems under the terms of an omni-license. Alternatively, these frequencies can be used without licensing, if they are low power and use spread-spectrum coding.

5.15 GHz-5.25 GHz, 5.25 GHz-5.35 GHz and 5.75 GHz-5.85 GHz spectrum was made available by the FCC in January 1997. These bands, which are part of the Unlicensed National Information Infrastructure (U-NII) spectrum, are relatively free of interference and offer the potential for transmission at much higher speeds than the currently specified 2 Mbps maximum [11-49].

18 GHz-19 GHz are sometimes employed in a wireless LAN environment, at low-power levels. The same frequencies are used in commercial microwave systems, thereby offering the potential for interference unless spread-spectrum coding is employed.

Infrared light systems require no licensing. The potential for interference between systems is very limited as line-of-sight is required. Transmission rates of 4 Mbps are common, with some systems providing transmission of 10 Mbps and 16 Mbps; typical applications include inter-building connectivity. Infrared LAN bridges commonly operate at rates of T-1 and T-3, and less commonly at 155 Mbps and even 622 Mbps.

A number of *Special Interest Groups* (*SIGs*) also have made progress on non-standard specifications, many of which are directed at the seamless interconnectivity of a wide variety of devices such as cellular telephones, portable computers, PDAs, and peripherals. These groups and specifications include the Bluetooth Special Interest Group with its Bluetooth specification (named after the 10th century king who unified Denmark), the Home RF Working Group with SWAP, and the Wireless LAN Interoperability Forum (WLIF) with OpenAir [11-50] and [11-51].

Wireless LANs: Applications and Futures

While wireless LANs have gained a foothold in the United States, their future is less certain elsewhere. In 1997, it was estimated that the United States accounted for approximately 70 percent of the global WLAN market of $496 million; that market is expected to grow to just over $2 billion in 2001 [11-5]. Traditionally, ETSI has endorsed DECT as the standard, providing up to 1.14 Mbps. However, the 2.4 GHz (U.K.) and 18 GHz (Germany) bands also are being promoted. The concern of ETSI and the EC seems to be that the use of those frequencies will favor U.S. manufacturers. As the saying goes, *Think global; buy local!* ETSI also has made progress on a standard known as *HiperLAN*, which runs at speeds up to 24 Mbps in the 5 GHz range.

An interesting application for wireless LANs is that of certain grocery stores in northern California. Some shopping carts are equipped with wireless terminals that communicate with servers through hub antennae, using unlicensed radio frequencies and spread-spectrum technology. The shopper can key into the terminal the general categories of items on the shopping list, and be guided through the store with the aid of a map displayed on the terminal screen. Scattered throughout the store are special in-store coupon offers, which can be accepted through wireless acknowledgement. Once the shopper reaches the checkstand, the coupon acknowledgement is communicated to the intelligent point-of-sale device (cash register) and is credited against the purchase – without any paper changing hands.

Wireless LANs in the ISM band also commonly are used in warehousing and distribution applications. In an extreme example, a forklift equipped with a RF client terminal device might be directed to a truck at a receiving dock. As it enters the truck, the client terminal might scan a magnetized bar-coded tag on a pallet of merchandise, sending that information to a server; it then might instruct the forklift to transport that same pallet to the loading dock for immediate shipment. Thereby, the pallet is checked into inventory and immediately checked out, without ever resting on a shelf in a warehouse. It's not exactly *data warehousing* in the contemporary sense of the phrase, but it's a great application for WLAN technology.

Wireless Local Loop (WLL)

The local loop is the access circuit from the customer premises to the service provider's closest *Point of Presence* (*POP*). In traditional terms and generally speaking, we think of the service provider to be a LEC (Local Exchange Carrier), and the POP to be in the form of a Central Office (CO) switch, which sits at the edge of the cloud of the PSTN (Public Switched Telephone Network). In contemporary terms, the carrier just as easily can be an IXC (IntereXchange Carrier) or a data service provider. The POP just as easily can be a Frame Relay Network Device in the form of switch or router, or even an ATM switch. The cloud just as easily can be a Frame Relay network, the Internet, or an ATM network. Regardless of the nature of the service provider, the POP, and the cloud, access is a must, and access is gained through the local loop.

Local loops have several problems. First, the vast majority of them are a twisted pair — a very old twisted pair — which tends to offer relatively little in terms of bandwidth and error performance, and which is highly distance-limited, especially at the higher frequencies required to boost the bandwidth. Second, a twisted pair is a cabled medium, and cabled media (i.e., twisted pair, coax, and optical fiber) are expensive and time-consuming to deploy. Right-of-way must be secured, trenches must be plowed and conduits placed, poles must be planted, and crossarms must be hung, splices must be made, amplifiers and repeaters must be connected, and so on. Third, the LECs own most of the local loops. (CATV providers own the coaxial cable network, but that's another story). The Telecommunications Act of 1996 set the stage for competition in the local loop, by requiring that the LECs cooperate with the CLECs (Competitive LECs). Essentially, they must unbundle the cost of the loop, and must make it available to their competitors on a cost-based basis, and they must do so with reasonable speed. The primary incentive to the ILECs (Incumbent LECs) is that they will be permitted to offer interLATA voice and data services within their home states of operation once they satisfy the FCC that they have co-operated with their competitors. It's only one point of a 14-point checklist, but it's an incredibly powerful point.

The cost of copper local loops in North America ranges from approximately $1,000 to $7,500, with the upper end of the range applying where terrain is especially difficult (e.g., rocky soil or high water tables) or where population density is low (e.g., Loma Alta, Texas or Ojo Caliente, New Mexico). The cost of an optical fiber loop is much higher, but they are deployed in support of high-volume business in high-density areas. Since local-loop revenues generally are low and costs are high, there really are no profits in the local loop business. Rather, the profits are in the capabilities of the networks to which they provide access. And whoever controls the local loop controls access to the network.

As a CLEC (voice or data), therefore, you have two basic choices. First, you can lease local loops from the ILEC, which has mixed emotions about assisting its competition. The ILEC executive in the blue suit has one, very formal, position, while the union craftsman in the tool belt has quite another position, which is much less formal. Secondly, you can build your own local loops. It comes down to a basic *build or buy* decision.

When considering building local loops, twisted pair is almost out of the question, unless you are an ILEC extending a last-mile legacy network. Coaxial cable is out of the question, unless you are a CATV provider extending a last-mile legacy network. Fiber optics really is the only cabled choice, for reasons of bandwidth, error performance, distance, and resiliency. Fiber is the optimum choice, whether in the trunk facilities or to the premises, but it's just too expensive now for low-capacity applications (e.g., small business, home office, or residential). Again, however, the deployment of cabled transmission systems is an expensive and lengthy process.

In building local loops, the advantages of *Wireless Local Loop* (*WLL*), also known as *fixed wireless,* are fairly obvious at this point in our discussion of communications systems and networks. First, WLL systems can be deployed much more quickly and much less expensively. Second, the aggregate bandwidth of the system can be apportioned to end users on a channelized basis. Third, the system can be configured and reconfigured, and can be managed on a remote basis. The disadvantages of WLL also are fairly obvious. First, interference always is an issue, and one that in many ways is out of the control of both the service provider and the user organization. While licensed frequency bands are protected from direct interference from others that might covet the same frequencies, unlicensed bands are available for all to share. Regardless of whether the band is licensed or not, Radio Frequency Interference (RFI) and ElectroMagnetic Interference (EMI) remains an issue. Such interference can be caused by electric motors, radio systems transmitting out of their assigned bands or in excess of their prescribed power levels, and by the forces of nature (e.g., lightning, static electricity, and solar flares). Additionally, the quality of the airwaves is always an issue because dust, smoke, pollution, temperature, precipitation, and humidity can negatively affect the quality of the signal. Second, distances are limited due to factors such as quality of the airwaves and the frequencies used; remember that higher frequency signals suffer attenuation to a much greater extent than do lower frequency signals. Third, line-of-sight is preferable, and absolutely is required at the higher frequencies. Fourth, the process of licensing can be lengthy and expensive, especially given the great demand for licensed spectrum. Finally, security is always an issue with radio systems. Note that WLL comprises radio frequency (RF) systems – infrared (Ir) is just too limited in its capabilities to be considered a viable WLL technology.

The WLL options available are many, including non-standard and standard approaches, and licensed and unlicensed frequency bands. This discussion includes the most significant and interesting, at least now. Regardless of the specific technology, WLL configurations include centralized antennae, which support RF connectivity to matching antenna at the customer premises, as illustrated in Figure 11-10. The reach of the centralized antennae may be extended through cabled connections to remote antennae. As a local-loop technology, the centralized antennae either are located at the edge of the carrier network or are connected to the network edge via optical fiber.

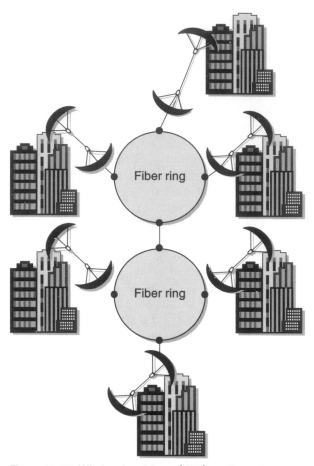

Figure 11-10 Wireless Local Loop (WLL) configurations

Local Multipoint Distribution Services (LMDS)

Bernard B. Broussard developed *Local Multipoint Distribution Services* (*LMDS*). Together with Shant and Vahak Hovnanian, they formed CellularVision, a New York wireless cable TV firm that provided 49 TV channels, and later added high-speed Internet access. The technical rights to LMDS technology later were spun off into a separate company. The FCC auctioned licenses for LMDS radio in early 1998. The 104 successful bidders yielded revenues of approximately $578 million, which underscores the interest in WLL. Notably, and in consideration of the emphasis on competition in the local loop, the RBOCs and CATV providers were not permitted to participate, and further were prevented from holding any LMDS licenses for a period of three years. Licenses were awarded in two blocks for each of 492 markets known as *Basic Trading Areas* (*BTAs*). The *A Block* has a width of 1.15 GHz in the frequency ranges of 27.5-28.35 GHz, 29.1-29.25 GHz, and 31.0-31.15 GHz. The *B Block* has a width of 150 MHz in the spectrum between 31.15 GHz and 31.3 GHz. Given the range of frequencies used in the GHz range, LMDS requires line-of-sight, and generally is limited in distance to a cell diameter of 10 miles—although cell sizes generally are much smaller. LMDS can carve a 360(cell into four quadrants of alternating polarity, thereby improving traffic capacity. As a digital microwave system, LMDS offers excellent error performance, with rain fade compensation through the use of adaptive power controls. LMDS is flexible enough to support local loops ranging from T-1 (1.544 Mbps) to 155 Mbps, and in either symmetric or asymmetric configurations. Individual subscribers in office complexes or multidwelling units (MDUs) can gain access to bandwidth in DS-0 (64 Kbps) increments. Spectrum bandwidth efficiency is achieved through a variety of modulation techniques including QAM (Quadrature Amplitude Modulation). Outside the United States, LMDS is expected to operate in the 20 GHz and 45 GHz bands [11-52-11-54].

Multichannel Multipoint Distribution Services (MMDS)

Operating in the 2.5-2.7 GHz range, *Multichannel Multipoint Distribution Services* (*MMDS*) has enjoyed limited success for one-way TV transmission. While line-of-sight is required, distances of up to 35 miles can be achieved in the relatively low range of the microwave spectrum. MMDS also has been tweaked for two-way applications. Currently, MMDS has stalled, primarily to the limited bandwidth of 200 MHz [11-55] and [11-56].

Licensed Microwave

In the frequency ranges of 24 GHz and 38 GHz, the FCC has licensed microwave to a number of service providers for point-to-point WLL applications. The licenses are for aggregate channel capacity of 100 MHz, which can be subdivided into local loop channels of T-1 (1.544 Mbps), 8 T-1s (12.352 Mbps), T-3 (44.736 Mbps), or even 155 Mbps. Some carriers hold multiple licenses, which yield aggregate bandwidth of 400-500 MHz or more. In these microwave frequency ranges, line-of-sight is required and distances are limited to approximately five miles. Typically, the cells are much smaller, in consideration of the advantages of frequency reuse. Error performance for these digital microwave systems is in the range of 10^{-13}, which compares very favorably with UTP-based T-1 at 10^{-7}; in fact, and under optimal conditions, it compares with optical fiber. The paired transmit/receive typically are about one foot in diameter, with a pair currently costing in the range of $10,000-$12,000. Larger antennae and variable power levels are employed to compensate for *rain fade* in areas of heavy and prolonged rainfall. Teligent (previously Associated Communications) is the most notable license-holder in the 24 GHz range, having shifted from the 18 GHz range based on agreements with the FCC and Teledesic. Winstar is the most notable license-holder in the 38 GHz range, and also holds a number of LMDS licenses. AT&T

acquired a number of 38 GHz licenses through the acquisition of Teleport Communications Group (TCG) in 1998. Advanced Radio Telecom also holds licenses in the 38 GHz range [11-56-11-58].

Personal Communications Services (PCS)

Personal Communications Services (*PCS*) is the U.S. term for the *Personal Communications Network* (*PCN*) concept originally developed in the United Kingdom. PCS is a service concept, which is technology-dependent and which operates on a set of frequencies set aside for its purpose. PCS ultimately intends to provide a full range of enhanced services through a single device and utilizing one telephone number, which will work *anywhere and anytime, for life.* Earlier in this chapter, I discussed the use of the term *PCS* for a digital cellular telephony alternative, using analog AMPS bands in the 800-900 MHz range. Actually, , *PCS* now means just about anything. At this point, let's explore PCS in the context of the FCC licenses, with a focus on WLL.

While the spectrum allocation varies by country or region, the designated U.S. frequencies include Narrowband, Broadband, and Unlicensed PCS. Actually, much of the PCS spectrum already was spoken for by high-band microwave systems; clearing that spectrum is the responsibility of the PCS licensees, at an estimated cost of at least $70 million [11-3]. For the first time in U.S. history, that spectrum was auctioned (and re-auctioned in some cases, after default on downpayments...a long story) by geographic area. The 1995 auctions of two frequency blocks brought in $7.7 billion, and the 1996 auctions accounted for another $10.22 billion.

Unfortunately, the competing PCS providers are not expected to provide interconnectivity, except through the PSTN – much as is the case with cellular providers. Additionally, different technologies will be deployed in support of PCS, from region to region. This translates into a lack of portability, or roaming capability. In other words, the PCS terminal used in San Francisco may well not be able to access a PCS network in Dallas so, the concept of PCS as an anytime, anywhere wireless network will not be realized.

Narrowband PCS	has been allocated spectrum in the ranges of 900-901 MHz, 930-931 MHz, and 940-941 MHz. That AMPS spectrum extends the capabilities of pagers and cell phones to include acknowledgement paging, two-way messaging, and digital voice.
Broadband PCS	is allocated 120 MHz in the 1.85-1.91 GHz and 1.93-1.99 GHz ranges. This spectrum is intended for the delivery of next-generation, high-tier wireless communications including WLL, voice and data services, and cellular-like services for pedestrian traffic in high-density areas [11-59].

Unlicensed PCS   spectrum serves low-tier applications such as wireless
                                  LANs, wireless PBXs, PDAs, and PCS voice and data
                                  services with a building or campus environment.
                                  Unlicensed PCS spectrum has been set aside in two
                                  ranges, with 20 MHz in the 1.91 GHz to 1.93 GHz
                                  range, and 10 MHz in the 2.39-2.40 GHz range.

Low-Earth Orbiting Satellites (LEOs)

Low-Earth Orbiting and *Middle-Earth Orbiting* satellites (*LEOs* and *MEOs*) are satellites
that operate at low altitudes of several hundred miles or so, in a variety of non-equa-
torial orbital planes. This compares with *Geosynchronous Earth Orbiting* satellites
(*GEOs*), which always are placed in equatorial orbital slots at an altitude of approximately 22, 300 miles (Chapter 2). LEOs operate at altitudes of 644-2,415 kilometers.
Although the term is not tightly defined, *Little LEOs* involve a relatively small number
of satellites, and operate at frequencies below 1 GHz in support of low bit-rate data
traffic (e.g., telemetry, vehicle messaging, and personal messaging). *Big LEOs* are bigger networks that operate at higher frequencies in support of voice and higher-speed
data communications. MEOs operate at altitudes of 10,062-20,940 kilometers.

LEOs & MEOs systems are configured as constellations of small, low-power
satellites. In combination, the satellites in such a constellation at least provide
full coverage of major land masses, and often are designed to provide full coverage of every square inch of the earth's surface. The various proposals include
from 12 to 840 satellites, and are intended to provide various combinations of
voice and data services. These systems also are known as *Mobile Satellite Systems*
(MSSs), as opposed to the *Fixed Satellite Systems* (*FSSs*) in geostatic orbit.
Whizzing around the earth like electrons whizzing around the nucleus of an atom
(see Figure 11-11), LEO & MEO networks are designed so that a satellite is always
within reach of a terrestrial terminal.

The origin of this incredible concept is worth exploring. According to legend, the
wife of a Motorola executive was vacationing in the Bahamas and was irritated by
her inability to place a certain telephone call (probably from some secluded beach).
She complained to her husband, and captured his imagination. In any event,
Motorola named its proposed 77-satellite constellation *Iridium*, after the element
iridium, which is Number 77 in the Periodic Table of Elements. Subsequently, the
proposal was pared down to 66 satellites, although the name *Iridium* stuck. After
all, *Iridium* seems to roll off the tongue better than *Dysprosium*, the rare earth element which is number 66. *Iridium* also translates from the Greek as *rainbow*, which
can describe a rainbow of bandwidth. The Iridium constellation is now fully
launched. Eleven operational satellites, and one spare, are placed in each of the six
orbital planes, at altitudes of 421.5 nautical miles.

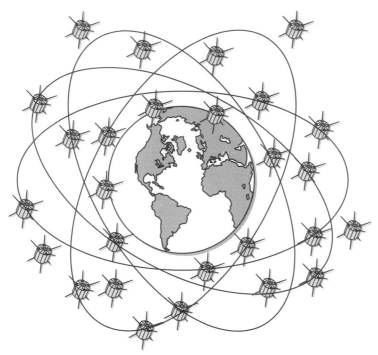

Figure 11-11 Low-Earth Orbiting (LEO) satellite constellation

How LEOs Work

Now, let's discuss how LEO constellations work. First, we'll focus on Iridium (refer to Figure 11-12), which is the most significant operational constellation at the present. From an Iridium phone, you might initiate a voice call to another Iridium phone, using a special international telephone number in a block allocated to Iridium. The telephones are a slightly supersized version of a cellular phone. Since it is a satellite call running in the GHz range, you need line-of-sight, so you either need to be out in the open or you need to stick a little satellite dish on top of your automobile. (Please do NOT try this while seated in a taxicab in New York City or Hong Kong.) Your Iridium phone, by the way, is equipped with an antenna the size of a good cigar, which you first must unfold. Your connection to the satellite is supported over the L-band, at frequencies of 1.616-1.6265 GHz. Through a gateway, Ka-band frequencies are used, with 29.1-29.3 GHz on the uplink and 19.4-19.4 GHz on the downlink. Once connected to the satellite, the inter-satellite links operate in the Ka-band, at frequencies of 23.18-23.38 GHz. (See Table 11-2 for a listing of satellite frequency bands.) The satellite constellation finds the target Iridium phone just like a cellular network finds another cell phone — each active (powered-up) phone maintains a signaling and control link with the satellite network — just like your cell phone keeps in touch with the cellular network when it powers-up. Presto, you're connected, and the quality resembles that of an analog AMPS network, which is pretty good for a satellite call. Propagation delay isn't much of an issue for several reasons. First, the satellites are in Low-Earth Orbits of approximately 485 miles, so the uplink and downlink propagation delays are not significant. Second, the satellites communicate directly over inter-satellite links, so only one uplink and one downlink are required. As the satellites whiz around the earth like electrons whiz around the nucleus of an atom, however, you can't maintain contact with any given satellite for very long, and neither can the other party involved in this telephone call. Therefore, the satellites with which you established the connection must pass that call off to another satellite before it gets out of view, and so must the satellite at the terminating end — and so must every satellite in between. Think of it as a cellular network in reverse. In a cellular network, the antennae at the cell sites are stationary. As you whiz through the cellular network in your high-speed vehicle, the cellular network maintains the connection through a hand-off process between cell sites. In an Iridium environment, you are the one who is (relatively) stationary, while the cell sites whiz around you. Iridium also, by the way, supports pagers, and airplane communications, via the same L-band frequencies. If you call a device that is not on the Iridium network, your call can be connected to the existing PSTN and cellular networks via 12 regional gateways.

Table 11-2 SATELLITE FREQUENCY BANDS

IEEE Band Designation	Frequency Range (Upper-Lower Limits)
L-band	1-2 GHz
S-band	2-4 GHz
C-band	4-8 GHz
X-band	8-12 GHz
Ku-band*	12-18 GHz
K-band	18-27 GHz
Ka-band**	27-40 GHz
Q-band***	33-50 GHz
U-band****	40-60 GHz
V-band*****	40-75 GHz
W-band	75-110 GHz

*Ku = under K-band
**Ka = above K-band, commonly designated as 20-30 GHz
***FCC designation
****FCC designation
*****FCC designation, 50-75 GHz

Iridium is an incredible network, and it should be – the total capital investment was in the neighborhood of $4.7 billion. The system went fully operational on November 1, 1998. On May 28, 1999, Iridium LLC received a waiver until June 30 of certain financial covenants from all its lenders, to enable it to restructure its capitalization. Those covenants required that the company have at least 27,000 customers by May 31. It seems as though the actual numbers fell far short of that requirement. At a cost of $3,000 or so for an Iridium phone, $3,795 for a dual-mode phone that also works on existing cellular networks, $500 or so for a pager (one-way, so no guaranteed message delivery), a considerable monthly charge, and $3-$7 a minute for the connect time (depending on which press releases and articles you believe), Iridium's pretty pricey – unless you want to call from the summit of Mt. Everest (true story) to the jungles of New Guinea. (It's possible, if the canopy of the rain forest isn't too thick.) The bleak beginnings of Iridium have given pause to the other eight or so remaining proposed LEO networks [11-60-[11-64]. , Iridium soon announced deep price cuts for both terminal equipment and airtime, although this action was too little, too late – Iridium defaulted on its loan payments, and ownership reverted to the creditors in mid-1999.

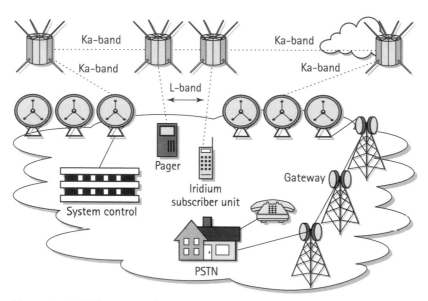

Figure 11-12 Iridium network

Let's now turn our attention to the Teledesic LEO network, dubbed the *Internet-in-The-Sky*. *Teledesic* is a combination of *tele*, meaning over a distance, and *geodesic*, meaning the shortest distance between two points that lie on a given surface (i.e., the earth). Before we identify the two points involved, let's examine the origins of Teledesic, the concept, and the underlying technologies. Teledesic is the brainchild of Bill Gates of Microsoft fame, Craig McCaw of McCaw Cellular (now AT&T Wireless) fame, and Boeing of Boeing aircraft fame. Gates knows a lot about computers and the Internet, McCaw knows a lot about wireless, and Boeing knows a lot about satellites and launch vehicles. Motorola joined this group and now owns a 26-percent stake in the venture; Saudi Prince Alwaleed Bin Talal also has invested some $200 million. (By the way, they all know a lot about making money.) The idea behind Teledesic is to launch a constellation of 288 (pared down from 840) broadband LEOs, plus spares, for Internet access. These two-way satellites are intended to support high-speed Internet access from any business or residence on the face of the earth. The satellites would whiz around your inexpensive, two-way satellite dish at low altitudes (about 700 kilometers), thereby avoiding the aggravating issues of propagation delay that might otherwise have you yelling at your computer. From your computer, you would have a connection to your dish, to the satellite, from satellite to satellite, and down to a portal, which would be your gateway to the Internet and the World Wide Web. The costs of your access to this $9 billion network are expected to be competitive when it becomes operational in 2003 or so. Your asymmetric access speeds are expected to be up to 2 Mbps on the uplink (Ka-band at 28.6-29.1 GHz, using FDMA), and up to 64 Mbps or more on the downlink (Ka-band at 18.8-19.3 GHz, using TDMA). Optional symmetric speeds of 64 Mbps or more also are expected to be available [11-60], [11-61], and [11-65]. That's the basic idea, and it's an incredible one ... if the technology falls into place ... and there's no reason that it can't. There are a lot of very smart people behind this project, with very deep pockets, at very big stakes. If you stop to think about Teledesic for just a minute, you will realize that it will bypass your modem (e.g., conventional, IDSN, xDSL, and CATV), your local loop (e.g., analog voice-grade, ISDN, xDSL, CATV, T-1, and T-3), your LEC (ILEC or CLEC), your ISP, the wired Internet backbone and all its pieceparts, and your current portal. Teledesic will bypass everything conventional. (Referring back to the definition of *Teledesic* at the beginning of this discussion, you now understand that the term means that the shortest distance between your computer and the Teledesic portal is the Teledesic network.) Now, I may not be as smart as the Teledesic folks, and I certainly don't have pockets nearly as deep as the least rich of the lot, but I'll bet my next royalty check from this book that the Teledesic portal won't be optimized for Netscape Navigator — if it even works. As I said before, it's an incredible idea. Note, however, that Teledesic was conceived in 1986, when there were no optical fiber backbones, no xDSL, and no cable modems, and when Internet access typically involved modems that ran at the blazing speed of 19.2 Kbps, best case. Table 11-3 provides a view of the key characteristics of some of the most notable LEO and MEO constellations either in service or currently proposed.

Table 11-3 PROPOSED LOW EARTH ORBITING (LEO) AND MIDDLE EARTH ORBITING (MEO) SATELLITE CONSTELLATIONS

	Globalstar	ICO	Iridium	Odyssey	Teledesic
Services	Voice, data, fax, paging, position location	Voice, data, fax, short message service	Voice, data, fax, paging, position location	Voice, data, fax, paging, position location	Voice, data, fax, paging, video, Internet access
Modulation Technique	QPSK	QPSK	????	QPSK	QPSK
Orbital Class	LEO	MEO	LEO	MEO	LEO
Altitude (km)	1,410	10,390	780	10,354	695–705
Number of Satellites (Active/In-orbit Spares)	48/8	10/2	66/6	12/3	288/??
Visibility Time, or Dwell Time in Minutes	16.4	115.6	11.1	94.5	3.5
Roundtrip Propagation Delay in Milliseconds Minimum/Maximum)	4.63/11.5	34.5/48.0	2.60/8.22	34.6/44.3	2.32/3.4

Personal Digital Assistants (PDAs)

Personal Digital Assistants (PDAs), also known as *Personal Communicators*, are multifunction devices, most of which have wireless communications options. The first PDA generally is recognized as having been the Linus Pen Computer, which was introduced in 1987, but faded from the scene in the early 1990s [11-66]. Next on the scene (1993) was Apple Computer's Newton, which was discontinued in 1998. Proprietary operating systems generally are employed, although the Windows CE operating system, introduced in 1995, is a considerable step toward an open platform. A Graphic User Interface (GUI) is a standard, and vital, characteristic of PDAs. Data entry is via a combination of handwriting and soft keys, with some devices supporting external keyboards. The devices will accommodate one or two PCMCIA cards for wireless networking, with most also supporting infrared communications, and with some boasting internal wireless modems. The PCMCIA slot(s), of which there are one or two, support wireless modems, flash memory, applications, and attachable keyboards. PDAs are networked through the use of modems, which may be external or in the form of a PCMCIA card. Supporting network technologies include CDPD, PCS, and packet radio. Transmission rates vary from 2.4 Kbps to 14.4 Kbps, although throughput generally is much less. The PalmPilot VII from 3Com Corporation, for instance, supports Internet access at speeds up to 9.6 Kbps over BellSouth's packet radio network.

PDAs are intended to perform a wide range of functions in support of personal and business use; hence the term *Personal Digital Assistant*. Current functions include handwriting recognition and handwriting-to-text conversion. These functions, coupled with limited data networking capabilities, offer excellent support for sales and delivery people. Federal Express and other delivery companies use such devices to great advantage.

Extending these functions a bit further, PDAs also can be used for e-mail access, facsimile networking, and access to information services – and then to the Internet. The information contained in the PDA, perhaps downloaded from the Internet or from a facsimile server, can be uploaded via an infrared link or hard-wired line to a workstation, which may be LAN attached. The devices also typically provide calendaring and scheduling applications, with alarming. They generally support the management of to-do lists, as well.

References

[11-1]   Brooks, John. *Telephone: The First Hundred Years*. Harper & Row, 1975.

[11-2]   Calhoun, George. *Digital Cellular Radio*. Artech House, 1988.

[11-3]   Williams, Veronica A. *Wireless Computing Primer*. M&T Books, 1996.

[11-4]   Gasman, Lawrence. *Manager's Guide to the New Telecommunications Network*. Artech House, 1988.

[11-5]   "Warning: sharp growth ahead!" *Communications News*, May 1998.

[11-6]   Baldwin, Thomas F. and McVoy, D. Stevens. *Cable Communications*. Prentice-Hall, Inc., 1988.

[11-7]   Feuerstein, Marty. "Controlling RF coverage." *America's Network*, February 15, 1998.

[11-8]   Newton, Harry. *Newton's Telecom Dictionary, 15th Edition*. Miller Freeman, Inc., 1999.

[11-9]   Bates, Regis J. *Wireless Networked Communications*. McGraw-Hill, Inc., 1994.

[11-10]   Paetsch, Michael. *Mobile Communications in the U.S. and Europe: Regulation, Technology, and Markets*. Artech House, 1993.

[11-11]   Emmett, Arielle. "Paging FLEXes its muscle." *America's Network*, November 1, 1997.

[11-12]   "Pager Protocols." RTS Wireless.www.rts-inc.com/pager.html

[11-13]   "FLEX Family of Protocols Q&A." Motorola, Inc., www.mot.com/MIMS/MPSG/CTSD/white_papers/flex_q&a.html

[11-14]   "FLEX Protocol Fact Sheet." Motorola, Inc. www.mot.com/MIMS/MPSG/CTSD/white_papers/FLEX-old/promo/tech_sheet.html

[11-15]   Karmer, Matt. "Going Beyond The Beep." *PC Week*, December 11, 1995.

[11-16]   Carey, Anne R. and Parker, Suzy. "Explosive Business." *USA Today*

[11-17]   Levy, Doug. "Satellite's death puts millions out of touch." *USA Today*, May 21, 1998.

[11-18]   "SkyTel 2-Way: Paging Dick Tracy." *Information Week*, December 18, 1995.

[11-19]   Moore, Mark. "Paging Net Off To Bumpy Start" *PC Week*, December 18, 1995.

[11-20]   Brown, Margaret J. "Major Pagers." *Mobile Computing & Communications*, April 1998.

[11-21]   "A Wristful of Messages." *Mobile Computing & Communications*, April 1998.

[11-22]   Muller, Nathan J. "Wireless PBX Systems." *IT Continuous Services*. Datapro Information Services, September 9, 1998.

[11-23]   Velasquez, Sonina and Trivett, Diane. "Wireless Telecommunications Office Systems: Overview." *Datapro Communications Analyst*, September 1994.

[11-24]   "IS-136: TDMA Technology for Cellular and PCS Wireless Communications." Communications Plus! www.comm-plus.net/ATTWS/tech.html

[11-25]   "IS-54B Overview." Texas Instruments Incorporated. www.ti.com/sc/docs/wireless/cellsys/is54over.html.

[11-26]   "Cellular CDMA Standard: IS-95A." Qualcomm Incorporated. www.qualcomm.com/cdma/phones/whatiscdma/95a.html

[11-27]   "CDMA Technology & Benefits." Motorola, Inc. www.mot.com/CNSS/CIG/Technology/cdma.html.

[11-28]   Sharrock, Stuart. "CDMA/TDMA from fists to facts."www.ericsson.se/Connexion/connexion3-93/techno.html.

[11-29]   Dempsey, Michael. "Not-So Saturation Coverage From GSM." *Global Telecoms Business*, October/November 1994.

[11-30]   "The Telecommunications Industry at a Glance." www.itu.int/ti/industryoverview/top20cellular.html.

[11-31]   "Frequently Asked Questions & Fast Facts." www.wow-com.com/consumer/faqs/faq_general.cfm#one.html

[11-32]   "European Cellular Market Forecasts:1998-2003." www.analysis.com/publish/titles/eurocell.html.

[11-33]   Lucas, Jerry. "Next Generation Systems for Wireless Service Differentiation." *Billing World*, February 1998.

[11-34]   Shankar, Bhawani. "3rd Generation 4th Dimension." *Telecommunications*, June 1998.

[11-35]   Holley, Kevin and Costello, Tim. "The Evolution of GSM Data Towards UMTS." www.gsmdata.com/artholley.html. February 1998.

[11-36]   Wallace, Bob. "AT&T to Ship PCMCIA Cellular Modem." *InfoWorld*, November 7, 1994.

[11-37]   Moore, Mark. "Data-Ready Cell Phones To Debut." *PC Week*, January 1, 1996.

[11-38]   Velazquez, Sonina. "How CDPD Works." *Internetwork*, July 1995.

[11-39]   Barney, Doug. "McCaw Rolls Out CDPD Service." *InfoWorld*, November 28, 1994.

[11-40]   Mason, Charles. "Bursting at the seams." *America's Network*, February 15, 1998.

[11-41]   Cholewka, Kathleen. "Web Connections Without the Wires." *Data Communications*, September 21, 1997.

[11-42]   Barney, Doug. "Third-Party Cellular Mobile Apps Readied." *InfoWorld*, November 21, 1994.

[11-43]   Greene, Tim. "Reason to Roam With Your Cellular Phone." *Network World*, July 10, 1995.

[11-44]   Hills, Alex. "CDPD Puts IP Networks on the Move." *Business Communications Review*, May 1995.

[11-45]   Wexler, Joanie. "McCaw Activates CDPD Service, Details Pricing." *Network World*, April 17, 1995.

[11-46]   "Remarks by William E. Kennard, Chairman, Federal Communications Commission, to Personal Communication Industry Association of America." www.fcc.gov/Speeches/Kennard/spwek828.html. September 23, 1998.

[11-47]   "Ardis gets new lease on life." *America's Network*, March 1, 1999.

[11-48]   Sweeney, Daniel. "In the shadowlands of data." *America's Network*, February 1, 1999.

[11-49]   Karve, Anita. "The Wide World of Wireless." *Network Magazine*, December 1997.

[11-50]   Ruber, Peter. "Wires Not Included." *Network Magazine*, December 1997.

[11-51]   "About the WLI Forum." www.wlif.com/about/index.html.

[11-52]   Sweeney, Daniel. "LMDS: Finally ready for prime time?" *America's Network*, August 1, 1998.

[11-53]   Sweeney, Daniel. "LMDS: How Competitive?" *America's Network*, August 15, 1998.

[11-54]   Willis, David. "LMDS: Is It a Little Too Much, a Little Too Late?" *Network Computing*, February 8, 1999.

[11-55]   Dunlop, Amy. "Wireless Access Enters Real-World Trials." *Internet World*, May 1997.

[11-56]   Bernier, Paula. "Carriers Charge Ahead with 38 GHz." *X-Change*, February 15, 1998.

[11-57]   Lawyer, Gail. "Air Wars?" *X-Change*, January 1999.

[11-58]   Dawson, Fred. "AT&T To Use Wireless Licenses." Inter@ctive *Week*, February 22, 1999.

[11-59]   Mathias, Craig and Rysavy, Peter. "The ABCs of PCS." *Network World*, November 7, 1994.

[11-60]   Hughes, Tom. "Pie in the Sky?" *Global Technology Business*, January 1999.

[11-61]   Ingley, Carol. "Global Vision: Making the Right Connections." *Satellite Communications*, February 1999.

[11-62]   Louderback, Jim. "Iridium Phones Give New Ring To Satellite Communications." *PC Week*, February 1, 1999.

[11-63]   Louderback, Jim. "Iridium Pager Hits Growing-Pains Stage." *PC Week*, February 1, 1999.

[11-64]   Alleven, Monica. "Iridium Gears Up For New Strategy." *Wireless Week*, June 7, 1999.

[11-65]   "Fast Facts." Teledesic LLC. www.teledesic.com/overview/fast-facts.html.

[11-66]   "Not just a bunch of toys." *LAN Times*, April 13, 1998.

Chapter 12

The Internet and World Wide Web

As a net is made up of a series of ties, so everything in this world is connected by a series of ties. If anyone thinks that the mesh of a net is an independent, isolated thing, he is mistaken. It is called a net because it is made up of a series of interconnected meshes, and each mesh has its place and responsibility in relation to other meshes.
Buddha

From its early beginnings as DARPANET, linking a select few military and R&D facilities, the Internet has grown to comprise thousands of networks and millions of users in virtually every country in the world. The Internet is the *kudzu* of networks, growing like the uncontrollable weed of Southern infamy.

The Internet truly *was* the *Information Superhighway*, long before the term was coined. While actually more of a private road, it was characterized by a sense of truly unparalleled freedom. That early network stood apart by virtue of its providing free and open access to information – that characteristic remains today as the hallmark of the Internet. The Internet is a network of networks, and has become a *Global Village*, much as envisioned by Marshall McLuhan. In some sense, at least, the Internet *is* the Information Superhighway!

The Internet Defined

The Internet is a global *network of networks* currently linking over 60,000 networks and spanning over 150 countries. According to Network Wizards Inc., the number of connected hosts increased by about 45 percent in 1998, to over 43 million (see Table 12-1). According to the ITU-T, approximately 150 million people on the face of the planet have Internet access. That's about 2.5 percent of the total population of 6 billion, which comprises about 1 billion households. About 56 million (37.3 percent) of Internet users reside in the United States, and the vast majority are in industrialized nations [12-1]. International Data Corp. figures that the number of users will increase to 320 million by 2002, and that they will use more than 515 million computers and other devices to do so [12-1]. Figure 12-1 provides a graphic view of the growth of the Internet; notably, there were only four hosts in 1969. E-mail, the most popular application, is estimated to account for well over 2 billion messages and over 2 trillion bytes (2 TB) of data per month.

Table 12-1 INTERNET DOMAIN SURVEY, JANUARY 1999: NUMBER OF HOSTS, DOMAINS, AND NETS. *SOURCE: NETWORK WIZARDS (HTTP://WWW.NW.COM)

Date	Hosts	Domains	Replied To Ping*	Network Class A (Large)	B (Medium)	C (Small)
Jan 99	43,230,000	Not available	8,426,000	Not available	Not available	Not available
Jan 98	29,670,000	Not available	5,331,640	Not available	Not available	Not available
Jan 97	16,146,000	Not available	3,392,000	Not available	Not available	Not available
Jan 96	9,472,000	240,000	1,682,000	92	5,655	87,924
Jan 95	4,852,000	71,000	970,000	91	4,979	34,340
Jan 94	2,217,000	30,000	576,000	74	4,043	16,422
Jan 93	1,313,000	21,000	Not available	54	3,206	4,998

*Estimated by pinging 1 percent of all hosts

The Internet is grounded in the U.S. Department of Defense *ARPANET* (*Advanced Research Projects Agency NETwork*), which began in 1969 as a means of linking personnel and systems involved in various computer science and military research projects. ARPANET, and its successor, *DARPANET* (*Defense Advanced Research Projects Agency NETwork*), were developed to be totally *fail-safe*. The distribution of computing power and the redundancy of the data switches and computer links all were intended to provide a meshed computer network that could withstand a nuclear strike.

In the early 1970s, work began at Stanford University on a set of internetworking protocols designed to prove connectivity among the ARPANET computers. In May 1974, Vinton G. Cerf (Stanford University) and Robert E. Kahn (Advanced Research Projects Agency, U.S. Department of Defense) published "A Protocol for Packet Network Intercommunication" in the IEEE *Transactions on Communications* [12-3]. That concept became known as TCP/IP (Transmission Control Protocol/Internet Protocol). They completed development work on the protocols in 1980, and in 1983 the Office of the Secretary of Defense mandated that ARPANET users accept the new set of computer protocols, which became the standard for ARPANET. In order to encourage colleges and universities to transition to TCP/IP, DARPA eased the implementation process for *Berkeley Software Distribution*, commonly known as *BSD UNIX* or *Berkeley UNIX* — a version of the UNIX operating system which they mostly ran at the time. Toward that end, DARPA funded Bolt Baranek and Newman, Inc. (BBN, now GTE Internetworking) to implement the TCP/IP protocols with Berkeley UNIX; this approach filled an internetworking protocol void and formed the foundation for the Internet [12-4].

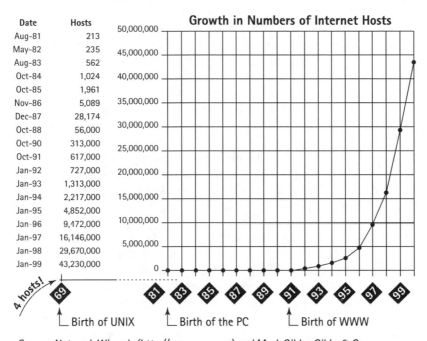

Date	Hosts
Aug-81	213
May-82	235
Aug-83	562
Oct-84	1,024
Oct-85	1,961
Nov-86	5,089
Dec-87	28,174
Oct-88	56,000
Oct-90	313,000
Oct-91	617,000
Jan-92	727,000
Jan-93	1,313,000
Jan-94	2,217,000
Jan-95	4,852,000
Jan-96	9,472,000
Jan-97	16,146,000
Jan-98	29,670,000
Jan-99	43,230,000

Source: Network Wizards (http://www.nw.com) and Mark Gibbs, Gibbs & Co.

Figure 12-1 Growth in Internet hosts. Source: Network Wizards (http://www.nw.com)

In late 1983, ARPANET split into two unclassified networks: DARPANET (Defense ARPANET) and *MILNET* (*MILitary NETwork*). Although ARPANET officially was retired in June 1990, the Internet has survived. TCP/IP has been enhanced recently and currently enjoys wide popularity in education, research and development, and commercial applications.

The National Science Foundation founded *NSFNET* (*National Science Foundation NETwork*) in 1985 to link its supercomputer centers, and to provide access to the Internet. NSFNET was a high-speed backbone network consisting of point-to-point links in a mesh configuration. The network was deployed fully in 1988, initially at 56 Kbps. In 1986, NSFNET partially funded a number of regional networks, tying into the backbone. In 1992, the backbone was upgraded to T-3, operating at 45 Mbps. More recently, major portions portion of NSFNET were upgraded to OC-3 (155 Mbps) and beyond. NSFNET officially was retired in 1995, and was replaced by the *MERIT* network. MERIT originally was a statewide network operated by the University of Michigan, and a regional component of both NSFNET and the Internet.

Internet Physical Topology

The physical topology of the Internet, ultimately, is not that important, as long as connectivity is achieved. That topology also changes from day to day, and varies considerably from place to place. However, and for those of you who, like me, absolutely must know at some level, the Internet physical topology consists of leased lines that connect various major computing centers through switches and routers. This leased line network is a partially-meshed network for purposes of redundancy and network resiliency. Initially, ARPANET consisted of approximately 50 BBN *Packet Switching Nodes* (*PSNs*), which were custom-built and scattered around the United States and Western Europe. NSFNET (1985) consisted of 56-Kbps leased-line circuits that connected the NSF supercomputer centers in San Diego, California; Boulder, Colorado; Champaign, Illinois; Pittsburgh, Pennsylvania; Ithaca, New York; and Princeton, New Jersey. During this time, a great deal of Internet traffic over the NSFNET backbone became commercial in nature, prompting a number of private commercial Internet backbone providers to establish a point for the exchange of this traffic. This point was established at Wiltel offices in Santa Clara, California, and became known as the *CIX* (*Commercial Internet Exchange*).

The original NSFNET was replaced in 1988 by an expanded version through a partnership of MERIT, IBM, and MCI (now MCI Worldcom). Sites were added in San Francisco, California; Seattle, Washington; Houston, Texas; Ann Arbor, Michigan; and other cities that housed large computer centers. The third version of the NSFNET backbone was deployed in 1989, increasing backbone speed, and adding some circuits while deleting others. In 1996, NSFNET officially was retired and replaced with the MERIT network, which has expanded and evolved considerably. That network consisted of *Network Access Points* (*NAPs*) in San Francisco (Pacific Bell), Chicago (Ameritech), and New Jersey (Sprint), as well as a *Merit Access Exchange* (*MAE*) in Washington, D.C., and was built by MFS Datanet, which MCI Worldcom later acquired. Subsequently, *MAE* variously became an acronym for either *Metropolitan Area Exchange* or *Metropolitan Area Ethernet* (the exact definition is lost in the mists of time, as best I can determine), and now is just *MAE*, a service mark of MCI Worldcom. Tier 1 MAEs, which are regarded as national points of interconnection, are located in San Francisco (MAE West) and Washington, D.C. (MAE East). Tier 2 MAE sites currently are located in Chicago, Dallas, Houston, Los Angeles, and New York. The NAPs and MAEs are locations (see Figure 12-2) where ISPs can exchange traffic at high speeds. Each MAE comprises a Gbps-ATM switching platform, which supplements legacy switched-FDDI technology. ISPs seeking to interconnect through the NAPs and MAEs do so through their own routers, which may be collocated at the NAPs and MAEs. The ISPs must maintain their own routing tables. The interface from the ISP to the NAP/MAE typically is on the basis of Ethernet, FDDI, or ATM. ISPs also can exchange traffic at local or regional private peering points [12-5-12-7].

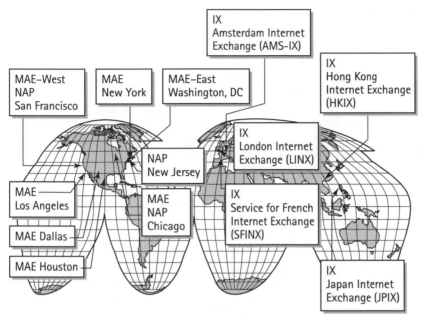

Figure 12-2 Network Access Points (NAPs) and MAEs

Aside from the backbone network, NSFNET funded a number of mid-level networks at the state and regional levels. Access networks also have been funded in various networks to support backbone connections for specific organizations or consortia. Campus networks also connect to the backbone through dedicated lines leased from various carriers [12-4]. In an interesting recent development, universities have become distressed over the degradation in Internet performance as traffic levels have increased because of its commercialization. In fact, a number of them petitioned The National Science Foundation to build a new, separate NSFNET intranet (private Internet) just for them – it seems as though success comes at a price [12-8]. In October 1996, this concern translated into action in the form of Internet2, which I discuss later in this chapter.

In addition to the basic Internet backbone structure spawned by NSFNET, the major incumbent interexchange carriers — AT&T, MCI Worldcom, and Sprint – have built national backbones. These carriers also have made a number of acquisitions to either enhance those backbones or, more typically, they have acquired backbones that they then enhance. A clear example is the acquisition of MFS and its UUNET subsidiary by MCI, which then became MCI Worldcom. MCI also acquired Advanced Networks and Services (ANS), a consortium to which MCI was a party. Similarly, AT&T acquired Teleport Communications Group (TCG), which previously acquired the CERFnet backbone. The emerging competitive interexchange carriers (e.g., Level 3 and Qwest) also support Internet traffic, as do the LECs, both incumbent and competitive. A number of less well-known regional carriers transport Internet traffic, as well.

So far, our discussion has focused on the U.S. topology, which is appropriate, as the Internet is a U.S. invention. For all practical purposes, it exclusively was a U.S. network until the 1990s. As the Internet gradually extended outside U.S. borders, all traffic initially was routed through the U.S. infrastructure. That meant, for instance, that local traffic from one user in Hong Kong to another in Hong Kong was routed through MAE West in San Jose, and back to Hong Kong. In order to confine regional traffic and, thereby, correct this obvious inefficiency, NAPs now exist in a number of international locations. The Hong Kong Internet Exchange (HKIX) serves 50 ISPs in Hong Kong; the Japan Internet Exchange Co., Ltd. (JPIX) serves 20 ISPs in Japan; the Amsterdam Internet Exchange (AMS-IX) serves 52 ISPs in The Netherlands; the Service for French Internet Exchange (SFINX) serves 36 ISPs in France; and the London Internet Exchange (LINX) serves 50 ISPs in The United Kingdom. Overflow traffic stills loops back through the U.S. NAP/MAE access points [12-9].

In order to put this physical topology in some sort of reasonable order and context, let's consider the concept of levels. While these levels are not defined absolutely, they do serve to put the topology of the Internet in perspective. At Level 1 are the interconnect points, and at Level 5 are the end users. In a long-haul, coast-to-coast communication, you might well work up through all five levels, and back down through all five.

- ◆ Level 1 includes all of the NAPs and MAEs, both domestic U.S. and international. Again, these NAPs are the major points of interconnection where national, and perhaps regional, carriers exchange traffic. The NAP provider may be independent of other levels (e.g., the international NAPs), or may be a Level 2 provider (e.g., MCI Worldcom or Sprint).

- ◆ Level 2 is the national backbone level. At this level are the national service providers such as AT&T, Cable & Wireless (which purchased MCI's backbone when the latter merged with Worldcom in September 1998), GTE Internetworking, UUNET (an MCI Worldcom company), and Sprint. Level 2 providers are facilities-intensive, as they own long-haul, high-speed transmission facilities that serve to interconnect their various high-speed switches and routers.

- ◆ Level 3 comprises the regional carriers. Such carriers typically operate a backbone in a single state, or perhaps several states. Level 3 service providers also are facilities-based, but at a lesser level than the Level 2 service providers. The RBOCs operate at this level, although they are restricted to an intraLATA presence.

- ◆ Level 4 comprises Internet Service Providers (ISPs). ISPs can be small *mom-and-pop* companies, or they may be intraLATA (i.e., RBOCs), regional, or national in nature. In any event, the ISPs do not own transport facilities. Rather, they connect their customers to the Internet backbone at Level 3 or Level 2, or perhaps even Level 1, through leased circuits. A Level 3 or Level 2 service provider may operate at Level 4 in areas where they do not have facilities in place; examples include America Online, CompuServe, Prodigy, PSINET, and UUNET.

◆ Level 5 consists of the end users. Level 5 connection to the Internet may be through a Level 4, Level 3, or even Level 2 provider. Access techniques run the full range of network options discussed in previous chapters, and discussed again later in this chapter. Such techniques include leased lines, dial-up, xDSL, Frame Relay, and ATM [12-10].

Internet Access

While the number of Internet users is growing at unbelievable rates, not everyone has access. In this Information Age, there is great concern about creating a new class system of the *information haves* and *have-nots*. In an attempt to address this issue, a great debate has arisen about subsidizing some level of universal service, much as was assured in the 1930s for the PSTN. With the goal of providing access to every American school by the year 2000, $36 million was raised from private sources in 1995 — with matching funds from the U.S. government sources and donations. Additionally, various carriers have offered special access rates and some manufacturers have donated equipment or offered special discounts [12-11].

Access to the Internet can be accomplished through a variety of means. Access from the customer premises can occur over a dial-up connection, either analog or ISDN in nature; xDSL, CATV modem, or a dedicated circuit. The local loop portion of the access circuit might be provided by the ILEC, the CATV provider, or a CLEC, and may be either wireline or wireless in nature. The connection might be supported over the circuit-switched PSTN, a packet-switched Frame Relay network, or even a cell-switched ATM network. Access from the user premises to the Internet can be through a Level 4 ISP, a Level 3 regional provider, or a Level 2 national backbone provider — with access at Levels 3 and 2 generally on the basis of a dedicated circuit. The performance of the connection between the user premises and the service provider depends on the nature of the underlying technologies and the level of bandwidth provided. Through the service provider and across the Internet, the level of performance depends on the specifics of the networks at Levels 4-1. Congestion, loss, and error may occur anywhere in the network. As is always the case in the networked world, the least capable element of the network defines the maximum level of performance, which can be realized, end to end. According to Telecommunications Reports International, Internet Service Providers (ISPs) claimed 28.2 million customers at year-end 1998; their definition of ISP included local, regional, and national providers. Of that total, 26.9 million (95.4 percent), were dial-up accounts, and 530,000 (1.9 percent) accessed the Internet via CATV modems [12-12].

Dial-Up Access

Terminal access via dial-up connection clearly is the most common means of Internet access – certainly for the residential, or consumer, and SOHO (Small Office/Home Office) markets. Whether through an analog modem or an ISDN modem, dial-up access makes use of the PSTN which, if you recall, is a circuit-switched, TDM-based network.

The most common dial-up access technique (refer to Figure 12-3) is through an analog modem, as most consumer and SOHO local loops are analog in nature. You explored the process of conventional dial-up modem access in quite some detail in Chapter 6, with respect to V.34 (28.8 Kbps) and V.34+ (33.6 Kbps) symmetric modems, and the more recently developed V.90 (56 Kbps) asymmetric modems. I do not repeat that discussion here, although I must make several points of significance. First, the analog local loop is a source of difficulty because it affects error performance and, therefore, affects throughput in a decidedly negative way. Second, consider the fact that the PSTN is a circuit-switched network. As such, bandwidth is provided on demand and as available, through the originating Central Office circuit switch, across the network, and through the terminating Central Office switch. Call set-up takes some amount of time, and the quality of the connection can vary considerably from connection to connection, depending on the physical path of the connection, and the nature of other activity taking place in local-loop cables and other elements of the network. Third, bandwidth is constrained to 2,400 baud over the analog local loop, and to an absolute maximum of voice-grade 56 Kbps (actually 53.3 Kbps) in the network cloud and across the channelized T-carrier local loop that terminates at the ISP or other access provider. Finally, the circuit-switched, TDM-based network provides bandwidth on a temporary basis, which is continuous and exclusive in nature. In other words, that capacity is provided for the use of that one connection, for the entire duration of the connection – whether it is used or not. This approach is extraordinarily wasteful of limited and, therefore, precious network resources in an interactive, packet-oriented data session such as that of Internet access.

ISDN, discussed in Chapter 7, offers the advantages of a digital local loop, which certainly improves performance and, therefore, throughput. Further, through a Terminal Adapter (TA), ISDN BRI (Basic Rate Interface) provides fully symmetric bandwidth at either 64 Kbps or 128 Kbps. ISDN must be supported by the ISP or other access provider, typically in the form of PRI (Primary Rate Interface) at an aggregate rate 1.544 Mbps, divided into 23 B (Bearer) channels. ISDN certainly is an improvement, but it's also more costly, and more limited in availability. As ISDN also is a circuit-switched access technology, it remains a very wasteful approach.

In order to overcome the inherent wastefulness of the circuit-switched PSTN for Internet access, the major Central Office manufacturers have developed a device that front-ends the CO. This device logically is positioned between the local-loop access port and the CO's internal switching matrix. Should the terminating telephone number be recognized as one associated with an ISP or other Internet access provider, this device shunts that traffic away from the CO and toward a packet-based data network. This obviates any issues of congestion that might be caused by the decidedly inappropriate use of the circuit-switched PSTN for packet data transfer.

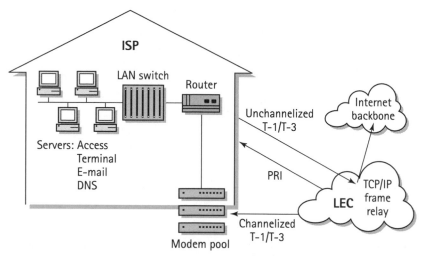

Figure 12-3 Internet Access via dial-up PSTN connection to an Internet Service Provider (ISP)

Dial-up access is supported by virtually all Internet Service Providers (ISPs), which focus largely on that method of access. All Information Service Providers (e.g., America Online, CompuServe, Microsoft Network, and Prodigy) — national ISPs that also provide content as well as access — support dial-up modem access because they largely are focused on consumer-level services. As I noted, ISPs are by far the most popular means of consumer access to the Internet, with approximately 28.2 million customers in the United States at year-end 1998, according to Telecommunications Reports International. Table 12-2 lists the top 12 ISPs in order of subscriber base.

Table 12-2 LEADING DOMESTIC U.S. INTERNET SERVICE PROVIDERS
           (ISPS), YEAR-END 1998 [12-12]

Internet Service Provider (ISP)	Subscriber Base (Year-End 1998)
America Online (AOL)	15,000,000
CompuServe	2,000,000
MSN Internet	1,500,000

Continued

Continued

AT&T WorldNet	1,400,000
EarthLink Sprint	1,000,000
IBM Internet	1,000,000
GTE Internet Solutions	824,000
MindSpring	650,000
Prodigy	643,000
RCN.net	500,000
SBC Internet	455,000
NetCom	400,000

xDSL Access

As discussed in great detail in Chapter 9, xDSL (generic Digital Subscriber Line) is an incredibly powerful network access technology. While still in development, xDSL access is becoming widely available throughout major metropolitan areas in the United States. A wide variety of xDSL technologies exist, some are standardized, some are in the process of standardization, and others are proprietary in nature. The only purely standardized version is ADSL (Asymmetric DSL), which is problematic in terms of its unyielding demands on the twisted-pair local loop. Since IDSL (ISDN DSL) is based on ISDN standards, it can be characterized as standardized, but it also is fairly demanding of the local loop. RADSL (Rate-Adaptive DSL) is very forgiving in that respect, but is proprietary in nature. G.lite, also known as ADSL Lite, is in the process of standardization, although early versions are available for end-user consumption. IDSL and RADSL are data-specific, while ADSL supports voice, data, and video, and G.lite supports both voice and data. While the data speeds vary by technology, they are much greater than the speeds offered by even the most sophisticated modem technologies. In many cases, the access speeds are definable, and the cost to the end user is sensitive to speed rating. In most cases, access speeds are asymmetric, with much greater bandwidth provided downstream. This asymmetry, generally speaking, is entirely appropriate for purposes of access to either the Internet or an intranet, regardless of the size of the user organization (i.e., an organization of one, several, or a great many). In addition to the greater level of bandwidth, xDSL access is *always-on*. In comparison to a dial-up connection, therefore, xDSL yields the advantages of no delays associated with call set-up, and no blockage at the originating CO circuit switch. While issues of congestion from the DSLAM (DSL Access Multiplexer) forward remain, congestion is a fact of life in a shared packet network. Remember that the lowest common denominator always rules in the networked world.

Cable Modem Access

Access to the Internet also is offered by a number of CATV (Community Antenna TeleVision) providers, as discussed in some detail in Chapter 9. Since the mid-1990s, a number of CATV providers aggressively have begun to upgrade their traditional coax-based networks with optical fiber, thereby increasing overall network performance considerably. Even in the absence of optical fiber upgrades, coax can support not only downstream TV delivery, but also two-way Internet access and other data applications. With the upgrade of the electronics to support two-way transmission, and the dedication of upstream and downstream data channels, high-speed Internet access can be provided at end-user costs that generally compare quite favorably with xDSL. The development of the *DOCSIS* (*Data Over Cable Service Interface Specification*) standard for cable modems has encouraged the deployment of this access option, although availability currently remains limited because of the cost of the required network upgrades. Note that older CATV systems use the *telco-return* approach, whereby upstream access to the Internet is provided via dial-up connection to an ISP through the PSTN; downstream access is provided over a shared channel over the coax CATV network.

As is the case with most xDSL technologies, cable modem access is asymmetric in nature – which generally is quite agreeable for consumer use. Notably, cable modem access usually is limited to consumer or SOHO application, as the CATV networks themselves are oriented toward the consumer, rather than the business, market. Unlike xDSL technologies, cable modem access bandwidth is shared among all users, as the CATV network itself is a shared network. Therefore, the bandwidth available to any individual user at any given time is sensitive to the number of subscribers active on any given CATV network segment at any given time, as well as the level of intensity of their usage. The shared nature of the CATV network also poses significant security issues in the absence of effective access control and encryption mechanisms.

Encouraging the deployment and acceptance of cable modem access are not only the development of DOCSIS specification, but also changes in regulation. The Telecommunications Act of 1996 opened the local exchange to competition, and clearly stimulated the CATV providers to position themselves as CLECs (Competitive Local Exchange Carriers) – initially focusing on the data market, with an emphasis on Internet access. Although the support of voice communications over a shared CATV network is somewhat more problematic, some providers offer that service, as well.

Perhaps the most dramatic factor that affected the availability of cable modem access to the Internet was the 1999 acquisition by AT&T of both TCI and MediaOne. AT&T acquired these networks and thereby became the largest domestic CATV provider largely to secure the ownership of local-loop systems that bypass the more limited local-loop networks controlled by the ILECs (Incumbent LECs). AT&T and other CATV providers also have the advantage of a gap in regulation. While the Telecom Act of 1996 effectively opened the door to competition in the LEC networks, there is no such requirement in the CATV domain. CATV providers largely are unregulated at the national level, and regulated only to a relatively modest extent at the local level. In fact, federal law specifically prevents the 30,000 or so local CATV government franchising authorities from requiring that the CATV providers offer telco-style interconnection [12-13] and [12-14]. Nonetheless, several municipalities announced in 1999 that they will require AT&T to open those CATV local loops to competitive ISPs; AT&T immediately announced its plans to appeal those decisions.

Satellite TV Access

Satellite TV networks offer yet another option for Internet access. While Iridium promises to offer direct, two-way access via a constellation of LEO (Low-Earth Orbiting) satellites, as discussed in Chapter 11, currently available offerings are based on GEO (Geosynchronous Earth Orbiting) satellites. As discussed at some length in Chapter 2, GEOs are effective for broadcast applications because their footprints, or areas of coverage, are substantial and stable. In terms of the downstream path from the Internet, GEOs offer considerable bandwidth, although it is shared — much like the bandwidth provided over a CATV network. The upstream channel is the real obstacle, as two-way home satellite dishes currently are prohibitively expensive. Further, a two-way connection via a GEO in equatorial orbit at an altitude of approximately 22,300 miles would impose aggravating delays due to roundtrip signal propagation of at least .64 seconds. Those of us who are impatient quickly would develop an uncontrollable case of *clickitis*, which undoubtedly would cause our PCs to lock up. In order to overcome this limitation, GEO-based Internet access services make use of the same telco-return access technique for the upstream channel; this technique involves dial-up access through an ISP over the PSTN. The market for Internet access through GEOs, which is estimated by some to grow from the current level of 200,000 subscribers to over 1 million by 2002, is dominated by DirecPC and WebTV.

◆ DirecPC is a service offered by Hughes Electronics, which also offers DirecTV — a satellite TV service. Unfortunately, each service requires a separate receive-only satellite dish. DirecPC offers downstream speeds of up to 400 Kbps, with the telco-return upstream channel limited to conventional modem speeds. SpaceWay, a proposed two-way system, is planned for introduction in 2002. DirecPC currently boasts approximately 100,000 subscribers; about half are located in the United States. In June 1999, America Online (AOL) announced a $1.5 billion investment in Hughes Electronics; this investment involves $500 million each for DirecPC and DirecTV, with approximately $150 million earmarked for marketing DirecTV to AOL members. The remaining $500 million is intended for a DirecTV/AOL interactive TV service. Of the total, $100 million will be spent to develop DirecDuo, a single dish technology supporting both DirecPC and DirecTV [12-15]. The AOL investment largely is viewed as a competitive counter to Microsoft's acquisition of WebTV.

◆ WebTV Networks, formed in 1995, is the pioneer in this space. The company was acquired by Microsoft in 1997, and now operates as a Microsoft subsidiary. WebTV also is a leader in this market, currently claiming a subscriber base of approximately 1 million. Given Microsoft's ownership interest in the Teledesic LEO project, the company clearly is heavily invested in satellite technology. WebTV offers Internet access through either a standalone satellite dish, or one that supports both Internet and TV access. In either case, the upstream channel is via a dial-up 56-Kbps modem connection through the PSTN. In many areas, the serving ISP is affiliated with WebTV, although other ISPs also can be utilized. Notably, access to WebTV is not supported through either AOL or CompuServe – according to WebTV, this limitation is due to reasons of *incompatibility* [12-16] and [12-17]. I suspect that this is an issue of business incompatibility, rather than technical incompatibility.

Dedicated Access

Direct connections to the Internet, in this context, are considered to be those that connect to a regional or national backbone provider (i.e., Level 1, 2, or 3), bypassing a local ISP (Level 4). Dedicated access arrangements are cost-effective for large user organizations, and for those who use the Internet intensively. Direct access can be on the basis of any number of alternatives, including DDS, T-carrier (e.g., Fractional T-1, T-1, Fractional T-3, and T-3); any of these service offerings might be provided over SONET at the Physical Level. Direct SONET access also is offered at speeds up to 155 Mbps (OC-3) by UUNET and select other providers. Such direct connections commonly are in the form of leased lines provided by the ILEC, although a facilities-based data CLEC (e.g., UUNET) also might provide such access. Typically, the T-carrier facilities are unchannelized, running TCP/IP protocol inside Frame Relay.

Access Anywhere

The Internet is an incredible network of networks that enables you to access from your machine virtually any other machine and any database and any type of information, anywhere in the world ... as long as you have access to the Internet. From your residence, your SOHO, and your corporate office, you have that access through a dial-up connection, a CATV provider, a wireless link, or a satellite provider – and this access involves an ISP or a direct connection to a backbone provider. The trick is for the *road warrior* to gain access from some place other than home or office. The national ISPs solve that problem for travelers who confine their roaming ways to the domestic United States and Canada, as they provide local number access from just about anywhere; the plug interfaces conform to the same specifications. The trick is to gain access elsewhere in the world, where their ISPs have no presence, and where the plug interfaces can vary as widely as the languages and the currencies. External modems and plug adapters can solve the physical problems. Some ISPs (e.g., AT&T, GTE, and IBM) have significant international presence, but most do not. Over the past several years, companies such as iPass Alliance (www.ipass.com) and consortia such as GRIC (Global Roaming Internet Connection at www.gric.com) have developed international presence to fill that void through arrangements with large numbers of local ISPs around the world. However, developing countries largely remain unwired for Internet access, as I am constantly reminded during my regular business trips to Africa – where even the best *business class* hotels often fail to provide dataports in the guest rooms.

Internet Access Costs

The costs of Internet access and usage generally are quite reasonable in the United States, although costs can be considerable in other countries. Access and usage usually are free for college and university students and faculty, and a few privileged others, although nominal charges sometimes apply. Still, someone pays for everything. Tax dollars funded much of the Internet and still do, although private enterprise has taken over in large part. Access can be either on a dial-up or dedicated basis, with costs varying widely between and within those options.

Dial-up access charges for information service providers such as America Online (AOL), CompuServe (now owned by AOL), Microsoft Network (MSN), and Prodigy historically were usage-based and speed-dependent. In the 1997 time frame, competitive pressure forced virtually all service providers to a flat-rate model, which generally is in the range of $19.95-$21.95 per month now. Limited-usage plans remain available, at lower monthly costs and with hourly surcharges applying above threshold usage levels. Slight discounts also may apply to users who access these services through a traditional ISP. MSN currently boasts approximately 1.5 million users, while AOL leads the pack with about 17 million users – including the 2 million CompuServe customers. (Note: I distinguish information service providers from Internet Service Providers, or ISPs; the former provides content, as well as Internet access.) ISPs generally offer Internet access at roughly the same rates as the information service providers.

Notably, Gateway and several other computer manufacturers offer a year of free Internet access with the purchase of a computer, usually at a minimum cost of $500 (reconditioned) to $1,000 (new). Office Depot offers a free PC (actually a PC for $599, with a coupon for a $400 rebate), assuming that you are willing to sign a three-year contract for Internet access through CompuServe. A small number of ISPs have offered Internet access for a one-time fee, generally in the range of $100-$150. At least one company has offered free Internet access for qualified users willing to watch a constant parade of advertisements on a fixed portion of their computer screens.

In many countries outside the United States, local calls are not free; rather, they are metered, and all calling is on a usage-sensitive basis. That includes local calls to the ISP for Internet access. In 1998, AOL lost its spot as the #1 ISP to BT Clickfree, an offering of British Telecom — one of the LECs. While BT may be losing money on the ISP service, it clearly is making money on the local-calling portion of the access.

User Equipment Requirements

At a minimum, the full-fledged Internet user requires a 486 PC capable of support-ing a Windows Graphical User Interface (GUI); a Macintosh computer does the trick, as well. Lots of memory (both RAM and hard drive) are most helpful. As speed is important, a 56-Kbps modem is ideal for access over analog lines. To get the full benefit of sound and color graphics, it is necessary to equip the terminal with a color monitor, speakers, and a sound card. You can obtain such a PC for $1,000 or so, although a full multimedia, Pentium-class PC with a large color monitor, CD-ROM, and all the other niceties easily is in the range of $2,500. If ISDN circuits are to be employed (better quality and higher speed), an ISDN Terminal Adapter must be added in the form of either an internal PC card or standalone unit — the additional cost begins in the range of $100-$250, plus the additional cost of the cir-cuit. Even better is xDSL, but it adds to the cost of the line, and it may involve ad-ditional equipment cost in the form of a modem/splitter. Large users, of course, also require the appropriate routers and other devices, which they may well have in place. Conversely, access to the Internet requires more equipment, as another net-work is being added to the mix in support of additional applications and associated traffic. The router also should include security in the form of a firewall (discussed later in this chapter) to provide protection against hackers and the like. Clearly, this is not an inexpensive proposition.

Having said all this, Apple Computer introduced in late 1997 the iMac computer. At a very attractive cost of $1,199 (July 1999), the iMac includes a 333 MHz processor, 32 MB RAM, 6 GB hard drive, 24x CD-ROM drive, built-in 56-Kbps modem, 10/100BaseT interface, two built-in Universal Serial Bus (USB) ports, Mac OS (Operating System), and a substantial software suite [12-18]. The iMac comes Internet-ready directly out of the box. While the iMac is a sealed unit, and, there-fore, not upgradeable, it is an incredibly attractive unit for the average home user. Adding to its attractiveness is the fact that is comes in five colors: strawberry, blue-berry, grape, tangerine, and lime. In May 1999, iMacs were the 3rd best-selling desktop computers in the domestic retail market, according to *PC Data*. Blueberry is the most favored flavor [12-19]. Several other manufacturers offer similar computers.

A number of manufacturers in recent years have proclaimed the emergence of much less expensive devices known variously as *diskless workstations*, *Net devices*, *Net readers*, *Internet terminals*, and *Net stations*. Reminiscent of the dumb termi-nals of the old mainframe days, these devices would have little or no processing power or storage capacity. Rather, they would have the ability to access the Internet and World Wide Web, and support a highly pleasing GUI. All of the serious processing power would reside in the network, as would all storage capacity. Serious computer users are unlikely to embrace such a device, although casual users might accept it at a low enough price. Costs are anticipated to be in the range of $500, although there is discussion of terminals at half that price. Around 1995-1996, a number of manufacturers announced development efforts toward such devices. Those announcements came from companies including Oracle Corp., Sun Microsystems Inc., Apple Computer Inc., IBM, Web Book Inc., SunRiver Corp., and Japan Computer Corp [12-20] through [12-26]. Currently, no serious products have made their way to market.

Free-PC in 1998 offered free Internet-ready computers to 10,000 qualified users who were willing to endure a deluge of advertisements. In a very short period of time, over 1 million people applied (over the World Wide Web, of course) for the right to a free PC. While I don't have any idea of the specifics of the qualification process, I suspect that family income, home and automobile ownership, buying habits, purchasing plans, and other similar demographics that might appeal to prospective advertisers were part of the mix. The interesting thing about this process is that you have to be able to afford a PC to qualify for a free one.

Internet Standards, Administration, and Regulation

You should note that the Internet is most unusual as a network. Virtually any entity can connect to the Internet to offer resources or to access them. Virtually any type of information can transverse the Internet, and without much in the way of regulatory interference. There is no central authority that regulates the Internet, although there are organizations that set certain fundamental standards and guide its operation. The Internet, by design, is autonomous and even anarchistic; in the end, this is both a strength and a weakness.

There exist a number of organizations that are involved in various Internet administrative and support activities. Those organizations include CERT, IAB, IETF, IESG, IRTF, ICANN, and The Internet Society (also known as ISOC).

The *Computer Emergency Response Team* (*CERT*) is a group of computer security experts at Carnegie-Mellon University that is charged with the responsibility for responding to Internet security issues. CERT was formed by DARPA in November 1988, in response to several incidents involving *worm viruses*.

The *Internet Architecture Board* (*IAB*), originally the *Internet Activities Board*, is a voluntary board comprising 12 expert individuals who use the resources of their sponsoring companies to further the interests of the Internet [12-27]. The IAB supervises the activities of two task forces: the IETF and the IRTF. In combination, those organizations set policy and direction.

The *Internet Engineering Task Force* (*IETF*) identifies, prioritizes, and addresses short-term issues and problems, including protocols, architecture, and operations. Proposed standards are published on the Internet in the form of RFCs (Requests for Comment). Once the final draft of a standard is prepared, it is submitted to the *Internet Engineering Steering Group* (*IESG*) for approval.

The *Internet Research Task Force* (*IRTF*) deals with long-term issues, including addressing schemes and technologies [12-28].

The *Internet Corporation for Assigned Names and Numbers* (*ICANN*) is a not-for-profit organization formed in 1999. ICANN was formed to assume the responsibilities from the federally-funded *Internet Assigned Numbers Authority* (*IANA*) for assigning parameters for Internet protocols, managing the IP address space, and assigning domain names. Internet protocol parameters managed by ICANN include the assignment of TCP *ports*, which are logical points of connection in the context of TCP (Transmission Control Protocol) — a part of the TCP/IP protocol suite developed for what we now know as the Internet. Port numbers are 16-bit values that range from 0 to 65,536. *Well-known ports* are numbered 0 to 1,023, for the use of system (root) processes or by programs executed by *privileged users*. Examples of well-known ports include 25 for SMTP (Simple Mail Transfer Protocol), 80 for HTTP (HyperText Transport Protocol), and 107 for Remote Telnet Service. In the Internet TCP/IP-based client/server environment, the server assigns the ports in consideration of the application-level protocol exercised at the client level. ICANN also assigns IP addresses to organizations desiring to place computers on the Internet, with the number of addresses depending on the size of the organization.

The *Internet Society* (*ISOC*) is a voluntary organization that acts to lend some formal structure to the administration of the Internet. The Internet Society has granted the IESG formal authority to make decisions on standards.

IP Addressing

The vast majority of networks currently make use of *IPv4 (Internet Protocol version 4)*, although IPv6 is available and used in some large, recently deployed networks. The specifics of IPv4 and IPv6 are discussed in some detail later in this chapter. Now, let's focus our attention on the specifics of the addressing scheme, with emphasis on IPv4, which was defined in RFC 791.

IPv4 provides an address field size of 32 bits, which yields the potential for 2^{32} or 4,294,967,296 distinct addresses. The addressing architecture includes five address formats, each of which begins with one, two, three, or four bits that identify the class of the network (either Class A, B, C, D, or E). The Network ID space identifies the specific network, and the Host ID space identifies the specific host computer on the network.

 ◆ Class A addresses are identified by a beginning *0* bit. The next seven bits identify the specific network, with only a possible 128 (2^7). The remaining

24 bits identify the specific host computer on the network, with as many as 16,777,216 (2^{24}) possible machines. Class A addresses are intended for very large networks supporting a great number of host computers. As of January 1988, the 51 assigned Class A addresses included Bolt, Baranek and Newman (BBN), IBM Corporation, Hewlett-Packard Company, Ford Motor Company, and Computer Sciences Corporation.

◆ Class B addresses are identified by a beginning set of two bits in a *10* sequence. The next 14 bits identifies the network, with 16,384 (2^{14}) possible networks. The remaining 16 bits identify the specific host computer, with as many as 65,536 (2^{16}) possible machines. As of January 1988, about 12,000 Class B addresses were assigned.

◆ Class C addresses are identified by a beginning set of three bits in the binary sequence *110*. The next 21 bits identifies the network, with 2,097,152 possible networks. The remaining eight bits identify the specific host computer on the network, with as many as 256 (2^{8}) possible machines. Most organizations hold Class C addresses. As of January 1988, about 800,000 Class C addresses were assigned.

◆ Class D addresses are identified by a beginning set of four bits in the binary sequence *1110*. Class D addresses are intended for multicast purposes, with the remaining 28 bits specifying the multicast address.

◆ Class E addresses are identified by a beginning set of four bits in the binary sequence *1111*. Class D addresses are reserved for future use [12-28].

Dotted decimal notation is the manner in which all IP addresses are written. Each 32-bit address field is divided into four fields, expressed as *xxx.xxx.xxx.xxx*, with each field given a decimal number value of 0-255, expressed as a single octet (2^{8}=256, or 0-255). Class A addresses begin with 1-127, Class B with 128-191, and Class C with 192-223. As, Northwest Link (my ISP) has an address of *199.xxx.xxx.xxx*, it's easily identified as holding a Class C address.

As noted above, the *Internet Corporation for Assigned Names and Numbers (ICANN)* assigns IP addresses to organizations desiring to place computers on the Internet; the IP Class, and the resulting number of available host addresses, depend on the size of the organization. The organization assigns the numbers then can reassign them on the basis of either static or dynamic addressing. *Static addressing* involves the permanent association of an IP address with a specific machine. *Dynamic addressing* assigns an available IP address to the machine each time a connection is established. For instance, an Internet Service Provider (ISP) may hold one or more Class C address blocks. Given the limited number of IP addresses available, the ISP assigns an IP address to a user machine each time the dial-up user accesses the ISP to seek connection to the Internet. Once the connection is terminated, that IP address becomes available to other users [12-6]. This dynamic IP address assignment usually is accomplished through a router running the *DHCP* (*Dynamic Host Configuration Protocol*) protocol. Conversely, an ISP offering xDSL access generally assigns one or more static IP addresses to the user. As the xDSL connection is *always on*, dynamic addressing is not appropriate for this class of users.

As noted earlier, IPv4 provides an address field size of 32 bits, which yields the potential for 2^{32} or 4,294,967,296 distinct addresses. That's not quite enough to address every man, woman, and child on the face of the Earth, but it's close — give or take a billion or so. And it seemed adequate for many years. The popularity of TCP/IP, especially given the commercialization of the IP-based Internet, has led to the exhaustion of the IPv4 numbering scheme — much as the popularity of networked fax machines, cell phones, pagers, computer modems, and even copy machines has led to the exhaustion of the numbering scheme used in the PSTN. Adding to the problem is the fact that the very substantial Class A and Class B addresses were parceled out to large organizations that really didn't need them. As only a small percentage of the addresses were actually used, a huge number of available addresses were wasted. This is not unlike the wasteful way in which telephone numbers are parceled out to U.S. LECs — in CO prefix blocks of 10,000 at a time, regardless of whether they actually need 1, or 10, 100, or 10,000.

To alleviate this problem, at least partially, the IETF documented *Classless InterDomain Routing* (*CIDR*) in the early 1990s in RFCs 1518 and 1519. CIDR builds on the concept of *supernetting*, which allows multiple Class C subnet address blocks to be grouped under a single address. For example, an ISP needing 1,000 IP addresses could get four consecutive Class C blocks, and all addresses in those blocks could be routed to the same host. CIDR simply uses shorthand to specify the *subnet mask* (the number of 1s bits in the network address). CIDR reduces the number of routes and, therefore, the size and complexity of the routing tables that the Internet switches and routers must support. While CIDR adds flexibility to the IP addressing scheme, it does not solve the basic problem of the lack of IP addresses into the future.

IPv6 resolves this issue through the expansion of the address field to 128 bits, thereby yielding 2^{128} potential addresses. That's a total address potential of 340,282,366,920,938,463,463,374,607,431,768,211,456. According to my neighbor's 11-year old son, that's more than a gazillion. According to Christian Huitema, that's enough to assign 32 addresses per square inch of dry land on the Earth's surface — which should just about do the trick [12-29]. Given the proposals for assigning IP addresses to network coffee pots, refrigerators, heating and air conditioning systems, automobiles, and virtually every imaginable device, IPv6 clearly adds value. IPv6 also provides additional functionality, although CPE upgrades are required.

Domain Name System (DNS)

The Internet is divided into logical domains, which are identified as a 32-bit portion of the total address, under the terms of IPv4 (Internet Protocol version 4). Addresses in the *Domain Name System* (*DNS*), the administration of which is the responsibility of ICANN, follow a standard convention: *user@organization.domain*. The vast majority of the 45 million or so registered Top Level Domains (TLDs) are commercial in nature. TLDs, which are identified as the domain address suffix, are of two types: *generic Top Level Domains* (*gTLDs*) and country codes.

gTLDs include the following:

.com   commercial organizations

.edu   educational institutions

.gov   government agencies

.int   organizations formed under *inter*national treaty

.mil   *mi*litary

.net   *net*work access providers

.org   non-profit *org*anizations

For example, *ray@contextcorporation.com* is the e-mail address for Ray Horak (user) at The Context Corporation (organization providing the connection), a commercial enterprise. (Note that the domain name (e.g., contextcorporation), is limited to 26 alphanumeric characters.) In 1998, serious consideration was given to the establishment of a new set of gTLDs, including .arts (entities emphasizing cultural and entertainment activities, .firm (businesses or firms), .info (entities providing information services), .nom (individual or personal nomenclature, i.e., a personal nom de plume, or pen name), .rec (entities emphasizing recreation and entertainment activities), .shop (businesses offering goods to purchase), and .web (entities emphasizing activities related to the World Wide Web). Currently, new gTLDs are not under active consideration.

Top Level Domains also identify the country, in the form of a two-character *country code*. Country codes are appended to the standard address, and are necessary only if the target country domain differs from the country domain of origin. For example:

.au   Australia

.jp   Japan

.nz   New Zealand

.sw   Sweden

.us   United States

.za   South Africa

Note that ray@contextcorporation.com does not carry the suffix *.us*; this country code generally is assumed. In the event that *.us* were appended, *.us* would be defined as the Top Level Domain and *.com* would be defined as the *Second Level Domain.*

ICANN assumed the responsibility of administering Internet addresses from IANA. Under IANA administration, the responsibility for TLD assignment was contracted to the *Network Information Center* (*NIC*) *Internet Registry*, commonly known as *InterNIC*. InterNIC is a commercial enterprise of Network Solutions Inc., previously a business unit of SAIC that also acquired Bellcore, now known as Telcordia Technologies. For the first few decades of the Internet, domain assignments were free for the asking. More recently, InterNIC began to charge for *.com* domains, at the rate of $70 for the first two years and $35 for each one-year renewal. In 1999, InterNIC lost its monopoly over domain assignment, as four competing entities were approved in April 1999 for a testbed period to extend through June 25, 1999. ICANN also announced that a number of other applicants met its accreditation criteria, and are expected to gain accreditation upon completion of the testbed phase. Coordination of domain name assignment is intended to be accomplished through the *Shared Registry System* (*SRS*), so duplicate names are not assigned. Currently, all domain names are maintained in a database on a centralized *domain name server*, which periodically downloads database updates to ISPs and other networks and network access providers.

Now for a word of warning from the author: During April 1999, I was on the road (as usual) for a public seminar tour. I logged onto the Internet and accessed the World Wide Web to find www.internic.org in order to register several domain names. Somehow, and I'm not quite sure how, I wound up at www.internic.com. I registered the domain name, and wound up with credit charges of US$217.94 and US$219.21, after conversion from Australian $342.00 and $344.00, respectively. I tried to cancel the domain names, but was unsuccessful. I did not want to do business with an Australian company that considerably overcharged me for a US$70.00 service. I suspect that my access to www.internic.com was *pirated*, although I can't prove it. Currently, I'm lodging a protest with my credit card company andwaiting for final resolution. I quite simply won't pay! So much for my doing business over the Internet, but I'll discuss e-commerce later in this chapter, when I've cooled down a bit. Note: www.internic.com since has changed its domain address to www.oznic.com. The company also reached agreement with the Australian Competition and Consumer Commission, in conjunction with the US Federal Trade Commission, to establish a fund of A$250,000 to reimburse people who were similarly duped.

Address Translation: Domain Name to IP Address, and Vice Versa

The Internet works on the basis of IP addresses, as already discussed. You certainly can access another host computer on the basis of an IP address, but IP addresses are hard to remember, and hard to type correctly. Domain names are much easier to remember and enter, but a translation must take place to covert domain names to IP addresses; the various routers and switches depend on this in order to route the data to the correct destination device. This process of translation takes place through the *Address Resolution Protocol* (*ARP*), and takes place through an address resolution database that resides on a server and is accessed by the originating router.

For example, let's assume that you want to send e-mail to *ray@contextcorporation.com*, thanking me for the writing this book, and sharing with me the fact that it has changed your life for the better. (This also is an acronym test. The answers are provided at the end of this little tale.) You might access your ISP from your PC at your SOHO through a xDSL line over a UTP local loop, which the ISP has leased for resale from the ILEC. As the DSL line is *always on*, you are assigned anIPv4 address on a static basis. Your client PC runs against the ISP's server, both of which run TCP/IP. Your e-mail message makes use of SMTP, an applications-layer extension of TCP, and is placed on the UTP local loop in serial mode using PPP. As the message reaches the CO, it is uplinked to the ISP through a DSLAM over an unchannelized T-carrier circuit leased from the ILEC. At the ISP location, an e-mail server receives the e-mail message. It then consults a DNS database on another server, translating *ray@contextcorporation.com* into ray@nwlink.net – which is the TLD of the e-mail server of Northwest Link, the ISP that hosts my TLD as a virtual domain on a logical partition of their domain server. That TLD then is translated into the IPv4 address 199.xxx.xxx.xxx, which is the IP address of the Northwest Link server. The DNS at your ISP is updated periodically through downloads from InterNIC. At your ISP, your e-mail message also is converted into a Frame Relay format and forwarded to a NAP over an unchannelized T-carrier circuit, perhaps leased from a CLEC, at which point it enters the Internet backbone. In the core of the Internet backbone, the e-mail message travels in an ATM format, in AAL 3/4. At the destination edge of the Internet backbone, the process is reversed to Northwest Link, which translates the IPv4 address into my domain, and deposits the incoming e-mail into my mailbox. When I check my e-mail over a dial-up connection and through a 56-Kbps modem, I also use PPP and a TCP/IP client/server connection-oriented communications mode. As I connect to my ISP, I am dynamically assigned an IPv4 address through DHCP once I enter my password. I then access the e-mail server, and the message is downloaded to my PC at my SOHO. You just put a big smile on my face. Thank you!

Now for the acronym decoder:

AAL:	ATM Adaptation Layer
ATM:	Asynchronous Transfer Mode
CLEC:	Competitive Local Exchange Carrier
CO:	Central Office
DHCP:	Dynamic Host Configuration Protocol
DNS:	Domain Name System
DSL:	Digital Subscriber Line
DSLAM:	Digital Subscriber Line Access Multiplexer
ILEC:	Incumbent Local Exchange Carrier
InterNIC:	Network Information Center Internet Registry
IP:	Internet Protocol
IPv4:	Internet Protocol version 4
ISP:	Internet Service Provider
NAP:	Network Access Point
PC:	Personal Computer
PPP:	Point-to-Point Protocol
SMTP:	Simple Mail Transfer Protocol
SOHO:	Small Office Home Office
TCP/IP:	Transmission Control Protocol/Internet Protocol
TLD:	Top Level Domain
UTP:	Unshielded Twisted Pair
xDSL:	generic Digital Subscriber Line

Internet Protocols

Internet protocols include TCP and IP, as well as application-level protocols. TCP/IP is fundamental to the operation of the Internet, while the application-level protocols serve to support specific user applications.

TCP/IP

Transmission Control Protocol (*TCP*) and *Internet Protocol* (*IP*), as discussed in Chapter 7, are specific, layered protocols that operate within a protocol stack typically referred to as the TCP/IP protocol suite. TCP/IP is a public domain protocol, as it was developed with public funds for use in a public network — the Internet. The TCP/IP networking protocol suite operates at Layer 3 (Network) and Layer 4 (Transport) of the OSI reference model. TCP/IP has been enhanced continuously and used extensively in a variety of computer networks, including X.25 and Ethernet. Additionally, some vendors have layered ISO *FTAM* (*File Transfer and Access Management*), X.400, and X.500 applications protocols (Layer 7) above TCP/IP. Its advantages certainly include its high level of documentation, ease-of-use, stability, and broad applicability. TCP/IP provides a means of passing datagrams among virtually any networks capable of sending and receiving bits — it is a highly effective *lowest common denominator* protocol.

INTERNET PROTOCOL (IP): CONNECTIONLESS DATAGRAM DELIVERY

Internet Protocol (IP), the basic building block of the Internet, is a Layer 3 (Network) internetworking protocol for the routing of datagrams through gateways connecting networks and subnetworks. IP is a connectionless protocol, as no true connection is established between the source and destination devices. Rather, the IP packets are presented to the network by the originating device and handled through the network with no knowledge of either the existence or the availability of the destination device. IP can be characterized as datagram-oriented because each IP packet works its way through the network independently, with no thought of an individual packet belonging to a larger stream of packets. Therefore, IP packets are not numbered, and packet resequencing is not supported. IP also can be characterized as a *best effort* protocol, as it offers no guarantees of delivery, no sequencing, and no error detection and correction mechanism.

IP provides for packet segmentation and reassembly and provides specific addressing conventions in the form of dotted decimal notation, as previously described. IP supports routing control, as well as status translation and communications. While IP has no concept of the specific content of the packet or of its service requirements, it also supports multiple service types, including low-delay, high-bandwidth, and high-reliability paths. Dial-up IP access protocols include SLIP and PPP.

The total size of the IP datagram, including the IP header, can be up to 65,535 octets in length. The minimum size, which all networks must support, is 576 octets. As illustrated in Figure 12-4, the minimum size of the IP header is 20 octets. Note that the IP datagram is viewed in terms of a 32-bit (i.e., 4-octet) width, as the original processors that implemented the IPv4 protocol had 32-bit word (value) lengths [12-28]. The IPv4 datagram contains the following fields:

◆ **VERS:** 4 bits identifying the IP version number. The version number is 4.

◆ **IHL:** 4 bits of Internet Header Length. The minimum value is five 32-bit words, or 20 octets. The IHL also provides a measurement of where the TCP header, or other higher-layer, header begins.

◆ **Service Type:** 8 bits indicating the quality of service requested for the datagram. While TCP/IP networks do not provide guaranteed Quality of Service (QoS) currently, the networks will attempt to honor QoS requests in terms of parameters that include packet precedence (i.e., priority), low delay, high throughput, and high reliability.

◆ **Total Length:** 16 bits describing the total length of the datagram, including the IP header. The maximum size is 65,535 octets ($2^{16}-1$, with 0 not considered as it has no value), and all network hosts must be able to handle a datagram of at least 576 octets.

◆ **Identification:** 16 bits that are used in fragmentation control. In the event that the receiving network cannot accommodate a datagram of the specified *total length*, that datagram must be fragmented. Each fragment must contain a copy of the *identification* field and certain other fields in the IP header so they can be reassociated and the datagram can be reconstituted.

◆ **Flags:** 3 bits that define the manner in which the fragmentation occurs. The first bit always is set at 0. The second bit defines whether fragmentation is permitted. For example, fragmentation may not be permitted in certain applications where only the entire datagram is useful. The third bit is used to identify the last fragment in a series of fragments.

◆ **Fragment Offset:** 13 bits that identify where the fragment fits in the complete set of fragments that comprise the original datagram. This field is used to sequence the fragments correctly, as they may arrive at the destination device out of sequence.

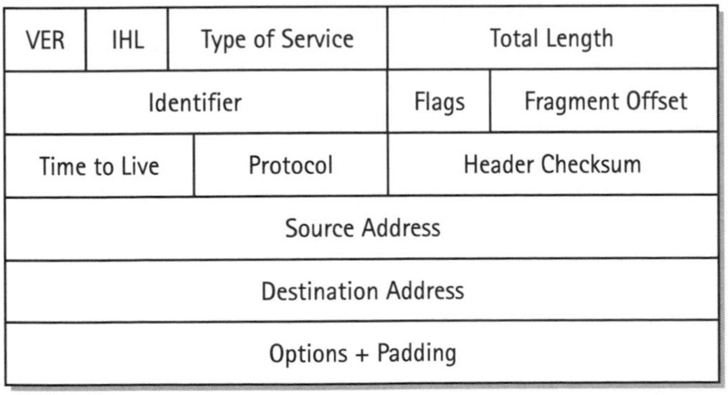

VER	IHL	Type of Service	Total Length	
Identifier			Flags	Fragment Offset
Time to Live		Protocol	Header Checksum	
Source Address				
Destination Address				
Options + Padding				

Figure 12-4 Internet Protocol version 4 (IPv4) datagram format

◆ **Time To Live (TTL):** 8 bits that specify the length of time in seconds that the datagram can live in the Internet system. The maximum length of time is 255 seconds (2^{8-1}, with 0 not considered, as it is the official time of death), or 4.25 minutes. From the instant the IP datagram enters the Internet, each gateway and host that acts on the datagram decrements the *TTL*. When the *TTL* reaches 0, the datagram is declared dead and is discarded. The *TTL* mechanism prevents packets from wandering the Internet for eternity, at which point they would have no value, and would only contribute to overall network congestion. The default *TTL* is 64.

◆ **Protocol:** 8 bits identifying the higher-layer protocol that created the message contained in the Data field. Examples include TCP and UDP.

◆ **Header Checksum:** 16 bits used for error control in the header. The process is that of *CRC* (*Cyclic Redundancy Check*), as described in Chapter 6.

◆ **Source IP Address:** 32 bits containing the IP address of the source host

◆ **Destination IP Address:** 32 bits containing the IP address of the destination host

◆ **IP Options, If Any:** An optional, variable-length field used by gateways to control fragmentation and routing options

◆ **Padding:** A variable-length field used only when necessary to ensure that the IP header extends to an exact multiple of 32 bits

◆ **Data:** A variable-length field that contains the actual data content [12-4] and [12-28]

SLIP *Serial Line Interface Protocol* (*SLIP*) – the original – remains the most basic protocol for handling IP packets in a serial bit stream across a voice-grade telephone connection. Installed on both the user's workstation and the provider's server, SLIP forwards packets created by TCP/IP software.

PPP *Point-to-Point Protocol* (*PPP*) performs the same basic functions as SLIP. Additionally, it performs fairly sophisticated compression in order to eliminate unused or redundant data in the headers of long sequences of packets in a transmission stream. Further, PPP supports multiple native machine and network protocols and supports subnet routing. For instance, PPP installed on a telecommuter's home PC enables communication with the home office through a router connecting to an Ethernet LAN. PPP also supports IP packet communication through the Internet [12-30].

INTERNET PROTOCOL VERSION 6 (IPV6): BETTER YET

The IPv6 specification (RFC 1883, replaced by RFC 2460) grew out of the efforts of the IETF IPng (IP next generation) Working Group to define a successor protocol to

IPv4. As you discovered in our examination of IPv4, that protocol is highly limited in the context of contemporary packet networking. Limitations of IPv4 include the facts that its addressing scheme is too limited at 32 bits, its address assignment is not flexible enough, application-level protocols are not tightly integrated, Quality of Service (QoS) is not supported, and security is lacking. IPv6 addresses all of these shortcomings, and more, through a header of 40 octets (compared to the 20 octets of IPv4) that can be extended as necessary through optional headers.

◆ **Addressing:** IPv6 expands the address field from 32 bits to 128 bits, thereby providing plenty of room for growth well into the 21st century.

◆ **Address Assignment:** IPv6 offers much improved flexibility of address assignment through two approaches, both of which offer automatic address assignment and discovery. *Stateful* autoconfiguration resembles Dynamic Host Control Protocol (DHCP), as the configuration servers dynamically assign unique addresses to devices as they require them, drawing from a pool of such addresses. *Stateless* autoconfiguration employs two IP addresses, and is particularly advantageous in mobile applications. One address is assigned permanently to the mobile device, and another address is used to route data to the network to which the mobile device is connected at the time. This stateless approach is much like sending a datagram to a device *in care of* a network, and is useful in the context of mobile devices that move among pager, cellular, packet radio, wireless LAN, and other wireless networks.

◆ **Address Types:** IPv6 supports multiple address types, including unicast, multicast, and anycast (which is a new mode). *Unicast* supports communications between source-destination pairs. *Multicast* involves the communication of data to multiple hosts, each with its own IP address. Rather than the traditional approach of copying a packet stream at the originating router, and then transmitting that stream to each device on a sequential, unicast basis, multicast involves a single transmission into the network. Based on its knowledge of the general physical direction in which the individual devices lie, the network fans out the packet stream to its peers, and the process continues until such time as all destination devices are located and the data is presented to them. *Anycast* is a new scheme that supports the communication between a source host and the closest member of a group of destination devices, with the group sharing a single anycast IP address. In this mode, the network routes the packet stream to the *nearest* device in the group sharing the address, based on the routing protocol's measure of distance. That device then assumes responsibility for forwarding the data to the group.

◆ **Priority:** IPv6 includes a 4-bit priority field that enables a source host to assign delivery priority to packets. For example, stream-oriented voice or video might be assigned a very high priority, network management data a slightly lower priority, routing table updates a lower priority still, and e-mail data the lowest of all. This priority designation permits the data with the lowest tolerance for latency to be treated on a preferential basis. Further, a 24-bit *Flow Label* is available to identify real-time data applications that are stream-oriented. Development work continues on protocols that would provide Quality of Service (QoS) guarantees.

♦ **Efficiency and Flexibility:** The IPv6 header includes a field that identifies additional, optional headers that can be associated with TCP, or one of the six IPv6 extension headers. The *Hop-by-Hop* extension includes information that must be examined and processed by each network node, including the destination node. The *Destination* extension includes information that need be examined only by the destination node, and not by the intermediate nodes in the network. The *Routing Header* specifies the intermediate nodes through which the packet must pass from origin to destination. The *Fragment Header* is used to fragment large packets into smaller ones that can be processed by the intermediate nodes, in recognition of the fact that the least capable device (i.e., an IPv4 node) may not be able to process packets of more than 576 octets. Where packets must be fragmented, the Fragment Header must be copied into each fragment so the fragments ultimately can be reassembled. Assuming that all nodes, from source to destination, can run IPv6 in native mode, the 16-bit Payload Length field can be used to identify a *Jumbo Payload Option*, which extends the size of the packet beyond the IPv4 limit of 65,535 octets.

♦ **Security:** IPv6 includes an option for IP security in the form of *IPsec*, which is identified through the use of optional *Authentication* and *Encapsulating Security Payload* headers. The *Authentication* header is used to verify the validity of the originating address in the header or every packet, thereby ensuring that the originating device is privileged to access the destination network, its internal resources, and rendering session-stealing programs ineffective. The *Encapsulating Security Payload* (*ESP*) encrypts the entire datagram, with the specifics of the encryption algorithm left up to the implementer. IPsec is a standards-based security suite that operates transparently; it may eliminate the need for proprietary firewall mechanisms in some applications. IPSec also provides for encapsulation of the secured IPv6 payload in IPv4 packets, in consideration of both the increasing need for security and the long-term transition process to IPv6.

In total, IPv6 offers significant advantages over its predecessor IPv4. Through *tunneling* (i.e., the encapsulation of IPv6 packet in IPv4 packets), IPv6 is backward compatible. The real advantages of IPv6 only can be realized, however, if all nodes from source to destination are capable of running IPv6 in native mode. Therein lies the problem. For the most part, IPv6 requires a forklift upgrade. Therefore, IPv6 is finding its way fairly slowly into the domain of internetworking. While the emerging IP-based networks, both private (e.g., Internet2) and public (e.g., Level 3 and Qwest), are building from the ground up, they easily can implement IPv6. They also must run dual protocol stacks to support both versions in native mode. Similarly, new backbone router implementations in large enterprise networks can support both versions easily. Gradually, IPv6 will supplant IPv4, as it works its way from the backbone to the desktop, but the full process may well take decades [12-28], [12-29], and [12-31] through [12-35].

TRANSMISSION CONTROL PROTOCOL (TCP): RELIABLE DATASTREAM TRANSPORT

Transmission Control Protocol (TCP) is a Layer 4 (Transport) protocol that evolved from the Network Control Protocol (NCP) of ARPANET. NCP was developed to provide reliable transmission across the essentially unreliable media of analog UTP and packet radio (e.g., AlohaNET). In support of higher level applications, TCP can be characterized as making use of virtual circuits in support of byte-stream oriented communications. As a connection-oriented protocol, TCP supports status exchange and synchronization over virtual circuits. TCP provides for file segmentation into packets on the transmit side, and for reassembly on the receiving end. TCP (see Figure 12-5) also provides for packet sequencing, end-to-end flow control, and error control, [12-36] and [12-37] thereby guaranteeing delivery. Each packet in a stream of packets received by the destination device is either acknowledged as having been received correctly, or is requested to be retransmitted in the event of corruption. Packets that are not acknowledged or requested for retransmission are considered unacknowledged, and are retransmitted by the source host.

The TCP unit of data transfer between two host computers is known as a *segment*. Segments are used to establish connections, transfer actual data, acknowledge packet receipt and request retransmissions, and terminate connections. Figure 12-5 provides a view of the TCP header, and its constituent fields. The standard size of the TCP header is 20 octets, although four additional octets may be used to accommodate options. The TCP header fields are defined as follows:

◆ **Source Port:** 16 bits that define the TCP port number used by the source application program. As discussed earlier in this chapter, TCP *ports* are logical points of connection. *Well-known ports* are numbered 0 to 1,023 for the use of system (root) processes or by programs executed by *privileged users*. Examples of well-known ports include 25 for SMTP (Simple Mail Transfer Protocol), 80 for HTTP (HyperText Transport Protocol), and 107 for Remote Telnet Service.

◆ **Destination Port:** 16 bits that define the TCP port number used by the destination application program

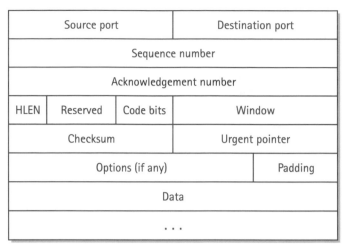

Source port		Destination port	
Sequence number			
Acknowledgement number			
HLEN	Reserved	Code bits	Window
Checksum		Urgent pointer	
Options (if any)			Padding
Data			
. . .			

Figure 12–5 Transmission Control Protocol (TCP) segment format

◆ **Sequence Number:** 32 bits that identify the position of the data in the TCP segment relative to the entire originating byte stream. This field is critical if data are to be sequenced properly at the destination host. It also is critical in order that positive acknowledgements can be sent to the originating host, and that retransmissions of segments can be requested.

◆ **Acknowledgement Number:** 32 bits that identify the acknowledgement number of the octet that the source expects to receive next

◆ **HLEN:** 4 bits that specify the length of the segment header, in 32-bit multiples

◆ **Reserved:** 6 bits reserved for future use

◆ **Code Bits:** 6 bits that define the purpose and contents of the segment. Examples include acknowledgement, connection reset, and end of byte stream.

◆ **Window:** 16 bits that advertise the size of the sender's receive window (i.e., how much data the host computer is willing to accept, based on buffer size)

◆ **Checksum:** 16 bits used for error control in the data field, as well as the header. The process is that of *CRC* (*Cyclic Redundancy Check*), as described in Chapter 6.

◆ **Urgent Pointer:** 16 bits that identify urgent out-of-band data (i.e., data not part of the information stream). Such data is treated on a high-priority basis, in advance of data-stream octets that might be awaiting consumption by the destination hosts. For example, urgent data might include a keyboard sequence to interrupt or abort a program.

◆ **Options, If Any:** 24 bits that address a variety of options, such as *Maximum Segment Size* (*MSS*)

◆ **Padding:** 8 bits in an optional field used only when necessary to ensure that the TCP header extends to an exact multiple of 32 bits. This field is used only when the *Options, If Any* field is used.

◆ **Data:** A variable-length field that contains the actual data content. As TCP is used in conjunction with IP, the minimum size of the data field is 536 octets — which is the minimum size of the IP datagram, less 20 octets each for the standard IP and TCP headers [12-4].

UDP

User Datagram Protocol (*UDP*) is a simplified host-to-host protocol that offers the same unreliable, connectionless datagram delivery as IP. Historically, UDP is used to send datagrams between application programs. Like TCP, UDP uses IP for addressing and routing purposes. Unlike TCP, UDP provides no sequencing, error control, or flow control mechanisms. An application program that uses UDP assumes full responsibility for all issues of reliability, including data loss, data integrity, packet latency, data sequencing, and loss of connectivity. UDP is used extensively in VoIP (Voice over Internet Protocol) applications, where compression techniques are designed to mitigate such issues over a highly shared packet network.

UDP source port	UDP destination port
UDP message length	UDP checksum
Data	
. . .	

Figure 12-6 User Datagram Protocol (UDP) datagram format

The standard size of the UDP header is eight octets; it comprises the following fields, as illustrated in Figure 12-6:

◆ **Source Port:** 16 bits that define the UCP port number used by the source application program

◆ **Destination Port:** 16 bits that define the UCP port number used by the destination application program

◆ **UDP Message Length:** 16 bits that identify the length of the message in the Data field

◆ **Header Checksum:** 16 bits used for error control in the header, only. This checksum need not be used; if the value is set to 0, it is disregarded. This lack of regard for header control is possible because it also is accomplished in the IP header. The checksum process is that of *CRC* (*Cyclic Redundancy Check*), as described in Chapter 6.

◆ **Data:** A variable-length field that contains the actual data content [12-4]

TRANSMISSION FRAMING

Now that we've discussed the header formats and functional characteristics of IP, TCP, and UDP, it's time to view the transmission-framing format used in an Internet context, as illustrated in Figure 12-7. This format generally follows the generic data format in Chapter 6. The IP header comes first, as it is required for routing purposes. Next, is the UDP or TCP header. Finally, comes the actual application data. The entire transmission frame is considered to be either a UDP datagram or a TCP segment. If you consider this in the context of an Ethernet 802.3 LAN, the datagram or segment becomes the payload of the Ethernet frame, and is limited to 1,500 octets. The encapsulating Ethernet header and trailer add another 18 octets, and the framing process is complete.

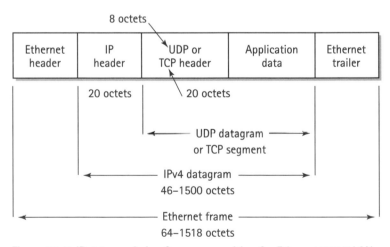

Figure 12-7 IPv4 transmission frame composition for Ethernet 802.3 LAN

Note that the entire IPv4 datagram has a minimum length of 576 octets, and a maximum length of 65,535 octets. The IP header consumes 20 octets, the TCP standard TCP header 20 octets, and the UDP header 8 octets. The balance is available for application-layer data, subject to any limitations of the local network.

Application-Level Protocols

Application-level protocols (Layer 7 of the OSI Reference Model) function above the TCP/IP protocol suite in support of specific Internet applications. Examples include TELNET, FTP, SMTP, and SNMP.

TELNET

Telecommunications Network (TELNET) is perhaps the oldest Internet application protocol. *TELNET* provides terminal emulation over a TCP connection, enabling the user to assume control over the applications that reside on a remote system. Virtual network terminal services permit the DTE to emulate other terminal devices, transparently, in a client/server environment.

FTP

File Transfer Protocol (FTP) supports the exchange of files between two hosts across the Internet. FTP also supports interactive user interface in which humans must interact with a remote host. The specifics of the file type and format (e.g., ASCII, EBCDIC, or binary; and compressed or uncompressed) of data can be determined from client to server. FTP also requires clients to satisfy security authorization in the form of login and password.

SMTP

Simple Mail Transfer Protocol (SMTP) is an extension of UDP, and provides the underlying capabilities for networked electronic mail. While SMTP does not provide the user interface, it supports text-oriented e-mail between any two devices that support *MHS (Message Handling Service)*. *Multipurpose Internet Mail Extension (MIME)* is a SMTP extension that permits the attachment to textual e-mail of other types of files, including audio, graphics, and video. Thereby, compound mail can be transmitted across the Net. SMTP is simpler that its predecessor, *Mail Transfer Protocol (MTP)*.

SNMP

Simple Network Management Protocol (SNMP) supports the exchange of network management information between hosts, typically including one or more centralized network management consoles that manage larger numbers of network elements in real-time. SNMP operates over UDP, thereby avoiding the overhead associated with TCP.

Internet Applications

Internet applications are growing as fast as the imagination, and technology, will support. These applications include e-mail, file transfer, Bulletin Board Systems (BBSs), library catalogs, online banking, video and radio broadcasting, and even voice telephony.

E-mail

Electronic mail (e-mail) clearly is the most popular application. Billions of e-mail messages comprising trillion of bytes transverse the Internet each month. It is estimated that well over 100 million people currently use e-mail applications over the Internet. E-mail transport through the Internet makes use of the Simple Mail Transfer Protocol (SMTP). E-mail messages commonly are sent with attachments, which may be in the form of compressed images, video clips, and audio clips.

File Transfer

File transfer is accomplished through the File Transfer Protocol (FTP) and in support of topical research. Through 8,000 FTP servers, any of the thousands of Net servers can be accessed and the resident file resources can be accessed and transferred in ASCII or binary code. While many FTP resources are privileged, others are unrestricted and available for public consumption; you can access such unrestricted resources via the use of the account name *anonymous*. Large files (equal to or greater than 50 KB) generally are handled in compressed format using compression techniques specific to the computer operating system. Examples include *.Z* or *.tar* (UNIX), *.zip* (MS-DOS), and *.hqx* (Macintosh).

Bulletin Board Systems

Bulletin Board Systems (*BBSs*) are specific to a region or area of topical interest; each supports numbers of subcategories. Network News, or Usenet News, formed in 1979, is a collection of over 6,000 special-interest Bulletin Boards (BBSs). Example BBSs include the following:

com	Computer, including specific LAN technologies
biz	Business
K12	Topics of interest to primary and secondary school educators (Kindergarten-12th grade)
Rec	Recreation
Sci	Sciences, such as biology, chemistry, and physics
Soc	Social issues such as religion and politics

Library Catalogs

Library catalogs for over hundreds of libraries are available through the Internet. Such catalogs include the U.S. Library of Congress, the Research Libraries Information Network, and many major colleges and universities. Through the Interlibrary Loan program, Internet users can have the document loaned to their local library.

Real-time Applications

Real-time applications are growing at significant rates. There are a number of legitimate applications, and many that are less so. Real-time applications include collaborative design and development, interactive role-playing, interactive remote education, and chat lines (real-time BBSs). Other applications include voice and videoconferencing, network games, gambling, and radio and video broadcasting (*cybercasts*).

Financial Services

Online banking has received a good deal of interest. While security issues abound, there is little doubt that this application has great promise. In the area of financial services, online stock trading has made a huge impact, having taken significant market share away from conventional brokerage houses. The downside of online stock trading is that several of the Internet-based brokerages have experienced numerous short-term system failures that have resulted in the total loss of their ability to execute trades on behalf of their customers.

Video

Although it is terribly bandwidth-intensive and the quality is poor, you can transmit packet video over the Internet. Videoconferencing also is possible with a SLIP/PPP connection and a high-speed modem. A black-and-white video camera can be had for under $100 from a number of manufacturers. In either case, connection is provided through a video server known as a reflector.

Radio

Radio broadcasting makes use of packet radio systems such as RealAudio from Progressive Networks. AM radio quality is possible with a 10-second delay. As is always the case with packet-switched networks, streaming audio is subject not only to delay, but also to data loss with no opportunity for recovery. In other words, the general quality is not great, but the price is right. I had a number of students from Asia at a graduate-level course I taught at the University of San Francisco. Several students from Japan, in particular, regularly listened to radio broadcasts from Tokyo over the Internet. Again, the quality was not great, but the price was right (read *free*). Additionally, they really had no other means of hearing such a broadcast, or getting information from home on a timely basis. My wife, Margaret, also a consultant, several years ago had a long-term engagement with a large wireless company. For the first few weeks, she complained about the fact that the office was as quiet as a tomb. Not only was there none of the usual water cooler conversation, but people seldom ventured out of their cubicles. One evening when we were shopping at the local office supply store, she stopped to buy an expensive headset, which puzzled me. It seemed as though she had figured out the reason for the dead silence in the office. Margaret was about to join the other hundred or so staffers who listened to radio broadcasts on the Internet while working. Quality wasn't much of a problem because the company had several T-3 circuits directly to the Internet backbone.

Internet Telephony

Internet telephony, also known as *Internet Voice*, is a means of transmitting voice over the Internet, bypassing the traditional PSTN and saving money in the process. While I discussed VoIP (Voice over Internet Protocol) at some length in Chapter 5, dealt with the detailed specifics of IP earlier in this chapter, and will deal with the subject again in Chapter 15, VoIP merits further discussion here, in the context of the public Internet. Internet telephony is accomplished through the use of special software residing on a multimedia PC equipped with a microphone, speaker, and modem (14.4 Kbps or better). Initially, most such software worked on a half-duplex basis, enabling only one person to talk at a time using a *push-to-talk*, *over-and-out* protocol reminiscent of CB radio. Through appropriate modems and using more recently developed software, full-duplex communications also can be supported. In every case, a voice conversation is supported only through the use of matching software residing in both transmit/receive devices.

Whether full or half-duplex, voice is not well supported over the public packet Internet due to issues of packet delay and loss. As discussed previously, the Internet is a packet network optimized for interactive data communications, specifically in support of time-share applications. Such applications are designed to tolerate packet delay and packet delay variability. Further, they tolerate packet loss and data corruption, as retransmissions of affected data can be accomplished relatively easily and without affecting the integrity of the data stream. Such data applications variously make use of IP, TCP, or UDP, and applications-level TCP extensions such as SMTP and FTP. Internet telephony is an Internet-based VoIP (Voice over IP) application that does not make effective of TCP's reliability mechanisms. There simply isn't time to recover from loss or error conditions, should they occur. In order to improve on the variable and unpredictable delays associated with Internet telephony, various service providers employ early versions of *RSVP* (*Resource Reservation Protocol*), *RTP* (*Real Time Protocol*), and other protocols that effectively set aside bandwidth on a best-effort basis for voice and other demanding, stream-oriented applications.

Depending on the software in use, it may be necessary that both parties schedule the call in advance, typically either via e-mail over the Internet or through a short, preliminary telephone call. Current software/hardware technology also enables the caller to *ring* the target PC, or even a telephone set over the Internet. While voice over the public Internet is far less than agreeable in quality, it is free if you are lucky enough to be a college student or faculty member. End users connecting through an Internet Service Provider (ISP) also can make use of this application essentially for free in the contemporary climate of flat-rate pricing. In any event, the cost of Internet voice compares quite favorably with long-distance charges imposed by traditional PSTN carriers.

As you might expect, some of the PSTN carriers are very upset about this application because it threatens to shift large volumes of traffic away from the conventional PSTN. Other issues abound, including reduced tax revenues at the local, state, and federal levels. The Universal Service Fund will be threatened unless ISPs and backbone carriers are required to contribute – the upshot will be an increased burden on PSTN users in support of local service cross-subsidies to maintain a high level of network access to rural areas at reasonable cost to those end users. In February 1999, the FCC ruled that dial-up Internet calls are interstate in nature, rather than local. This ruling may open the way for new fees for ISPs and users. ISPs long have contended that they support the Universal Service Fund through charges embedded in the circuits they and their subscribers lease from the ILECs. Clearly, however, these fees do not come close to matching the USF contributions that apply to voice, fax, and data traffic over the PSTN. While the FCC's decision may set the stage for future taxation of the Internet, it has no immediate impact, as the Internet Tax Freedom Act became law in October 1998. That act places a three-year moratorium on taxation of Internet access at the state and local levels, at least. The act also protects e-commerce from taxation (e.g., sales taxes) for out-of-state transactions. In effect, the Internet and World Wide Web have been reaffirmed as a tax-free zone.

ISPs face increased costs for servers, modems, local loops, and links to the backbone networks in support of increased traffic, which yields no additional revenues under a flat-rate pricing scheme. The backbone networks, which often are under stress from more appropriate and more conventional applications, will experience extra pressure on scarce and expensive bandwidth. In turn, this will force additional investment in support of an application that clearly is inappropriate for the Internet and negatively affects the performance of the applications for which it was intended.

Internet telephony actually offers more than just low cost in return for low quality, however. Consider a convergence scenario in which you access the Internet and the World Wide Web through your ISP to view a Web site to make a reservation or order a product or service. As you click your way around the Web site through your browser, you have a question about the specifics of a product. You click the *Talk to An Agent* button, and are connected to a real person with whom you can carry on a conversation over the public Internet using VoIP technology. While you are talking, you both view the same information on the Web site. The agent can take control of the Web site to present you with the proper information, which saves you a lot of mouse clicks, thereby improving communications and enhancing your Internet experience. The voice quality may be horrible, but the convergence of voice and data has added considerable value, overall.

Now, take this experience to the next level. If you access your ISP over a xDSL local loop, and if your ISP supports connection to a next-generation IP-based carrier such as Qwest or Level 3, then your converged voice and data communications might transport over an improved IP-based backbone optimized for voice, as well as data. Your voice communication will be improved. Your data communication probably will be more satisfactory, as well. At this level, Internet telephony really isn't Internet telephony at all, except perhaps at the very edges. Rather, the majority of your experience is one of voice and data communications over a finely –tuned, IP-based network. While Internet telephony may remain the province of the hobbyist, NetHead, and college student, VoIP is to be taken seriously.

Integrated Messaging

Integrated, remote messaging over the Internet is a relatively new concept, but one that is technically feasible and has been translated into real products. A number of companies active in the messaging business have developed system software that enables a remote user to access the office messaging platform. After satisfying the necessary security challenges, the remote worker can download e-mail, voicemail, and fax mail over the Internet. The messages can be played on the user's multimedia PC, for instance, and responses can be created and uploaded over the Internet to the office platform. The centralized office system then forwards those messages to the originators in their native format — e-mail, voice, or fax. Although the voice quality is a bit rough, of course, the concept is solid, the products work, the cost of the systems and software are justifiable, and the cost of the call is negligible.

Internet2

In an interesting recent development, universities have become distressed over the degradation in Internet performance as traffic levels have increased because of its commercialization. In fact, a number of them petitioned The National Science Foundation to build a new, separate NSFNET intranet (private Internet) just for them — seems as though success does come at a price [12-8]. In October 1996, this concern translated into action in the form of Internet2, which is discussed later in this chapter. Internet2is a project of the *University Corporation for Advanced Internet Development* (*UCAID*), a not-for-profit entity created specifically to develop and manage the network. Internet2 is a collaboration of the NSF, the U.S. Department of Energy, more than 110 research universities, and a number of private businesses. Internet2 is intended as a private Internet for the benefit of its member organizations, although it will connect to the present Internet, as required. Internet2, which is still in the deployment phase, makes use of GigaPOPs (i.e., Gbps Points of Presence, or switches and routers positioned as access points), which are interconnected over optical fiber transmission facilities initially running at speeds up to 10 Gbps (SONET OC-192). Initially, Internet2 will make use of existing networks such as the NSF's *vBNS* (*very-high-speed Backbone Network Service*), although separate transmission facilities eventually will be deployed in some cases. Each participating university has committed at least $500,000 to fund the project, and each will be required to make substantial capital investments on-campus. In consideration of the experimental nature of Internet2, substantial funding and contributions of technology have been made by the likes of Cisco, IBM, Qwest, and MCI Worldcom (which is the vBNS service provider). Internet2 also falls under the auspices of the Clinton administration's *Next Generation Internet* (*NGI*) initiative, which includes over $300 million of available funding to universities on the basis of government grants. Applications under development for Internet2 include collaborative surgery and other collaborative environments, broadcast quality video and videoconferencing, multimedia virtual libraries, telemedicine, distance-independent instruction, weather forecasting, and military-troop-movement monitoring. While only member organizations will have access to Internet2, the underlying technologies being developed to support these applications are intended to form the basis for the next generation of the public Internet. The TCP/IP protocol stack is run in Internet2, as in the original Internet. Internet2 largely runs IPv4 (Internet Protocol version 4, the traditional version), although it also supports native IPv6 traffic [12-38-12-40].

Having introduced the *vBNS* in the context of Internet2, I had best define it. MCI (now MCI Worldcom) announced in March 1995, a five-year, $50 million relationship with the NSF to build a *very-high-speed Backbone Network Service* (*vBNS*) running over an ATM/SONET backbone at 155 Mbps (OC-3), with plans to upgrade to 622 Mbps (OC-12) and higher. The SONET backbone transmission system connects GigaPOPs, which are switches and routers running at speeds in the Gbps range. The network connects the Pittsburgh (Pennsylvania) and San Diego (California) Supercomputing Centers, the Cornell Theory Center, the National Center for Supercomputer Applications, and the National Center for Atmospheric Research. Access service also is offered in San Francisco, Los Angeles, Seattle, Denver, Chicago, Cleveland, New York, Boston, Atlanta, and Washington, D.C. [12-41] and [12-42]. The vBNS also supports IPv6 traffic over ATM, both in native mode and tunneled in IPv4 connections. The vBNS takes advantage of the very substantial backbone network built by MCI over the years, as well as the network it acquired through the merger with MFS, and most especially the UUNET network, which MFS acquired previously. In 1998, MCI Worldcom acquired Advanced Networks and Services (ANS) and merged it into the UUNET subsidiary. ANS was a consortium of IBM, MCI, and Merit Network, Inc., which owned a substantial part of the backbone network. ANS also provided access to NSFNET and was the access provider of choice for many *Fortune 1000* companies.

World Wide Web (WWW)

The World Wide Web (WWW), also known as *The Web*, is the Internet's first *killer application*. Mr. Tim Berners-Lee developed the WWW at CERN, the European Laboratory for Particle Physics in Geneva, Switzerland. The Web is a multiplatform operating system that supports multimedia communications on the basis of a *Graphical User Interface (GUI)*. The GUI provides *hypertext*, which enables the user to click a highlighted text word and search related files, across Web servers, and through *hot links*; in other words, the Web is *hyperlinked*. In addition to text, The Web supports graphics, audio, and video, with various levels of quality and speed depending on the bandwidth available.

While CERN served to conceive the Web, its home has moved to the W3 Consortium (W3C). W3C is a cooperative venture of CERN, The Massachusetts Institute of Technology (MIT), and Institut National de Recherche en Informatique et en Automatique (INRIA). The primary focus of W3C is that of the World Wide Web Core Development (WebCore) project, which is intended to develop Web standards [12-49]. You can monitor progress through the W3C Web site (of course) at http://www.w3.org.

Web Sites and Home Pages

Organizations or individuals can develop a *Web site*, consisting of a computing platform (server) connected to the Web on a full-time basis. Although the typical business approach involves the deployment of a dedicated server, smaller users may achieve the same end through renting Web site capability from an ISP — which logically partitions a server in support of multiple users and multiple home pages.

Home pages effectively provide a *point of presence* on the Web for businesses, typically supporting advertising and informational purposes. Within each Web site is a *home page*, or multimedia informational document, which may contain graphics, animated graphics, video clips, and audio clips, as well as text. Individuals may develop personal home ages, which may offer updates on personal life along the lines of a cyberspace version of the ever popular, *What I did on my summer vacation.*

Uniform Resource Locators (URLs)

Uniform Resource Locators (URLs) are unique WWW addresses assigned to each Web site and to each home page. The structure of the URL follows a standard convention that is *method://host_spec{port}{path}{file}{misc}*. By way of example: http://info.cern.ch/hypertext/WWW/MarkUp/MarkUp.html, where *http = hypertext transport protocol* and *html = hypertext markup language*.

HTTP is the default protocol for transmitting HTML content over the Internet. It advises the browser to use the http protocol in accessing Web documents. HTML was the first programming language for creating compound documents for Web sites, and for supporting hot links to other sites. HTML has the clear advantage of device independence; in other words, the specifics of the user terminal (e.g., Macintosh, IBM-compatible PC, or Sun workstation) do not affect the presentation of the file [12-30].

Clearly, URLs are of great value in the world of e-commerce. For instance, IDG Books Worldwide, the publisher of this book, has the Web site http://www. idgbooks.com, which is very important to its online business. (Unabashedly self-serving Hint #1: You order large quantities of this book from that Web site.) Microsoft reportedly paid $5 million for the rights to www.internetexplorer.com, which was the property of another company that made legitimate use of it [12-43]. Some companies have filed lawsuits against *squatters*, who had registered Web sites mimicking the copyrighted, trademarked, or service-marked names of other companies specifically for the purpose of selling them to the rightful owners for substantial sums of money.

Some companies and individuals have secured rights to attractive, unclaimed URLs with the intention of selling them. For example, Marc Ostrofsky of Houston, Texas, owned the URL www.eflowers.com. In 1999, he sold it to Flowers Direct for $25,000, plus $0.50 for every transaction generated over the Web site — plus free flowers for his wife, Sarah, for the rest of her life. Given the projections of 500,000 transactions per year, that's not a bad return on an investment of $70.00.

Standards

Standards for the WWW are set by the *W3 Consortium*, which is run by The Massachusetts Institute of Technology (MIT), *Intitut National de Recherche en Informatique Et En* (*INRIA*) in Europe, and in collaboration with CERN. Tim Berners-Lee, creator of WWW, serves as the group's coordinator.

Applications

WWW applications are in a world of their own, including advertising, publishing, micromarketing, catalogs and direct sales, entertainment, and e-commerce. The great hope is that the Web will become a significant tool for commerce, enabling customers to access a home page on a Web site, gain information about a product or service, and actually make a purchase online.

ADVERTISING: HOME PAGE SPONSORSHIP
Home page sponsorship is offered by several directories and frequently hit portals and home pages. Virtually all browser portals and home pages for publishers of periodicals, for example, sell sponsorships at rates that easily can run as high as $100,000 per quarter. In return for this rather princely sum, your home-page banner will appear on their home page; users can click your banner and hyperlink to your home page. Simba Information estimated Internet advertising revenues to be $2.1 billion in 1998, growing to $5.5 billion in 1999, and $7.1 billion in 2002 [12-44].

Zima once advertised its home page on six different home pages. The Marin Institute for the Prevention of Alcohol and Other Drug Problems (San Rafael, California) and others complained loudly about such *cyberbooze* encounters. Zima countered by suggesting that it is a responsible *cybercitizen*, clearly asking that the user be at least 21 years of age to join *Tribe Z*. There no longer is a www.zima.com – which definitely is a good thing.

PERSONAL HOME PAGES

Personal home pages exist by the hundreds of thousands, at least. Text describing collections of airsick bags, photos of the children, audio clips of the growls and screeches of family pets, and video clips of summer vacations – all of these are possible and all of these are present on Web. Truly bored NetHeads can while away their time with such home pages as:

- *Mr. Potato Head*: Revealing data about everyone's favorite starchy vegetable toy (http://www.cyberstreet.com/users/lynn).

- *The Uselessness of Pi and its Irrational Friends*: Calculate the value of *Pi* to as many decimal places as you desire (http://www.go2net/internet/useless/pi.html).

- *Strawberry Pop-Tart Blow-Torches*: A step-by-step guide to the process of using this popular breakfast food as an incendiary device (http://www.sci.tamucc.edu/%7Epmichaud/toast). I do not recommend that you try this at home.

- *Lost in Space*: A guide to every episode of this popular TV show. (http://dangerwillrobinson.lycos.com/lois_splash.html).

E-commerce

Electronic commerce, or *e-commerce*, has grown to incredible proportions over the past several years. According to the U.S. Department of Commerce, the e-commerce and IT industries accounted for one-third of the U.S. real economic growth between 1995 and 1998 [12-45]. According to Forrester Research, total Web purchases in 1999 will total approximately $51 billion, $43 billion of which will be business-to-business, and $8 billion of which will be business-to-consumer. Forrester estimates that e-commerce will reach $1.438 trillion in 2003, with $1.331 trillion of that total being business-to-business. Key transaction categories in the 2003 business-to-business services market will be financial services ($80 billion) and business travel ($38 billion). The business-to-business goods market forecast includes key categories of computing and electronics ($395.3 billion) and motor vehicles ($212.9 billion) [12-46].

E-commerce essentially involves the purchasing of goods and services over the Web, usually through a secure credit card transaction. Examples of Web-based businesses include online booksellers, some of which have expanded into sales of music, videotapes, toys, and electronic games. Online auction houses recently have gained a good deal of attention, as well; online auctions of airline tickets, cruises, and hotel rooms currently are especially popular. Application software routinely is sold over the Web, and then downloaded over it. Using the MP3 (Moving Pictures Experts Group, Audio Layer 3) compression algorithm, near CD-ROM quality music also can be purchased over the Web, and then downloaded over the Internet, although there are significant concerns relative to copyright infringements and avoidance of royalty payments. Some companies even distribute the music for free, in anticipation of increased revenues from concerts and T-shirts. Electronic brokerage houses have made a significant dent in the overall stock brokerage market; although they are plagued by occasional router and server failures, electronic trades are accomplished at a fraction of the commissions paid to conventional stock brokers.

As noted earlier in this chapter, the Internet Tax Freedom Act became law in October 1998. One of the provisions of that Act protects e-commerce from taxation at the state and local levels, in effect declaring the Internet and WWW a tax-free zone in terms of sales taxes for interstate transactions. In other words, your online purchases from a company in Rhode Island are not taxed, assuming that you live outside the state. Technically speaking, no taxes apply as long as the seller does not maintain a physical presence in the buyer's state. This step is grounded in tradition, as mail-order catalog companies long have enjoyed the same advantage. For that matter, the purchases that you make in New York City are exempt from state and local sales taxes if you have them shipped back to Seattle, rather than taking them back to your hotel and hauling them back home yourself. And, as most people know, the cost of postage easily can be less than the sales taxes. Now, buyers are required to pay levies on their online and mail-order purchases when they file their state income tax returns, assuming that there is an income tax in the state of residence, but it's unlikely that any but the most right-minded consumer actually would do such a thing. The risk, of course, is that the increasing popularity of e-commerce can undermine the state and local tax bases, which fund a wide variety of social and other services. In the meantime, the debates continue in the hallowed halls of Congress.

Search Mechanisms and Browsers

The huge number of servers and incredible amount of information available on the Internet and Web quickly made it difficult to find the desired resource. In other words, you couldn't find the information unless you knew pretty much where to find it — sort of like having to know at least the approximate spelling of a word in order to look it up in the dictionary to determine the exact spelling. This problem was addressed in the early 1990s through the development of search mechanisms and, more recently, Web browsers.

Search mechanisms are in the form of client/server software that supports the search for Internet informational resources, through the development and maintenance of resource directories. The first primitive text browser appeared in 1991, courtesy of CERN. In 1993, the first graphical browsers appeared: Viola for X windows, Mac browser from CERN, and Mosaic for X Windows [12-47]. Early browsers that remain widely used include Archie, Gopher, Veronica, Jughead, and WAIS. Currently, the most popular browsers are Netscape Communicator (which contains Netscape Navigator), Netscape Navigator, and Microsoft's Internet Explorer.

Archie a corruption of *archive*, is a FTP search mechanism first deployed in 1991. Archie enables you to search for a file (exact name unknown) on a file server (name unknown) somewhere on the Net. Archie servers contain directory listings of all such files, updated on a monthly basis through a process of file-server polling. Archie provides a user-definable number of file hits, as well as file names, server names, and directory paths to access each listed file. Archie capabilities are limited to specific search *strings*, thereby providing little flexibility. Currently, Archie is often integrated into Gopher or WWW clients, to be activated when the user accesses an Archie server.

Gopher was developed at the University of Minnesota, where the Golden Gopher is the school mascot. Developed as a user interface to provide easy access to server resources in educational institutions, Gopher has become a de facto user interface standard. Gopher servers enable the user to access a directory of over 1,800 Gopher server sites, click the name of the server, and browse its file resources on the basis of nested menus. Gopher requires that the user know the server on which the subject file is located, somewhere in *gopherspace.*

VERONICA (*Very Easy Rodent-Oriented Net-wide Index to Computerized Archives*) is an Archie variation that supports an index of Gopherspace titles on which a search can be performed. The selected resources are then delivered to the user in the form of a Gopher menu.

JUGHEAD (*Jonzy's Universal Gopher Hierarchy Excavation And Display*) is similar in operation to Veronica, although it limits the search to a specific organization. Jughead also delivers a custom menu of available resources located on the basis of the *keyword* search. Playing off Archie and Gopher, subsequent developers of search mechanisms tried to stay with the Archie comic book/rodent theme, proving once and for all that even acronyms can be fun. Alas, the more recent and more powerful browsers were not named with a noticeable sense of humor.

Mosaic is a browser developed at the National Center for Supercomputing (NCSA) at the University of Illinois Urbana-Champaign campus. Mosaic provides a consistent user interface available in versions to support Macintosh, Microsoft Windows, and UNIX-X Windows. Mosaic can be used over dedicated or dial-up Internet connections; the dial-up access provider must support either SLIP or PPP. Mosaic enables the easy browsing of WWW resources through menus that support hypertext. Through a simple process of mouse-clicking, the user can select menu options. Selected files can include audio and graphics, both of which can be viewed without the requirement to download the subject file. Mosaic technology is licensed by the NCSA for commercial application. Spyglass, Inc. (Naperville, Illinois) has licensed well over 12 million copies of Mosaic to IBM, DEC, and others who intend to resell the company's Enhanced Mosaic; Enhanced Mosaic includes enhanced security mechanisms based *on S-HTTP (Secure HTTP)*.

WAIS (*Wide Area Information Service*) servers enable the user to specify the databases requested for search, and to conduct a subject-matter search on the basis of *keywords.*

Netscape Navigator was developed by Netscape Communications Corp. — since acquired by America Online (AOL). The software, built by a team led by Marc Andersen (creator of the original Mosaic), features simultaneous image loading and continuous document-streaming speed performance. Navigator quickly became the top browser choice, and is included in Netscape Communicator. Navigator includes a number of search engines, which currently include Excite, Google, GoTo.com, HotBot, Infoseek, LookSmart, and Lycos.

Internet Explorer (*IE*) is a highly capable browser, which has the advantage of being packaged with Microsoft's Windows suite of software. IE currently includes the following browsers: AltaVista, GoTo.com, Infoseek, Lycos, and MSN (Microsoft Network). Now, Microsoft remains in an antitrust legal battle with the U.S. Justice Department, which alleges that the company used its dominance in personal computer operating system software to force Internet Explorer on customers, while shutting out its competitors, mainly Netscape.

Intranets and Extranets

Intranets are the concept of the Internet turned inward — an unexpected turn, perhaps, but a very significant one. Intranets essentially are mini-Internets deployed within organizations or groups of organizations. They can be in the form of internal Internets, functioning to provide access to information resources within the company, university, or other organization. They can be confined to a campus environment or can extend across the wide area to link together multiple, geographically dispersed locations. They also can function as a closed subnet of the Internet, much as is intended for Internet2 in the college and university market. Although conceived as recently as 1995, intranets have spread quickly to the point that most medium-to-large user organizations have them in place. Intranets use the same browsers as used for Internet application, thereby avoiding the training and support requirements imposed by another application software package such as groupware.

Intranets can be used for communications to and between employees for just about any purpose imaginable. A number of corporations use intranets to keep their employees advised of company policies, job postings, company events, product literature, press releases, and so on. With the proper password for security purposes, of course, privileged users can access sensitive internal company information, including customer billing records and network usage data. As is the case with the Internet and World Wide Web, images, video clips, and sound clips can be associated with textual information. Hypertext links can be included to *hot link* to other sites and databases, and even to the Internet and WWW.

Health care organizations have made fairly extensive use of intranets to link remote clinics, reducing paperwork and abbreviating communication time. Kaiser Permanente has put the intranet concept to use in order to keep employees abreast of changes in health legislation and insurance law, as well as to provide access to company telephone directories and human resources manuals [12-48]. Eli Lilly uses its intranet to schedule clinical trials of new drugs and to speed the process of regulatory submissions in 120 countries. The company's initial implementation of 3,000 desktops was accomplished at costs of about $80,000; plans are to hook up approximately 16,000 employees, or about 1/3 of its entire staff. The company considered groupware products such as Lotus Notes, but found the costs unfavorable and the training and support requirements relatively extreme in comparison to the intranet alternative [12-49].

Cisco Systems should be a big fan of intranets, and they are. The company reportedly conducts virtually all IT development via its intranet, which it feels increases productivity dramatically. Cisco claims that the technology yields a ROI (Return on Investment) of $3.5 million annually [12-50].

Extranets are intranets opened to select groups of users outside the company. Access generally is provided to groups of vendors, suppliers, customers, and others who have a requirement to access select databases and processes, perhaps for EDI (Electronic Data Interchange) applications. For example, extranets can enable customers to place orders electronically and to track them to fulfillment, and vendors can track retail sales of their products, perhaps store-by-store.

Internet Security: A Special Issue

The Internet is inherently insecure. It is, after all, an open network. Its openness certainly is one of its major strengths and, at the same, perhaps its major weakness. While e-commerce is promoted as the future of The Net, this lack of security certainly has slowed development of commercial applications. However, it is worth noting that providing your credit card number over the Internet is probably as secure as giving your credit card to a server at a restaurant.

Beyond security concerns over Internet commerce, you must remember that access to the Internet is a two-way door — just as users can get out, others can get in. All too often, those others have no legitimate right to do so. Although few organizations admit to having had their systems breached via the Internet, it is clear that such occurrences are all too common.

Security Risks and Countermeasures

The Internet is rife with risks. *Hackers, crackers*, saboteurs, and other unsavory characters abound, eagerly attacking the Net and its users at every opportunity. The risks certainly include system intrusion, unauthorized data access, system sabotage, planting of viruses, theft of data, theft of credit card numbers, and theft of passwords. While the Internet and WWW can't be blamed for the concepts and practice of mischief, fraud, theft, and other socially unacceptable forms of behavior, they certainly provide another high-tech cyberalley on the Information Superhighway. As noted by Panchatantra in the 5th century B.C., *Not a cow, nor a gift of land, nor yet a gift of food, is so important as the gift of safety, which is declared to be the great gift among all gifts in this world.*

CERT (*Computer Emergency Response Team*) at Carnegie-Mellon University comprises a group of experts, which are responsible for overseeing security issues on The Net. While it is highly doubtful that a single security measure or standard will prevail in the near and distant future, there exist a number of options, including message encryption, authentication, and authorization. Firewalls, incorporating much of the above, recently have gained the spotlight in terms of a defense mechanism.

ENCRYPTION

Encryption involves scrambling and compressing the data prior to transmission; the receiving device is provided with the necessary logic in the form of a *key* to decrypt the transmitted information. Encryption logic generally resides in firmware included in standalone devices, although it can be built into virtually any device. For instance, such logic now is incorporated into routers, which can encrypt/decrypt data on a packet-by-packet basis. Encryption comes in two basic flavors: private key and public key.

Private key	encryption, also known as single-key or secret-key encryption, uses the same key for both encryption (encoding) and decryption (decoding). This approach requires that the key be kept secret through some form of secure key transmission prior to the ensuing data transfer.
Public key	encryption involves the RSA encryption key that can be used by all authorized network users. The key for decryption is kept secret. Public key encryption is much slower than private key, but the dissemination of the key is accomplished much more quickly. Public key encryption is available freely on the Net via a program known as PGP (Pretty Good Privacy), developed by Philip Zimmerman. PGP was under a cloud for some time because there was concern that it was so powerful as to violate U.S. technology export laws. By the way, encryption technology technically is classified under U.S. law as a form of munitions.

The commercial version of PGP is known as ViaCrypt PGP, offering an improved user interface.

DATA ENCRYPTION STANDARDS

Data encryption standards include *DPF* (*Data Private Facility*), DES, RSA, and Clipper. *DES* (*Data Encryption Standard*), which uses a challenge-response approach and intelligent tokens, was formulated by the U.S. National Bureau of Standards. *RSA*, named after its developers, Rivest, Shamir, and Adleman, is the standard for public key encryption. *Clipper*, an encryption standard developed by the U.S. government, uses escrowed keys to permit government deciphering through a *back door*. Clipper, which is non-exportable, is used extensively by the U.S. government and those who wish to do business with it. Encryption programs used on the Net include SSL, S-HTTP, and combinations of them.

Secure Socket Layer (SSL) from Netscape negotiates point-to-point security between client and server, including type of encryption scheme and exchange of encryption keys. SSL sends messages over a socket, which is a secure channel at the connection layer and existing in virtually every TCP/IP application. While SSL can accommodate a number of encryption algorithms, Netscape has licensed RSA Data Security's BSafe to provide end-to-end encryption, as well as key creation and certification. Netscape's Netsite Commerce Server technology, including SSL, has been licensed by the likes of DEC, Novell, the Bank of America, and Delphi. *Socket*, by the way, is an operating system abstraction that permits application programs to access communications protocols automatically. Bolt Beranek and Newman developed this concept in conjunction with the company's early work on TCP/IP.

Secure HyperText Transport Protocol (S-HTTP) from Enterprise Integration Technologies also negotiates point-to-point security between client and server, although at the application layer. EIT has licensed RSA Data Security's BSafe TIPEM (Toolkit for Interoperable Privacy-Enhanced Messaging). S-HTTP is a superset of HTTP and, therefore, is specific to the Web; several manufacturers of Web servers have announced plans to include S-HTTP in their products. S-HTTP has gained the support of the WWW Consortium, and looks to be moving toward acceptance as a de facto standard.

AUTHENTICATION

Authentication provides a means by which network managers can authenticate the identity of those attempting access to computing resources and the data they house. Authentication consists of password protection and intelligent tokens.

Password protection should be imposed to restrict individuals on a site, host, application, screen, and field level. Passwords should be of reasonably long length, alphanumeric in nature, and changed periodically. There is a current trend toward the use of dedicated password servers for password management. *Password Authentication Protocol (PAP)* is a commonly used mechanism for password protection in support of remote users. While PAP is easy to use, passwords typically are sent to the Remote Access Server (RAS) in *plain text* (i.e., *in the clear,* or unencrypted).

Intelligent tokens are hardware devices that generate one-time passwords to be verified by a secure server. They often work on a cumbersome *challenge-response* basis. *Challenge Handshake Authentication Protocol (CHAP)* is an example of this improved approach. CHAP involves the RAS's challenging the remote user with a random number. The user responds with a *digest,* which is an encrypted password based on the random number challenge. The RAS then decrypts the password using that same random number key to verify the identity of the remote user.

AUTHORIZATION

Authorization provides a means of controlling which legitimate users have access to which resources. Authorization involves complex software that resides on every secured computer on the network; ideally, it provides *single sign-on* capability. Authorization systems commonly used in support of Internet security include Kerberos, Sesame, and Access Manager.

Kerberos draws its name from *Kerberos* (also known as *Cerebrus*), the three-headed monster that guarded the entryway to the infernal regions in Greek mythology. Perhaps the best-known authorization software, it was developed by the Massachusetts Institute of Technology (MIT) and is available free, although more powerful commercial versions exist, as well. As Kerberos uses DES, it is not easily exportable. IBM's Kryptoknight is a Kerberos variant — weaker but exportable. By way of example, EIN uses Kerberos in its Secure Server product. Although Hercules defeated Kerberos, according to Greek legend, a hacker of Herculean proportions has yet to emerge victorious over this powerful software.

Sesame (*Secure European System for Applications in a Multivendor Environment*) was developed by the ECMA (European Computer Manufacturers Association). It is flexible, open, and intended for large, heterogeneous network computing environments. It also is highly complex and not effective for smaller applications.

Access Manager approved by the IETF, uses an API for application development, employing scripting. *Scripting* involves a process of mimicking the log-on procedures of a program, providing basic levels of security for small networks.

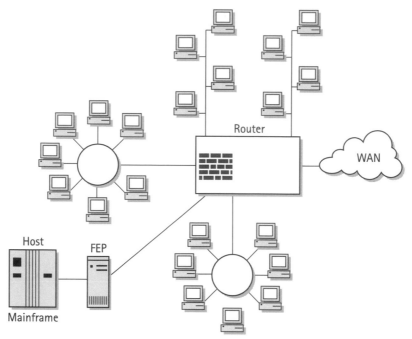

Figure 12-8 Firewall implementation in a router

FIREWALLS

Firewalls comprise application software that can reside in a communication router, server, or some other device. That device physically and/or logically is a first point of access into a networked system (see Figure 12-8). On an active basis, the device can block access to unauthorized entities, effectively acting as a *security firewall*. Firewalls provide logging, auditing, and *sucker traps* to identify access attempts and to separate legitimate users from intruders. Firewalls can be in the form of a programmable router or a full set of software, hardware, and consulting services.

SATAN, A SPECIAL ISSUE

SATAN (Security Administrator Tool for Analyzing Networks) is software designed to identify and report security weaknesses, including unauthorized access and virus contamination. Through mimicking an intruder, the software was designed to identify security holes and to alert the system administrator of their presence. Very easy to use as a result of its Mosaic interface, SATAN unfortunately also can be employed to crack the very security it is intended to ensure. Dan Farmer of Silicon Graphics and Wietse Venema, of the Netherlands University of Eindhoven developed SATAN. When Farmer made SATAN available, free-of-charge, on the Internet on April 5, 1995, he separated from Silicon Graphics officially by mutual consent.

CERT issued a SATAN advisory warning on April 10, 1995. That warning suggested that SATAN posed significant risk of intrusion when run with certain Web browsers, including Netscape and Lynx – but not Mosaic. The danger is presented if a user moves immediately from a session running SATAN to browsing the Web, without first quitting the browser. The very next day, Dan Farmer posted SATAN V1.0 on the Web; that version offers tighter security and warns users of the potential for system vulnerability. *Sometimes/The Devil* [Satan] *is a gentleman* (Percy Bysshe Shelley, "Peter Bell the Third," 1819).

Virtual Private Networks (VPNs)

The term *Virtual Private Network* (*VPN*) has many definitions, all of which are valid. In Chapter 5, we explored voice VPNs, also known as Software Defined Networks (SDNs). In Chapter 7, we explored classic data VPNs. Both of these conventional VPNs are circuit-switched in nature. In subsequent chapters, we examined X.25 and packet switching, Frame Relay, and ATM, all of which also are characterized as VPNs. In contemporary usage, the term most commonly refers to the creation of a virtually private network over the public Internet, or over a public IP-based network.

At the center of all definitions is the fact that the VPN has some of the characteristics of a private, leased-line network without being one. True private networks are distinguished by the fact that dedicated, leased-line circuits, or channels, or channel capacity, interconnect multiple sites in an enterprise network. Therefore, the bandwidth always is available and without any usage charges, and there are no issues of access and congestion control, as least not at the network level. Performance essentially is guaranteed, and security never is an issue. The disadvantages of private networks include long configuration and reconfiguration times, high installation costs and recurring charges, lack of scalability, and susceptibility to catastrophic failure. Private networks are optimized on the side of performance, rather than raw efficiency.

Virtual Private Networks reverse these factors to some degree. VPNs are fast and easy to configure and reconfigure, and are highly scalable, with a solid relationship between cost and functionality. As VPNs make use of a public network that is shared in terms of access, switching, and transport, and which is highly redundant, issues of catastrophic failure are much reduced. Their shared nature, however, creates ever-present issues of access control and congestion control. Therefore and particularly in the case of IP and Frame Relay packet networks, issues of latency, jitter (variability of latency), loss, and throughput always must be considered. Further and particularly in the case of the IP-based Internet, security is a considerable concern. In the current context of the Internet-based VPN, security issues are mitigated through the use of a combination of authentication, encryption, and tunneling.

AUTHENTICATION

Authentication, as previously discussed, is a means of access control that ensures that users are who they claim to be. Whether through password protection or intelligent tokens, the authentication process is intended to avoid the possibility that unauthorized users might access internal computing or network resources.

ENCRYPTION

Encryption, as also discussed previously, is the encoding, or scrambling, of the data for security purposes. In order to decode the data, the destination device must have the correct key. In the VPN context, data encryption and decryption can occur either at the user end points, or at the edge of the service provider's network. In the first case, the user end point devices can include workstations or other host computers, routers, or Remote Access Servers (RASs). In the second case, the carrier's or service provider's (e.g., ISP) equipment is responsible for encryption and decryption.

TUNNELING

Tunneling is the process of encapsulating an encrypted data packet in an IP packet for secure transmission across the inherently insecure Internet. The four leading tunneling protocols are SOCKSv5, PPTP, L2TP, and IPsec.

- ◆ SOCKSv5 is an authentication technique that runs at the Session Layer (Layer 5) of the OSI Reference Model. Through the use of secure sockets negotiated between client and server over a virtual circuit and on a session-by-session basis, SOCKv5 supports the security of UDP datagrams as a data stream, rather than on a packet-by-packet basis. SOCKSv5 also supports protocol-specific communications, such as SMTP, to prevent hackers from extracting e-mail data through the use of an alias. SOCKSv5 is a cross-platform technique, working across multiple operating systems and browsers. SOCKSv5 also interoperates on top of IPv4, IPsec, PPTP, L2TP, and other lower-level protocols.

- ◆ **Point-to-Point Tunneling Protocol (PPTP)** operates at the Data Link Layer (Layer 2) of the OSI Reference Model. Initially conceived by Ascend and developed by Microsoft and embedded in Windows NT, PPTP is a proprietary technique that encapsulates Point-to-Point Protocol (PPP) frames with IP packets. Packet filters provide access control, end-to-end and server-to-server.

- ◆ **Layer 2 Tunneling Protocol (L2TP)** is an IETF standard that evolved from a combination of PPTP and Cisco's *Layer 2 Forwarding* (*L2F*) protocol. L2TP is used for secure, node-to-node communications by ISP and other VPN service providers, in support of multiple, simultaneous tunnels in the network core. End users gain access to the service provider on an unencrypted basis; the service provider assumes that responsibility at the edge of the packet network.

♦ **IP Security (IPsec)**, as I noted earlier in this chapter, is the security mechanism developed for IPv6. In a dual-stack mode, IPv4 frames are encapsulated for transport within encrypted IPv6 frames. IPsec runs at the Network Layer (Layer 3). IPsec is a standards-based solution from the IETF.

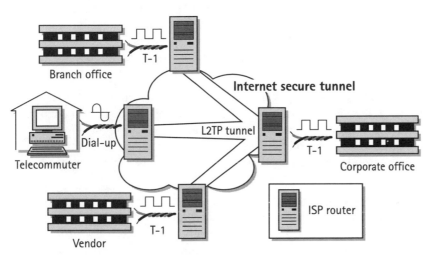

Figure 12-9 Virtual Private Network (VPN) through the Internet, illustrating the use of tunneling

Applications Scenarios

VPNs really are all about cost-effectiveness, with the emphasis on cost, rather than raw performance. Especially in the context of the IP-based VPN, the reduction in costs can be very significant, indeed. Such VPNs currently are based on the public Internet, although the emerging IP-based networks from the carriers such as Level 3 and Qwest likely will challenge that model. Access techniques include all of the options I have detailed, including dial-up modems, ISDN, xDSL, Frame Relay, and ATM. The applications scenarios include remote access, intranets, and extranets. Note that VPNs can be incredibly cost-effective in support of the multinational enterprise, as truly private networks often are prohibitively expensive, if even available, on an international basis.

♦ **Remote Access VPNs** are highly cost-effective in support of telecommuters, and mobile and remote workers. Assuming that the worker can reach the Internet or other IP-based network over a dial-up or other form of connection, reasonably secure communications can be accomplished with the home office, or any branch office on the VPN. The level of bandwidth provided, of course, depends on the speed of the remote access link; the speed of the link to the home or branch office, and the total volume of traffic over that link; and the level of congestion currently experienced over the shared IP backbone network. Significant cost savings can be realized when you compare VPNs to dial-up PSTN costs, whether based on DDD or toll-free access numbers. Each client PC, of course, must be equipped with software that supports the necessary tunneling protocols. Savings also can be realized at the branch, regional, or corporate location, as both T-carrier circuits connected to the PSTN and associated *RADIUS* (*Remote Authentication Dial-In User Service*) routers can be either eliminated or consolidated, in favor of shared T-carrier circuits connecting to the VPN.

♦ Intranet VPNs serve to link branch, regional, and corporate offices. Access to the VPN generally would be on the basis of dedicated circuits, usually in the form of unchannelized T-carrier, which might run the Frame Relay protocol or, perhaps, ATM. In this scenario, the elimination of, or consolidation of, access circuits can yield significant cost benefits at all connected sites.

♦ Extranet VPNs serve to link vendors, customers, affiliates, and distributors into the main corporate office. An extranet VPN often must be extremely flexible in terms of access techniques and security mechanisms, as the corporate sponsor may have little control over the specifics of the external users' systems and processes.

Cost savings can be extreme if access to and usage of the VPN is based on a flat rate, with no usage charges — although performance may be less than totally satisfactory. Large ISPs offering enhanced VPN services typically offer service-level guarantees that address overall network throughput, which can be cruciai in a mission-critical and time-sensitive application environment. While such enhanced performance contracts are based on an additional usage-based pricing algorithm, the overall costs still compare quite favorably with those of DDD and toll-free, dial-up access. Providers of such enhanced VPN services include AT&T, GTE, MCI Worldcom's UUNET, PSINET, and Sprint. The popularity of the VPN concept is evidenced by the following footnoted sources for this discussion [12-51-12-61].

MISUSE AND CONTENT

There have been a large number of highly publicized cases of the Internet and the Web being misused for illicit and immoral purposes. The Internet has been used for transmitting stolen credit card numbers, cellular telephone ID numbers, and such. While any communications medium can be used for such purposes, the Net creates another set of difficulties for law enforcement because communications are virtually instantaneous and multiple parties can gain access to the illegal data through a bulletin board. Further, it is difficult, if not impossible, in many cases to track down the offenders.

More significant from a social perspective is the fact that Internet *chat rooms* have been used to lure minors into the clutches of pedophiles and others who wish to take advantage of them. The offenders generally seem to mask themselves as minors, striking up an electronic conversation and suggesting a meeting somewhere. While there have been only a few such cases uncovered and publicized, the risks exist and the consequences can be terrible.

Also of great concern is the issue of content and access to it. Numerous Web sites contain sexually explicit material, including photographs. While adults have a constitutional right to view such material, minors generally do not; the Internet and the Web really have no effective means of controlling access, since the users are anonymous and their ages and other characteristics are unknown. Most of the truly explicit Web sites (so the author is told) offer very little for free; full access to the offending material generally is provided only on the basis of paid subscription.

The U.S. Federal Communications Commission (FCC), however, is seriously considering regulating the content of the Internet. While censorship can go too far, there are numerous and clearly documented cases of beasts who prowl the Internet. (Author's humble opinion: At the risk of lapsing into a discussion of morals, there should be a method for constraining those who would use the Internet and the Web for immoral purposes, as defined by law. At the very least, there should be a means of blocking access of minors to such material. There also should be stiff penalties imposed on violators.) The Electronic Frontier Foundation, Electronic Privacy Foundation, and Voters Telecommunications Watch are battling the FCC and U.S. Congress in this regard, citing freedom of speech; petitions were passed (you guessed it) over the Internet. Although a Communications Decency Act was passed in 1996, it was overturned in Federal District court, citing violation of free speech as guaranteed by the First Amendment to the Constitution; the federal government is expected to appeal to the U.S. Supreme Court. Should the Act be upheld, the issues remaining to be addressed concern who would assume the role of *cybercop*, and the extent to which the service providers would be held liable for the transgressions of their subscribers. While we may never see Internet content censored at the network level, there do exist a number of commercially available software filters that enable parents to deny access to Internet sites that might contain unsavory content, as defined by the filter developers. Those filters run against Web servers, which are updated on a regular basis in order to keep pace with the dynamics of the Web sites and their content.

Outside the United States, very tight content controls have been exercised in some countries; as you might expect, those nations include Singapore and the Peoples Republic of China (PRC). As recently as January 1999, an Internet e-mail broker in the PRC was sentenced to two years in prison for "inciting the overthrow of state power" by supplying 30,000 e-mail addresses to a pro-democracy magazine in the United States. The sentence was considered by many to be light, as three leaders of the China Democracy Party received sentences of 11, 12, and 13 years after being found guilty of the same charge in December 1998.

Internet Oddities, Screwball Applications, and Some Really Good Ideas

As mentioned previously, only technology and the human mind can limit the applications for the Internet and the World Wide Web. There have been a number of recent announcements of Internet oddities and screwball applications, as well as some really good ideas. I've got my own ideas about which are which. Other judgements I'll leave entirely up to you.

◆ *Package tracking* is offered on the Web by Federal Express, UPS, USPS, and other carriers. Customers can access the Web sites and get the latest status of packages, based on package tracking numbers. The savings easily are in the millions of dollars, compared to the costs of handling voice calls through an incoming call center. UPS reportedly handles an average of about 750,000 package tracking requests per day on its Web site, in addition to 60,000 requests for information about shipping prices, and 40,000 requests for information about transit time. USP estimates that about 2.1-3.2 percent of all Internet traffic stops at its site [12-62].

◆ *Document delivery* over the Internet is being promoted by UPS, through its Document Exchange service known as UPS OnLine Courier. Senders upload documents to the secure UPS server, then, UPS sends e-mail notifications to the recipients, advising them of documents awaiting delivery. The recipient uses the URL provided in the notification to download the document from the secure server via a Web browser. An option enables the sender to require that the recipient use a password known only to the sender and recipient. Security is provided via 128-bit encryption on the server, and 40-bit Secure Socket Layer (SSL) encryption during transport. Pricing is attractive, especially when compared to U.S. Postal Service (USPS) Registered Mail and traditional courier services. This service resembles a plan hatched by the USPS for a service dubbed Dossier, which has yet to be introduced [12-63].

◆ *Distribution of software, upgrades, and bug fixes* is a really good idea. In many cases, software is provided free-of-charge as a public domain release, with subsequent, enhanced versions provided commercially.

◆ *Online publishing* has really taken off in recent years. A large number of major newspapers have developed Web sites to test the medium. Most of the technology publications, of course, have developed Web sites for online access to published articles and late-breaking news. While associated advertising revenues are not made public, they are very substantial. According to the Internet Advertising Bureau, online ad revenues for the 1998 hit $1.92 billion, an increase of 112 percent over the previous year [12-64].

◆ *CyberFairs* are job fairs that enable companies to post job listings and recruit applicants online. Interactive communications are supported.

◆ *CyberGambling* (Now there's a constructive idea!) is now offered by casinos. The casinos can circumvent U.S. gambling laws by placing their servers offshore. Users are required to have offshore bank accounts, as well, in order to deposit their winnings. imho (that's netspeak for in my humble opinion. note the lack of capitalization. that's also an e-mail convention. it's in the style of e.e. cummings.), we do not need a Virtual Vegas. The U.S. government appears to agree.

◆ *CyberSex* is not worthy of comment. Shame on you! Go back to "Go" and get a life!

◆ *Music distribution* over the Internet currently makes use of MP3 (Moving Pictures Experts Group, Audio Layer 3) compression algorithm. As each minute of uncompressed digital music requires a file of roughly 10MB, it takes a very long time to download an entire CD-ROM album, even over a xDSL connection. MP3 compresses a 600MB CD-ROM music album down to about 50MB. In March 1999, Lycos claimed to have a library of over 500,000 MP3 files available for download. Issues of copyright infringement are significant with respect to this application.

◆ *Online auction* houses offer electronic auctions for just about everything imaginable – from airline tickets, hotel rooms, and cruises to sporting goods and antique china. The risks are several: you don't get to see the goods before you buy, and you have no real assurance of delivery. In other words, you buy on faith. Personally, I don't get it. I can get much better fares, much better flight schedules, and much better service from my travel agent. Conversely, it seems that the airlines are doing everything they can to put the travel agents out of business, so I may not have that option forever.

◆ *Bill presentment* is the rendering of a bill on a Web site. A number of large voice and data communications providers (e.g., AT&T, MCI Worldcom, and Nextlink) offer this service via secure Web sites, also providing for electronic payment in the form of authorizations for wire transfers.

◆ SETI@home is a means of harnessing the power of hundreds of thousands of home PCs to assist in the SETI (Search for ExtraTerrestrial Intelligence) project. SETI involves sifting through billions and billions of radio signals captured by large radiotelescopes, in the hopes of finding a pattern that could represent a message from an intelligent life form on another planet. SETI@home screen saver can be downloaded across the Internet, along with samples of radio signals for analysis. During periods of idleness, the software searches for patterns. Once the analysis is complete, the results are uploaded to the SETI server, and another sample is downloaded for analysis. This is a cool idea! Carl Sagan would be proud. No question about it!

The Dark Side: An Editorial

It has been said that the Internet is the electronic equivalent of the Gutenburg printing press in terms of its impact on the Information Age. That quite likely is an understatement. Certainly, the Internet and the World Wide Web support an unprecedented level of information access for the electronically privileged. In contrast to the printed word, however, much of the content on the Internet and the Web essentially is self-published. Therefore, there are no guarantees of either its objectivity or its accuracy. It is up to the reader to sort out the bias, the subjective, the self-serving, the inaccurate, and the outright lie in order to get the truth. Similarly, it is up to the reader of the text, and the viewer of the image or video, to sort out the ugliness of racial hatred and pornography that assault the senses and sensibilities of the vast majority of us in the global society.

Take this book, for example. It is based on 30 years of experience, countless hours of research, and an unyielding commitment to the objective truth. It has been written with all the skill at my disposal. A highly skilled team, including a consulting editor, a technical editor, a development editor, and a copy editor has reviewed it. For what it is, it is the best that we can make it. If my drafts contained any obviously and blatantly biased, subjective, self-serving, inaccurate, or untrue statements, the team eliminated them. If my drafts overly emphasized the ugliness of Web sites that promote racial, ethnic, or religious hatred, or that of pornography, my editors would have struck it, and rightfully so. Compare that with your own experience on the Internet and the Web. I make that comparison every day, as I do my research and sort through the tens of thousands of sources of information and misinformation.

You may recall the horror of the TWA Flight 800 incident. You also may recall the statements of Pierre Salinger, who was the press secretary for President John F. Kennedy. Salinger claimed to know on national news that Flight 800 was, in fact, shot down by an errant missile fired from a U.S. Navy warship. Salinger got this bogus information from a Web site.

You may remember the *Good Times* virus, and a host of other viruses. While there are many real viruses that pose real threats, many of them are absolute hoaxes – the rumors of which spread like wildfire over the Internet. Virtual panic resulted.

You may remember that in June 1998, an Associated Press reporter mistakenly posted a prepared obituary for Bob Hope on that wire service's Web site. While the error was discovered virtually immediately and the obituary was removed within 15 minutes or so, a U.S. congressman saw it and eulogized Bob Hope from the floor of the House of Representatives. Mr. Hope's response was somewhat along the lines of Mark Twain's, "Reports of my death have been greatly exaggerated."

Perhaps Sir Walter Scott said it best: "Oh, what a tangled web we weave when first we practice to deceive."

The bottom line is that it is your responsibility to seek the true and the beautiful. There are no filters on the Internet or the Web that truly will protect you. Please protect yourself, and please protect our children. Please support legislation to help us all protect each other.

References

[12-1]   Kalin, Sari. "The Worldlier Wider Web." *CIO Web Business*, March 1, 1999.

[12-2]   The Editors of PriceWaterhouseCoopers' *Technology Forecast: 1999.* "Internet backbone and service providers: A market overview." *America's Network*, April 15, 1999.

[12-3]   Cerf, Vinton G. and Kahn, Robert E. "A Protocol for Packet Network Interconnection." *IEEE Transactions on Communications.* Institute of Electrical and Electronics Engineers, 1974.

[12-4]   Comer, Douglas E. *Internetworking with TCP/IP, Second Edition.* Prentice Hall, 1991.

[12-5]   "MCI Worldcom MAE Services." www.wcom.com/tools-resources/about...services/mae_services_defined/tiers.shtml.

[12-6]   Garfinkel, Simson. "Where Streams Converge." *Hotwired.* www.hotwired.com/packet/garfinkel/96/37/geek.html.

[12-7]   Pappalardo, Denise and Gittlen, Sandra. "Is it too late for WorldCom's MAEs?" *Network World*, August 24, 1998.

[12-8]   Metcalfe, Bob. "Coming Internet Collapse Spurring Shortsighted Proliferation of Intranets." *InfoWorld*, May 20, 1996.

[12-9]   "A Day in The Life of The Internet." *Network World*, March 1, 1999.

[12-10]   Rickard, Jack. "Internet Architecture." *Boardwatch Magazine,* 1996. www.boardwatch.com/isp/fallisp/archi.html.

[12-11]   Carl, Jeremy. "Universal Access to Internet: Who Pays?" *Web Week,* May 20, 1996.

[12-12]   "Industry Spotlight: ISPs Struggle With Customer Growth." *The Industry Standard,* March 22, 1999.

[12-13]   Rohde, David. "More trouble for AT&T cable plan." *Network World,* June 28, 1999.

[12-14]   Bannan, Karen J. "Cable Access Remains Open Question." *Inter@ctive Week,* June 21, 1999.

[12-15]   Roberts-Witt, SarahL. "Big Investments Go to Satellite, Wireless Services." *Internet World,* June 28, 1999.

[12-16]   www.webtv.net

[12-17]   Moran, Susan. "Step by Step, 'Internet Anywhere' Approaches." *Internet World,* April 12, 1999.

[12-18]   www.apple.com/imac

[12-19]   www.macnn.com/features/9906mayhits/shtml

[12-20]   Andrews, Paul. "Could This Be The End Of The PC As We Know It?" *The Seattle Times,* March 31, 1996.

[12-21]   Andrews, Paul. "Out With The PC, In With The Net Reader?" *The Seattle Times,* April 7, 1996.

[12-22]   Gates, Bill. "Proposals For Cheap Internet Terminal Are Misguided, Computer History Shows." *Skagit Valley Herald,* April 10, 1996.

[12-23]   Lee, Yvonne L. "Japan Computer Corp. Unveils Internet Device." *Infoworld,* February 26, 1996.

[12-24]   Melford, Bob. "Are $500 Internet Terminals In Your Future?" *Digital News & Review,* March 1996.

[12-25]   Silwa, Carol and Messmer, Ellen. "'Net Devices Coming...but what are they good for?" *Network World,* May 20, 1996.

[12-26]   Weston, Rusty. "The Survey Says: Internet Terminals Hold Little Appeal." *PC Week,* November 27, 1995.

[12-27]   Muller, Nathan. "Dial 1-800-Internet." *BYTE,* February 1996.

[12-28]   Miller, Mark A. *Implementing IPv6.* M&T Books, 1998.

[12-29]   Miller, Mark A. "Finding Your Way Through the New IP." *Network World,* December 16, 1996.

[12-30]   Miller, Robert and Keeler, Elissa. *Internet Direct: Connecting through SLIP and PPP.* MIS:Press, 1995.

[12-31]   Messmer, Ellen. "Making the move from modem bank to IPSec." *Network World*, November 23, 1998.

[12-32]   Thayer, Rodney. "Bulletproof IP." *Data Communications*, November 21, 1997.

[12-33]   Moskowitz, Robert. "IPv6 For VPNs: It's Looking Better All The Time." *Network Computing*, January 15, 1998.

[12-34]   Moskowitz, Robert. "IPSec for Communities of Interest." *Network Computing*, April 1, 1998.

[12-35]   Karve, Anita. "Lesson 115: IP Security." *Network Magazine*, February 1998.

[12-36]   Saho, L. Michael. "Transmission Control Protocol/Internet Protocol (TCP/IP)." *Datapro Communications Analyst.* Datapro Information Services Group, March 1994.

[12-37]   Muller, Nathan J. "Using the Internet." *Datapro Communications Analyst.* Datapro Information Services Group, December 1994.

[12-38]   Smith, Veronica. "Internet 2: Building The Next Backbone." *Internet Week*, February 16, 1998.

[12-39]   Rendleman, John. "Internet2 to Go Live, Act as Testbed for New Technologies." *PC Week*, February 8, 1999.

[12-40]   "About Internet2." www.internet2.edu/html/about_i2.html.

[12-41]   Wilder, Clinton. "The Net on The Edge." *Information Week*, April 29, 1996.

[12-42]   "MCI to Upgrade Internet Backbone." *Information Week*, March 25, 1996.

[12-43]   Driscoll, Paul A. "What's in a name? For 'Internet Explorer,' $5 million." *Seattle Post-Intelligencer*, July 2, 1998.

[12-44]   "Net Ads to Break $7 billion in 2002." *The Industry Standard*, March 29, 1999.

[12-45]   www.ecommerce.gov

[12-46]   "Spotlight: Corporate E-commerce Kicks Into Gear." *The Industry Standard*, March 29, 1999.

[12-47]   Blum, Adam. *Building Business Web Sites.* MIS:Press, 1996.

[12-48]   "Intranets: An Inside Look At Real-World Applications." *Internetwork*, May 1996.

[12-49]   Gross, Neil. "Oh, What a Tangled Web." *Business Week*, February 26, 1996.

[12-50]   McCreary, Lew and Horgan, Tim. "On the Inside, Looking Out." *CIO Web Business*, July 1, 1999.

[12-51]   Kovac, Ron. "VPN basics." *Communications News*, April 1999.

[12-52]   Stephenson, Ashley. "The VPN Gold Rush." *X-Change*, December 1998.

[12-53]   Kim, Gary. "VPNs: The Future of Remote Access." *X-Change*, January 1999.

[12-54]   Henthorn, Alex. "Sorting through the VPN protocols." *Network World*, March 3, 1997.

[12-55]   Fratto, Mike. "unlocking virtual private networks." *Network Computing*, November 1, 1997.

[12-56]   Higgins, Kelly Jackson. "Safer Nets?" *Communications Week*, March 17, 1997.

[12-57]   Hervey, Joyce. "The VPN puzzle." *America's Network*, April 1, 1998.

[12-58]   "Does Everybody Really Know What a VPN Is?" Internet Week, December 14, 1998.

[12-59]   "VPN's Defining Moment: What Exactly Is It?" Internet Week, December 14, 1998.

[12-60]   "VPN Implementation Calls For a Tunnel Trip." Internet Week, December 14, 1998.

[12-61]   "Now's The Time to Start Looking at VPN's Benefits." Internet Week, December 14, 1998.

[12-62]   "Deliverance." *CIO Web Business*, July 1, 1998.

[12-63]   www.ups.com

[12-64]   www.iab.com

Chapter 13

Video and Multimedia Networking

"It's a success, Ned! I've struck it!" cried Tom, in delight.
"Ouch! You struck 'me,' you mean!" replied Ned, rubbing his shoulder, where the young inventor had imparted a resounding blow of joy.
"What of it?" exclaimed Tom. "My apparatus works! I can send a picture by telephone! It's great, Ned!"
"But I don't exactly understand how it happened," said Ned, in some bewilderment, as he gazed at the selenium plate.
"Neither do I," admitted Tom.

Excerpted from *Tom Swift and His Photo Telephone or The Picture That Saved a Fortune*, by Victor Appleton. Gross & Dunlap, 1914.

Tom Swift certainly had a great idea, although he didn't understand quite how his *photo telephone* worked. Tom used his invention to save Mr. Damon from Messrs. Peters and Boyman, kidnappers and swindlers who were close to cheating him out of a fortune. While the dastardly pair had poor Mr. Damon kidnapped, they called Tom to arrange for the ransom. Tom took a picture of them with his *photo phone*. That photo ultimately was used as evidence to convict the dastardly duo. While Tom may have saved Mr. Damon a fortune, there is no mention of the cost of the *photo phone*. However, we must assume that the cost was reasonable, as the young inventor was featured in an entire series of books in which he also invented the motor cycle, the motor boat, the air glider, the airship, the submarine, the wireless telegraph, the electric rifle, and a giant cannon—all funded with his modest allowance. Since Tom invented the *photo phone*, the concept has been refined by other young inventors, and now is used in a variety of applications, including law enforcement. In the right applications, the technology clearly has the potential to save a fortune, but the costs tend to be more than typical teenagers can afford out of their allowances. After all, Tom Swift's invention was just a simple image transmission over an analog telephone circuit. This chapter deals primarily with interactive video and multimedia networking.

On the whole, you may wonder how critical interactive video and multimedia networking are to our daily lives. The answer is not clear. While we all understand that a picture can be worth a thousand words and we clearly benefit from one-way video and multimedia, the ability to engage in an interactive video or multimedia communications is not necessarily that important to most of us, either personally or professionally. Such interactive networking currently is expensive in terms of both bandwidth and equipment, although those costs certainly will come down over time. Many of the highly touted benefits have yet to be proven, although a compelling case is developing.

Certainly, video and multimedia have application in education. People tend to have different learning styles. Some are *visual* learners and need to see something in order to process the information. Some are *auditory* and need to hear about it Still others tend to be more *kinesthetic* and need to touch it. In any event, the addition of the visual information stream certainly assists in the educational process, as it does in the communications process, in general. A fascinating application is in the world of health care. As discussed later in this chapter, telemedicine has proved itself to be of great importance in the delivery of high-quality medical care to remote areas where specialists, and even general practioners, may not be available.

Video Communications: Defined and Evolved

What's past is prologue, wrote William Shakespeare in *The Tempest*. So it is in video, as it is in all of life and all of technology – without history, there is no future. Video (from the Latin *video*, meaning *I see*) communications has its roots in broadcast TV (TeleVision), from the Greek *tele*, meaning *far off*, and the Latin *vision*, meaning *to see*. Broadcast TV is transmitted over the airwaves, and remains the primary source of TV in many areas and in most countries. The first true television mechanism was developed in 1884 by Paul Nipkow, a German engineer, using a scanning disk, lenses, mirrors, a selenium cell (as did Tom Swift), and electrical conductors. Doing so, he was able to transmit images in rapid succession to a lamp, which changed in brightness according to the strength of the currents received. Using this mechanical scanning technique, Nipkow demonstrated that portions of a full image viewed in rapid succession (15 images or more per second) created the illusion of viewing the full image [13-1]. It later was discovered that viewing 15 or more images per second created the illusion of full motion, due to electrochemical processing delays in the human eye. While this mechanical scanning approach was abandoned in later years, the concept of *persistence of vision* remains valid. Psychologist and film theorist Hugo Munsterberg explained a second process, known as the *phi phenomenon*, in 1916. This process explains the fact that we hallucinate, or believe that we see, a continuous action rather than a series of still images – the mind, in effect, fills in the blanks [13-2]. Modern TV and video systems create the illusion of motion by refreshing screens in rapid succession, a dot at a time and a line at a time.

The development of modern television (TV) largely was due to the efforts of Herbert E. Ives, a scientist at Bell Telephone Laboratories. As the son of Frederick Eugene Ives, who in 1878 developed the first practical process for making halftone-printing plates, Ives was oriented toward the visual world. In 1923, he and his associates combined the photoelectric cell with the vacuum tube repeater to produce the first commercial system for the rapid transmission of pictures over telephone wires, for application by the daily press. Using a scanning beam developed by Frank Gray, another Bell Labs scientist, multiple real-time images of people were transmitted in rapid succession – television was born. The first public demonstration, on a black and white TV, was conducted in April 1927; color TV first was demonstrated in June 1929 [13-3]. That experimental color transmission included the transmission of pictures of an American flag, a watermelon, and a bunch of roses. The transmitting system had three sets of photoelectric cells, amplifiers, and glow-tubes, with each filtering out one color – red, green or blue (RGB). At the receiving end, mirrors superimposed the monochromatic images to create a single color image [13-1]. In the 1930s, the first commercial TV stations began operation over the radio waves.

Coaxial cable entered the world of TV in 1936. The first experimental transmission took place between New York and Philadelphia. Jointly conducted by AT&T and the Philadelphia Electric Storage Battery Company (Philco), the experiment proved highly successful in terms of transmission performance, as multiple frequencies could be transmitted over the same shielded (read *noise-free*) medium. In 1950, AT&T opened the first coaxial cable for coast-to-coast TV transmission [13-4]. Community Antenna TeleVision (CATV), generally based on coaxial cable, largely has supplanted broadcast TV in the United States. Somewhat recently, CATV has spread to a number of other developed countries, including England and Australia.

Now, only two key evolutionary concepts remain – those of the iconoscope and kinescope. Vladimir Zworykin, a Russian immigrant, built on his graduate work in Russia where he had studied the nature of fluorescence under Boris Rosing. On January 1, 1939, Zworykin received patents for his iconoscope (transmitting) and kinescope (receiving) tubes, which formed the basis for modern cameras as well as cathode ray tubes used as display devices (TV sets and computer monitors) [13-1] and [13-5].

Video communications extends well beyond Broadcast TV and CATV, into videoconferencing, multimedia communications and, ultimately, interactive TV. In this chapter, we will explore the nature of the equipment and networks that support video and multimedia collaborative communications, as well as related standards and costs.

Video Basics

In order to fully understand the nature and implications of advanced video communications, it is necessary to comprehend the basics of video. The basic concepts are frame rate, scanning, resolution, aspect ratio, luminance, chrominance, and synchronization.

Frame rate

refers to the rate at which frames of still images are transmitted. Video is a series of still images that are transmitted in succession to create the perception of fluidity of motion. If transmitted in rapid succession, the perception is one of complete fluidity; 24 frames per second (fps) is considered to be motion picture quality, and 30 fps is considered to be broadcast quality. If the frames are transmitted at a slow rate, the result is a poor quality, herky-jerky video that creates a strobe-light effect reminiscent of 1970s discos. Particularly below 15 fps, quality suffers quite noticeably.

Scanning

refers to the process of refreshing the screen; the scanning rate is a function of the power source of the receiver. Interlaced scanning, which is used with most analog TV systems, involves two fields. Odd lines (fields) are refreshed in one scan, and even lines in the next. Each set of odd and even lines refreshed constitutes a frame refreshed. For example, the American NTSC standard provides for 30 fps, involving 60 scans, which relates directly to the 60 Hz of the U.S. power source. Progressive scanning involves displaying all vertical scan line in one frame at the same time, which avoids the problem of interline flicker. While the refresh rate varies, most contemporary PC monitors operate at 60-90 frames per second. The difference between the two techniques is imperceptible to most of us, until we see a broadcast TV news show that includes a video clip of PC monitors.

Resolution

refers to the definition, or sharpness, of the image. Resolution is determined by the number and density of the pixels, or pels (picture elements), which essentially are dots of picture. The greater the number and density of the pixels, the better the resolution. If the same number of pixels is spread over a greater area, the result is a grainier picture, as you can readily see by sitting close to a big-screen TV.

Aspect ratio

refers to the relationship between the width and the height of the image. The 4:3 (4 wide to 3 high) aspect ratio specified by the American NTSC standard is rooted in the early days of TV, when round picture tubes made effective use of this approach.

Luminance

refers to intensity, or brightness, which can vary within an image. An analog video transmission varies the luminance by varying the power level, or amplitude, of the signal.

Chrominance	refers to color, with different standards permitting varying levels of color depth. Clearly, the video image is more pleasing and life-like when the range of color is as broad as possible.
Synchronization	includes vertical and horizontal synch, both of which are critical. Vertical synch is required to keep the picture from scrolling, or flipping. Horizontal synch keeps the picture from being twisted.

Analog TV Standards

Television standards are several and incompatible. The initial standards were set in the United States, where broadcast TV originated. In 1945, the FCC set the initial VHF (Very High Frequency) transmission standards at 4.5 MHz. The *National Television Standards Committee* (*NTSC*) was formed in 1948 to standardize the characteristics of the broadcast signal. Ultimately, the Radio Corporation of America (RCA), which was owned by AT&T, lobbied the Electronics Institute of America (EIA) and set the initial black-and-white TV standards. Color TV was commercialized some years later. Among the first live color TV broadcasts were the Cotton Bowl and Rose Bowl football games on January 1, 1954 [13-1]. As the cost of color TV sets was quite high, color didn't really take off until the 1960s when sets became affordable for the masses. Table 13-1 compares the major analog standards – NTSC and PAL – with digital HDTV.

Table 13-1 TELEVISION STANDARDS COMPARED: NTSC, PAL, and HDTV

	NTSC (National Television Standards Committee)	PAL (Phase Alternate Line)	HDTV (High Definition TV)
Analog/Digital	Analog	Analog	Digital
Horizontal Scanlines	525	625	640, 704, 1280, or 1920
Synchronization	40	49	N/A
Resolution (pixels per line)	640	640	480, 720, or 1080

Continued

Continued

Frame Rate (fps)*	30i	25i	24p, 30p, 60p and 60i
Aspect Ratio	4:3	4:3	4:3 and 16:9

i = interlaced, p = progressive

NTSC (National Television Standards Committee), was established in the United States as the first standard (1953), setting the tone for broadcast TV. NTSC is defined in ITU-R Recommendation 1125. While other standards have since been developed, they all derived from the NTSC baseline. NTSC is characterized as analog in nature, with 525 interlaced scanlines. There are 640 pixels per line, 485 of which are dedicated to the active picture. The frame rate is 30 fps, interlaced, and the aspect ratio is 4:3. An early analog standard that is viewed as overly complex and ineffective in the contemporary digital world, NTSC also is said to mean *Never The Same Color* [13-6].

PAL (Phase Alternate Line) was established in Western Germany, The Netherlands, and the United Kingdom in 1967. PAL addresses problems of uneven color reproduction thatwhich plague NTSC due to phase errors associated with electromagnetic signal propogation. PAL inverts the color signal by 180(on alternate lines, hence the term *Phase Alternate Line* [13-6]; it currently is used in much of Western Europe, Australia, and Africa. PAL is characterized as analog, with 625 interlaced scanlines. There are 640 pixels per line, with 576 dedicated to the active picture. The frame rate is 25 fps, and the aspect ratio is 4:3.

SECAM (Systeme Electronique Couleur Aven Memoire) is a variation of PAL, was developed in France. In addition to its use in France, it also is the standard in regions once under the influence of France, including areas of the Middle East.

Digital TV (DTV) and High Definition TV (HDTV)

Digital TV (DTV) transmission offers the same advantages as any other form of digital communications, including enhanced bandwidth efficiency through compression, improved signal quality, and more effective management and control. Additionally, digital video must be recognized as nothing more than data. As a result, it offers advantages in terms of processing, storage, and manipulation. Those advantages include editing, alteration (e.g., *morphing*), reproduction, compression, transmission, storage, and store and forward capability.

TV and all video, for that matter, in their native forms comprise synchronized analog voice and analog image information. Digital video requires that the information be digitized through the use of a video codec. A broadcast quality video signal is extremely bandwidth intensive, and storage intensive. For example, the resolution of a digital video might require 640 horizontal pixels and 480 vertical. Chrominance and luminance require 24 bits/pixel; and the frame rate is 30 fps. Therefore, the video signal, alone, requires 7,372,800 bits per frame. At a frame rate of 30 fps, the bandwidth requirement is 221,184,000 bps. Clearly, it is not within the realm of reason to transmit a broadcast quality video signal requiring 221+ Mbps. Additionally, it is evident that the storage requirements are incredible. It is therefore and equally clear that compression is critical if the networks are to support digital TV.

Despite all the advantages of digital technology as applied to TV production, storage, transmission, and reception, all of the TV sets were analog. A conversion from analog to digital broadcast TV is revolutionary and completely unthinkable, unless there exists a compelling reason for the changeout of untold millions of TV sets. According to the manufacturers and the FCC, that compelling reason is in the form of HDTV (High Definition TV).

The definition of HDTV standards caused a debate that raged for a number of years between Japanese analog standards and digital standards proposed by the United States. The U.S. digital standards proposals focused on those offered by the *Grand Alliance*, which was formed by the FCC in May 1993, and which comprised AT&T, General Instruments, Zenith, The Massachusetts Institute of Technology (MIT), Thompson Consumer Electronics, Philips Consumer Electronics, and the David Sarnoff Research Center. The efforts of the Grand Alliance led to a set of recommended DTV (Digital TV) standards for HDTV and *SDTV (Standard Definition TV)*. Those recommended standards were tested and documented by the *Advanced Television Systems Committee (ATSC)* in the summer of 1995 and approved by the FCC in December 1996. Table 13-2 presents the specifics of the ATSC scanning formats.

Table 13-2 SCANNING FORMATS: ATSC DIGITAL TELEVISION STANDARDS

	Vertical Lines	Horizontal Pixels	Aspect Ratio	Frames per Second (fps)**
HDTV	1080	1920	16:9	24p, 30p, 60i
	720	1280	16:9	24p, 30p, 60p
SDTV	480	704	16:9, 4:3	24p, 30p, 60p and 60i
	480	640	4:3	24p, 30p, 60p and 60i

*[13-7] and [13-8]
**i = interlaced, p = progressive

The ATSC standard also specifies the compression algorithm as MPEG-2, which is discussed later in this chapter, and the transport subsystem as that of ISO/IEC 13818. Packet transport involves a serial data stream of packets of 188 bytes, one byte of which is a synchronization bit and 187 bytes that are payload. This packet approach is suitable for ATM switching, as each 188-byte MPEG-2 packet fits nicely into the payload of four ATM cells, with only 4 bytes of padding required. Forward error correction (FEC) is employed in the form of Reed-Solomon coding. RF modulation is accomplished using 8 *VSB* (*Vestigal Sideband*), which supports a bit rate of 19.28 Mbps over a 6 MHz terrestrial broadcast channel through the use of eight discrete amplitude levels. Audio compression is based on the AC-3 specification from the ATSC. The audio sampling rate is 48 kHz, and the system supports six channels in the Dolby Digital surround format. That format specifies multiple channel outputs, including center, left and right center, left and right surround, and *low-frequency enhancement* (*LFE*), also known as subwoffer13-7].

The FCC also set a timetable for DTV transmission. Beginning on November 1, 1998, 42 stations (including non-commercial stations) in the top 10 markets, began voluntary DTV transmissions, in addition to analog NTSC transmissions. All stations in those markets were required to transmit DTV by May 1999. By April 2003, all public television stations must convert fully to digital. By April 2005, all stations must *simulcast* (i.e., simultaneously broadcast) 100 percent of NTSC programming on their DTV channel, and by December 2006, all stations must turn off their analog signals [13-8] and [13-9]. Each broadcast television station in each market is required to bear the substantial capital expense of the equipment upgrade to DTV. The FCC made available the DTV RF spectrum at no cost to the broadcaster; the logic is that the analog spectrum will be returned for reassignment in 2006. Later, the deadline for returning that spectrum was pushed out to the vague date at which 85 percent of the designated viewers in a given market have access to the digital channels, whatever that means. In any event, each station is responsible for any costs associated with clearing DTV spectrum of other users – these costs are indeterminable, but can be significant. The costs of converting the several hundred million analog TV sets are the responsibility of the viewers. Currently, DTV sets are in the range of $8,000 to $10,000, if you can find one. These expensive sets currently weigh in at about 300 pounds, giving new meaning to the term *forklift upgrade*. Should the viewer still have analog TV sets in 2006, the thought is that inexpensive digital-to-analog converters will be available. By the way, your analog VHS VCR won't work, either. The costs of adding 200 million or so analog TV sets and 100 million or so VCRs to existing landfills has not been addressed, as far as I know, but I'll bet that they will be substantial and that we consumers will pay the tab. Assuming that we were to use a single landfill, just imagine its size and the bewilderment of future archaeologists when they excavate it.

Now, you may wonder why I have spent so much time discussing broadcast TV technology and standards, and their evolution. The reasons are several. First, most of the same technologies and standards apply to interactive videoconferencing and multimedia. Second, and although broadcast DTV and CATV don't necessarily have to follow the same rules of the road, it is likely that the CATV providers will carry broadcast TV signals in a digital format. Indeed, the FCC has imposed *must carry* rules on the CATV providers, thereby forcing them to carry local broadcast TV channels and to fairly compensate the local stations for that content. When you consider our previous discussions of CATV-based Internet access and hybrid digital fiber/coax CATV networks, the circle is complete. But, we can't forget our discussion of Internet access via satellite – the same satellites that carry digital TV signals. Extend that logic to Iridium and its Internet-in-the-Sky, and the other proposed LEO constellations, and we've completed another circle.

Bandwidth and Compression

The bandwidth required for video transmission is very significant, affected by frame rate, resolution, color depth, aspect ratio, and audio. Broadcast quality TV requires about 6 MHz in analog form, of which the signal occupies about 4.5 MHz. As little can be done to compress an analog signal, analog TV is limited to airwave broadcast or CATV transmission over analog coaxial cable . . . in other words, analog is doomed!

Conversely, digital video can be compressed fairly easily. As uncompressed, broadcast quality video requires between 90 Mbps and 270 Mbps, compression is critical. Without compression, a 1-Gbps fiber optic network could accommodate no more than 11 digitized NTSC channels. To digitize and compress the video information stream, the analog video and data signal first must be digitized through the use of a codec. Clearly, the amount of bandwidth required to transmit digital video, and the amount of memory required to store it, can be reduced by reducing the frame rate, resolution, or color depth. However, the result is less than pleasing. In order to maintain the quality of the video presentation, therefore, the data must be compressed using an appropriate and powerful data compression algorithm.

Lossless compression enables the video signal to be reproduced faithfully, with no data loss; compression rates are in the range of 10:1. *Lossy* compression results in a degraded picture, but permits compression at rates up to 200:1 [13-10]. Actually, compressed video currently can be transmitted with quite acceptable quality at T1 speeds of 1.544 Mbps or less. MPEG uses lossy compression in the form of *DCT (Discrete Cosine Transform)*. There are a number of steps involved in video compression, including filtering, color-space conversion, scaling, transforms, quantization and compaction, and interframe compression.

Filtering   also known as *image decimation*, reduces the total frequency of the analog signal through a process of averaging the values of neighboring pixels or lines. For instance, a black pixel and a white pixel becomes a gray pixel. *Taps* are the number of lines or pixels considered in this process; MPEG, for instance, uses a 7-tap filter.

Color-space conversion	also known as *color sampling*, simply involves the reduction of color information in the image. As the human eye is not highly sensitive to slight color variations, the impact is not noticeable. Black and white, however, is prioritized because the human eye is very sensitive at that level.
Scaling	addresses the creation of the digital image according to the presentation resolution scale. Rather than digitizing the video signal in large scale, the codec is tuned to the scale of presentation in terms of horizontal and vertical pixels, thereby reducing the amount of data that must be digitized. In consideration of this factor, the aspect ratio must be standardized.
Transforms	convert the native two-dimensional video signal into data dimensions. Although beyond the scope of this book, the various approaches include *Discrete Cosine Transform* (*DCT*), *vector quantization, fractal transform,* and *wavelet compression.*
Quantization and compaction encoding	simply reduce the number of bits required to represent a color pixel. Again beyond the scope of this book, compaction techniques include *run-length encoding, Huffman coding,* and *arithmetic coding.*
Interframe Compression	considers and eliminates redundant information in successive video frames. For instance, the background of a movie scene might not change, although the actors move around the set. While the motion of the actors must be reflected, the background need not be transmitted over the network — it can be compressed out of each frame until background changes must be reflected.

Video Standards

According to an anonymous, but very wise, man, *The nice thing about standards is that there are so many from which to choose!* Video compression standards are no exception — they are numerous and incompatible. Early standards were developed for specific purposes, such as motion picture production (MPEG) and photographic editing (JPEG). Only recently has the ITU-T become involved in the development of international standards towards B-ISDN. In the videoconferencing world, numerous proprietary standards have been developed that require that the network involve equipment from only a single vendor.

As of late, a number of true standards (as opposed to proprietary, or ad hoc "standards") have developed. Those video compression standards of significance include Px64, JPEG, and MPEG and its variations. Virtually all manufacturers of significance have embraced these standards, incorporating one or more of them into their systems alongside a proprietary compression technique. Generally involving Px64, this approach provides at least a minimum level of communication between systems of disparate origin – at least between fairly substantial systems. The world of desktop videoconferencing is much more parochial; proprietary solutions long predominated, yielding incompatibility all too often [13-11]. As is always the case in networking, the lowest common denominator rules – lacking a common denominator, anarchy rules. The lowest common denominator currently, and thankfully, is Px64, a standards-based solution that virtually all manufacturers support.

Px64

Px64 is an ITU-T standard designed to support videoconferencing and various levels of bandwidth, in increments of 64 Kbps up to a maximum of 2.048 Mbps (E-1). Note: In *Px64*, p = 1-30 channels of 64 Kbps, with the maximum of 30 bearer channels supported by E-1. Px64 specifies various frame rates and levels of resolution. Most manufacturers of videoconferencing equipment support Px64 as a lowest common denominator, although they each prefer their own proprietary standards in promotion of their own equipment and unique feature sets. Px64 also is known as H.261, referring to the specific ITU-T video-coding standard, as well as the video formats. Those formats include *CIF* (*Common Intermediate Format*), which is optional, and *QCIF* (*Quarter-CIF*), which is mandatory in compliant codecs. H.261 CIF supports 352 x 288 = 101,376 pixels per frame and 30 frames per second (fps), although lower frame rates also are supported. QCIF supports 176 x 144 = 25,344 pixels per frame, exactly 1/4 the resolution of CIF.

Actually, H.261 is an element of the ITU-T H.320 umbrella standard for video telephony over circuit-switched ISDN; it addresses narrowband visual telecommunications systems and terminal equipment. Related ITU-T standards include H.221, which defines a frame structure in support of audiovisual teleservices in 64-Kbps channels; and H.222, which defines the frame structure for such services in an ISDN environment. While these umbrella standards truly are international in nature, the U.S. and European camps unfortunately (and not surprisingly) are divided over certain implementation aspects of the ITU-T standards. Specifically, those differences deal with the manner in which audio and still-frame graphics are handled. For example, the Europeans have adopted JPEG (ITU-T T.81) for graphics, which is compatible with most PC-based graphics software. That approach is totally incompatible with the H.261 standard implemented in the United States, although it does provide a bridge to true multimedia applications [13-12]. H.320 is discussed in greater detail later in this chapter.

JPEG

JPEG (*Joint Photographic Experts Group*) was developed *jointly* by the ISO and ITU-T. JPEG is a compression standard used for editing still images, as well as color facsimile, desktop publishing, graphic arts, and medical imaging. A symmetrical compression technique, JPEG is equally expensive, processor intensive, and time consuming in terms of both compression and decompression. *Motion-JPEG* is used in the editing of digital video. JPEG is not appropriate for video transmission, as the compression rate is in the range of only 20:1-30:1. JPEG transmission in support of videoconferencing requires bandwidth in the range of 10-240 Mbps.

MPEG

MPEG (*Moving Picture Experts Group*) standards are several and still in final development stages. MPEG standards provide very high compression levels and excellent presentation quality. MPEG is a joint technical committee of the International Standards Organization (ISO) and the IEC (International Electrotechnical Commission). MPEG offers the critical advantage of asymmetric compression and decompression. Additionally, the standard is supported by IBM, Apple, AT&T, and a host of other manufacturers and carriers. While the compression of the video signal is time consuming and expensive, the decompression process is rapid and involves relatively inexpensive equipment. MPEG compression is as high as 200:1 for low-motion video of VHS-quality; broadcast quality can be achieved at 6 Mbps. Audio is supported at rates from 32 Kbps to 384 Kbps for up to two stereo channels.

MPEG-1   was standardized in November 1992, as ISO/IEC 11172; it provides VHS (videotape) quality at 1.544 Mbps and is compatible with single-speed CD-ROM technology. In fact, it was designed as the standard for storage and retrieval of moving pictures and audio on storage media such as compact disc. MPEG-1 integrates synchronous and isochronous audio with video, and permits the random access required by interactive multimedia applications. Intended for limited-bandwidth transmission, it provides acceptable quality and output compatible with standard televisions. Current applications include video kiosks, video-on-demand, and training and education. Compression of about 100:1 is supported by MPEG-1.

MPEG-2	defined in November 1994 as ISO/IEC IS (International Standard) 13818, is the standard for digital television at 4-100 Mbps over transmission facilities capable of such support (e.g., fiber optics, hybrid fiber/coax, and satellite). While MPEG-2 requires much more bandwidth than MPEG-1, it provides much better resolution and image quality, and at much greater speed. MPEG-2 already has found application in Direct Broadcast Satellite (DBS) services, also known as Direct Satellite Systems (DSS). Such services employ Ku-band satellites and VSAT dishes in competition with CATV, running MPEG at rates of about 3 and 7.5 Mbps [13-12]. In a convergence scenario (refer to Chapter 14), MPEG-2 is the standard of choice, supporting compression rates of about 200:1. MPEG-3, designed for HDTV application, was folded into MPEG-2 in 1992.
MPEG-4	Version 1 was approved in October 1998 as ISO/IEC IS 14496, as the standard for multimedia applications. It is a low bit-rate version intended for application in videophones and other small-screen devices, and in both client/server and mass storage-based playback scenarios. MPEG-4 deals with the coded representation of audiovisual objects, both natural and synthetic (e.g., computer-generated), and their multiplexing and demultiplexing for transmission, playback, and storage. Version 2 is anticipated to be approved in December 1999.
MPEG-7	scheduled for approval in July 2001, officially is known as the Multimedia Content Description Interface. MPEG-7 is intended to be the content representation standard for multimedia information search, filtering, management, and processing.

The H.320 Family of Multimedia Standards: With A Special Focus on H.323

The ITU-T has developed a number of Standards Recommendations for videotelephony and multimedia communications. These recommendations fall under the umbrella of H.320, which was defined in 1990 for systems operating over Narrowband ISDN (N-ISDN). Table 13-3 details the range of standards under the H.320 umbrella. Each standard was developed for a specific network environment, and includes standards for video and audio coding, signaling and control, and multipoint control units.

H.320

Also known as *Px64*, *H.320* supports videoconferencing and multimedia communications over N-ISDN B (Bearer) channels at bit rates from 64 Kbps to 1.920 Mbps, in increments of 64 Kbps. Video compression makes use of H.261, discussed earlier in this chapter. H.261 supports image resolutions – both the optional *CIF* (*Common Intermediate Format*) with a resolution of 352 x 288 pixels, and the mandatory *QCIF* (*Quarter-CIF*) with a resolution of 176 x 144 pixels. Frame rates are 30 frames per second (fps), or lower. Audio coding and compression recommendations include G.711, which is PCM (Pulse Code Modulation) at 64 Kbps, thereby requiring a full ISDN B channel. G.722 is ADPCM using a 7 kHz range and operating at 48/56/64 Kbps. G.728 specifies LD-CELP at 16 Kbps. The balance of the specification (H.221, H.230, and H.242) addresses techniques for call setup and teardown, data framing and multiplexing, and various other operational and administrative functions [13-13]. Table 13-4 details these various recommendations; the audio compression element largely is a restatement of the data provided in Table 10-3, which supports the discussion of packet Voice over Frame Relay (VoFR).

H.321

H.321 is the ITU-T Standard Recommendation for the adaptation of H.320 visual telephone terminals to B-ISDN environments. B-ISDN depends on ATM switching, which offers the considerable advantage of guaranteed Quality of Service (QoS), as discussed in Chapter 10. H.321 also involves H.310, which is the recommendation for broadband audiovisual communications systems and terminals.

H.322

H.322 is the ITU-T Recommendation for visual telephone systems and terminal equipment for local area networks, which provide a guaranteed quality of service. This specification is limited to IsoEthernet.

H.323

H.323 is the ITU-T Recommendation for packet-based multimedia communications systems. Annex D describes real-time facsimile. The recommendation addresses LANs, which do not provide a mechanism for guaranteed QoS; Ethernet and Token Ring are the most prevalent. H.323 also is used for service over the Internet and other IP-based networks, as illustrated in Figure 13-1. H.323 offers the advantage of supporting various compression techniques for packet-based voice communications, which yields much more efficient utilization of network resources than does the traditional G.711 approach of PCM over circuit-switched networks, as discussed in several preceding chapters. Interoperability of products (e.g., terminals and switches) can be achieved across the LAN and WAN domains. As H.323 is not linked to any specific hardware device or operating system, it can be deployed in a

Table 13-3 OVERVIEW OF ITU–T VIDEOTELEPHONY AND MULTIMEDIA STANDARDS*

	H.320	H.321	H.322	H.323 V1/V2	H.324
Approval Date	1990	1995	1995	1996/1998	1996
Network	N-ISDN PSTN	B-ISDN PSTN, ATM LAN	Packet Network with Guaranteed Bandwidth (e.g., IsoEthernet)	Packet Network, with No Guaranteed Bandwidth (e.g., Ethernet, Token Ring, and Internet)	Analog PSTN
Video Compression	H.261 H.263	H.261 H.263	H.261 H.263	H.261 H.263	H.261 H.263
Audio Compression	G.711 G.722 G.728	G.711 G.722 G.728	G.711 G.722 G.728	G.711 G.722 G.728 G.723 G.729	G.723
Multiplexing	H.221	H.221	H.221	H.225.0	H.223
Control	H.230 H.242	H.242	H.230 H.242	H.245	H.245
Multipoint	H.231 H.243	H.231 H.243	H.231 H.243	H.323	
Data	T.120	T.120	T.120	T.120	T.120
Communications Interface	I.400	AAL I.363 AJM I.361 PHY I.400	I.400 & TCP/IP	TCP/IP	V.34 Modem

Source: [13-13] and [13-14]

wide variety of devices, including PCs, telephone sets, and cable modems and set-top boxes. H.323 supports multicast communications, thereby avoiding the requirement for specialized Multipoint Control Units (MCUs) — although MCUs can improve communications. The four major components specified for H.323 include terminals, gateways, gatekeepers, and Multipoint Control Units.

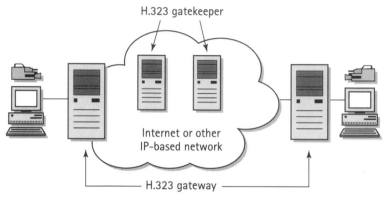

Figure 13-1 H.323 networking over IP-based network

Terminals	are the client endpoint devices on the LAN. While all terminals must support voice, data and video are optional. H.245 must be supported for negotiation of channel usage and capability. Q.931 is required for signaling and control. The *RAS* (*Registration/Admission/Status*) protocol communicates with the gatekeeper. Sequencing of audio and video packets is supported through *RTP/RTCP* (*Real Time Protocol/Real Time Control Protocol*). Terminals optionally may include video codecs, T.120 dataconferencing capabilities, and MCU functionality.
Gateways	are optional elements in the H.323 environment that serve as protocol converters between devices and networks that have native H.323 capability and those that do not. The gateway also may translate between audio, video, and data formats.
Gatekeepers	are optional elements that act as the central points in H.323 *zones* (zones of control). Endpoints may communicate directly, in either a unicast or a multicast environment, if no gatekeeper is present. If a gatekeeper is present, all endpoints in its zone must register with it. Gatekeepers serve to translate LAN addresses into IP or IPX addresses, as defined in the RAS specification. Gatekeepers also can act to route H.323 calls. Gatekeepers may

be distinct network elements, or gatekeeper functionality can be incorporated into terminals or Multipoint Control Units.

Multipoint Control Units (MCUs) support conferencing among three or more participating terminals. The MCU comprises a *Multipoint Controller* (*MC*) and optional *Multipoint Processors* (*MPs*). The MC is responsible for call control negotiation to achieve common levels of communication. The MP may process either a single media stream or multiple media streams, depending on the nature of the conference.

H.324

H.324 is the ITU-T Recommendation for low bit-rate multimedia communication over the analog PSTN through V.34 modems. As such, modems are limited to maximum transmission rates of 28.8 Kbps; voice must be highly compressed in order to make room for video and other visual information streams [13-13] through [13-16].

Table 13-4 H.320 RELATED STANDARDS RECOMMENDATIONS*

ITU-T Standard Recommendation	Description
G.711	Pulse Code Modulation (PCM) voice coding at 64 Kbps
G.722	Adaptive Differential Pulse Code Modulation (ADPCM) voice coding and compression at 64/56/48 Kbps based on 7 KHz audio sampling
G.723	Dual rate speech coder at 5.3 and 6.3 Kbps for multimedia communications
G.728	Low-Delay Code Excited Linear Prediction (LD-CELP) coding and compression of 3.3 KHz voice at 16 Kbps
G.729	Conjugate-Structure Algebraic-Code-Excited Linear-Prediction (CS-CELP) voice coding and compression at 8 Kbps
H.221	Frame Structure for channel of 64-1920 Kbps in audiovisual teleservices
H.223	Multiplexing protocol for low bit-rate multimedia communication. Annexes address mobile communications over low, moderate, and highly error-prone channels.
H.225	Call signaling protocols and media stream packetization for packet-based multimedia systems

Continued

Continued

H.230	Frame synchronous control and indication signals for audiovisual systems
H.242	System for establishing communications between audiovisual terminals using digital channels up to 2 Mbps. Addresses call setup and teardown, in-band signaling and control, and channel management
H.245	Call control procedures for multimedia communications
H.261	Video codec for audiovisual services at p x 64 Kbps
H.263	Video coding for low bit-rate communication at rates less than 64 Kbps
T.120	Multipoint transport of multimedia data

*Source: ITU-T

T.120

The ITU-T Recommendation for the multipoint transport of multimedia data is T.120, which data can include whiteboarding or binary files. This series of recommendations supports a broad range of underlying network technologies, and can work either alone or under the H.320 umbrella. T.120 is entirely platform independent, and can run in a variety of network environments, involving either reliable or unreliable data transport. Unicast and multicast modes both are supported [13-13] and [13-17].

Videoconferencing Systems

Videoconferencing systems consist of cameras, monitors, video boards, microphones, and speakers. Videoconferencing can be accomplished in the workplace over a LAN, although such applications are unusual — it generally is more effective, easier, and less costly to walk across the hall and hold a face-to-face meeting. Videoconferencing over the WAN, however, offers great benefits in terms of reduced cost and increased availability for meetings. Systems for videoconferencing can be quite substantial, or can be PC-based. Videoconferencing has increased significantly over the past few years, as the cost of equipment and bandwidth have decreased — systems are made up of room systems, rollaboutt systems, and PC-based systems.

Room systems are complex and quite expensive systemsintended for videoconferencing among groups of people. While a specially designed room and equipment easily could cost $250,000 in the 1980s, a room system can be configured for less than $25,000 today. AT&T, MCI Worldcom, and Sprint have provided room-based conferencing services for years from select locations. These IXCs also provide network-based videoconferencing services for large corporations. Those services include access and transport services, as well as network-based MCUs. Virtually all of the ILECs offer some form of videoconferencing service. While many of them in the late 1980s or early 1990s announced plans for *video dial tone*, those announcements clearly were way ahead of both the technologies and the market. All of those plans have been abandoned or delayed. Pacific Bell's plans in the late 1980s to provide what it calls *visual dial tone* were based on FTTP (Fiber To The Premise), and clearly were ill conceived. Pacific Bell currently offers no video service to the premise. Ameritech and SNET (Southern New England Telephone), a business unit of SBC Communications, offer videoconferencing over their CATV networks. BellSouth and US West offer integrated videoconferencing, Internet access, and voice services over xDSL. All of these various offerings are limited in availability, of course [13-18].

Kinko's Copy Centers began deploying services in 1994, and in April 1999 they announced plans to expand the current 100 locations to 150 in the United States and Canada. Kinko's has improved quality to 30 fps through an alliance with Sprint for high-speed access and transport, and VTEL for room systems. Point-to-point service is priced at $225 per hour per location; multipoint conferencing, available in select locations, is priced at $265 per hour per location

Rollabout systems essentially are portable and much less expensive versions of room systems — also intended largely for group-to-group conferencing. Such systems account for the preponderance of the standalone equipment market.

PC-based systems, or desktop systems, are intended for person-to-person conferencing. PC-based systems are enjoying increased popularity, with the systems generally working over LANs or ISDN circuits. Analog transmission also is accommodated by some systems, through modems at speeds up to 33.6 Kbps. As you might expect, the cost of the system and the network are directly related to the frame rate supported and the elegance of the compression technique employed. Inexpensive PC-based systems can be had for as little as several hundred dollars today. The cost is that of camera and codec, the latter of which fits into the expansion slot of a PC (486 or better) or Macintosh computer, with the monitor serving as the video presentation device. Inexpensive PC-based systems are used for Internet videoconferencing, although quality is poor due to latency and data loss associated with packet switching.

Great strides are being made in the support of PC-based videoconferencing systems that can be supported over LANs and, in the near future, through PBXs. As noted by Bob Metcalfe, five out of six calls handled by a PBX never reach the

WAN; rather, they are station-to-station. Although videoconferencing originally was touted as a means of reducing travel expenses, it eventually may save more shoe leather than gasoline [13-19].

Videoconferencing Equipment

Videoconferencing equipment includes transmit (camera) and receive (display) equipment that operate in concert with and through various intermediate devices to format the signal properly and otherwise treat it for effective transmission over a network. Those intermediate devices include codecs, inverse multiplexers, servers, and control units. Figure 13-2 presents a simple videoconferencing arrangement.

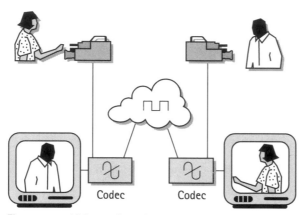

Figure 13-2 Videoconferencing network employing cameras, codecs, and monitors

Codecs accomplish the process of digitizing, or coding, the analog signal on the transmit side and *de*coding it on the receive end. The codecs also accomplish the process of data compression and decompression, according to the specifics of the compression algorithm used. Additionally, codecs may include encryption features for security purposes.

Inverse Multiplexers (Inverse MUXs) are used in commercial videoconferencing systems where dedicated bandwidth is not available for relatively bandwidth-intensive communications. An inverse MUX splits the video signal into two or more component parts that are transmitted over separate circuits or, perhaps, separate channels of multiple DS1 circuits. The inverse MUX on the receiving end reassembles and resynchronizes the complete video signal for proper presentation.

Servers are extremely high-capacity storage devices, containing many GBs (GigaBytes), or even TBs (TeraBytes) of memory. Servers store video and audio data for delivery to clients, on demand. While some video servers have found their way into business applications in a LAN environment, they are expensive and, therefore, unusual. Server technology primarily is aimed at a convergence scenario, in which video-on-demand will be delivered over ATM-based, fiber optic networks.

Multi-point Control Units (MCUs) are digital switching and bridging devices that support multipoint videoconferencing, with up to 28 parties (sites) supported. MCUs must be compatible with the compression standards employed with the codecs; H.231 describes ITU-T MCU standards and T.120 describes generic data-conference control functions. MCUs may be found in the carrier network in support of a carrier videoconferencing service, or on the end user premise in support of a videoconferencing network based on leased lines.

Videophones originated with the AT&T Picturephone, which was demonstrated at the New York World's Fair in 1964. Never intended for legitimate application, the Picturephone was extremely bandwidth-intensive, requiring about 90 MHz, and weighing about 26 pounds [13-6]. During the past few years, AT&T, BT, and others developed videophones that sold for less than $1,000. As the cost was high, as each party was required to have a videophone of the same manufacture, and as the picture quality was poor (2 fps), videophones were stunning failures.

But hold the phone, literally! Matsushita, the parent company of Panasonic, in 1999 developed and demonstrated the first version of a wireless videophone for use in Japan's cordless phone system. The phone used ITU-T standard video compression techniques to squeeze video down to a 32-Kbps channel for display on a 2.5-inch color LCD display. A 1/3-inch camera also was built into the device for video transmission at 3-7 frames per second [13-20]. That cordless phone never made it into commercial usage, although the Japanese since have developed and demonstrated other versions of the same concept. It's just a matter of time!

WAN Videoconferencing Networks

Video networking can be accomplished over a number of facilities and service offerings, depending on the application and the amount of bandwidth required (see Figure 13-3). Analog circuits will support videoconferencing at low speeds, although the results are less than completely pleasing. The failed videophones offered by AT&T, BT, and others made use of dial-up analog circuits. As always is the case, digital circuits offer better performance than do analog circuits.

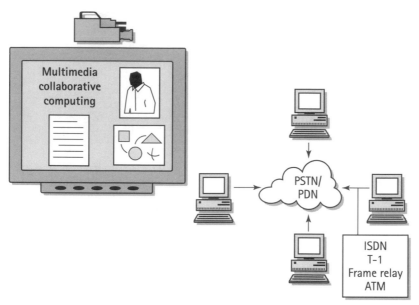

Figure 13-3 Videoconferencing across the Wide Area Network (WAN)

ISDN circuits are preferable to analog circuits because they provide more bandwidth and better transmission quality; however, the greater cost and less availability of ISDN has slowed the acceptance of videophones based on ISDN technology. Switched 56/64 Kbps circuits can be used for videoconferencing — generally aggregated or *bonded* to provide multiple channels. Switched 384-Kbps connectivity can be provided on the basis of Fractional DS1 or through ISDN PRI channels in a channel group known as H0.

DS-1 facilities support full-motion, high-quality videoconferencing over dedicated networks at rates up to 2.048 Mbps for E-1 and 1.544 Mbps for T-1. However, such facilities are costly and not widely deployed in such applications. Large user organizations with dedicated DS-1 backbone networks make highly effective use of videoconferencing; the video communications contend with voice and data for network access through intelligent MUXs.

Broadband networks are much more capable of supporting the demands of videoconferencing. Frame Relay supports video, although that clearly is not the primary reason for its existence. While Frame Relay performs well under normal circumstances, it is likely to yield herky-jerky video should the network suffer severe congestion. SMDS provides much better video performance than Frame Relay, due to improved congestion management and lesser latency, but SMDS (refer to Chapter 10) is almost an historical footnote. ATM undoubtedly will be the network technology of choice in a convergence scenario. ATM will offer tremendous bandwidth over fiber optic or hybrid fiber/coax networks and in support of voice, image, facsimile, and data traffic, as well as video.

LAN-Based Video Networks

LANs were not designed with video in mind, but neither were existing WANs, for that matter. In any event, LAN technology has developed to the point that it will support video, although such implementations remain unusual and problematic. By way of example, a 10 Mbps Ethernet LAN may provide only 4 Mbps throughput; sharing that bandwidth among 20 or 25 users reduces the available bandwidth to unacceptable proportions. Additionally, LANs generally impose delay on the signal; this is especially true of Ethernet, as explained in Chapter 8.

The basic problem is that video is isochronous, or stream-oriented, traffic. LANs were not developed to support continuously streaming data. Additionally, video is highly bandwidth intensive. Even 100 Mbps LANs have trouble supporting high-quality video intermingled with more traditional and legitimate LAN data traffic. Traditional (relatively speaking) LAN options for videoconferencing include Fast Ethernet, Switched Ethernet, and FDDI. More recent technologies and standards include ATM and IsoEthernet.

Multimedia

Multimedia is a combination of voice, data, video, and image information—blended into a single, coordinated and synchronized presentation—with strong emphasis on the visual. Multimedia systems consist of a combination of monitors, speakers, software, cameras, microphones, and very significant amounts of computer memory. Multimedia, in the purest sense, typically is supported on a stand-alone basis. Multimedia PCs are commonplace, supporting voice clips, data, video clips, and images for access to CD-ROMs. As such multimedia systems are effective only in limited applications (e.g., training, education, and research) and as costs have remained high, the market has yet to develop to significant proportions.

Multimedia networks, currently in their infancy, must support this demanding blend of data. The difficulty of multimedia networking is twofold. First, the data stream is highly bandwidth intensive, due to the impact of video and image information. Second, multimedia is isochronous in nature, since the voice and video elements are stream-oriented. Therefore, the networks that support multimedia must provide substantial bandwidth; they also must accept and deliver the data stream on a regular, continuous, and reliable basis. Such network performance is found only in a few instances, including circuit switched (expensive), dedicated (expensive), or cell-switched (expensive) networks. In case you missed it, *expensive* is the operative word. While multimedia can be supported at lower cost through ISDN BRI, the bandwidth available is not sufficient to support high-quality video; additionally, ISDN is relatively expensive (compared to analog circuits) and certainly is not ubiquitous. Multimedia networking in the LAN environment also is problematic — LANs just weren't designed for the task. To be truly effective, multimedia must be networked — and on an interactive basis. Therein lies the problem!

Software: Focus on Collaboration

Software must be in place to support electronic text, image, audio, and video information in a multimedia conference. While the voice and video aspects of the conference are supported in a fairly straightforward manner, the real and distinct advantage of multimedia conferencing is that of enabling multiple parties to collaborate on textual and graphic documents. Special software enables each party to contribute to such documents, in collaboration with the other parties; hence the term *collaborative computing*. During such a collaborative session, the original text document is saved, while each party contributes changes that are identifiable as such and are identified by contributor. Once the parties agree to the collaborative edits and enhancements, the entire text file is refreshed and saved.

Similarly, a design or a concept can be developed graphically and on a collaborative basis through *whiteboarding*, much as the parties would do on a physical whiteboard in a face-to-face meeting. Typically, each party to the conference has access to a special whiteboard pad and stylus, which is used to draw. Each party can modify the initial drawing, with each individual's contribution identified by separate color. Again, and once the group has agreed on the final graphic rendition, the graphic is saved and all screens are refreshed.

The clear benefits of such a collaborative process, conducted on a logical basis over a wide area network, include reduced travel time, reduced travel expense, and increased speed of collaborative effort. Even in a LAN environment, shoe leather is conserved and productive time is maximized.

LAN Networking

Multimedia over LANs, as noted previously, is problematic. Bandwidth certainly is an issue, as is flow control. Multimedia is not tolerant of delay, due to its isochronous voice and video elements. Current options for LAN video and multimedia collaboration include Fast Ethernet, IsoEthernet, FDDI, and ATM; in any case, you must be cautious in supporting multimedia over a LAN.

Isochronous Ethernet (IsoEthernet) Was formalized by the IEEE 802.9a committee. As illustrated in Figures 13-4 and 13-5, IsoEthernet runs over Cat 5 UTP at 16 Mbps, with 10 Mbps reserved for standard Ethernet packet streams and 6 Mbps available for isochronous video/multimedia. Through this process of frequency division multiplexing, isochronous data (voice and video) is supported effectively and without interfering with the basic reason that LANs are deployed — data communication. The advantage is that Ethernet is everywhere; the drawback is that it is a solution limited to a LAN (read *single-site* environment). While IsoEthernet did a very nice job of supporting voice and data in a LAN environment, its limitations have relegated it to little more than a historical footnote.

Switched Ethernet at 100 Mbps certainly provides enough raw bandwidth, but contention at the switch remains an issue. Assuming that the Ethernet is used for its intended data communications purposes, the performance of data applications easily can be compromised if bandwidth-intensive video is prioritized. Gigabit Ethernet provides a solution to that issue, at least at the backbone level.

FDDI clearly, is a multimedia-capable LAN standard, although it also is expensive to deploy and support. FDDI's sheer bandwidth of 100 Mbps and its token-passing access method (see Figure 13-6) can support multimedia applications reasonably effectively, although it is possible that an intensive multimedia conference can speak to all of the available bandwidth.

ATM -based LANs in the workplace can support multimedia quite nicely, running at speeds of 155 Mbps and 622 Mbps as a backbone technology. ATM offers low latency, prioritized cell transport, and seamless WAN connectivity. However, ATM deployment in the LAN domain has developed more slowly than anticipated due to its relatively high cost and technical challenges.

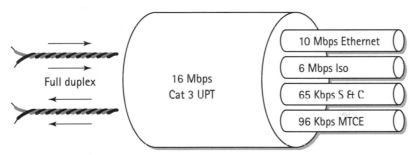

Figure 13-4 IsoEthernet bandwidth allocation

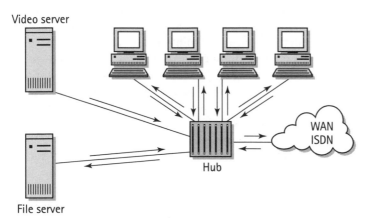

Figure 13-5 IsoEthernet network in support of videoconferencing

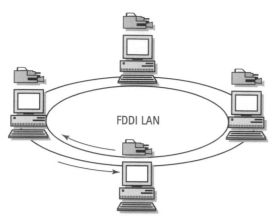

Figure 13-6 Videoconferencing over FDDI

WAN Networking

ATM offers the greatest potential for multimedia over the WAN. Now deployed at Gbps backbone rates and with DS1-DS3 access rates, ATM supports multimedia nicely. ATM, however, is expensive. The ultimate solution is B-ISDN, which is based on ATM network technology and which employs SDH/SONET as the physical infrastructure. B-ISDN can support a wide range of services, providing bandwidth-on-demand.

The Internet

The Internet also supports videoconferencing and multimedia; the latter is the purpose behind the World Wide Web (WWW). Although it is slow and rough, the presentation of true multimedia is routine and inexpensive. Clearly, there is a significant issue in terms of bandwidth, as well. The Internet really wasn't designed to support voice or video, much less multimedia. Heavy use of the 'Net for such applications places great strain on the backbone networks, causing brownouts (access delays and slow response times) and even threatening mcltdown. Internet Service Providers sometimes discourage or even forbid videoconferencing, as it requires enough bandwidth to freeze out other users. Additionally, the bandwidth limitations of the typical local loop further affect the viability of such applications, particularly in the case of analog local loops — regardless of the speed of the contemporary modem. As always, the strength of the chain is limited by the weakest link.

The Internet supports multipoint videoconferencing through the MBone (Multicast backBONE), which enables a variety of shared, real-time, collaborative applications to interact with reasonable efficiency. Videoconferencing, in specific, is supported by the CU-SeeMe software, which was developed at Cornell University and quickly became a de facto standard. Future, serious use of the Internet for such applications depends heavily on improved compression technologies and increased bandwidth in the backbone.

Multimedia Standards

At the international level, the ITU-T's series of H.32x video and T.12x conferencing standards set the stage for at least a minimal level of interoperability. Related compression standards include H.323 for Ethernet and H.310 for ATM. The International Multimedia Teleconferencing Consortium (IMTC) sponsors a number of test events in support of ITU-T standards.

The Future of Video and Multimedia

There can be little doubt about the value of enhancing a communication with visual information. Pictures add another and very important element to the process of learning and comprehension. Moving pictures enable us to see the person to whom we are talking, thereby creating a more natural and effective person-to-person communication. Taking it one step further, a truly collaborative effort is enhanced greatly when multiple persons can work on a document. Supporting all of this over a network can save a lot of money, time, shoe leather, and gasoline. Serving to supplement, but never replace, face-to-face collaboration, video and multimedia networking has a legitimate place in the networked world.

The development of videoconferencing has been much slower than many of us projected. Terminal and network technologies haven't developed to the point that videoconferencing is affordable at any reasonable level of quality. The recent development of standards for IP video promise to change that, especially given the emergence of special purpose IP-based networks such as those of Level 3 and Qwest. Large organizations just can't deny its value, and the costs of the systems technologies are becoming quite reasonable for video-intensive applications. As costs continue to drop, small business, home business, and even consumer markets for multimedia equipment will expand greatly. The hope is that videoconferencing will be commonplace by 2010 or so.

An application in point is that of *telemedicine*, which supports consultation and even remote diagnosis and treatment. A number of projects have experimented successfully with this concept, largely in support of remote clinics. Through a videoconferencing system and network, a nurse or medical technician in a remote clinic can gain the assistance of a doctor (even a specialist) located at a major urban hospital. The doctor can guide the technician through the process of diagnosis and treatment, viewing the patient over a videoconferencing network and perhaps viewing x-rays transmitted over the same high-quality, digital network. For that matter, a multipoint conference can be established so the physician might consult with distant colleagues on a particularly difficult diagnosis and treatment plan. Taking the scenario one step further, the physician can even guide the technician through an emergency surgical procedure! Prescriptions, clearly, can be transmitted electronically to a local pharmacy. While such an application scenario currently is a bit unusual, it is possible, has been accomplished, and is in daily use. Although the typical commercial enterprise might not find videoconferencing or multimedia networking to be a lifesaving application, they will be critical elements of the technology mix for those firms seeking to gain or maintain competitive advantage.

Another interesting application for videoconferencing is in the justice system. Judges around the country, including in my little town of Mt. Vernon, Washington, make use of videoconferencing systems for video arraignments and other court appearances required for suspected criminal defendants. The clear advantage is that a video communication among the judge and lawyers in the courtroom and the defendant in the jailhouse eliminates the costly and sometimes dangerous process of transporting the accused and convicted. Tom Swift would have been proud, indeed, of the evolution and application of his *photo phone.*

References

[13-1]　Settel, Irving and Laas, William. *A Pictorial History of Television.* Grosset & Dunlap, Inc., 1969.

[13-2]　Mast, Gerald, revised by Kawin, Bruce F. *A Short History of the Movies, Fifth Edition.* Macmillan Publishing Company, 1992.

[13-3]　Brooks, John. *Telephone: The First Hundred Years.* Harper & Row, 1975.

[13-4]　Mayer, Martin. *About Television.* Harper & Row, 1972.

[13-5]　Oslin, George P. *The Story of Telecommunications.* Mercer University Press, 1992.

[13-6]　Trowt-Bayard, Toby. *Videoconferencing: The Whole Picture.* Flatiron Publishing, 1994.

[13-7]　ATSC Standard. Doc A/53. September 16, 1995.

[13-8]　Outler, Elaine, Baker, Ron and Barr, Tracy. *DTV For Dummies.* IDG Books Worldwide, 1998.

[13-9]　FCC 96-493 December 27,1996.

[13-10]　Minoli, Daniel. "Videoconferencing." *Datapro Communications Analyst,* May 1994.

[13-11]　Bort, Julie. "Standards Compliance won't Ensure Interoperability." *InfoWorld,* October 16, 1995.

[13-12]　Halhead, Basil R. "Videoconferencing Standards." *Datapro Communications Analyst,* September 1994.

[13-13]   Kupst, Shirley, Mehravari, Dr. Nader, Olson, Mark & Rush, Scott.
           "Designing Virtual co-Location and Collaborative Environments via
           Today's Desktop Videoconferencing Technology." http://www.arch.
           usyd.edu.au/kcdc/conferences/VC97/papers/kupstlhtml.

[13-14]   "A Primer on the H.323 Series Standard. Version 2.0." Databeam Corp.
           http://gw.databeam.com/ccts/t120primer.html.

[13-15]   "Demystifying Multimedia Conferencing Over the Internet Using the
           H.323 Set of Standards. Intel Corporation, 1999. http://www.
           andygrove.com/technology/itj/q21998/articles/art_4a.html.

[13-16]   "Videoconferencing Standards." FVC.COM. December 1997.
           http://www.fvc.com/whitepapers/stndards.html.

[13-17]   "A Primer on the T.120 Series Standard. Version 2.0." Databeam Corp.
           http://gw.databeam.com/h323/h323primer.html.

[13-18]   Wilson, Carol. "Bells Turing To Video Again." Inter@active *Week*,
           April 26, 1999.

[13-19]   Metcalfe, Bob. "Video Telephones Will Arrive in Businesses First –
           Connected to LANs." *InfoWorld*, April 10, 1995.

[13-20]   "Handy-Dandy Video Phone." *Network World Collaboration*,
           March/April 1996.

Chapter 14

Network Convergence

We have now reached the stage when virtually anything we want to do in the field of communications is possible. The constraints are no longer technical, but economic, legal, or political. Arthur C. Clarke. *United Nations Telecommunications Day,* 1983. Source: Heather E. Hudson, *Communications Satellites,* The Free Press, 1990.

While Arthur C. Clarke may have overstated things a bit in 1983, there is no question that technology has developed very quickly, and continues to do so. Virtually anything is possible, short of *teleportation*, and scientists are working on that, or so I'm told. Ultimately, of course, technology really is just an enabler of applications, and people keep dreaming up new and exciting applications, many of which are highly demanding technically. Many of these applications are extremely bandwidth intensive, including high-speed data, video, and even multimedia. Billions of dollars have been spent in the development and deployment of new network infrastructure in an attempt to satisfy our seemingly insatiable desires to communicate instantly and in a variety of formats, from audio to data to video to multimedia.

Analog has given way to digital technology. Copper has yielded to glass, at least in the backbone. Wireline networks have given way to wireless, at least in support of mobile communications, and wireless technologies do a wonderful job of supplementing the wireline backbone networks. Circuit switching is challenged by packet switching across all applications types. While cell switching looked to be the ultimate solution, at least in the backbone, some suggest that advances in packet-switching technologies make ATM unnecessary. Satellite constellations support communications anywhere on the face of the Earth. The Internet and World Wide Web provide access to virtually any type of data in any database residing on any networked computer anywhere in the world — issues of security not withstanding. Electronic commerce promises to change forever the way we shop for everything from books to music to clothing to automobiles to groceries. Telephone calls are so inexpensive that we no longer give any thought to picking up the phone and calling across the country and even across continents. Telephone calls, inexpensive as they are, and snail mail, and even faxes have given way to electronic mail, which is virtually free. Plain old telephone sets are yielding to PCs and cell phones, and the size of the cell phones we use seems to be related inversely to the size of the *SUVs* (*Sports Utility Vehicles*) we drive. By the time you buy your next Chevy Subdivision, your cell phone may well fit in your ear and be activated by your brain waves, so be careful what you think.

The U.S. economy has changed in the last 200 years from agrarian to industrial to one based on information technology. Ten years ago, we lamented the fact that we no longer *make* anything in this country, and that our having lost our industrial edge would be the ruination of the American way of life. In fact, Generation X could look forward to being the first generation in our history to enjoy a lower standard of living than the previous generation. Today, our economy is as strong as it has ever been, unemployment is near all-time lows, and top college graduates in the right fields routinely are offered signing bonuses and starting salaries in the six-figure range. We may no longer make every part that goes into every car that we assemble, buy, and drive, but we much of the information technology that drives the rest of the world that makes the parts that go into the Chevy Subdivisions and other vehicles that are assembled in Mexico or Canada or who knows where, and shipped to the United States and bought over the WWW, that runs on technology that was developed mostly in the United States, and embedded in machines that we were at the forefront of inventing, and which include components we invented, and bought over the WWW, and the same goes for the cell phones that soon will fit in our ears so that we're not distracted while driving our Subdivisions – and on and on and on. How's that for a long, complex sentence Ms. Vanderford? (She was my freshman college English professor. If you find any grammatical errors in this book, don't blame them on her – she tried her best, and she was wonderful.) But I digress, Mr. Dunton. (He was my sophomore economics professor, and he taught me how to think. If my logic is flawed, don't blame it on him – he also tried his best, and he also was terrific.)

In any event, this network infrastructure is being developed to deliver something that a few years ago was known widely as the *Information Superhighway*. Initially conceived in the United States as the *National Information Infrastructure (NII)*, heavy sponsorship was proposed by the federal government. That government commitment was withdrawn in favor of commercial development of the concept, which still enjoys government endorsement and encouragement. Internationally, the concept also goes under the names *International Information Infrastructure (III)* and *Global Information Infrastructure (GII)*.

Although the term *Information Superhighway* has fallen out of favor, the concept remains sound. The applications are exciting and even compelling. Many of the enabling technologies are available and are being deployed and many of the necessary standards have been defined, at least in their early versions; examples include SDH/SONET, Frame Relay, and ATM. B-ISDN, the ultimate service offering, remains very much in the early stages of development. Despite the publicity that surrounded the Information Superhighway, it is a broad, sweeping, and troubled concept. Its form is not well defined, its applications are not entirely clear, its funding is uncertain, regulatory issues abound, and implementation is by no means assured. *Highway* or *Hypeway*? Only time will tell. Now, it is worth reflecting on the content of a letter sent in 1829 from Martin Van Buren, Governor of New York, to President Andrew Jackson:

Dear Mr. President:
The canal system of this country is being threatened by the spread of a new form of
transportation known as railroads. The federal government must preserve the canals
for the following reasons.
One: If canal boats are supplanted by railroads, serious unemployment will result.
Two: Boat builders would suffer and tow-line, whip and harness makers would be left
destitute. Three: Canal boats are absolutely essential to the defense of the United
States.
As you may well know, Mr. President, railroad carriages are pulled at the enormous
speed of 15 miles per hour by engines which, in addition to endangering life and limb
of passengers, roar and snort their way through the countryside, setting fire to crops,
scaring the livestock, and frightening women and children. The Almighty certainly
never intended that people should travel at such breakneck speed.
(signed)
Martin Van Buren
Governor of New York

The Information Superhighway is not a *thing*, and it will not be an *event*. Rather,
it is a concept that will unfold in various ways and with various levels of functionality. In India, for example, the I-Way might mean placing a single payphone in
every village, while urban dwellers gained Internet access. In the United States,
select business and residential users in affluent areas likely will have access to multiple providers of high-speed networks in support of voice, data, video, entertainment, and multimedia. U.S. schools and libraries, with government support, perhaps
will have universal access to the wisdom of the scholars since the beginning of
recorded history. In rural U.S. markets, such capabilities will be spotty, if available at
all. The development of the I-Way, certainly in full form, will be gradual and driven
by market forces, more than by social interests and government policy.

Convergence Defined

Convergence is defined as *the moving toward union or one another*. In the context
of the Information Superhighway, the concept of convergence cuts across a number
of dimensions, including a wide range of applications and the underlying technologies. In full form, convergence represents the coming together of every technology
and application discussed in the previous 13 chapters.

Applications

Applications, truly, are at the very crux of convergence. The only conceivable reason for investing billions of dollars in network technologies is to serve legitimate,
revenue-producing, profit-generating applications. There appears to be no single
killer ap driving the Information Superhighway — although the World Wide Web

comes close. Certainly, a number of interesting and productive niche applications exist which, in various user-specific combinations, constitute a killer ap suite. One of the most compelling applications is that of Web-enabled call centers, as discussed previously. Multimedia, in full form, currently is viewed as the ultimate in terms of presentation mode, although compelling applications of real substance have yet to be defined.

Network Technologies

The network technologies under the umbrella of the Information Superhighway already are being put in place. Analog switches and transmission facilities rapidly are being replaced with digital network elements. This process largely is complete in the carrier backbone networks and the Central Office Exchange networks. The local loop, of course, remains largely analog, at least in the voice domain, as well as the residential and small business market segments. Digital ISDN never enjoyed much success in either the residential or business markets. T-carrier is used widely as an access technology in the medium and large business markets. SONET/SDH optical fiber transmission systems remain unusual in local-loop applications, but are used widely in the carrier backbone networks. The incumbent voice carriers' networks are based on digital circuit-switches and time division multiplexing (TDM).

Data networks are digital in the backbone, and have been so for years. While residential and small business users typically access the network on a dial-up basis through modems, larger users typically make use of digital local loops in the form of T-carrier. xDSL local-loop technology will have a huge impact. Data networks certainly are being upgraded to provide higher-speed services over optical fiber backbones. Additionally, new switching technology is being put in place to support Frame Relay, ATM, and IP networking.

CATV networks, also, are experiencing significant upgrades. The old one-way coaxial cable distribution systems are being converted to two-way. The larger CATV providers in many cases are replacing the old analog coaxial cable distribution systems with analog fiber, upgradeable to digital fiber. While the coax connection to the premises remains in place, the effect of a hybrid fiber/coax system is significant in terms of bandwidth and, therefore, deliverable applications.

Terminal Technologies

Terminal devices are evolving at a rapid pace, as well. Multimedia PCs are widely available to support synchronized data, video, image, and audio applications. While multimedia is useful for games, education, and WWW access, it largely remains a standalone application for PCs. True multimedia over the WAN awaits the deployment of broadband network technologies and cost-effective service offerings.

So, What's The Big Deal?

The big deal about convergence is integration. If a single terminal device can access multiple applications through a single local loop and across a single network, there are advantages to be gained. Those advantages can include both cost and performance.

COST

The cost of an integrated terminal device certainly can be less than the cost of multiple devices. Assuming that you have a requirement for a telephone set, a computer, a videoconferencing unit, and a television set, the cost of a single, multifunctional device can be less than the total cost of the individual devices. The cost of a single, multifunctional local loop can be less than the cost of multiple, application-specific loops. And the cost of a single, multifunctional network can be less than the cost of multiple, application-specific networks. A basic assumption is that the technology is in place to enable such an integrated scenario – and that enough people are sufficiently interested to buy enough integrated terminals, rent enough loops, and subscribe to enough network services to enable the manufacturers to build and sell enough devices and develop and sell enough application software to bring the unit cost down to an affordable level. Only then can the network providers offer such services at affordable cost.

PERFORMANCE

The performance of an integrated suite of applications certainly is an improvement over that of multiple, disconnected applications. This is the essence of multimedia. We don't necessarily need to view text, or image, or video information in connection with every telephone call – but it often is advantageous to do so. When you talk to a realtor in another city about an impending house-hunting trip, it is helpful to see images of houses that meet your criteria, see a map of the city to get a sense of the house's location, view the proposed contract with the realtor, and even see the realtor through a videoconference. You certainly can do most of these things through a combination of a telephone call, a fax transmission, and an e-mail transfer, but combining them all together in a single, interactive, multimedia presentation enhances the overall performance of the communication.

Driving Forces

The evolution of the network moved at a relatively glacial pace for the first hundred years or so. With the exception of Step-by-Step (SxS) electromechanical switches and rotary dial telephones, little in the way of technology was introduced for the first 50 years. The introduction of Crossbar (Xbar) switching in 1937, Direct Distance Dialing (DDD) in the 1950s, and tone dialing in the 1960s were considered absolutely revolutionary. The pace accelerated, relatively speaking, with DDS,

Switched 56 Kbps, and T-carrier services in the 1960s, 1970s, and 1980s. Toward the mid-1980s, the pace picked up considerably, and ISDN deployment began to make an impact in the early 1990s. A number of forces are driving the development of the Information Superhighway. Those forces include deregulation, privatization and competition, applications, and technology.

Deregulation and Competition

Deregulation, perhaps, was the primary driving force. Beginning with the FCC's Carterphone decision in 1968, end users were presented with a wide variety of options for terminal equipment. The Modified Final Judgement (MFJ), which took full effect on January 1,1984, was the next step, dictating the breakup of the AT&T Bell System and ending what had constituted a virtual monopoly over communications in the United States — from research and development, to network equipment manufacturing, to service delivery. Competition developed as a result of the actions of the FCC and the federal courts. That level of competition has intensified by orders of magnitude since the passage of the Telecommunications Act of 1996 (see Chapter 15), even though aspects of that act remain challenged in the courts, and now includes competition for local service, as well as equipment and long-distance services.

CPE (Customer Premise Equipment) and long-distance competition developed quickly after the Carterphone Decision and the MFJ. CPE competition is widespread, with literally thousands of manufacturers competing for the voice, data, video, and image systems markets. Competition in the long-distance business is intense in the United States, with well over 400 facilities-based carriers vying for the interLATA market. Some level of competition for intraLATA long distance also now exists in every state. The Telecommunications Act of 1996 is intended to increase the level of competition, nationwide, once the Regional Bell Operating Companies (RBOCs) can freely compete for interLATA services in their states of operation.

Local service competition exists, at some level, in most states. Alternative Access Vendors (AAVs) provide high-speed, fiber optic facilities in major industrial and commercial areas, largely for the purpose of providing direct access to the IXCs, and bypassing the Incumbent Local Exchange Carriers (ILECs). While some of the AAVs already had begun to offer a limited set of local services, The Telecommunications Act of 1996 virtually eliminated state regulatory barriers, which had prevented such activity. Many of the AAVs became CLECs (Competitive LECs), and now operate successfully in most states, with emphasis on the larger and more lucrative geographic markets, and on larger businesses. In addition to voice CLECs, a number of data CLECs also operate successfully, with emphasis on Internet access, Frame Relay, and dedicated private-line services.

Local loop competition, as such, has not existed to any great extent in the United States or other developed nations until very recently — literally, about the time of this writing in late 1999. The primary exception, of course, has been that of the AAVs, which extended their optical fiber facilities directly to the customer premises. A number of Wireless Local Loop (WLL) providers did just the reverse, building optical fiber backbones. The Telecommunications Act of 1996 required that the ILECs lease local loops to the CLECs, and provide space in their Central Offices so the CLECs might collocate their termination facilities in a convenient and cost-effective Point of Presence (POP). The Act also required the ILECs to *unbundle* the cost of those loops, thereby charging the ILECs only for the loop and not for the various Operations Support Systems (OSSs) and other network elements that are bundled into the overall cost of a loop for purposes of calculating the rate base for regulatory purposes. CATV providers also are providing data communications services, most especially Internet access, in an increasingly large number of areas. As discussed previously, CATV upgrades are progressing at a rapid pace in support of two-way data communications. Voice communications also can be supported over coax-based CATV networks, although currently it is unusual. A few electric power utilitiesalso compete in the local loop through the deployment of optical fiber networks, and in support of voice, data, and entertainment TV services.

Applications

Applications, clearly, are the primary force driving the concept of The Information Superhighway. Users have developed a real appetite for bandwidth-intensive applications, lacking only the network infrastructure to support them. The capability of a single provider to deliver a full range of voice, data, video, image, and even multimedia services across the full spectrum of meaningful applications is a compelling feature of a converged network. Basic telecommunications applications certainly must be supported, including voice and data communications, as well as Internet access. A convergence scenario also adds TV to the basic service mix, resulting in the blending of voice, data, and entertainment applications. The more exciting applications include videoconferencing, distance-delivered learning, music- and video-on-demand, home shopping, publishing, and integrated messaging.

VOICE COMMUNICATIONS

Voice communications, including both the provisioning of local loops and the delivery of local service, certainly is part and parcel of convergence. While local service is not stunningly profitable now, competition and relaxation of regulation over local service rates are likely to go hand-in-hand. Additionally, the successful local service provider has a competitive edge in the highly profitable long-distance market. Bundled with other voice services (e.g., enhanced custom calling features) and with data services such as Internet access, such a package can be most attractive to the user and highly profitable to the service provider – especially when delivered over a single local loop using xDSL technology. In a full convergence scenario, IP-based carriers such as Qwest can offer a full range of voice, data, fax, video, and multimedia services over a single, integrated backbone network.

DATA COMMUNICATIONS

Data communications services tend to be highly profitable. The historical growth of – and the growth potential for – bandwidth-intensive data services is well documented. In the competitive market for data communications services, emphasis is on highly profitable dedicated services such as native LAN-to-LAN connectivity and Packet Over SONET (POS), as well as on enhanced services such as Frame Relay, IP-based Virtual Private Networks (VPNs), and Asynchronous Transfer Mode (ATM). Many of these services are not regulated.

INTERNET ACCESS

Internet access is a natural for a convergence scenario. A vast number of large end-user organizations have dedicated Internet access, often provided over unchannelized T-carrier service delivered to the premises through a SONET local loop. Additionally, millions of small businesses and individuals have dial-up access to the Internet, generally over dial-up, analog lines through a conventional modem. This dial-up approach quickly is yielding to xDSL and even CATV cable modem access, which is *always on*. Further, the single xDSL or CATV local loop can support other applications. Depending on the specifics of the technology, those applications can include voice, LAN-to-LAN, entertainment TV, and videoconferencing. For the most part, the Internet is not regulated.

TELEVISION

Currently, CATV providers offer television on a highly profitable basis, especially since CATV rate regulations were lifted in recent years. In fact, CATV providers essentially are unregulated at the federal level, and only marginally regulated at the local level. In addition to basic offerings, premium channel subscription and pay-per-view are growing in popularity and profitability. As I discussed in previous chapters, CATV networks rapidly are being upgraded in support of Internet access and voice communications. Videoconferencing, multimedia, and other applications also can be supported over CATV networks.

While CATV is likely to continue as the primary means of TV delivery, Direct Broadcast Satellite has grown in popularity, offering greater choice of channels at reasonable cost. Employing digital satellites and MPEG 2 compression, transmission quality is excellent, although propagation delay remains an issue with traditional Geosynchronous Earth Orbiting (GEO) satellites. Developing Low-Earth Orbiting (LEO) satellite constellations such as Teledesic promise to eliminate this problem of propagation delay, and to enable cost-effective, two-way Internet access over broadband space platforms.

VIDEOCONFERENCING

Videoconferencing expands to *Video Dial Tone*, or *Visual Dial Tone*, on The Information Superhighway. This application appeals to some, and borders on the ridiculous to others. Affordable bandwidth and terminal equipment remain major issues.

DISTANCE-DELIVERED LEARNING

Distance-Delivered Learning has long been accomplished through the media of broadcast television or CATV. More recently, there have been numerous applications of special educational programs over satellite TV, such as the Jason project. Additionally, a number of technical seminars are delivered routinely on a commercial basis over Business TV (BTV) channels. A number of colleges and universities now offer Bachelors and Masters degree programs over the Internet, thereby extending the advantages of higher education to those unable to take advantage of an on-site educational program.

VIDEO-ON-DEMAND (VOD)

Video-on-Demand (*VOD*) offers potential, although its future is very uncertain. A number of field trials have surfaced technological problems and limitations, mostly related to server capacity and performance. Additionally, it is not at all clear that a market for VOD will be strong enough to justify the cost of deployment of high-capacity local loops and VOD servers. *Near-VOD* (*NVOD*) is a variation on the VOD theme, providing access to a predetermined set of video offerings. Those videos run at frequent intervals, perhaps beginning every 15 minutes, with the user reserving access to the video channel at the desired viewing time. Despite the enormity of the investments required, the technical problems remaining, the uncertainty of the demand, and the low probability of short-term profits, a number of VOD trials were conducted in the mid- to late-1990s. All trials were canceled due to lack of demand. It seems as though people prefer the larger selection available at the local video store.

MUSIC-ON-DEMAND (MOD)

Music-on-Demand (*MOD*) provides access to a wide variety of music over high-quality local loops. MOD involves access to an audio server, much like a CD-ROM jukebox. For some years, this application was forecast to be highly attractive, but the technology didn't evolve sufficiently until 1999 when the MP3 (Moving Pictures Experts Group, Audio Layer 3) compression algorithm was developed. MP3, as discussed in Chapter 12, supports the downloading of near CD-ROM quality music over the Web. Significant concerns remain relative to copyright infringements and avoidance of royalty payments.

INTERACTIVE GAMES

Interactive games are networked video games that enable multiple players to engage in a competitive game experience. The CD-ROM program is housed in a server residing in the network. This application is highly popular in some circles, and currently is supported over the Internet and WWW.

HOME SHOPPING

Home shopping already is experiencing considerable success over the Internet, as I discussed in the context of electronic commerce. This application likely will grow significantly, not only on the Internet, but also on the basis of catalog servers residing at regional locations in the converged network. Localized home shopping catalogs likely will be developed on servers in a convergence scenario. Thereby, local shopping malls and department stores could effectively provide the same type of service, but on a regional or localized basis and provided over a converged network with TV or even HDTV quality. Significant issues of credit card security can be resolved through encryption.

PUBLISHING
Publishing already is experiencing limited success on the Internet. A wide variety of technical papers long have been distributed in this fashion; additionally, Web home pages provide substantial vehicles for the publishing and distribution of certain types of documents. A critical remaining issue is that of copyright laws that effectively would govern the subsequent use of documents published electronically. (Don't look for this book to be published over the Internet in the near future, even though my contract with IDG Books Worldwide covers the possibility, and they actually do publish excerpts on the Web.)

MULTIMEDIA AND INTEGRATED MESSAGING
Multimedia standards, as discussed in Chapter 13, already are specified in H.320 and H.323. Multimedia services are not available widely, however, due to issues that include bandwidth and upgrade costs for both networks and terminal equipment. Into the future, however, integrated messaging offers great potential, extending well beyond the boundaries of voicemail and e-mail — with image attachments. Integrated messaging will include video mail and image mail. The compound mail technology, in effect, will render *multimedia mail*. In general, multimedia has great potential, although not in the foreseeable future — at least, not for most of us.

Technology

The technology to support the current vision of the Information Superhighway largely is in place, or in various stages of development. Certainly, a wide variety of voice and data communications technologies are well developed. Yet, real technology issues remain, and they cut across network domains from end-to-end. Keep in mind, of course, that the vision of convergence will continue to evolve with ever greater visions of applications and ever more capable enabling technologies.

TERMINAL EQUIPMENT
Terminal equipment currently provides excellent support for individual voice, data, video, and image applications, but through separate devices — telephones, computers, and TV sets. Multimedia PCs will support voice, data, and video, but their voice and video capabilities still aren't all that great. Cable-ready PCs are available now, although at higher cost; in fact, many Apple computers have been cable-ready for years. While this can be useful for video editing, few people are excited about

watching TV on a PC. About the only converged device that has been successful is that of a combined telephone and fax machine.

In a convergence scenario, terminal equipment likely will not be in the form of a single, multifunctional device. Rather, it likely will take the form of modular computers, telephones, displays, cameras, and other devices to be snapped together as desired. In this manner, the user will realize the advantages of modular functionality, which then theoretically can be upgraded on a modular basis. In different rooms of a residence, different individuals might use these devices in different combinations. For example, the SOHO (Small Office/Home Office) might be equipped with a multiline telephone and headset, computer keyboard and mouse, a CPU and hard drive, and flat panel display with attached camera mounted on the wall – all wireless. A wireless connection might be provided to a combined color printer/fax machine/copier. The family room might focus on a large, flat-screen display device. The master bedroom might contain a smaller display. The playroom and children's rooms, as well as the kitchen and bathrooms, also could feature smaller displays. In every case, wireless connectivity might be supported among the display unit and a remote control, keyboard and mouse, camera, and telephone. The end result is that of a modular, wireless *Home Area Network* (*HAN*). Any and all applications could be accessed, conceivably from any room. While this scenario might seem a bit exotic, it currently is technically feasible. The remaining issues, of course, center on standards and costs.

We actually can take this scenario quite a bit further. Given the expansion of the IP addressing scheme through IPv6, every device might have its own static IP address assigned. Your home control unit also might have an IP address so that you can access it remotely from your cell phone or two-way pager in order to disable the security alarm and unlock the front door for your children, make sure that you turned off the iron and other appliances before you left the house, or perhaps turn on the air conditioner before you get home so that the house is at a comfortable temperature.

In my humble opinion, the highly-touted NetStation (refer to Chapter 12) will not take the world by storm. This concept, once again, is that of a dumb terminal with a keyboard, mouse, display, and communications software; all processing power and all storage of any significance would reside in the network. There certainly are applications for such a device – now available for as little as $500. However, those who take our computing even remotely seriously will continue to favor premise-based solutions. I wouldn't even have considered writing this book and developing the graphics on the basis of network computing, and it's my guess that the typical reader of this book wouldn't make use of such a concept either. I also doubt that the typical *couch potato* has much of an inclination to compute, at all. As a small indication of the intense speculation over the future of the information appliance, note references [14-1] through [14-6], which date to 1996. During the intervening years, the level of interest in this concept has declined considerably, although the Internet-ready iMac computer from Macintosh has experienced great success. The iMac currently (August 1999) is priced at $1,199, attractively packaged in five colors, and includes many traditional personal computing components (e.g., monitor, CPU, hard drive, 56-Kbps modem, and CD-ROM drive) packaged in a single case. The iMac, however, does not include a floppy disk drive and is not backward compatible with legacy Macintosh peripherals because of its reliance on the USB (Universal Serial Bus) architecture, rather than the traditional SCSI (Small Computer Serial Interface). Further, the iMac is a sealed unit and, therefore, is not upgradeable. Despite its shortcomings, it is a powerful machine and deservedly has experienced considerable success. It's not a NetStation, but it's close and it's better.

USER INTERFACES

The user interfaces for the converged terminal device remain very much in the development phases. The primary effort focuses on highly intuitive Graphic User Interfaces (GUIs) that yield an effective *navigator*, much like the concept of a Web browser. Perhaps through a wireless remote, you will be able to select application options from menus presented on a converged device consisting of a big-screen display, supporting video applications, as well as serving as the display for a multimedia computer system.

NETWORK INTERFACES

Various network interfaces have been developed in recent years, and others are in final stages of development and standardization, as discussed in Chapter **9**. In the xDSL domain, ADSL (Asymmetric Digital Subscriber Line) splitters have been standardized for several years in support of voice, data, and video. It is unlikely, however, that ADSL will experience great success in support of this full range of applications, largely because of the incredible demands on the local loop made by the high-frequency TV channel. The G.lite DSL specification is in final stages of standardization by the ITU-T. Although G.lite will support only voice and data, and not entertainment TV, it undoubtedly will have a significant impact.

CATV networks hold more promise for a full convergence scenario, at least at the consumer level. The DOCSIS (Data Over Cable Service Interface Specification) standard is finalized, although only a small number of products have been certified as compliant. DOCSIS provides a standard interface to a coax-based CATV system in support of two-way voice and data, as well as downstream entertainment TV. However, and as we previously discussed at great length, CATV systems involve a shared medium that presents significant issues in terms of performance and security.

There certainly is the potential for another interface to a converged network, and that's in the form of a VSAT (Very Small Aperture Terminal) satellite dish that would provide connectivity between the users' premises and a broadband LEO network such as that under development by Teledesic. Although I consider this scenario highly unlikely, it certainly is technically feasible; this fact must make Arthur C. Clarke very proud, indeed.

The ultimate network interface, imho (Netspeak for *in my humble opinion*) will be in the form of a centralized terminating multiplexer that will interface both coax and UTP inside wiring systems to an optical fiber terminating at the premises. The optical fiber local loop will run the ATM protocol over SONET, and in support of all of the applications I just mentioned. That interface is years in the future – perhaps many years in the future.

LOCAL LOOP: NETWORK ACCESS

Local-loop technologies are developing rapidly, with emphasis across the full range of wireline and wireless. Wireless, as I have discussed on numerous occassions, is limited in terms of spectrum, and therefore bandwidth, although advanced compression algorithms mitigate this drawback to a considerable extent. Wireless also is suseptible to poor performance because of inclement weather; is distance-limited, particularly at the higher frequencies; and is inherently insecure. Terrestrial wireless local loops are viable only because they permit the CLEC to avoid dealing with an uncooperative ILEC through bypassing the embedded local loop, and doing so quickly and cost-effectively. Non-terrestrial wireless technologies (i.e., satellites) suffer from many of the same limitations, although Teledesic and other proposed LEO constellations anticipate overcoming many of them.

The UTP-based local-loop networks owned by the ILECs are limited by virtue of the laws of physics as they apply to high-frequency electrical signals propagated over thin copper conductors. However, recent xDSL developments have extended their capabilities well beyond what most of us would have thought possible only a few years ago. Nonetheless, there are limits to what even the brightest scientists can devise. While coax-based CATV networks inherently are more capable than their UTP cousins, they remain limited by the laws of physics as they apply to electricity and copper. Again, CATV systems also are limited by the fact that a shared local loop is involved.

The ultimate solution is Fiber-To-The-Premises (FTTP), although it is unlikely that a wholesale upgrade will ever occur. In fact, the development of xDSL and CATV technologies may well make that conversion unnecessary, at least in support of consumer and small business applications. More likely, we will see the continuing development and deployment of Fiber-To-The Neighborhood (FTTN). Current plans and trials largely focus on hybrid systems that involve high-capacity, optical fiber trunk facilities to a neighborhood, where they terminate in a ngDLC (next generation Digital Loop Carrier) system, as illustrated in Chapter 9. The ngDLC performs multiplexing functions, as well as the optoelectric conversion process in support of the Physical-Layer interface between the optical fiber and the embedded copper-based local loops, which may be in the form of either UTP or coax. The incumbent CATV providers will use existing coaxial cable for the last few hundred meters or so, segmenting the traditional CATV network much as LAN switches serve to improve performance by segmenting a single logical LAN and, thereby, isolating collision domains. The ILECs, of course, will deploy xDSL over UTP for the last few hundred meters or so. Having said all of that, it wouldn't surprise me a bit to see fiber gradually work its way out to even the residential premises on an as-needed basis, of course. The time will come in the early 21st century when copper and coax just won't do the trick for some of us – the development of new applications will drive the need, and the cost of fiber will decrease along with the cost of fiber connectors and optoelectric interfaces. While I doubt that the result will be a Tpbs in every living room, 51 Mbps (OC-1) 155 Mbps (OC-3), or even 622 Mbps (OC-12) certainly is possible in the next decade or so. Note that digital transmission and MPEG 2 compression can squeeze as many as 10 video channels into the bandwidth required by only one channel in the analog coax world of CATV [14-7].

Now, it seems to me that we have to consider that the CATV providers are replacing a lot of coax trunks with fiber, but the ILECs don't seem to have quite as much interest in extending fiber to the neighborhood. We also have to consider that there must be a reason for that imbalance, and that the reason must be more than cost, for the ILECs have very deep pockets. It must involve more than technical expertise, for the ILECs are perhaps the most technically competent builders of infrastructure in the world. It also must involve more than just applications because the ILECs would dearly love to provide TV service, in addition to voice and Internet access, to the premises. To solve this puzzle, we have to think forward to Chapter 15, which deals with regulation and deregulation. The CATV providers are not affected by the Telecommunications Act of 1996. For that matter, they are hardly affected by any sort of federal or state regulation. The CATV providers are regulated at the municipal or county level, and not very much, at that. As a result of the lack of regulation, they don't have to open their local loops to competition. Therefore, they can upgrade those analog, coax-based loops for their own benefit. The ILECs, on the other hand, are unlikely to make such investments because they would then be forced to make those incredibly expensive facilities available to their competitors, and on a cost-plus basis. If I were an ILEC, I wouldn't do it, and I'll bet my next paycheck that you wouldn't either.

TRANSPORT

The transport transmission facilities in the core of the converged largely have been upgraded to optical fiber, and that trend will continue. As discussed in several previous chapters, optical fiber offers tremendous advantages in terms of bandwidth, error performance, distance, security, and cost. Also discussed in Chapter 9 was the debate over SONET/SDH (Synchronous Optical Network/Synchronous Digital Hierarchy) versus DWDM (Dense Wavelength Division Multiplexing). SONET/SDH is a TDM (Time Division Multiplexing) approach, while DWDM is a FDM (Frequency Division Multiplexing) technique at the optical level. Now, I must reiterate my position that there is not necessarily a direct conflict, and that the two techniques will coexist, for the most part. The backbone carriers will continue to deploy SONET at rates up to 10 Gbps (OC-192), and higher speeds as the standards and technologies evolve. Further and as required, they will open up windows to 32 DWDM in order to achieve speeds up to 320 Gbps per fiber, and open more windows to achieve higher speeds as the standards and technologies evolve.

The exception to this forecast is that of satellite networks, and particularly those proposed by Teledesic and other companies that intend to deploy constellations of broadband LEOs. Those networks, assuming that they live up to their press clippings, will provide broadband voice, data, image, and perhaps video services, bypassing the conventional landline network in the process. However, those networks largely will be subnetworks. Access from your premises to a Teledesic Internet portal is only part of the story. From the Teledesic portal through the Internet and WWW, the conventional landline network will be used, and that network will be based on optical fiber — likely employing both SONET/SDH and DWDM.

SWITCHING AND NETWORK PROTOCOLS

The last major technological issue to consider in a network convergence scenario is that of switching and network protocols.

At the switching level, we must deal with the raging battle between circuit, packet, and cell switching. As previously discussed, circuit switching is very effective, but it's also very inefficient for anything other than traditional, uncompressed voice and video. TCP/IP-based packet switching is very efficient, but isn't very effective for other data applications that are tolerant of variable levels of delay and loss. While the IETF and other standards bodies are working diligently on Quality of Service (QoS) mechanisms to address this shortcoming, packet networks remain *best effort* networks. Conversely, cell switching in the form of Asynchronous Transfer Mode (ATM) was designed from the ground up to provide guaranteed QoS to all applications, simultaneously. This is another classic trade-off between cost and performance, and one that provides no clear-cut answer, in my very humble opinion.

ATM is the ultimate solution, or so it appears. At the moment, however, ATM is just too expensive and too technically demanding for anything other than backbone data networks. Packet switching is very efficient and affordable, but just doesn't do the job in terms of QoS. The cost of circuit switching is dropping considerably in the face of competition from cell and packet switching, but just isn't efficient enough in the long run — bandwidth remains limited, at some level. The incumbent IXCs (AT&T, MCI Worldcom, and Sprint) all have stated that they no longer will make investments of consequence in circuit switching. Rather, they will invest in ATM in the network core, and gradually work that technology out to the network edge, and ultimately to the premises. Some of the competitive IXCs (e.g., Qwest) have committed to packet switching, mitigating the inherent *best effort* nature of the TCP/IP protocol suite by turbocharging the TCP/IP gateway routers and servers, and by deploying multi-Gbps optical fiber transmission facilities in the form of SONET and DWDM.

Into the foreseeable future, what we likely will see is a hybrid of all of the above. Circuit switches will remain at the edge of the incumbent networks until they either have been fully depreciated or have outlived their functional lives, whichever comes last. Packet switches running the TCP/IP protocol suite will comprise the edge of the network for competitive IXCs (e.g., Qwest and Level 3), and increasingly so for the incumbent IXCs, which are very quietly experimenting with IP voice. ATM cell switching is being dropped into the core of all networks, also at this very moment. The initial focus on ATM is in the data networks, for they are in the greatest need because of the incredible growth in traffic. Voice traffic gradually is shifting to ATM core switches, very quietly and as required.

Providers of the Toll Roads

The Information Superhighway is not free. It is anticipated that well over $100 billion will be required to construct the *I-Way* in the United States, alone. That investment by no means ensures that every U.S. business and residence will have high-speed access; rather, deployment will be driven by market potential. Likely, results will resemble that of the road system, with urban areas having access to high-speed, multilane freeways, loops, and the like (hopefully without the congestion that characterizes this analogy) — all of which will be as smooth as glass, in addition to *HOV* (*High-Occupancy Vehicle*) lanes for power users. High-speed, multilane interstate highways, as smooth as glass, will interconnect the major urban centers. Smaller towns and cities will have lesser access, and rural areas will be relegated to access via even more modest and bumpy farm-to-market roads. Voice-grade, unpaved roads will connect to the farms and ranches. The potential providers of the toll roads include providers of telecommunications, data communications, CATV, electric power, and wireless services. Table 14-1 provides a comparison of telecommunications, data communications, CATV, wireless, and Internet networks along a number of key dimensions.

Telecommunications Networks

Telecommunications networks were developed expressly to support voice communications. They virtually are ubiquitous in developed nations, supporting bidirectional communications on a circuit-switched basis. The national networks are fully interconnected to provide complete international calling capabilities, subject to bandwidth limitations and issues of national security. As voice is not particularly demanding in terms of bandwidth or error performance, local loops for access to the networks from residential and small business premises typically remain analog in nature. Although ISDN finally is making an impact, xDSL may overwhelm it, at least in residential and SOHO applications. T-1 and T-3 facilities commonly are used for network access in support of PBX and ACD systems with approximately 100 station lines or more. Very large end-user enterprises sometimes connect multiple sites via dedicated leased lines in the form of T-1 or T-3. The local loop terminates in a local Central Office Exchange, or Class 5 exchange, which traditionally is a circuit switch.

Table 14-1 COMPARISON OF TYPICAL, CONTEMPORARY TELECOMMUNICATIONS, DATA COMMUNICATIONS, CATV, WIRELESS, AND INTERNET NETWORKS

	Voice	Data	CATV	Wireless	Internet
Presence	Ubiquitous	Widely Available	Ubiquitous	Virtually Ubiquitous	Ubiquitous
Transmission Mode	Analog/Digita	Digital	Analog	Analog/Digital	Analog/Digital
Bandwidth (Access)	4 KHz to 45 Mbps	56 Kbps–45 Mbps+	500/750 MHz	Voice Grade to 45 Mbps	4 KHz to 45 Mbps+
Call Direction	Two–Way	Two–Way	One–Way	Two–Way	Two–Way
Switching Technology	Circuit	Circuit, Packet, Frame, Cell	N/A	Circuit, Packet	Circuit/Packet
Transmission Medium	UTP Loop, Fiber Backbone	UTP Loop, Fiber Backbone	Coax	Radio	UTP or Coax Loop, Fiber Backbone
Interconnectivity	Total	Varies	Rare	Cellular – Yes, through PSTN; Data – No	Total
Network Management	Strong	Strong	Poor to Non-Existent	Moderate to Strong	Poor
Market Perception	Excellent	Excellent	Poor	Spotty to Poor	Spotty to Poor
Cost	Highly Affordable	Reasonable to High	Reasonable to High	Moderate to High	Free to Reasonable

The backbone telecommunications networks largely have been upgraded to fully digital switches and digital fiber optic facilities, which are being upgraded to SONET/SDH. Such upgraded backbone networks certainly provide additional bandwidth, performance, and economies of scale for voice carriers through high-capacity, multichannel facilities. Additionally, they provide the side benefit of supporting certain data communications applications through a common transmission infrastructure.

Telecommunications carriers bring a lot of strength to the table in terms of their network design, deployment, and management skills. The telecom networks are known for their reasonable cost and high degree of reliability. Additionally, the carriers have strong customer service reputations and are used to transaction-based billing. Perhaps their biggest weaknesses are lack of flexibility, lack of market responsiveness, historically weak marketing skills, and complete inexperience in the dimension of content. As previously discussed, *content* is key in the Internet and TV domains, and certainly will be so in a full convergence scenario. As some have noted, the telcos have developed and redeveloped numerous convergence strategies that quickly backfired – sort of like the *Wile E. Coyotes* of a convergence cartoon [14-8].

The telecommunications networks have changed quite a lot since 1996, thanks in large part to the Telecommunications Act of the same year. A large number of competitive carriers have entered the local exchange market with aggressive service offerings and very aggressive pricing. These CLECs (Competitive Local Exchange Carriers) have enjoyed a great deal of success, although their market share pales by comparison to that of the ILECs (Incumbent LECs). At the IXC (IntereXchange Carrier) level, not only have a host of new carriers arisen, but also several IP-based carriers – Qwest is most notable in this regard – have begun to offer attractively priced packet voice, although quality issues are at least modest in magnitude. Given the advent of VoIP (Voice over Internet Protocol), the telecommunications network isn't necessarily the conventional PSTN anymore. Rather, the PSTN just as easily can be a packet data network optimized for voice applications. If VoIP network providers succeed in balancing cost and performance, this shift will be more than just interesting – it will be dramatic ... and all appearances are that such will be the case early in the 21st century.

Data Networks

Data communications traditionally involves modems for dial-up, circuit switched transmission over analog circuits, dedicated T-carrier leased lines, or switched digital services (e.g., Switched 56/64 Kbps). Additionally, ISDN is a thoroughly acceptable circuit-switched network technology for data communications, although transmission speed is limited. All of these alternatives essentially involve data over voice networks, as these services are provided over the public voice network or a partition thereof.

The first data-specific network was the X.25 packet-switched network, which evolved into what we currently know as the Internet. During the 1990s, packet switching reached new levels with the development and deployment of Frame Relay, which has enjoyed significant success; SMDS, which has faded away; and ATM, which is finding acceptance in backbone applications. In some cases, these data-specific networks and network services involve totally separate infrastructure. In many cases, however, the infrastructure is shared with voice, video, and fax traffic. SONET transmission systems certainly are capable of supporting multiple traffic types, as are ATM switching systems.

CATV Networks

Entertainment networks, for the purposes of this discussion, are those of the CATV providers. As discussed in Chapter 9, and with rare exception, those networks are isolated islands of entertainment based on analog coaxial cable facilities. Bandwidth is substantial, but is Frequency Division Multiplexed into fixed video channels of 6 MHz. Further, CATV networks generally are one-way. Finally, CATV networks are dedicated, multipoint broadcast networks, rather than switched and interconnected. Developing the necessary convergence infrastructure will be difficult for many of the smaller CATV providers, as they typically are undercapitalized, private companies with relatively small cash reserves and lacking access to capital (debt and equity) markets. Further, the CATV companies do not have transaction-based billing systems in place, and generally lack a high level of network management capability, as well as customer service and support systems and staff. Not only must they expand their technological capabilities and skill sets, but they also must enhance their public perception.

A number of CATV providers recently have made major commitments to upgrading existing facilities. Those commitments are most clear in the cases of TCI and MediaOne; once the MediaOne merger is complete, these properties will make AT&T the largest CATV provider in the United States. The TCI and MediaOne networks, along with some other select networks, are upgrading as fast as possible, given the limitations of technology, manpower, and capital. Those upgrades include:

- Dedication of upstream and downstream channels in support of Internet access and voice communications

- Conversion from analog to digital transmission

- Placement of optical fiber in the backbone trunk facilities

- The addition of packet switches for IP-based voice and data (some CATV providers are using proprietary TDM-based systems for voice)

- The addition of network management and other back-office support systems.

Regardless of the level of system upgrades, however, you must remember that CATV networks are shared networks. As discussed previously, shared networks involve shared bandwidth, which can degrade response times under heavy load. Shared networks also pose issues of security. Clearly, there are ways to mitigate these negative factors, but ignoring them is not an option.

Wireless Networks

Wireless networks include those of cellular telephony, paging, and voice-grade data. These networks all essentially are terrestrial in nature, although paging networks often employ a satellite element. Wireless Local Loop (WLL) technologies, of course, offer an excellent alternative for gaining high-speed access to both voice and data wireline networks. As I noted previously, wireless networking suffers from limited spectrum, which translates directly into limited bandwidth. Regardless of the sophistication of the compression technique, this limitation remains an issue. Wireless technologies always are distance-limited in consideration of frequency reuse and, therefore, limitations on power levels. Line-of-sight is best, and is required at the higher frequency levels, and error performance is subject to the quality of the airwaves. On the positive side, wireless technologies offer the advantages of portability and even mobility. In a fixed wireless application (i.e., WLL), additional advantages include speed and low cost of deployment.

You must consider wireless technologies as one element of a convergence scenario. In other words, WLL is just an alternative access technology with severe limitations. Cellular, paging, and packet radio networks are attractive only because of their incredible advantage of mobility. It's not that these technologies don't have merit, but wireless does not have the potential to serve as a backbone network. WLL certainly can support voice, data, fax, video, entertainment, TV, and multimedia. Cellular, paging, and packet radio networks support low-speed Internet access. Some paging networks support highly compressed voice messaging, although the messages are limited in length. Although currently experimental, some cellular networks even support low-speed, highly compressed videoconferencing. Two-way paging networks widely deployed in Norway and some other Scandinavian countries enable the user to do things such as unlock doors, start automobiles, and turn coffeepots on and off — all from a wireless device such as a cellular phone or pager.

Satellite Networks

Satellite networks, as discussed in several previous chapters, essentially are non-terrestrial microwave networks. Traditional GEO (Geosynchronous Earth Orbiting) satellites certainly have a place in broadcast applications such as TV and radio, and in certain data communications applications such as retail transaction processing. WebTV and DirecPC (refer to Chapter 12) use GEOs for various Internet and WWW applications, although there certainly are limits in terms of shared bandwidth, limited bandwidth, propagation delay, line-of-sight, rain fade, and antenna cost. GEOs just don't have the potential to serve as the backbone in a convergence scenario, at least not unless you have the good fortune of living on a remote desert isle, in which case this discussion (and this entire book) is totally irrelevant. So put this book down and go catch a wave, Dude!

LEO (Low Earth Orbiting) satellite constellations may be quite another matter, although I have my doubts, especially given Iridium's early lack of success (refer to Chapter 11). Although the proposed Teledesic constellation is intended to a broadband Internet-in-the-Sky, it certainly has its share of technical challenges ahead, as discussed previously. Teledesic may turn out to be a highly profitable venture as an alternative means of accessing the Internet and WWW, but it likely will be limited to that niche, at best.

Electric Power Utilities

In the face of competition in their own industry, many electric power utilities are building, or planning to build, fiber optic networks, at least to the neighborhood. Ostensibly, in many cases, these networks are intended to provide a network-based means for load control management of electric power and other utilities. Clearly, many of the power utilities intend to lay a fiber optic grid and to lease capacity to providers of the Information Superhighway. While some of the major power utilities likely intend to become Highway providers, themselves, none have announced such intentions. In any event, it is highly unlikely that they will do so *en masse*. Their cautious approach is because of the fact that the communications business is foreign to them, at least in a commercial sense. While the utilities are experienced in the design and deployment of cable systems, they generally don't have experience in terms of transaction-based billing, media content, and other areas critical to the provisioning of voice, data, and video services.

Heated discussions are taking place relative to pole and conduit access. Traditionally, the telcos and power companies each have enjoyed reciprocal rights to use the facilities of the other for hanging or pulling cables; CATV providers also traditionally have been provided access. Pole and conduit usage fees apply, of course, although the level of such fees has remained quite reasonable. As the competition for the Highway grid intensifies, traditional logic no longer applies. The debate already has ensued and is likely to reach significant proportions before it is fully resolved.

A number of small power utilities have deployed CATV networks that support Internet access, as well as entertainment TV. Some of them have been highly successful, although in small markets. Notable in this regard is MWR Telecom, a spin-off of Midwest Power Company in Iowa. The company built its own 110-mile fiber optic network to serve internal needs, and since has resold excess capacity to the incumbent interexchange carriers (i.e., AT&T, MCI Worldcom, and Sprint) and over 70 large user organizations. Glasgow Electric Plant Board in Kentucky has deployed a two-way coax system that supports CATV, Internet access, and telecommunications in competition with the incumbent providers in its serving area of about 13,000 customers. The Glasgow offering has been well received, particularly in terms of Internet access and cable TV [14-9] and [14-10]. Central and Southwest

Corporation in Texas, Pacific Gas & Electric in California, Entergy Corporation in Louisiana, The Southern Company in Georgia, and Portland General Electric in Oregon are among the other investor-owned utilities experimenting with the technology and service concepts that will position them as I-Way providers [14-9]. Generally speaking, the power utilities are building and operating these networks in small and rural markets, thereby avoiding direct confrontations with the larger and more experienced voice and data carriers. For example, Central and Southwest Corporation is focusing its initial efforts on Austin, Laredo, and Georgetown, Texas, rather than on the larger and more intensely competitive markets of Dallas and Houston. In other cases, the power utilities are partnering with incumbent carriers. An example is the partnership of Duke Power, BellSouth, and Carolina Power & Light in Charlotte, North Carolina for the provisioning of wireless PCS services [14-11]. In general, it is unlikely that the power utilities will be a major force in the world of the I-Way. While they may function as providers of the grid, they unlikely will be successful as providers of services or content.

As a footnote that might become more than just a footnote, an old technology has resurfaced that might change the prediction that I just made. NORWEB, based in the United Kingdom, announced in 1997 the development of a *power line carrier* system for the transmission of IP-based multimedia data over that country's power lines. The transmission system involves complex arrangements of power transformers and noise filters. In support of NORWEB's efforts, Nortel announced its agreement to develop PCMCIA cards to interface PCs to the power line carrier network [14-12]. And, while the concept has merit, its quality implementation will be difficult. Power line carrier has been around for many years and without much success. Rural telephone companies and cooperatives have used it for provisioning voice-grade telephone service to remote farms and ranches. A few manufacturers offer residential key telephone systems that plug into electrical outlets – the ultimate *information appliance*, I suppose – and which interface to the telephone network through a key service unit (KSU) in the traditional manner. On a limited basis, electric power utilities have deployed packet-based *SCADA* (*Supervisory Control And Data Acquisition*) systems that use power line carrier for remote meter reading, remote energy control, and other power management functions. Power utilities also long have used power line carrier for voice and low-speed data communications with remote power stations. Power line carrier works, but the quality remains marginal, at best. However, it's all too easy to discount such a technology, and it's all too easy to be wrong in doing so. A case in point is that of the Internet and other IP-based networks, which most industry pundits have long discounted as totally inappropriate for voice and video — we quite likely are on the verge of seeing at least some of those judgements reversed.

The Internet and IP Networks

Some suggest the Internet is the Information Superhighway, at least for the present and, perhaps, well into the future. While the Internet and the WWW are constrained by network limitations of bandwidth and packet delay, they certainly deliver many of the applications currently envisioned in a convergence scenario. Those applications, which are available and growing, certainly include shopping-at-home and distance-delivered learning. As I noted in Chapter 12, voice communications, videoconferencing, and radio broadcasting also are supported, but not very effectively; these applications truly are inappropriate for the Internet and place great strain on the available resources.

The Internet and the Web certainly are not the ultimate vision of the Highway, but they do deliver a fair amount of functionality . . . and now, rather than later. As the ultimate vision of the ATM-based, Fiber-To-The-Premise (FTTP), multimedia-ready Information Superhighway is years away, the Internet likely will continue to enjoy a very substantial niche in the I-Way market. Since the Internet became commercialized, it has experienced its share of ups and downs. It became so popular that many predicted brownout or even meltdown in the 1996-1997 time frame. That didn't happen. Rather, the backbone service providers added capacity in the form of SONET, and Tbps routers and switches. However, the public Internet likely will never have the ability to support full convergence with guaranteed, or even acceptable, Quality of Service across all applications types. In fact, the Internet will continue to serve the same functions it largely serves today – that of an application-oriented packet data network – one which will be accessed by a converged local network in the not-too-distant future.

The real potential for Internet technology in a convergence scenario is in the form of the next-generation IP networks deployed by Qwest and others. These new carriers are building broadband backbone networks from the ground up (actually from the ground down is more accurate, I suppose), including SONET and DWDM transmission, Gbps-Tbps IPv6 routers at the edge, and Gbps-Tbps ATM switches in the core. This combination is incredibly powerful, and has the potential to support a full convergence scenario, across all information types. Subject to advances in IPv6 standards, these networks may not offer fully guaranteed QoS, but can come very close to it.

The Converged Network

Figure 14-1 illustrates the converged network, at least one likely version of it. Digital local loops will be SONET optical fiber directly to the large business enterprise. Residences and small businesses will take advantage of SONET trunk facilities that will terminate in a ngDLC (next generation Digital Loop Carrier) to the neighborhood, with a copper-based last mile or less of the local loop. That last copper portion of the local loop will be in the form of coaxial cable for the CATV providers, terminating in a DOCSIS CATV modem. The ILEC local loop will be in the form of UTP, running some form of xDSL, and connecting to a xDSL modem or splitter. The CLECs will lease those local-loop facilities from the ILECs or perhaps the CATV providers (assuming changes in regulation), deploy their own fiber facilities, or use some form of WLL technology to connect to the users' premises. The local loop may even run the ATM procotol, and connect to an ATM chipset embedded in the modem or splitter, or even in the individual terminals.

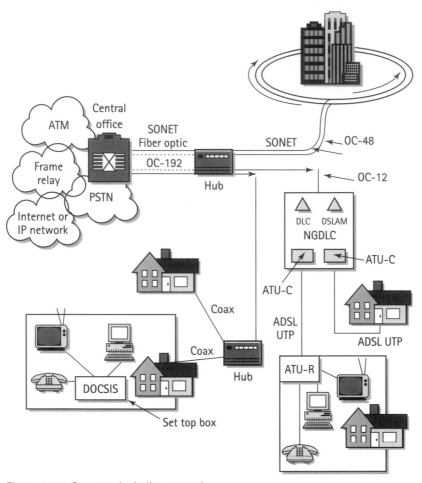

Figure 14-1 Converged wireline network

At the edge of the carrier network will be positioned a Central Office that will house POPs (Points of Presence) for multiple carriers. In addition to traditional circuit switches for access to the conventional PSTN, the Central Office will house SPOT (Single Point Of Termination) frames for Internet access through conventional ISPs, ATM switches for end-to-end ATM users, Frame Relay switches and routers for users of that service, and IPv6 routers for those end users of next-generation, IP-based networks. The Central Office location also may boast one or more satellite antennae for access to broadcast TV and audio programming.

In the core of each of the carriers will be optical fiber transmission facilities running both SONET and DWDM protocols. The core switches will be ATM in nature.

Admittedly, this scenario is extreme and may be many years into the future. It also is based on the very large assumption that new technologies don't develop in the meantime to overwhelm this charming little story.

Highway Issues

A number of significant issues must be overcome if the Information Superhighway is to become a reality. Those issues include standards, regulation, taxation, addressing, and interconnectivity.

Standards

Standards (read *standards recommendations*) enable manufacturers and service providers to build and deliver to a common set of specifications, with options they can exercise to maintain a reasonably high level of differentiation. Assuming that standards develop quickly, manufacturers will build to them while complaining about stifled creativity. If they develop slowly, manufacturers will develop their own ad hoc *standards* in order to get products and services to market and remain competitive.

Standards are well in place for some aspects of the Information Superhighway. In terms of Physical Layer standards, SDH/SONET is well developed, although work remains to be done at the higher levels (above OC-192). DWDM is developing rapidly, as are xDSL standards. WLL enjoys a wide range of standards, and a number of nonstandard approaches. At the switching level, ATM standards are well developed, although that work will continue for many years. Broadband ISDN (B-ISDN) clearly needs attention, and it relies on ATM. IP networks enjoy the advantage of the highly mature TCP/IP protocol suite, which recently was enhanced through the development of IPv6 and the H.320 umbrella standard. In an IP-based convergence scenario, however, QoS issues remain unresolved. CATV networks do not enjoy the same level of standardization, with the exception of DOC-SIS cable modems.

Regulation

Regulatory issues are not trivial in the context of the I-Way. At the federal, state, and local levels, a number of issues loom large. Regulatory issues include franchise rights, right-of-way, universal service, provider of last resort, and censorship.

FRANCHISE RIGHTS

Geographical franchise rights largely are regulated at the local level. Local loops and local telecommunications services generally remain the domain of the

Incumbent Local Exchange Carriers (ILECs). Municipal and county governments originally granted such exclusive franchises. Currently, a mix of state and federal oversight prevails, although the Telecommunications Act of 1996 provides for competition in the local loop. The various municipal and county governments grant franchises to the CATV providers on a local level. Local governments are used to being rewarded by CATV providers for franchise rights, generally on the basis of gross receipts taxes. Telcos have balked at the suggestion of paying such local taxes for I-Way franchises, claiming already to be heavily taxed at all levels. Additionally, they hold the position that their rates and services are regulated at the national and state levels, not at the local level.

RIGHT-OF-WAY

Right-of-way, referring to the legal right of passage over the property of another, also is a local issue. Municipal and county governments tend to take a very keen interest when a telephone company of a CATV provider wants to dig up streets and walkways to bury cables, or to punch holes in the ground to plant poles. On more than one occasion, local governments have taken strong exception to cabling projects aimed at laying redundant information grids. Local governments also recently have taken strong exception to the placement of cellular, WLL, and PCS antennae and enclosures. In fact, a cell phone tower along I-25 near Colorado Springs is disguised to look like a very tall pine tree. In rural areas, some wireless antennae are disguised as windmills, and some have been hidden in church steeples – all to make them less obtrusive. In addition to issues of aesthetics, health concerns remain relative to EMF (Electromagnetic Frequency) emissions, whether or not those concerns are grounded in scientific fact.

UNIVERSAL SERVICE

Universal service is a concept that has influenced telecommunications policy in developed nations for many years. The best possible service, universally available at the lowest possible cost, is a basic precept on which telecommunications networks developed since the 1930s. Currently, all incumbent telecommunications providers (LECs and IXCs, alike) contribute to a *Universal Service Fund* (*USF*), which is administered at the federal level. CATV providers, power utilities, CAPs/AAVs, ISPs, next-generation VoIP providers, and others do not contribute to the USF. Their lack of participation poses a serious threat to the concept of universal service.

PROVIDER OF LAST RESORT

Provider of last resort is a concept closely tied to both universal service and competition. In order to be universally available, some company must assume the responsibility for providing service under the worst possible circumstances. From the standpoint of pure profit motivation, there is no incentive for a carrier to provide products and services such as lifeline service or Telecommunications Devices for the Deaf (TDDs). Nonetheless, there is a social obligation to provide them, and some service provider must be held accountable. Although the ILECs currently are the providers of last resort, the various regulatory authorities have not addressed this issue fully — at least not in a fully deregulated environment.

CENSORSHIP

Censorship, increasingly, is the focus of a good deal of government attention, particularly at the federal level, and some degree of regulation is virtually inevitable. Recent instances of Internet *cyberporn* have led to government investigations and numerous arrests. Internet Bulletin Board Systems (BBSs) and *chat groups* have been used for illegal activities such as child abductions, posting of illegally-obtained credit card numbers and cellular telephone ID numbers, and various other illegal activities. Law enforcement is at work, making occasional arrests of violators, although the difficulty of tracking down and prosecuting the offenders is difficult, given the anonymity of the medium.

Debates also rage over issues of television content. While the V-Chip (Violence-Chip) was settled on as a solution, apparently there is little demand for TV sets so equipped. Assuming that all TV and VOD (Video On Demand) content is rated and assuming that the TV set is equipped with the V-Chip, parents automatically can reject the access of minor children to certain scenes, programs, or even entire channels. That assumes, of course, that the same parents who can't program the VCR (or even reset the VCR clock) can figure out how to program the V-Chip. Similarly, software filters are commercially available for the Internet. Such filters block access to Web sites of unseemly content, and the filters regularly are updated through downloads from centralized servers maintained by the software providers.

Taxation

Municipal and county governments long and heavily have relied on taxation of traditional utility companies to balance their budgets. The shift to wireless communications has left the cities in something of a lurch. Cellular telephony and satellite TV, certainly, have required that the tax codes be rewritten. They also have made the job of calculating and collecting revenues much more difficult. The Internet poses a similar problem with respect to both voice communications and electronic commerce, which threatens to undermine the revenues realized from sales taxes.

Assignment and Portability of Logical Addresses

Logical addresses come in a variety of forms and relate to physical addresses in various ways. Telephone numbers, URLs (Uniform Resource Locators), and IP addresses are examples of logical addresses. Ultimately, of course, those addresses translate into something physical, whether it is a location or a device, and the data is routed to that location or device on the basis of the logical address. In this dynamic Information Age, you move around a lot, and you move your devices around a lot. Unfortunately, your logical addresses aren't as portable as your equipment and you are.

A telephone number is a logical address that ultimately translates into a physical address in the form of a switch port and local loop circuit; these connect to a physical location such as a residence or a place of business, and ultimately to a physical device in the form of a telephone set. With the exception of your toll-free In-WATS number (800, 888, or 877), your telephone number is not highly portable. The North American Numbering Council (NANC) assigns telephone numbers in North America to carriers on the basis of geographical areas, and in blocks of 10,000. Depending on the manner in which your metropolitan area of residence is numbered (i.e., overlay versus split area codes), you may not be able to move from one suburb to a neighboring suburb without changing your area code. And you almost certainly will have to change your telephone number if you move more than a few miles. Also with the exception of toll-free numbers, you could not switch your local service from an ILEC to a CLEC, for example, without changing your telephone number. The Telecommunications Act of 1996 came to the rescue with a provision for Local Number Portability (LNP) between LECs within a given geographic area. In July 1996, the FCC mandated that LNP be in place by January 1, 1998, although that deadline slipped quite a bit in various state jurisdictions. Generally speaking, LNP takes advantage of the Advanced Intelligent Network (AIN) infrastructure, as discussed in Chapter 10. The FCC mandated that the various wireline and wireless LECs cooperate in the implementation of LNP through the establishment and synchronization of regional number databases that reside in Signal Control Points (SCPs) in the AIN control network. Lockheed Martin currently is responsible for running all seven Number Portability Administration Centers (NPACs), which serve as national clearinghouses for local service operators in North America. (Note: Lockheed Martin also is the primary administrator for the North American Numbering Plan, or NANP). As each state is responsible for overseeing LNP implementation, however, the timetables for full implementation vary considerably, as do the specific methods for accomplishing it.

URLs (Uniform Resource Locators), as discussed in Chapter 12, are unique logical addresses in the form of domains on the World Wide Web. Domain Name Servers (DNSs) translate URLs, which you do *own* as long as you pay the annual charge for them, into unique logical IP addresses that also are *owned* by you, your company, or your service provider. While your IP address isn't portable across companies or service providers, your URL is portable through a relatively simple change in the master DNSs. For example, I could change my ISP from Northwest Link, which hosts my virtual domain, to Hypothetical Link. The new ISP would simply change the master DNS in order to point my URL, *contextcorporation.com,* from the Northwest Link IP address 199.xxx.xxx.xxx to the IP address associated with Hypothetical Link. Within a day or two, at most, that new IP address would be downloaded to all of the DNSs in the Internetwork, and my e-mail would be routed correctly to the new physical device in the form of the e-mail server at Hypothetical.

Unfortunately, not all Internet addresses are so portable. For example, some years ago I subscribed to America Online (AOL), and selected the e-mail address *contextcrp@aol.com. Contextcrp* is unique to me on the AOL network, but the domain is AOL's. Therefore, that address by no means is portable to CompuServe, Prodigy, MSN, or any other service provider. I still use AOL on the road, because it's almost always a local call — I just forward my mail ray@contextcorporation by gaining access to my ISP's UNIX server through TELNET. My daughter also uses my AOL account, under her own *screen name*. The Context Corporation effectively is wed to America Online, unless I'm willing to change my e-mail address as I switch providers. As some of us are well aware, divorces are far more difficult and expensive than weddings. Besides, my daughter wouldn't tolerate my forcing her to change her e-mail address, as well. (If you are financing the college education of an adult child, you will understand. If not, I could write a book about it, and then you *might* understand.)

The concept of PCS (Personal Communications Services), also known as PCN (Personal Communications Network), takes the issue of address assignment and portability to the extreme. PCS, in full theoretical form, enables a single logical address to follow you for life, across the full range of applications (e.g., telephony telephony, paging, facsimile, e-mail, and video mail), across carrier domains, and around the world. While no one has specified just exactly how this is to be done, IPv6 might well be the answer. Recall that the IPv6 128-bit addressing scheme is wide enough to support the assignment of 32 addresses per square inch of dry land on the Earth's surface, which seems wide enough to permit you to have one or two of your own.

Interconnectivity

Interconnectivity is critical in telecommunications networks and the Internet. Some data networks provide for interconnectivity on the basis of privilege and other factors; examples include the Internet, X.25, and Frame Relay networks. Other data networks are not intended necessarily to support high levels of interconnectivity. Regardless of the provider, the converged network must support full interconnectivity, at least for voice, videoconferencing, and certain types of data ... and on an equal access basis.

One Potato, Two Potato, Three Potatoe, Four...

Potato(e) can be spelled more than one way, as Vice-President Dan Quayle illustrated several years ago. There also is more than one way to build an I-Way. There is a very serious question as to just how many wires (hard wires and *wireless wires*) should be extended to provide access to the I-Way in a convergence scenario. After all, the very word *convergence* means *coming together*. You have to wonder how much redundant infrastructure is reasonable, and at what cost. Perhaps the electric utilities have the right idea — build one information grid and provide access to a wide variety of service providers. Of course, this idea is not new. Utilities tradition-ally have provided a single grid for telecommunications, data communications, CATV, electric power, gas, water, and sewer services. The fundamental economic concept of a *natural monopoly* still has merit.

Rochester Telephone (Rochester, New York), well known as an innovator, several years ago hit upon a variation of the same theme. The New York PUC approved the separation of the company into R-Net, the grid provider, and R-Comm, the service provider. R-Net acted as an information grid wholesaler, providing access to service providers, including R-Comm. On January 1, 1995, the people of Rochester became the first U.S. citizens to have a choice of local telephone service providers since 1919 [14-13]. Rochester Telephone is now part of Frontier Corporation, which has announced that it will merge with Global Crossing, an international submarine fiber optic carrier.

In all likelihood, a *natural duopoly* or *triopoly* will prevail in many areas. Telecommunications and CATV local-loop networks already exist; they need only to be upgraded. While the level of capital investment is not trivial in either case, it is quite likely that two grid providers can survive quite comfortably and profitably. If you add a wireless carrier or two to the equation, perhaps that number expands to three or four, given the flexibility of wireless network configuration. But it is highly unlikely in the foreseeable future that there will be more than two or three wireline grids.

Content Is the Key

As standards develop, technologies evolve, applications find favor, and the builders of the grid lay pipe, it will become increasingly clear that service providers must find a means of differentiation. Service quality, reliability, responsiveness, and other factors, certainly will help to differentiate one provider from another. However, that differentiation must extend beyond price, promotion, and place ... *Product*, the fourth *P* of the classic marketing definition, is critical.

In a full convergence scenario, content is the key. *Content* includes music, movies, games, educational programming, and a host of other things that entice business and personal users to access the I-Way and use it. Clearly, the industry has realized the importance of content, as numerous mergers, acquisitions, and strate-gic alliances attest.

The Race Is On: Mergers and Acquisitions (M&As)

The race is on and here comes pride up the backstretch. Heartaches are goin' to the inside...and the winner loses all. From *The Race Is On*. Composed by Don Rollins and first recorded by George Jones in 1965.

ILECs, CLECs, IXCs, CAPs/AAVx, CATV providers, PCS licensees, electric utilities, and others all jockey for the pole position to lay the grid and provide the services that will make them rich. In recognition of the fact that convergence is the name of the game, and that no one company has all of the answers, hardware manufacturers, software developers, and carriers are gobbling each other up at a record pace. The race definitely is on! The following is a small, but representative sample of the scope and scale of such activity.

The Evolution of the Bell System

Breakup to make up, that's all we do. First you love me, then you hate me. It's a game for fools. The Stylistics, 1973.

The evolution the old Bell System is an interesting case in point. It may not be a game for fools, but there has been an awful lot of breaking up and making up. Now, let's reflect on the breakup of the Bell System, which I discussed at length in the context of the Public Switched Telephone Network (refer to Chapter 5). On January 1, 1984, AT&T spun off its 22 wholly-owned *Bell Operating Companies* (*BOCs*) under the terms of the *Modified Final Judgement* (*MFJ*), also known as the *Divestiture Decree*. These BOCs were reorganized into seven *Regional Bell Operating Companies* (*RBOCs*), also known as *Regional Holding Companies* (*RHCs*), as noted in Table 14-2. Over time, the RBOCs fully absorbed the individual BOCs, creating a single legal entity with a centralized management structure. Cincinnati Bell and Southern New England Telephone (SNET) were not affected by the MFJ, as they were not wholly-owned subsidiaries of AT&T.

Table 14-2 BELL SYSTEM OPERATING COMPANY ORGANIZATIONAL STRUCTURE, BEFORE AND AFTER THE MFJ, AND TO THE PRESENT

Bell Operating Companies (BOCs), Pre-divestiture	Regional Bell Operating Companies (RBOCs), Post-divestiture
Illinois Bell	Ameritech (IL). Proposed to merge with SBC Communications
Indiana Bell	

Continued

Continued

Michigan Bell	Ameritech (IL). Proposed to merge with SBC Communications
Ohio Bell	
Wisconsin Telephone	
Bell of Pennsylvania	Bell Atlantic (PA)
Diamond State Telephone	
The Chesapeake and Potomac Companies (DC, MD, VA, & WV)	
New Jersey Bell	
South Central Bell	Bell South (GA)
Southern Bell	
New England Telephone	NYNEX (NY). Merged into Bell Atlantic (August 14, 1997)
New York Telephone	
Pacific Bell	Pacific Telesis (CA). Merged with SBC (April 1, 1997)
Nevada Bell	
Southwestern Bell	Southwestern Bell Corporation (TX), now SBC Communications
Mountain Bell	US West (CO). Proposed to merge with Qwest Communications.
Northwestern Bell	
Pacific Northwest Bell	

THE BOCS BREAK OUT OF THE BOX

While the MFJ had incredible impact on the telecommunications environment in the United States, the resulting landscape was neat and orderly. That's no longer quite the case. Southwestern Bell Telephone Company changed its name to Southwestern Bell Corporation and then to SBC Communications. The last name change was a bit puzzling until the merger (read *acquisition*) with Pacific Telesis was announced—*Southwestern* no longer had any positive value. Pacific Telesis ceased to exist, but Pacific Bell and Nevada Bell retained their identities. Subsequently, SBC also merged with Southern New England Telecommunications (SNET), a Connecticut LEC once partially owned by AT&T. SNET also retained its identity. A key advantage to SBC of the SNET merger is the fact that SNET was not affected by the MFJ; therefore, SNET could freely develop a small, but successful position as an IXC. SBC potentially can build a much more substantial IXC business on the SNET foundation, once it can do so under the terms of the Telecom Act of 1996. SBC also announced (May 1998) its intent to merge with Ameritech; this merger is still pending.

Bell Atlantic also has been busy, announcing (July 1998) its merger with GTE. GTE previously (May 1997) had acquired Internet Service Provider (ISP) BBN Planet, which then became GTE Internet Solutions — a very substantial, nationwide ISP. While the GTE merger currently remains pending, Bell Atlantic's merger with NYNEX was completed in August 1998. NYNEX ceased to exist.

US West reached a definitive agreement in 1999 to merge with Global Crossing, an upstart international submarine fiber optic carrier. Global Crossing also reached a definitive agreement to merge with Frontier Corporation, a LEC and IXC that began life as Rochester Telephone. Qwest, an upstart IP-based IXC, then made a hostile bid for both US West and Frontier, and a war broke out. Actually, it was more of a skirmish, as Qwest very quickly (July 1999) was declared the winner with respect to the US West merger. Global Crossing walked away with the Frontier Corporation merger agreement remaining intact. Global Crossing and Qwest were attracted to US West since a good deal of long-distance traffic either originates or terminates in US West territory. While Frontier's properties in Rochester, New York, are not particularly attractive, its status as a second-tier IXC was very attractive. The bottom line is that both Global Crossing and Qwest spend billions of dollars *laying pipe* (i.e., building backbone infrastructure), and they need to fill those pipes with minutes of traffic. It's faster and easier, and often less expensive, to buy the minutes than it is to take them away from the competition. Qwest has a history of this sort of activity, having merged with LCI in June 1998; LCI previously (September 1997) acquired USLD Communications. US West previously spun off its CATV business, US West Media Group, which became MediaOne, which is in the process of merging with AT&T.

SO WHAT HAS AT&T BEEN UP TO?

Speaking of AT&T, the company reorganized into two business units at the time of divestiture in 1984. AT&T Long Lines became AT&T Communications, operating as an Interexchange Carrier. AT&T Technologies was formed of Western Electric, the manufacturing arm of AT&T, and AT&T Bell Telephone Laboratories (Bell Labs), the research and development organization. For the next 13 years, AT&T did very well focusing on its core businesses, although it did acquire NCR Corp. in a failed attempt to get into the computer business. With all of the hype that surrounded the merging of voice and data at the time, it apparently seemed to AT&T management that AT&T Technologies and NCR Corp. would make a great match, and a great launching pad for computer telephony systems. That seemingly great idea just didn't work. IBM previously experienced a similarly dismal failure with its acquisition of ROLM Corp., an almost legendary PBX manufacturer, which it subsequently sold to Stromberg-Carlson.

On January 1, 1997, AT&T effected the largest voluntary breakup in history. The $75 billion company split into three market-focused companies, also selling AT&T Capital Corp., its captive financing business. Approximately 8,500 employees, all in the Global Information Solutions (GSI) computer business, lost their jobs fairly immediately. GSI resulted from the NCR acquisition, which did not live up to expectations. Tens of thousands of others lost their jobs over time. The post-divestiture AT&T boasted assets of $79.2 billion, annual revenues of $75.1 billion, and a total workforce of 303,000. Table 14-3 provides a view of AT&T, both post-divestiture and post-spinoff.

Table 14-3 AT&T, POST-DIVESTITURE AND POST-SPINOFF. SOURCE: AT&T 1995 ANNUAL REPORT

AT&T, Post-Divestiture	AT&T, Post-Spinoff
AT&T Communications Services (formerly AT&T Long Lines)	AT&T Corp.
Role: Long Distance Service, Universal Card, AT&T McCaw Cellular (acquired 1994)	Role: Long Distance, Universal Card, AT&T McCaw Cellular, Wireless, Internet Services, AT&T Laboratories. Revenues: $51 billion. Assets: $56 billion. Employees: 127,000
AT&T Bell Telephone Laboratories	Lucent Technologies
Role: Research & Development	Role: Research and manufacturing of CPE/DTE. Includes Bell Laboratories and AT&T Technologies. Revenues: $21 billion. Assets: $20 billion. Employees: 131,000
AT&T Technologies (formerly Western Electric)	
Role: Manufacturer of CPE/DTE	
AT&T Global Information Solutions (formerly NCR Corp.)	NCR Corp.
Role: Manufacturer of Computers, Automatic Teller Machines (ATMs), Electronic Cash Registers	Role: Data Processing Systems, ATMs, and Electronic Cash Registers. Revenues: $8 billion. Assets: $5 billion. Employees: 38,000

Since the time of the voluntary breakup, AT&T has been busy, of course. In February 1996, AT&T announced its Internet access service, which was an instant hit. Although the AT&T WorldNet service hasn't experienced the same level of growth as others since that time, it currently ranks fourth, behind AOL, CompuServe, and MSN Internet.

In January 1996, AT&T purchased a 2.5 percent stake ($137 million) in DirecTV, a provider of entertainment TV via DBS satellite. AT&T marketed DirectTV to its customer base, billing for the monthly services through its standard long-distance billing system. Purchase and installation of the dishes also could be financed through AT&T credit cards. Subsequently, AT&T divested its stake in DirecTV, which Microsoft now owns.

In July 1998, AT&T merged with TCG (Teleport Communications Group), a large CAP/CLEC that previously (January 1997) acquired Cerfnet, a large Internet backbone provider. AT&T also completed the acquisition of TCI (Tele-Communications Inc.) in early 1999, about the same time it announced its intent to merge with MediaOne. These two mergers will make AT&T the largest CATV provider in the United States. TCI previously (October 1993) announced a merger with Bell Atlantic, although that merger later (February 1994) was called off for *financial reasons*. AT&T is rebranding the TCI to AT&T Broadband & Internet Services (AT&T BIS). MediaOne, as discussed above, was spun off from US West in June 1998. As a sample of activities prior to that time, MediaOne and its predecessor company, US West Media Group, merged with Comcast, a large CATV provider, partnered with TCI in the formation of the Telewest broadband service company in the U.K., developed an alliance with Time Warner, merged with Continental Cablevision, and acquired two CATV systems in Atlanta, Georgia.

In July 1998, AT&T and British Telecom (BT) announced the formation of Global Venture, an international alliance that expects revenues of $10 billion in its first year of operation. BT contributes to Global Venture its concert services, which it previously linked with MCI. BT, at one time, owned 20 percent of MCI, which subsequently merged with Worldcom to become MCI Worldcom. AT&T's link with BT required that it dissolve its WorldPartners WorldSource international alliances, which involved a large number of partners all over the world.

IN OTHER NEWS

MCI Worldcom formed in September 1998 by the merger of MCI and Worldcom, the 2nd and 4th largest U.S. IXCs, respectively. Worldcom formed by the acquisition of Wiltel by LDDS (Long Distance Discount Service), which began life in 1983 as a long-distance reseller in Mississippi. In order to gain approvals from the various regulators who feared that the combined company would dominate the Internet backbone market, MCI sold its Internet backbone business to Cable & Wireless. British Telecom reached an agreement to merge with MCI, of which it owned 20 percent, but lost interest when the high cost of MCI's entry into the CLEC business exceeded its expectations. Part of the fallout of that failed bid was the breakup of the international concert relationship between MCI and BT. As previously mentioned, BT then formed Global Venture with AT&T. Worldcom previously (October 1997) merged with Brooks Fiber, a large CAP. Worldcom also acquired CompuServe (September 1997), a large ISP, from H&R Block; as part of that deal, Worldcom shed CompuServe's interactive services division off to America Online (AOL), and acquired ANS Communications from AOL. Earlier in time (January 1997), Worldcom merged with MFS (Metropolitan Fiber Systems), a large CAP, to form MFS Worldcom, which then changed it name to just Worldcom. While MFS lost its identity, UUNET, which it previously (August 1996) acquired, has retained its identity as a highly reputable Internet access provider.

Cisco Systems acquired Stratacom in April 1996, adding significant Frame Relay and ATM switching technology to its product line.

3Com Corp. acquired U.S. Robotics in February 1997, adding a powerful modem product line to its portfolio.

Ascend Communications acquired Cascade Communications in March 1997, thereby adding significant Frame Relay and ATM switching technology to its product line.

America Online Inc. (AOL) announced in November 1998 its intention to acquire Netscape Communications Corp., thereby putting it in a better position to address Microsoft's entry into the Internet domain through MSN (Microsoft Network) and IE (Internet Explorer). Interestingly, AOL had exclusive rights through January 1, 1999, to market Microsoft's IE browser, which provided serious competition versus Netscape Navigator.

References

[14-1]   Buerger, David J. "The Inter-Personal Computer Is A Trojan Horse That Will Only Benefit Vendors." *Network World,* November 20, 1995.

[14-2]   Meade, Peter. "Crossing The Lines." *Information Week,* August 21, 1995.

[14-3]   Metcalfe, Bob. "Faster, Easier, Cheaper Information Appliances Looking for New Identity." *InfoWorld,* October 23, 1995.

[14-4]   "PCs: 'Ridiculous' or Wave of Future?" *San Francisco Examiner,* September 9, 1995.

[14-5]   Smith, Gina. "NC: An Idea Whose Time Has Come. *San Francisco Examiner,* December 10, 1995.

[14-6]   Yamaguchi, Mari. "Apple Tests Simpler, Cheaper Computer." *Seattle Post-Intelligencer,* March 15, 1996.

[14-7]   Hargadon, Tom. "The State of The Info Highway." *New Media,* October 1995.

[14-8]   Birkhead, Evan. "Reality Check." *Internetwork*, September 1995.

[14-9]   Lockwood, Judith. "Utilities Energized for Telecom Business."
            Convergence, November 1994.

[14-10]   Jones, Kyle F. "Electric Power, Cable TV, and Technology: The Glasgow
            Electric Plant Board Experience." Presentation at ComNet '96,
            February 1, 1996.

[14-11]   Cooper, Lane. "Utilities open the door on a new market." *Telepath*,
            October 1996.

[14-12]   Freymuth, Casey and Reed-Smith, Judy. "Power Telephony." *X-Change*,
            January 1998.

[14-13]   "Rochester Telephone's New Frontier." *Convergence*, April 1995.

Chapter 15

Regulation: Issues And (Some) Answers

Order marches with weighty and measured strides; disorder is always in hurry.
Napoleon I (Napoleon Bonaparte, also Napoleon The Last). *Maxims.* 1804-1815.

Regulations, from Latin *regula* meaning *rule*, are rules or orders established by governmental bodies and having the force of law. As generally is the case in matters of government, regulations are not developed quickly. Like standards, they develop slowly, based on human experience and setting the stage for the next cycle of experience. Generally written by groups of lawyers, they are characteristically lengthy and complex to the extent that it takes other groups of lawyers to interpret them. Where there are disagreements or disputes, lawyers appeal to the regulators and all too often litigate those matters through the court systems. As noted by Karl Shapiro in *Reports of My Death* (1990), "Lawyers love paper. They eat, sleep and dream paper. They turn paper into gold, and their files are colorful and their language neoclassical and calligraphically bewigged." While current regulations also are available electronically, the size of the files to be downloaded reflects the size of the official paper documents, and you'll wind up printing them out anyway.

This chapter isolates discussion of recent developments in U.S. regulation, as well as pending regulatory issues. As I have dealt with specific regulatory events and issues in a number of previous chapters to the extent that they were germane to the particular network at hand, let's not repeat those discussions. Rather, let's focus on the Telecommunications Act of 1996 (*The Act*), and how it will shape the future of communications in the United States. We also will discuss remaining issues of decency, rates and tariffs, and number portability. You may obtain information relative to The Act and other regulatory and legislative information from the FCC and Congress over the Internet as follows:

◆ Federal Communications Commission: http://www.fcc.gov

◆ United States House of Representatives: http://www.house.gov

◆ United States Senate: Senate: http://www.senate.gov

Regulations tend to build on one another, for without the experience of history the future tends to be a bit uncertain. Over time, a complex fabric of regulation has been woven at the international, national, state, and local levels. While the seams are generally well stitched, there are significant overlaps in some cases and the patterns don't always match up quite right. In the United States, the weave of the fabric traditionally has been tight and has covered the body of communications from head to toe. The clear trend is one of a much lighter and looser weave, and for less coverage – in other words, *deregulation*. As deregulation takes hold and the competition heats up, comfort and freedom of movement become increasingly important. The risk, of course, is that those unused to the full sun of a competitive environment (read *ILECs*) may suffer from sunburn for a short time. Those same companies would claim to have sharpened their market skills in the cellular radio market over the past 10 years or so. As with all things, only time will tell.

Full deregulation, however, is unlikely. At the risk of stretching the fabric analogy to the tearing point, the telecom world of New Zealand is virtually threadbare. Some years ago (the late 1980s), the government completely deregulated telecommunications abolishing the regulator in the process. As a result, any legal disputes among carriers must be addressed through the courts, as must any other commercial civil dispute. Over the years, the carriers have engaged in several such disputes. The issue of interconnection, for instance, worked its way through the entire national court system and then was appealed to the Privy Council in England for final resolution. Australia took much the same approach as New Zealand during the late 1990s when it abolished AUSTEL, which was the equivalent of the FCC. As best as I can determine, no other nation has taken deregulation quite to this extreme.

For the most part, the United States sets the regulatory model for the rest of the world. This has been the case traditionally, and continues to be so, with notable exceptions such as those of New Zealand and Australia. Following the U.S. lead, CPE and long-distance competition has been introduced in much of the world, and regulation generally has been relaxed in favor of permitting market forces to determine which products and services will find success, and at what price. Quite a few countries have privatized their government-owned networks, either completely or partially. Numerous others have plans in that regard, and in some cases the proceeds of privatization have been earmarked for specific purposes such as education. Table 15-1 provides a chronology of selected key regulatory and legal events in telecommunications history.

Table 15-1 SUMMARY OF SELECTED KEY REGULATORY AND LEGAL EVENTS IN TELECOMMUNICATIONS HISTORY

Year	Event
1865	ITU (International Telegraph Union) created to establish rules for interconnectivity of national telegraph networks.
1876	Alexander Graham Bell granted patent for telephone.
1910	*Mann-Elkins Act* grants Interstate Commerce Commission (ICC) interstate regulatory authority.

1913	Department of Justice (DOJ) considers antitrust action against Bell System, based on commitment by President Woodrow Wilson to break up monopolies.
1913	*Kingsbury Commitment* causes DOJ antitrust action to be dropped in return for AT&T's agreement to interconnect with independent telcos, stop acquiring them, and divest its stock in Western Union.
1918	Post Office assumes interstate regulatory authority for telephone and telegraph by executive order of President Wilson.
1921	*Graham-Willis Act* establishes telephone companies as natural monopolies.
1924	ITU forms CCIR (International Radio Consultative Committee, now ITU-R) to set standards for international connectivity of radio networks.
1927	*Radio Act of 1927* establishes Federal Radio Commission to regulate all radio spectrum, except bands owned by federal government.
1934	*Communications Act of 1934* establishes Federal Communications Commission (FCC) to regulate interstate, international, and maritime communications, with universal service stated as the goal. DOJ begins major antitrust action against Bell System, which is delayed due to issues of national interest during WWII.
1935	First state Public Utility Commissions (PUCs) formed to assume intrastate regulatory authority from municipal and city governments.
1945	Supreme Court rules in *Ashbacker Radio Corporation vs. the FCC* that radio spectrum allocation is to be on the basis of comparative hearings.
1949	DOJ files antitrust action against AT&T, -which action had been delayed by W.W.II. This action results in 1956 Consent Decree.
1955	FCC's *Hush-a-Phone Decision* supports AT&T's contention that even acoustically -coupled foreign (non-telco provided) devices cannot be connected to the network without special arrangement.
1956	*Consent Decree* negotiated as settlement between AT&T and DOJ, permittingallowing AT&T to retain ownership of Western Electric if it manufacturers only for Bell companies. Also prevents Bell System from offering data processing services and other services not related to functions of a common carrier. Requires that Bell System patents be licensed to others on basis of reasonable fees.
1959	FCC's *Above 890 Decision* grants private microwave access to a dedicated portion of radio spectrum. Also permits construction of such networks, regardless of economic impact on the established common carrier.

Continued

Continued

1962	*Communications Act of 1962* places authority with FCC to assign commercial satellite frequencies. Act establishes *Communications Satellite Corporation* (*Comsat*) to act as a carriers' carrier (wholesaler) for international satellite service and in conjunction with Intelsat. *Intelsat* (*International Telecommunications Satellite Organization*) established as international financial cooperative that owns and operates satellites for international communications.
1963	Microwave Communications Inc. (MCI) files application to operate as a Specialized Common Carrier (SCC).
1968	FCC's *Carterphone Decision* counters Hush-a-Phone decision, enablingallowing interconnection of foreign equipment through standard protective coupling device provided by telco.
1971	FCC's *SCC Decision* clears way for MCI and other SCCs to construct and operate networks.
1972	FCC's *Domsat Decision* permits domestic satellite market. AT&T excluded from market for three years.
1975	FCC establishes *Part 68* registration program for certification of foreign equipment, eliminating requirement for coupling devices.
1978	FCC's *MTS/WATS Decision* permitsallows MCI and others to offer switched MTS voice services.
1980	Second Computer Inquiry (Computer Inquiry II) requires AT&T to offer enhanced communications and CPE/DTE through separate subsidiary.
1982	*Modified Final Judgement* (*MFJ*) negotiated between DOJ and AT&T as a modification to 1956 Consent Decree. MFJ forces divestiture of Bell Operating Companies (BOCs) and establishes equal access. Also removes restrictions on AT&T against computer and related businesses. AT&T retains Long Lines (long distance) Bell Telephone Laboratories (R&D) and Western Electric (manufacturing). AT&T retains embedded CPE base. AT&T files reorganization plan with Federal District Judge Harold H. Greene.

Congress grants FCC authority to award radio spectrum licenses on basis of lottery, rather than comparative hearings. Cellular radio licenses are granted on this basis. |
| 1983 | Judge Greene files order based on AT&T reorganization plan. Order specifies seven RBOCs, with Bellcore for common R&D support. LATAs established, with AT&T and other IXCs permitted to provide interLATA service. BOCs and other LECs granted exclusive rights to provide local and intraLATA long-distance services. |

1984	MFJ takes full effect January 1.
1985–1996	MFJ relaxed through series of waivers (e.g., permitting RBOCs to offer enhanced services such as voicemail). Several PUCs permit intraLATA and local competition.
1993	*Omnibus Budget Reconciliation Act* provides for creation of new class of wireless services, PCS. FCC authorized to auction PCS spectrum.
1994	First PCS auctions held, raising $8.3 billion.
1996	*Telecommunications Act of 1996* passed by Congress and signed into law February 8, allowing full and open competition across all dimensions, including manufacturing, local service, and long distance. Conditions established for RBOC entry into long distance market within home states. FCC begins process of establishing rules for implementation of act. Implementation specifics in process of full definition; ultimate impact remains unclear.
	Communications Decency Act enacted to hold both creators of content and service providers responsible for access of minors to indecent or offensive material over the Internet. The act was ruled unconstitutional, in violation of *free speech* guaranteed by the First Amendment. DOJ is expected to appeal to the Supreme Court.

Sources: [15-1], [15-2], [15-3], [15-4], [15-5], and [15-6].

Telecommunications Act of 1996

On February 8, 1996, the administration signed into effect a law that passed both houses of Congress by overwhelming majorities and that, once again, will dramatically redraw the landscape of telecommunications. The *Telecommunications Act of 1996 (The Act)* effectively supersedes the 1982 MFJ, removing line-of-business restrictions and promising to permit full and open competition in virtually every aspect of communications – from radio broadcasting to CATV to local exchange and long distance. Ownership restrictions in large part are lifted, enabling the carriers to invest, relate, merge, and acquire. Over time, rates will be deregulated, tariffs may be eliminated, and the regulator may well take a back seat. The Act also effectively deregulated CATV, opened spectrum for broadcast TV stations to introduce HDTV, and established a Universal Service Fund to keep rates low in rural areas and to subsidize telecommunications and Internet services to schools and libraries.

Lines of Business

The Act effectively removes the line-of-business restrictions imposed by national regulations since the early part of this century and strengthened by the MFJ. Some of the major reversals include allowing the RBOCs to enter the long-distance business, permitting AT&T and others to compete as LECs, enabling them all to own and operate CATV businesses within and without their home states, and permitting them all to manufacture products. In some cases, restrictions apply, at least until certain tests are satisfied.

Mergers and Acquisitions

The Act largely lifts restrictions on ownership — in other words, LECs and IXCs. CATV, satellite, radio, TV, and wireless companies are free to merge, acquire, and otherwise invest in each other without much in the way of restriction, although both the FCC and the DOJ must be satisfied that such activities are in the public interests. As discussed in Chapter 14, there has been a flurry of such activity since The Act was signed into law. SBC acquired (whoops, I mean *merged with*) Pacific Bell, Nevada Bell, and SNET, and is awaiting final approvals to merge with Ameritech. Bell Atlantic merged with NYNEX, and plans to add GTE to the fold. US West is set to merge with Qwest, and Frontier with Global Crossing.

AT&T merged with TCG (Teleport Communications Group), a large CAP/CLEC with a considerable Internet backbone. AT&T also completed the acquisition of TCI, and has announced its intent to merge with MediaOne. These two mergers will make AT&T the largest CATV provider in the United States. AT&T also has made a number of acquisitions of wireless providers, including McCaw Cellular (now AT&T Wireless). In total, the optical fiber facilities of TCG, the coax-based CATV networks of TCI and MediaOne, and its WLL spectrum (including its PCS licenses), will present AT&T with considerable local loop options. These options will enable AT&T to largely avoid having to deal with its disowned children, the RBOCs, for local loop access to its prospective customers. AT&T's position as a CLEC will be enhanced considerably once these acquisitions are developed fully and the necessary network upgrades have been accomplished.

Media ownership restrictions were eased, as well. However, a company is still restricted, in a single local market, from owning two TV stations, or a newspaper and TV station, or a newspaper and CATV operation, or a CATV operation and broadcast TV station in a single market. On the other hand, The Act does increase the number of TV stations that any company can own, up to a maximum of 35 percent of the total national market.

Rules and Implementation

The FCC, despite budget cuts, has a truly overwhelming task ahead; this task is made more difficult by the fact that many of the provisions of The Act remain under the cloud of legal challenges. Included in the issues of significance are the

Universal Service Fund, rules under which the LECs will be permitted to offer long-distance service in their home states, interconnection between incumbent and competing carriers, and rights of way.

UNIVERSAL SERVICE

Universal service remains an issue without a complete answer. The concept of universal service was established by the Communications Act of 1934, and the Universal Service Fund (USF) was formally created some years later — although it was not codified until the Telecommunications Act of 1996. The USF traditionally was intended to subsidize the cost of providing service to *high-cost* areas, defined as areas where the cost of providing service is at least 115 percent of the national average. Thereby, the USF ensured that even the most remote, sparsely populated, and impoverished areas of the United States had access to good quality basic telephone service at reasonable cost. In effect, it was a national cost-averaging scheme designed for the benefit of society, in general. The USF extended over time to support the provisioning of *lifeline* service to those who can't afford the cost of basic telephone service. The Telecommunications Act of 1996 codified the USF, extending its benefits to subsidize Internet access to schools and libraries. The USF currently involves about $5 billion a year paid by IXCs and end users. Under the direction of the FCC, the *National Exchange Carriers Association (NECA)* governs the USF, which actually is administered by the *Universal Service Administrative Company (USAC)*, which NECA operates. USAC accepts the collected funds from the LECs and the IXCs. The LECs collect USF fees that are embedded in the access charges to the carriers and their subscribers, net out their USF requirements, and pass any remaining monies to USAC. The IXCs, under orders from the FCC, have added a surcharge of up to 4.9 percent to customers' bills, which they pass to USAC. USAC redistributes the funds in support of USF objectives. Specifically, USAC distributes designated funds to the *Schools and Libraries Corporation (SLC)* to the tune of approximately $2.25 billion, and to the *Rural Health Care Corporation (RHC)* at a level of approximately $400 million. The FCC set up these organizations under the terms of The Telecom Act of 1996. Remaining funds are parceled out to qualifying LECs in support of high-cost subsidies ($1.7 billion) and lifeline subsidies ($500 million) [16-7] and [16-8].

This policy of universal service worked exceptionally well for 60 years, until certain provisions of the Telecommunications Act of 1996 and advances in technology combined to undermine it. Voice over IP, whether it travels over the Internet or a next-generation IP network such as that under construction by the likes of Qwest, travels over networks that do not fully participate in the USF, if at all. To the extent that VoIP network access involves local loops provided by the ILECs, marginal contributions are made to the USF. The actual VoIP traffic itself, however, is not subject to USF contributions. CATV local loops providing access to VoIP networks do not contribute, either. The risk of VoIP is that if enough voice traffic shifts from the conventional PSTN to IP or other data networks, the USF will collapse. If that happens, basic service rates will increase in consideration of the actual cost of providing basic service, which in high-cost areas can cost upwards of $45 a month. So, while VoIP may save me a few pennies a month, it will force someone living on Social Security in Truth or Consequences, New Mexico, for example, to pay the consequences by disconnecting service.

LEC LONG DISTANCE

Effective immediately on passage of The Act, the RBOCs and *GTOCs* (*GTE Operating Companies*) were free to offer long distance services, but only outside their home states of operation. Several did just that, initially reselling long-distance service to their cellular customers. Otherwise, the ILECs have made little effort to develop interLATA long-distance networks. SBC's acquisition of SNET, which is unconstrained by The Act, and of GTE, which has a substantial long-distance network, clearly signals its intentions.

The Act prevents the RBOCs from competing in the interLATA market within their home states of operation, however, and the stakes are huge. Clearly, the RBOCs are eager to leverage their brand recognition in their home states, where they are best known and where they enjoy long-standing relationships with customers. Additionally, their in-region intraLATA networks can be interconnected very easily. In order to offer in-region long-distance service, however, the RBOCs must satisfy a 14-point competitive checklist. Each point on the list is intended to prove that they offer competitors free and easy access to local facilities, and at fair and reasonable rates that are cost-based. For the first three years after authority is granted, in-region long distance can be offered only on the basis of a separate subsidiary; after that time, the requirement disappears. Interestingly, the GTOCs can freely enter the interLATA market immediately and without restriction, even in-region. With the exception of Los Angeles, however, GTE does not serve any truly significant markets, although it does serve a number of major market suburbs (e.g., Irving, a suburb of Dallas, Texas). As GTE's far-flung serving areas likely don't generate enough traffic among them to support in-region networks, this issue likely is moot for GTE. However, GTE's long-distance network, limited though it might be, appears to be highly attractive to Bell Atlantic. Combined with its original network and its acquired NYNEX network, the GTE network clearly could serve as the foundation for a very substantial interLATA network, particularly along the East Coast.

INTERCONNECTION: THE QUID PRO QUO

Interconnection is an issue of great significance. The voice world always has been fully interconnected, while the data world has been less so, and the CATV world never had much use for the concept. In the world of convergence, all the competing carriers will offer some combination of voice, data, and content/entertainment. *Voice* and *interconnection* are the operative words here, as any viable service package must include voice and Internet access, which absolutely require interconnection through local-loop facilities.

Interconnection issues cut several ways. Clearly the IXCs, CATV providers, and other competing carriers are concerned about the terms under which they can connect to the existing local-loop infrastructure in order to reach the customer quickly. While many of them are building or rebuilding infrastructure to do that independently, that process will take time and will be on a highly selective basis, addressing areas where market potential justifies the investment. On a wireless basis, the costs will be in the range of $750-$1,000 per premise, with uncomfortable bandwidth constraints. On a wired basis, the minimum costs will be more in the range of $2,000-$5,000 per premise for new plants and $500-$750 for CATV and telco rebuilds and retrofits. Clearly, this level of investment is not trivial. In the meantime, the competing carriers must have access to the embedded local-loop plant owned by the incumbent carrier. The terms of that interconnection are the immediate issue.

As previously discussed, the RBOC ILECs must satisfy a checklist of 14 points in order to provide interLATA long distance within their home states. Most especially, they must satisfy the state PUCs, DOJ, and FCC that interconnection is a significant reality or, at least, is significantly available on reasonable terms. Further, the costs of interconnection must be at levels that reflect real costs so the competing carriers can buy local-loop access at compensatory wholesale rates that enable them to retail those loops at competitive prices. Those costs must be unbundled so switch costs, for instance, cannot be applied to non-switched facilities, and that the costs of support systems cannot be included.

The Act identifies a minimum set of network elements to which access must be provided on an unbundled and non-discriminatory basis; the individual states may add to that list. The list of elements include the following:

◆ Network Interface Devices

◆ Local Loops

◆ Local and Tandem Switches (including software features)

◆ Interoffice Transmission Facilities

◆ Signaling and Call-Related Database Facilities

◆ Operations Support Systems (OSSs) and Information

◆ Operator and Directory Assistance Facilities

On one hand, the ILECs have an interest in being agreeable so they speed the process and wrest themselves free of the restrictions. On the other hand, they have an interest in delaying the process until such time as they can solidify their market positions. You could argue either way ... and many do. The ILECs suggest that their costs are very close to their tariffed retail prices for local loops and that wholesale discounts in the range of 5 percent are appropriate, based on the actual cost of provisioning the loops. AT&T and others suggest that the discounts should be more in the range of 25-40 percent, and should be based on the subsidized costs in consideration of rate and tariff cross-subsidies of residential service by business customers.

Aside from cost issues, the CLECs complain that the LEC processes are too slow in providing the loops to the CLECs; meanwhile, the ILECs claim that they are doing all they can to cooperate. The CLECs complain that they have to fax their orders to the ILECs, which then process them manually, rather than providing direct interfaces into the appropriate OSSs for order placement and tracking, and for trouble reporting. The ILECs are concerned about system security, of course — their OSSs intentionally are closed systems.

The CLECs also complain that the ILECs make unreasonable demands with respect to the collocation of termination facilities, or POPs (Points of Presence). Most of the ILECs require that collocated POPs be physically distinct and secure, so neither the ILEC nor the CLEC have free access to the others' facilities. That requirement for physical partitioning sometimes requires only separate equipment cages, while in other instances the ILECs insist on separate entrance facilities (i.e., doors). In either case, the CLECs bear the costs; sometimes reaching levels in the area of $400,000 per Central Office POP.

The battle lines appear to be drawn — the PUCs, the DOJ, and the FCC will sort it all out, the courts will get involved, and so on. This issue is far from resolution.

Note that the CATV providers are not required to provide interconnectivity — at least federal regulations do not require that they do so. Recall from our detailed discussion of CATV networks in several previous chapters that the CATV providers are regulated largely at the local level only. At the federal level, they largely are unregulated, except for issues of content, which were restated and redefined by the Telecommunications Act of 1996. The Act focused on opening the RBOC's local networks to competition, never considering the CATV monopolies. As a result and for example, AT&T's CATV networks, (one of which it acquired from TCI and another that it is acquiring from MediaOne), are not required to be opened to CLECs of any sort. In January 1999, AT&T and TCI filed suit against Portland, Oregon, Multnomah County and eight local cable regulators. Those local regulators placed an open access condition on their approval of the AT&T/TCI merger, insisting that competing ISPs be provided open access to the network. This first challenge to the closed nature of CATV networks likely won't be the last, as AT&T seeks permissions from hundreds of local regulators in connection with its TCI and MediaOne mergers.

ACCESS TO RIGHT-OF-WAY

The Act contains provisions relative to pole attachments. The FCC amended those provisions in its August 1, 1996 preliminary implementation rules. Specifically, The Act and its FCC interpretation provide for non-discriminatory access by CATV providers and telcos to poles, ducts, conduits, and rights-of-way owned by power utilities and incumbent LECs.

Rates and Tariffs

Rates and tariffs have been part and parcel of telecommunications regulation for many years, as previously discussed in Chapter 5. Beginning with the MFJ, the posture of the FCC gradually relaxed to the point that interstate long-distance tariffs largely are optional. Actually, the FCC prefers that they not be filed at all, and is considering eliminating them altogether. Such a move would enable carriers to bundle services, perhaps including CPE in a package of cellular, PCS, long distance, and local service. At last report, 10,000 annual long-distance tariffs filed with the FCC account for 4 million pages of paper! In fact, there is discussion about eliminating local service tariffs, as well, in favor of permitting market forces to dictate prices in the soon-to-be competitive market. No doubt the spotted owl and other forest critters are looking forward to the outcome of this debate!

CATV providers have been up and down the regulatory path – first regulated at the federal level, then deregulated, then re-regulated, and now de-regulated again, in 1999. However, it is quite possible that the hundreds of local regulatory authorities will follow the lead of those in the Portland, Oregon area and bring pressure on the CATV providers to open their networks much as the Telecom Act of 1996 forced the dominant ILECs to do. It also is quite likely that the FCC will step into the middle of this issue at some point.

The Internet

The Internet and, especially, the World Wide Web remain both hot topics and open issues. As part of the government's initiatives in telecom reform, Congress passed the Communications Decency Act (CDA) in February 1996. That act provided for sentences up to two years and levies of fines up to $250,000 for those who made indecent or offensive material available to minors on the Net. Not only were the creators of such content liable, but also the Information Service Providers (e.g., American Online, CompuServe, and Prodigy). A number of coalitions and groups led by the American Civil Liberties Union (ACLU) and Electronic Frontier Foundation (EFF) challenged the law. A panel of federal judges struck down the CDA in June 1996, citing violation of *free speech* as guaranteed by the First Amendment to the Constitution. Judge Stewart Dalzell, who wrote the opinion, stated that *The Internet may fairly be regarded as a never-ending worldwide conversation. The government may not, through the CDA, interrupt that.* Numerous appeals have been unsuccessful, so far.

Regardless of the outcome, the issue of censorship of the Net and the Web will continue unabated for many years. It is clear that measures of some sort must be taken to limit access of minors to certain material. It may well be that the government will require installation on newer PCs of something akin to the V-chip (Violence-chip), which will be required to be included in new TV sets under provisions of The Act. Software filters currently are available that enable parents to impose some level of restriction, although the cost is additional and the filters must be updated continuously.

Other remaining Internet issues include the extent to which Internet Service Providers (ISPs) will be required to contribute to the Universal Service Fund. As the FCC develops rules and implementation strategies for The Act, the Internet, itself, may benefit through classification as an essential service. Thereby, its availability will increase at low cost to libraries and schools, further encouraging its continuing and expanding use by future generations. More than just a footnote is the fact that the expanding use of Internet telephony (refer to Chapter 12) certainly threatens to impact the Universal Service Fund in a very negative way unless some measures are taken. In October 1998, the Internet Tax Freedom Act was signed into law, imposing a moratorium until October 21, 2001 on federal and state taxation of the Internet, and on taxation of electronic commerce. In February 1999, however, the FCC ruled that Internet calls are long distance, rather than local, in nature. This ruling sets the stage for a new round of rule making (and subsequent litigation), if Internet traffic, and particularly Voice over the 'Net (VON) is subjected to participation in the USF.

Number Portability

As noted in Chapter 5, the PSTN relies on a standard logical addressing scheme known as a numbering plan. Based on the U.S. numbering scheme (the first, if not the best approach), it includes country codes, area codes, Central Office prefixes and extensions. Various combinations of leading 1s and 0s advise the network of things such as a request for operator assistance, or the crossing of an area code boundary or national border. These logical addresses always were oriented geographically in the voice world, and oriented by customer and carrier in the data world; further, those numbers were not portable. The sole exception to this rule was that of toll-free (800/888/877) numbers in the United States, which became portable some years ago.

The lack of portability of local telephone numbers became a considerable issue with the introduction of deregulation and competition in the local-exchange domain. As discussed in Chapter 14, the Telecommunications Act of 1996 came to the rescue with a provision for Local Number Portability (LNP) between LECs within a given geographic area. In July 1996, the FCC mandated that LNP be in place by January 1, 1998. Generally speaking, LNP takes advantage of the Advanced Intelligent Network (AIN) infrastructure, as discussed in Chapter 10. The FCC mandated that the various wireline and wireless LECs cooperate in the implementation of LNP through the establishment and synchronization of regional number databases that reside in Signal Control Points (SCPs) in the AIN control network. Lockheed Martin currently is responsible for running all seven Number Portability Administration Centers (NPACs), which serve as national clearinghouses for local service operators in North America. (Note: Lockheed Martin also is the primary administrator for the North American Numbering Plan, or NANP). As each state is responsible for overseeing LNP implementation, however, the timetables for full implementation vary considerably, as do the specific methods for accomplishing it.

So, What This Means To Me Is . . . ?

What all of this means to all of us is yet to be determined — or as my stepdaughter, Kristin Goodman, would say, *So, what this means to me is?* However some things are certain. First, carrier and service options will increase as telecom carriers, ISPs and other data service providers, CATV providers, cellular and PCS carriers, and others compete for business. Second, products and services will be bundled in interesting ways in order to capture all of that business. Third, costs will drop, drop again, and probably again as competition heats up. As an indication, long distance dropped about 40 percent in the last decade, and the new IP-based carriers such as Qwest now undercut their circuit-switched competitors considerably. Fourth, there will be a major shakeout in the industry over the next five years and, most probably, another five years later. Those with the deepest pockets (read *RBOCs* and *IXCs*) will continue to invest in or acquire their weaker rivals, including CATV providers, cellular and PCS providers, WWW content providers and Internet software developers, manufacturers of LAN internetworking products, and DBS satellite carriers. They also will continue to invest in or strike strategic alliances with large content providers, such as Hollywood studios. They will continue to acquire each other, in the vein of the SBC/PacTel and Bell Atlantic/NYNEX mergers. And, new competitors will continue to come out of nowhere, must as did Qwest, Level 3, and Global Crossing, and they also will play in the M&A game until there are perhaps three or four major network and service providers in the United States. Fifth and finally, companies such as Nextlink, Level 3, Nextel, Teledesic, and Microsoft will build on their interrelationships.

Using these tightly linked companies as an example, they will link together optical fiber networks (Nextlink in the metropolitan area and local loop, and Level 3 in the long-haul domain). Next up, these companies likely will link together Wireless Local Loop (WLL) access technologies (Nextlink), wireless mobile networks (Nextel), and broadband satellite networks (Teledesic and WebTV) into wide-ranging, all inclusive voice, data, Internet, video, TV, and multimedia networks, bypassing the incumbent carriers in the process. Hanging off the edges of the network will be information appliances running on a common operating system (Microsoft) and using a consistent graphic user interface (Microsoft). From desktop to desktop, an integrated suite of applications will be supported through the TCP/IP (IETF), and specifically the IPv6 protocol, with Quality of Service improvements.

As the competition heats up, bundling of products and services promise to work to the advantage of the consumer, as we all witnessed in the cellular world. Creative packages might include CPE and a full range of such services as cellular, PCS, long distance, In-WATS, Internet access, facsimile, and local service. Also, don't be surprised when carriers begin to offer flat-rate long distance within a given area, such as a LATA, a state, a region, or even nationwide. Larger companies will get commodity-level voice for free, bundled in with data services, which are more desirable (i.e., profitable) from the carriers' perspective.

The end result is impossible to predict, but it is certain that those who keep their options open will find it to their advantage. As the old Chinese saying goes, *May you live in interesting times.* There is no doubt that the next few years will be very interesting, indeed!

References

[15-1]   Williams, Veronica A. *Wireless Computing Primer.* M&T Books, 1996.

[15-2]   Parker, Edwin B. and Hudson, Heather E. *Electronic Byways: State Policies for Rural Development Through Telecommunications.* The Aspen Institute, 1995.

[15-3]   Bates, Bud and Gregory, Donald. *Voice & Data Communications Handbook.* McGraw-Hill Inc., 1996.

[15-4]   Tunstall, W. Brooke. *Disconnecting Parties.* McGraw-Hill, 1985.

[15-5]   Hudson, Heather E. *Communications Satellites.* The Free Press, 1990.

[15-6]   Snow, Marcellus S. *Marketplace for Telecommunications.* Longman Inc., 1996.

[15-7]   Lawyer, Gail. "Rural Retreat." *tele.com*, June 1998.

[15-8]   Gareiss, Robin. "Why Jonny Can't Surf the 'Net." *Data Communications*, November 21, 1998

Appendix A

Acronyms, Abbreviations, and Symbols

"The question is," said Alice, "whether you can make words mean so many different things." Lewis Carroll. *Through the Looking Glass and What Alice Found There*, 1872.

*+$^*&@%&**$!	Encryption (get it?)
2B1Q	2 Binary 1 Quaternary
AAL	ATM Adaption Layer
AAV	Alternative Access Vendor
ABR	Available Bit Rate
ACD	Automatic Call Distributor
ACELP	Algebraic Code-Excited Linear Prediction
ACK	ACKnowledgement
ACLU	American Civil Liberties Union
ADM	Add/Drop Multiplexer
ADML	Asymmetric Digital Microcell Link
ADPCM	Adaptive Differential Pulse Code Modulation
ADSL	Asymmetric Digital Subscriber Line
AGC	Automatic Gain Control
AIN	Advanced Intelligent Network
AM	Amplitude Modulation
AMPS	Advanced Mobile Phone System
ANI	Automatic Number Identification
ANSI	American National Standards Institute
AO/DI	Always On/Dynamic ISDN

AP	Adjunct Processor, Application Processor
APD	Avalanche PhotoDiode
API	Applications Programming Interface
APPN	Advanced Peer-to-Peer Networking
APS	Automatic Protection Switching
ARCnet	Attached Resource Computer network
ARP	Address Resolution Protocol
ARPANET	Advanced Research Projects Agency NETwork
ARS	Automatic Route Selection
ASCII	American Standard Code for Information Interchange
ASIC	Application-Specific Integrated Circuit
ATM	Asynchronous Transfer Mode, Automatic Teller Machine
ATMS	Advanced Traffic Management System
ATSC	Advanced Television Standards Committee
ATU-C	ADSL Termination Unit-Centralized
ATU-R	ADSL Termination Unit-Remote
AWG	American Wire Gauge
B-ICI	Broadband-ISDN InterCarrier Interface
B-ISDN	Broadband-Integrated Services Digital Network
B-TA	Broadband-Terminal Adapter
B-TE	Broadband-Terminal Equipment
B-UNI	Broadband-User Network Interface
BBN	Bolt, Beranek and Newman
BBS	Bulletin Board System
B_c	committed Burst (size)
B_e	excess Burst (size)
BECN	Backward Explicit Congestion Notification
Bellcore	Bell Communications Research
BER	Bit Error Rate

BFT	Binary File Transfer
BHCA	Busy Hour Call Attempts
BICI	Broadband InterCarrier Interface
BOC	Bell Operating Company
bps	bits per second
Bps	Bytes per second
BRA	Basic Rate Access
BRI	Basic Rate Interface
BSC	Binary Synchronous Communications
BSD UNIX	Berkeley Software Distribution UNIX
BSS	Broadband Switching System
BT	Burst Tolerance
BTA	Basic Trading Area
BUS	Broadcast and Unknown Server
C/R	Command/Response
CAC	Carrier Access Charge
CAI	Common Air Interface
CALC	Customer Access Line Charge
CAP	Competitive Access Provider
CAPI	Common ISDN Applications Programming Interface
CAS	Centralized Attendant Services
CATV	Community Antenna Television
CB	Citizens Band
CBDS	Connectionless Broadband Data Service
CBR	Constant Bit Rate
CCIR	Consultative Committee on International Radiocommunications
CCITT	Consultative Committee on International Telegraphy and Telephony
CCLC	Carrier Common Line Charge
CCS	Common Channel Signaling, Centum Call Seconds

CDA	Communications Decency Act
CDDI	Cable Distributed Data Interface
CDMA	Code Division Multiple Access
CDPD	Cellular Digital Packet Data
CDR	Call Detail Recording
CDSU	Channel Digital Service Unit
CDV	Cell Delay Variation
CDVT	Cell Delay Variation Tolerance
CE	Circuit Emulation
CELP	Code-Excited Linear Prediction
Centrex	Central exchange
CEPT	Committee on European Posts and Telegraph
CER	Cell Error Ratio
CERT	Computer Emergency Response Team
CES	Circuit Emulation Service
CHAP	Challenge Handshake Authentication Protocol
CICS	Customer Information Control System
CIDR	Classless InterDomain Routing
CIF	Common Intermediate Format
CIR	Committed Information Rate
CISC	Complex Instruction Set Processing
CIX	Commercial Internet eXchange
CLASS	Custom Local Access Signaling Services
CLEC	Competitive Local Exchange Carrier
CLID	Calling Line IDentification
CLNP	ConnectionLess Network Protocol
CLP	Cell Loss Priority
CLR	Cell Loss Ratio
CMR	Cell Misinsertion Rate
CMISE	Common Management Information Service Element

CMTS	Cable Modem Termination System
CO	Central Office
COE	Central Office Exchange
CoS	Class of Service
CPE	Customer Premise Equipment
CPU	Central Processing Unit
CRC	Cyclic Redundancy Check
CS	Convergence Sublayer
CS-ACELP	Conjugate Structure-Algebraic Code Excited Linear Prediction
CSA	Carrier Serving Area
CSMA	Carrier Sense Multiple Access
CSMA/CA	Carrier Sense Multiple Access/Collision Avoid
CSMA/CD	Carrier Sense Multiple Access/Collision Detect
CSTA	Computer Supported Telephony Applications
CSU	Channel Service Unit
CT	Computer Telephony, Cordless Telephony
CTD	Cell Transfer Delay
CTI	Computer Telephony Integration
CTS	Clear To Send
CUG	Closed User Group
CVSD	Continuously Variable Slope Delta
D-AMPS	Digital-Advanced Mobile Phone System
DAC	Dual Attached Concentrator
DACS	Digital Access Cross-connect System
DAMA	Demand-Assigned Multiple Access
DARPANET	Defense Advanced Research Projects Agency NETwork
DAS	Dual Attached Station
DBS	Direct Broadcast Satellite

DCC	Data Communications Channel
DCCH	Digital Control CHannel
DCCS	Digital Cross-Connect System
DCE	Data Communications Equipment
DCT	Discrete Cosine Transform
DCTE	Data Circuit Terminating Equipment
DDD	Direct Distance Dialing
DDS	Dataphone Digital Service
DE	Discard Eligibility
DECT	Digital European Cordless Telecommunications
DES	Data Encryption Standard
DHCP	Dynamic Host Configuration Protocol
DID	Direct Inward Dialing
DISA	Direct Inward System Access
DLC	Digital Loop Carrier
DLCI	Data Link Connection Identifier
DNIS	Dialed Number Identification Service
DNS	Domain Name Server, Domain Name Service
DOCSIS	Data Over Cable Service Interface Specification
DOD	Direct Outward Dialing
DOJ	Department Of Justice
DPCM	Differential Pulse Code Modulation
DPF	Data Private Facility
DPLC	Digital Port Line Charge
DPMA	Demand Priority Media Access
DQDB	Distributed Queue Dual Bus
DQPSK	Differential Quaternary Phase Shift Keying
DS	Digital Signal (level), Direct Sequence
DSA	Digital Switched Access
DSI	Digital Speech Interpolation

DSL	Digital Subscriber Line
DSLAM	Digital Subscriber Line Access Multiplexer
DSMA/CD	Digital Sense Multiple Access/Collision Detect
DSP	Digital Signal Processor
DSS	Direct Satellite System
DSSS	Direct Sequence Spread Spectrum
DSU	Digital Service Unit
DTE	Data Terminal Equipment
DTMF	Dual Tone Multi-Frequency
DTV	Digital TeleVision
DWDM	Dense Wavelength Division Multiplexer
DXC	Digital Cross-Connect
DXI	Data eXchange Interface
E-Carrier	European-Carrier
E-TDMA	Enhanced-Time Division Multiple Access
EA	Address field Extension
EBCDIC	Extended Binary Coded Decimal Interchange Code
EC	European Community
ECC	Electronic Common Control
ECMA	European Computer Manufacturers Association
ECN	Explicit Congestion Notification
ECSA	Exchange Carriers Standards Association
ECTF	Enterprise Computer Telephony Forum
EDFA	Erbium-Doped Fiber Amplifier
EFF	Electronic Frontier Foundation
EHF	Extremely High Frequency
EIA	Electronic Industries Alliance, Electronic Industries Association
EKTS	Electronic Key Telephone System
ELAN	Emulated Local Area Network

ELF	Extremely Low Frequency
EMI	ElectroMagnetic Interference
EPABX	Electronic Private Automatic Branch Exchange
ERMES	European Radio MEssage System
ESF	Extended SuperFrame
ESMR	Enhanced Switched Mobile Radio
ETSI	European Telecommunications Standards Institute
EVRC	Enhanced Variable Rate voCoder
FCC	Federal Communications Commission
FCS	Frame Check Sequence
FDD	Frequency Division Duplex
FDDI	Fiber Distributed Data Interface
FDM	Frequency Division Multiplexer
FDMA	Frequency Division Multiple Access
FDX	Full DupleX
FEC	Forward Error Correction
FECN	Forward Explicit Congestion Notification
FEP	Front-End Processor
FEX	Foreign EXchange
FEXT	Far-End CrossTalk
FH	Frequency Hopping
FHSS	Frequency Hopping Spread Spectrum
FM	Frequency Modulation
FOD	Fax-On-Demand
FoIP	Fax over Internet Protocol
fps	frames per second
FRAD	Frame Relay Access Device, Frame Relay Assembler/Disassembler
FRND	Frame Relay Network Device
FSK	Frequency Shift Keying

FSS	Fixed Satellite System
FTAM	File Transfer and Access Management
FTP	File Transfer Protocol
FTTC	Fiber-To-The-Curb
FTTH	Fiber-To-The-Home
FTTN	Fiber-To-The-Neighborhood
FTTP	Fiber-To-The-Premise
FUNI	Frame User Network Interface
FX	Foreign eXchange
gTLD	generic Top Level Domain
G	Generation, Giga
GE	Gigabit Ethernet
GEO	Geosynchronous Earth Orbiting
GFC	Generic Flow Control
GII	Global Information Infrastructure
GO-MVIP	Global Organization for Multi-Vendor Integration Protocol
GoS	Grade of Service
GPS	Global Positioning System
GSM	Global System for Mobile communications
GTOC	GTE Operating Company
GUI	Graphical User Interface
HAN	Home Area Network
HCV	High Capacity Voice
HDLC	High-Level Data Link Control
HDSL	High bit rate Digital Subscriber Line
HDTV	High Definition TV
HDX	Half DupleX
HEC	Header Error Control
HF	High Frequency

HFC	Hybrid Fiber-Coax
HLEN	Header LENgth
HPPI	High-Performance Parallel Interface
HSTR	High-Speed Token Ring
HTML	HyperText Markup Language
HTTP	HyperText Transport Protocol
Hz	Hertz
IA	Implementation Agreement
IAB	Internet Architecture Board
IAD	Integrated Access Device
IANA	Internet Assigned Numbers Authority
IAP	Internet Access Provider
IBC	Integrated Broadband Communications
ICANN	Internet Corporation for Assigned Names and Numbers
ICF	Interexchange Compatibility Forum
ICN	Implicit Congestion Notification
IDSL	ISDN Digital Subscriber Line
IDU	Interface Data Unit
IEC	InterExchange Carrier, International Electrotechnical Commission
IEEE	Institute of Electrical and Electronics Engineers
IETF	Internet Engineering Task Force
IGF	International Gateway Facility
IHL	Internet Header Length
ILEC	Incumbent Local Exchange Carrier
ILMI	Interim Local Management Interface
IMA	Inverse Multiplexing over ATM
imho	in my humble opinion
IMT	International Mobile Telecommunications

IMTS	Improved Mobile Telephone Service
IN	Intelligent Network
INP	Interim Number Portability
INRIA	Intitut National de Recherche en Informatique Et En
InterNIC	Network Information Center Internet Registry
IP	Intelligent Peripheral, Internet Protocol
Ipsec	IP security
IPX	Internet Packet Exchange
Ir	Infrared
IRC	International Record Carrier
IRTF	Internet Research Task Force
IS	Interim Standard, International Standard
ISDN	Integrated Services Digital Network
ISM	Industrial/Scientific/Medical
ISO	International Organization for Standardization
ISOC	Internet SOCiety
ISP	Internet Service Provider
ISSI	Inter-Switching System Interface
ISU	Integrated Service Unit
ITU	International Telegraph Union, International Telecommunications Union
ITU-R	International Telecommunications Union-Radiocommunications
ITU-T	International Telecommunications Union-Telecommunications Standardization Sector
IVD	Integrated Voice/Data
IVR	Interactive Voice Response
IXC	IntereXchange Carrier
JDC	Japanese Digital Cellular
JPEG	Joint Photographic Experts Group
JTACS	Japanese Total Access Communications System

JTAPI	Java Telephony Application Programming Interface
JUGHEAD	Jonzy's Universal Gopher Hierarchy Excavation And Display
k, K	kilo, Kilo
KTS	Key Telephone System
KTU	Key Telephone Unit
λ	lambda
L2TP	Layer 2 Tunneling Protocol
LAN	Local Area Network
LANE	Local Area Network Emulation
LAP	Link Access Procedure
LAP-B	Link Access Procedure-Balanced
LAP-D	Link Access Procedure-Data (or Delta) channel
LATA	Local Access and Transport Area
LCR	Least Cost Routing
LD-CELP	Low Delay-Code Excited Linear Prediction
LEC	Local Exchange Carrier, LAN Emulation Client
LECS	LAN Emulation Client Server
LED	Light Emitting Diode
LEO	Low-Earth Orbiting
LES	LAN Emulation Server
LF	Low Frequency
LFE	Low Frequency Enhancement
LLC	Limited Liability Corporation
LLPOFYNILTATW	Liar, Liar Pants On Fire, Your Nose Is Longer Than A Telephone Wire (hee hee!)
LMDS	Local Multipoint Distribution Services
LMI	Local Management Interface
LNP	Local Number Portability
LNPA	Local Number Portability Administration

LOH	Line OverHead
LRC	Longitudinal Redundancy Check
LRN	Local Routing Number
LSB	Least Significant Bit
LU	Logical Unit
LUNI	LANE User-to-Network Interface
μ	micro, micron
m	milli
M	Mega
MAC	Media Access Control; Move, Add and Change
MAE	MERIT Access Exchange, Metropolitan Area Exchange
MAN	Metropolitan Area Network
MAT	Maintenance and Administration Terminal
MAU	Media Access Unit, Multistation Access Unit
MBS	Maximum Burst Size
MC	Multipoint Controller
MCR	Minimum Cell Rate
MCTD	Mean Cell Transfer Delay
MCU	Multipoint Control Unit
MDP	Motorola Data Protocol
MEO	Middle Earth Orbiting
MF	Medium Frequency
MFJ	Modified Final Judgement
MHS	Message Handling Service
MILNET	MILitary NETwork
MIME	Multipurpose Internet Mail Extension
MMDS	Multichannel Multipoint Distribution Services
MMF	MultiMode Fiber
MOD	Music-On-Demand

MOS	Mean Opinion Score
MP	Multipoint Processor
MPEG	Moving Picture Experts Group
MPI	MultiPath Interference
MPLS	MultiProtocol Label Switching
MPOA	MultiProtocol Over ATM
MPOE	Minimum Point Of Entry
MPPP	Multilink Point-to-Point Protocol
MSS	Mobile Satellite System
MTP	Mail Transfer Protocol
MTS	Message Telecommunications Service
MTSO	Mobile Traffic Switching Office
MTSX	Mobile Traffic Switching eXchange
MUX	MUltipleXer
MVIP	Multi-Vendor Integration Protocol
N-AMPS	Narrowband-Advanced Mobile Phone System
N-ISDN	Narrowband-Integrated Services Digital Network
NAK	Negative AcKnowledgement
NANC	North American Numbering Council
NANP	North American Numbering Plan
NAP	Network Access Point
NCC	Network Control Center
NE	Network Element
NECA	National Exchange Carriers Association
NEXT	Near-End CrossTalk
NGDLC	Next Generation Digital Loop Carrier
NGI	Next Generation Internet
NHRP	Next Hop Resolution Protocol
NIC	Network Information Center (NIC) Internet Registry, Network Interface Card

NII	National Information Infrastructure
NIU	Network Interface Unit
NMT	Nordic Mobile Telephone
NNI	Network-to-Network Interface
NOC	Network Operations Center
NOS	Network Operating System
NPA	Numbering Plan Administration
NPAC	Number Portability Administration Center
NREN	National Research and Education Network
nrt-VBR	non real-time Variable Bit Rate
NSFNET	National Science Foundation NETwork
NT	Network Termination
NTSC	National Television Standards Committee
NTU	Network Termination Unit
O&M	Operations and Maintenance
OA&M	Operations, Administration and Maintenance
OADM	Optical Add/Drop Multiplexer
OC	Optical Carrier
OCC	Other Common Carrier
OPX	Off-Premise eXtension
OSI	Open Systems Integration
OSPF	Open Shortest Path First
P-phone	Proprietary phone
PA	Pre-Arbitrated
PABX	Private Automatic Branch eXchange
PAD	Packet Assembler/Disassembler
PAL	Phase Alternate Line
PAM	Pulse Amplitude Modulation
PAP	Password Authentication Protocol
PBX	Private Branch eXchange

PC	Personal Computer
PCB	Printed Circuit Board
PCM	Pulse Code Modulation
PCMCIA	Personal Computer Memory Card Industry Association
PCN	Personal Communications Network
PCR	Peak Cell Rate
PCS	Personal Communications Services
PDA	Personal Digital Assistant
PDC	Personal Digital Cellular
PDN	Public Data Network
PDU	Protocol Data Unit
pel	picture element
PGP	Pretty Good Privacy
PHY	PHYsical layer
PID	Pager IDentification number
PIN	Personal Identification Number, PhotoINtrinsic diode,
PM	Phase Modulation, Physical Medium
PN	PseudoNoise
PNNI	Private Network-to-Network Interface
POCSAG	Post Office Code Standardization Advisory Group
POH	Path OverHead
POP	Point Of Presence
POS	Packet Over SONET
POTS	Plain Old Telephone Service
PPO	Private Paging Operator
PPP	Point-to-Point Protocol
PPTP	Point-to-Point Tunneling Protocol
PPV	Pay-Per-View

PRA	Primary Rate Access
PRI	Primary Rate Interface
PSC	Public Service Commission
PSK	Phase Shift Keying
PSN	Packet Switching Node
PSTN	Public Switched Telephone Network
PTE	Path Terminating Equipment
PTI	Payload Type Indicator
PTT	Post, Telegraph and Telephone
PU	Physical Unit
PWT	Personal Wireless Telecommunications
PWT-E	Personal Wireless Telecommunications-Enhanced
PUC	Public Utility Commission
PVC	Permanent Virtual Circuit
QA	Queued Arbitrated
QAM	Quadrature Amplitude Modulation
QCIF	Quarter-Common Intermediate Format
QoS	Quality of Service
QPSK	Quadrature Phase Shift Keying
QPSX	Queued Packet Synchronous eXchange
RACE	Research for Advanced Communications in Europe
RADIUS	Remote Authentication Dial-In User Service
RADSL	Rate-Adaptive Digital Subscriber Line
RAM	Random Access Memory
RAS	Registration/Admission/Status, Remote Access Server
RATT	R1022 ATM Technology Testbed
RBOC	Regional Bell Operating Company
RCC	Radio Common Carrier
RD-LAP	Radio Data-Link Access Protocol

RF	Radio Frequency
RFC	Request For Comment
RFI	Radio Frequency Interference
RGB	Red, Green, Blue
RHC	Regional Holding Company, Rural Health Care Corporation
RIP	Routing Information Protocol
RISC	Reduced Instruction Set Processing
RM	Resource Management
RPC	Remote Procedure Call
RS	Recommended Standard
RSVP	Resource reSerVation Protocol
rt-VBR	real-time-Variable Bit Rate
RTCP	Real Time Control Protocol
RTP	Real Time Protocol
RTS	Request To Send
S-HTTP	Secure-HyperText Transport Protocol
SAA	Systems Application Architecture
SAR	Segmentation And Reassembly
SAT	Subscriber Access Terminal
SATAN	Security Administrator Tool for Analyzing Networks
SCC	Specialized Common Carrier
SCE	Service Creation Element, Service Creation Environment
SCP	Signal Control Point
SCR	Sustainable Cell Rate
SCSA	Signal Computing System Architecture
ScTP	Screened Twisted Pair
SDH	Synchronous Digital Hierarchy
SDLC	Synchronous Data Link Control

SDN	Software-Defined Network
SDSL	Symmetric Digital Subscriber Line
SDTV	Standard Definition TeleVision
SEAL	Simple and Efficient ATM Adaptation Layer
SECAM	Systeme Electronique Couleur Aven Memoire
SECBR	Severely Errored Cell Block Ratio
Sesame	Secure european systems for applications in a multi-vendor environment
SFTP	Shielded Foil Twisted Pair
SHF	Super High Frequency
SIG	SMDS Interest Group, Special Interest Group
SIM	Subscriber Identification Module
SIP	SMDS Interface Protocol
SLC	Schools and Libraries Corporation, Subscriber Line Charge
SLIP	Serial Line Interface Protocol
SMDR	Station Message Detail Recording
SMDS	Switched Multimegabit Data Service
SMDSU	Switched Multimegabit Data Service Digital Service Unit
SMF	SingleMode Fiber
SMR	Switched Mobile Radio
SMS	Service Management System, Short Message Service
SMTP	Simple Mail Transfer Protocol
SNA	Systems Network Architecture
SNMP	Simple Network Management Protocol
SNI	Subscriber Network Interface
SOH	Section OverHead
SOHO	Small Office/Home Office
SONET	Synchronous Optical NETwork
SPE	Synchronous Payload Envelope

SPOT	Single Point Of Termination
SPX	Sequenced Packet eXchange
SRC	Spiral Redundancy Check
SRDL	SubRate Digital Loop
SRF	Special Resource Function
SRP	Source Routing Protocol
SRT	Source Routing Transparent
SS	Spread Spectrum, Switching System
SS7	Signaling System 7
SSL	Secure Socket Layer
SSP	Service Switching Point
STDM	Statistical Time Division Multiplexer
STM	Synchronous Transfer Mode
STP	Shielded Twisted Pair, Signal Transfer Point, Spanning Tree Protocol
STS	Synchronous Transport Signal
SUV	Sport Utility Vehicle
SVC	Switched Virtual Circuit
SxS	Step-by-Step
T	Tera, Measurement Interval (time)
T-carrier	Trunk-carrier
TA	Terminal Adapter
TACS	Total Access Communications Systems
TAPI	Telephony Application Programming Interface
TASI	Time Assigned Speech Interpolation
T_c	Time-committed (Rate Measurement Interval)
TC	Transmission Convergence
TCP	Transmission Control Protocol
TDD	Time Division Duplex
TDM	Time Division Multiplexer

TDMA	Time Division Multiple Access
TE	Terminal Equipment
TELNET	TELecommunications NETwork
TIB	Tag Information Base
TLD	Top Level Domain
TM	Terminating Multiplexer
TMR	Trunk Mobile Radio
TO	Telecommunications Organization, Transport Overhead
TOH	Transport OverHead
TPDDI	Twisted Pair Distributed Data Interface
TSAPI	Telephony Services Application Programming Interface
TSR	Terminate-and-Stay-Resident
TTL	Time To Live
TV	TeleVision
U-NII	Unlicensed-National Information Infrastructure
UBR	Unspecified Bit Rate
UCAID	University Corporation for Advanced Internet Development
UCD	Uniform Call Distributor
UDP	User Datagram Protocol
UHF	Ultra High Frequency
UIFN	Universal International Freephone Number
UMTS	Universal Mobile Telecommunications System
UNI	User Network Interface, Universal Network Interface
UNICODE	UNIversal CODE
URL	Uniform Resource Locator
USAC	Universal Service Administrative Company
USDC	United States Digital Cellular
USF	Universal Service Fund

UTP	Unshielded Twisted Pair
V-chip	Violence-chip
vBNS	very-high-speed Backbone Network Service
VBR	Variable Bit Rate
VAN	Value-Added Network
VC	Virtual Channel, Virtual Circuit
VCI	Virtual Channel Identifier
VDSL	Very high Data rate Subscriber Line
VDU	Visual Display Unit
VERONICA	Very Easy Rodent-Oriented Net-wide Index to Computerized Archives
VERS	VERSion number
VG	Voice Grade
VGE	Voice Grade Equivalent
VHF	Very High Frequency
VLAN	Virtual Local Area Network
VLF	Very Low Frequency
VoATM	Voice over Asynchronous Transfer Mode
VOD	Video-On-Demand
VoFR	Voice over Frame Relay
VoIP	Voice over Internet Protocol
VON	Voice Over the 'Net
VP	Virtual Path
VPI	Virtual Path Identifier
VPN	Virtual Private Network
VQC	Vector Quantizing Code
VRC	Vertical Redundancy Check
VSAT	Very Small Aperture Terminal
VSB	Vestigal SideBand
VSELP	Vector Sum-Excited Linear Prediction

VT	Virtual Tributary
VTAM	Virtual Telecommunications Access Method
VTOA	Voice Telephony Over ATM
W-CDMA	Wideband-Code Division Multiple Access
WAIS	Wide Area Information Service
WAN	Wide Area Network
WARC	World Administrative Radio Conferences
WATS	Wide Area Telecommunication Service
WMBTOTCITBWTNTALI	We May Be the Only Telephone Company In Town But We Try Not To Act Like It (Ho ho!)
WDM	Wavelength Division Multiplexer
WLAN	Wireless Local Area Network
WLL	Wireless Local Loop
WOTS	Wireless Office Telecommunications System
WWW	World Wide Web
XBar	CrossBar
xDSL	generic Digital Subscriber Line
XNS	Xerox Networking System

Appendix B

Standards Organizations and Special Interest Groups (SIGs)

There is no useful rule without an exception. Thomas Fuller. *Gnomlogia,* (1732)

ADSL Forum
39355 California Street, Suite 307
Fremont, CA 94538
Tel: 510-608-5905
www.adsl.com

ANSI
American National Standards Institute
11 West 42nd Street
New York, NY 10036
Tel: 212-642-4900
Fax: 212-398-0023
www.ansi.org

ATSC
Advanced Television Systems
Committee
1750 K Street, N.W., Suite 800
Washington, D.C. 20006
Tel: 202-828-3130
Fax: 202-828-3131
www.atsc.org

ATIS
Alliance for Telecommunications
Industry Solutions
1200 G St. NW, Suite 500
Washington, D.C. 20005

Tel: 202-628-6380
www.atis.org

ATM Forum
2570 West El Camino Real, Suite 304
Mountain View, CA 94040
Tel: 415-949-6700
Fax: 415-949-6705
www.atmforum.com

Bellcore
See Telcordia Technologies

BICSI
Building Industry Consulting Service
International
8610 Hidden River Parkway
Tampa, FL 33637
Tel: 813-979-1991 or 800-242-7405
Fax: 813-971-4311
www.bicsci.org

CableLabs
Cable Television Laboratories, Inc.
400 Centennial Drive
Louisville, CO 80027-1266
Tel: 303-661-9100
Fax: 303-661-9199
www.cablelabs.com

CDG
CDMA Development Group
650 Town Center Drive, Suite 820
Costa Mesa, CA 92626
Tel: 714-545-5211, or 888-800-2362
Fax: 714-545-4601
www.cdg.org

CDPD Forum
401 North Michigan Avenue
Chicago, IL 60611
Tel: 800-335-2373
Fax: 312-321-6869
www.cdpd.org

CEMA
Consumer Electronics Manufacturers
Association
2500 Wilson Blvd.
Arlington, VA 22201
Tel: 703-907-7600
Fax: 703-907-7601

CEN
European Committee for
Standardization
rue de Stassart 36
B-1050 Brussels, Belgium
Tel: 32-2-519-68-11
Fax: 32-2-519-68-19

CENELEC
European Committee for
Electrotechnical Standards
rue de Stassart 35
B-1050 Brussels, Belgium
Tel: 32-2-51-96-871
Fax: 32-2-51-96-919

CTIA
Cellular Telecommunications Industry
Association
1250 Connecticut Ave., NW, Suite 200
Washington, DC 20036

Tel: 202-785-0081
www.ctia.org

ECTF
Enterprise Computer Telephony Forum
303 Vintage Park Drive
Foster City, CA 94404
Tel: 415-578-6852
www.ectf.org

ECMA
European Computer Manufacturers
Association
114, Rue de Rhone CH-1204
Geneva, Switzerland
Tel: 41-22-846-60-00
www.ecma.ch

EFF
Electronic Frontier Foundation
1550 Bryant Street, Suite 725
San Francisco, CA 94103-4832
Tel: 415-436-9333
Fax: 415-436-9993
www.eff.org

EIA
Electronic Industries Alliance
2500 Wilson Blvd.
Arlington, VA 22201
Tel: 703-907-7500
Fax: 703-907-7501
www.eia.org

EMA
Electronic Messaging Association
1655 North Fort Myer Drive, Suite
500
Arlington, VA 22209
Tel: 703-524-5550
Fax: 703-524-5558
www.ema.org

ETSI
European Telecommunications
Standards Institute
Route des Lucioles
F-06921 Sophia Antipolis Cedex
France
Tel: +33 (0)4 92 94 42 00
Fax: +33 (0)4 93 65 47 16
www.etsi.fr

FCC
Federal Communications Commission
1919 M Street, NW
Washington, DC
Tel: 202-418-0200
www.fcc.gov

Frame Relay Forum
303 Vintage Park Drive
Foster City, CA 94404
Tel: 415-578-6980
Fax: 415-525-0182
www.frforum.com

Gigabit Ethernet Alliance
20111 Stevens Creek Boulevard,
Suite 280
Cupertino, CA 95014
Tel: 408-241-8904
Fax: 408-241-8918
www.gigabit-ethernet.org

GO-MVIP, Inc.
3220 N Street, NW, Suite 360
Washington, D.C. 20007
Tel: 508-650-1388
Fax: 508-650-1375
www.mvip.org

ICSA
International Computer Security
Association
1200 Walnut Bottom Road
Carlisle, PA 17013-7635

Tel: 717-258-1816
www.ncsa.com

IEC
International Engineering Consortium
549 W. Randolph Street, Suite 600
Chicago, IL 60661
Tel: 312-559-4100
Fax: 312-559-4111
www.iec.org

IEC
International Electrotechnical
Commission
3, rue de Varembe
1211 Geneva 20
Switzerland
Tel: 41-22-919-02-11
www.iec.ch

IEEE
Institute of Electrical and Electronics
Engineers, Inc.
445 Hoes Lane
Piscataway, NJ 08855-1331
Tel: 908-981-0060
www.ieee.org

IMC
Internet Mail Consortium
127 Segre Place
Santa Cruz, CA 95060
Tel: 408-426-9827
Fax: 408-426-7301
www.imc.org

IMTC
International Multimedia
Teleconferencing Consortium, Inc.
Bishop Ranch 2
2694 Bishop Drive, Suite 105
San Ramon, CA 94583
Tel: 925-277-1320
Fax: 925-277-8111
www.imtc.org

InterNIC
P.O. Box 1656
Herndon, VA 22070
www.internic.net

IrDA
Infrared Data Association
P.O. Box 3883
Walnut Creek, CA 94598
Tel: 510-943-6546
Fax: 510-943-5600
www.irda.org

ISO
International Organization for
Standardization
One Rue de Varembe CH-1211
Case Postale 56
Geneva 20
Switzerland
Tel: 41-22-749-0111
www.iso.ch

ITU
International Telecommunications
Union
Place des Nations
CH-1211 Geneva 20
Switzerland
www.itu.ch

NAB
National Association of Broadcasters
1771 N Street, NW
Washington, D.C. 20036
Tel: 202-429-5300
www.nab.org

NARTE
National Association of Radio and
Telecommunications Engineers
P.O. Box 678
Medway, MA 02053
Tel: 508-533-8333

Fax: 508-533-3815
www.narte.org

NARUC
National Association of Regulatory
Utility Commissioners
P.O. Box 684
Washington, D.C. 20044
Tel: 202-898-2200
Fax: 202-898-2213
www.erols.com/naruc

NCTA
National Cable TV Association
1724 Massachusetts Avenue, NW
Washington, D.C. 20036
Tel: 202-775-3669
www.ncta.com

NECA
National Exchange Carriers
Association
100 South Jefferson Road
Whippany, NJ 07981-8597
Tel: 973-884-8000
Fax: 973-884-8469
www.neca.org

NIST
National Institute of Standards and
Technology
Gaithersburg, MD 20899
Tel: 301-975-2000
www.nist.com

NMF
Network Management Forum
1201 Mt. Kemble Avenue
Morristown, NJ 07960
Tel: 973-425-1900
Fax: 973-4251515
www.nmf.org

NTIA

National Telecommunications and
Information Administration
U.S. Department of Commerce
Washington, D.C. 20230
Tel: 202-377-1880
www.ntia.doc.gov

NTIS

National Technical Information
Service
Technology Administration
U.S. Department of Commerce
Springfield, VA 22161
Tel: 703-605-6000
Fax: 703-321-8547
www.ntis.gov

PCIA

Personal Communications Industry
Association
500 Montgomery Street, Suite 700
Alexandria, VA 22314
Tel: 703-739-0300
Fax: 703-836-1608
www.pcia.com

PCMCIA

Personal Computer Memory Card
International Association
2635 North First Street, Suite 209
San Jose, CA 95134
Tel: 408-433-2273
Fax: 408-433-9558
www.pcmcia.org

SCTE

Society of Cable Telecommunications
Engineers, Inc.
140 Philips Road
Exton, PA 19341-1318
Tel: 610-363-6888
Fax: 610-363-5898
www.scte.org

SIF

SONET Interoperability Forum
c/o Alliance for Telecommunications
Solutions
1200 G Street, NW, Suite 500
Washington, D.C. 20005
Tel: 202-628-6380
Fax: 202-393-5453
www.atis.org/atis/sif/index.html

SMPTE

Society of Motion Picture &
Television Engineers
595 W. Hartsdale Avenue
White Plains, NY 10607-1824
Tel: 914-761-1100
Fax: 914-761-3115
www.smpte.org

TCIF

Telecommunications Industry Forum
c/o Alliance for Telecommunications
Industry Solutions
1200 G Street, NW, Suite 500
Washington, D.C. 20005
Tel: 202-628-6380
Fax: 202-393-5453
www.atis.org

Telcordia Technologies

8 Corporate Place
Piscataway, NJ 08854-4156
Tel: 908-699-2000
www.bellcore.com

TIA

Telecommunications Industry
Association
2500 Wilson Boulevard
Arlington, VA 22201
Tel: 703-907-7700
Fax: 703-907-7727
www.eia.org

UL
Underwriters Laboratory
333 Pfingsten Road
Northbrook, IL 60062
Tel: 847-272-8800
Fax: 847-272-8129
www.ul.com

W3C
World Wide Web Consortium
Massachusetts Institute of Technology
Laboratory for Computer Science
545 Technology Square
Cambridge, MA 02139
Tel: 617-253-2613
Fax: 617-258-5999
www.w3.org

WLI Forum
Wireless LAN Interoperability Forum
1111 W. El Camino Road, #109-171
Sunnyvale, CA 94087
www.wlif.com

WLANA
Wireless LAN Alliance
2723 Delaware Avenue
Redwood City, CA 94061
www.wlana.com

WTO
World Trade Organization
154, rue de Lausanne
CH-1211 Geneva 21
Switzerland
Tel: 41-22-739-5111
Fax: 41-22-739-5458
www.wto.org

Index

The corporations which will excel in the 1980's will be those that manage information as a major resource. John Diebold as quoted in Infosystems, October, 1979.

In an attempt to help you manage the information in this book, this index points you to the pages on which topics are discussed. Each term and subject is spelled out completely, with the acronym or abbreviation following in parentheses. If you know only the acronym or abbreviation, please consult the Acronyms and Abbreviations appendix, which serves as a cross-reference to this index, and which immediately precedes it. The numbers in *italics* point you to the pages on which each term is defined and discussed in most complete detail, or the treatment of the subject is most significant. The numbers not in italics point you to the pages on which the term or subject is discussed either in lesser detail or is placed in application context. Pages on which the term or subject is mentioned only peripherally are not listed.

continued

NOTES

NOTES

NOTES

NOTES

my2cents.idgbooks.com

Communications Systems and Networks, Second Edition